The Journals of

WOODROW WYATT

Volume Two

Edited by Sarah Curtis

PAN BOOKS

First published 1999 by Macmillan

This edition published 2000 by Pan Books
an imprint of Macmillan Publishers Ltd
25 Eccleston Place, London SW1W 9NF
Basingstoke and Oxford
Associated companies throughout the world
www.macmillan.com

ISBN 0 330 39007 4

1 3 5 7 9 8 6 4 2

A CIP catalogue record for this book is available from
the British Library.

Phototypeset by Intype London Ltd
Printed and bound in Great Britain by
Mackays of Chatham plc, Chatham, Kent

Contents

List of Illustrations

SECTION ONE

SECTION TWO

Introduction

Margaret Thatcher is the tragic heroine of this second volume of Woodrow Wyatt's journals, and the survival of Thatcherism is its political theme. In the first volume, spanning the years 1985–8, WW noted but dismissed the early rumblings of discontent in Tory ranks against their leader who had led them to election victory. Now we watch the rift with her chancellor of the exchequer, Nigel Lawson, over her economic adviser, Alan Walters; the preliminary 'stalking horse' challenge to her leadership of the Conservative Party by Sir Anthony Meyer in 1989; the assault which toppled her in the 1990 leadership contest; and the emergence of John Major, carrying the banner of what might be called 'the acceptable face of Thatcherism'.

WW makes it clear that he gives Mrs Thatcher his fervent support in his columns in the *Times* and the *News of the World* because he approves of her political philosophy and most of her policies in practice. It is their identity of purpose about Europe, about privatization, and about individual freedom world-wide which binds him to her. But beyond the political there is the personal: WW cannot understand why either the Tories or the country should want to change such a strong, successful and in his view sensitive leader.

The journals, recorded contemporaneously and not in retrospect, show that John Major was Mrs Thatcher's preferred successor, though his succession came too soon for either her or WW. 'I think he seems to be the sort of person who would carry on with her ideas,' he says in May 1989 when she has made a point of introducing Major to him at her private lunch to celebrate ten years of her premiership. In October 1990, just before Sir Geoffrey Howe resigned from the government, precipitating the decisive leadership contest, WW sets out his own position about supporting the Conservative administration if there were a change: 'Unless I was satisfied,' he says at The Other Club, 'you had got somebody who was carrying on with her objectives, I would start attacking the Tory Party very strongly.'

Some of WW's friends wondered whether his influence would continue now that he could no longer pick up the telephone and speak to the Prime Minister whenever he wished. 'So long as I go on with these columns,' he says in July 1991, 'the Tory government is going to be very polite to me.' He told Rupert Murdoch during the final leadership contest that he would 'be able to keep contact with Major all right', and so he did, having supported Major in the final round, but not as closely as he did with Mrs Thatcher. He cogitates much about the change and concludes in June 1991, 'I don't get the same reception but Major is still a good egg.'

WW had other people on whom to press his causes, notably Norman Lamont, his close friend whose rise in the Cabinet we now see. Loyalty to friends was a quality WW prized with Forsterian resolve, and his loyalty to Lamont would be demonstrated across the years (though this did not stop him confiding to his journal, as about all his friends, any defect he saw from day to day). He also had dealings with successive home secretaries through his position as chairman of the Tote and established close relationships with two in this period, Douglas Hurd and Kenneth Baker.

As Mrs Thatcher grows increasingly critical of her successors, WW sees his task as acting as a bridge between her and the new administration, sympathizing with her predicament but trying to temper her interventions. There is no overt rift – he continues to telephone her regularly when she is not abroad, and he offers her advice about her memoirs – but their former harmony is tinged by suspicion when he claims Major is being loyal to her legacy.

Why before her fall did WW not take the dangers to her more seriously and why did he continue to believe she would win through? His failure to anticipate events was partly due to his optimistic temperament. Tim Bell jokes in June 1989, 'If a third world war broke out, Woodrow would ring her and say, "Don't worry, Margaret, I'll put it all straight in the *News of the World* on Sunday." '

However, the main reason was his unshakeable belief in her ability and charisma; that belief was so strong that it blinded him. In addition, he was exceptionally busy during this period. In the crucial months of 1989, including Geoffrey's Howe transfer from the Foreign Office and leading up to Nigel Lawson's resignation, he was immersed in the tortuous negotiations to cast and stage his play, then called *The Division Belle*, at the Theatre Royal, Margate.

In the selected extracts from his journals which form this volume, there has been space for only a taste of the pages of agonizing as theatre after theatre, actor after actor turn down the play, and then the pages of anxious euphoria as WW writes and rewrites scenes and dialogue during the rehearsals and run of the play. His tribulations will strike a chord with every would-be playwright. Mitty-like he dreams of starting yet another career at over seventy. Always one to 'bond' (a word he would abhor) with groups, his final worry when the play folds is almost as much for the actors' next jobs as for his own future as a dramatist.

The play itself is about a rising Tory MP who has an affair with his secretary, whose daughter sniffs what she thinks is cocaine at her élite school and whose socialist son has a fight with the police. He is faced with exposure by the *News of the World*. It contains references to many of WW's hobby horses, from the importance of eating unsaturated fats to the transitory nature of sexual attraction.

WW's formidable energies were also channelled into defending the Tote and himself against attacks. The government was investigating the possibility of privatizing the Tote. This investigation entailed scrutiny of the Tote's affairs, first by Lloyds Merchant Bank and then by the House of Commons Home Affairs Select Committee, chaired by Sir John Wheeler. WW passionately defended the Tote's record, citing the successful introduction of advanced technology under his stewardship and the increase of its turnover and profits (and hence its subventions to racing) in difficult years for the industry. He vehemently opposed the dismemberment of the Tote, thinking it essential to keep under one umbrella its on-course, credit and betting shop operations. He believed privatization would put its profits into the pockets of the bookmakers rather than the racing industry, and supported the solution of a racing trust taking over the Home Office's responsibilities vis-à-vis the Tote, as long as the existing arm's-length relationship with the board (and its chairman) was maintained. The problem was shelved by the then Home Secretary, but it is interesting that a similar future for the Tote to the one then envisaged was forecast at the time this book went to press.

Some of WW's most vitriolic attacks are on people in racing organizations and journalists who opposed him and in his view failed to recognize his achievements and those of the Tote. However, a kind word at a later date often enables him to revise his opinion of an erstwhile enemy. He records lengthy negotiations, which in the end failed, for the Tote to purchase Coral's betting shops, but the subsequent agreement for Coral to have Tote computer terminals was something of a triumph.

WW's activities also included his strenuous efforts as a crossbencher in the House of Lords to persuade the government to give more passports to the citizens of Hong Kong, threatened with an uncertain future by the imminent take-over by China, and to amend the Broadcasting Bill to ensure the political balance of programmes. He appreciates earlier than Mrs Thatcher the need to recognize the independence of former members of the Soviet Union and sees the vulnerability of Gorbachev. The way he operates, using his network of contacts to gain information, campaigning in his newspaper columns and constantly putting before the Prime Minister and other ministers the facts as he sees them, shows again the processes of lobbying and the relationship between government and the press.

WW's final, ever-present preoccupation was the need to make more money to support his household and his way of life: a lord he is, but a millionaire he is not. His expenses range from the vintage wines at his dinner parties, to the annual holiday entertaining friends in Italy, to his part share in a racehorse (which, alas, is not a winner). In this volume we see him taking on another consultancy, for the US firm of lawyers Skadden Arps, and toiling to bring together suitably high-powered industrialists who might be able to use their services. He confides to his journals more than before his misgivings about having to take such work – 'I find it a bit grubby' – while maintaining his integrity and his ability to keep separate the various strands of his life. He sees no problem in lobbying for Rupert Murdoch to be able to develop his satellite television holdings as well as his newspapers, telling Murdoch in March 1990, 'Margaret is very keen on preserving your position. She knows how much she depends on your support. Likewise you depend on hers in this matter.'

A recurrent vein of introspection is an attractive feature of these years. Just when we think WW is unpardonably snobbish, rude or conceited, he lifts the veil of self-promotion and self-deception and shows that he is aware of his faults. Sometimes he is like the reverse of a press officer, fingering his own failings. He tells us in December 1989 that he doesn't think he has a talent for writing plays, he got nowhere in politics, his journalism is of variable quality and the real reason why his autobiography *Confessions of an Optimist* only sold 10,000 copies was that it wasn't good enough. When he watches old clips of himself from *Panorama* he is appalled at how boastful he was, as well as how fat. He goes into an aria of self-blame for his meanness when explaining how he counted the cost of the magnum of Winston

Churchill special cuvée 1979 champagne he gave Lord (Hartley) Shaw-cross for his ninetieth birthday. He reveals a touchingly vulnerable inner self behind the flamboyant front.

This volume of WW's journals, like the first, is only a selection from the entries he made for the period. The last volume contained about a third of all he wrote for the relevant years, this one less than a quarter. He wrote more and more as time went on, partly because of the momentous nature of the events he was witnessing, certainly in 1990, but perhaps too because the journals, which he began with the aim of providing some posthumous money for his heirs, became the means through which he could honestly express his dreams and anxieties. He wrote over a million words between January 1990 and April 1992, when this volume ends.

My aim throughout, as the editor making the selection for publication, has been to preserve the balance of what he wrote in the way I hope he would have wanted. There could have been one volume of this length devoted to politics, another on racing, another on the fortunes of his play and another entirely composed of gossip about friends and acquaintances. To have excluded any element would have been a distortion. I have tried to keep the flow running smoothly, without too much repetition of similar events. For example, WW attended many race meetings but not all are included. It was not possible to include every person WW met in his various roles but I have tried to keep the reader in touch with key characters.

As with the first volume, there have been difficult decisions of taste and discretion concerning what to include and what to omit. I have again resisted any pressures or temptation to bowdlerize WW or make him seem politically correct. His friends often reflect the prejudices of their generation and circle. Some make careless remarks about Jews which are offensive. WW is an advocate of equal opportunities for women, but his attitude and devotion to feminine charms have not been affected by feminism. The journals are valuable evidence of social as well as political attitudes.

WW had plenty to say about what is and is not acceptable for newspapers to publish. He repeats to Rupert Murdoch in 1990 what he had told the Queen Mother at Cheltenham in March 1989: 'It is only the élitists who don't want the people to know what goes on in high places because they know it already. They think the ordinary people, including the middle classes, are not capable of understanding the tittle-tattle without being put into a deep state of shock and disillusionment – though they themselves, who wish to curb and censor newspapers, are not at all disturbed by knowing who is sleeping with whom and what is going on with somebody's marriage and all that kind of thing.' He urges Murdoch, 'Remember your own belief that what you say in the *News of the World* and the *Sun* about naughty goings on are part of a morality play: "Look what happens to you if you misbehave." '

In these passages he seems to condone the revelations newspapers make (though sympathizing with his friends when they or their families caught the eye of the tabloids) but he left no guidance about his journals. Twenty or thirty years on, when the principals have died, it may be appropriate to tell all, but there must now be some discretion where marriages have survived, even when WW makes it clear that each partner knows what the other is doing. I have particularly tried to respect the privacy of younger people.

On a less serious level there may be some passages in this volume which will embarrass or upset WW's former friends (his remarks, for example, about people's appearances) but to have excised them all would have misrepresented the man they knew and whose quips they enjoyed in life.

Was WW accurate in his recollections? He did not keep a tape-recorder beneath his dinner table or fixed to his telephone, so obviously the conversations he relays are not verbatim. If you ask any two people to recall a discussion in which they took part a day or two previously, their accounts will nearly always vary; one will remember some aspects clearly, the second give a different slant. WW recorded his journals in his 'talking machine' at convenient moments, whenever he had the opportunity, but regularly when events must have been fairly fresh in his mind, even if the wine had been good. His secretary then typed up the tapes and he checked the manuscript. He made some alterations in his crabbed handwriting but they were nearly always merely to change a word; only occasionally would he add a line or two. (Maddeningly for his editor, he rarely checked the spelling of names, many of which were incorrect. I apologize if there are errors I have failed to spot.)

Sometimes a letter or document included with the manuscript confirms a conversation. For example, a letter from the Queen Mother in May 1990 repeats the verbal request he had recorded a fortnight before that he should take up with Lord Stevens, the proprietor of the *Express* newspapers, the attack on Prince Philip by Jean Rook. Such examples suggest that WW did record accurately the gist of what he heard.

Chips Channon in his diaries remarked, 'I feel caddish, even treacherous sometimes keeping this diary from the eyes of my wife.' Lady Channon knew he kept a diary, unlike Lady Wyatt – she did not see this book before its publication – but the point Channon made was that 'if she were to read it, and I knew she were, it would lose much spontaneity, and cease to be a record of my private thoughts'. These journals are Woodrow Wyatt's thoughts and his alone. He was definite – I asked him about this in 1995 on the third and last time I met him – that he did not want his journals to be edited by a member of his family. He did not say why, but I think one reason may have been that he would not have wanted to have exposed them to any responsibility for what he said.

Biographical details of some of the principal figures in the journals are given at the end of this volume on pp. 699–709. An asterisk at the end of a footnote refers the reader to the biographical notes the first time such a person is mentioned. I have also included a short appendix on racing and a chronology.

*

My thanks go to Lady Wyatt for her understanding of my role as editor; as before, to Diana Rawstron of Goodman Derrick, WW's lawyers, who introduced me to this project; to Mr Geoffrey Webster, public relations director at the Tote when WW was chairman, for answering my questions about racing; to Catherine Whitaker, my excellent editor at Macmillan; and to my family for their patience with my preoccupation with WW, especially my husband, Anthony Curtis, and son Quentin for their unfailing day-on-day encouragement and practical help.

SARAH CURTIS

May 1999

Woodrow Wyatt

Baron Wyatt of Weeford in the County of Staffordshire (knight 1983, life peer 1987) was born Woodrow Lyle Wyatt on 4 July 1918, son of Robert Harvey Lyle Wyatt (d 1932), founder and headmaster of Milbourne Lodge School, Esher, and Ethel, née Morgan (d 1974). He was descended from Humphrey Wyatt (d 1610), ancestor of the Wyatt architects, painters and sculptors.

Woodrow Wyatt was educated at Eastbourne College and Worcester College, Oxford, where he took a Second in Law.

He married 1 (1939–44) *Susan* Cox, an Oxford contemporary; 2 (1948–56) Nora (*Alix*) Robbins, later Coleman; 3 (1957–66) *Lady Moorea Hastings*, now *Black* (daughter of the 15th Earl of Huntingdon (*Jack*, d 1990) and his first wife (Cristina, d 1953, daughter of the Marchese Casati, Rome) by whom he had a son, *Pericles*, b 1963, m *Maria* (1989–91); 4 (in 1966) *Verushka* née Racz, widow of Baron (Hungary) Dr Laszlo Banszky von Ambroz, by whom he had a daughter *Petronella* (b 1968), and a stepson, *Nicholas Banszky von Ambroz* (b 1952), merchant banker, m (1984–95) *Caroline*, née While (two daughters – *Genevra*, b 1985, *Antonella*, b 1987). Verushka's mother Ilona (*Nadje*, d 1996) lived with the Wyatts.

Major Robert David Lyle, WW's older brother (d 1989), married Irene Joyce Francis (*Joy*, d 1984). He owned the family estate Bonython in Cornwall; his son and heir was WW's nephew *Robert Lyle* (b 1952, m (1991) Hon. *Tessa* Mayhew, solicitor).

After serving throughout the 1939–45 war (he was mentioned in dispatches in Normandy in 1944), during which time he founded and edited the series of books called *English Story*, WW entered Parliament in 1945 as Labour MP for Aston, Birmingham. He was personal assistant to *Sir Stafford Cripps* on the Cabinet Mission to India to prepare for independence in 1946. He lost the Aston seat in 1955 through redistribution, but was returned as MP for Bosworth 1959–70 and was Parliamentary Under-Secretary of State and Financial Secretary, War Office, from May 1951 until October 1951, when Labour lost power.

While still an MP he opposed his party on some issues, voting with Desmond Donnelly to hold up the nationalization of steel when Labour had a tiny majority, and once out of Parliament he moved further to the right. However, he never joined another party and when Mrs Thatcher made him a life peer in 1987 he sat on the crossbenches.

Throughout his career WW was an active journalist, on the *New Statesman*, 1947–8; as a weekly columnist on *Reynolds News*, 1949–61; at the *Daily Mirror* 1965–73; and the *Sunday Mirror*, 1973–83. He was under contract to BBC Television 1955–9 and a regular presenter of *Panorama* in the days of its early fame. It was through television as well as when an MP that he fought Communist domination of the unions, particularly the engineering union (AEU) and electricians' union (ETU). In the 1960s he owned a chain of Midlands newspapers and the Banbury Press, introducing non-heat-set web-offset colour printing to England in 1962. He was a member of the Council of the Zoological Society of London 1968–71, 1973–7.

In 1983 WW joined Rupert Murdoch's newspapers with a fort-nightly column in the *Times*, book reviews and a weekly column called 'The Voice of Reason' (not his title) in the *News of the World*. He was chairman of the Horserace Totalisator Board (first appointed by Roy Jenkins when Home Secretary) from 1976 until 1997, the year of his death. He wrote for the *Times* until the close of May 1997, when his contract was ended; his last column for the *News of the World* was on 30 November 1997. By then he was ill with cancer of the throat. He died of a burst artery on 7 December 1997.

His books include the ten volumes of *English Story* he edited (1940–50); an edition of the short stories of O. Henry (1967); *What's Left of the Labour Party?* (1977); *To the Point* (1981), a collection of short *causerie* pieces; two children's books about *Mr Saucy Squirrel* (1976 and 1977); his autobiographies *Into the Dangerous World* (1952) and *Confessions of an Optimist* (1985); a selection from *English Story* (*The Way We Lived Then*, 1989); and a play, *High Profiles* (1992).

Names in italics are of people WW mentions in this volume.

1989

Sunday 1 January

When I rang Mrs Thatcher at about 5.00 p.m. they said she had gone out. I left a message that I would myself have to go out at about half-past seven. At 6.00 she rang from Dulwich.

She said she was pottering around in her new house[1] which she has got to try to make feel lived in and unless she goes there sometimes it won't be. She shows no sign, as reported in the newspapers, that she wants to sell the Dulwich house.

I told her that I thought the *Sunday Times* MORI poll, putting her seven points ahead of her own government, was a sign that the public feel that they are not yet ready to see any change in Tory leadership.

We had dinner at the Connaught with Irwin Stelzer.[2]

Irwin has heard nothing more about the proposition that he should help Andrew Neil[3] run Rupert's[4] satellite adventure. He thought it was because of the amount he wanted as compensation for not doing his work in America which was perhaps too large for Rupert who, as I said, 'is not always an extravagant payer'.

Irwin is very worried about the whole enterprise, fearing Rupert may become over-committed with a billion million dollars at stake.

Pericles[5] rang from Philadelphia. He is going to marry Maria though she is twenty years older than him and already a grandmother. I wished them good luck. I thought it was useless to argue with him. She came

---

1. Bought for her eventual retirement.
2. American-born economist and journalist; *Sunday Times* columnist.*
3. UK editor, *Economist*, 1982–3; editor, *Sunday Times*, 1983–94; chairman, Sky TV, 1988–90; editor-in-chief, European Press Holdings, including the *Scotsman*, *Scotsman on Sunday*, *Sunday Business* and *Edinburgh Evening News*, since 1997 (and the *European*, 1997–8).
4. Rupert Murdoch, the newspaper owner, who had recently entered the satellite television field.*
5. Son of WW and his third wife (now Lady Moorea Black), b 1963, working in the US.*

on the telephone and said, 'We match each other as a team in every way.' I suppose she meant in bed and out of it.

Thursday 5 January

I was wanted on the telephone. I said, 'I'm watching *Newsnight*.' Verushka[6] said, 'It's a call from Number 10.'

I came down and there was an operator at the switchboard from No 10 saying, 'Did you just call the Prime Minister?' I said, 'No.' 'Well somebody has saying they were Lord Wyatt and they were put through to the Prime Minister. Would you like to speak to her now?'

She said, 'I thought if you were ringing me so late on a Thursday night it must be urgent so I asked for you to be put through. A high pitched voice came on and said something vaguely insulting and then rang off. I knew it wasn't your voice.'

I was disturbed. It's a creepy feeling that somebody is impersonating me and perhaps upsetting Margaret at the same time.

As she was on the telephone we talked about Libya and the possibility they have a chemical plant.

Friday 6 January

Irwin tells me that it seems Rupert is willing to pay for his services for Sky Channel. Andrew Neil was instructed to say, 'It's very expensive, can you not do it for less?' Irwin said, 'Tell him you've tried and I can't.'

Sunday 8 January

To Bowden Park[7] for lunch. Found Arnold [Weinstock] looking below par and tired. Also worried. Plessey, under the guidance of Sir John Nott,[8] the failed Defence Minister at the time of the Falklands, now Chairman of Lazards, is organizing an international consortium to bid for GEC.

---

6. WW's fourth wife (m 1966), née Racz, widow of Baron Dr Laszlo Banszky von Ambroz.*

7. Country house of Lord and Lady Weinstock (Arnold and Netta).*

8. Conservative MP, 1966–83; Secretary of State for Trade, 1979–81; Secretary of State for Defence, 1981–3; chairman and chief executive, Lazard Brothers, 1985–90; chairman, Etam, 1991–5; knight 1983.

Michael Heseltine[9] has been bouncing and jumping up and down. He is not interested in Arnold, but in making political capital. He, naturally, says that the Marconi business, which belongs to GEC, could not possibly be allowed to go to a consortium of foreigners.

Arnold said, 'I'm beginning to think that if the government don't stop this going any further, I don't mind if I just take my £25 million and go and live in Switzerland and just look after my racehorses.' 'And sell Bowden?' I asked. 'You can't do that. It was built by James Wyatt.'

He was upset by the attacks on him in the *Sunday Times*, particularly by Ivan Fallon[10] who only two weeks or so ago said that Arnold was doing frightfully well in his bid for Plessey in conjunction with Siemens, which was an act of great imagination.

He now says this morning that Arnold with GEC is on the way out and a jolly good thing, too.

People had been ringing since quarter past eight this morning. Arnold complained that he hadn't even had time to brush his teeth by twelve o'clock.

Arnold doesn't seem to me to have the fight in him that he used to have and maybe he means it when he says he would not mind so much if he lost, though he keeps saying they want to buy it in order to strip its assets: if it was sold bit by bit, the bits added together would be more valuable or would raise a higher price than the whole. 'I don't want that to happen after my twenty-eight years of building it up.'

He said he had agreed to one photographer coming from the *Guardian*. I said, 'Whatever for? It's got a minuscule circulation.' He said he was the only man on the telephone who was nice to him.

When we finished lunch I said, 'Let's go for a walk. Get out of this for the moment.' Lunch was done by the chef from the Gavroche, as usual at weekends, and began with some lobster which was pretty good in a salad. Then we had lamb, which of course is a killer with saturated fats but nevertheless was cooked very nicely, with French flageolets. There was Château Giscours 1966 which was excellent.

We debated whether he should approach Jack Welch who runs General Electric in America and is reputed to be one of the consortium

---

9. Conservative MP since 1966; Secretary of State for Defence, 1983–6, when he resigned over the Westland affair.*

10. Journalist; *Irish Times*, 1964–6; city editor, *Sunday Telegraph*, 1979–84; deputy editor, *Sunday Times*, 1984–94; chief executive officer, Independent Newspaper Holdings (S. Africa), since 1997.

trying to buy GEC. Arnold is willing to sell him his medical instruments company in America if he would withdraw from the consortium, though he has to put it very delicately now that a kind of semi-bid situation exists.

Instead of going back to London I stayed at Bowden, after asking Arnold whether he would like me to be there.

There is no doubt that many people don't like Arnold, who was the great predator a decade or so ago, and rejoice he is now at the receiving end. People are very envious and venomous. After supper, during which we had half a bottle of 1980 Haut-Brion white wine (it tasted musty, but very good) we drove back to London.

I decided to ring Margaret though it was fairly late by this time.

I didn't want her to think I was neglecting her on a Sunday because of the tiresomeness of somebody impersonating me earlier in the week.

I told her that I had been with Arnold. I briefly explained to her that under the joint Siemens-GEC bid for Plessey, Siemens would not get any part of Marconi which is the highly critical and sensitive defence business of GEC and vital to our national defence. On the other hand, GEC would get half of the Siemens defence business, and then we could export defence equipment much more freely to Germany.

She said, 'But who are these people?' I said, 'They are being organized by John Nott, Chairman of Lazards.' 'Oh,' she said, with meaning in her voice.

'Why are they doing it?' I said. 'It is a diversionary measure to try and foil the GEC-Siemens bid for Plessey.'

I said the reference to the Monopolies Commission or otherwise of the GEC-Siemens bid has got nothing whatever to do with this other consortium which they are trying to cook up. That ought to be stopped in its tracks in the national interest. But the other one, the GEC-Siemens one, ought to be allowed to go through.

After talking to Margaret I spoke to Arnold and told him what I had said to her.

Monday 9 January
Lunch at Claridge's with James Hanson[11] and Gordon White.[12] They are an engaging couple who have made vast fortunes. Unfortunately,

---

11. Chairman, Hanson PLC, 1965–97; life peer 1983.
12. (1923–95); chairman, Hanson Industries, 1983–95; board member, British Airways, 1989–93; knight 1979, life peer 1991.

they both think that Arnold is too old and too tired and are very downbeat about his chances of surviving with GEC intact and himself as the head of it.

The purpose of the lunch was to explore the possibility of Hanson's doing something about the Tote.[13]

In the upshot they were suggesting an arrangement by which they would put £100 million into the Tote in exchange for ninety per cent of the shares and would agree to all the conditions regarding guarantees for the percentage of profits going to racing sponsorship, help to the racecourses, etc.

Tuesday 10 January
A visit from the past. Michael Summerskill came to ask questions about his mother, Edith.[14] He is writing a biography of her. A mild, pleasant man. He asked me how much of a feminist I thought his mother was. I said not aggressively so but people were puzzled that her children were called Summerskill and not Samuel, their father's name, though you can understand she wanted to retain her maiden name.

He said they thought they would keep it like that because they were afraid that if the Germans succeeded in occupying Britain, they would be thought to be Jewish.

She was a stout supporter of Hugh Gaitskell[15] and anti-Nye Bevan.[16] She should have been in Wilson's Cabinet in 1964 but, because she disapproved of Harold Wilson[17] as much as Hugh Gaitskell and I did, she was not.

Wednesday 11 January
Arnold in a more cheerful and confident mood. The consortium from Lazards would appear to be receding in danger.

---

13. WW had been chairman of the Tote (the Horserace Totalisator Board) since 1976. The government was considering options for privatizing the Tote.
14. (1901–80); m (1925) Dr Jeffrey Samuel, a Welshman; qualified as doctor, 1924; MP, 1935–61; Parliamentary Secretary, Ministry of Food, 1945–50; Minister of National Insurance, 1950–1; life peer 1961. Michael Summerskill died before completing his book.
15. (1906–63); Leader of the Labour Party from 1955 until his untimely death.
16. Aneurin Bevan (1897–1960), left-wing Labour politician and creator of the National Health Service, famed for his Welsh oratory.
17. (1916–95); succeeded Gaitskell as Leader of the Labour Party in 1963; Prime Minister, 1964–70 and 1974–6.

He has spoken to Jack Welch who runs General Electric in America, and is doing a deal with him.

He says that I did a lot of good with my telephone call to Mrs T on Sunday night. She is now asking what it is all about and though she is not committing herself (she cannot in a quasi-judicial position), it looks as though her attitude is OK.

Thursday 12 January
Dinner party at 19 Cavendish Avenue.[18] I was annoyed with Verushka for having asked Andrew Devonshire[19] as the spare man we needed without consulting me first. I thought it was going to look a terrible dinner party with a Duke and the Duke's sister (Anne Tree)[20] and the Radnors,[21] as though we live with nothing but Dukes and ancient earldoms. Cecil Parkinson[22] presumably would like to talk seriously to at least one or two people. As it turned out the arrangement was a huge success with the guests because the non-peers and the non-ancient peers were cracking snobs.

James Hanson I like. He came from a little village in Yorkshire. He is now sixty-seven. His father had to leave school when he was fourteen and James at seventeen. He has worked pretty hard and sharply and made a great fortune.

When the men were alone there was some talk about Rupert Murdoch's *News of the World* and *Sun* and how horrible they were in their scandalous gossip, revealing the sex lives of people which has no public interest. Cecil Parkinson asked why Wendy Henry was no longer editor of *News of the World*. I said it was because she went too far – she didn't understand Rupert's dictum that the *News of the World*, and to some extent the *Sun*, are morality plays. Rupert is a son of the manse. He thinks it's absolutely right to expose all the details of people's goings on but there must be a moral at the end to say look how this

---

18. The Wyatts' house in St John's Wood, London.
19. 11th Duke of Devonshire.*
20. The Lady Anne Tree, née Cavendish, daughter of the 10th Duke of Devonshire, sister of the 11th Duke (Andrew); m (1949) Michael Tree (1921–99), painter, son of Ronald Tree, Conservative politician (d 1976).*
21. 8th Earl of Radnor (Jake), m 3 (1986) Jillean Pettit.
22. Conservative politician, Secretary of State for Energy since 1987; he resigned as Secretary of State for Trade and Industry in 1983, on the revelation that his secretary, Sara Keays, was pregnant with his child.*

has brought destruction upon them – this is what happens if you perform wicked acts. Andrew said he did it to sell newspapers.

Andrew was still bitter about the *News of the World* having bought from his butler his private telephone book.

The purloining of his telephone book led to various respectable women, friends of Andrew's, and of mine, including elderly ladies, being rung up to be asked whether the Duke of Devonshire had been giving them any presents and so forth with the inference that they were all his girlfriends.

Cecil Parkinson seems convinced that the consumer will get a better deal from the privatization of electricity. There will be genuine competition to supply the electricity to the companies distributing it to the population and to industry. He is also very keen, as I am, on developing nuclear power. However, despite his being extremely charming and intelligent and agreeable, I think basically he is a light-weight. He is often talked of as the next Chancellor of the Exchequer but it would be a mistake if she gave him the job.

You can see why Cecil Parkinson succeeds with Margaret. He is the great adaptable and adept courtier.

He is a great friend of Norman Lamont.[23]

Cecil hoped he wasn't about to get another black eye.[24] They get into similar scrapes.

Sunday 15 January

Allan Davis[25] rang that there was a gleam of light. The man who runs the Southampton repertory theatre was given his first introduction to a job by Allan years ago and they get on well together. He says he is longing to read the play.

He is still very worried about calling it *Thanks to Thatcher*.[26] He had been sounding his friends out and they say they would never go to see it because they hate Mrs Thatcher so much. I said, 'That's the

---

23. Conservative politician, Financial Secretary to the Treasury since 1986.*
24. The reference is to an incident in 1985 when Lamont was alleged to have received a black eye from a friend of Lady Olga Polizzi (née Forte). See Vol. 1, p. 18n.
25. Director designate of the play WW had written. Born 1913 in Sydney, Australia, he began his career as an actor; after war service in Britain he became a director and producer; his shows include *No Sex Please, We're British*. They were now seeking a theatre to try out the play.
26. Earlier titles were *A Thorough-going Woman* and *Knowing the Wrong People*.

trouble with your theatre. You've been putting on so many left-wing attacks on Mrs Thatcher and the establishment and all the rest of it that you have narrowed your audience to people who only like that kind of thing.'

I spoke to Margaret and told her Arnold wished that some hint would come from 10 Downing Street that he was not out of favour. She said, 'Of course he is not. Anybody who says that is absolutely wrong.'

She asked, 'Would the General Electric plus the GEC deal not cross competition lines in Europe?' I said, 'I don't think so. General Electric have already got a firm in Italy with which Arnold has now done a merger and there is plenty of competition for this kind of thing in Europe.' She is obviously not absolutely clued up about it.

I said, 'Can't we do more for our Hong Kong Chinese?'[27] I told her what the Portuguese were doing in Macau, issuing a hundred thousand passports.

She said, 'I get hopping mad with my two Ministers.[28] They say we can't do anything about the Hong Kong Chinese coming here because it would upset the Chinese and they would think we were going back on the arrangements we had made with them.' I said, 'If the Portuguese can do it, so can we.' She said, 'That is another matter altogether. I must look into that.'

When I rang Arnold later after speaking to her, he was cheered up by what she had said to me about him.

He was disappointed last week by some of the people for whom he had done great favours and who he had expected to ring up to say something in support of him, not doing it at all. Then he said to me, 'You have been through all that.' I said, 'Yes.' He was obviously thinking about what happened when the Banbury[29] collapse occurred in 1982.

He said the media were persecuting him, ringing him up all the time.

I said 'Why don't you turn the telephones off?' And he said,

---

27. With Hong Kong due to be returned from British rule to China in 1997, there was mounting concern about the future of Hong Kong citizens who did not have British passports.

28. Geoffrey Howe, as Foreign Secretary, and Douglas Hurd, as Home Secretary responsible for immigration.

29. WW's print and newspaper business.

'Suppose one of the children want to ring up in the middle of the night?' I said, 'I don't suppose they will. Anyway let Netta answer it. You shouldn't be answering the telephone yourself – it's ridiculous. Why don't you have a secretary at Bowden and at Grosvenor Square?' He said, 'Netta wouldn't like somebody in the house.'

Margaret began our conversation by saying, 'Nothing much to worry about last week – only the economy.'

Monday 16 January
I go to lunch with Abdul Al Ghazzi[30] at Claridge's.

He showed me correspondence they have had with Charles Brown, the architect supervising the restoration of the fire damage at Heveningham.

Various wrangles with Mary Ann Sieghart, in charge of the features page at the *Times*, wanting me to put in [my article defending Weinstock] some criticism about Arnold failing to succeed in the [business] computer market. I expect Arnold will be very displeased as he can't bear any slight adverse criticism. However, it looks better that way because if I don't acknowledge any faults, people won't take the rest of the article seriously.[31]

Tuesday 17 January
Arnold mildly irritated about the reference to business computers which the woman Mary Ann Sieghart insisted on putting in, or more or less insisted, saying she used to write for Lex [*Financial Times*] and knows about these matters.[32]

He said he had never made any business computers.

I told him she had asked whether I was a director of GEC or whether I had any shares and I told her no.

She also asked whether Arnold was on the Tote Board which I

---

30. Iraqi businessman and owner of Heveningham Hall in Suffolk, a fine example of the earlier classical work of James Wyatt (1746–1813), which he was restoring. See Vol. 1 for the history of the restoration and WW's evidence on 9 February 1988 at the public inquiry about Al Ghazzi's proposal to divert a footpath.

31. WW began the article, published 17 January, by declaring his interest: 'Lord Weinstock is an old friend.'

32. Mary Ann Sieghart, political journalist; Eurobond correspondent, then Lex columnist, *Financial Times*, 1982–6; political correspondent, *Economist*, 1986–8; op-ed page editor, the *Times*, 1988–91, now an assistant editor and political leader writer; m (1989) David Prichard.

thought was going it a bit. I wouldn't have had him on the Tote Board for anything – he'd have dominated it and argued and upset everybody, no doubt. Not that he would have wanted to waste his time on it in the first place.

About ten to ten Rupert rings from New York.

'I want to talk to you about the *Times*. Do you think there is a crisis there? Have I got to act immediately?' I said I wouldn't have thought so. 'What is the circulation doing?' He said, 'About 430,000. It's not going down.'

He said, 'What do you think of the home news?' I said, 'The home news is not badly done. Charles Wilson[33] has got fairly good news judgement.' Rupert commented that the foreign news was not good enough. I said, 'I think that is true. But the *Times* has improved a bit since we spoke last about it.'[34]

I said, 'You know the weakness of the *Times* is that the leading articles simply lack authority. Charlie Wilson is very nice and I like him very much and he no doubt has got a good sense of what is news value but he has no intellectual authority and the leaders don't give you that feeling. When Rees-Mogg[35] did them they did have a feeling of intellectual authority. I know he made a mess of the rest of the paper but the leaders were fine. Even when Charlie Douglas-Home[36] did them.' Rupert broke in to say, 'But he wasn't an intellectual.' I said, 'No but he had some presence and stability of depth and he knew where he was going.'

'Well who else should I have?' I said, 'I have suggested to you Charles Moore[37] in the past. He is very young but a very good editor for the *Spectator*.' He said, 'I don't like the *Spectator*.' I said, 'It's not

33. Editor, the *Times*, 1985–90; editorial director, Mirror Group, 1991–2, then managing director; editor-in-chief, *Sporting Life*, from 1990; member, Jockey Club, from 1993; member, Youth Justice Board, from 1998.

34. See 30 May 1988, Vol. 1, pp. 566–7, when WW criticized the features, the letters page, the gossip column and the obituaries page.

35. Editor, the *Times* 1967–81; chairman, Sidgwick & Jackson (publishers), 1985–9; vice-chairman, BBC Board of Governors, 1981–6; chairman, Arts Council of Great Britain, 1982–9, Broadcasting Standards Council, 1988–93; director, GEC, since 1981; chairman, Pickering & Chatto (publishers), since 1981; knight 1981, life peer 1988.

36. (1937–85), editor, the *Times*, 1982–5.

37. Born 1956; editor, *Spectator*, 1984–90, *Sunday Telegraph*, 1992–5, *Daily Telegraph*, since 1995.

at all bad and he has got some political news sense because he writes a good column in the *Daily Express* every Friday, a political one, and he would be on the right OK.'

He said, 'What about Bruce Anderson?'[38] I said, 'He is good and thorough but I think he is dull. I don't know anything about his ability to edit a newspaper. I wouldn't risk it.' He said, 'He's not quirky like Peregrine Worsthorne.'[39] I said, 'No, that is true, he is not. But you wouldn't want him or Max Hastings[40] editing the *Times*.' He said, 'No.'

Clearly he was expecting me to dream up a successor to Charlie Wilson who is nice enough but hasn't got the education or the depth to be a great editor of the *Times*. I said to Rupert, 'You need somebody like Delane who unfortunately died a hundred years ago – you can't get him now.[41] The *Times* wants to be the Thunderer, as Trollope used to call it in his novels.'

After we finished talking I thought to myself that Charlie Wilson has no idea of my relations with Rupert otherwise he wouldn't have been playing the fool and saying he only wanted to pay me £250 for the piece about the dock labour scheme when he had promised £500 and was quibbling that I should have done another article as well that week. Fortunately for him, I have my mind in two compartments. I think he is very silly not to be honourable about that, but I wouldn't let it influence my judgement in talking to Rupert about him.

Wednesday 18 January
Last night Petronella[42] and I started digging around in our minds who we could ask to have dinner with Queen Elizabeth [the Queen Mother] on February 23rd. Only the Rees-Moggs are coming so far. She suggested Graham Greene [the novelist]. We sent a telegram to him where he lives in Antibes. This morning he rang and said he couldn't come because he was going to be in Panama for two weeks at that period. I said, 'Are you writing something about it?' He said, 'No, just a visit.' I said, 'I'm sorry you can't come.' He said, 'It would have been very

---

38. Journalist; at this time on the *Telegraph* newspapers and a *Spectator* contributor.
39. Editor, *Sunday Telegraph*, 1986–91; knight 1991.
40. Editor, *Daily Telegraph*, 1986–95, *Evening Standard* since 1995.
41. John Thadeus Delane (1817–79) edited the *Times* 1841–77.
42. Daughter of WW and Verushka (b 1968).*

nice for me but I am not so sure it would have been nice for the Queen Mother.'

Diana and John Wilton[43] come to dinner. They are an exceptionally amiable and pleasant couple. Diana says that Miranda Morley, who has been David's[44] mistress for years, says that she'd rather carry on like that, only seeing David say one day in a week, than lose him altogether. He's given her a little house at Badminton where she is liable to bump into Caroline [Duchess of Beaufort] but it seems as though Caroline no longer bothers about that kind of thing. In fact David was saying to Verushka recently that he thinks he now loves Caroline more than she does him. Caroline has made her own life and is quite content with all her activities and trips abroad for botany and sight-seeing.

Diana said that occasionally John and she and Miranda Morley and David have dinner together. I said she had never been here because Caroline is such an old friend of mine.

I said, 'He's always had enormous charm and energy and he's done frightfully well with the picture business.' This is true. He has been able to spend much more money on Badminton from what he as made out of the Marlborough Art Gallery and his picture transactions than the old Duke ever could.

Thursday 19 January

I have been wondering whether to ask Ali Forbes[45] for dinner with Queen Elizabeth the Queen Mother on February 23rd. He is very amusing, talkative and personable but he is hopelessly unreliable. He would be quite likely to write his account of the dinner in the *Spectator* or elsewhere if he felt like it and I think she would very much dislike that, indeed I know she would.

But undoubtedly he is one of the most engaging people in English life and knows more stories and more gossip than anybody, beginning with Churchill, whom he met during the war years and saw quite a lot of.

---

43. 7th Earl of Wilton; m (1962) Diana, née Galway, previously married to David Naylor-Leyland.
44. David Somerset, 11th Duke of Beaufort; m (1950) Lady Caroline Thynne (d 1995), daughter of the 6th Marquess of Bath and the Hon. Daphne Fielding; chairman, Marlborough Fine Art, since 1977; the Beaufort seat is Badminton House, Avon.*
45. Alastair Forbes, journalist.

The Other Club.[46] Chris Patten[47] was in the chair. I talked to him and Michael Hartwell[48] before dinner about new possible members. Once again I advocated Charles Moore about whom Chris heartily agreed and so did Michael Hartwell. I said that I had put Charles Moore and A. N. Wilson[49] forward several times and nothing had ever happened. Later we thought of another potential [candidate] – Duke Hussey of the BBC.[50]

I had an argument with Roy [Jenkins][51] about Heveningham Hall. I said he'd never been there in his life. He said no, but he had heard about it from Jennifer.

He said he had given the go ahead as Chancellor of the Exchequer for buying the house at the end of 1969.

I said, 'It took a lot of pushing from me to get the government to do it.'

There was some speculation as to how the judges could have said that Lord Young[52] had no right to withhold the report on the Fayed brothers[53]

---

46. Churchill and F. E. Smith (later Lord Birkenhead) founded The Other Club in 1913 because they were not wanted at a club called 'The Club'. Its membership consists mainly of politicians from all parties.

47. Conservative MP, 1979–92; at this time Minister of State for Overseas Development; Secretary of State for the Environment, July 1989–November 1990; Chairman, Conservative Party, and Chancellor of the Duchy of Lancaster, 1990–2; Governor of Hong Kong, 1992–7.

48. Life peer 1968, formerly the Hon. Michael Berry; chairman and editor-in-chief, *Daily Telegraph* and *Sunday Telegraph*, 1954–87. Conrad Black, the Canadian newspaper proprietor, acquired control of the *Telegraph* titles in 1985 after sixty years of ownership by the Berry family.

49. Novelist, critic and journalist.

50. Marmaduke Hussey, managing director and chief executive (1971–80), director (1982–6), Times Newspapers; chairman, BBC Board of Governors, 1986–96.

51. Politician and historian; life peer 1987; m (1945) Jennifer, née Morris, DBE (1985), chairman, National Trust, 1986–91.*

52. Lord (David) Young of Graffham; Secretary of State for Employment, 1985–7, for Trade and Industry, 1987–9; deputy chairman, Conservative Party, 1989–90; life peer 1984. He set up the 1987–9 DTI investigation into the 1985 takeover of Harrods by the Fayed brothers; the report was published in 1989.

53. Egyptian-born owners of Harrods; Mohamed Al Fayed (father of Dodi who died with Princess Diana in 1997) was shown by the DTI report to have lied about the sources of his wealth which enabled him to buy the House of Fraser, including Harrods, for £615m; his brother Ali was granted a British passport in March 1999.

– Tiny Rowland[54] and they were in the Harrods take-over row – and he must refer the matter to the Monopolies Commission. Norman Tebbit[55] said they were totally wrong. He told me that he was then the operative Minister in the Department of Trade and Industry. From hearing the saga it emerged that to begin with Tiny Rowland was in cahoots with the Fayeds and he was making arrangements to sell and buy their shares etc. He was happy to collaborate with the people he now said were criminals and had a criminal record, and concealed the truth of their activities. He had known about them all the time and would have cheerfully had them as partners.

It sounded to me as though Tiny Rowland is as big a villain as the people he is attacking.

Friday 20 January

Bernard Levin[56] wants me to join a quiz programme. Some newspapers, daily ones, are engaging in a competition on the BBC wireless.

They have three specialist people in each team. Charlie Wilson and he want me to be the one on politics – the first period is thought to be the 1950s. I was rather doubtful as I know I can never answer these questions but Bernard was insistent so I reluctantly agreed.

He said comfortingly, 'We can always drop you after the first one if we get through into the next round and you were no good.'

Sunday 22 January

After his great victory Arnold is still not happy, or at least the original cheerfulness is dimmed. He says there are too many people anti-him out there. He hints at anti-semitism. Even the Prudential are asking him about the succession. He says they want to know who would take

---

54. (1917–98); chairman, Lonhro Group, which owned the *Observer* newspaper, 1981–93; described by Edward Heath as 'the unacceptable face of capitalism', he fought Mohamed Al Fayed for the ownership of the Fraser group.

55. Conservative politician; MP, 1970–92; Secretary of State for Employment (1981–3), for Trade and Industry, (1983–5); Chancellor of the Duchy of Lancaster, and Conservative Party Chairman (1985–7); life peer 1992.

56. Journalist, critic and author.

over if he goes. Simon [his son] is far the cleverest person he has there now.[57]

I said, 'He is shy and doesn't get on with people as well as you do. He has not got your charm or your touch of inspirational genius.' He said, 'Well, that's perhaps a matter of age.'

Arnold said he had thought of getting Harvey-Jones[58] in as Chairman but she, Margaret, would not have liked him there because he belongs to the SDP. I said, 'She might have preferred that to Prior,'[59] to which he replied that he went and spoke to her about Prior and she said he would be fine. I said, 'But you never understand her. If you had come and asked me about it first, I would have sounded her out and found out what she really thought.'

Now he is worried about Peter Levene who is the Chief Procurement Officer at the Ministry of Defence. He is going around saying that he would welcome Thomson of France getting involved in Marconi.

I told Arnold that he should not magnify the number of his enemies. He has some but he has many friends as well.

Tuesday 24 January
Gail Sheehy[60] of *Vanity Fair* and her husband, an American, came to lunch at the Lords. She is writing a piece about Margaret Thatcher for *Vanity Fair*. She wanted to pull out a dictating machine during lunch. I said, 'I don't think they would like that here.' So she took copious notes instead.

I told her my feelings about Margaret. She asked me how she treated personal attacks on her. I said, 'With controlled disdain.'

---

57. The Hon. Simon Weinstock, b 1952, died of cancer in 1996.*

58. Sir John Harvey-Jones; chairman, ICI (1982–7), Parallax Enterprises (1987–97), the *Economist* (1989–94); knight 1985.

59. James (Jim) Prior, Conservative politician; chairman, GEC, 1984–98; Parliamentary Private Secretary (PPS) to Edward Heath as Leader of the Opposition, 1965–70; Minister of Agriculture, Fisheries and Food, 1970–2; Lord President of the Council and Leader of the House of Commons, 1972–4, in the Heath government; then Secretary of State for Employment (1979–81), for Northern Ireland (1981–4, under Mrs Thatcher); life peer 1987.

60. Journalist and author; m Clay Felker (teacher, former magazine editor); she became well known in the US in the 1970s for her reports of the lives of prostitutes in New York; her latest book *Passages in Men's Lives: Directions for Men at Midlife* was published in 1999; her earlier books include *The Silent Passage*, about the female menopause, and an analysis of the Clintons' marriage.

I introduced Tam Dalyell[61] to Gail Sheehy and said that he sees Mrs Thatcher as the epitome of evil, with the devil standing over her as she burns, sticking his pitchfork into her.

Tam is an amiable crank, not in the main stream of the Labour Party but very much on the right wing ordinarily. He went to Eton and began as a Tory being, I think, President of the Conservative Association at Cambridge. He is a Scottish landowner. But he has made a parliamentary career of taking up with great thoroughness subjects with which he can discredit or seek to discredit the Prime Minister. Clearly she is not his kind of girl.

Tam said he was writing a biography of Dick Crossman for Weiden-feld. I told him what a marvellous man I thought him. A good friend, enthusiastic, unreliable but very penetrating. I shall always remember Dick with great affection for our tram rides[62] from the *New Statesman* when he explained politics to me when I was young and working with him on the *New Statesman*. He was a miraculous teacher with a generous heart, even though he could be bitter about many people and attack them spitefully as it seemed at the time.

Tam Dalyell said, 'Dick Crossman loved you, too.' I said, 'How do you know?' He said, 'I was living in the same flat with him during all the controversy over your preventing steel being nationalized in the 1964 parliament and he defended you always.' I said, 'I was right.' Tam said, 'I admit you were right and if I admit that now, will you admit Mrs Thatcher tells lies?'[63] I made no comment.

Wednesday 25 January
Dinner Cavendish Avenue.

Getting poor Mrs Tebbit[64] up the stairs and into the drawing-room and then into the dining-room was quite a performance. Norman is

---

61. MP since 1962; baronet but does not use his title; his *Dick Crossman: A Portrait* was published in 1989. Richard Crossman (1907–74), a former Oxford don, was a Labour MP and cabinet minister, and a prolific writer and journalist whose diaries gave insight into the relationship between cabinet ministers and civil servants.

62. The *New Statesman* offices were then at Great Turnstile, off High Holborn and Kingsway, where trams still ran.

63. Dalyell famously attacked Mrs Thatcher's veracity over the sinking of the *Belgrano* during the Falklands War.

64. Margaret, née Daines; m (1956) Norman Tebbit. She suffered serious injuries in the IRA bomb attack at the Grand Hotel, Brighton, during the 1984 Conservative Party Conference.

absolutely sweet with her, treats her most tenderly and makes sure that everything is comfortable for her. The poor girl is still crippled almost entirely, certainly from the waist down. She had very little movement in her arms. She can turn and move her head all right. She was looking very pretty and had got herself up pleasantly.

She sat next to Norman in the dining-room who had to cut her meat and other food.

There was ordinary white and pink champagne before dinner plus a bottle of Ayala 1949. At dinner we had a 1950 Pichon-Longueville des Lalandes.

Susan Hussey sat on my right and Mary Soames[65] on my left. I asked Mary how she came to be Chairman of the National Theatre. She said she didn't know but if I could find out she would be very interested. I said they must have realized what excellent taste you have and what knowledge of literary and artistic matters. Actually she does write very good books and is well clued up.

Mary does not like Mrs Thatcher, never has. She said it makes her ill every time President Reagan and Mrs Thatcher quote her father. I said, 'Your son Nicholas[66] likes her,' so she said, 'Yes I think he does.' I said I was sorry Nicholas was unable to accept the post in the government when he was offered it because of his separation from his wife and having to cut down his spending and earn some money.

I said to Duke Hussey after the women had left the room that his battle with the BBC was like the battle of the Somme in the trenches during the First World War. First of all you gain fifty yards, then you lose eighteen but you've still got thirty-two in hand: then you advance again and win fifteen yards and you lose seven but you've still got forty in hand and so it goes on, gradually pushing forward and losing a bit on each advance and coming back again. He said, 'That's exactly it. It's a hard slog and a slow slog but I think we're getting there.'

He then said that an opinion poll showed most people think that the BBC is Conservative biased. My reaction to that is it's probably because BBC staff on the air talk with posh accents. Conversely, polls always show the majority of readers thinking the *Sun* is a Labour newspaper.

The Tebbits had to go at ten because her nurse was waiting for her

---

65. Daughter of Sir Winston Churchill; widow of Christopher Soames (Conservative politician, life peer 1978); writer, chairman, Royal National Theatre, 1989–95.*
66. Conservative MP since 1983; m 1 (1981–90) Catherine, née Weatherall.*

to put her to bed. I went out with them to their specially constructed van/car.

How lucky one is not to be crippled for life.

How lucky one is not to have to nurse a crippled wife, as the noble Norman does without stint or complaint though, as he said to Verushka, temperamentally he is bad-tempered and impatient. He is a hundred per cent decent man and very funny as well.

During dinner David Montagu[67] made it clear again that he doesn't like Arnold. He always criticizes him for his cash mountain and so forth. But David was a hopeless failure as a banker and he is jolly lucky now to be Chairman of Rothmans.

Mary Soames smoked a cigar after dinner. It was quite a big one. She always smokes a cigar when she comes to my house. She said that Papa didn't smoke as many cigars as people thought.

Mary is a jolly girl.

She has a pleasant round face retaining some of the prettiness of forty-four years ago but she was never beautiful. She remains finely loyal to her father, reacting sharply to any criticism she reads or hears. Winston would be delighted.

Friday 27 January

Rupert rang at 7.35. He was in London for a couple of days working on his new Sky Channel [which is] beginning in early February.

He said he was having a lot of trouble with David Young's department. It's full of regulatory mechanisms for what he is trying to do with the Sky programmes by satellite. I said, 'If I can help, let me know.'

Rupert sounded very confident because his shares were moving up. I said, 'I can't think why with the enormous burden of the Sky Channel costing about a billion and a half pounds. You may lose the lot.' Rupert thinks he'll start to make it back in about two years' time.

Sunday 29 January

Her first words were, 'I missed you last week.' She always notices if I haven't rung up in a week.

We spoke about the Windlesham report on the *Death on the Rock* TV programme put out by Thames Television which suggested that the soldiers who killed the IRA assassins [in Gibraltar] were guilty of murder.

---

67. (1928–98); member of Tote Board.*

I told her that Ian Trethowan (Chairman of Thames Television)[68] had said to me that George Thomson,[69] who was Chairman of the IBA [Independent Broadcasting Authority] at the time, did not tell him that Sir Geoffrey Howe had asked that the programme should not be put out until after the inquest. Her response was: 'He should have known not to do it anyway.'

She raised the case of Paddy Ashdown, the Leader of the Liberals, making personal attacks on Alun Chalfont[70] who has been appointed Deputy Chairman of the new Independent Broadcasting Authority. That was my suggestion. Now Ashdown is trying to say that because he had connection with some security firms there is a conflict of interest. She was highly indignant about it.

I told her I was writing an article for the *Times* on Tuesday about Hong Kong.

I said, 'The real issue is that they want to have the passports so that they can use them to get out of Hong Kong if the Chinese break all their promises about leaving it as a free enterprise place with a democratic free press and all the rest of it. If they see that is happening, they can say to the Chinese government, "We've got these passports and we're going if you don't behave better." It's really to make the Chinese government behave properly.' Margaret said, 'You'll have to persuade Geoffrey about this.'[71]

Monday 30 January
Had dinner with Harold Lever[72] at the Portland Club. Before dinner I watched him play backgammon with Jimmy Goldsmith.[73]

---

68. (1922–90); Director General, BBC, 1977–82; chairman, Horserace Betting Levy Board, 1982–90; chairman, Thames Television, 1987–90; knight 1980.
69. Labour, later Lib Dem, politician; MP and minister, 1952–72; EEC Commissioner, 1973–7; chairman, Independent Broadcasting Authority, 1981–8; life peer 1977.
70. Journalist and expert on defence; life peer 1964; Minister of State, Foreign and Commonwealth Office, 1964–70; deputy chairman, IBA, 1989–90; chairman, Radio Authority, 1991–4. See Vol. 1, p. 629, for WW's suggestion about this appointment.
71. Sir Geoffrey Howe was at this time Secretary of State for Foreign and Commonwealth Affairs.*
72. (1914–95); Labour politician; Financial Secretary to the Treasury, 1967–9; Paymaster General, 1969–70; Chancellor of the Duchy of Lancaster, 1974–9; life peer 1979.*
73. (1933–97); industrialist, environmentalist, Member (for France) of the European Parliament; campaigner against political integration of Europe; Leader of the Referendum Party in the 1997 general election; knight 1976.

Jimmy Goldsmith must be one of the very richest men in the world. He is building two palaces in Mexico. He says they are in the mountains and distant from the capital of Mexico. Very beautiful. I asked him what was the point.

He said, 'I am making a most wonderful library.' I said, 'Yes but supposing you just want to see a few friends in the evening?' He said, 'I send for them with my aeroplane.'

I said, 'Once upon a time you used to send me blueprints for the disasters about to befall the human race. Why don't you do it any more?' He said, 'I've given it up. Anyway I think things are not so bad now. I think Margaret has done marvels and I think that if she goes on being Prime Minister long enough, she may have made an irreversible change.' I said, 'She has another ten years. She will go on. Politics is her life, her whole being and her care for her country also. She is full of energy. She won't be defeated,' and I gave all the reasons why she won't be.

I said to him, 'Would you come and have lunch with my Dr Sinclair? You know what it is all about, namely the International Nutrition Foundation.'[74] He said yes he would.

What a curious lot of people they are there. At dinner we had a very good 1966 Léoville-Las-Cases and a very good beginning [course], with wonderful wild mushrooms. But there they all are, wasting their time with massive gambling. I suppose they find it relaxing. I find it desperately worrying but then I haven't got the money.

Tuesday 31 January
Drinks at the house of Nick Lloyd and his wife Eve Pollard. He is the editor of the *Daily Express* and she is the editor of the *Sunday Mirror*.

Judy and Douglas Hurd were there.[75] I said to them, 'I think the Home Office is being taken for a ride by Lloyds Merchant Bank.[76] They ordered the cheapest and they've got the worst. It didn't seem very bright to me.' When I spoke to Douglas, he said that we at the Tote were still denying them documents they wanted to see. I said, 'I have heard nothing about that. They saw all the board papers and

---

74. WW was on the board of this organization, the life-work of Dr Hugh Sinclair, nutritionist.
75. Douglas Hurd was Home Secretary at this time.*
76. The Home Office in 1988 commissioned Lloyds Merchant Bank to make a feasibility study on privatization of the Tote (see Vol. 1, p. 624).

minutes. The only thing they weren't shown was the private minutes because they are private.'

Eve Pollard was very friendly. She said she missed Wendy Henry, her [former] opposite number at the *News of the World*. They used to exchange conversations on a Saturday about their lead stories. She now wishes she hadn't exploded with Rupert and was still there.

I feel vaguely guilty that I never got in touch with her.

From there on to the Lords where we had dinner with the Wolfsons.[77]

During dinner it came out that Leonard Wolfson doesn't have any living-in servant except an au pair girl. I think a cook comes in.

I said, 'You must be crazy. You've got paintings around your walls which must be worth over £50 million, all those French Impressionists and so on, and yet you don't live in any comfort. I've got no money but I've always had a butler and a cook in the house for as long as I can remember. All my life, even as a child, there were servants in the house. There is no luxury unless you can ring a bell and somebody answers it.' He said, 'Ruth answers when I call.' I said, 'That's not the same thing at all.'

'I said, 'I always leave my clothes on the floor and somebody picks them up.' Leonard said he doesn't do that.

---

77. Leonard Wolfson (life peer 1985) and his first wife, Ruth.*

Thursday 2 February
Tried to get the government to do something about Hong Kong at Question Time following on my article for the *Times* on Tuesday. Met with a brick wall, as I expected.

I sent a copy of *Confessions of an Optimist*[1] to Stephen Chan at the Hong Kong Government Office who helped me a good deal on Saturday and Sunday when I was getting material for the article.

Friday 3 February
Rupert rings from New York. He has a great idea that Mrs T should be persuaded to write the equivalent of Gorbachev's *Perestroika* for world-wide publication. It would be an international bestseller, better than Gorbachev's, explaining her philosophy.

I said to him, 'You are ringing me in your capacity as the new Chairman of Collins,' and he laughed. I said, 'The previous Chairman of Collins, Ian Chapman,[2] has already got me to try to persuade Mrs Thatcher to let Collins have her memoirs when the time comes. She has noted the proposal and seems favourable to dealing with Collins, if she does write her memoirs.'[3]

However, I said that I was not sure that she'd be willing to do as he says. First of all she hasn't got the time. Rupert interrupted, 'She could get John O'Sullivan[4] or somebody like that to write it for her and do the donkey work.'

I said, 'I'll be speaking to her this weekend and I'll put it to her as persuasively as I can.'

---

1. WW's 1985 autobiography.
2. Ian Chapman (senior), chairman and group chief executive, William Collins, 1981–9; publisher of *Confessions of an Optimist*.
3. Her memoirs, *The Downing Street Years*, were published in 1993 by Harper-Collins.
4. Journalist, now editor at large of the *National Review*.

Sunday 5 February

She began immediately by saying how good was the piece I had written about the NHS in the *News of the World* this morning. I thanked her but she said, 'No, it's I who thank you.' I said, 'We have a problem explaining to people that it is not going to be privatized.'

She said, 'How can something be privatized, if there is nothing being charged?'

I put to her Rupert's idea, which she might do, of a Gorbachev-type *Perestroika* book.

She said, 'My trouble is that I don't really have time.'

She then said, 'Perhaps I could do a number of speeches on a theme which then could be published in a book.' I thought to myself that this wouldn't be exactly what Rupert would want because it would hardly be an exclusive book. I then said to her, 'If you did that, which might be a good idea, you could expand the speeches and make them into a coherent whole for book publication and that would give it an originality and freshness.' She began to get slightly intrigued by this idea.

I told her that I was off to the launch of Sky this afternoon. 'How do I get it?' she asked. 'Which buttons do I have to press?'

I said, 'I think you press the one C6 that's got Sky on. Have you got Westminster Cable Television?' She said she didn't think she had. I said, 'We have it. We get CNN news on it.' She said, 'We get CNN news, too. It's the best news programme there is.'

I never did find out what button the Prime Minister should press. When I got to Syon House [for the launch party], there were Rupert Murdoch and Andrew Neil on the doorstep. Neither of them could tell me. Nobody quite knows what service she has and how she gets CNN news.

Syon House. Lovely inside. The Adam brothers. There was nowhere to sit and large numbers of people. Champagne and orange juice being served but no tea.

Then we were taken in a coach to the studios in Isleworth. When we got to the studios of Sky in Isleworth there was more champagne.

I met the new editor of the *News of the World*, Mrs [Pat] Chapman, who is having lunch with me this week. I said that I propose next Sunday to put in a piece saying I didn't see why people couldn't sell their kidneys if they wanted to. At this point the Deputy High Commissioner of Australia, Mr Evans, said, 'I have three kidneys.' It transpired that when he had a medical examination and X-rays they found he had three, one of them very small but all functioning. I said, 'You're in a very good position to sell one of them to a Saudi Arabian multi-millionaire.' Mrs Chapman got very excited about the three kidneys and took his name and telephone number and said would he mind if she put it in her news pages. He said, 'No not at all.'

When we had supper we sat at the same table as Ivan Fallon, Rupert Murdoch and Irwin Stelzer. Ivan Fallon said he did admire Arnold and did like him. I said, 'You made a charming retraction after I wrote the article in the *Times* defending Arnold.'

I told Rupert what Margaret had said about writing a book.

Rupert said, 'Why don't you do it with her and share the royalties?' I said, 'I am not sure about that, even if I would want to.' She is a very slow and painful composer in writing her speeches and other matters like that.

Charlie Wilson was there wanting to know what I thought the Home Secretary would do about the levy.[5] I said, 'I don't know but if Mrs Thatcher gets to hear about there being a levy – a hypothecated tax – it might be the end of the whole thing.'

Monday 6 February
Lunch with Irwin Stelzer at the RAC [Royal Automobile Club] and Bruce Buck who is a member of the biggest and most important legal firm in America. Skadden Arps have set up in London and want introductions, know-how to tackle English life and Whitehall and all that kind of thing. There is a proposition, initiated by Irwin, that they might pay me £25,000 a year to do this which would be delightful but I am not sure how much I could do for them.

Mr Buck seemed a pleasant enough man, highly intelligent and able. They are sending me some details of what his firm has done and how I could justify telling people that it is the best in America.

I ate an enormous crab salad. There must have been about four crabs in it. Dressed crab. It was very good and so was the asparagus before. It really is not a bad restaurant they have at the RAC.

---

5. The tax levied on betting to benefit horseracing, set annually by the Home Secretary.

Dinner at the French Embassy. It was in honour of William Waldegrave.[6] I don't know why embassies do these funny dinners but they do. I sat next to his wife who was quite pleasant but not all that easy to get talking to.

She said he gets hurt by some of the attacks on him. I said, 'So does Mrs Thatcher.' She was very surprised and said, 'Oh no, that can't be true.' I said, 'Of course she does. Though people put on a brave face, they are often very hurt by some of the things that are said.'

Mrs Waldegrave said, 'She rises above it.' I said, 'Exactly. It's the only way to deal with it if you're in politics. And William is doing very well.'

He is a brilliant boy. He got a First at Oxford and a Fellowship at All Souls; very bright indeed.

On my other side at dinner sat the elder daughter of the Countess Mountbatten. Her father is Lord Brabourne.

I told her how her grandfather[7] had asked me before he went to India what he should wear on arrival. I told him, 'You are semi-Royal. You are the last Viceroy and you should go in your best uniform, full of decorations, and be met by armed guards and massed bands, otherwise they will think you are slumming and they won't like it at all.' He had been afraid that they were rather left-wing in India and would want him to wear civilian clothes.

I said, 'I think your grandfather was naïve politically but your grandmother was not. She was very bright. I remember I often used to go and see her to talk about India and she had wonderful legs. She used to leap up on to sofas curling her legs up behind her. She was so light and graceful and intelligent.'

She [the granddaughter] is actually rather pretty. A very nice figure as well, like her grandmother, but I don't think she is quite so amorous. She said of course her grandmother had had an affair with Nehru, among many other people.

---

6. Conservative politician; life peer 1999; Minister of State, Foreign and Commonwealth Office, at this time; 2nd son of 12th Earl Waldegrave; m (1977) Caroline, née Burrows, who founded, with Prue Leith in 1975, Leith's School of Food and Wine.

7. Earl Mountbatten of Burma (1900–79), last Viceroy of India; m (1922) the Hon. Edwina, née Ashley (1901–60). The title Countess Mountbatten passed to their elder daughter who m (1946) 7th Lord Brabourne.

John Julius Norwich was there.[8] For some reason we have drifted apart over the years.

We pulled Tony Lambton[9] to pieces. John Julius stayed in La Cerbaia, the house we had from Tony [in Italy]. He said he rather liked it. I said, 'It was all decorated by Verushka.'

He said, 'Tony was very foolish to have a row with you because you were his link with politics in England.'

John Julius and I both agree that if anybody is sufficiently persistent, like Tony or George Weidenfeld,[10] who are always sending flowers and presents and giving unremitting attention and saying 'You are the only person in the world' and all the rest of it, they can succeed in the end if they wish, women being susceptible to that kind of flattery.

Tony of course was always rich and with plenty of time on his hands. John Julius thought it was odd of him to have gone to live in Italy after the great scandal. I said, 'Possibly he wouldn't have done so today but I think he correctly felt that his political career was at an end at the time, had it existed, and that he might as well take his fortune to a tax free place.'

John Julius thought he possibly quite enjoyed himself now being a writer, though not a very good one, and having this large house which is very handsome.

Tony has now written a book about Mountbatten which is highly insulting.[11] I don't suppose his friend Prince Charles will like it very much.

John Julius and I agreed that his little book of short stories wasn't bad but the book about Princesses in Russia was flawed by confusion between fact and fiction. I said, 'It would have been even worse if I hadn't cut large chunks of it out before it was published. That was when Tony was smothering me with affection.' John Julius said, 'But

---

8. Viscount Norwich, writer and historian of Venice, former diplomat; son of 1st Viscount Norwich (Duff Cooper) and Lady Diana Cooper; m 2 (1989) the Hon. Mollie Philipps, née Makins, daughter of 1st Baron Sherfield, former wife of the Hon. Hugo Philipps, now 3rd Baron Milford.

9. Viscount Lambton, m (1942) Belinda (Bindy), née Blew-Jones; MP, 1951–73; Parliamentary Under-Secretary of State, Ministry of Defence, 1970–3; he resigned from the Commons in 1973 after photographs of him with a prostitute were offered to the press.*

10. Publisher; life peer 1976.*

11. *The Mountbattens*, published 1989; his previous books include *Snow and Other Stories* (1983) and *Elizabeth and Alexandra* (1984).

why did he change?' and I said, 'He is like that. The novelty wears off and he then wants a row. He loves quarrels. He thinks they enliven his otherwise boring life. If he hasn't had one grow naturally, he will cause one like he did with me. I think he regrets it but it is too late. I suppose now I might forgive him if I saw him again but I don't feel particularly keen about it.'

Dinner was very poor considering it was the French Embassy.

Tuesday 7 February
Dinner at Mark's Club. Martin Laing, Chairman of John Laing the construction company, and Prince Michael [of Kent].

There was some very old champagne first, I don't know what it was, and then there was some Château Beychevelle 1982 which is pretty good. The food was utterly delicious and I got a very nice large Montecristo cigar at the end.

Opposite me sat Edwin Bramall, the Field Marshal.[12]

When I arrived I was offered a hard-backed chair and I said, 'No, the Field Marshal will sit in that; he needs some backbone,' referring to the decision by the MCC, of which he is this year's President, to give in to all the other countries about players who had played in South Africa being forbidden to play in Test Matches.

Actually he got the best deal he could manage.

Wednesday 8 February
Spoke to Margaret about Gail Sheehy and told her the questions she wanted to ask.

I told her that she was calling her the Queen of the West. 'Good Lord,' she said. I explained that *Vanity Fair* appealed to a lot of literary and opinion-making people and had a circulation of about a million.

I said I didn't think she would cut her up, in fact I was fairly confident she wouldn't.

So finally she agreed to see her when she comes back and she said she should ring Bernard Ingham.[13]

Saturday 11 February
To Newbury. Mrs Ann Parkinson came. Robbie [WW's chauffeur] picked her up and she came to the house and then we drove down.

---

12. Chief of the Defence Staff, 1982–5.
13. Chief Press Secretary, 10 Downing Street, 1979–90.

Norman Lamont and his wife were there.[14]

Mrs Lamont and Mrs Parkinson sat on either side of me, two wronged women but they still hold their husbands.

Richard Fries, a man from the Home Office in charge of the Tote affairs, was there. I told him what I thought about the weasel (Stephen Barrett of Lloyds Merchant Bank).

I explained about them trying to cause delays and blame them on us to get more money out of the government. He said, 'We have told him they have got to do it by early March, the report.' I said, 'I have got fed up with him complaining at delays.' He said, 'You didn't let him see some private minutes.' I said, 'They can have no relevance whatever to the business of the Tote and whether it is viable to be privatized. There is simply no connection. He was shown all the other minutes he wanted to see and he hardly looked at them.'

Norman asked me who I thought should succeed Nigel Lawson.[15] I said, 'What is this fellow John Major[16] like?' He said, 'He is good but I am not sure he is up to it.' He thinks Cecil Parkinson should succeed. I said, 'Do you think he is strong enough?' He said yes, he thought he was. They are great friends. I expect he thinks I should put in a word for Cecil for Margaret. I haven't quite made up my mind about it. He is certainly doing the Electricity Bill much better than the British Telecom one was done.

Sunday 12 February
I spoke to Margaret at about 4.00 p.m.

We discussed Leon Brittan who has gone as a Commissioner to Europe.[17] Immediately he has made a speech saying that we must join the EMS [European Monetary System] at once. 'They go native as soon as they get there. It's too extraordinary,' she said. She also added that his brother is Sam Brittan from the *Financial Times* who takes the same view.

I mentioned that Rupert is attracted by her idea of doing a series of speeches and then linking them together and expanding them into a book.

---

14. The Lamonts divorced in 1999, after twenty-eight years of marriage.
15. As Chancellor of the Exchequer.
16. Chief Secretary to the Treasury at this time.
17. He left Parliament in 1988, having resigned as Secretary of State for Trade and Industry over the Westland affair in 1986.*

She said, 'I have got so much to do but it is an idea that I should think about.' She said, 'How is it getting on, that Sky Television of his?' I said, 'I think it looks pretty good at the moment.'

She said, 'I believe they are bringing a [satellite] dish on Tuesday.'

Of course she loves the whole idea because it whittles down the influence of the BBC. It makes the area of choice more open and it is more difficult for people of left-wing persuasion to mount steady drip, drip campaigns against her.

I also told her about the great month, October 25th to November 21st, 'Britain salutes Hungary.' Would she be able to pop into the gala reception on April 25th? Immediately she said, 'I have got something that ends at seven o'clock with some Tory MPs.' So I said, 'If you can only come in for a few minutes I am sure they would be delighted. The Deputy Prime Minister will be there. Verushka is on the committee.'

Allan Davis now very gloomy about our play. He had heard nothing from Southampton.

Tuesday 14 February

Henry Keswick[18] came for a drink. He polished off three-quarters of a bottle of pink champagne.

He is enormously rich. He probably has got £100 million. He asked us to stay at Oare with them. His wife Tessa is the political adviser to Kenneth Clarke now.

I don't know that I would want to have a weekend there, though the house is beautiful.

He was giving me some advice on how to proceed with helping the Hong Kong Chinese. He wrote a very good letter in the *Times* after my article which Margaret commented on to me. He has seen her at a lunch recently and she had said, 'Go on with what you are doing. We have got to persuade the Foreign Office.' So it is all right to tell him her views.

Wednesday 15 February

Mr Buck [of Skadden Arps] and his friend Mr Kramer came in the evening.

---

18. Chairman, Matheson & Co. and Jardine, Matheson Holdings, Hong Kong; brother of Chips Keswick; m (1985) the Hon. Tessa, née Fraser, previously married to 14th Lord Reay.*

We discussed what I could do to help them. They agreed that I should try it for six months at the rate of £25,000 a year.

Friday 17 February
Up at six and had my breakfast. We depart at ten past seven for the airport [for Budapest].

The Ambassador, an oily creep called Leonard Appleyard,[19] makes himself known before we land.

We have a little suite [at the Atrium Hyatt Hotel]. I am sitting now in the sitting-room which overlooks the Danube which I have never seen blue on any visit to Hungary.

Unfortunately, there is piped music all around the whole time. We soon learn that gypsy music is out. The younger generation know nothing of it and dislike it and prefer discos. There is also a strong feeling against the gypsies who are ethnically different and who will soon be a fair number, 10.5 per cent of the population of 10.5 million.

The Ambassador comes to pick me up.

We drive off to the parliament building where I am to see Mr Pozsgay who is described as a Minister of State and is number two in the country. He is the flavour of the year. A great reformer who is partly at odds with Karoly Grosz, Secretary of the Communist Party and top man in Hungary. Mr Pozsgay (Imre) is in a high risk situation pushing away for more and more democracy.

The Ambassador in the car told me my questions should concentrate on the multi-party system and told me what other questions I should ask. Silly idiot, as though I didn't know what I want to ask. He is determined to be in on the interview.

Pozsgay is very friendly. Short and podgy, which more or less rhymes with his name and could pass as a pseudonym for it. We sit opposite each other at a long table in his office. It was an animated conversation. He brims with intelligence and enthusiasm but I was told later he is extremely lazy and doesn't really do his homework properly.

He says the Russians are very interested in Hungary's experimenting with the multi-party system and their attempt to introduce genuine private enterprise. They hope it goes well – that is Gorbachev does. If it does, it can act as a bit of a model for Russia, though the problems are quite different here. Hungary is far more developed than Russia

19. Ambassador to Hungary, 1986–9, to People's Republic of China, 1994–7; knight 1994.

and used to be ranked among the small countries only after Czechoslovakia in wealth and productivity before the war.

The Ambassador tries to interrupt from time to time with fatuous questions, holding out his hand and stretching his fingers as though to try and silence me – impertinent fellow.

I told Mr Pozsgay that if he really wants to attract private enterprise from abroad and get money from abroad, which he desperately needs, 'You should set up a private bank in Hungary. If bankers abroad felt that they were dealing with a privatized bank which could make decisions based on profits and commercial returns for the cash, they would be far more interested in providing money for joint enterprises in Hungary than if they were dealing with a state bank, with all its bureaucracy and inability to judge commercial risks and opportunities.'

I told him that it is no good trying to be part Communist and part private enterprise. He has to go the whole hog, though it doesn't matter if some basic services remain nationalized like the railways.

He agrees that it would be very difficult to shift the population now accustomed to full employment (mostly) on a very low level of pay but with security.

Mr Podgy says there will be a law officially allowing private enterprise newspapers and journals soon.

He says Rupert Murdoch could come and set up shop here now if he wanted to. The state television is allowed to take advertisements.

I was told later that they are at last allowed to have meetings – in fact Budapest is festooned with people booking halls for political meetings.

Last time I was here you were arrested if you attempted to have a meeting, even of only four people.

We were still talking animatedly when the Ambassador said, 'I know you are very busy,' to Mr Pozsgay and got up and said, 'We must go now.' He didn't look as if he wanted to stop talking at all.

Saturday 18 February

I was expecting a fax from the *News of the World* which Ron Pell [sub-editor] said he would dispatch overnight. When I asked for it in the morning I was told one hadn't been received.

I spoke to a girl who spoke moderate English but I couldn't get anywhere with her so I asked for somebody there who could speak English properly.

When I rang down again later to the fax room, Ron Pell having said he would send another one, a man answered and said, 'You have upset the lady here. She is crying. You must send her something.' I said, 'I might send her something if she finds my fax.' He said, 'Well there is nothing here, only something for someone called Woodrow.'

They are not always very efficient here and they are very touchy.

Livia [Verushka's sister] and ourselves went to the New York after dinner at the Intercontinental where we heard the gypsy music so little available in Budapest nowadays.

Livia said there were high priced girls in the hotels at about £100 a session. These were mainly used by foreigners, obviously. She said there was, however, a district in Budapest where the ordinary prostitute walked up and down. So we went to have a look in a taxi. There were a few. Some of them were quite pretty. I was told they cost anything from £10 to £30 a time. But they were not as plentiful as they are in some parts of London. Not very exciting.

Tuesday 21 February
Dinner with Andrew Knight.[20]

We had some interesting white New Zealand wine. It is very pleasant. I had never had New Zealand wine before.

The others were pleasant sort of business people [including] Ian Hay Davidson[21] who was in the great American accountants' firm and took over the running of Lloyd's, trying to clean it up. His wife said the corruption there was astonishing.

The Lloyd's people were amazed when he pointed out to them it was illegal for them as agents to use their clients' money for their own investments. Having made a profit with the investments, they put the money minus the profits back into their clients' accounts. I said I thought everybody knew that was against the law. They had asked Ian Hay Davidson where it said that in the new Act of Parliament regulating it. He said, 'It's not in that law. It's in the ten commandments.' Naturally they all hated him.

---

20. Editor, *Economist*, 1974–86; he became chief executive and editor-in-chief, *Daily Telegraph* and *Sunday Telegraph*, in 1986; m 2 (1975–91) Sabiha Malik; WW says later that he was born in New Zealand.

21. Managing partner, Arthur Andersen, 1966–82; deputy chairman and chief executive, Lloyd's, 1983–6.

Thursday 23 February

The guests were asked to come for the Queen Elizabeth dinner at 7.45 punctually. Instead, a number of them, including Willie Whitelaw and his wife,[22] arrived about half past seven while I was still decanting the 1940 Château Latour. This caused temporary confusion. Willie said, 'If you ask people to come punctually you must expect them to be punctual.' I forbore to point out that 7.45 would have been punctual, not earlier.

I waited, it was a little chilly, outside the gate for her car to arrive which it did on the dot of 8.00 p.m., she understanding better than Willie Whitelaw what punctuality is. She was looking very radiant in a flimsy white and blue long evening dress and wearing a necklace of what looked like diamonds and pearls. I said, 'How lovely your necklace is,' and she said, 'I always try to put something on for you. It was a present from Queen Mary.'

I made her the usual stiff dry martini with practically no martini and a hell of a lot of gin which I had soaked in ice while she was standing around talking to people. Once again she said it was much too strong so I added more ice to it. She said it was now better. She said, 'How lovely to have it in such a big glass. I can sip at it as much as I like and don't have to finish it.'

After ten minutes or so I asked her if she would like to sit down. She said no she was quite happy standing. I then produced Bernard Levin who was unaccountably shy and said, 'What do I do?' I said, 'Well go and stand by her where she can see you,' which he did. They then sat down in two chairs side by side and talked in some animation for a bit. When I thought Bernard had had long enough I produced Peter Shaffer [the playwright].

I greeted Peter Ustinov with a kiss on the cheek. He said, 'How very continental but it should be on both cheeks.' I said, 'All right,' and gave him another one on the other cheek. His wife[23] was dressed in some elegant embroidered concoction from Givenchy (about £1,000), bought for the occasion for which they had flown from France to be

---

22. Viscount Whitelaw (1918–99; created viscount 1983), Conservative politician, had in 1988 resigned as Leader of the House of Lords after suffering a stroke; m (1943) Cecilia, née Sprot.

23. Hélène du Lau d'Allemans m Peter Ustinov, the actor, dramatist and film director (knight 1990), in 1972, his third marriage.

at. She is French. She is a little plump. I thought Peter Ustinov had got thinner.

When Queen Elizabeth saw him she said, 'Oh I haven't seen you for a very long time,' which didn't exactly square with what he said to me when he said he had seen more of her than he had of me in recent years.

Because of the fourteen, not the usual twelve, we had lengthened the table with the introduction of a small table at one end. And put a table-cloth on. Queen Elizabeth said to me, 'I do like to see a table-cloth. One doesn't see them very often now and this is a very pretty one.'

We talked about Mrs Thatcher. She feels that people simply don't understand how compassionate and kind she is. I said, 'When she dashes off to scenes of disaster she does it because she feels she must because she feels so sorry for everybody.' She said, 'I know. We think she's wonderful.' I said how difficult it had been for her as a woman and a grocer's daughter becoming leader of the Tory Party with so many people who were both snobs and didn't like being run by a woman. She said, 'She has done it marvellously.' She recognizes, as obviously the Queen does, the terrific things she has done for the country.

She spoke of 'poor old Jim Callaghan'[24] and said of course he had got it all into a mess. She likes Jim Callaghan and he wants her to meet some of the younger brighter sparks of the Labour Party, the usual names. So I said, 'They won't be able to do anything unless they can change their defence policy and get a better policy about private enterprise.' But Jim is quite right in saying they have got some good ones now in the Commons.

She told me she was very cross with Nicholas Ridley.[25] His name came up when I said it was hard for people with his background, aristocratic and old family, and William Waldegrave's, to get into the government. She would only put them in strictly on merit. Queen Elizabeth said, 'They are putting up for sale to the highest bidder the beautiful Carolean Customs House on the quayside at Kings Lynn.'

She had written to Nicholas Ridley saying there was some society

---

24. Labour Prime Minister, 1976–9; life peer 1987.
25. (1929–93); life peer 1992; Conservative politician; Secretary of State for the Environment at this time; his father was 3rd Viscount Ridley, his mother the daughter of the architect Sir Edwin Lutyens.

who wanted to buy it but couldn't afford necessarily to match the highest bidder. She got a letter back – 'very bureaucratic', she said – turning her down.

He's a fairly graceless man, Nicholas Ridley. He banged on in his letter to her about this being the policy of the government to sell things to the highest bidder, irrespective of who or what they were.

She asked why Mrs Thatcher didn't go to the Derby because it would be a marvellous thing for her to do, a very popular action and everybody would be delighted. I said, 'The real reason is that she doesn't want to clash with the Queen. She thinks that's her day and she doesn't want to impinge upon her and she has a very great respect for the Queen,' to which Queen Elizabeth replied, 'Oh that wouldn't matter at all. The Queen wouldn't mind a bit. She would be delighted. Mrs Thatcher wouldn't be particularly seen. She would go to the Jockey Club area and to the Derbys' box and that kind of thing.' I said, 'Yes, maybe. I will ask her again,' which I will do.

I asked her if she knew Ali Forbes. She said yes and laughed a little. I said, 'He is a strange fellow and he repeats too much of what he hears. I nearly asked him to dinner but thought I wouldn't.' (I meant for tonight.)

'He has a story,' I said, 'that Harry Cust is Margaret Thatcher's grandfather. He lived at Belton a lot of the time near Grantham where the Brownlows live. (He was heir to the Brownlow barony at one point.) He used to go backwards and forwards to Belvoir as well and, as you know, Diana Cooper is reputed to have been his daughter.'[26]

She said, 'Yes, they always used to say about Ramsay MacDonald[27] that he was the illegitimate son of the Duke of Richmond which may have been the case.' I said, 'I thought it was a Scottish Duke.' She said, 'Well they are Scottish really. It's the Duke of Richmond and Gordon.' We speculated a little on the jolly possibility of Margaret Thatcher's grandmother, who worked in the house at Belton as some kind of a servant, being seduced by Harry Cust.

She liked the fish mousse very much but she only had a small helping. She eats like a bird. She didn't take much of the veal either.

---

26. Harry Cust (1861–1917) was a well-known philanderer, Conservative MP and editor of the *Pall Mall Gazette*. See Vol. 1, pp. 658–9.

27. First Labour prime minister, 1924 and 1929–35; he was the illegitimate son of a farm labourer and a servant girl, a fact made public in Horatio Bottomley's paper *John Bull*.

She was delighted though when the floating islands came – 'one of my favourites' – so she took a helping of that but not a large one and she ate it all.

She very much liked the claret and drank two or three glasses of it. The three bottles turned out to be just enough, though a number of people weren't drinking. She also liked the Chablis she had before which was a good one – my best, Alain Geoffroy 1984. Then came the question of whether she was going to have port. I told her it was Sandeman 1917 which I had just decanted or a 1943 bottle of Tokay Aszú (or both). She said throwing up her hands as in schoolgirl delight, 'You must tell me. I can't have both and I am not drinking port so much now these days.' That is certainly a new departure because not so long ago – perhaps less than a year – I saw her drinking quite a lot at a racecourse. So I had to choose for her that she would have the Tokay and she never had the wildly expensive bottle of Sandeman 1917.

During dinner we talked about the Duke of Edinburgh going to [Emperor] Hirohito's funeral.

She said did I know Laurens van der Post?[28] I said no but I knew what he had written about being in a prison camp and how the Japanese had treated our people like that because they thought they shouldn't be alive at all. It was a disgrace to surrender. They would have done the same to their own people. She said, 'Yes, that is what the difference is. But I do understand people's feelings about the Duke of Edinburgh going.'

I said, 'All the protesters almost certainly have Japanese cars and videos, television sets, radios, etc. made in Japan, so they are not exactly consistent.'

I talked to Queen Elizabeth about Amanda Cross, the Anglophile feminist American detective writer who is a professor in the Humanities at Columbia University.[29] I said I would send her some of her books.

At about half past ten Verushka hinted to her or gave her a look, as if to say, 'Would you like to leave the dining-room now?' She said,

---

28. (1906–96); South African-born writer, farmer, conservationist; mentor of Prince Charles.
29. Amanda Cross is the pseudonym of Carolyn Heilbrun, whose books published under her real name include studies of David Garnett and Christopher Isherwood, as well as *Towards Androgony* (1973) and *Representing of Women in Fiction* (1982).

'Oh I think Madame wants us to leave.' I said, 'Well not if you don't want to. You don't have to do what Verushka says.' She always calls Verushka 'Madame'. So off they trooped, the ladies.

We went back into the drawing-room at eleven.

Queen Elizabeth had been busy talking to all the ladies. She knows Hedwige's aunt[30] very well and stays with her in France.

At about twenty five to twelve she got up to go.

Friday 24 February
Went to see Gail Sheehy at her private hotel at 11 Cadogan Gardens. I had never been there before. Inside it was beautifully panelled, quiet and respectable, just like an Agatha Christie hotel.

I felt I had done about enough now but I was anxious to make sure that Gail got one thing in her head, that she [Mrs Thatcher] is not dictatorial but a great persuader. She likes arguments and she wants to convince people; and she won't move until she feels she has got enough conviction on her side and has persuaded them. No doubt people call her dictatorial but they are either bad arguers or can't stand up to her or she wins the argument – in which case they say she is dictatorial.

Mrs Sheehy gave me a cigar cutter from Asprey's to thank me for having arranged the interview with Mrs Thatcher. She had been prom-ised forty-five minutes and she actually got fifty-five minutes and she was amazed. She was very impressed with Mrs Thatcher, as well she might be.

Sunday 26 February
Allan Davis rang up very disconsolate. Windsor has turned the play down.

He is going to try Leatherhead.

Monday 27 February
I had a very jolly dinner at Pratt's where I haven't been for ages. I went with Alexander Hesketh[31] and together we took Hugh Trevor-Roper

---

30. Madame de La Barre de Nanteuil, wife of the French Ambassador.
31. 3rd Baron Hesketh; a government whip in the House of Lords at this time.*

(Lord Dacre)[32] who had never been there before. Ted Heath[33] was there and tolerably friendly, particularly when I complimented him on his great achievement of retail price maintenance being abolished and his inextricably getting us into the Common Market.

There was some talk about spirituality. I said you can't have a spiritual nature unless your material need is satisfied. How can you think about your soul if water is coming through the ceiling, you can't afford enough to eat, you can't pay the rent and you are going to the loo in an outside lavatory and wiping your bottom with old news-papers? Hugh Trevor-Roper said this is heresy. That is where spirituality is supposed to begin.

Martin Gilliat[34] came in and sat on my left.

He is seventy-five and wants to retire but can't because she [the Queen Mother] seems to like [him] going on for ever.

He said that she came the other night to Pratt's. The proprietor (the Duke of Devonshire) had said no one else should come to the Club that night but she should have a few friends to entertain, young people, her equerries and staff. She sat at the round table where we were sitting this evening and she drank quite a lot of port. I said 'That's very strange. She told me she had given up port.' So he laughed and said that it depends on her mood.

Tuesday 28 February
I decided to ring Margaret before leaving for Wigan because I didn't get her over the weekend as she had gone to see Mitterrand in France.

It was about ten to eight or just before when I rang her. I thought this would leave plenty of time to catch the train at 8.20 for the great opening of the new [Tote] Credit building by Douglas Hurd [in Wigan].

She said she gets on better with Mitterrand than she does with the others, meaning Kohl and co, though they are having an argument about the export of Nissan cars made in England to France. They are trying to resist them because they say there is not enough of the cars made in Britain.

I said Queen Elizabeth the Queen Mother had asked me, 'Why you don't go to the Derby?'

---

32. Regius Professor of Modern History, Oxford University, 1957–80; Master, Peter-house, Cambridge, 1980–7; life peer 1979.*
33. Mrs Thatcher's predecessor as Prime Minister.
34. (1913–93); he had been private secretary to the Queen Mother since 1956.

Margaret said, 'Oh did she really say that? When is the Derby?' and I said, 'Hang on I'll go and look in my racing diary.' Eventually I said, 'It's June 7th,' and she said, 'I'll see what I can do.'

She was amazed to hear that they were going so far [with democracy] in Hungary because she thought they were just going to have token parties.

It had got to nearly seven or eight minutes past eight. I dashed out of the house to arrive at the station when the train was just leaving.

I caught the 9.45. It was quite an amusing day. Douglas Hurd pulled the curtain from the plaque and I paid him a lot of compliments to which he replied, 'Flattery will get you nowhere.'

Sunday 5 March

Went to Bowden. Poor Arnold told me that he'd had a mild heart attack this morning. A great pain across his chest. I said, how did he know it wasn't indigestion? He said it might be a bit but it felt like the angina pain. I said, 'Haven't you got tablets for it?' He said, 'Yes, I've taken some. I don't look well do I?' I said, 'Not quite as good as you do sometimes.'

It is a lot to do with all these attacks on him, particularly the arrests they have made on Marconi[1] people, belatedly, for defrauding the government – which they have not been doing at all. It's only an accounting matter and any money which was due to the government has been paid to them. The real truth is the Ministry of Defence don't like GEC or Marconi making higher profits by their increased efficiency when they deal with a defence contract. In fact they often lose money and that particular branch of Marconi has been closed down because they have lost too much on defence contracts.

He said, how terrible it is to have worked all these years to build something up and then by implication to be accused of dishonesty. He said, 'I have never done a dishonest thing in my life.' I said, 'I know that's true. It was the same when the Tote was in trouble because some idiots, whom I knew nothing about, fiddled the dual forecast with no gain to themselves but because they thought they were doing something in the interest of the firm. But I just felt my conscience was clear and you should feel the same. I was very worried but that kept me bright in the circumstances.'

He said, 'Yes but I'm responsible for what goes on in the firm.' I said, 'You can't be responsible for everything. How can the National Westminster Bank Chairman be responsible for what a bank clerk may be doing in Penzance which is totally unauthorized? In any case, none of the people concerned with any mistakes at GEC/Marconi did it for personal gain.'

---

1. Marconi was a subsidiary of GEC.

During lunch we had been arguing about the Muslims' attempt to ban the Rushdie book [*The Satanic Verses*] and what religion meant.[2] He said he had now been drawn back into thinking of himself as Jewish again. I said, 'That's because you are getting older and you are affected by your upbringing. Your father was a very devout Jew and it's beginning to come back to you, even though you don't really believe in it.' He said no, he certainly didn't believe in any religion.

I think the argument and discussion cheered him up and got his mind going again. He was looking less in the dumps when I left.

When we got back at about six I rang Margaret but she was out.

At ten past eight she rang me. I said, 'Another dreadful train smash.'[3] She said, 'Yes, I thought I would go to the hospital and see the survivors and talk to people. I didn't want people to think that I only went to the very biggest crashes and neglected these smaller ones.'

I remarked that it had said on the news that the driver had admitted going through a red light. I said, 'You can't legislate for human error,' to which she agreed. Then she put her finger on the point immediately, as she always does: 'But why is it that, if the lights are against you, you can still go on?'

Tuesday 7 March
The Tote Annual Lunch.

There were about two hundred and sixty people this year, more than any other.

There was a good deal of laughter, particularly when I said I had known Ted Heath since I was at Oxford and that occasionally he disapproved of my admiration for a certain person. But otherwise we have never fallen out over a lady.

Roy [Jenkins] spoke very well as the guest speaker. Lots of jokes about me of the friendly kind. He said that he had appointed me in the first place[4] as he always thought, when he had the power of patronage, it was a good idea to appoint one's friends because you know all about them and if you don't have friends who are good, that is your look out.

---

2. The Ayatollah Khomeini's fatwa against Salman Rushdie had been issued on 14 February.
3. Four had died and more than eighty were injured in the Purley rail crash the previous day.
4. When Home Secretary in 1976.

Although I had a great deal of detail in about the Tote's stipulations on privatization, and what we would resist and what we actually favoured, I managed to get a few jokes in there, too.

Roy Jenkins made a joke about my humility to introduce one about Frank Longford.[5] He said he had even more humility than me. When he published a book on the subject of humility he was going past Hatchards in Piccadilly. He stopped, rushed into the shop and demanded to see the manager, to say angrily, 'Why aren't you displaying my book on humility in the windows of Hatchards?'

Wednesday 8 March

At last came the competition programme – the *Times* versus the *Guardian*.

I guessed that I was going to get Hungary and the October uprising. When it came to my turn for the specialist questions, I did better than anybody in either team of three. I answered every question correctly and got the maximum possible of sixteen points. That should have given us the means of winning because we were well ahead by this time. But then sadly, Sheridan Morley,[6] who is charming, fluffed one or two of his questions and Bernard [Levin] and he between them couldn't remember the music which Barbirolli wrote for some great occasion.[7]

Charlie Wilson came and sat in the audience which was very sweet of him.

Bernard said if he had the proverbial uncle who suddenly left him two or three million after dying in Australia, he would stop writing at once. I said, 'Good gracious why? Surely you want to say all the things you say.' He said, 'But that is not much now.' I said, 'Well I would go on writing, however rich I was, because I am a missionary and I just want everybody to do what I think they ought to do.'

Sheridan Morley is now writing Sir John Gielgud's biography but he doesn't want it to appear until after Gielgud is dead because it would be easier that way. He said he wrote one of Noël Coward. Noël

---

5. 7th Earl of Longford, Labour politician and prison reformer; *Humility* was published in 1969.
6. Author, journalist, broadcaster.
7. Sir John Barbirolli (1899–1970) was a conductor; though he made a few arrangements of classical music, WW here seems as confused as the rest of his team about the question.

Coward was very upset and said, 'I wish you hadn't put all that in about my being homosexual. Couldn't it have been left until after I was dead?'

Monday 13 March
She rang me back just before eight o'clock: 'I have been really upset and worried about all these little attacks on me saying, "We have become a grandmother." '

I said, 'It was only just an enthusiastic reaction to your being a grandmother. "*We've* become a grandmother" is a very normal thing to say. By the way I forgot to congratulate you on it. How is the boy?' She said, 'He is doing fine. The only thing is I can't see him because he's in America. But he is very well and so is the mother.'

She went on to A. N. Wilson's article in the *Spectator* this weekend. 'What is he complaining about? We are now being accused of being a nanny but if we don't do anything to regulate the things which he thinks should be regulated, we're told we are too much *laissez faire*.' I said, 'Take no notice of A. N. Wilson. I know him quite well and actually I have always liked him. He knows nothing whatever about politics. He writes good novels. He wrote a very good book about Tolstoy[8] and I am going to tell him off. He is just being silly.'

She was really very anxious that I spoke to her this morning. It was very much, 'Oh I am so glad you rang,' with her slightly schoolgirlish aspect which I am always very touched by. She needed some comfort.

Tuesday 14 March
Rang Andrew Neil last night to tell him not to worry about that bloody girl.[9] He wasn't married, he threw her out. It will only be a seven-day wonder and he shouldn't lose any sleep over it.

He said he was annoyed by the MP [Henry] Bellingham saying he gave the girl a Commons researcher's pass on the strength of a reference from an editor. People thought it was him but it was really Donald Trelford [editor of the *Observer*].

The girl, Pamella Bordes, tried to pursue Petronella at one time,

---

8. *Tolstoy*, published 1988, won the Whitbread Biography Award.
9. Pamella Bordes; see 30 January 1990 for the subsequent libel action Neil won because newspaper articles implied that he had known during his four-month affair with Mrs Bordes that she was a call-girl.

hoping to meet rich people through her. She actually came to the Tote Lunch some three years ago and sat at a table where she entertained various men who were much enthralled by her stunning looks. I never liked the look of her.

However, they are trying to make the Pamella girl a kind of Christine Keeler[10] which I don't think she is. Clearly the *News of the World*, when they taped her conversation when she turned up for one of their reporters, willing to go to bed with him for £500 and took off all her clothes, must be on pretty safe ground. Or they wouldn't have dared publish their scoop on Sunday. Certainly not after the *Star* lost half a million pounds to Jeffrey Archer by getting the facts wrong over his relationship with the tart.[11]

People are getting into a silly mood nowadays. Last night at Roy Jenkins' party for his book, Robin Day[12] said for the first time he thought she, Margaret, might not win the next election, she was losing her grip.

'Do you belong to the "Has Margaret gone mad group"?' I was asked several times.

Went to a party given at Carlton House Gardens by Douglas Hurd and his wife.

Nicholas Ridley introduced his wife to me. I thought she was very pretty. I said, 'You are prettier than he deserves,' in front of them both. He said he didn't agree with that but then he always is somewhat arrogant.

By the time we left to go to the River Café I had had too many little bits to eat but only one glass of champagne.

The food [there] was good as to the first course but not very nice as to the second course which was some kind of fillet of beef in a gravy, all very over-cooked. The third course included a zabaglione ice cream which was OK. I ate and drank too much and was quite woozy by the time we left.

---

10. The call-girl whose relationship with John Profumo, when Secretary of State for War in 1963, and his subsequent lie about it to the House of Commons, helped to discredit the Macmillan government.
11. Jeffrey Archer, Conservative politician and best-selling author, won his libel action over this matter in 1987.*
12. Television and radio journalist; knight 1981.

Margouch Gorky, widow of the painter,[13] now married to Xan Fielding,[14] said she remembered – I suppose it must have been something like thirty years ago – my driving her to stay with Mary Campbell[15] for a weekend. I had never stayed at the house before.

When I arrived I sat in the car blowing the horn and she said, 'Are you expecting somebody to come and collect the luggage?' I said, 'Yes,' and she said, 'Well you won't find that in this house.'

She seemed to think that was very funny.

It is just the physical blankness and weariness of it. These necessary tasks make me more tired, if I have to do them, than anything else. This is not just laziness, it is an incapacity for them.

Wednesday 15 March
Lunch at No 1 Carlton Gardens. The second function there two days running. This time Geoffrey Howe presided over a little luncheon for the Hungarian Foreign Minister.

On my left was Mr Appleyard from the British Embassy. He was the Ambassador who came with me to see Mr Pozsgay and I thought he was a tiresome little man then.

He said that my articles on Hungary were absolutely brilliant and he couldn't understand how I had discovered so much and understood so much in so short a time.

So I told him I had seen one or two of the people he had invited to his reception and thanked him for that.

I felt much better about him than I had before when I met him in Hungary.

Geoffrey Howe made a little speech. Fairly felicitous in his quiet droll way, making little jokes but speaking warmly of Hungary and his guest with whom he is having discussions. He referred to people longing for a small nation and the Welsh identifying themselves a little with the Hungarians. He is proud of being Welsh which I find attractive.

---

13. Arshile Gorky (1904–48), American abstract expressionist painter, born in Turkish Armenia.
14. (Major) Alexander Fielding (d 1991), travel writer, previously married to Daphne, mother of Caroline (Duchess of Beaufort).
15. Daughter of 5th Earl of Rosslyn, m 1 (1933–44) Sir Philip Dunn, m 2 (1945–59) Robin Campbell, and she remarried, her fourth marriage (1969), Sir Philip Dunn (d 1976).

I got a very tough letter from him over Hong Kong passports. He is by no means soft.

To Mickey Suffolk's.[16] He showed me four bottles of white wine before dinner. Which did I want? One was Chassagne-Montrachet; another was Pavillon Blanc which is the white wine of Margaux; one I can't remember and the fourth was Grillet, a fabulous wine sold at Les Pyramides. I plumped for that. It's about £60 a bottle but it's bloody good.

He also gave us La Conseillante 1970 and La Gaffalière 1970. They were both extremely good. I got a bit drunk as we had champagne first and of course I had had the Château Montrose 1970 at lunchtime, so it was a day for drinking 1970 claret of superb quality. We began with enormous helpings of caviar which was very agreeable. Really huge dollops, about double the size of the larger little pots one gets at Fortnum's.

The house was comfortable but our bedroom and the bathroom were blinding hot and I didn't know how to turn the heat off or down. I suppose if I hadn't been a bit woozy I might have found out how to do it.

Thursday 16 March

It was snowing on the way to Cheltenham and it was very likely the whole meeting was going to be called off. They made a decision at twelve and on we went.

We had a record take for the meeting. It came to £4.2 million which was £1.1 million up on the year before for the three days. The jackpot wasn't won at £119,000 and everything was a tremendous success. Ho ho ho.

I sat next to Queen Elizabeth [the Queen Mother] at lunch.

I told her about trying to get passports for the Hong Kong people and how they felt badly that we had let them down. When I said we had a debate coming up in the Lords, she was very pleased. I said to her, 'Don't say anything about it but she's egging me on. She [Mrs Thatcher] says to me that somehow she has to get her two Ministers to do something about it, the Foreign Secretary and the Home Secretary, but they are very difficult about it.' She just put her fingers to

---

16. 21st Earl of Suffolk and Berkshire; m 3 (1983) Linda Viscountess Bridport, née Paravicini.

her lips and said, 'No, I won't say a word,' in a charming conspiratorial way.

We talked about Rupert Murdoch a bit. She said, 'He's against us isn't he? He doesn't like us.' I said, 'He thinks you are absolutely marvellous and the Queen does a splendid job but it is the others he doesn't like.' 'Ah yes,' she said. 'That's why he runs so many scandals in his newspaper.' I said, 'Yes that is so. But of course he is really a puritan,' and I told her about him being a son of the manse and [how] he thinks that they should all behave themselves better.

I said I had had an argument with Norman Tebbit about Rupert Murdoch and the scandals and sensations they published about people's private lives. I had said, 'Of course you are taking a very élitist position. In the old days "everybody" knew what Palmerston was doing, chasing every girl into the bedrooms at every country house; and that no woman under fifty, if they were at all passable, was safe alone with Lloyd George in the room. Of course it wasn't generally known but everyone in top social circles enjoyed the gossip. Now you are saying that though democracy has widened and people are apparently better educated, they are not yet fit to be told what is going on, although it is very amusing.'

She thought I had a point there. But I said, 'I still don't like it. There is something rather distasteful about it. It was better when only a few of us knew about it.'

Then I said, about Princess Michael (I whispered to her because she was in the room on the other side) that she used to keep on ringing me up when she was in difficulties and saying couldn't I get Rupert to get the newspapers to lay off. And he would say to me, 'She'll have no trouble at all if she behaves herself.' Queen Elizabeth was quite amused. I said, 'I told her to pipe down, not make so many statements on television, and keep her head down for a bit, and I think she has been doing that.'

I said, 'I like her.' She said, 'She doesn't quite understand our ways but she is really quite good and has a good heart.'

We talked about books. She said had I read Evelyn Anthony who was a good detective writer.[17] I said, 'No.' She said, 'Ah well, there is

---

17. Evelyn Anthony writes espionage and psychological thrillers as well as historical romances (for example, *The Tamarind Seed*, made into a film).

one I have found for you.' I might have a look. And I told her about
S. S. Van Dine[18] and said I would send her one of those books.

I told her how wonderful she looked today with her very pretty
blue hat and her blue coat and dress. I said, 'I have seen that brooch
at the top before. What about that little one lower down?' It was
pinned on what I suppose you call her cleavage. 'Oh,' she said, very
sweetly, 'that was given me by the King. It was my engagement present
and it's got a naval insignia on it. He was in the Navy. He loved being
in the Navy. It's not valuable you know, not really. But I like to keep
it and I like to wear it on special occasions.'

During lunch I had been wondering whether to suggest asking
Rupert to dinner when she came one night but I thought perhaps she
wouldn't like it. She said, 'Oh yes, I think I would like it. I have only
met him once and he seemed interesting.'

So we will arrange for him to come to dinner.

After lunch Nicholas Soames came up. He had been staying with
Queen Elizabeth and they are quite friends. I said, his bookmaker's
suit was almost as good as my tie.

Desert Orchid ran a fabulous race. The crowd nearly went crazy.

If the second, Yahoo, had won the crowd would probably have
torn the horse to pieces.

Prince Michael did the rounds with me and Geoffrey Webster [Tote
public relations director] after the first race.

He is very good when talking to the staff and taking an interest. He
also came with me to the little tent which the BBC have to do interviews
and he listened to my being interviewed about privatization of the
Tote.

When I said to the Queen Mother that Princess Michael wasn't
such a bad girl, I quite like her and think she is jolly, Queen Elizabeth
said, 'Yes. I saw her give you two kisses.' 'Oh,' I replied, 'did you think
that one would have been enough?' She said, 'Yes. I think it would
have been,' and smiled as though much amused. She misses nothing.

---

18. The pen name of Willard Huntington Wright (1888–1939), American journalist,
    editor and critic whose first crime novel was *The Benson Murder Case*. Philo
    Vance was his rich, snobbish detective, with an affected British accent, notably
    portrayed in films by William Powell.

Saturday 18 March

William Golding[19] and his wife came to lunch [at Bonython in Cornwall, with WW's brother Robert].

He said he was thinking of another book but he doesn't work to a regular pattern, so many words a week like Trollope. He said he thought Trollope wasn't very good and thought C. P. Snow[20] was better on politics. I said, 'Good gracious I don't think he is anywhere near the mark of Trollope. Trollope really understood politics and I don't think C. P. Snow understood them at all with his "corridors of power" stuff.' I knew Snow quite well and considered him naïve and ill-informed about politics, no insight at all.

John St Levan[21] was there with his agreeable wife.

St Levan said, 'Can't we get something done about A. L. Rowse?[22] He is a great Cornishman writer, historian, etc.' I said, 'What do you mean?' He said, 'Something like a Companion of Honour.' I said, 'I doubt if they would give him that, or the OM. But why doesn't the Lord Lieutenant do something about it?' (He is coming to dinner tomorrow evening – Lord Falmouth.)[23]

When we were sitting in the drawing-room after lunch, I asked William Golding whether he would sign my books of his and he said yes. I decided to read chunks of his address on getting the Nobel Prize out loud. Some of it was very funny and everybody was shrieking with laughter, himself, William Golding, included.

He only came to live in Cornwall, though he was born in Cornwall, to get away from journalists and reporters and the media who would pester him the whole time when he lived in Hampshire. It is much

---

19. (1911–93); author; awarded Nobel Prize for Literature 1983; m (1939) Ann, née Brookfield; knight 1988.
20. (1905–80); civil servant, author and Labour politician (Parliamentary Secretary, Ministry of Technology, 1964–6); life peer 1964. His 1964 novel *Corridors of Power* was one of a sequence under the general title 'Strangers and Brothers'.
21. 4th Baron St Levan, owner of St Michael's Mount, Cornwall; m (1970) Susan, née Kennedy.
22. (1903–97); Cornish-born historian and author; Fellow of All Souls College, Oxford. He identified from the Forman papers the dark lady of Shakespeare's sonnets as Emelia Lanier, daughter of an Italian musician. With his many interests and decided opinions, he was a controversial figure among academics. He was appointed Companion of Honour in 1997, shortly before he died.
23. 9th Viscount Falmouth; Lord Lieutenant of Cornwall, 1977–94; m (1953) Elizabeth Price Browne.

more difficult for them to come to Cornwall. They can't descend on him to have lunch or try to. (He felt he had to give them some lunch sometimes.)[24]

He is very pleased with the house where he is now. He said it used to belong to Princess Bibesco[25] and did I know anything about her. I said, 'Yes, I knew her and her daughter who was a journalist.' He said the Princess had a reputation for promiscuity but [people] didn't mind it in so grand a lady as they do in someone like Pamella Bordes.

I told Golding how encouraging it was that he was writing books at such a great age, even older than me. I said I keep looking up the people who went on writing well, very late, like Bernard Shaw and so on. Golding was forty-three (now seventy-seven and a half) when he wrote his first novel. He is very lively, rather short, a quizzical face, darting eyes, grey beard. He moves quickly, a little like a bird.

He started as a schoolmaster. It lasted for ten years and he hated it. So I said, 'Don't you understand children from that?'[26] He said, 'Not really. I understand children because I was a child,' and I said, 'You have remained one. You strike me as somebody who never grew up really. Remains young, however old.'

We parted on terms of some affection.

When he went down the steps, he said, 'I hope we shall have some more nice quarrels.' He enjoys an argument, fighting back when I said that Mrs Thatcher was the leader of the environmentalists both national and global, a thought which had not really occurred to him before. He is not too keen on her.

David Harris MP[27] and his wife came to Bonython at about twenty-five past seven. We drank some excellent Piper Heidsieck 'Rare' 1976 champagne. Then we went out to dinner.

During dinner and afterwards he had talked about life in the Commons and being PPS to Sir Geoffrey Howe. Geoffrey Howe takes enormous care when writing a speech; he sits with about four people

24. Golding described the unwelcome attentions of an aspiring biographer in *The Paper Men* (1984).

25. Née Elizabeth Asquith (d 1945), daughter of Asquith the Prime Minister; author of plays, poems, short stories and novels; m (1919) Prince Antoine Bibesco (1878–1951), from the Romanian former royal family.

26. Golding's first novel (1954), *Lord of the Flies*, was about schoolboys surviving on a desert island.

27. For St Ives, 1983–97.

and they go through it over and over again. It's just like Mrs Thatcher but the result is not so good, though it's not wholly dim.

He said, 'I do hope you tell her not to go around saying things like "We're a grandmother." ' I said, 'That was a very natural, girlish expression and she has got a charming girlish side.'

He said, 'Some of the colleagues are a bit wobbly but there is nothing serious. They have been worried about water privatization.'

They lived just outside the constituency, not in it, because they didn't want to have the constituents on top of them all the time but wanted to be near enough to be available when needed. They are all involved tremendously in these ghastly surgeries these days.

Sunday 19 March

Rang Margaret and I was put straight through this time, without any ringing back to make certain it was me and not an impostor.

I congratulated her on her Saturday's speech.

She said, 'I'm glad it's out of the way now. I always feel a bit edgy when I have got a big speech to make. It hangs like a little weight at the back of one's head.'

I know that very well. I have got the Hong Kong speech sitting on the back of my head now. I talked to her about Hong Kong and said that Peter Carrington[28] had promised to come down and may even say something.

We briefly discussed the Budget.

She said she thought it was very much a time for caution: 'After all, paying back the National Debt of £14 billion means we save one and a half billion interest a year which can all be used to reduce taxes later.'

She said, 'John Smith[29] was an awful flop on the Budget.' I replied, 'I think Gordon Brown[30] is quite effective in a low level way.' She said, 'Yes but there is no real thought content in it,' and I agree with her about that. She also dislikes Robin Cook[31] for his destructive approach with nothing solid as an alternative.

---

28. 6th Baron Carrington, Conservative politician; Foreign Secretary, 1979–82.
29. (1938–94); he succeeded Neil Kinnock as Leader of the Labour Party and the Opposition in 1992 but at this time was principal Opposition spokesman on Treasury and Economic Affairs.
30. At this time shadow Chief Secretary to the Treasury.
31. At this time shadow spokesman on health.

No one came to lunch so we treated ourselves to a Château Lafite 1966, one of the very great years. We decanted it with loving care.

The cook they got for the weekend is fabulous.

My brother has been using her from time to time over the past few years and, as it was his birthday weekend and I was on what was jokingly called 'a state visit', she was produced for the occasion.

After lunch Robbie [WW's nephew] and I walked round to the lake.

Robbie said, 'I suppose you will retire some time. Would you like to come and live here?'

I said, 'Well where would I put my books?' He said, 'We'd move them to the library we'd make. You would have everything you wanted here.'

He said that after all the harum scarum he would settle down in a more level course. He is taking a great deal of interest in Cornish Spring Water which we may have a chance of developing into something really worthwhile. Robbie with his usual enthusiasm talks of making half a million profit a year which I feel is not very likely, at least for a long time.

The little piece of land he sold at the Lizard, the opening bid for it was £330,000 but he thinks he may get £400,000, clear off his debts and have something left behind.

I wonder whether I would really like to live at Bonython. It's a hell of a long way away. I suppose I could live in one of the little houses where the old stables or mews were, though it would need a good deal of alteration. I should think Verushka would hate it but it is not an impossible notion as a fall-back.

I have been thinking of my old cousin Molly.

In the dining-room I see again the curious church harmonium which she had on the right, facing as you come in. She used to play hymns on it very badly on a Sunday and even on other days.

In the walled garden I thought of Cousin Molly again, doing her gardening at half past six in the morning in the summer and then coming and eating her breakfast, beginning with porridge and huge lashings of wonderful Cornish cream which I am afraid I ate some of today at lunch – it was so good. Then she would have steak. Then she would have bacon and eggs and sausages and then she would have large quantities of toast and marmalade. She was as round as she was tall, fairly short. But she lived until around ninety.

George Falmouth who is coming to dinner in a moment[32] is the largest landowner in Cornwall.

He is building a £100 million airport (not all his own money of course) to be near Redruth. It would be convenient if it were to be built in my lifetime.

The airport is to be built on a spot of waste land, derelict tin mines. The idea would be to have some new industries coming there and be able to service them and all the rest of it. But the local people are protesting because they say they are a part of history. The tin mines are deep in the consciousness of the Cornish. Indeed, the very house I am staying in only came into our family through the activities of Captain Lyle and his brothers and cousins who were all tin mine owners.

George Falmouth, the 'Lord Loot' as he calls himself, is podgy and a bit deaf. It was difficult to get him to hear everything I was saying. But his wife was pleasant enough, an expert on gardens. Rather plain but with a mild amount of animation.

Falmouth said, that he had written to No 10 about giving A. L. Rowse an honour last October but got a brush off. He asked me to write via Margaret.

Rowse has irritated people quite a lot but he is clearly a considerable Cornishman. The Cornish feel that London always neglects them.

Monday 20 March
There was a board meeting for Cornish Spring Water. I think it is getting on reasonably well and it may be a big success. The question is whether to spend a lot more money to develop the production.

Party at the Garrick Club given by Peregrine Worsthorne. Moyra Fraser was there with her husband. She is Mrs [Roger] Lubbock in real life. She looks far older than he. She is a one-time successful actress who can't find a play.

Catherine Amery[33] was there. She had limped up the stairs with her stick. Julian arrived later. Catherine is looking fairly bright but she was almost totally crippled.

---

32. WW did not regularly record his diary at the end of each day but would pick up his 'voice machine' to fill in a few minutes if he was alone, continuing the story later, if necessary.
33. Lady Catherine Amery (d 1991), daughter of Prime Minister Harold Macmillan, m (1950) Julian Amery, Conservative politician.*

Paul Johnson[34] was there but he barely deigns to speak to me. He doesn't like me because he is jealous of my connection with Mrs T.

Wednesday 22 March

It seems that David Stevens'[35] wife, Melissa, did not have a massive heart attack as I had thought. The coroner's inquest showed that she choked on a small piece of peach when she was sitting on the loo at about 6 in the morning. David Stevens heard her breathing very heavily, went in and thought she was looking strange and rang for an ambulance. By the time they had got to the hospital she was about dead. Very odd.

[I was told] he lived a very strange life with Melissa.

She much preferred her ex-husband to David, according to [the] story, and she only married David because he was rich.

I find it hard to believe this story in its entirety. I remember seeing them when it was not known that anyone was watching them, walking along hand in hand at Cagnes-sur-Mer looking very happy and cheerful. She must have been a very good actress if this is all true.

There is a little trouble with Mr Pozsgay. He doesn't want to come to England unless he can have half an hour alone with Mrs Thatcher. I suppose I had better ask her if she is willing to do that but I can't do it until next weekend when I speak to her again.

Mrs Tamborero[36] very kindly stayed until extremely late while we hacked out the speech [on Hong Kong].

Irvine of Lairg,[37] who is going to speak for the opposition at the House, asked me for a copy of it and they collected it for his barristers' chambers so he could read it that evening.

Thursday 23 March

About twenty or so peers came to the chamber [for WW's question on Hong Kong] and eight spoke.

What was interesting was that of all those that spoke, not one

---

34. Writer and journalist (editor, *New Statesman*, 1965–70), he moved from left to right of the political spectrum.
35. Chairman, United Newspapers, since 1981, Express Newspapers, since 1985; m 2 (1977) Melissa Milicevich (d 1989); life peer 1987.
36. Wendy Tamborero, WW's secretary since the beginning of 1989.
37. QC; shadow Lord Chancellor, 1992–7; Lord Chancellor since 1997; life peer 1987.

supported the government except the Minister, Glenarthur, who is a drip and doesn't understand the situation. That poor fellow was only retailing what the Foreign Office said he was to say.

Friday 24 March
Yesterday in the House, while I was waiting to make my speech, Baroness Blackstone[38] came in and sat talking for a few minutes to Irvine of Lairg who was waiting to support me. I saw her look across at me once or twice, as did he. When she got up to go, she handed me a little note which said, 'Thank you so much for the nice review of *Inside the Think Tank*. William Plowden and I were very pleased when we read it. I am glad you enjoyed the book. Thank you too for the nice things you said, about me. You flattered me more than I deserve. Tessa B.'

That was the bit when I referred to her as beautiful and brilliant Baroness Blackstone. Both the adjectives were correct. I think she must have been very surprised at my being so favourable to her activities in the Think Tank, considering that she is an ardent Thatcher hater.

Also the other day in the Lords, Ted Short thanked me for my review of his book about being Chief Whip to Wilson. He said he was very surprised and pleased that I wrote so kindly about it. I don't know why people are surprised when I disagree with their views but write nice things about their books.

Saturday 25 March
Went to stay with the Trees for the night.

It is always difficult ringing Margaret when staying away. Eventually I left a message for her. She rang at about 8.00 a.m. I had to stand in a passage but nobody could overhear.

She is going to Africa to visit six countries on Monday early in the morning. That's why I wanted to catch her on Saturday because I thought she would be very busy on Sunday.

She asked me how I got on with my debate about Hong Kong.

---

38. Tessa Blackstone, life peer 1987. At this time Master, Birkbeck College, University of London; Opposition spokesman in the Lords for education and science; chairman, Institute for Public Policy Research (IPPR), of which William Plowden, at this time Visiting Professor in Government, LSE (London School of Economics), became senior research associate, 1992–4. Their book was *Inside the Think Tank: Advising the Cabinet 1971–83*.

She was interested, very, that MacLehose, a former governor of Hong Kong [1971–82], supported me on the passport issue. 'Did he really?' she said, with pleased surprise. I shall have to continue this fight.

I told her that Mr Pozsgay would very much like to have half an hour alone with he when he comes on April 25th. I didn't tell her he wouldn't come if he didn't get that because of his loss of face in Budapest without an interview with her.

She said, 'I will find half an hour for him but please don't tell my staff until I come back.'

I asked her about the Derby. She said, 'Oh, I felt I had to refuse because it's in the middle of the Euro elections and I have got a speaking campaign for the Euro MPs; it would look very bad if I went to the Derby.'

I said, 'Perhaps you will come next year?' She said, 'We'll see what things are like then.' I think that somebody must have put her off but I don't know who. It's a pity because it would identify her with ordinary people in a very telling way if she were seen enjoying herself at the Derby.

Tuesday 28 March

At last I did my boring chore for the Conservative Central Office publication commemorating ten years of Mrs Thatcher's government in May. It is so irritating having to write 1,600 words, first of all for nothing, and secondly to think it all out. They wanted me to deal with the egghead attacks on her and how she had disposed of them. I don't know why people think you should give your time for absolutely nothing. If I had written this for a magazine, I would have charged at least £1,000 to £1,500 for it.

Wednesday 29 March

Lunch with Swires. Sir Adrian Swire is the head man. They have been at it since the 18th century.

They employ twenty thousand people in Hong Kong, the largest employers. They also employ three thousand in Taiwan. They are frightfully pleased with my endeavour to get something done for the poor old Hong Kong Chinese about passports. They think that they will not feel so badly abandoned by the British after my efforts. But why was I interested?

I said I was interested since I went to the opening of the Shah Tin racecourse and found what a marvellous place Hong Kong was. I have always been concerned about injustice and the way the Hong Kong Chinese had been treated by having their rights and passports taken away from them was gross injustice.

In the afternoon Rupert rang saying had he read correctly that Gorbachev is coming to London on April 5th? I said, 'Yes that is right.' He said nothing but I think he was wondering whether to ask me if I could get an invitation for him to a reception at 10 Downing Street. But I didn't propose to offer that. I had had enough trouble doing it last time when the Gorbachev visit was cancelled.[39]

Friday 31 March

Jack Logan repeated a bit out of a previous *Sporting Life* 'Weekender' suggesting that Lloyds Merchant Bank are going to recommend selling the betting shops and 'giving the Tote back to the racecourses'. This, added Logan, in his rather nasty little piece, will give Lord Wyatt a shock. Well it certainly would if it were carried out.

There could well be some trouble coming up at the Tote and for myself. It is a bit depressing but I suppose there is no point in worrying about it until there is something I have to oppose.

In the evening we saw *The Vortex*. Anne Lambton[40] was the second principal girl, Maria Aitken being the principal one. Anne performed very well. I hadn't realized how good an actress she was.

I could see gleams of the wit that was to develop in Noël Coward peeping through.

[The play] was only a success originally because for the first time people openly talked about mothers having lovers the same age as their sons and the sons taking drugs. That hadn't been done on the English stage before.

---

39. In December 1988. See Vol. 1, pp. 673 and 681.
40. Actress daughter of Tony Lambton.

Sunday 2 April

Spoke to Margaret. It was just after five o'clock in the afternoon. She had got back from her great African trip this morning.

I asked her whether she thought that South Africa would change now that President Botha is retiring.[1] She said, 'They know they've got to.' I said, 'But I don't think one man one vote is necessarily the answer.' She agreed but she thought there was some way of doing it.

On the issue of releasing Mandela I said, 'Its quite absurd. It's a matter of pride on both sides. Mandela won't agree to non-violence if he is released and the South African government won't release him unless he does agree to it.' She quickly said, 'They lose all sympathy if they start violence again.'

We talked about Gorbachev's visit on Wednesday. 'That is very important,' she said. I said, 'I don't think he has been harmed by the way the elections went in Russia.' She answered, 'They strengthened his hand.' I said, 'But he still doesn't want multi-party elections.' She said, 'No, he wants a Socialist state still.' I said, 'But they must know that is impossible. They will never get anything done unless they have private enterprise.' She said, 'But the difficulty is to persuade them all to understand about private enterprise. It is just like here. A lot of people don't want to be entrepreneurs. They just want safe secure jobs.'

I said, 'I've been wondering how much money we ought to give them from the West to help them.' She said very firmly, 'Not too much.' I agree with her. She went on, 'If we give them too much money or lend them too much, they will never do it all for themselves and they will rely on us to help them out the whole time.'

---

1. P. W. Botha had been President since 1984 and Prime Minister, 1978–84; he was succeeded by F. W. de Klerk.

Monday 3 April

Andrew Neil was disappointed Willie Whitelaw had not said more about Mrs Thatcher, his difficulties with her, in his book which the *Sunday Times* is serializing. So he is sending Brian Walden[2] along to interview him. Willie thinks that Andrew Neil wants to get some political and excitingly damaging remarks about Mrs Thatcher from him. But he said to send Brian Walden to interview him on the subject of Mrs Thatcher is ridiculous because Brian Walden is so pro Mrs Thatcher.

Tuesday 4 April

On the committee stage of the Official Secrets Bill, Hugh Thomas[3] moved an amendment which would allow those who had been engaged in secret service work to write about it if they got the permission of the Secretary of State who could not refuse such permission unless he was reasonably satisfied that it would be a danger to security.

I like Hugh Thomas. He is unctuous in an agreeable Welsh way. Not quite so much as George Thomas, the ex-Speaker, and not as good as he at the flattery and 'subject people' Welsh approach. He spoke hesitatingly, fumblingly but he got in a number of good points.

He was appointed to the Lords by Mrs Thatcher because he was working in the Conservative Party Policy Centre or some such Conservative organization, having previously been an ardent Labour supporter. I remember well his writing about the Spanish Civil War from a left angle and about John Strachey in an admiring manner in his biography.[4]

Once again I thought how much I like Hugh Trevor-Roper who speaks with a boyish charm though he was head of a Cambridge college and a Regius Professor of History at Oxford. He looks slight and perky as though his remarkable brain is not quite matured and he is using it not as a man of wisdom but as a man of jokey provocation. He had a long analogy between people who broke through security barriers and moths breaking through a hole in a blanket, finishing with

---

2. Former Labour MP; television journalist and presenter, ITV's *Weekend World*.
3. Historian; chairman (1979–90), Centre for Policy Studies, a conservative 'think-tank' founded by Sir Keith Joseph in 1974; life peer 1981.
4. *The Spanish Civil War* was published in 1961; his biography of John Strachey (1901–63; Minister of Food, 1946–50; Secretary of State for War, 1950–1, with WW his Under-Secretary, May to October 1951) was published in 1973.

the strong migratory moth which sometimes goes right through the hole to distant parts, referring to Peter Wright.[5]

Spoke to Alan Hare.[6] I decided almost to give up drinking Latour because of the sale by Pearsons of Château Latour to Allied Lyons. Alan Hare, I thought, must have been deposed as Chairman of Latour. On the contrary, he is continuing under the new ownership to go on being Chairman and living in the house.

The part that Pearsons had in it twenty-six years ago cost them £600,000. They have now sold it for £56 million.

At about 11.30 p.m. Rupert rang. He has been heavily engaged in London. He is planning to raise money for his new world-wide media venture. He is going to see Arnold [Weinstock] tomorrow. I said, 'I don't know if he will be interested.' To which he replied, 'He has got plenty of money hasn't he?' But I was thinking that he hates the *Sunday Times* and Andrew Neil because he feels they are all against him and cause a lot of trouble for him. However, maybe he might think this is the way of neutralizing Rupert's newspapers so that he will put some money into one of his ventures.

Thursday 6 April
Suddenly the government announce in a special statement that they are going to abolish the National Dock Labour Scheme forthwith. They have published a White Paper and the introduction of the Bill will follow tomorrow. Labour is caught on the hop, defending a ludicrous out-of-date restricted practice system whereby dockers are paid even while doing nothing.

I think I have had a lot to do with it. I wrote a big article in the *Times* in mid December[7] and kept pressing Margaret about it: why on earth be afraid of there being a strike if they were to announce ending such an appalling scheme?

---

5. In 1986 the British government failed to persuade the Australian courts to ban Wright's autobiography *Spycatcher*, with its revelations about British security services.
6. The Hon. Alan Hare (1919–95), chairman, *Financial Times*, 1978–84; director, Pearson Longman, 1975–83, the *Economist*, 1975–89; president, Société Civile du Vignoble du Château Latour, 1983–90.*
7. 14 December 1988, headed 'Unload These Passengers'; see Vol. 1, p. 679.

Michael Tree rang up and said, 'I've got a marvellous piece of gossip for you. Charlie Benson[8] says that the *Daily Mail* got hold of pictures of Colin Moynihan[9] with Pamella Bordes and rang him up and said they had these pictures. He said, 'What are you going to do with them?' They said, 'Publish them.' He said, 'Do you think that would be wise?' When they asked why he replied, 'I've got pictures of Lord Rothermere[10] naked with Pamella Bordes.'

On the television this evening – *Sky News* – there was a fascinating discussion with Sir Bryan Carsberg.[11] He explained better than I have ever heard it explained how a government publicly owning an industry cannot regulate it properly. He is the head of OFTEL and he has done amazing things to improve British Telecom because it is outside the government and outside the industry and can compel them to do things which they didn't do before.

I think I must tell Margaret what a splendid man he is and to keep an eye on him for something far better.

In the evening Isabel Derby[12] rang at half past ten. Would I go to have lunch with them at the Grand National? I said I doubted it. It was so wet and cold, the ground was so soft they might even call the race off and I had too much to do. She went on pressing away. She is such a jolly girl and I was very happy to talk to her, spreading her little brightness on the wintry evening here.

She was very excited about going to Venice on Monday.

She said, 'They told me to bring flat walking shoes but I hate sight-seeing.' I said, 'Take no notice. You can do all the sight-seeing you want by sitting in St Mark's Square. Napoleon said it was the finest drawing-room in Europe.'

Friday 7 April

Went to the Lords. I wanted to hear the barristers and the judges complaining about the Lord Chancellor's sensible reform proposals.

---

8. Racing journalist.
9. Conservative MP, 1983–92; Minister for Sport at this time.
10. 3rd Viscount Rothermere (1925–98); chairman, Associated Newspapers (*Daily Mail*, *Mail on Sunday* etc.), from 1970.
11. Arthur Andersen Professor of Accounting, LSE, 1981–7; Director General of Telecommunications, 1984–92; Director General of Fair Trading, 1992–5; knight 1989.
12. Countess of Derby (1920–90).*

They sounded like the Transport and General Workers enraged by the end of the National Dock Labour Scheme. Arnold Goodman[13] was one of the few who spoke balanced sense.

Sunday 9 April
Rather irritating. In Bruce Anderson's *Sunday Telegraph* weekly political article he writes about the idea that Roy Jenkins might have become Chancellor of the Exchequer in her (Mrs Thatcher's) first government.

He goes on, 'About that time, I asked Woodrow Wyatt – then as now a confidant of Margaret Thatcher's – whether Geoffrey Howe would be Chancellor. "I believe he will, and I'll tell you why. She used to say to me: 'What am I going to do about Geoffrey's wife, and that dreadful Commission of hers?' She wouldn't be worried about Elspeth being on the Equal Opportunities Commission unless she thought of Geoffrey as her Chancellor." So it proved; on Sir Geoffrey's appointment to the Treasury, Lady Howe resigned from the EOC.'[14]

I hope she either hasn't seen that or is not bothered if she has. I don't recollect the conversation. I hardly knew of Anderson at the time except that he was something to do with the research centre at the Conservative Office which Mrs Thatcher had removed and he was then anti-Mrs Thatcher. If I did say anything of that kind, and certainly what he says is true in essence, it would have been on a strictly confidential basis.

We had discussed it quite frequently and she was very interested in it, having some doubts about Geoffrey Howe at the time and recognizing how good Roy Jenkins had been at cutting expenditure.

Today nothing is held secret. Poor Princess Anne had some letters stolen written to her by an equerry at the Palace. They are very personal and intimate we are told. Possibly they were love letters and dealt with some romance she had been having with him. I don't blame the poor girl married to that dim fellow Mark Phillips. It is appalling that she can't do anything without some beastly person stealing her private letters. They were sent anonymously to the *Sun* who made a great boast that they had given them to the police or returned them to the Palace and hadn't revealed their contents. If they had really been noble,

---

13. (1913–95); solicitor; Master of University College, Oxford, 1974–86; chairman, Observer Editorial Trust, 1967–96; life peer 1965.*
14. Lady Howe was deputy chairman, Equal Opportunities Commission, 1975–9.

they would have said nothing about the letters and simply returned them quietly.

Now today it is all over the Sunday newspapers who her correspondent was. He was actually present at Windsor Castle for the lunch on Friday when Gorbachev came. He had to go into hiding. This could not have happened fifty years ago.[15]

All that the popular press do now is to reveal scandals and start rumours on a wider scale than was the custom in the past. Scandals in high places then were kept to the *cognoscenti*. Democracy has advanced and now everybody wants to be in on them. Hence the current furore about Pamella Bordes whose maiden name was Singh. Her father was an officer in the Indian Army and was killed in border fighting with the Chinese. She has operated as a high class *poule de luxe*, though far more varied in her patrons, more speedily changing them, than the normal lady of that type.

'Another triumphant week and you looked beautiful on television,' I said [to Margaret].

This was at about twenty to eight on Sunday evening. She went on talking for the best part of half an hour, bubbling away.

I said, 'I am sorry that Leon Brittan said on TV about Bernard Ingham and Charles Powell leaking the Solicitor General's letter over Westland and reviving all that controversy.'[16]

I said, 'He is quite a decent fellow but he made himself look cheap.'

She said, 'He won't face up to the fact that it was his responsibility and that it was his fault.'

I said, 'I watched Michael Heseltine on television, on *Newsnight* with Denis Healey.[17] He was defending you strongly and saying

---

15. Buckingham Palace issued a statement on the evening of 8 April naming Commander Timothy Laurence, equerry to the Queen, as the author of letters addressed to the Princess Royal which had been reported as stolen from the Palace. The *Sunday Times* of 9 April ended its news story: 'The publicity surrounding the letters and their theft will add to speculation that all is not well with the marriage of the Princess Royal and Captain Mark Phillips.' The Princess Royal and Captain Mark Phillips divorced in 1992; she married Commander Timothy Laurence RN in 1992.

16. See Vol. 1, pp. 56–74, for the 1986 Westland helicopter affair and responsibility for the leaked letter; Bernard Ingham was the PM's Press Secretary and Charles Powell her Private Secretary.

17. Labour politician; Chancellor of the Exchequer, 1974–9; at this time Opposition spokesman on foreign affairs; life peer 1992.

your policies were right and had been right all along with regard to Russia and defence and so forth.' She said, 'He didn't always say that at the time. But now he is behaving very honourably and refusing to get drawn into trying to revive the stale old Westland affair.' I said, 'Perhaps you may feel it is possible to reclaim him for civilization at some point.' She murmured something not very emphatic.

I think it will be a long time before he is able to work his passage, if he is able to at all. Gently I am trying to persuade her he might be useful to have back on our side but she won't readily forgive him. She hardly ever has anybody back once they have gone unless they had to go, as Cecil Parkinson did, in non-political circumstances.

I said, 'Do you know Sir Bryan Carsberg?'

I then went on, 'He is extremely good and if you are thinking of anybody for higher and better things, he is your man.'

Tuesday 11 April

Dinner at 8 Lord North Street given by Jonathan Aitken[18] for Julian Amery's seventieth birthday. There were about forty people.

Jonathan Aitken has made quite a lot of money and has a large house. I was sitting at the top table with Julian, on his left. On his right he had Alec Douglas-Home[19] who made a charming little speech about Julian and on my left was young Winston Churchill.[20] On his left was Quintin Hogg.[21]

Immediately we got into an animated conversation, Quintin, Winston and myself, about the law reforms. 'Are you not in favour of any single one of the proposals, Quintin, not even that the solicitors should be allowed to appear in the higher courts?' I asked. He said, 'No, not one. There are no solicitors good enough. They should stick to their cushy jobs. We barristers have worked hard. We know what we are doing,' etc. etc. etc.

---

18. Conservative politician, journalist and businessman; MP, 1974–97; convicted of perjury for his evidence in his libel action against the *Guardian*, 1999.
19. Conservative politician; Prime Minister, 1963–4; life peer 1974, having disclaimed his peerages as 14th Earl of Home.
20. Grandson of the Second World War statesman; Conservative MP, 1970–97.
21. Lord Hailsham, Conservative politician; Lord Chancellor, 1970–4 and 1979–87; life peer 1970.

Winston said to me, 'It cannot be right to annoy all one's friends at once,' meaning the professions like the lawyers and the doctors, though he was on the side of reform.

Young Winston was bewailing his fate at having been sacked once as a front bench spokesman for the Tory Party when in opposition, for refusing to conform with the Tory Party's decision to abstain on the question of sanctions against Rhodesia. She fired him then for not performing as one of the team. I said, 'She never forgives anyone who breaks ranks even though it is only a little thing.'

He says she showers him with attention and warmth and he and his wife are always being asked to Chequers and Number 10 Downing Street but nothing ever comes to him by way of a job.

Before dinner I was talking to Ian Gow, one of Mrs Thatcher's staunchest allies and a former PPS who foolishly resigned over the issue of Northern Ireland.[22] I said, 'Are you worried?' He said, 'A little bit. It reminds me of going through France in 1968 with signs and posters all down the roads saying "Ten years are enough".'[23] That was when De Gaulle's demand – that a referendum on the constitution should go his way or he would resign – was defeated and so he was.

Wednesday 12 April

Robbie rang from Bonython at a quarter past one in the morning. My brother had died a few minutes before. They think it was a massive heart attack. The poor fellow had been in great pain for years and was worn out by long drawn Parkinson's which was getting worse not better and by diabetes as well.

Maybe death affects one differently as one grows older. I cried for two weeks when Hugh Gaitskell died, thinking he would never be able to see Regent Street again and other familiar places. I cried quite a lot when Stafford Cripps[24] died. I even wept a little for Churchill when he

---

22. He resigned in December 1985 in protest at the Anglo-Irish Agreement; he was murdered by the IRA, 1990.

23. It was almost ten years since Mrs Thatcher had become Prime Minister after the May 1979 general election.

24. (1889–1952); Solicitor General in the first Labour administration, 1930–1, and Chancellor of the Exchequer in the second, 1947–50; he chose WW when a young MP to be one of his two personal assistants on the 1946 Cabinet Mission to prepare for Indian independence.

died. Michael Ham, who was killed in 1940 flying, made me weep with memories of him at Oxford, with his tall body and proudly held head and his painting and his love of Eric Gill [the artist and sculptor]. There have been others who I would weep for years ago but I merely felt sad about my brother and did not get moved to tears.

Yet the memories come trudging in. The days at Milbourne Lodge[25] as children and when he went to Eastbourne [public school] and I followed him. There was a time when I thought he was the most marvellous person in the world. That was when I was around eleven or twelve. He was a kind of hero. I suppose all small boys make a hero of someone. I began to see that though there was a generous and kind side, he was limited. Never read. Did well in the City but was no intellectual or ingenious and clever person like my step-son Nicholas [Banszky]. After the war or during it entered his wife Joy.

She divided my brother and myself somewhat. I could never get on with her.

After Joy died I was immediately able to get on much better with him again and something of my feelings of brotherly affection that I had earlier, before I went to Eastbourne and which I even retained until I was about seventeen, returned.

How glad I was that I went for the weekend which culminated in his birthday on March 20th. It was a very jolly weekend.

For dinner came Count and Countess Pejacsevich plus the Wiltons. She is a Hungarian Countess who is still quite attractive. An ancient Hungarian family which came from Croatia when that was a part of the Austro-Hungarian Empire.

He is now quite well off, having gone into business.

We drank a magnum of Grand-Puy-Ducasse 1973. I decanted it at a quarter past seven and we were drinking it by a quarter to nine. It was very good.

After which we had an agreeable game of bridge.

Thursday 13 April
Told Charlie Wilson how good I thought his recent leaders were. Strong and authoritative. He was very touched. 'Would you tell Rupert the

---

25. The school in Esher, Surrey, which their father had founded and where the family lived.

next time you speak to him? He is inclined to think they are too wimpish.' I said I certainly would.

The *News of the World* want me to write a special article about Mrs T which I have got to do, not for this weekend but the next, by Thursday. At least they will pay me £700 extra for it.

A large evening party at Julian Amery's. It is a house I have known since I was nineteen when I first knew Julian at Oxford and I went to lunch etc. with him and his father. It is about the only house left in Eaton Square still completely in private occupation.

Talked to Peter Walker, recently in the news making a speech which is somewhat at variance with the accepted philosophy of the Thatcher government. He is the Secretary for Wales. He was a tiny bit tipsy but very friendly. He said that he had done a little deal with Margaret when he was made Secretary for Wales after the last election. At first he didn't want to do it and then he said, 'Well if I do it, will you let me do it my way and [with] regional aid and all that kind of thing?' and she said, 'All right.' He got a special dispensation from the Treasury and they got on very well.

But he thinks Lawson is doing it all wrong and that interest rates are not the right or the sufficient way of getting inflation down.

He didn't mind if he left the government because he had plenty of money and anyway he had been there a long time; and Wales was not a great area. He said, 'I have only ruled three and a half million people.'

On the way out I saw Michael Heseltine. I said to him, 'I am so glad you didn't have anything to do with reviving that boring old Westland affair.' He replied almost with a snarl, 'It is not boring to me.'

Friday 14 April
Johnnie Henderson[26] has a beautiful house which is probably not by Inigo Jones though some people say it is.

The house inside was bitterly cold.

I thought I would freeze.

We had Gruaud-Larose (second growth St Julien) 1966 for dinner. It was good but it would have been much better if it had been properly

---

26. Chairman, Henderson Administration, 1983–90; Lord Lieutenant of Berkshire, 1989–95.

decanted. I am always amazed by these very rich people who have very expensive wine and then treat it badly so that it is not at its best.

Saturday 15 April
We went to Newbury [races].

Next to me [at dinner] was a girl called Mrs Spence[27] whose sister is Miranda Morley, David's [Beaufort's] girlfriend. We talked briefly about her and how she was absolutely resigned to never marry him and just lived her life for him for whenever he wanted to see her.

The sister started twenty-three years ago a kind of Dame's School in Pimlico called Miss Morley's.

Her husband was also a lively man.

He was much interested in helping the Tote through its privatization with the aid of Jockey Club, of which he's a new member, and racing money. That is why he had been asked to the dinner primarily. He is shrewd and very interested in horses, obviously owning some himself. He seems to be a valuable ally. When we talked after dinner I told him that Jimmy Hanson had offered to buy the Tote for £100 million. He said, 'I suppose that is what you really do need.' I said, 'Yes but we can't do that straight away,' and I didn't want to go into the Hanson situation because I thought we'd lose our identity.

Sunday 16 April
I talked to Johnnie about the guarantees we must have from the racing industry and the availability of the £20 million. He said he was organizing the Racecourse Association and the Jockey Club and a guarantee of at least the first £10 million. I said, 'We have got to have clear indication the other £10 million would be forthcoming.' So he is going to reword the letters he is going to send us or make available to the Home Office to see.

We went over to [see] Nicky Henderson, his son who is a trainer. He has about seventy horses.

We looked at Isaac Newton which I once had a twelfth share in but no longer do. He is still coming in second or third and is unlikely ever to win a race.[28]

---

27. Susan, née Morley, m (1970) Christopher Spence.
28. See Vol. 1, pp. 361, 474, for WW's hopes and disappointment in this horse.

Margaret had been to Hillsborough to see the football ground where the disaster was yesterday and to see and talk to survivors.[29]

She said, 'It must be the end of terraces. We must have seats and tickets only. There is no leadership in the Football Association any more.' I said, 'They spend millions on buying players from each other but not on their grounds.'

We talked about the judges and Quintin Hogg. She said he had become a cantankerous old man. She said, 'I suppose he thinks he still ought to be Lord Chancellor but he couldn't go on being that for ever. When his wife died, I said to him, "If we win the election (this was before 1979), you will be Lord Chancellor if that is any comfort to you." I wanted to give him something to latch on to because he was terribly distressed about his wife. But I didn't think of him being Lord Chancellor for more than one parliament.'

When we finished talking and we had been talking for about twenty minutes she said, 'Bless you for ringing, dear.'

I rang her particularly this evening because I knew she had had a terrible day. She feels it all very keenly for the families who have suffered losses, and the fear that those who survived would have permanent brain damage. People are absolutely mad to think that she doesn't care.

Wednesday 19 April
Got up very early to have breakfast at seven so as to catch the aeroplane from Heathrow. Managed to get myself into a rage because the collar that Flavio and I put out the night before was the wrong size for the shirt so I couldn't get the tie tucked in. I don't remember so easily how to tie a long tie any more. The long black tie is very thick. I had to take another collar to change when I got to Cornwall.

It was just on one by the time we got to Bonython. The funeral was due to begin at two. On the aeroplane were a number of people who had worked with Robert in the City.

I read the last chapter of Ecclesiastes, the King James I version. There had been some awkwardness about this because they only have

---

29. Ninety-six were crushed to death and 170 injured after fans surged into the enclosure at the FA Cup semi-final played at the Sheffield Wednesday ground between Liverpool and Nottingham Forest.

the new modernized version in the church now but I took Robbie's Bible from Bonython and read from that.

The funeral went on for a very long time.

There must have been over five hundred there. My brother was very well known locally, as the clergyman said in his address, for his generosity and hospitality.

Back at the house even more people turned up for tea than there had been at lunch before the funeral. I saw William Golding at the funeral but he didn't come back to the house. A. L. Rowse was there.

He said we must meet and arrange the past.

I said, 'You mean rearrange the past.'

The most interesting person to me who came back for tea was my first cousin whom I had never seen before. Very Welsh with a strong Welsh accent and her husband likewise. She said, 'I am Tudor's daughter. The black sheep of the family, not at all respectable.' So I laughed and said, 'I never said that about your father.' But she said that was what the family thought. That was true.

He was my mother's brother and was always wasting and losing money. He finished up owning a public house in which he hanged himself because his older brother Arthur, who was very rich, refused to pay his debts. He had done so several times before but had now ceased to do so. I said, 'You remind me of my mother. You have a little bit of the looks of her,' and she said, 'That is the nicest thing that has been said to me for years.'

Sunday 23 April

Margaret is upset by the nasty things being said about her in many newspapers, including those she thought were on her side, as the ten-year anniversary of her being Prime Minister approaches on May 4th.

Obviously Brian Walden scratched around to find some unpleasant things which he could draw from Willie [Whitelaw]. I said, 'All that stuff that you would never meet socially, well that is ridiculous.'

It was the main story on the front page of the *Sunday Times*. One of the quotes at the top said, 'I would never dream of going to stay with her.' 'And that is a Murdoch paper,' she said, 'which is supposed to be in support.'

She said she didn't think Willie really meant to be unpleasant but that was how they picked out the pieces to be nasty. I agree. She was really a little bit upset.[30]

I had just been speaking to Arnold Weinstock who had got this new smart card which you lay on top of a box and it takes one tenth of a second for the machine to pass or reject the person with the card. They have discussed it with the government. I told her I was writing something about the football problem tomorrow morning for Tuesday's *Times*. She was very pleased.

She said about the attacks on her, 'This hurts.' I said, 'Don't be depressed about them. I have always told you that the fashion is to say you are frightfully good at one moment and then they get bored with that and have to publish something different.'

I really love that girl. She has got such terrific guts.

I know she is the best Prime Minister of my lifetime and if I can help to strengthen and comfort her when things look bleak, I will do it.

Tuesday 25 April

Went to listen to Margaret at Question Time in the Commons. She was in splendid form, winning every point. But when a Labour MP asked whether those who got payments from the Hillsborough disaster funds would lose their social security benefits, she was suddenly very kind and sympathetic and said she would look into it all. There were certain rules which governed these situations from previous disasters and also it depended on how these charities were arranged. She spoke so warmly and humanely that I find it difficult to understand why people attack her for being hard.

We went to the launch party for the Britain Salutes Hungary month in October. All the arrangements had gone well. Mr Pozsgay is now Deputy Prime Minister. He had his talk with Mrs Thatcher at Number 10 at a quarter to five. They both came to the reception.

On the way out she came over to me and gave me a kiss. Somebody said to me afterwards, 'You have got lipstick on your face.'

At dinner at the Hungarian Embassy Mr Pozsgay was immensely pleased.

---

30. Whitelaw, portrayed as 'the public school representative of the Tory Party's landed gentry' in contrast to 'the grammar school girl, born above her father's shop', was reported as saying, 'Ours is only a political friendship, and I have never been someone who has shared her life in any way.'

I sat on the left of Mr Pozsgay and Robert Maxwell, who speaks excellent Hungarian, sat on his right.[31]

During dinner I explained how he had won the Military Cross for bravery under a Czech name during the war fighting for us. Then people thought he hadn't got it because they couldn't find a Robert Maxwell with the MC in the War Office records. They got themselves into trouble by querying his bravery.

I then explained how good he was at business and so forth and he began to glow a bit.

Before the reception began at the Barbican, David English, editor of the *Daily Mail*, was asking me about the prospects for Mrs Thatcher. He is getting worried. I said, 'I wouldn't worry,' and explained why not. Peter Stothard, the deputy editor of the *Times*, also took the same view as David English. He then said, 'Of course in the *News of the World* I suppose you spend your time, as you feel you have to, attacking her critics.' I said, 'Yes, because I have nothing particularly critical to say about her so why should I say it?'

Thursday 27 April

Had a jolly lunch at Claridge's with Abdul Al Ghazzi. But it all takes so long. I got there dead on time. He was sitting there having a drink. That was after he said he was glad about the message I didn't want any alcohol because it was Ramadan.

It's strange that so many people like Abdul have a belief in the mysterious abilities of the English to manoeuvre their way successfully internationally. I pointed out all the errors we had made in Egypt up to and including the ludicrous attack on Egypt over the Suez Canal [in 1956]. 'How can you say,' I asked, 'that we have got more experience than the Americans and are therefore better able to behave wisely in the Middle East?'

I think things are beginning to move at Heveningham. By the time he has completed the new repairs it will have cost him seven and a half million pounds.

I said I had been rather busy as I had been having to write more articles than usual and make more speeches in the Lords and [was] trying to make some money.

He said, 'Oh do you need money? Let me help you make some.' I

---

31. (1923–91); the Mirror Group chairman and former Labour MP was born in Hungary.

quickly said no because I don't mean that at all. It would be a very bad idea if he was making money for me and then everybody would say I was in his pocket.

However, I did say did he need American lawyers. He said he did need them, in fact he had a big case on now but unfortunately he had got lawyers already. I said, 'Well I am asking you because I am trying to represent these American lawyers.' I must send him their brochure and tell them about him. I think it is perfectly respectable to act for my little consultancy.

Saturday 29 April
Went to Sandown.

Queen Elizabeth the Queen Mother was there for lunch. She always comes on Whitbread Gold Cup Day to present the prize. Before we went in to lunch Martin Gilliat was telling people around us that I had written a play and that he had saved up £2,000 to put into it, more than he had ever put into any other play. He was going to get on to Allan Davis as soon as he got back and tell him he has got to get this play done. 'It has certainly got to be done in time for Queen Elizabeth's ninetieth birthday, if not before.'

Then he said to me, 'She will come you know. She will come to the first night. She has been wanting to come.' Then he whispered, 'But is there any foul language, words like shit?' I said, 'No. Nothing like that at all.'

Queen Elizabeth said, 'I always agree with [your articles] but I didn't with one the other day when you were attacking the judges.' She talked about centuries of building up the English legal system and it was all being destroyed. I said, 'It is not true. Do you know Lord Mackay the new Lord Chancellor?' She said she had just met him. I said, 'He is brilliant, he is kind and he knows the law. But one of the arguments they use against him, certainly in private – they have done it with me – is that he is Scottish and he is trying to make us conform with Scottish law. You, Ma'am, ought to be on his side. That must be the best argument for it for you, that he wants to introduce something from Scotland here – if the argument were true.' She said, 'But Scotland is a very small country.'

I said, 'Never mind about that. They have got a very good legal system and ordinary people get better access to the law.'

Afterwards Johnnie Henderson and company expressed great

surprise at the vigorous argument I had had with her. I said, 'Oh we often do that. We never fall out but she doesn't mind an argument.'

When I said goodbye to her she said, 'When shall we meet again?' 'On the racecourse. Or perhaps we could have another dinner,' I said. 'Oh good,' she said and gave a little skip and a laugh. I said, 'You look wonderful as always.' When she gives that little skip and laughs she is like an eighteen-year-old girl, and she raises her hands up with glee. She has dazzling charm. She likes it when I kiss her hand.

Sir Gordon White was there.

I was hesitant about Gordon White before but I think I like him. He is tall and lean and keen. Mad keen as he may be on making money, he must have some altruism in the way he backs the Derby. I said, 'Is there any evidence that more Ever Ready batteries are sold now as a result of your sponsorship and calling it the Ever Ready Derby?' He said he didn't think so.

Sunday 30 April
Margaret gave a lengthy explanation of why we have got nearly eight per cent inflation which she now calls eight per cent. She said it was all Nigel Lawson's fault. 'He tried to keep us in line with the Deutschmark by keeping it at 3.14 to the pound.'

She said, 'They didn't tell me they were doing this for months. The result was, when we had to stop keeping the pound in line with the Deutschmark, interest rates went shooting up because we couldn't afford putting any more money into the situation.' I said, 'What about the October [1987] crash? There was an element of lowering interest rates in case there was going to be a recession.' She said, 'Yes, but that was only a small part of it. It was Nigel's fault really by trying to keep matching the Deutschmark.' I said, 'It was a kind of back door way of joining the EMS?' She said, 'Exactly. I hadn't realized what they were doing. It was an own goal.'

She said, 'We don't want to tie ourselves to the Deutschmark. That would put up our inflation and cause unemployment again. Also, there may be a Socialist government there and we don't want to be tied to that.'

She went on at some length about this and is not at all pleased. She is still dead against joining the EMS. I said, 'Your instincts are always right.'

Talking about the various polls, I said that they overwhelmingly say 'that people respect you even if they don't like you'. She said, 'I don't know why they don't like me.' I said, 'Nor do I. They don't know you well enough. And it's because of all the unpleasant stories put out by people who are against you. But don't worry. There are more like me that love you.'

There is a great myth that she has no sense of humour. At the end of the interview with Kohl she was given some of the local wine which is supposed to be very good. She said, 'Its just right for me, dry with just a little sweetness.' I wish people could understand what a human and humorous person she can be and so full of care for others.

Monday 1 May
Went to Arnold's.

He said he thought Margaret was on her way out. He sensed it. I said, 'That is simply not true. People have often been sensing that in the past.' He said, 'Yes but she is getting tired and she has nothing new to say.' I said, 'Of course she has got lots of new things to say.' 'Well people want her changed.' 'That is something else that has been said. Like Queen Victoria they have got used to her and they couldn't accept such a gap in their lives now.'

He then said he had been helping Peter Jay[1] with his programme on ITV last night on Channel 4 in which he called witnesses in the first part of a two-part series, saying how all her economic miracles had been a total mirage. So I said, 'You helped him? You amaze me.' He said, 'I told him that the manufacturing base had gone down, we weren't doing any better now than we were in 1979.' I said, 'Arnold, how could you do such a thing?' He did look a bit ashamed. He talks about people not being loyal to him but I can't say that was a particularly loyal act.

I told him his public relations at GEC were very bad. It was not until I told the Prime Minister about his smart cards that there was government interest.

He said, 'But I wrote to her myself and she took no notice.' I said, 'Well that is because you never got any public steam up behind it.'

He had a joke. An Irishman applied for a job in construction work. He was given a sort of test. One question was 'Do you know the difference between joist and girder?' He said, 'Yes. The first wrote *Ulysses* and the second wrote *Faust*.'

We had an excellent Château Batailley, fifth growth Haut Médoc. It was 1966. That is really getting into a superb year.

The moment I walked in Allan Davis rang up.

---

1. Writer and broadcaster; Ambassador to the US, 1977–9; chief of staff to Robert Maxwell, 1986–9; economics and business editor, BBC, since 1990.

He has heard from Bromley that if it only reached a fifty-five per cent audience in a three weeks run, my play would then lose £13,500. Did I think that was too much to guarantee? I said I would like to hear more about it. But I don't need to. I am sure I could get one or two people to help, if they got special terms for special higher rates of share in the profits if it came on in London.

Actually I was thinking I wouldn't mind doing it myself. I can get it off tax if I lose it all and in any case I wouldn't mind just once in my life spending some money on something I really want to see. Other than expensive dresses.

Thursday 4 May
Spent a lot of time in the morning getting ready for my speech for the committee stage of the Water Bill.

I don't do it for the government. I do it in support of Mrs Thatcher as she was very worried about the bad presentation that water has had for its privatization.

Dinner party at Cavendish Avenue.

Princess Michael came gushing along. From the very moment she started coming up the steps she was hugging people and giving them great kisses. She looked quite splendid in her Junoesque way. She wore an attractive black dress in the latest fashion.

At dinner I said to Princess Michael I was glad she was keeping out of the news now and keeping a low profile. I said also it must help that you are not the only one who gets into trouble, now that Princess Anne is. She said she doesn't like Princess Anne at all. When they were at Cheltenham for the Tote Cheltenham Gold Cup, Princess Anne wouldn't even speak to her though she went up to her in a friendly way. I said, 'Queen Elizabeth the Queen Mother likes you.' She said, 'Why do you think that?' I said, 'Because she has told me so.' She said, 'I am not sure about her. She doesn't always say what she really thinks, you know.' Then she said she thought the Queen liked her.

It was a part Hungarian evening. Count and Countess Pejacsevich were there. They say that Princess Michael's claims about her family's aristocratic connections in Hungary are absolutely true.

When the ladies had gone the Prince was very interesting. He is not a fool. He sat next to Gorbachev at the Guildhall who was surprised at his fluent Russian. He said, when he was talking to Gorbachev about the terrible things that President Ceauşescu was doing in

Romania, Gorbachev said that we, the Soviets, can't interfere with the internal affairs of other countries which Michael thought was a bit rich.

Ed Streator, who used to be Minister at the American Embassy in London and did all the work because US Ambassadors are never clever enough to understand what is going on properly[2] – he later became Ambassador to the OECD in Brussels – said he thought that Gorbachev had only a one in ten chance of surviving.

Nicholas Shakespeare was one of the guests but a last minute one because Mark Weinberg,[3] who said he was coming, suddenly found a business engagement.

He is descended directly from Shakespeare's grandfather. He is the closest living relative of William Shakespeare. He is allowed specially by the College of Heralds to use Shakespeare's coat of arms because his grandfather would have been entitled to it as well.[4] He was very pleasant. He is the literary editor of the *Daily Telegraph* and will soon be of both the *Sunday* and the *Daily Telegraph*. He can't make out what these great changes are that Andrew Knight has made, whether they are going to save anything or not.

So it all seems absurd, the merging of the two papers into a seven day a week paper.

Friday 5 May
Margaret rang. There had been a misunderstanding about Rupert Murdoch. She had thought that as he was unable to go to the Gorbachev do which I had arranged for him, he and Anna might like to come to her buffet luncheon on Sunday.[5] Somebody (Tim Bell)[6] had met him and said he was sorry he wasn't able to come. He said, 'Oh but I haven't had an invitation.' There had been a mix up. She was

---

2. WW is referring to the fact that most US ambassadors are political appointments rather than career diplomats on the British model.

3. Chairman, Allied Dunbar Assurance, 1984–90, J. Rothschild Assurance, since 1991; m (1980) Anouska Hempel, fashion designer and hotelier; knight 1987.

4. A variant version of William Shakespeare's arms was granted to Nicholas Shakespeare's family in 1946 as there is no direct connection between his family and the playwright.

5. For her tenth anniversary.

6. Public relations consultant; chairman, Lowe Bell Communications, since 1987; knight 1990.

personally asking for his telephone number in New York etc. I said, 'Don't bother. I will deal with it.'

More spin-offs from the dinner party. David Metcalfe[7] told me he had a long conversation with Marie-Christine. He was wearing cufflinks which the Duke of Windsor had given to his father. She had received gifts from the Duchess of Windsor of jewellery. They compared notes. She naturally had buttered up the Duchess when the rest of the family took no notice of her and was given and left quite a nice lot of items of jewellery. That is her general manner of approach.

Rupert is so keen to come with Anna [to the party] that he is flying over on Concorde on Saturday evening and going back at six on Sunday after going to Chequers.

Rupert is very keen on power and being near to power. I suppose it does his adrenaline good.

Saturday 6 May

It was a beautiful day at Newmarket. The 2,000 Guineas was won by Nashwan, trained by Dick Hern.[8] There were great cheers and a throng surrounding the crippled Dick Hern. There was high feeling that the Queen had behaved very badly in not renewing his lease at the end of this year at the West Ilsley stables. He has been ousted by the Queen's racing manager, Lord Carnarvon.[9]

At lunch time in our room I said to Isabel [Derby], 'The Queen has done something I thought was impossible. She is turning the Jockey Club and the racing world into republicans.'

After dinner at Stanley House we were talking in the drawing-room about the Hern situation. Isabel was denouncing the Queen. I said, 'Of course you never have liked the Hanoverians. You don't like their Jewish blood.' I could have bitten off my tongue because there was David Montagu sitting listening. So I hastily added, 'You don't think it is suitable for royalty,' rather lamely. But David took no notice or

---

7. Son of Major Edward 'Fruity' Metcalfe, who was best man at the Duke of Windsor's wedding; director, Sedgwick James Management Services (insurance brokers); m 3 (1979) American-born Sally Cullen Howe.

8. Principal private trainer to the Queen until this time, and trainer for other owners including the Makhtoum brothers; he was seriously injured in 1984 when fox-hunting.

9. Henry Porchester, 7th Earl of Carnarvon. See Vol. 1, pp. 642 ff. for the controversy.

seemed not to. I never think of him as being a Jew and nor do I bother about it. But it seemed a trifle anti-semitic what I said.

I went for a little walk in the garden with Isabel and said how awful I felt about it and she said, 'Never mind, I've made remarks like that before and it doesn't matter.' I said, 'I remember David Somerset telling me how they used to tease him when he was at school and call him a dirty little Jew boy. Boys can be very nasty.' She said, 'So can grown-up boys. Look what they are doing to Dick Hern.'

At the end of the race, the 2,000 Guineas, Willie Carson [jockey] said it was the team that mattered, that the Major [Hern] was the head of the team and that of course the win could not have come at a better time. It was quite brave of him because he often rides for the Queen. He is a nice, impish, Puckish-looking fellow with a lot of cheek and guts.

Sunday 7 May

It was down to Chequers today for the little celebration luncheon. There were fifty-nine people there. They were nearly all those who had helped her through thick and thin.

Before lunch I talked a little bit to Mrs Mark Thatcher. She is extraordinarily pretty.

Mark Thatcher said how surprised and delighted he was last Tuesday when he brought his son over. Margaret stopped work for the whole of Tuesday morning, which he thought must have been a record, to play with and be with her grandson. He was brought out on the terrace by his Norland Nurse and all the women gurgled over him.

Mark told me he is getting on very well in America with his business. Then he said, 'We shall all have to help when she retires because she won't have much money.' I thought that was a bit odd and I wondered why he didn't realize he could sell her memoirs for millions. Also his father has plenty of money.

He said to me, 'It is so wonderful that you go on helping her and ringing her up. She is very lonely. She is very upset at the moment and she needs to be revved up.' Naturally he would use a motoring term, having been a racing driver. He said, 'Did you notice that there is only one of the younger ones here, John Major. The others seem to be semi plotting against her and she is feeling rather low. She hasn't got real support in the Cabinet and they are all quarrelling, which they shouldn't be.'

Another thing Mark said was that after the next election she would be able to get a Cabinet more loyal to her. She would be able to get rid of Geoffrey Howe and Douglas Hurd. Certainly Douglas Hurd doesn't like her and she knows that and she doesn't like him which is not exactly helpful to me over the privatization or otherwise of the Tote. Obviously she talks pretty freely to Mark.

Although it was a buffet, we all had our tables and our place names in front of them.

After I had had some curry and rice, which was pretty good, Margaret came round and said, 'You have got to go and eat some more because there is masses of food out there and the chefs will be very upset if it is all wasted.' John Major and Alastair Burnet[10] and I with Bill Deedes[11] dutifully got up and went to get some more food.

The wine was good. There was Château Latour 1972.

At lunch I talked to John Major about my proposition that all taxation is theft. He said, 'I think it is not quite like that. I think all excessive taxation is theft. I would agree with that.'

On my left was Lady McAlpine.[12] She said to me the first time I had met her at dinner I had extolled to her the virtues of her husband's previous wife. I said, 'I'm sure I couldn't have done that. Or I couldn't have realized that you were his wife.' She said, 'I was rather upset at the time.' But she was laughing now.

Tim Bell was looking rather fat and his wife was looking pretty.

I can see why Margaret likes him. He is such a cheerful soul, full of optimism, even though he exaggerates somewhat his own part in what goes on.

Sitting at my table, and I didn't recognize her to start with, was Arabella Lacloche.[13] She used to live in Cavendish Avenue. I am looking out of the window towards her house now. She is a great gardener.

I said I used to lust after her when she was working in her garden. She said, 'I used to lust to be invited into your house.'

---

10. Editor, *Economist*, 1965–74; news presenter, ITN, 1976–91; director ITN, 1982–90; director, United Racecourses Holdings, 1985–96; knight 1984.
11. Conservative MP, 1950–74; editor, *Daily Telegraph*, 1974–86; life peer 1986.
12. Romilly Thompson m (1980) Alistair McAlpine, Hon. Treasurer, Conservative Party, 1975–90, life peer 1984; he married 1 (1964–79) Sarah, née Baron.
13. Italian born garden designer; gold medallist at Chelsea Flower Show, 1998; m (1974) the Hon. Mark Lennox-Boyd, Conservative politician, MP, 1979–97, knight 1994.

She is not quite so pretty now, having thickened out a bit, but it is a long time ago when I used to know her and talk to her a bit.

She is now married to Mark Lennox-Boyd. He is Margaret's PPS. He hasn't known her all that long but he is counted as a loyal supporter, as he certainly is in his present role.

John Junor[14] was there. I was delighted to see him. He was the person who told Margaret she ought to get hold of me in 1975 and see whether I would be willing to support her. So he performed a great service to her and naturally to me. He has always been a stalwart supporter. I congratulated him on his column in the *Sunday Express*.

Rupert was delighted at being there. Willie Whitelaw said to me that he had come up to him and said, 'I think our papers have done you very well,' and he, Willie, thought he should have replied to say they had nearly done *for* him because of the interview with Brian Walden in which he was made to look very ungracious about Margaret Thatcher.

I said to him that Rupert probably didn't realize the effect of it and maybe hadn't even read the interview. He has so many papers and so much to do that I don't think he knows as much as he used to about what goes in his newspapers.

Rupert said he had read my words of wisdom this morning and seemed quite pleased with them. I said, 'I want to speak to you in private but not here. It is something to do with Collins.'

I was of course talking about this manuscript. It has been put into some confusion by Ian Chapman disappearing.[15] He told me that he hasn't told his successor anything about it and although he told me I mustn't trust anybody, not even Rupert, I have got to trust somebody so it must be Rupert. So I will tell him about it and hope it all goes well and that I can do it for Collins. But it would be disastrous if a word gets out.

I didn't recognize poor Jock Bruce-Gardyne.[16] He seemed to be completely bald or almost so. He had a beard. I said, 'Why have you got a beard?' without thinking. What an ass I am because then I looked more closely and he had a great scar on his head. He had a tumour from his brain removed.

---

14. (1919–97); he edited the *Sunday Express*, 1954–86; knight 1980.

15. See Vol. 1, p. 675 and 683 ff., for Ian Chapman's resignation as chairman of Collins after Murdoch took the firm over in 1988.

16. (1930–90); Conservative politician and journalist; life peer 1983.

Marcus Sieff[17] was there and I complained to him about Marks & Spencer. 'You don't sell braces any more.'

Margaret was very solicitous moving around from table to table. When I came in she was at the door and I had my straw hat which Mary Rothermere[18] gave me in Italy. I said, 'Can I leave it here in case we go outside afterwards into the garden and it is sunny?' She said, 'Oh yes, put it just there,' which I did on some oak chest or whatever in the hall.

Later when we were in the garden to my astonishment she brought my hat out which I put on. Everyone else was then astonished and those who hadn't noticed me wearing a hat before came up and said, 'Only you would do that. You are the only person who would go to Chequers and after lunch put on a hat as though you were at a race meeting or on the beach.' I said, 'As the Prime Minister went and fetched it for me, I had to put it on.' Denis Thatcher took a photograph of me in it and so did Lady Thorneycroft.[19]

At the end of the lunch Willie Whitelaw got up and made a nice little speech saying how marvellously well Margaret had done in her ten years and how much everybody admired her and how she had transformed Britain and all the usual sort of stuff. But he did it nicely. Mark Thatcher got up and said a few words and he did that nicely, too, and there was a good deal of loud applause.

Margaret is frightfully sharp. I said in a very low voice to Alastair Burnet, 'What job does John Major do?' She was about ten yards away and came bouncing over and said, 'He is Chief Secretary at the Treasury.' She particularly wanted me to meet him and that is why she had put me close to him on that table. I talked to him at considerable length and found him very solid and sensible. I think he is exceptionally bright and he seems to be the sort of person who would carry on with her ideas.

As we went we all had to sign our names in the visitors' book which was out in the garden in front of the arch from which we could rejoin our cars without going back into the house. Margaret said to

---

17. Chairman, Marks & Spencer, 1972–84; life peer 1980.
18. Daughter of Kenneth Murchison of Dallas, Texas, Mrs Mary Ohstrom m (1966) 2nd Viscount Rothermere (Esmond, 1898–1978), his third marriage; d 1993.
19. Countess Carla Roberti, m (1949, his second marriage), Peter Thorneycroft (1909–94, Conservative politician; MP, 1938–66; Chancellor of the Exchequer, 1957–8; life peer 1967).

me, 'Are you driving?' rather anxiously, thinking I might be a little tipsy. I said, 'No it's all right, I have got a chauffeur.' She said, 'Good.'

I rang Margaret [later] and told her it was a lovely party, English and summery and beautifully organized by her, and 'You were so solicitous as a hostess, making sure that everybody was meeting people and going round seeing that they had what they wanted. I don't know where you get the energy from.'

She said, 'I wanted to get people meeting those they hadn't met. You hadn't met John Major before.' I said, 'He told me that he is the only person at the Treasury who hadn't got a double First.' She said, 'He would have got a double First if he had been able to go to a university. But they were very poor. His father was a circus performer and he had to leave school when he was sixteen.' I said, 'He has got a first-class brain and he is a very solid person, very sound and very good.' She said, 'I am glad you like him because I think he is splendid.'

I said, 'I thought Kenneth Clarke[20] got quite a good bargain with the doctors.' She said, 'When I first saw it I thought, "Good Lord. Only twenty-six hours dedicated to seeing patients," and he said, "Well it was only twenty hours or much less for many before so it is a great improvement." ' I said, 'It won't get them all off the golf course,' and she replied, 'But they will be less on it than they were before. It was a good agreement.'

We talked for about fifteen minutes.

Twenty past ten. Michael Tree rings up. Would I speak to David [Beaufort] who was with him in a terrible state. He thinks Margaret is going to screw us at the next election and the whole thing a disaster. He was talking to Charles Morrison[21] who said that Michael Heseltine was going to stand against her in the autumn and split the party and/or, win the leadership from Margaret.

I said, 'Don't be daft. Let me speak to him,' and I did. I told him not to be an ass and that everything was all right and we were better placed now than we were at the same time in the last parliament.

Monday 8 May
Dinner party at 19 Cavendish Avenue. The day began well because Charles and Irene Forte[22] couldn't come. That reduced the number to

---

20. Secretary of State for Health at this time.
21. The Hon. Sir Charles Morrison, Conservative MP, 1964–92; knight 1988.
22. Charles Forte, at this time chairman, Trusthouse Forte; m (1943) Irene, née Chierico; life peer 1982.*

twelve. A much more manageable party and it meant that three bottles of the 1960 Domaine de Chevalier would be enough. The Fortes, though very sweet and nice, are heavy-going in conversation and they never say anything really exciting and they always leave early.

The following came: Viscount Norwich and Mrs Hugo Philipps.[23] Lord Ampthill,[24] Sir Alex and Lady Alexander,[25] Lord and Lady Wolfson,[26] Mr and Mrs Peregrine Worsthorne.

John Julius (Viscount Norwich) has great vigour.

He himself acknowledged that his grandfather was not the Duke [of Rutland] but Harry Cust.[27]

John Julius is absolutely convinced that he and Mrs Thatcher are cousins. He said he would be very proud to be so. He said had I ever asked her. I said, 'No. I didn't think it would be appropriate.' He said, 'Well if you will ask her to dinner with me, I will say to her, "I think I may have the great honour, Prime Minister, of being your cousin." '

I am not certain that I ever will arrange this dinner party at which John Julius will claim to be Mrs Thatcher's cousin.

It might end a beautiful friendship.

I now believe the story is true. How lucky for England there were no contraceptives for women and no abortions when Harry Cust was seducing Margaret's grandmother. We would never have halted our national decline.

After the ladies had left the dining-room, there were energetic conversations. I set one off by asking Perry Worsthorne what he thought would be Mrs Thatcher's rating in history. He said, and all agreed, that no one would deny that she had made dramatic changes in attitudes over the whole country during her ten years. Perry said she is now hopelessly out of touch. She has forgotten all about the professional people. All those people who don't want to be entrepreneurs but just want nice professional jobs.

Geoffrey Ampthill is more or less against Mrs Thatcher and against

---

23. They married in 1989.
24. 4th Baron Ampthill (Geoffrey), at this time Deputy Speaker, House of Lords.
25. Alex Alexander (1916–94); chairman, J. Lyons, 1979–89; then managing director, Lehman Brothers International; knight 1974.
26. Leonard Wolfson, son of Sir Isaac Wolfson, chairman, Great Universal Stores; chairman and founder trustee, Wolfson Foundation; m 1 (1949–91) Ruth, née Sterling; life peer 1985.
27. See 23 February 1989 for this story.

the privatization of water. He is Chairman of the Kitchen Committee
of the Lords. I gave him some of our Cornish Spring Water to try and
he said it was very good and that he would buy it, if the price was
right.

I was very sorry for poor old Peregrine Worsthorne. He talked to
Petronella of nothing but his hatred of Andrew Knight with whom we
are having dinner on Tuesday – and Conrad Black[28] who he thinks is
extremely unpleasant. On Monday Max Hastings takes over as joint
editor of the *Daily Telegraph* and the *Sunday Telegraph* and Perry will
cease to be the proper editor of the *Sunday Telegraph* and have only
three opinion pages to look after. He looked suddenly aged and stressed
last night. I shouldn't really have teased him so much but I had forgotten in a way and I had thought it was better to behave as though
he was in his normal state which he clearly wasn't.

Tuesday 9 May

Dinner at Andrew Knight's. To my surprise, as we were getting out of
the car, there were Peregrine Worsthorne and his wife arriving,
having the night before said how much he hated Andrew Knight. It
seemed odd to me that he was there. But I suppose he can't help it.
He looked a bit brighter than he had yesterday evening.

I met Hugo Young for the first time. He once said very nastily about
me that I should never have been made a peer. That was in his column
in the *Guardian*. However, we had a long talk and I liked him a good
deal.

He has a grudging admiration for Mrs Thatcher. He has written a
best-selling book about her.[29]

He asked me how long she would go on for. I said, 'Ten years, I
expect, but she will take it one election at a time.'

Wednesday 10 May

Petronella is in a great state of distress. She couldn't be persuaded to
come to dinner to eat her asparagus just up from Cornwall. Eventually
she came in. 'What happens if I don't get a First? All my friends and
people like Bernard Levin will think I am not brilliant.'

I was searching through *Who's Who* to show her who hadn't had
a First among the distinguished intellectuals. It was surprising how

---

28. Canadian proprietor of the *Telegraph* newspapers.
29. *One of Us*, 1989.

many notable people clearly hadn't got a First. It looks as though Bernard Levin hasn't got one either. I left a message on his answering machine to ask him.

Auberon Waugh[30] didn't get a First. Evelyn Waugh only got a Third. John Betjeman didn't get a First and so on and so on. Conrad Russell[31] – I assumed he didn't because he didn't say he had got one, as an academic would. Likewise Noël Annan[32] and likewise Hugh Trevor-Roper. Likewise Victor Rothschild.[33] But Jacob [Rothschild] did and puts it in *Who's Who*.

Thursday 11 May
Bernard said, 'The answer to your question is I got an upper Second. What about you?' I said, 'I got a Second.' He said, 'Isn't that good enough for her?' I said, 'No, she has the utmost contempt for my brain.'

I have now told Petronella to say, if she doesn't get a First, that the fault is not in her stars but in her examiners.[34] She said, 'Yes, they ask stupid questions,' and I said, 'And they couldn't understand your answers because they were so brilliant.'

It had just gone 8.00 a.m. when Michael Tree rang. David Somerset [Beaufort] was seeing Alan Walters at 9.30 this morning. What questions should he ask him? Alan Walters is the top economic adviser to Mrs Thatcher whom she trusts greatly and he at times differs with Lawson about the EMS and such matters.

I rang David and he said, 'How on earth did you know?' I said, ' "Radio" Tree told me.'

David rings back after having seen Alan Walters. He has asked him to stay for the weekend at the same time as we are going to Badminton.

---

30. Novelist, journalist, editor and wine connoisseur; son of Evelyn Waugh.
31. At this time Astor Professor of British History, University College London, where Petronella was reading History; he did get a First and so did some of the others, but see later.
32. Provost, King's College, Cambridge, 1956–66; Provost, University College, London, 1966–78; Vice-chancellor, University of London, 1978–81.
33. 3rd Baron Rothschild (1910–90); scientist and banker; Prize-Fellow, Trinity College, Cambridge, 1935–9; father of Jacob.*
34. 'The fault, dear Brutus, is not in our stars/But in ourselves, that we are underlings' – Shakespeare, *Julius Caesar*, Act I scene ii. Petronella got an upper Second.

The Other Club. A good turnout. Before dinner I talked to Jack
Profumo.[35] I told him not to be bothered by this film [*Scandal*].

I asked, 'Are you still bothered about all that?'

He said, 'Yes, very much so.' It was clear as he talked that he
seemed to think of nothing else.

He had been trying to resign for some time before the thing blew
up – which he never expected to happen. It didn't blow up until
eighteen months after he had last seen Christine Keeler. He wanted to
resign because he didn't think he had much further to go in politics
and he would have preferred to look after his family fortune and do
something else. But he was asked not to go by the Chief Whip,
Redmayne, who had said he would be likely to get into the Cabinet if
he stayed, which he never did. After it all blew up, people in the
government thought he had only been trying to resign to avoid the scene
which would occur when the Christine Keeler and the Russian Naval
Attaché affair blew up.[36]

He admitted that he did behave badly by misleading the House and
I reminded him of my having written to him at the time that people
have always lied about things like collusion with Israel – Selwyn Lloyd
and Anthony Eden did that[37] – but I never thought the House would
mind about lies about women. He said he had always been grateful to
me and for what I wrote in the leading article of the *Banbury Guardian*
at the time.

He said it was far worse for Valerie, his wife, who is still much hurt
and cast down by it. He said it was very bad for his family and they
still brood over it, the disgrace. I said, 'You must tell them to grow
up. Everyone fully respects you, more so than ever before. It is bound
to be mentioned. It will go on being mentioned because it is such a
good story, as you must realize. But for them to hold it against you
and feel that you let them all down at this stage is ridiculous. You can
hold your head high, particularly after all you have done for Toynbee
Hall.'

---

35. John Profumo, Conservative politician; Secretary of State for War, 1960–June
    1963, when he resigned over his lie to the House of Commons over his affair with
    Christine Keeler; president, Toynbee Hall, since 1985; m (1954) Valerie Hobson,
    actress (d 1998).
36. She had previously been having an affair with Ivanov, the Russian Naval Attaché,
    and concerns were mooted about security.
37. Over the Suez invasion in 1956.

I said, 'You might think of writing your whole version of the story at some point.' He said he thought his son David[38] probably would do it when he is dead. He had been telling him quite a lot about it now.

I said to Noël Annan, 'Did you get a First?' He said, 'Yes of course.' I said, 'Well you didn't say so in your *Who's Who* entry. It just went on to say you were a professor and a Fellow and all that kind of thing.' So he said, 'I didn't think it was necessary.'

I sat opposite Leon Brittan. He looked at me a bit warily, obviously having read what I said about it being cheap of him to resurrect the Westland case again in my article in the *News of the World*. We then got talking in a friendly manner. He is still very keen on the EMS (Britain joining it). He says that is the way of avoiding a proper European common currency. I said, 'She is much against it for the reasons you probably know and thinks it was a mistake to have tied ourselves to the German mark.' He said, 'She is wrong about that. I am seeing her early next week.' I said, 'Don't burn your boats with her. You may want to come back into politics here.'

I told Noël Annan who was sitting between Jacob and myself that Jacob was one of the richest men in England now he had inherited another £40 million from his aunt.[39] Noël was very startled. Jacob started telling me about the horses he had inherited. I said, 'I thought you didn't like horse racing?' He said, 'Well I do now. We won quite a good race with one of them yesterday. Will you come and see my stud?' I said I would be delighted.

I asked him why he didn't subscribe to 'Britain Salutes Hungary' in October, seeing that he has a Hungarian grandmother.[40] He said, 'You must ask my father about charities now. I pass them on to him.' I said, 'Are you on good terms with him again?' He said, 'Yes, very.' I said that was very good news and that perhaps Victor would subscribe, as it is he that has the Hungarian mother.

I never quite know were I am with Jacob. I think that since the Banbury crash he regards me as hardly worth knowing because I am

---

38. Author and journalist.
39. Dorothy, née Pinto, always known as Dollie, m (1913) James de Rothschild (eldest son of Baron Edmond de Rothschild of Paris, Liberal MP 1929–45, owner of Waddesdon Manor); she died in 1988, aged ninety-three, leaving £92m; see 7 October 1989 and 25 February 1990.
40. Rozsika, daughter of Captain Alfred Edler von Wertheimstein of Nagy-Varad, Hungary, m (1907) the Hon. Nathaniel Charles Rothschild.

not rich any more. On the other hand, I have known him for a very
long time and it was I who arranged in the end for his marriage to
Serena who inherited a nice property from her father and for that time
a lot of money.[41]

Friday 12 May
Brian Walden rings at a quarter to six in the evening. He talked for
three quarters of an hour. 'I am very angry with you.' This was because
I had said, in my review of Willie Whitelaw's book, that it was a pity
that the *Sunday Times*, which bought the serialization of this excellent
book, felt it needed jazzing up with ungracious nuances of hostility
towards Mrs Thatcher extracted in a contrived interview.

He said, 'I want you to know that every word that I printed he
said. It wasn't my fault that the *Sunday Times* took some quotes out
and put them at the top of the front page. I had a complete transcript
of the interview. I left out a number of things which would have been
even more damaging to him and his relationship with Mrs Thatcher.
Willie's secretary checked it all and agreed it was an absolutely fair
transcript. I warned Willie each time he said something damaging that,
"You realize what you are saying and do you really want to say it?"
and he said, "Yes." Willie's great concern was to protect the £100,000
fee he was due to get from the *Sunday Times* which they weren't going
to pay him because they thought his book was dull.'

Brian went on, 'You and I are genuine Thatcherites. They don't like
us because we were previously in the Labour Party.'

He said, 'He doesn't like her and it was clear that he doesn't like
her as he talked to me. Then, by the way, he said about you, "That
dreadful old Lord Wyatt. He keeps ringing her up and giving her bad
advice." '

He said would I tell Mrs Thatcher what the truth is. I said I was a
bit reluctant to because I don't want her to be upset any more. My
whole aim was to prevent a breach between Willie and her and I was
trying to mollify the situation a bit in my review, as I had been doing
in private.

Brian then said, 'Will you tell her that when the next election
campaign comes I am prepared to come over from the Channel Islands,

---

41. WW was best man at the 1961 marriage of Jacob to Serena, elder daughter of Sir
    Philip Dunn (1905–76) and granddaughter of the Canadian steel magnate Sir James
    Dunn.

without any fee and without any other recognition, to be a part of her team to help her win the next election?'

We appear to have rung off on good terms. I hope so. I like him and he has been jolly good in his support of her; and of course it is also true that the Tory wets like Pym[42] and Whitelaw and the others don't like us. But I was surprised to find that Willie Whitelaw is so two-faced and that he was saying something unpleasant to Brian about me whereas he always comes up and congratulates me on the speeches I make in the Lords and says what a marvellous support I have been to Margaret and all that kind of thing.

I raised with Arnold about my play at Bromley. He wants to put in £3,000. I said I wouldn't ask him for more. He said, 'I'll do that and maybe I'll have the chance of meeting the leading lady.' So with Abdul Al Ghazzi saying he will produce £3,000 to £4,000 we are really about halfway to getting the money we need.

Petronella and I went to see the Rose Theatre remains by Southwark Bridge. It has to be covered up on Monday though the developers say it may one day be made visible to spectators.

Sunday 14 May
Spoke to Margaret.

She wasn't altogether surprised by Willie. I also told her what Willie had said about my ringing her up and giving her bad advice. She said, 'That is because you and I are fighters and you and I are exactly alike,' and I told her I agreed. Willie wants to compromise on the consensus and a quiet life and nothing to be ever a battleground.

I am glad I told her what Brian had said. It is much fairer to him and she has to realize what some of these people are like, even though it is hurtful. I still regard Willie as a very good-natured fellow and very loyal but not quite as much as he appears. She also thought it was something to do with her being a woman. That may be true.

I told her about Brian Walden's offer.

She said, 'That's a very good offer but he would have to come over two or three times before to make sure he knows how we are thinking at the moment.'

So I shot both the barrels.

I then spoke to her about the new management of Collins and how

---

42. Foreign Secretary, 1982–3; life peer 1987.

they would like her to write her memoirs when the time came. She didn't make much comment.

At half past nine Arnold Goodman rings. Would I speak to the Prime Minister as I am the only person who can do something to help. The Rose Theatre. Mr Biddle, the American archaeologist, thinks that putting gravel and sand on the site will make the site deteriorate and will not preserve it.

She said, 'If Arnold Goodman is not satisfied, why doesn't he ring Sieferts himself?' I duly rang Arnold and gave him the message.

Tuesday 16 May
Rang Margaret 8.00 a.m. to thank her for her action in saving the Rose Theatre. She said the difficulty was that previously the architects and archaeologists had seemed to agree that what they were doing would preserve the Rose Theatre.

There is no doubt that if I hadn't rung Margaret on Sunday night, the police would have removed the crowd and gravel would have been put upon the Rose Theatre on Monday.

All the jokes bar one which I made at the United Newspapers lunch [today], apart from my asides and spur of the moment inventions, came from Arnold Weinstock. I rang him early in the morning and he said, 'Give me time to think.' A little later on he rang back. That shows great tycoons running huge industrial companies always find the time to do something frivolous. It cheered him up thinking of the jokes.

Wednesday 17 May
Dinner at Alan Hare's.

Duke Hussey was there.

I asked him why he didn't step in and stop the BBC *Today* programme being run for Socialist propaganda by Brian Redhead[43] and reiterating totally untruthful reports from the Child Poverty Action Group and the Low Pay Unit, pretending that one-third of the country was in poverty. He said it was very difficult. I thought to myself that if I had been the Chairman as long as he has, by this time I would have sorted it all out.

On my right sat Tessa Keswick.

---

43. (1929–94); journalist and broadcaster; presenter, *Today* (BBC Radio 4), 1975–94.

She is very happy at being an assistant to Kenneth Clarke, political, though she is paid by the civil service.

She says the Conservative government, which she supports, is very bad about single parent families and women and enabling women to go out to work.

I said, 'I am very fond of women and I don't think they should be unfairly treated. You had better send me some material.'

Sunday 21 May

I was nervous about ringing Mrs Thatcher. Gail Sheehy in her profile of her for *Vanity Fair* had described visits to an Indian lady, ex-wife of Sir Frank Price.[44]

Apparently she gives some strange treatment with baths and tiny electric shocks. Gail Sheehy said that was how Margaret rejuvenated herself and why she looked so young. Naturally this was the only part of the article which was reproduced in Britain. It was all over the popular papers with jokes and cartoons.

I decided to ring Margaret at just on 11 p.m. She was working as usual. When I referred to the Gail Sheehy article I said, 'I don't know where she got that stuff about electric baths from. Was it true?' She was, I think, a little brusque. She said, 'I never read that sort of thing about myself and I disregard it.' From which I deduced it was true and she was pretty annoyed.

I said, 'The profile itself was remarkably good about you.'

Margaret replied, 'I thought she probably would write well. She seemed a very nice woman and a very intelligent woman and I thought sincere. But it is typical. They would never reprint anything nice about me over here.' She is getting very perturbed by the feeling that the media is against her.

I asked her about her row with Lawson. Just before the weekend she had said that the reason why we had this eight per cent inflation was that he had tried to maintain the pound at three Deutschmarks in early 1988. It was impossible and we had had to sell a great deal of sterling in order to keep the pound high.

She said, 'Nigel likes to take the credit when everything goes right. But he won't take the blame for any failure.' I said, 'But isn't inflation

---

44. Sir Frank Price, Lord Mayor of Birmingham, 1964–5; m 2 (div 1984) Veronica, daughter of Zubadri Singh; knight 1966.

coming down now? Isn't the medicine working?' She said, 'Well there is not much sign of it yet.'

She was a little terse about it.

I told her I would be writing in the morning for the *Times* on Tuesday about the Common Market.

I said, 'I wouldn't mind betting that we are the only country which actually honestly hands over our percentage of VAT to the Community.' She said, 'I wouldn't say that, Woodrow. It might be dangerous.'

I felt that Margaret did slightly blame me for the *Vanity Fair* article, writing something which could be used against her in England and to make fun of her. No woman likes her aids to beauty or youth being relayed in the press. Ladies who have face lifts, which she never has, try desperately to keep it secret.

Thursday 25 May

Dinner party at Cavendish Avenue. As Chips had been particularly helpful arranging lunch for the Skadden Arps people, I said he could have some exceptionally old champagne. It was Pommery 1929. There was very little life in it but a glorious taste and golden colour like nectarine. We also had Boyd-Cantenac 1964.

William Shawcross[45] was there with Olga Polizzi. We talked about how he was getting on with his book about Rupert. He came wearing a rather grubby, crumpled, light-coloured suit. Not how to arrive at a smart dinner party. Olga of course was beautifully dressed as ever. She thinks she is going to marry him. She said her father was wondering about it and said that he had been very tolerant about her love affairs. I thought for Charles Forte, a strict moralist, that is certainly true.

Olga is very important now in the Trusthouse Forte organization, ordering specifications and designers and builders and architects and so forth for new hotels. She is a competent girl, more competent than Rocco [her brother], but she doesn't think so. I have always liked her.

Lord King[46] was quite irritated. I had put a little tiny individual tub of Flora poly-unsaturated margarine in front of his place and said, 'This is what you must serve to your passengers on British Airways. Americans are very food conscious and you will get more if you do that.' He said he would certainly look into it.

---

45. The Hon. William Shawcross, writer; m 3 (1993) Olga Polizzi, née Forte.*
46. John King, chairman, British Airways, 1981–93; life peer 1983.

Friday 26 May

We left at about ten to drive to Bonython. On the way we stopped at the Cornish Brewery at Redruth to meet Mr Smith, the Managing Director. We were shown all the latest equipment they have which I find is very boring but he was anxious for us to approve of it. He has a marvellous bottling plant which would do for Cornish Spring Water.

I think we may be able to do a deal which will help Robbie [Lyle] with the death duties of the estate and give him a good income. It would also provide the shareholders, namely himself and myself as the main shareholders (myself with 26.3 per cent) with a reasonable income.

Saturday 27 May

A. L. Rowse came to lunch. He is eighty-six. Very friendly, enthusiastically so. He kept asking me to send his love to Margaret and tell her how much he admires her.

He said, 'We are going to rearrange history.' He then proceeded to explain how he came to think the Labour Party was no good but had been very bright during the time of Attlee and before the war. We both agreed that we had similar reactions to Labour because of the unforgivable injustice of before the war and we both agreed how good Attlee was. We both agreed that we had followed much the same course away from the Labour Party.

He brought me a copy of his *Cornish Childhood*, proudly saying it had sold half a million copies. That is tremendous. My poor little autobiography only sold ten thousand.

Unfortunately, he is rather deaf at the moment but he leans forward and cocks his ear and asks you to repeat things and talks merrily away. He has a narrow, alert, enquiring face with a Celtic head which is why the Cornish are known by the Saxons as the West Welsh.

Sunday 28 May

A lunch party for twenty-five people, all arranged around the pool.

William Golding was there and I asked him to sign my first edition of *Close Quarters* which he did.

Lady Golding is rather a jolly lady. She said she used to be pretty. I said, 'You are very attractive now,' which she is in her way. Nice round face and pleasantly plump.

John St Levan is an active seventy. Very keen on all things Cornish and helping the Cornish people. A good man and a nice man. He is much put out by Peter de Savary[47] and his Land's End concrete jungle which is attracting many visitors who stay looking around at Land's End instead of coming on to his house where, though it is owned in a sense by the National Trust, he gets revenue from the visitors. He said he had had four hundred there that day.

At 5.15 we left Bonython to go to St Michael's Mount.

It is like a fairy-tale castle; it has lovely alcoves and windows to look out at the sea; and it has its cannons which pooped off at the Spanish Armada. Recently, though, about a month ago, a party of French came in a yacht and stole two of the cannons, later ones [which] had been captured from the French in the Napoleonic Wars. They thought they should have them back. He was much annoyed about it. Nobody can trace them.

There is a portrait of Dolly Pentreath, buried at Penzance (pronounced Penzarnce by John St Levan so I suppose that must be right), the last woman to speak Cornish. John Opie, described by Reynolds as the 'wondrous Cornishman', painted her when she was very old. She looked dark and Welsh – a brooding spirit. There is a painting of my great-great etc. grandmother at Bonython by John Opie.

Wednesday 31 May
Dinner with Mark and Anouska Weinberg at Addison Road, meeting Henry Wrong[48] from the Barbican on the doorstep.

I sat on Anouska's left. She wore a dress which slit down the back. I put my hand on once or twice and it felt very pleasant. She seemed to be not displeased. She is very attractive and is also an exceedingly clever businesswoman.

---

47. International entrepreneur in the energy, property, finance, maritime and leisure fields.
48. Director, Barbican Centre, at this time.

Sunday 4 June

Rupert rang. He had just been to Hungary and was full of it. As though he was the first to discover the changes there. But he had not met Mr Pozsgay, the real power. He said they were asking whether he would like to start some newspapers as only foreigners could do it properly. One like the *Sun* and one like the *Times*. They are also interested in having him open television stations there.

He was then very worked up about China and all these murders taking place.[1] He said we should break off diplomatic relations at once and cancel the agreement with China over Hong Kong. I said, 'Steady on, steady on. We don't quite know how it is going to turn out yet.'

Just as I was going to bed Mrs Thatcher rang back. I had been cleaning my teeth and my false teeth were out so I had to jam them back in again otherwise I would have sounded strange. I said to her that if she was going to have to look for a successor to Nigel Lawson, Parkinson would be a good choice. They understand each other. He has done the Electricity Bill extremely well and he has got a good manner and he could manage it. She agreed but she said, 'I don't want Nigel to go. He has got to finish what he started first.' That is in total contradiction of all the rumours put out by the papers and the media that she wants to get rid of him.

She was horrified by the murders in Peking by the Chinese military and the old die-hard government.

I said, 'It all points that we have got to do something about Hong Kong. We cannot desert them like this and just say things are going to be all right.'

Monday 5 June

I received further income tax demands and I don't know how these are all being settled.

---

1. The Tiananmen Square massacre of Chinese students and others marching for democracy took place on 3 June; about 2,600 were killed.

However, I rang the watch shop where Robbie [the chauffeur] had taken my gold watch to be repaired. They had offered me to my amazement £4,000 on Friday for it and I had got them up to £4,500; and they said the cheque was in the post. So that will just be swallowed by income tax immediately. It is rather sad really that my last relic from Emil Bustani,[2] an old Rolex which now has got antiquarian value after thirty years, with its wonderful movement of the moon and the dates and the month, has gone.

Tuesday 6 June

Charles Moore rang to say how good my article was in the *Times* this morning about passports for the Hong Kong Chinese. He is doing a great double-spread editorial in the *Spectator* which he has never done before, going around the wrapper and supporting me. He said I am the only person who has really taken their case up properly. All the rest of the papers have been very mealy-mouthed about it.

Wednesday 7 June

She said, 'The extraordinary events in China have given us a chance now to do something about passports for Hong Kong residents. I have been trying for three years against the Home Office and the Foreign Office. I have sent for all the papers. I am going to sit down and go through them and see what we can do.'

I said, 'I have asked in the *Times* for the whole lot to be allowed passports to get something moving but I understand that is asking for a lot, though they will never come. It is an insurance [for them] to be able to get out if they want to.'

To the Derby. I find it always an anti-climax. I cannot get so worked up about the actual race. Again today I wasn't quite clear what came second and third. Nashwan won. But of course it is so much better on the television. When I saw the replay I knew what had been happening.

At lunch on our table was Sir Peter Middleton, the Secretary of the Treasury.

I told him I was seeing Alan Walters at the week-end and wondered how he would react. Surprisingly, he said he was very pleased. He likes Alan Walters and he thought it was very useful for the Prime Minister to have an economic adviser like that whom she could talk to easily and without difficulty of access. He, Sir Peter, thinks Alan Walters is

---

2. Lebanese politician, killed in an aeroplane accident in 1963.

very sound. So much for the notion that Nigel Lawson, or at least the Treasury, hate him.

Thursday 8 June
To lunch with Robin Janvrin, the Queen's Press Secretary, at Overton's.

I said, 'I feel very sorry for Princess Diana who can't even have dinner with a few friends without them being photographed and told she is in love with one of them or whatever. It is much harder on her in a way than it is on the Prince of Wales who ought to stop complaining that he doesn't like being the Prince of Wales because people can't understand it when he says he has nothing to do.'

I said, 'I have suggested to the Prime Minister that he should be put in charge of celebrations of the Year 2000 as Prince Albert took charge of the Great Exhibition in 1851.'

When we got in there it was very funny: there were the Prince of Wales' Secretary and the Princess of Wales' Secretary having lunch, just the two. I said, 'That's very good. Those two are talking to each other at least, even if their principals aren't.'

But I don't believe that their principals are not talking to each other. It is all much exaggerated by the press who get so much wrong.

Evening. Dragon Boat Hong Kong Association dinner. I sat next to the Governor of Hong Kong. David Young made a speech as the Cabinet Minister present. It was a sombre evening.

I liked Tim Renton[3] on my left. He told me he had been staying in Suffolk with the Mahmoud who owned the Derby winner. He took him on a shoot and they shot 1,600 birds in a few hours.

He told me that he was on my side but he explained quite reasonably that he had difficulties about immigration. He is having trouble with the Kurds who are coming here now, not because they are refugees from persecution but to get work, and they were being coached by the people who organize them in Turkey to say the right words to get past the immigration.

Saturday 10 June
At Badminton, staying with the Beauforts.

The legendary Sir Alan Walters, Mrs Thatcher's guru. Tall, thin, sharp, intelligent face. Grey hair but not bald. An enthusiastic jogger.

---

3. Conservative politician; MP, 1974–97; at this time Minister of State at the Home Office; life peer 1997.

Utterly charming and modest on the face of it but utterly convinced his views have no viable alternative. Open and not hesitant to say what he thinks or what has gone wrong.

He said he, too, used to vote Labour at one time. He hadn't realized that I had abandoned the party, or it had abandoned me, in the early seventies.

He says that it was really true that Lawson was trying to shadow the Deutschmark and pumping all the printed money into the economy by so doing. The interest rates had stayed low too long and the money supply had got out of control. It had wasted two years unnecessarily. He agreed that it was an endeavour to prove, without her knowing it, that entry into the EMS was desirable and would work.

When I asked him why she didn't sack him and didn't she know what he was doing, he said, 'Yes. I told her but I was away for two years, relevant years, in America. But I did warn her. She didn't know what to do about it. She couldn't very well sack Lawson and anyway she is a bad sacker.'

He said there is no real alternative to the high interest rates.

I said, 'Is this another stop-go?' He said, 'It looks like one but it isn't really. It's just a mistake that was made by Lawson. An unnecessary mistake.'

He said we should not join the EMS. It is a pity that there is so much talk about 'doing it at the right time'. I said, 'What would be the right time?' He said, 'We could say that when the European countries allow our insurance houses and our banks and our mortgage facilities to operate in exactly the same way in their countries as they do in Britain and as we allow any European countries to do here. You have got to really get the market open.'

He said the European common currency wouldn't be so bad if it wasn't for the Delors plan where they would be controlling our budgets. It should be more like the USA where the local states have their own tax systems. Then it might be possible. But the more you open up the Common Market in the world, the less necessary such things become.

I asked why he thought Nigel did it and he said he thought it was very difficult to tell people's motives but perhaps he wanted to have his achievement of joining the EMS to crown his successful career as a Chancellor which he had been very good at, as a tax reformer and in other ways.

He, Alan, thinks we should not have more than a flat rate of tax of twenty to twenty-five per cent and [should] abolish the higher rates. We wouldn't get any less revenue. We might even get more.

I said, 'She won't do that because she is still stuck with the Socialist notion that while encouraging people to earn more you must punish them when they do, even though they have been creating wealth for the nation as a whole. It is not part of her system yet or part of the British system. That is why there is no chance that any large number of people would come from Hong Kong to a place where there is a forty per cent top rate tax and Kinnock promises fifty per cent plus nine per cent for national insurance with no limit, making fifty-nine per cent.'

After lunch Caroline [Beaufort] had taken Alan Walters on a short tour and I went too. In the hall she explained that the ladies of the house in 1863, fed up with their men always being out hunting and they didn't always want to go, devised this game of badminton. She pointed out the places on the walls from which the net was hung and showed us the original bats which were used and the shuttlecocks. In tournaments, international and otherwise, the court is still the same size as the hall at Badminton.

Sunday 11 June
Victor [Rothschild] came to lunch, flown over by David's aeroplane and pilot from Cambridge, who also picked up Michael Tree. Victor looked very shaky and grey. I hadn't seen him for a couple of years. He seems to have lost most of his sparkle and caustic wit.

He said I hadn't got it quite right about Jacob's inheritance at the bank. He said the shares were lost further back to Evelyn's family. He thinks that Evelyn[4] must be worth £1,000,000,000 now.

He said that his relations with Jacob had never recovered since the great bust-up when Jacob had a tremendous row with Evelyn and left the bank. He doesn't think Evelyn is at all nice. But at the time he was the Chairman of the bank and he felt he couldn't intervene. Jacob bitterly upbraided him because he should have protected him as his son.

He was afraid that Jacob would throw him out, Tess and himself, from the rent free apartment they had in St James's when he inherited

---

4. Evelyn de Rothschild, second cousin of Victor (their grandfathers were brothers); succeeded Victor as chairman of N. M. Rothschild & Sons; knight 1989.*

it from his aunt. But he didn't. He has made a deal with Jimmy Goldsmith who has taken the rest of the house.

Victor was sad. I asked him who was the fifth man[5] but he said he didn't know.

Now he says he considered suing the *Daily Express* which had a headline saying, 'Is Lord Rothschild the Fifth Man?' But his solicitor had said, 'Don't because it will cost you a lot of money. You would no doubt win but you would be asked lot of questions in the witness box. Somebody like Bob Alexander[6] might appear for the newspaper and you would find it very unpleasant.'

There had been some talk last night about the Dick Hern affair. Arnold [Weinstock] was quite emphatic that Dick Hem had been extremely ill and said he couldn't go on and that was why the arrangement had been made with William Hastings Bass.[7] He then said later that he had made a very good recovery, when Hastings Bass had already been invited to take over as the Queen's trainer there, and he wanted to stay put. Everything, according to Arnold, had been done to accommodate him, including this arrangement by which he is sharing the stables though that doesn't seem altogether satisfactory.

There seem to be two sides to this strange story and I swayed back to the Queen's and Porchester's side after this conversation.

I had left a message when I got back from Badminton for Margaret to say I had rung and if she wanted to speak to me I would be there. At about twenty past seven she rang. She was delighted to hear that I had been talking at great length to Alan Walters. She said he is absolutely brilliant and how modest he was.

We talked about Hong Kong. She surprised me. She said that what she is worrying about and is most exercised about is how can we hand over Hong Kong at all to these dreadful people who do these awful things to their own subjects.

It is very curious. At one moment she goes even further than me by even contemplating an arrangement whereby Hong Kong is never handed over to China because of their unreliability and in the next she

5. Victor Rothschild was a member of MI5 during the Second World War; there had been newspaper rumours in 1986 that he might be the fifth man involved with the Soviet spies Burgess, Maclean, Philby and Blunt.

6. Eminent QC; life peer 1988.

7. Son of Mrs Priscilla Hastings, member of the Tote Board; in 1990 he succeeded his kinsman as 16th Earl of Huntingdon.

is not so keen as me on all these passports involving so many potential immigrants here.

When I told her that Alan Walters thought that we could get inflation down to four per cent by the next election she said, 'Only if we do what he says.'

Margaret said there is a lot of jealousy of him. I said, 'Not from Peter Middleton whom I sat next to at the Jockey Club on Wednesday at the Derby.'

She said, 'Yes, he's not jealous and he gets on well with Terry Burns.[8] But some of them are jealous of him.'

At about half past eight Norman Lamont rang. I told him I had been staying in the same house as Alan Walters and he was rather glum. I said he thought very highly of Nigel Lawson and he seemed not to believe me so I said he'd said, 'He is a very great reforming Chancellor.'

Then he told me he would give me an inkling of what was going on about the report [on the Tote] from Lloyds Merchant Bank. He said one of the strong options they suggest is either selling or having a management buy-out of the Tote Bookmakers. I said, 'That is quite mad as you can see from the papers I sent to you.' He said, 'I understand your position but Douglas Hurd is not necessarily very strong on this. He wants the whole thing to be discussed in quite a quick committee, perhaps an internal one, in relation to how racing should be funded.' I said, 'That would be an absurd thing to do, to get rid of our betting shops. In any case he can't order us to. He can't have an Act of Parliament saying that.'

Monday 12 June
In the evening Geoffrey Ampthill gave us dinner in his new grill room [at the House of Lords]. It is called the Barry Room.

It has the functional purpose of supporting weight of floors above; with lovely arches and the old stonework cleaned it looked absolutely charming.

He gave us no end of 1981 Château Batailley fifth growth, extremely good.

---

8. Chief economic adviser to the Treasury at this time; knight 1983.

Tuesday 13 June

Went to a lunch given by the Chairman of Lloyds and his Council.

Before lunch in came Mary Archer looking very delicious.[9] She is such a pretty girl. She wore a green, flowery top or bodice and a white skirt. Her hair was beautifully in place. She wore elegant but not flashy jewellery.

She represents the external people in the syndicates. Marcus Kimball,[10] who is on the same committee, said at first they were worried that she would be letting Jeffrey Archer know what was going on through pillow talk. I said, 'I don't think there is any fear of that. She is the most competent girl. She was at one time Fellow of two colleges and she still is of one. She is a scientist and a researcher.'

She told me that she was writing a book about solar energy – not DIY but a serious study into the possibilities of it from a scientific angle.

She has perked up no end since the great libel action. It is quite clear that she is tough in an acceptable way and I said, 'There is a marvellous brain lurking behind those beautiful eyes of yours.' She also has very nice legs though her bottom is getting a tiny bit wider these days. But her figure and weight remain as trim as ever.

After lunch I went to the Lords and then on to the Commons to listen to Margaret dealing with her questions. She was harried about the rift between Lawson and herself. She denied it and Lawson sat beside her nodding his agreement with her. She said they were all united in the policy to bring down inflation.

Dinner at the Connaught with just Rupert and Anna and ourselves, Anna looking in full beauty and I like her much better again now. She has become warmer again, not so self-conscious. We both gave poor Rupert the going over. I said about privacy, 'Is it really necessary to do a thing in the *News of the World* whereby the wretched Robson, who was the manager of the English football team, was pilloried by some woman he had had an affair with who told it all to the *News of the World* with vivid detail?'

So Rupert said, 'He shouldn't have done it.' I said, 'No, but people

9. Mary, née Weeden, scientist; Fellow of Newnham College, Cambridge, and Lector in Chemistry, Trinity College, Cambridge, 1976–86, Bye-Fellow of Newnham since 1987; member, Council of Lloyd's, 1989–92; m (1966) Jeffrey Archer.*

10. Conservative politician; MP, 1956–83; external member, Council, Lloyd's, 1982–90; life peer 1985.

do that, you know very well. I know you don't because you are very strait-laced,' at which point Anna said, 'I would be after him with a knife if I found him straying.' She looked as though she meant it.

Wednesday 14 June
Arranged for Alan Walters to come to a late dinner on Friday to talk to Rupert at Cavendish Avenue.

Friday 16 June
Rupert immediately warmed to Alan Walters whom he had never met before.

The more I see of Alan Walters the more I like him but the less certain I am that he is as modest as it is claimed.

He told us how he had argued with Margaret before the 1981 Budget that it must be a tight Budget otherwise she would never get the direction to growth which she wanted. She had turned him down again and again. Then ten days or so before the Budget was about to be made her Economic Private Secretary rang up and said the Prime Minister wanted him to tell him that she thinks he is right and the Budget would be on the lines he had proposed. It seems she had seen Geoffrey Howe and said it had got to be like that and he had agreed. Geoffrey only had about two weeks to readjust his Budget. Alan Walters was amazed because she had been arguing vehemently against him, Alan, and then she suddenly changed course. I said, 'It is often the way with her. She may argue against you to hear the arguments from you and she gets convinced. She then takes them on board and acts.'

Saturday 17 June
The Queen's Club. Lendl[11] was in the semi final. Tim Bell, Margaret's great public relations chum, was giving the party and providing the seats.

I stayed to the end and then set out to go back by tube. I took the wrong way out of the Queen's Club first and had to be redirected by passers-by, who were very amiable, to Barons Court tube station. It took about a quarter of an hour to walk there in the heat. I then went into a tube station for the first time, I suppose, in about twenty years.

---

11. Ivan Lendl, no. 1 seed for Wimbledon in 1989 but defeated by Becker in the semi-final.

I found the escalators absolutely filthy and I am not surprised about the fires.[12] I also found them menacing as they went down from a steep height. I had a little panic moment, thinking there might be a black man behind me when I was alone on the escalator about to hit me on the head.

The trains came surprisingly quickly. They weren't as bad internally as I had expected. There were some Coca-Cola tins empty on the seats. There were a good deal more non-whites than there used to be but I didn't see any sign of menaces.

There were a number of black people and elderly whites, some much older than myself, on the tube trains who didn't seem frightened.

Sunday 18 June
Margaret.

She said, 'It will be a difficult week but I shall have to bear it.' I said, 'Don't be despondent about the low Euro polls for you. It will all come back by the next election. You will make it so. You always will. As you said, you have done the unpopular things or are doing them first so by the time we get to the election they will have become popular.'

Margaret said, 'I am not going to be pushed into a reshuffle. I shall only do it when I am ready.'

Dinner at the Lamonts.

I asked young [Mark] Lennox-Boyd, who is very pleasant, what they were going to do about Ernest Saunders, the disgraced Chief Executive of Guinness.[13] 'He made you all very rich, about four times richer than you were, and now he is being carted. I know he was doing things which were illegal. I went to see him and I realized that when I said, "Are you telling the truth about your innocence?" and I didn't believe him when he said that he had done nothing wrong. Nevertheless, the poor fellow is absolutely ruined. He has been hanging about

---

12. A reference to the Kings Cross underground fire in April 1988.
13. Ernest Saunders, Sir Jack Lyons and four others were charged in 1987 with various offences connected with the takeover of the Distillers' Company, but the first Guinness trial did not open until February 1990. In the end Saunders was found guilty of twelve offences, Lyons of four. In December 1996 the European Court of Human Rights ruled that Saunders' trial had been unfair because of the use of evidence given before the inspectors without the right of silence. Mark Lennox-Boyd's mother was a Guinness, hence WW's probing.

for three years awaiting a trial which never arrives. He is destitute. Will you do something about him when it is all over?'

He said he thought perhaps they ought to try and do something about that though it was a bit difficult at the moment, which I understood.

Mrs Lamont had taken enormous trouble with the dinner, having cooked it herself. It was very good. The wine we drank was Grand Cru Chablis. It was excellent. I drank too much of that and of the magnum of Fortnum's house champagne which he was giving us before dinner.

Monday 19 June
I spoke at length to my new telephone pal, Dr Martin Holmes, a senior Visiting Research Fellow at Mansfield College [Oxford]. He had written a splendid article in the *Wall Street Journal* on June 6th. I was intending copiously to crib from it but I wanted to know a number of extra points and what he meant.

When I had finished my article [for the *Times*], Charlie Wilson rang up and said he wanted me to do a much longer piece all about the Euro elections. I said I had just written about the EMS.

That was twelve o'clock. I asked him for some extra money. He said, 'You have only got to write another two hundred words,' and I said, 'Well I want another £300,' and he said, 'No, £200,' so I said, 'Make it £250.'

Dinner with Elizabeth Harris[14] who still looks very young.

She seemed to be having some success with her business promoting hotels and whatnot. She is moving to a small house in Fulham.

We had some very good Léoville Barton 1975. She said it was from the remains of the Richard Harris cellar, one of her previous husbands who she says is very good to her and has helped her with this new house in Fulham.

After the ladies left the dining-room Peter Rawlinson[15] said he still goes on disliking Margaret, thinking she prevented him from becoming

14. The Hon. Elizabeth Aitken, née Rees-Williams, daughter of 1st Baron Ogmore (Liberal politician); m 1 (1957–69) Richard Harris, actor; m 2 (1971–5) Rex Harrison, actor; m 3 (1980) Peter Aitken, grandson of 1st Lord Beaverbrook.
15. Lawyer and Conservative politician; Solicitor General, 1962–4; Attorney General, 1970–4; life peer 1978. His autobiography *A Price Too High* was published in 1989.

Lord Chancellor. I said, 'You did treat her rather roughly, didn't you, when you were together in the shadow Cabinet. What do you expect? Actually she has never said to me anything other than favourable things about you.' I didn't add that I think she always thought that Peter was not quite the lawyer he is cracked up to be. His book has had a terrific success and he is now going to write one about F. E. Smith.

Petronella has walked straight into this trial job for two months at the *Daily Telegraph*. She is going to be on the 'Peterborough' diary, writing paragraphs as well as articles and generally learning the trade as well as getting a salary.

Tuesday 20 June
Rang Margaret at 7.15 a.m.

I sent round to her by hand the article from the *Wall Street Journal* by Dr Martin Holmes because she said she wanted to read it. She seemed to be in good spirits and inclined to go on talking for a bit longer but I was unable to do so because I was in too much of a hurry with having to leave for Ascot at ten o'clock.

Wednesday 21 June
Again Ascot.

I found the girl in the grandstand at the bottom who had said to me yesterday morning she could do with some cold drinks or words to that effect, whereupon I had got Mark Kershaw to organize them for all the four hundred and fifty staff on duty. That was to be repeated again today. So that shows that something worthwhile happens when I do go around.

Isabel and John Derby for lunch. Isabel is most put out. Baroness Trumpington (Jean),[16] the large and wonderful Minister from the Lords, was wearing exactly the same dress as herself but of course many sizes larger. Isabel was very annoyed. I said, 'Where has your dress come from?' She said, 'Lanvin,' after I had teasingly asked if it had come from Marks & Spencer. Others thought perhaps it didn't really come from Lanvin as Baroness Trumpington seems unlikely to be in that class of spending.

Tim Bell, when he was talking about Mrs Thatcher, said she was very interested in the peccadilloes of her entourage. When it was

---

16. Parliamentary Under-Secretary, Ministry of Agriculture, Fisheries and Food, at this time; life peer 1980.

announced that Cecil Parkinson's girlfriend Sara Keays was pregnant, she sat there looking very puzzled. She worked it out on her fingers and said, 'It must have been during the election campaign that he did it. I can't think how he found the time.' Cecil Parkinson was then Chairman of the Conservative Party, running a successful campaign and apparently non-stop on the job.

He [Bell] was telling stories about his and my relations with Mrs Thatcher. He said, 'Woodrow always reassures and bolsters her. If a third world war broke out, Woodrow would ring her and say, "Don't worry, Margaret. I'll put it straight in the *News of the World* on Sunday." ' Everybody roared with laughter.

While we were having lunch Piers Bengough came in.[17] He came over to me and said would Verushka and I have tea with the Queen after the fourth race. I could hardly have said no but I thought it was a bit of a nuisance as we had so many people coming in later as well.

I said nothing to the Queen except, 'Good afternoon Ma'am,' and then came the Queen Mother who was as usual very bubbly.

We were taken to sit at her table. I sat next to her on her left.

When the liveried flunkies brought round sandwiches, filled rolls and so forth, she kept saying would I like this one or that one. I didn't really want one and said, 'Well I don't know.' So she said, 'I'll try them for you.' She tried several things and said, 'Oh no, don't have that one,' took another one and said, 'No, don't have that one.'

I was laughing and she was laughing and I said, 'This reminds me of Eddie Cantor in *Roman Scandals*. Do you remember how he was the Royal food taster for the Roman Emperor and he was in the plot to poison the Emperor? They gave him some fish in the kitchen and he was told the one without the parsley was the one without the poison. He kept muttering this to himself the whole way to the place where the Emperor was sitting and then he saw that both the fishes had pieces of parsley on and there had been a mistake. So he was in an absolute frenzy and didn't know which one to taste first. Now it seems that you are doing the tasting for me which appears to be the wrong way round.'

I told her about my new discovery in well written detective novels.

---

17. Colonel Sir Piers Bengough, Her Majesty's Representative, Ascot, 1982–97; Jockey Club steward, 1974–7 and 1990–2; former amateur jockey riding in four Grand Nationals; knight 1986.

They are books by Roy Lewis about a detective called Eric Ward who retired from the police and became a solicitor.[18]

We still went on talking, the Queen Mother and I, after everybody else had gone. Then she said, 'Come and watch the race,' so we went up to the big chairs lined right in front of the Royal Box.

We thought that the race was just starting. She got her glasses [binoculars] and we couldn't find the horses. I said, 'How very odd.' The television was on behind describing the race.

After a bit the Queen came up and said, 'What are you doing?' and the Queen Mother said we were watching the race. The Queen said, 'But it's finished,' I said, 'What!' and she said, 'Yes. That's a repeat going on the television.'

Then the Queen began to laugh and I had never seen the Queen laugh so much before.

I said to the Queen that we thought the horses must have disappeared behind some hitherto undiscovered bushes. I said, 'You had better not employ us to look after your horses for you, Ma'am.' The more this idiotic situation went on, the more the Queen laughed, and then she went on still laughing, with a lovely smile on her face, and the Queen Mother said, 'We are not very good at the flat racing. We prefer the jumping.'

Then we went out to dinner with Stanley and Hilda Rubin. Hilda is Netta Weinstock's sister. The Mortimers were there.[19] He said, 'Margaret is yesterday's woman. She is finished. She won't win the next election.' I said, 'John, you are far too clever to be so optimistic.'

I like John Mortimer. He told me he is writing a sequel to his book *Paradise Postponed* called *Titmus Revisited*. Titmus was modelled on Norman Tebbit. I said, 'You have fallen in love with Norman Tebbit,' and he said, 'Yes. The more I write this book, the more I see of Norman Tebbit and the nicer I think he is.'

Thursday 22 June
Last day of Royal Ascot.

Willie [Whitelaw] was saying how he and Peter Carrington didn't

---

18. Lewis also wrote other crime novels featuring a Northumbrian planning officer called Arnold Landon.
19. John Mortimer, lawyer, novelist and playwright; *Paradise Postponed* was published in 1985, televised in 1986; *Titmus Regained* was published in 1990, televised in 1991.

like Mrs Thatcher but decided to back her loyally which they did. He said he then became firm friends with her and devoted to her. He said, 'She does bend from time to time when she thinks it's necessary. She is not as intransigent as it is made out.' He accepts how difficult it was for her to enter these male chauvinist portals of the Tory Party as the Leader. It was bound to make her seem tough and aggressive, taking command of the show.

David Metcalfe brought Kenneth Tynan's widow.[20] She wrote a book about her husband and told the world his sexual peculiarities. She was once very pretty, obviously. She still has reasonable looks. In her book I read for the first time, I said to her, that my [second] wife Alix[21] had had an affair with her husband: 'I knew nothing about it but you have a signed confession.' She replied, 'Yes, but not from Ken, from your previous wife.'

She wore a badge which said 'Mrs David Metcalfe' which she clearly wasn't. That was very risky. If David Metcalfe had been found out by Piers Bengough as having done that, he would never be allowed to go to Ascot again.

In the afternoon yesterday, sitting in our Tote room, I suddenly felt somebody tickling the hair at the back of my head. I turned round and it was Princess Michael. She was very beautifully dressed in white and I complimented her on that. Prince Michael was with her. I said, 'Don't worry about all that stuff in the *Sun.*' A nasty story was told to the *Sun* by Barrett, the man who were their Private Secretary after Mountbatten died and whose Private Secretary he had been.

I said, 'Why don't you have proper contracts with these people so that they can never reveal anything – legally enforceable ones?' She said, 'We were so innocent at the time we didn't realize it would be necessary, particularly as he had been Mountbatten's Private Secretary.' I said, 'I don't think anybody is going to take any notice.' She said very honestly, 'Some of it is true. There is always a grain of truth in these things.' The article was all about her being difficult and treating Michael badly and doing all kinds of things to get money which I know to be true because she has said so to me.

I must say I like her despite her strange flamboyant ways. The truth

---

20. Kathleen Halton, m (1967) Kenneth Tynan (1927–80, drama critic and National Theatre literary consultant, his second marriage). *The Life of Kenneth Tynan* was published in 1987.
21. Née Robbins, m WW 1948–56; m 2 John Coleman, journalist.

is they haven't got any money, or at least very little, and she has always thought they ought to have more to keep up the role of a Royal Princess.

It was a little sad, curiously, leaving the Tote room as we did before the last race. We had quite a lot of jolly people in during the week. Next year could be my last year if my term is not renewed either by the racing trusts or by Hurd who will never do it if he is still Home Secretary.

Friday 23 June

After hearing blares of hostility against Margaret on the wireless, even including Nicholas Soames who says that she will have to bend and make concessions, and having heard also Leon Brittan quoted as saying she must join the EMS, and Lord Cockfield[22] saying the same, I felt I must ring her up and find out if she was going to stand firm as everybody was saying she was not going to. So I duly did and she is going to stand firm.

She said she didn't give a damn about what Cockfield said – he was previously a European Commissioner appointed by her who went native. And as for Leon Brittan, well, that was a sad case. Nicholas Soames wasn't always steady under gunfire.

Allan Davis brought Linda Thorsen [actress] to Cavendish Avenue. We sat in the garden. They drank champagne but I began with tea. She is tall, elegant. A woman with a very good figure.

She loves the play but thought that smoking marijuana for the Hyacinth set would seem very tame so could it be crack?[23]

We discussed this and she said, 'In America the schoolchildren often try to take coke. Sometimes they are sold baby powder and they don't realize until twenty minutes afterwards or so that they have been sold the wrong stuff.' I said, 'That is a brilliant idea. I will work that in.'

She was a jolly lady full of spirit and go. She has been married four times. She complained that one paper said she was forty-three but she was only forty-two. 'That's when a woman is at the height of her sexual and other powers,' I said. She promptly agreed.

---

22. Former managing director, Boots, and chairman, Price Commission; government minister in House of Lords; then a Vice President, European Commission, 1985–8; life peer 1978.
23. Hyacinth is the teenage daughter of Philip, the MP hero of WW's play; she attends a smart London school.

Sunday 25 June

The *Observer* Harris Poll showed Labour fourteen points ahead.

I thought I must ring her to say she must 'accentuate positive'. I couldn't remember the rest of the words. Petronella knew them: 'You've got to accentuate the positive/eliminate the negative/latch on to the affirmative/and don't mess with Mr In Between.' I rang Anthony Quinton,[24] the great expert on lyrics of this period. He was cutting wood at the time at his house in the country. It was written by a man called Harold Arlen in 1945.

When I rang her I said, 'You are too young to remember this but you must put the sentiment in when the EEC issue some communiqué at the end of the Madrid Summit.[25] You must accentuate the positive.' She knew some of the lines, too.

Allan Davis rang. Great excitement. Bruce Montague, who just finished last night at Wolverhampton doing a year's tour with a play by Neil Simon, a very good playwright, had read the play between the time he got back last night and this morning.

He is very keen on the play because he says it is so witty and very funny and he would very much like to do the part of Philip.

Then we went off to Smith's Lawn, the Guards Polo Club, where David Montagu was giving a big lunch because Rothmans (he's the Chairman)[26] have been sponsoring the finals there all this week up until Sunday.

Mrs Johann Rupert, a South African girl who was exceedingly pretty, worked for Rothmans and her husband ran Cartier in South Africa.[27] I thought she would be really right-wing but no, not at all. She had voted for Dennis Worrall who was the previous Ambassador in London and went back for the last election. He was quite against

---

24. Philosopher; President, Trinity College, Oxford, 1978–87; chairman, British Library, 1985–90; life peer 1982.*

25. To be held on 26 June.

26. Since 1988.

27. Rothmans International was controlled by companies owned by the South African Rupert family until January 1999 when they became a minority shareholder in an enlarged BAT (British American Tobacco). Johann Rupert's father, Anton, started a drycleaning business in 1941, and moved into liquor and tobacco, buying the original Rothmans company from its founder in the mid 1950s. In 1988 Johann Rupert put the international interests of the family holding company, Rembrandt, into the Swiss-based company Richemont which controlled Dunhill and Cartier. BAT paid £5bn for Rothmans.

the government, which he had been representing in London, as a candidate.

She said next time, when the election comes up in September, she is going to vote for de Klerk's National Party. She thinks there really is a genuine attempt going forward now to get a solution on a political basis. She hopes and believes that de Klerk will protect the minorities, including the white minority, and give them some reserve power as well.

The polo I found more interesting than I had expected. It is amazing how they can hit the ball with considerable accuracy while their heads are moving and their horses are moving and while holding the horses with one hand.

A few of David Montagu's directly personal party had seats in the Royal Box after lunch.

I now find myself almost human talking to the Queen whereas previously I had been tongue-tied.

She said to me, 'David Montagu says that if the Arabs were to go on dominating British racing, we would be left with the kind of horses pulling those little carriages and dog carts we have just seen.' I said, 'Yes, the Arabs won twelve out of twenty-four races at Ascot. But nothing can be done about it. It's the weight of money.' She agreed that nothing could be done about it but she seemed slightly put out at the idea.

The mother of the Duchess of York turned up.[28] She had been the wife – I think they have now separated – of an Argentine polo player. Though she had some moles on her cheeks, she looked very much more elegant than her daughter, much more attractive and she was pleasant enough.

Robin Tavistock[29] said he thought that Henry Porchester and Arnold Weinstock had behaved disgracefully towards Dick Hern and he didn't believe the excuses made. He said Porchy can do anything with the Queen. When she was very young she was much in love with him and wanted to marry him. But he wouldn't marry her. She then fell in love with Prince Philip.

But she still loves Porchester in a way and, for her, he can do no wrong.

---

28. Susan, née Wright, m 1 Major Ronald Ferguson, m 2 Hector Barrantes; d 1998.
29. Marquess of Tavistock; director, United Racecourses, 1977–84.

Tuesday 27 June

Levy Board meeting. It was Stoker's, the Marquess of Hartington's,[30] last meeting before becoming Senior Steward [of the Jockey Club]. I said I thought he would make one of the best we have had for many years. I can't say that tonight when I go to the Levy Board dinner for Fairhaven, the departing one, and for Stoker, the new one.

Arnold said this morning that they had a nice holiday in Sardinia except that it had been spoilt by reading my article about not joining the EMS. He said I didn't know what I was talking about and that I shouldn't write about economics. I said, 'Don't be absurd.' He said, 'It is all Walters.' I said, 'Nonsense. It is also Dr Martin Holmes and Patrick Minford[31] who know a great deal more about it than you do.'

In the Lords, Frank Longford came up to me and said, 'You are the last person left supporting Mrs Thatcher so what will you do when she is thrown out?' I said, 'Nothing. I only support her because she is not a Tory and I am not a Tory either. She's a Manchester Liberal.' Then he said, 'You wrote in your book that you were in love with her.' I said, 'I am a bit, platonically.'

He said, 'Of course you have moved so much to the right.' I said, 'Have I? Am I on the right when I attack the government for not giving passports to Hong Kongers? I think these terms of right and left are out of date.'

Wednesday 28 June

Rang Margaret to tell her I was proud of her. She did the Common Market Summit at Madrid brilliantly.

She is very pleased that she has got it stated that the Delors report was only one approach to greater economic union.

Thursday 29 June

I went to the Lords where I popped up to ask a supplementary on a question about Hong Kong and told Glenarthur that he should warn Geoffrey Howe, who is going to Hong Kong over the week-end, that unless he proposed something more positive than he has so far he might well be lynched. This got quite a lot of attention in the newspapers the next morning and in the *Evening Standard* on Friday as well.

---

30. Eldest son of the Duke of Devonshire.*
31. Edward Gonner Professor of Applied Economics, University of Liverpool, since 1976.

In the evening we drove to Cliveden. William Astor[32] and his wife were giving a dinner for about thirty-five people. It is the family house and reverts at some point from the National Trust to William's estate. He is the owner or part owner of the hotel now operating in it. Before dinner we had champagne on the terrace. It was a sunlit evening and the grounds stretching out beyond with hills and fields, miles and miles from London, were green and beautiful.

I sat at Annabel Astor's table on her right.

Annabel wanted to talk to me about her mother and the past. She said she remembered me as a child when I used to go to Bruern Abbey when her mother was married to Michael Astor.[33] I said, 'Good Lord. Was your mother Pandora Jones?' She said, 'Yes.' I said, 'Now I see why your face reminds me of somebody.' She said, 'But I am nothing like so beautiful,' and I said, 'You are very attractive,' which she is, though she is right in thinking herself far short of the beauty her mother was. We talked at some length about Pandora and Michael and also Pandora's next husband, a plastic surgeon whom Annabel described as being Jewish. She said he made her mother very happy. She died of cancer very young.

I told her about the malacca walking stick, with the silver top inscribed, which her mother had given me at Christmas 1964. I thought to myself, 'Perhaps I should arrange to leave it to her with its nice inscription.' I told her everybody was a bit in love with her mother including myself.

John King was there. I said, 'I am told you have already started putting tubs of poly-unsaturated margarine on your aeroplanes.' He said, 'Yes, I did give that instruction after I came to dinner with you.'

Friday 30 June
Allan Davis rings to say that Michael Medwin, who is apparently quite a good actor, wants to do the part of Jack [a friend of the hero, also an MP] but Bromley was not available.

32. 4th Viscount Astor, m (1976) Annabel Sheffield, née Jones.
33. Hon. Michael Astor (1916–80), son of 2nd Viscount Astor, m 2 (1961–8) Pandora, née Clifford (d 1988), her second husband; she had married 1 Timothy Jones, son of Sir Roderick Jones of Reuters and the writer Enid Bagnold.*

He is now seeking to get Greenwich which will be very good, if he can get it.

It seems the place is run by a left-wing feminist but Allan Davis says they have a right-wing audience.

Monday 3 July

Spoke to Margaret at 7.40 a.m. She is in much better spirits now, after her success at Madrid has been realized.

Lunch kindly arranged by Chips Keswick at Hambros. I thanked him for the enormous salmon he sent. I said it was the size of a policeman. Verushka [had] said she couldn't get it into her deep freeze but she managed it all right in the end.

The object of the lunch was to help Joe Flom of Skadden Arps, and Maurice Kramer and Bruce Buck from their London office, to meet people who might be interested in doing legal work in America.

Joe Flom spoke very well about the difference between the cultures in America and in Britain and how things didn't mean the same thing though the language was the same. He agreed that they were certainly very expensive but he pointed out that their rent in the City of London was twice as much as their New York rent.

He is small with grey hair and elderly but very keen, sharp, bright eyes, fluent and persuasive.

The young South African, Johann Rupert from the Rembrandt Group, said they are the biggest shareholder in Rothmans, owning forty-three per cent, and David Montagu was an old family friend. That is obviously how David got the job of Chairman.

Michael Blakenham[1] came in at the end and I asked him, to get him going in the conversation, what his experience of American lawyers was. He spoke at some length and agreed that they were very expensive but that you couldn't do anything without them. It seems that Joe Flom's right when he says they play to a large extent the role of the investment banker here.

Blakenham always puzzles me.

He has a not very alert face. His hair is tousled, his face is large and hangs down, the stubble grows fast and dark, making him look

---

1. 2nd Viscount Blakenham; chairman, Pearson, 1983–97, *Financial Times* Group, 1983–93.

as if he hasn't shaved properly which I am sure he has. I think he is more shrewd than he appears but I don't think he is a ball of fire.

I went back with the Skadden Arps people to their offices and talked for a while. I pointed out a flaw in their offer document for sea containers which they are doing on behalf of an American and an English firm. It was that they said that it was only their *present* intention not to dispose of the ferries.

I said, 'I will write to David Young [Secretary of State for Trade and Industry] about it for you but it would be much better if you could give me a note in which you said that you are prepared to make that stronger, such as not for five years or something to that effect.' Flom said that was a very good point and they were going to look into it straight away.

We discussed their seminar for November 16th. Would I get Arnold Weinstock or Hector Laing?

I think they may feel that I am worth having as a consultant.

I was feeling sad yesterday about Dora Gaitskell who has just died at the age of eighty-eight. She was a great fighter, like a fighting bantam, small. She was younger than Hugh. She was furious about Annie Fleming[2] and his love for her but she was deeply loyal and she fought like mad against his enemies. Alas, she had been a bit gaga for some years.

How different it would have been if he hadn't died in 1963 when he was about fifty-six. The Labour Party would have won much more easily in 1964. I would have been in his Cabinet and I might never have left the Labour Party because it would never have gone down the slippery slope towards extremism as it did under Harold Wilson.

I rang Brian Walden in the Channel Islands, telling him that Margaret would be asking for him to come over and he was very pleased.

He said he thought she should get rid of Kenneth Clarke because he didn't seem to be a caring man in charge of the NHS. He said never mind the rights and wrongs of the NHS but you just have to have the

---

2. (1913–81); Anne, née Charteris, m 1 (1932–44) 3rd Baron O'Neill (d 1944), m 2 (1945–52) 2nd Viscount Rothermere (Esmond, d 1978), m 3 (1952) Ian Fleming, the writer.

image right. Some wet lady like Virginia Bottomley[3] would do it very well, weeping over the patients, and no one could say she was hard-hearted like they do about Kenneth Clarke. Maybe he has got something there.

So the great debate [House of Lords] about whether a divorcee could be ordained or whether they could stay in the Church as a priest if they married a divorcee.

I said to several people, and several said to me, that it is none of our business what the Church of England does about its priests. My own view is that the Church should be disestablished anyway. I had promised the Archbishop I would come and support him because he had been so pleasant about Robert Law being a candidate for the Bishopric of Truro. Now he had asked me in return to do so and I kept my word.[4]

I arrived at the Griersons[5] for dinner very late.

Jimmy Goldsmith was there. He talks a combination of rubbish and sense.

He criticized Margaret for her style in approaching Europe. He said he agreed with the Bruges speech[6] but what these people on the Continent want is a vision, an idealistic vision. I said, 'You should be supporting her. She has got the real vision of a flexible evolution of Europe. Not some ridiculous federal government.'

After dinner I sat next to Mrs Black who is very pretty. She is not

---

3. A former psychiatric social worker and Inner London juvenile court magistrate, she was at this time Parliamentary Under-Secretary, Department of the Environment; she was appointed Minister for Health later in 1989, then Secretary of State for Health, 1992–5.

4. WW had been asked to write to Runcie to support Law. Runcie had replied on 26 June that Law would be an outsider as a candidate as there were others with more experience: 'I can only promise to see that he is considered.' In a postscript he said, 'One good turn deserves another,' and would WW support him in the Clergy (Ordination) Measure?

5. Ronald Grierson, vice-chairman, GEC, 1968–91; chairman, GEC International, since 1992; member Arts Council of Great Britain, 1984–8; chairman, South Bank board, then South Bank Centre, 1985–90; m (1966) Heather (d 1993), née Firmston-Williams (m 1 (1947–66) 3rd Viscount Bearsted); knight 1990.

6. On 20 September 1988, when she defined Britain's attitude to the EC: 'We have not successfully rolled back the frontiers of state in Britain only to see them reimposed at a European level, with a European super-state exercising a new dominance from Brussels.'

coming to dinner [at Cavendish Avenue] tomorrow for some reason or other but Conrad is coming. Her children are at school in America though one child has entered the American School in London. I said, 'I thought you were going to send them to English schools,' but she had changed her mind.[7]

Tuesday 4 July

Rang Arnold, having decided not wait until he came to dinner, to ask him whether he could do the Skadden Arps seminar on November 16th.

After a bit he said, 'Tell them to write to me because I might do it for you but I won't do it for them.'

Ben Pimlott[8] came to the Lords.

We wished each other a happy birthday.

He asked me whether I had been given some nice presents and I said, 'One or two. What about you?' He said his wife had framed for him a family pedigree chart on his American side, the origin of which was a witch in Salem. I thought that perhaps was the reason for his rather odd left-wing views.

He was very pleasant and we chatted away about Harold Wilson.

Wednesday 5 July

When I got home last night there was a birthday card delivered by hand from Prince Michael, a comical one with a black man wearing a white thingamajig, some tribesperson from Africa, on the head. He wrote, 'A good place for a Tote badge.'[9]

There was also a parcel with two tickets, a sticker for the car park and the debenture holders' lounge, for Wimbledon the next day at the Centre Court. I thought, 'Gosh, how am I to go to that, but why not?'

The tickets had come from Pat Chapman, editor of the *News of the World*.

I wondered whether they had any connection with the telephone call I had, as we were finishing dinner last night, from Rupert and Anna and Irving and Cita [Stelzer] who were ringing up from Aspen

---

7. See discussion in Vol. 1, p. 599, 7 July 1988.

8. Professor of Politics and Contemporary History, Birkbeck College, University of London, since 1987; former political journalist and Labour parliamentary candidate; his biography of Harold Wilson was published in 1992.

9. July 4 was also Prince Michael's birthday.

where they were sitting looking over the hills and having a barbecue lunch. They all rang up to wish me a happy birthday.

We watched McEnroe and Wilander, the Swede. Though McEnroe behaves abominably still at times, I have grown rather fond of him.[10]

All day I have been in a state of terror about my left eye, the only good one. When I woke up in the morning I found that it was a bit sore and I couldn't see out of it properly. I couldn't read the [Tote] board papers properly at the meeting or the newspapers on the way there. Not even my own article in the *Times*. I said that at the board meeting and Frank Chapple[11] said, 'Why did you want to read it? Didn't you know what was in it?' I said, 'I like to read them and see if they have mucked them up at all.'

Dinner party.

Robin Day arrived with his lady friend, Barbara Thornhill.

When he was introduced to the Duchess [of Marlborough], he introduced his lady friend and said, 'This is my friend Barbara Thornhill, Your Grace,' and I was very amused at his using that form of address, like a butler.

She was very elegant. She has got a business in New York and a very nice house there. She had a pretty dress on and I asked her where it came from. She said, 'Chanel.' So she must have plenty of money.

I think he feels a bit finished now that he is no longer the presenter of *Question Time*. His behaviour at dinner was strange. He kept asking me questions about what I thought about this, that and the other and the Prime Minister and so on. I said, 'But Robin, you know the answers to these questions. You are not on *Question Time* now.' He can't seem to get out of the habit and have a normal conversation.

With all his braggadocio Robin is unsure of himself. I asked him if he wore a black bow tie when he went to a funeral because I never did in case I looked like a waiter. He said he wore a black tie with little stripes or stars to make it look not like an ordinary one but a tie of mourning.

Nicholas Ridley refused to comment on who will be the next Chancellor of the Exchequer and he particularly wouldn't discuss himself.

---

10. John McEnroe, Wimbledon champion 1981, 1983 and 1984, as famous for his tantrums as his tennis, won this quarter-final but was beaten in the semi-finals by Edberg.
11. General Secretary, Electrical, Electronic, Telecommunication and Plumbing Union (EETPU), 1966–84; member, Tote Board, 1976–90; life peer 1985.

In discussing drink and politicians and the effect on people's lives, he said that when he was very young, about ten or eleven, Winston Churchill came to stay at his parents' house. The next day he was due to make a speech, an important one, to some Conservative conference or other. His mother asked him what he would like for his lunch and he said, 'Will you send up a tray of some eggs or something simple like that, a bottle of champagne and some of that excellent brandy you gave me last night.' So Nicholas was told to take it up to his room.

When he came back to collect it later, the whole bottle of champagne had gone and half the bottle of brandy. Winston then proceeded to dictate to his secretary the speech he was going to make which Nicholas said was brilliant, and he said it was marvellous to be in the room while this was going on.

Before Netta [Weinstock] went, she said to me, 'We must go now. There has been a very unpleasant thing which has happened,' so I said, 'What is it?' and she said, 'I will tell you later.'

I got her outside as they were on their way out to go and she said, 'Nicholas Ridley sat next to me, as you know, at dinner and he began to attack Arnold and said he had made money only by being a monopoly and he made money out of government and that the whole business was a terrible one. He, Nicholas Ridley, had been connected with the Board of Trade, trying to sell these exports, and everything that came from GEC didn't work and was delivered late and was no good. What really ought to happen was that Sir John Clark at Plessey should run the whole of GEC because Arnold was not any good at it.' She was naturally very upset.

I found it amazing that Nicholas Ridley could be so rude or so silly because half of what GEC make is sold overseas. All the other countries and their private customers can't be so foolish as to be buying because it is a British monopoly. They just buy the best from all the varieties they have on offer. Likewise the American defence industry places huge orders with GEC and they have their own great armament manufacturers and electronic manufacturers to choose from as well.

Later Arnold was saying that it was because he is anti-semitic, but I don't think that is true either. I think it is just rather foolish of Nick Ridley. Though Arnold says it is the sort of thing that goes on in the Treasury and there is a group of people who have been peddling this line for a very long time.

Netta said that as Nicholas Ridley went, he said he apologized for getting so steamed up.[12] The next morning, when I spoke to Arnold, he said he was going to sue him for libel. I said, 'You can't do that. It's slander anyway. It would be a ridiculous thing to do. You couldn't prove it and you would need something in writing. I don't know why you say he is anti-semitic or the government is anti-semitic. What about David Young and Nigel Lawson? They are both Jews.'

Allan Davis just before the dinner party rang to say we couldn't get Greenwich because the lady in charge, the feminist, didn't like it.

Friday 7 July
Allan tells me he has slightly more hopeful news.

There may be some possibility by starting it at Guildford and going to Windsor or the other way around.

No wonder Allan calls his lecture on getting plays put on and theatre and play-writing, 'On the Roller-coaster'.

A copy [came] of the letter which Arnold had sent to Bruce Buck who had written to him at my suggestion.

Arnold had written that Buck was quite right in assuming that he never did things of this kind and he wasn't going to do this one either so he had to decline the invitation.

I rang Arnold and said, 'Why have you done that? You said you were prepared to do it.' He said, 'Because I am a member of the Merrill Lynch International Trust and I will probably have to go there to America at that time.'

I am trying to get hold of Bruce Buck to tell him what has happened because Arnold has made a fool of me. I know why. It's because he wrote that letter the night after the dinner party with Nicholas Ridley. He was furious with Nicholas Ridley and presumably with me because I had happened to ask them both to the same house for dinner.

I think it is very mean of him. When he got a £500 million order for a torpedo or something of that kind, I forget the details, Margaret only gave it him on my extracting from him his assurance that it would be delivered on time, that it would work and that we would get exports for it. I pushed it hard for him.

----

12. Ridley did not mention this episode in his short, handwritten thank-you letter to WW. He praised the wines, said, 'I think you rather enjoyed knocking Arnold & Robin Day about politically. I certainly did listening to you,' and thanked WW for his support 'in slightly difficult times'.

People are extraordinarily petty. I suppose I am, too, but I thought that was really going it a bit.

Sunday 9 July
Grantchester [the Archers'].

The lunch was in the garden. Somewhat cold. I had two Pimm's, warm. I had two glasses of champagne, cold, but not the Krug he likes to have at his London parties.

John Gummer[13] asked me about Heveningham Hall. I told him about John Martin Robinson.[14] He said would I get John Martin Robinson to ring him up or give him his telephone number? His constituents are always asking about it and it would be nice to be able to say something sensible was being done about it.

Jeffrey said, 'The Tories will recover. Everything will go well and you and I will be in high office.' What he meant by that I had no idea except that perhaps he is hoping to become Deputy Chairman of the Tory Party again or maybe to get into the House of Lords, or get some official post.

In his lavatory there were lots of jolly cartoons. He had put up three front pages of *Private Eye*.

One showed him and Mary. He was saying to her, 'My reputation is spotless' (that was after the successful conclusion of his libel action) and Mary was replying, 'So is your back.' That was a reference to the tart saying he has a lot of spots on his back and she saying in the witness box it was not true because his back was spotless.

After getting back Harold Lever rang. He wanted to tell me my article in last Wednesday's *Times*, about the reasons for not joining the currency union or having a central European bank and explaining Margaret's vision of Europe, was the best he had ever read on the subject.

I was glad to have his approval, particularly as Arnold said I don't understand anything about economics. He can't say that about Harold Lever.

---

13. MP for Suffolk Coastal since 1983; Minister of State, Department of the Environment, at this time.
14. Librarian to the Duke of Norfolk since 1978; appointed Maltravers Herald of Arms Extraordinary in 1989; author of *The Wyatts: An Architectural Dynasty* (1980) and introduced in 1987 by WW to Abdul Al Ghazzi as a possible adviser on the restoration of Heveningham Hall (see Vol. 1, p. 416).

Spoke to Margaret.

On the NHS I mentioned what Brian Walden had said about somebody like Virginia Bottomley, though I said I thought Kenneth Clarke was very good

I said, 'You sound in very good heart.' She said, 'Yes. I'm thinking about Bastille Day and the French Revolution. I am thinking of [getting] some scarlet pimpernels to tie round my neck.'[15] I said, 'It is terrible you have got to go there and celebrate it.'

Monday 10 July

Seventeen-year-old Lachlan Murdoch came to lunch in the Lords. He is doing a fortnight for the *Times* on how politics work and he has got passes into the Lords and the Commons. He is a very nice boy and wants or is thinking of going to Worcester College, Oxford.[16]

Lachlan is very keen to be a newspaper man.

He wants to succeed Rupert in the way that Rupert succeeded his father, Sir Keith. He is inclined at the moment, Lachlan, to want to stay British but his mother said, 'Why don't you come with me and be an American when you are eighteen?' He can choose either and will wait for the time being.

Tuesday 11 July

A disturbing lunch with Sir Robert Haslam, Chairman of British Coal.

On the whole, I had always thought that nuclear power was the safest and the cleanest, least polluting energy one could have and that is why I have been advocating it.

Now there is a new factor. The consumer of electricity is going to have to pay all the costs of decommissioning ancient nuclear power stations, like the Magnox ones. None of them has ever been decommissioned before so no one knows what will happen.

We are at a very late stage. The Electricity Bill has gone through its final stages.

Oh dear, oh dear, what am I to do? I must speak to Parkinson and get some more satisfactory answers from him both on the cheapness

---

15. A reference to the hero of Baroness Orczy's books who opposed the Terror following the overthrow of the French monarchy.
16. Rupert Murdoch, Lachlan's father, was at Worcester, like WW, but Lachlan went to Princeton.

of nuclear power and how we are going to eliminate its side effects over the centuries when nuclear power stations are decommissioned.

Went to see Eric Arnott, the eye specialist. He said I might have slept with the pillow in my eye but he thought it was more likely that my lens for the left eye (the other one is no good at all) is now too strong because my left eye is improving. He said it is a very healthy eye. So he gave me a prescription and I went to get a new lens and it was perfectly true, it was better than with the stronger lens.

Wednesday 12 July
Allan Davis came to lunch.

We discussed at length whether the references to Mrs Thatcher should be left in now that we no longer call the play *Thanks to Mrs Thatcher* and have reverted to the original title, *Knowing the Wrong People*. My feeling is that the mention of her name, even if people don't like her, and the feeling that she is around and about the place, would add a spark of force and interest.

Winston and Minnie Churchill's twenty-fifth wedding anniversary party in Charles Street.[17]

I talked to Robert Armstrong.[18] He said he remained devoted to Mrs Thatcher. I asked him if he had got a First but he said no. I turned to Petronella who is terrified of what her results may be and said, 'There. Robert Armstrong didn't get a First and look at him. Nobody could have gone higher as a mandarin, being in charge of the whole civil service as he was.'

Before I got into bed Arnold rang.

He is clearly a bit contrite of his pettishness as displayed in the letter to Bruce Buck.

Arnold is now worried that Nicholas Ridley may be made Secretary for Industry and that would be an end to his hopes of doing a take-over of Plessey.

I said again I thought Nicholas Ridley's behaviour to Netta was absolutely extraordinary and unforgivable and I think he must have been a bit drunk. He said, 'No. It's what really underlies some of these people, anti-semitism.' But he is now embattled with Levene at the Ministry of Defence, who does the buying and the making of contracts

---

17. They divorced in 1997.
18. Secretary of the Cabinet, 1979–87; Head of the Home Civil Service, 1983–7; life peer 1988.

with big firms like GEC, Plessey and American firms, all the arms we buy. I said, 'Well he is Jewish.'

He said, 'I have to invite him to lunch at home and dinner and so on, and pretend to get on with him, and I know very well he is two-timing me all the while. But there is nothing else I can do. And if Ridley becomes Secretary for Industry, I will emigrate.' But I doubt it.

Thursday 13 July
Lunch at Sedgwick House. Sedgwick's are a huge insurance brokers. The other guests were Arnold Weinstock, the American Ambassador and myself. I had not met the American Ambassador, Catto, before.[19] He seemed a polished and civilized man. His brain is much sharper than that of his predecessor though he doesn't have so much jollity about him. But he had a sense of humour.

I went to the French Embassy to celebrate the fall of the Bastille two hundred years ago.

It is all Mitterrand's vanity, that idiotic display in celebration of a reign of terror which did not lead to democracy, quite the reverse.

The American Ambassador said how entertaining the lunch had been in the City.

He told me was a Texan and didn't I realize that from his accent. I said no, 'You sounded quite civilized,' and he laughed and put on a Texan accent.

Went on to dinner at George Weidenfeld's apartment on the Chelsea Embankment.

Again the American Ambassador was there.

He said, 'Where shall we meet for breakfast?'

Jimmy Goldsmith was there plus Annabel, his English wife. He keeps a kind of wife in Paris and in New York. Three establishments of substance.

Friday 14 July
Allan Davis says it now could be possible – but not to throw my hat in the air yet – that the play could be starting in Margate in October with rehearsals in September.

---

19. Henry Catto, US Ambassador, 1989–91.

Saturday 15 July

The newspapers and magazines are still awash with assessments, tributes and obituaries of Laurence Olivier.[20]

His son told me that he was very unkind to him and wouldn't see him for years or take an interest in his life. That was because the son, Tarquin, was the son of Jill Esmond. Apparently he, Laurence Olivier, found her in bed with the nanny and he was deeply shocked.

In the country today at Bowden it was very warm. We swam about a lot, at least I did. Arnold didn't much but he says he is going to have the swimming pool made more shallow by eighteen inches. He doesn't like to swim where he can't stand up because it puts him in a state of anxiety. He is strange in his phobias.

I said, 'What about this dinner you gave the Queen?' 'How did you hear?' I said, 'Lucian Freud [the artist] told me at the French Embassy. He said that Robert Alexander, the QC, was there and Giovanni Agnelli, the Fiat man from Italy, and O'Reilly,[21] the man from Ireland who owns Irish newspapers and is president of Heinz world-wide.'

Arnold said, 'Peter Ustinov was also there with his wife. How did Lucian Freud know?' I said, 'It's obvious. Agnelli rings David Somerset every day. David speaks with Michael Tree every day and Michael Tree speaks with Lucian Freud every day.'

He said they were told the Queen didn't eat any shellfish. I said, 'That is probably because of her Jewish ancestry, Prince Albert being the son of his mother and a Jewish music master.'[22] Arnold laughed.

Later there was some talk about Sir Michael Sobell, Netta's father who is ninety-seven. Netta is very shocked because he asked his nurse whether she would like to go to bed with him. I said, 'That sounds very encouraging.' She said, 'He's in excellent shape. He then complained that the butler was keeping a brothel; that he was going to

---

20. The great actor; m 1 (1930–40) Jill Esmond (d 1990), m 2 (1940–61) Vivien Leigh (d 1967), m 3 (1961) Joan Plowright; life peer 1970.

21. Tony O'Reilly's newspaper group obtained a controlling interest in the UK *Independent* titles in 1998.

22. In his 1997 biography, *Prince Albert: Uncrowned King* (p. 25), Professor Stanley Weintraub refutes as having no substance the posthumous allegation, made in a 1915 German pamphlet and repeated by Lytton Strachey in his 1921 *Queen Victoria*, that Albert's mother's involvement with a court chamberlain, Baron Ferdinand von Meyem, made Albert 'a half-Jew'.

bed with the nurse in the next room to him.' I said, 'It seems to me he wants to be part of the brothel.'

Margaret was jolly and lively on her return from Paris. She said there had been no friction between herself and Mitterrand over her remarks about the rights of man not beginning in France and the French Revolution leading to the terror and the dictatorship of Napoleon etc.

I said, 'I am worried about nuclear power. Why have the public got to pay for that on their electricity bills?'

She said, 'I am looking at it. The point about the old Magnox power stations, which are the first to be decommissioned, is that they were built in nationalized times and I think something should be done about it.'

I then said, 'I don't know about your reshuffle but I hope that David Young isn't going. He is very good in the Lords. He is very clear and he seems to be able.' She said, 'I think so, too.' 'But I hear that he was saying and telling his friends he thought he was going,' I said, and she made no particular comment on that.

She then said to me, 'What are your views on the reshuffle?'

I said, 'I think you should bring up some of your new younger ones like John Major. John Major should have a department now. I think Paul Channon is very nice but he is not a leader,' and she said, 'I'm afraid that is true.'

She said she hadn't really given her mind to the reshuffle yet but she would have to do so shortly.

I said, 'Nicholas Ridley is very good but he is not very good on presentation.' She said, 'He has brilliant ideas,' but she agreed with me about his failure on presentation. I didn't tell her about Arnold threatening to announce that it was a disaster if he was made Secretary for Industry. I thought that might only make matters worse.

Arnold had said to me that Tim Bell spoke to Margaret about what Nicholas Ridley said to Netta.

According to Tim Bell, Margaret said, 'It is simply not true and if he does it again, I shall have to speak sharply to him about it.'

Arnold said that he had to go specially to Salzburg during August to give Margaret dinner there and take her to the opera: 'What a nuisance.' But I thought to myself he didn't really mean that at all because he is delighted to get a chance to entertain her, even if he does have to fly out there specially.

Monday 17 July

I went to a strange dinner at the Metcalfes. There was Charles Forte and his wife. He had been told the dinner was in honour of him. There was Conrad Black and his wife. He had been told the dinner was in honour of him. There was James Hanson and his wife. James thought it was in honour of him and was very grumpy.

There was Michael Heseltine and his wife. Strange. There was Alistair McAlpine and his wife, Romilly; and there was the Earl of Westmoreland whose wife had to cry off because she was ill and Petronella came in her place.

I thought David can't know much about politics to bring two stout adherents to Mrs Thatcher, Alistair and myself, face to face with Michael Heseltine who seemed distinctly displeased to see me, at least.

When the men were alone, I asked James Hanson what he thought of the bid by Jacob Rothschild, Jimmy Goldsmith and Kerry Packer[23] for BAT [British American Tobacco]. He said he thought it was not a creative bid at all. It was just asset stripping without wanting to create or run a business.

I can't remember before being in a room with so many megalomaniacs. There was Conrad Black saying how powerful he was and how he was going to outdo Northcliffe. There was James Hanson saying he was a creative businessman and the best in the country; and he was buying Consolidated Goldfields because he had mining interests at heart and it is similar to what he does making bricks. There was Charles Forte preening himself when Hanson said he owned more hotels than anyone else in the world. There was Michael Heseltine who thinks he ought to be Prime Minister and his ambition pops out of his dyslexic eyes. I felt that only Alistair McAlpine and I were sane in the room.

Tuesday 18 July

There was a tremendous gathering at Drue Heinz's[24] where we were asked for a belated birthday party for Isaiah Berlin.[25]

Serena Rothschild was sitting at the same table as me. She said, 'Do you know why I am sitting next to you?' I said no and she said, 'Because I changed the places round. Perhaps it was your favourite

---

23. Australian entrepreneur.
24. Philanthropist widow of Henry John (Jack) Heinz II (1908–87).
25. Sir Isaiah Berlin OM (1909–97), philosopher.

lady, the French Ambassadress, but I put her on another table while no one was looking and gave you myself.' They were too literary at the table she was at.

We were talking beforehand to Andrew Devonshire. I told him how well Stoker was doing as Senior Steward [of the Jockey Club]. He said, 'It's terrible when one's son becomes God.'

After we left 43 Hay's Mews I waved to Carla Powell[26] who was looking rather luscious on a bicycle, just leaving by the back. Shortly, she overtook us at a traffic light and I called out to her and said, 'You are not pedalling hard enough.' She said, 'I ought to be wearing trousers.' I said, 'No, not at all. I wouldn't have been able to see your beautiful legs.' She is a very jolly girl and waved merrily as she cycled on, saying it was much the quickest way to get about in London.

I went into the Lords when there was a division and saw David Young.

He said yes, he is going to leave the government but he hopes to come back later. He is going to help whoever is Chairman of the Party in organizing the Central Office to try and get them better on the job of doing their research and propaganda. He said she still had wanted him to do the job of the Chairman but he said it was impossible for him with the atmosphere in the Tory Party, the backbenchers and elsewhere. I said, 'They are only jealous because you have gone straight into the Lords but you have always been very effective and I think you have done brilliantly here.'

My evening was badly interrupted by ringing up all the [Tote] board members about the appalling statement which Douglas Hurd had wanted to issue to the press, including recommendations from Lloyds Merchant Bank which were supposed to have been kept confidential in a confidential report. They would have utterly wrecked the morale of the Tote. There was a recommendation about selling off the Tote Bookmakers and there was also heavy criticism of the Tote Board, saying it immediately needed restructuring.

I rang Douglas Hurd in the evening and got him on his car telephone: 'You can't do this. This is ridiculous. Though you say you are doing it to end speculation, you will increase the speculation. In any case the Tote Board would never agree to sell the Bookmakers before

26. Carla née Bonardi, from Domodossola, Italy, m (1964) Charles Powell (diplomat, at this time Private Secretary to the Prime Minister, knight 1990); supporter of Goldsmith's Referendum Party in the 1997 general election.

privatization nor would they restructure the Board. It is ridiculous to say the Board is no good when we get record profits over and over again and again each year, etc. etc.' Douglas said would I let him know which bits I wanted left out.

I had seen Douglas at 5.30 and when I left he handed me the statement which he intended to publish on Thursday morning. Intolerable.

Wednesday 19 July
In the morning I rang Douglas Hurd at about 7.20 and said, 'I think nothing should be published. It is a breach of confidentiality. I shall have to attack the Home Office and Lloyds Merchant Bank and so on. The Board are horrified and it could be an unseemly wrangle.' He said afterwards, 'You have made your point and I will ring you at lunch time.'

We went ahead with the 9.30 board meeting at 19 Cavendish Avenue which I had arranged last night. David [Montagu] arrived armed with a fearsome draft of an attack on the merchant bank and the Home Office and so on. I thought it was very good but it needed a lot of modification and we discussed it for a longish time.

I was just finishing the redraft after the only two board members who had been able to come – Priscilla Hastings and David Montagu – had gone, when the telephone rang at twenty past twelve. It was a Mr Walters, Senior Private Secretary to Douglas Hurd. He said there would be no release of anything to the press by the Home Office or by the bank. He said, 'You can write your views to the Home Secretary taking it at your leisure. You can have discussions in September about what should be done and proper consultations.'

If Douglas had insisted on his press release, I would have said to him, 'Then I suppose I shall have to ring the Prime Minister.' I didn't want to do this except as an utter last resort. He had said he had consulted the Prime Minister about my not taking my increase of salary because it was bad timing. But I am not sure that I believe him or that she would worry. By bad timing I think he simply referred to the fact that the Board and I had been criticized in the report.

However, Douglas caved in, realizing that I was going to create the most ghastly scene, as Richard Fries had gathered when he rang and said he understood that 'the atmosphere was incandescent'. Brian [McDonnell] had replied to this senior civil servant overseeing the Tote affairs, 'That is an understatement.'

In the midst of it all I had to write a blurb for my play for the Margate manager.

Everybody has suddenly turned now to thinking that it is a frightfully good play. Laurence Fitch, the old agent who had always said to me that it would get on in the end, said, 'This happens very much in the theatre. Once people begin to smell success the whole thing turns because you have got your cast together.'

Also during the day, in which I was extremely tired, I followed up the Skadden Arps business and their speaker for November 16th. I got on to Bruce Buck at last. He had rung Arnold and Arnold had said that if he had done it for anybody, he would have done it for me but he didn't think he could be reliable enough because of this ridiculous Merrill Lynch thing in New York.

We then canvassed who should be the person to substitute for him and he said, 'What about Jacob Rothschild? Do you know him?' 'Yes. He is one of my oldest friends.'

So I rang Jacob.

I asked him if he would do the speech and he said no because he was so bad at it, he was hopeless at it. But Jimmy Goldsmith was the man. I said, 'But he has already turned it down.' He said, 'I will ask him again and he may be in a different mood now as he will have something to talk about regarding mergers and acquisitions.'

Thursday 20 July
Spoke to Margaret.

I went through the people who might be promoted or removed.

I suggested that Edwina Currie[27] should be brought back to give a little sparkle. She is very popular. She said, 'But she did do awful things about the eggs and it all cost a lot of money.' I said, 'To make a pun, she certainly over-egged it. But in fact she was right and probably did a lot of good in making egg production safer.'

I said I thought Major ought to go to the Department of Trade and Industry. I said I thought Nicholas Ridley perhaps could go to Defence.

I said, 'Douglas Hurd is certainly no friend of yours and I always regard him as a potential traitor.' She said, 'Yes but he has been doing the job quite well and it is a very difficult one.'

---

27. Parliamentary Under-Secretary of State for Health, 1986–8; she resigned over her outspoken remarks about the risk of salmonella poisoning from British eggs; see Vol. 1, pp. 690–2.

I said, 'You have got Michael Howard. I think he is good. Lamont is good. Portillo is good.'

I suggested there might be a change in the Lords, that Bertie Denham would be better to lead it than Belstead. 'I can't do that because they are very devoted to each other and I don't think that Bertie would agree to take Belstead's place. He is not very good at speaking either.'

I said, 'Why not bring back Cecil Parkinson as Chairman [of the Conservative Party]?' She said, 'No. I can't do that. I never believe in going back on what has happened before.'

A jolly dinner at the Connaught. Unfortunately the food is very rich. But the claret, 1961 Calon-Sègur, was superb.

Irwin is very worried about the attack on Sky. People are ganging up to try and make Rupert get rid of it on the grounds he owns newspapers in Britain. There is no legislation to that effect yet but it could well happen with the Broadcasting Act which is now being cooked up. Rupert is anxious to know what I can do to help.

I have told Irwin the only thing I can do is to put the case to Mrs Thatcher. There was an amazing interview, which they gave me a record of, which Sky had had with the Office of Fair Trading. They complained that Rupert's newspapers were too far to the right and supported Mrs Thatcher. Therefore the implication was he shouldn't be allowed to run Sky Channel or to have so many newspapers. It is a most extraordinary attempted censorship. I think she will be pretty annoyed when she hears it from me.

Irwin Stelzer promised to put £3,000 into my play. He was reluctant to begin with and then his wife said, 'Oh go on, you must.' She also declared she was coming for the first night and she would make him go as well. That is at Margate on October 4th.

Allan rings up two or three times a day. The manager likes it at Margate, everybody likes it, but now there is this worry about Linda Thorsen. She may be offered an important, that is to say valuable, television series in America.

Monday 24 July
Talking to Duncan McEuen of Christie's about some cigars, old ones which I would like him to bid for this evening at South Kensington, he said would I like to come to lunch today at Christie's even though at such short notice.

The champagne was Gosset 1973. First class. There was a Mâcon white wine which was excellent. There was Château Giscours 1975.

Then we had Château Climens, an excellent sweet wine. Then we had a very good Vargellas Taylor port 1967.

If one had a little more money and didn't feel under stress of working desperately to make enough to keep the household going, not die a pauper and to leave something for one's wife, one could have a very agreeable time.

Tuesday 25 July
Margaret's great reshuffle in the newspapers.[28]

She didn't take much notice of me. Though I think my emphasizing how excellent Norman Lamont is could well have tipped the balance in his becoming Chief Secretary in the Cabinet.

I rang Margaret and told her I thought the reshuffle was pretty good, not a night of long knives. She seemed to think it was better than pretty good and that I might have been more enthusiastic.

I said I thought Major was an inspired choice. They were complaining about him being too young but Anthony Eden was only thirty-seven when he became Foreign Secretary. I said I was glad about Christopher Patten who has been moving towards 'us'.

I said, 'I suppose it doesn't matter Nicholas Ridley being rough with industrialists at the Department of Industry.' She said, 'Oh yes, it does matter.' I hope she understands the point I was trying to make (an oblique reference to what Nick said to Netta about Arnold).

Then I mentioned to her the question of Sky Channel. I said, 'Do you realize there is a move to get Rupert dispossessed of it? It would be a terrible misfortune after so much money had been spent on it.'

Then I began to read her extracts from the meeting with the Office of Fair Trading. When I got to the bit about the *Times* moving to the right and so forth, she cried out, 'But this is censorship.'

She said, 'I am very glad you have told me. I shall enquire into it.' So I think that may very well put a stop to Sky Channel being squashed.

I rang Norman Lamont to congratulate him. He said, 'I know I

---

28. John Major replaced Geoffrey Howe as Foreign Secretary; Howe became Deputy Prime Minister and Leader of the House of Commons; Hurd remained Home Secretary; Lawson remained Chancellor of the Exchequer, with Lamont promoted to Chief Secretary to the Treasury, in the Cabinet; Ridley went to the Department of Trade and Industry; Parkinson returned to the Cabinet at Transport; Chris Patten took the Environment; Baker became Party Chairman.

owe a lot to you. You have been backing me for years and I am deeply grateful to you.'

Norman followed in to see Mrs Thatcher some time after John Major on Monday. He, John Major, came out from her looking absolutely shaken and had to sit down in a chair to recover himself. Norman said he thought to himself, 'My God, what has happened? Has he been given the sack?'

Bad news this morning. Allan Davis said Linda Thorsen had been given a three year contract by ABC in America for a great television film series. I said, 'She would be mad not to take it.'

Wednesday 26 July
Saw Willie [Whitelaw] in the Lords. He thinks that the hurt has gone very deep with Howe.

Willie told me the trouble really started at Madrid.

But she told nobody, not even her staff, not a soul, what she had in mind about Geoffrey.

Jim Prior said, 'Our lady, or I suppose I should say your lady, has made an absolutely monumental mess of everything. How could she be so disloyal to Geoffrey Howe when he has always been loyal to her?' I said, 'Perhaps she didn't like being outnumbered two to one on things like the EMS.' He said, 'She has got to realize she is wrong about that.'

I spoke to Rupert earlier in the morning and told him that I had spoken to Mrs Thatcher and she had been horrified about the Office of Fair Trading approach.

Unfortunately I woke Anna up. It was seven o'clock in the morning. She told me he was in the shower and when he came out, I said, 'Please apologize to Anna for my waking her up.' He said, 'Not at all. It is time she got up.'

I am worried that she has made a bitter enemy in Geoffrey Howe and her relations are not too good with Nigel Lawson.

Saw Allan Davis to look at the set design for the play.

Thursday 27 July
I asked Margaret how the leak arose about Geoffrey Howe and Douglas Hurd and the offer to Geoffrey Howe of the Home Secretaryship. She said, 'There were only two people in the room and it certainly wasn't me who leaked it. I suppose he told Elspeth straight away.'

She said she was fed up of people attacking her about the Geoffrey

Howe and Hurd incident.[29] I said, 'You couldn't have possibly have said anything to Douglas Hurd until you had made an agreement with Geoffrey first.'

She said, 'No. I told him he was a very good minister and I have told him that before.' I am not sure that I altogether agree with that but I am probably prejudiced because of the way he is behaving over the Tote privatization.

I went down to the Lords.

I talked to Lord Fanshawe (Tony Royle).[30] He was in great dismay about John Major. Tony used to be a Vice Chairman of the Tory Party and is rather senior in the whole operation though he is not active there now. He thought that Major would either be her creature or be taken over by the Foreign Office. Either way he had no future.

He said Geoffrey Howe had behaved disgracefully. He had lost for ever any chance he once had of being offered the leadership of the Tory Party by breaking confidence in this way and how awful it is that the new changes have been overshadowed by squalid squabbles about houses. He said, 'Why didn't he keep his own house?'

I said, 'Probably because he didn't have any money and maybe he needed the money when he sold it. You don't realize how few of them have got any money.'

Friday 28 July

Rang Margaret to say goodbye and wish her a jolly holiday. 'I hope you are going to relax,' I said. 'At the moment I don't feel like relaxing at all,' she said. 'I feel an anger or a deep disgust at the way I have been battered. I can't answer back. Naturally I talk to my most senior Minister first about possible changes. At one time Prime Ministers used to ask for everybody's resignation and everybody used to hand in their portfolios when there was a reshuffle. That didn't happen this time but

---

29. See *The Downing Street Years* by Margaret Thatcher (1993), p. 757, for her account of what happened. She says she first offered Howe the Leadership of the House ('he looked rather sullen and said he would have to talk to Elspeth first'), then the Home Office ('knowing in advance that he would almost certainly not accept'), then use of Dorneywood, the house the Chancellor of the Exchequer had, and finally the title of Deputy Prime Minister 'which I had held in reserve as a final sweetener'. Previously Howe had use of Chevening in Kent, when Foreign Secretary and before when Chancellor of the Exchequer.

30. Conservative politician; MP, 1959–83; life peer 1983.

I am entitled to make a reshuffle. And then there is all this business about houses.'

I said, 'Did Douglas Hurd know anything about the possibility he might be asked to be Leader of the House if Geoffrey took over the Home Office?' She pushed straight through that one and said, 'I was talking to my most senior person and was entitled to think he would keep his own counsel.'

I have never known Margaret so upset as she was this morning. She was railing at the unfairness of it all.

Kenneth Baker, the new Chairman of the Tory Party, rings. He was very anxious that I should know he has set the Cabinet on the course of fighting the next election now. He had got Mrs Thatcher at a Cabinet meeting to say the team would remain the same and this was going to be the winning team of the election.

He was very full of himself which was all to the good.

I must try to give them the best advice I can. I am sure they can get it right and, as I said to Kenneth, get that inflation rate down and the rest will be comparatively easy.

Abdul Al Ghazzi came to lunch. He has already sent the £3,000 to Allan Davis. Irwin Stelzer has sent his £3,000. Neither of them quibbled. It is only Arnold who has quibbled as he always does, but I am sure he will be sending his £4,000 promptly. Allan Davis is everlastingly wanting to add things to the letter he is writing in answer to Arnold's asking for the details of the financial plan etc.

Abdul at lunch said he had this problem with Virginia Bottomley who has just left the Department of the Environment. Before she left she started saying why isn't the house going to be open during August? That was the covenant at Heveningham Hall. He had been trying to explain to her and the Department that there is not much point in visitors coming to see it with workmen all over the place and most of the rooms locked and the furniture removed.

I rang Virginia Bottomley and I was told, as I had forgotten, that Alexander Hesketh had taken her place.

On the way to the airport I spoke to Alexander Hesketh.

He said, 'I know all about it. I will look into it straight away.'

When we got to Perignano, Gingo [Count Sanminiatelli] was waiting up for us and helped carry the bags up. In fact he did carry the bags up. I was very feeble about it as they were very heavy.

Tuesday 1 August
Arnold rang in the evening.

'You are a dog,' he began. He was using the word in the sense that you would use of a horse that has turned rogue. His complaint was that I had said in the *News of the World* that Nicholas Ridley had been 'monstrously maligned'.[1] 'Not enough,' said Arnold.

He complained that I said he was an original thinker, that he had other good assets. He said, 'How could you say that?' I said, 'First of all I think it is true. Secondly, I was defending Margaret in her choice of people which I think was very good,' at which point he broke in and said, 'There is a lot of trouble about it in the Tory Party and she won't be able to survive it.' I took no notice of this because he always talks in these dramatic terms and it probably comes from Sara Morrison[2] and people like her and her ex husband, Charles Morrison.

Wednesday 2 August
Rang Margaret to see if she was all right. I was worried about her when we spoke last Friday.

This morning she was bright and lively again. She thanked me for my article in the *News of the World*. 'Pure joy', she called it.

She said the *Sunday Times* had been awful about the changes. I said, 'I don't know what the matter is with Andrew Neil. But he will be all right on the day and will tell everybody to vote for you. He has got a slightly twisted approach. However, he does let Brian Walden write every week in the most prominent position.' At which point she said, 'I must have him over.'

I was much relieved that the note of frustration and anger had gone.

---

1. WW was answering criticisms of Mrs Thatcher's new team.
2. Director, GEC, since 1980; vice–chairman, Conservative Party Organization, 1971–5, when Heath was Conservative Prime Minister; chairman, National Council for Voluntary Organizations, 1977–81; née the Hon. Sara Long, m (1954–84) the Hon. Charles Morrison (Conservative MP, 1964–92, knight 1988).

Allan Davis rings. He is full of a long letter from Arnold still quibbling away about his £4,000 contribution to *The Division Belle*[3] launch at Margate. He would like to know the corporate structure of the people he is dealing with. He said the money is available but goes on asking question after question of an absurd nature. It must be out of irritation over what I have said about Nicholas Ridley.

Sunday 6 August
The Worsthornes arrived. She is French, fat and with only a glimmer of the possibility she was once pretty.[4]

It is transparent that she and Perry do not get on well.

Peregrine himself is engaging. He looks younger than his sixty-five years. He is tall with a wonderful mane of white curly hair, curling down on to his shoulders. He has a distinguished-looking face and his profile is almost noble from every angle.

In fact he is something of a noble by descent. His cousin has recently become Commander of the Order of St John (Knights of Malta). This is the most noble of the relics of the great guilds or companies or charters left from the Crusades. He [the cousin] is entitled to wear a cardinal's hat and is treated as a head of a state.

Perry is a jolly conversationalist. We have been talking like under-graduates into the night about politics, philosophy and the meaning of life. I have been telling him he must read the small print and be more exact in his leading articles in the *Sunday Telegraph*. I tell him that they are excellent but they are only thought pieces and often perverse at that.

I said also it is about time that his writers, in the four pages of opinion and comment he has left to him as editor of the *Sunday Telegraph*, began to take Labour's policies apart. 'Have you read Labour's policy review? It is a long document,' I asked. Perry admitted that he had not. I said, 'You are neglecting your duty. You have got to get down to the nitty-gritty.' He said he would but I wonder.

Monday 7 August
Arnold is behaving in a ridiculous manner.

He is upsetting Allan Davis and treating him as though he was a

---

3. The title eventually agreed for the play's Margate run.
4. Claudie, née de Colasse, m 1 Geoffrey Baynham, m 2 (1950) Peregrine Worsthorne; d 1990.

crook. That is Arnold's attitude to everybody. They are all dishonest except for him. They are all plotting against him. They are all trying to swindle him. If necessary, I will have to put up the £3,500 which is still missing from the £10,000 the Margate theatre want.

I am not going to tell him that I have had a letter read to me from London which came back from Nicholas Ridley saying that he will treat Arnold with scrupulous fairness, but he is very offensive and he must expect people to be offensive to him. This is true of course. And Arnold got immediately the go-ahead from Nicholas Ridley for the bid with Siemens for Plessey. He might not have got that if I hadn't said to Nicholas Ridley in my letter about not underestimating Arnold.

Tuesday 8 August
Last night Gino Corsini[5] and his wife came to dinner. He is delighted at my intervention with Kew Gardens. The Curator has written to him several times and they have now arranged that a young man who is on a scholarship will come out in the spring and stay in one of Gino's houses and identify the trees, some of which are unique in Europe, and list them all correctly.

Perry was much impressed that I had written a play which is going to be performed. He says it is the highest form of writing and thought to be by many people. I said, 'I don't think a play can ever match a novel by Dickens or Trollope or Jane Austen.' He thought it could because one has with a few words, as in Chekhov, to depict the characters and atmosphere.

Perry doesn't think much of Allan Davis.

I said, 'He has been my mentor and he has taken me to all kinds of plays; he knows things which can be done which you can get away with on the stage, different approaches.'

He tries to find out how much I see of Mrs Thatcher and said, 'I haven't noticed you having lunch there lately.' He meant what they put in the newspapers about the lunches at Chequers and Number 10. I said I hadn't been, not for a year, and tried not to be drawn on the subject, though I had been to her tenth anniversary lunch at Chequers not long ago.

It was with some shock that I realized on getting to Italy that I had

---

5. Marchese Corsini; see Vol. 1, pp. 617 ff., for WW's offer to help to get Kew Gardens' aid over the trees in his arboretum whose labels were removed by the Germans during the Second World War.

forgotten to send Queen Elizabeth the Queen Mother my usual book for a birthday present for her August 4th, eighty-ninth birthday. I got Mrs Tamborero to send a birthday greetings telegram. Yesterday a telegram came back from the Queen Mother with warmest thanks etc. etc. for my good wishes on her birthday.

The heat is mounting. I am swimming forty lengths of the swimming pool every day at the moment. That must be over six hundred metres a day. Perry says I am thinner and looking very well. I am not quite sure why I am because I am worried not merely about the Tote but about the income tax and all the many things I have to do, including having to sort out Hevengingham Hall.

However, there is good news from Cornwall. Devenish Brewery definitely are making an agreement with us.

Cornish Spring Water will get half the profits with Devenish in the enterprise which they will market and manage and run.

It would be slightly romantic if Bonython, which I have always loved and had as a centrepiece in my mind as the only stable house throughout my life, started to earn money on a reasonable scale.

The arm, the right one, which Verushka fell on and thought she had broken the bone of again as she did last year, now seems to be mending though it is painful. She fell over an iron clamp in a car park in Porto Ercole the day after we got here. I was in terror that the holiday would be a repeat of last year with her in agony and feeling that her holiday had been wrecked again – the one she looks forward to so much.

The Sinclairs[6] arrived. Andrew is much more mellow and less chippy. He was a friend of Philip Howard, the literary editor of the *Times*, at Eton. Maybe that explains why he is so frequently used by Philip as a novel reviewer.

Sonia looks very elegant and stylish. Slim. Some of us went naked bathing in the pool lit up after dinner.

I said to Sonia it recalled the days when we used to go swimming in the sea in the moonlight at their house in Majorca and Julian would lead a party of naked bathers.

Sonia and Andrew left after a few days to stay with John Vestey

---

6. Andrew Sinclair, writer and former academic, m 3 (1984) Sonia Lady Melchett, novelist and board member, Royal Court Theatre, from 1974, Royal National Theatre, 1984–94. She married 1 (1947) the Hon. Julian Mond (later 3rd Baron Melchett, grandson of the founder of ICI, d 1973).*

and Judy Bathurst.[7] Andrew quite properly didn't want to go at all but Sonia, who is still socially slanted, likes the atmosphere of the rich or the very rich and the jet-setting sort. That despite her holding herself out as some kind of a Socialist which she is not because she doesn't know what one is. Her pretence is merely to cover some feeling of guilt about preferring the frivolous and the gossip columnists to the serious.

Thursday 10 August
Get through to Pericles after a lot of struggle. I tried to find him at home or at his restaurant. He is very rushed because it is the middle of lunch time. He tells me he is getting married at 12.00 noon Philadelphia time on Sunday 13th.

Sunday 13 August
I get through to Pericles at The Old Guard House, Philadelphia, the restaurant where he is the manager and where his wedding reception is. I get him just after the marriage service has been completed in that strange American way in the restaurant.

I wish him luck and speak to Maria and wish her luck. Then I say to him, 'And a great big hug for you.' There were sobs in both our voices at this point. He used to say to me, when he was at school, why didn't I like other boys' fathers give him a hug when he came home.

I had always supposed it would have embarrassed him if I had done that. Later I regretted it.

I told Pericles that my wedding present to him was sixty-seven shares in Cornish Spring Water and he had better start ordering it for his restaurant.

The Wiltons and the Metcalfes arrived. The conversation dropped like a stone.

Monday 14 August
David Metcalfe wants to speak only of the very rich people he knows and ask fatuous questions about will Jimmy Goldsmith bring off his bid for BAT and how much money David Somerset has put into the bid.

I think poor David, who has no money, has to bring in the clients to Sedgwick's, the brokers where he works.

---

7. Judith, née Nelson, m (1959–76) 8th Earl Bathurst.

We go on an outing on a fishing boat again. When we get to the seaside in Porto Ercole David Metcalfe and Sally are horrified. 'How can we go in a boat like this?' It was almost the same as the boat we had before except not quite so comfortable and there was no cabin you could go down into.

We had taken a lot of trouble finding these boats. True they only cost a hundred thousand lire (£50) for the outing. But I wasn't prepared to pay £600 for a slightly larger one and a crew nor a fortune to take them all out in some John Vestey type yacht.

Diana didn't grumble at all because she is a lady. Anyway she liked it. Nor did John complain in the least.

I prefer Sally Metcalfe to David. She is pretty, forty-eight or so and has been married before. She has been making out a career for herself. She is a partner in an antique shop on Long Island (*Great Gatsby* land).[8] She has a design business in London with an office in Battersea and a shop in Belgravia from where the materials and so forth are sold. Her dinner parties are often angled at getting customers for doing up offices or for rich people who want their houses done up. I find that quite acceptable and do the same myself in a minor way. She is determined not to be poor. She uses her skills and considerable charm to that end.

We have been playing bridge, Diana, Verushka, Sally and myself. We have jolly games. I play with Diana who mostly taught me what little I know about bridge.

Allan Davis has been ringing me with emendations and notes, will I bring in this bit and put in a line about that. He is delighted he has got this lady, Caroline Blakiston.[9] He has also got the girl who was the wife in *No Sex, Please, We're British*. I remembered her, very pretty and lively and exactly suitable for Jane.[10]

Allan had rung in great excitement about a piece by Ned Sherrin in the Saturday *Times* of August 12th. It had a great headline over his whole piece saying, 'The Baron and the Belles'. He then began, 'I have a scoop. Did you know Woodrow Wyatt had written a play?'

There was then a fatuous observation that I 'affected' a bow tie and bounders always wore bow ties. There was a huge cartoon with

---

8. Gatsby was the eponymous, rich hero of F. Scott Fitzgerald's 1926 novel, set in Long Island.
9. To play Victoria, the wife of the MP hero.
10. The actress Wendy Padbury, to play Jane, the MP's mistress in the play.

Churchill and Cecil Beaton, Robin Day, Jeffrey Archer, Ian Fleming and so forth and myself, all wearing bow ties. Allan says the publicity is quite good.

Wednesday 16 August
David Metcalfe again ringing his secretary in London. He is furious with me because I didn't tell her to hold on while I looked for him down at the swimming pool. He has no consideration for anybody.

It will be surprising if he offers to make any payment for his telephone calls which by this time must have come to £70 worth.

He is strange-looking man. Six foot, four inches, very lean and thin, with an enormously long nose and a narrow, long head and face.

He is a grandson of Lord Curzon, once Foreign Secretary and once Viceroy of India. Diana said, 'Does that make you feel more respect for David now you know how well connected he is?' I said, 'I don't think it makes much difference.'

What it does make me wonder is how he could be so brainless.

I have been thinking about Pericles. How can it be sensible to marry a woman twenty years older than himself, a grandmother?

But he has got charm and he has got guts. He will be twenty-six in a few days, August 22nd. We used to play a lot of chess together. I used to go with him to his athletic meetings at London Harriers when he was away from school. He was always delighted when I would hold the stop watch and time the various competitors in a race and take part in something he was interested in.

Thursday 17 August
We had dinner with John Vestey and Judy Bathurst (Countess of Bathurst). He has lived with her for fourteen years now.

He says he doesn't have all that much money as he is a younger son of a younger son. But he has quite a lot. He spends nine months out of England in order to avoid paying taxes. They travel a lot.

Once she was beautiful. I said, 'You were a friend of Maurice Macmillan's,[11] weren't you?' when I sat next to her at dinner and she said wistfully, 'Yes.' They had a considerable walk-out emanating from

11. Viscount Maurice Macmillan (1921–84), Conservative politician; son of Harold Macmillan, former Prime Minister, 1st Earl of Stockton; m (1942) Katherine, née Ormsby-Gore.*

the hunting field. Katie Macmillan had been pretty furious. At that time Judy was the scourge of Wiltshire wives.

Sunday 20 August

Allan Davis said he has now decided on Sasha York, daughter of Susannah York [actress], for Hyacinth.[12] She laughed a lot when he said her mother would have hysterics when he told her she was playing a part which is so anti-left-wing. She is ditching her A level preparations for the time being.

Caroline Blakiston's father was at school [Eton] with Cyril Connolly and they wrote letters to each other which were published.[13] She is connected to the Russells and according to Allan looks very aristocratic. Now he wants a party for them at Cavendish Avenue on September 10th, the Sunday night before the rehearsals begin. Twenty people but we ought to meet each other. Oh dear. This will be something of a problem with the servants still away.

The Sanminiatellis came to lunch. Anna Lu[14] was looking very handsome for her age. She and Gingo have been married for thirty-seven years or thereabouts.

Gingo said that a hundred and forty thousand cows in Sicily are getting subsidies from the European Agricultural Policy but actually the cow population in Sicily is only around twenty thousand. Corruption is all over the place. No wonder Margaret is nervous of getting immersed with people who don't keep the rules.

Tuesday 22 August

Anna Lu read my play.

She called it brilliant and said it would run for years. I hope she is right.

They went off after breakfast, stopping on the way to see relations. When her mother once gave a party for Corsini relations there were a hundred and twenty of them and they didn't know them all. They have cousins all over the place. As a member of the senior part of the family, with a trio of palaces in Florence, a castle in Umbria and her father the Prince Corsini, she is very attentive to the cousins who clearly

---

12. Hyacinth is the teenage daughter of the MP in the play.
13. *A Romantic Friendship: The Letters of Cyril Connolly to Noel Blakiston*, published 1975.
14. Princess Anna Lucrezia Corsini.

adore her whenever they see her. She hadn't actually met Gino for over a year so it was a great reunion.

Wednesday 23 August

I had just poured out my coffee and was having breakfast after swimming twenty lengths of the pool when the telephone rang. Rupert Murdoch on the telephone from London. I abandoned my coffee but I had finished my boiled egg (which I get from the cook just about right now by timing it myself and standing over the saucepan towards the end so that they don't take it out too soon).

I asked Rupert about the party for mega-rich publisher Malcolm Forbes' eightieth birthday at Tangiers. He pretended to have enjoyed it but he clearly didn't.

I can't think why Rupert goes to such ridiculous parties other than to please Anna who wants to be seen as a member of the greatest jet set ever.

Rupert is almost in a panic. Tim Bell has told him that Gordon Borrie, head of the Office of Fair Trading, will recommend next week to the Department of Trade and Industry that Rupert's ownership of newspapers should be referred to the Monopolies Commission on the grounds that he has too many and also that he gives too much space to Sky Television. Rupert's comment on the last point was that the others don't give any space to it at all.

He said he had tried to get hold of Nick Ridley, now Secretary for Trade and Industry, but he was away shooting in Scotland. He tried to get hold of Kenneth Baker but he wasn't at home.

I rang Margaret about half an hour later when I had finished my breakfast and cleaned my teeth and put my little false teeth in my mouth so that I would sound reasonably all there.

I explained to her the situation.

The reason why Tim Bell doesn't report to her about these matters is, as he said to Rupert, she is very difficult to talk to on these quasi judicial issues.

She said, 'Oh Lord, this is terrible.' Then after a while she said, 'I shall have to think how to tackle it.'

I also told her that Rupert says that if they want him to close newspapers or not have them, he would close down the loss-making ones and that would include the *Times* and *Today*, both of which are still making huge losses.

I rang Rupert back again and said it was absolutely confidential.

He said he wouldn't even tell Irwin Stelzer. I reported to him what she had said, that she would think how to tackle the matter and that she was greatly shocked and concerned about it.

Several times he said, 'I am very grateful to you,' and indeed he might be. I hope he will bear that in mind when I ask for my annual pay rise, though I would have done it anyway because it would be a shocking thing to try and smash up the Rupert newspaper empire, being the only sure supporters in the media the government has.

The Pejacsevichs are very pleasant. We played bridge last night. But this morning they insisted on coming down to swim when I was about to get in naked for my pre-breakfast swim, listening to the six o'clock news on the BBC overseas world service. It meant I couldn't swim naked as I like to. They also talked during the news so I couldn't hear all of it properly.

Wednesday 30 August
I am too idle. I lack a determined routine to write steadily at the new play. Three hours in the morning I should do at least. I swim first and fool about reading the odd detective story or a novel after breakfast, sitting in the sun which is gentle early in the morning. I fear I am incurably lazy and always have been.

Now the holiday tails off.

I have written one act and about a third of the second act of the new play.

Sunday 3 September

Allan Davis comes and we go over all the new bits I had written that he wants for the play

Caroline Blakiston didn't want to say as Victoria, 'I would vote for her any day,' meaning Mrs Thatcher. She had said she couldn't say that. I said, 'Why ever not?' and Allan said, 'She is too left-wing.' I said, 'That is ridiculous. She is acting a part in a play.' But I did alter it to, 'That's why non-Tories vote for her.'

Tuesday 5 September

There was a picture of me very young, in uniform in my army days during the War, in the *Times*. It was accompanying my article refuting the new historians who say we should never have declared war on Hitler.

Underneath the photograph it said that a collection from *The Way We Lived Then: The English Story in the 1940s*, which I had edited and introduced, had been published yesterday. So Joanne Robertson was very pleased from Collins.

She came to the party organized by Collins at Cavendish Avenue. It was a very small gathering. But Stephen Spender[1] came and so did Elizabeth Berridge.[2] They are the two walking, living, active survivors of all those writers of stories which appeared in the collection now out which was derived from the ten books I did, *English Story*, between 1940 and 1950 for Collins.

Stephen said it was all very nostalgic and he described some of his efforts [during the war] as a fireman, saying that when he left the Hampstead station there had been no fire in the area for three years. He was then sent off to some Ministry and there was immediately a fire. He said they looked after him rather well in the fire service,

---

1. (1909–95); poet and critic; Professor of English, University College, London, 1970–7; knight 1983.
2. Novelist and book-reviewer; m Graham (Reginald) Moore (d 1990) who worked with WW on *English Story*.

describing him correctly as incompetent to perform any difficult fire-fighting duties.

A. N. Wilson was there. I said, 'I see you have now written in the *Spectator* that you would rather be governed by Ron Todd[3] than Mrs Thatcher.' So he shifted about a bit. He brought his girlfriend with him, Mrs A. N. Wilson having been disposed of. She was dark and sultry. Probably left-wing and maybe the reason why he decided he didn't like Mrs Thatcher any more. She was not unattractive.[4]

Petronella had been told by Peterborough on her second day of work at the *Daily Telegraph* that she should cover the party.

Milton Shulman[5] was there. He was very discouraging about my play. He said the cast was not sufficiently well known and had not been stars in theatre or television.

Arnold has agreed to pay the £4,000. Allan Davis is very pleased. I had wronged Arnold, though I had thought that in the end he would cough up.

I must face it about the play: we could only get into Margate by offering to pay something towards the production. They were the only management willing to have it, though Bromley had been when the dates unfortunately fell through.

Wednesday 6 September
A huge dinner party at Brooks' Club given by Hollinger which is the holding company of Conrad Black's interests including the ownership of the *Daily* and *Sunday Telegraph*. There must have been eighty people there.

On my left was Sabiha Knight who said she very much liked the married state, in fact she couldn't live without Andrew. He had to go to a funeral in America and could not be there tonight.

Sabiha said this was only the second time she had been out anywhere without Andrew.[6]

Jimmy Goldsmith said he was going to speak at the Skadden Arps seminar. He had done what I had asked him by talking to Joe Flom and all was set. He also said he didn't think his BAT bid had much hope of succeeding.

---

3. General Secretary, Transport and General Workers' Union, 1985–92.
4. Andrew Wilson m 1 (1971–89) Katherine Duncan-Jones, m 2 (1991) Ruth Guilding.
5. Journalist and author; drama critic of the *Evening Standard*, 1953–91.
6. The Knights had married in 1975.

Peter Carrington is now on the Hollinger Board.

He said that there had been a party with Conrad Black to see Margaret at Downing Street today. He said she claimed she had made Argentina democratic by defeating them over the Falkland Islands. He thought that was going rather far.

He then said she was marvellous and we must all support her and though she was difficult, she was indispensable. He refers to her as 'the mistress'.

Sunday 10 September

The party at Cavendish Avenue for the actors and stage manager and the designer. The design of the set is really beautiful. The model had been made with loving care by the stage designer, Mr Page. The curtain material had been provided by Tom Parr of Colefax & Fowler and it is very pretty.

Deeply worried about the nice Caroline Blakiston. She looks nearly sixty, not at all pretty. She wore rather shabby clothes and didn't look in the least bit elegant. Moreover she is not even famous, apart from her appearances in the rather awful television series on Channel 4 called *Brass*.

The little girl for Jane, who was the wife in *No Sex, Please, We're British*, is pretty with a little pert face. I thought she was going to be blonde in the play but she says she can be if required.

The man playing Philip, Bruce Montague, is nice enough but not a very exciting ace, a bit dour. He said he couldn't understand some of his speeches which made me think he was also dim. Michael Medwin, who is to do Jack, is perfect for the part and is a man who seems to be very much with it.[7] He said he had met me at the Turf Club at

---

7. Jack is another MP in the play, friend of Philip and admirer of Victoria. The play is about scandals threatening Philip (played by Bruce Montague), a Conservative MP aspiring to office in the Cabinet. He is married to Victoria (Caroline Blakiston), with teenage children, Julian (Ian Targett) and Hyacinth (Sasha York), and a mistress, Jane (Wendy Padbury). His wife discovers his affair, his daughter is suspended from school for snorting cocaine, his socialist son is involved in a brawl with the police and the *News of the World* discover his dalliance. A distinguished solicitor, Sir Edgar Wiseman (Richard Caldicot), helps them sort it all out. There is also a maid called Maud (Fanny Carby). Directed by Allan Davis, designed by John Page, presented by Allan Davis Ltd in association with Lee Menzies and Nick Salmon at the Theatre Royal, Margate, in October 1989, it was subsequently published by Samuel French Ltd under the title *High Profiles*.

Ascot when I had lunch there with Sarah Keswick one day. He also is a Tote Credit member and proudly produced his card.

Little Sasha York, Susannah York's daughter (and I say little but she is quite tall, only gives the impression of being little) seems pretty and is lively and will do very well. The boy for Julian hasn't got a very good accent but I don't think it will be too much noticed.

Curiously, seeing the four of them together – mother, father, boy and girl – they looked as if they could have been a genuine family.

Allan talks about not bringing it to London till we have reshaped the cast but of course this is dead secret because they would all be put off if they thought they were going to be reshaped.

For fourteen people we drank nine bottles of champagne, with me having a small glass and a half and the leading lady only half a glass because she was driving herself home. So the others must have tucked in a pretty good lot.

It seems that I have been wronging poor Arnold Weinstock. The reason why he delayed answering Allan Davis' letter of August 7th was that my secretary put Grosvenor Gardens on the envelope instead of Grosvenor Square. It therefore took twenty-two days for it to arrive.

Monday 11 September
The first reading at first rehearsals of the play at the Challoner Club, Pont Street.

There were lots of photographers from the *Daily Mail*. They were particularly interested in Sasha York who is pretty and for obvious reasons as she is the daughter of Susannah York. I thought the cast read the play pretty well.

Out to dinner with Irwin Stelzer at the Connaught.

I told Irwin I was extremely worried about Sky Television. I said, 'People like Napoleon and other great entrepreneurs often overreach themselves. They can't stay where they are and run the empires they have got. I do hope Rupert is not going to fail on it.' I think Irwin is a little worried about it.

Tuesday 12 September
I rang Irwin early in the morning. I thanked him for the delicious dinner.

I then said could he arrange some publicity in the *Sunday Times* for my play – in which he has an investment so I called it our play. He is going to try.

I asked him next what he thought about my arguments with Rupert about the salary I get from News International. It's only £65,000. I write book reviews in the *Times*, a fortnightly article for the *Times* and my weekly article in the *News of the World*.

I get offers from Conrad Black and the *Express* and so forth and they would all leap at the chance of my writing for them. Also, I do a lot of extra things to help Rupert. I have asked for £80,000. Irwin said he didn't think that sounded unreasonable but he didn't really know what the going rate was. I said John Junor gets more than I do for doing less work.

I have stopped taking Neuromet, the new brain pill recommended by Giovanni Ricci.[8] I am now not taking any brain pills at all. I find myself feeling better in the mornings, more alert and far less irritated. Maybe I should never have taken the things in the first place.

Wednesday 13 September

Attend rehearsals again of the play. It is just as well I pop in because we had to redo the long soliloquy by Philip before the Jack and Victoria seduction scene.

Got a message that Nigel Lawson would be happy to ring me about his proposals last weekend that currencies should be freely accepted in each other's countries in the European Common Market in order to avoid a single currency. I had been enquiring about it. Very civil of him.

Thursday 14 September

Stinking cold. I had tried on coming back from Italy not to put on weight again. So I slept with only a sheet over me so I would be cold and use energy in calories which would take the fat off. Instead I got a cold and my weight went up.

Went to a party given by Ralph Harris (Lord Harris of High Cross). He is Chairman of IEA (the Institute of Economic Affairs). He instigated many of the policies Mrs Thatcher implemented.

Ralph Harris and his Director of the IEA, John Wood, are approaching sixty-five. They thought they would give a party to celebrate their becoming pensionable. I said it wasn't very Thatcher-like to spend the proceeds of your pensions before you have got them.

Rupert was there. Geoffrey Howe was there. I thought he might be

8. Italian neurologist, father of Aliai Forte.

rather cross with me for having been so rude to him in my last article before going to Italy. On the contrary, he came over when he spotted me and we had a long talk about Hong Kong and the government generally.

Rupert asked me to give him a lift back to his flat in St James's which of course I did. When he had rung me earlier, he had said he wanted to see me for lunch or dinner over the weekend. I thought it was to talk about my demand for £90,000 a year.[9] Maybe it still is but in the car we talked about nothing except for his problems about people wanting to refer him to the Monopolies Commission for his ownership of too many newspapers and his ownership of Sky Television.

Saturday 16 September
I rang Rupert to find out if we were going to see him and he invited us over to lunch tomorrow. Anna was just going off with some girlfriend to the Lake District where she is going to bicycle with her for a week.

I asked him if Peter Stehrenberger had spoken to him about my money from News International. 'Oh yes,' he said, 'that's agreed. £80,000.' I said, 'No, that's not the figure. It's £90,000.' He said, 'I won't quarrel with you about that. You do an awful lot for us so we'll make it £90,000.'

It was quite a pleasant start to the morning.

I went along to the Challoner Club.

We did the whole of the first act. Some of them had interesting suggestions, quite sensible. I rewrote some bits on the spot.

The young man is rather bright, the very young one. He had been going to Marxist meetings and he suggested a phrase to describe what they had in Russia now. He said one of them had said what they have got there is really controlled capitalism, which I thought would do very well for Julian to say.

Sunday 17 September
Last night Norman Lamont rang me. He was very fussed at the Treasury. Those like Kenneth Baker and Chris Patten, now at the Environment Ministry, may succeed in making headway in getting

---

9. Two days previously, on Tuesday 12th, WW gave £80,000 as the salary he wanted, and Murdoch seems to have thought it was £80,000 on Saturday 16th.

£650 million spent by the Treasury to provide a safety net in the areas where councils will be gainers at the end of the four years.

The idea is to lower the community charge in such areas. This would take away the whole point of trying to make people see that it is the local councils who are responsible for the community charge and not the government. Would I say something to Mrs T about it?

I rang Margaret earlier on Sunday than I usually do – about half past seven.

She was quite adamant that she was not going to have the Treasury dishing out all this money.

When I rang Norman, he said it was extremely good news. Only the other day she had been saying, 'We are not free agents,' and she had said it several times, meaning the 1922 Committee was putting a lot of pressure on.

Margaret and I talked about a number of other things.

I told her I was having lunch with Rupert Murdoch today. Then I said, 'What is happening about that referral to the Monopolies Commission?' She said, 'Has he seen Nicholas Ridley?' and I said, 'Yes. He had quite a satisfactory conversation with him and also with Kenneth Baker whom he had to dinner the other night.'

I also pointed out to her that it was only due to Rupert at Wapping and what he did there that new newspapers have been able to start. There have been two recently, the *Independent* and the *Sunday Correspondent* which was out this morning. She said she felt that the *Independent* was seventy to thirty per cent against her and looking at the *Sunday Correspondent* she thought that was even worse against her. I said, 'Yes but the competition is there. If it hadn't been for Rupert, he himself would have got nearer to a monopoly position on newspapers.'

She was in really good heart, trilling away.

Rupert was in high form. He said, '*Today* has got a circulation of six hundred and fifty thousand now and it should be making break-even point in profit before long.' He has already spent £120 million on Sky Television and was convinced it would be making a profit in three years' time.

He thought the immediate danger about the Monopolies Commission was off though he thought there might be a little inquiry by the Office of Fair Trading which they could cope with, he felt.

Rupert is very thorough. On the way out I noticed a copy of the *Sunday Times*. I said, 'Why do you mark those football match reports?'

He said it was because he was trying to get them to put more and more in because they have very big club attendances outside London and it was no good just doing the London clubs, though there were different local editions.

I said, 'How on earth do you manage all these enterprises in America and Australia and Britain and elsewhere?' He has even got an evening newspaper and a magazine in Hungary now. He said that he didn't really manage them as well as he should. I think he is beginning to realize he shouldn't take on anything very big any more now.

The question of Douglas Hurd came up. Rupert had seen him and he had been very friendly and amiable. Rupert said, 'Beware of him. He hates Mrs Thatcher. Take care.' I said, 'That is true. He may not exactly hate her but he doesn't like what she does or why she does it or how she does it and he would be delighted to get rid of her.'

I said, 'It is rather extraordinary that there are three bordello lady keepers in the Sunday press.' He said, 'What do you mean?' I said, 'There is Wendy Henry with the *People*, there is Eve Pollard with the *Sunday Mirror* and there is Pat Chapman with the *News of the World*.' He didn't seem to think that was as funny as I did.

I do wish our leading lady was younger and more sexually attractive. I also wish she didn't have her hair all frizzled up and curled on the top of her head which is quite wrong. She wears clothes quite elegantly but what is wrong is her hair. Allan says he is beginning to talk obliquely to her about it and he will sell her the idea that she has got to do something about it and he would get on to saying, 'Perhaps you might have to wear a wig.'

Tuesday 19 September
In the *Times* my article about the writing of my play. I thought I must drum up some publicity. Immediately Monty Court, the editor of *Sporting Life*, rang the Tote wanting to know which year it was I spoke to Rachel Douglas-Home at Ascot.[10] I rang back when I went to the rehearsals to tell Geoffrey Webster to be sure to let Monty Court know that one of the characters – that's Jack right at the beginning of the play – comes in carrying *Sporting Life*.

---

10. Wife of the playwright William Douglas-Home. WW recalled in his *Times* article that he had said to her, half jokingly, 'If William can write successful plays it must be quite easy.'

Wednesday 20 September

In the evening Allan came to see me. He wanted some big cuts at the end. I said, 'But some of these are my best jokes.' He replied that they were holding up the completion of the story.

He does understand the theatre, at least I hope he does.

Allan said that he must be kinder to the manager at the Theatre Royal, Margate.[11] He has mortgaged his house to get the production on. I said, 'Oh my God. Have I got that burden on me too?' He said, 'He may not be called upon for it because some people will go and see it.' But I know already that the production will cost £30,000 and we are only putting up £10,500. It shows the manager believes in it, though Allan had spent a lot of time saying, 'He's a fool and incompetent.' He had better stop saying all that because he seems to be a noble fellow.

I told Allan again I was very worried about the cast and what would happen to them. He said, 'This is the theatre. Of course they long for it to go on tour.' Allan got on to Lee Menzies and Nick Salmon[12] and they are going to come to our first run through. It all depends on how they feel about it.

Thursday 21 September

Lunch with Philip Howard at the Garrick. I found him in the alcove which will turn up in my play.

Philip once had ambitions to be editor of the *Times* but thinks he is now too old and in any case he likes writing books about the English language and about English words in his articles. And he likes having his own chunk of the book pages.

There were a number of jocular remarks about my play. Robin Day said several times they were going to take a bus load from the Garrick to come and see it. He also talked about his book[13] and how nervous he was about the reception for it. He asked if I had been presented with a copy and I said, 'Yes, I have got one.' He said, 'Is anyone going to ask you to review it?' I said yes that somebody had but I didn't tell him who. I didn't think Philip Howard would have been very pleased if I had said that and he was sitting with me.

I have only glanced at Robin's book so far. It seems a little bit dull

---

11. Jolyon Jackley.
12. The play's producers, in association with Allan Davis who also directed it.
13. *Grand Inquisitor: Memoirs*, 1989.

and stereotyped but Robin assured me that everyone at the BBC will be up in arms about it. I said, 'That means it is very good.'

I asked Robin had he seen his successor (that is the man who is his successor on *Question Time* on the BBC).[14] He said no but he had heard he had done disappointingly well.

I am not sure it is worth my bothering to apply for membership [of the Garrick] because I shall be too old, though Philip says there is an inside track. I expect Peter Jenkins[15] would blackball me.

Saturday 23 September
Plug, plug, plug at my play at rehearsals.

One good thing about Sir Edgar [Richard Caldicot] is he is always in long runs. He was in *No Sex, Please, We're British* for four years. He was the successful butler in *Me and My Girl*. He did the part of the Colonel friend of Higgins for years in *My Fair Lady* when it had a revival. Maybe he's our lucky mascot. So I mustn't bully him about not knowing his lines. When he does remember them as the solicitor at the end, winding up the legal matters, he is very effective and has a great sense of timing and humour.

Sunday 24 September
Spoke to Mrs T at about twenty to six. I congratulated her on making a dent on the Japanese about their restrictions on foreign imports.[16]

I said also that it was a great thing that she backed Gorbachev on her stopover on the way back and he must have been very pleased that she spoke on television telling the Russians to back him. She said, 'Yes. I had to tell them that because they have got openness and glasnost, it doesn't mean to say that their economy suddenly improves. You have to work hard and you have to do it yourselves. He can only get the framework right.'

After Margaret and I had been talking for about twenty minutes I said, 'Denis must have been enthralled by this Ryder Cup thing.' She said, 'Yes. We won, didn't we?' and I said, 'No we didn't. We managed to prevent them winning. It was a tie and we didn't actually

---

14. Peter Sissons.
15. (1934–1992); political columnist; see Vol. 1, pp. 445 and 668, for WW's unfavourable review of Jenkins's book.
16. Mrs Thatcher visited Japan 19–22 September.

win.' 'Oh,' she said. 'I must go and see Denis on BBC2. He's presenting the cup.'

I spoke to Andrew Knight and asked him if he was all right after the changes at the *Telegraph*. He is becoming Deputy Chairman and is no longer going to run the business which is going to be run by Conrad Black who is the eighty per cent shareholder. Andrew said he thought it was the right thing because otherwise they would be having clashes. He said he is now not going to spend so much time there. I said, 'You have come out of it pretty well, haven't you, in cash terms?' He said, 'Yes. But they are only shares. If I were to cash them, I would have to pay forty per cent capital gains on them.'

He said he didn't think Conrad Black was fully aware of what he had done. I said, 'Well you have been very good at business. You saved the RAC.[17] You certainly saved the *Telegraph* for him.' He said, 'You might tell him that when you see him in a tactful way.' I said I certainly would.

Tuesday 26 September

When talking to Mrs Thatcher on Sunday about her Cabinet I said there was one person I didn't fully trust because I didn't think he was really on our side and that was Douglas Hurd. She agreed without hesitation.

Went to the Savoy Theatre to see the *Mikado* as guests of Charles Forte.

Norman St John-Stevas, Lord St John of Fawsley, was there.[18] He took my hand and gravely said, 'Bless you, my friend.' I replied 'Have you got the authorization of the Pope to issue blessings?' He is a Roman Catholic. I like him.

At the dinner in the Waldorf afterwards I sat next to Aliai Forte, Rocco's wife. I am beginning to like her quite a lot now. She is developing poise and conversation. She is twenty-four. She looks very pretty and her skin is full of the freshness of youth.

I have been feeling inexplicably tired for quite long periods these days. When I went to see Dr Pounder on Tuesday morning he found

17. Knight was a committee member of the Royal Automobile Club in the early 1980s.
18. Conservative politician, lawyer and writer; Chancellor of the Duchy of Lancaster, Leader of the House of Commons and Minister for the Arts, 1979–81; at this time chairman, Royal Fine Art Commission; life peer 1987.

that my blood pressure was lower than it had been two years ago
when he last examined me at the Royal Free Hospital. I had a blood
test.

Wednesday 27 September

Today had a very jolly piece from Chris Hutchins, the columnist. It
said everybody would be scurrying off to Margate to find out who the
politician concerned is in the play. He said he found my explanation
that it was nobody in particular unconvincing. He phoned me and told
me he was going to say that and it would therefore help to get people
interested in the play.

I rang Nigel Dempster and read to him the lines in which his column
is mentioned. He was rather pleased so I think I may get a mention in
his column, too.

To the Garrick Club to a dinner given by the Quintons. It was a
large party. On my right sat Carla Powell. She is the wife of Charles
Powell, the Secretary to the Prime Minister. She told me she is forty-
six. She has been married since she met Charles Powell when she went
to Oxford.[19] She is dark and lively with the facial expressions of a
Latin plus the gestures. Very attractive and warm.

She talked about Charles' future.

He intends to stay with Margaret as long as she wants him and he
can get away with it at the Foreign Office, which no doubt she can
arrange. He absolutely adores her, as she does.

He is not interested in money and is quite prepared to live very
simply.

I said, 'He should stay with Mrs Thatcher until the end. She is
bound to give him a peerage.'[20] She asked me why I thought so and I
said, 'If Wilson could give Marcia Williams one, Charles has been far
more important to her and is far more worthwhile and umpteen times
cleverer.'

I also spoke to Paul Channon. I told him that I had been reading
his father's diaries and that they were very good.[21] He was an acute
observer. He said there were five million words. There was a gap of

---

19. She was studying at an English language school; he was an undergraduate at New
    College.
20. He received a knighthood in 1990.
21. *Chips: The Diaries of Sir Henry Channon*, ed. Robert Rhodes James, was pub-
    lished in 1967. The extant diaries covered the years 1918, 1923–8 and 1934–52.

four years, I think it was between 1918 and 1922, but he has got them up to 1958 when he died.

Then he said unexpectedly, 'He liked you very much, you know.' I said, 'Well he was always very kind to me. I wish I had known him better.' He said, 'Yes, he said kind things about you.' I wonder what on earth he meant by that. Maybe Paul Channon means it is in the part he can't print for years because so many people are still alive. There will be a later edition.

Friday 29 September
Went to the full rehearsal, not a dress rehearsal, at the Fortune Theatre. The sets won't be available till Margate next week.

Peter Saunders [impresario] was in the audience. So were Lee Menzies and Nick Salmon. Also Laurence Fitch, my agent. Laurence was ecstatic. Peter said it was a very good play and had lovely lines.

Saturday 30 September
To Ascot for the Festival of British Racing and the Tote Festival Handicap at which we had contributed £50,000 to the prize money.

We went up to the Royal Box where the Duchess of York was presiding. She wore the most awful clothes. However, she has a nice complexion, a fairly pretty face and attractive freckles. She behaved like a spoilt child, shouting and waving her fist in the air when she saw the horse she had backed in the race doing fairly well.

Earlier I had heard that Sonia and Andrew Sinclair are coming to Margate for the first night. I think that is very kind of them and I was greatly touched when Allan Davis told me.[22]

---

22. Sonia Sinclair had introduced WW to Allan Davis – see Vol. 1, p. 381, 26 June 1987.

Sunday 1 October

Frank Johnson has written a splendid long piece about my play, leading the Mandrake column in the *Sunday Telegraph*.

There seems to be a growing feeling that Caroline Blakiston is excellent as Victoria and is improving all the time. She is living the part and she makes very good suggestions and alterations, very small ones, which I would not agree to if they came from anybody else, but she is extremely knowledgeable. I am surprised she is not better known than she is. I hope we will be able to keep her if the play comes to London and I hope also she does something about that hair which is still unsuitable but it is very difficult to say anything at the moment. Allan said it would destroy her confidence before the first night.

Before I went out I talked to Margaret.

She said she was hoping that I would give her some thoughts for her speech at the Conservative Conference. 'You have a way of putting things,' she said. I said, 'I am sorry I have not done anything about it yet but I have been rather harassed by trying to get my play ready and altering it because the first night is on the 4th.' She said, 'Oh yes. That is much more important.' I said, 'No of course it is not more important. Trying to do things for you is far more important. I don't do them just because I love you but because you are so important to the country.' She gave a pleasant little laugh after I said, 'I don't do them just because I love you.'

She is more understanding about the pressures on me than anybody in this household though I suppose it is because she has so many on herself, far more than I ever have.

Dinner with Irwin and Cita Stelzer at Bibendum.

Very sweetly they had ordered a bottle of Château Latour 1966 as a send-off for my play.

Monday 2 October

By train to Margate, a fairly quick journey.

I did my filming for the BBC television lady and the crew. One of them met me at the station. It is extraordinarily pretty inside the theatre. Not so good outside but passable.

Tuesday 3 October
After a quick and early lunch, I am now off to Margate. I have been feeling terrible all day. I woke up at four in the morning and couldn't get back to sleep again.

I had said to the interviewer of the BBC, the pretty girl, when she asked me if I was nervous, that I was not particularly because there was nothing I could do about it. But I suppose at the bottom I am naturally worried about how the audience will receive it and what will happen to the actors who depend on it, I fear. It is a terribly precarious life. Before I left London I sent them all a telemessage.

The dress rehearsal was fairly good, a bit rough in places. They still get their lines wrong, some of them. Philip can't even remember the stanza from Byron.[1] He calls it 'the soul outwears its sheath' and of course it's 'the sword outwears its sheath', after Victoria says, 'Your sword's certainly worn out as far as I'm concerned.'

Wednesday 4 October
The audience was quite a good one as far as numbers are concerned. They had been attracted to some extent by the fact that it had been on ITV South, Channel 4 and on breakfast television.

There was not a cough or a sound during the whole of the first act. Everyone was intent on following the story. There was a lot of laughter. But there were not the belly laughs at the more subtle jokes because you are really meant to smile inside and I thought the audience were doing that.

Allan says that the first act must be cut by fifteen minutes as it's too long.

At the end we had a drink of my pink champagne which I had brought and some white champagne as well. Unfortunately, the Mayor and his wife and some other people not connected with the play were up in the circle bar and they were drinking it, too, so it didn't last as long as it would have done.

I cancelled Allan having breakfast with me at half past eight in my

---

1. For the sword outwears its sheath, / And the soul wears out the breast, / And the heart must pause to breathe, / And love itself have rest' from 'We'll Go No More a-Roving'.

room because I thought it would be too messy and also I wanted to think about the play more.

When Allan came I said, 'I am afraid I am going to be a bit difficult this morning. I hope you are not going to be upset. I don't want to hurt your feelings.' He said, 'Don't you remember when I said to you your turn will come and you will be able to round on me for mucking about with your play?' 'I don't want to do that at all,' I said.

I said I was afraid of the seduction scenes. I don't like it when Jack puts his hand up Victoria's skirt and it is altogether too overdone, the sexy part and very vulgar. 'If you remember when I first wrote it, when they were making love they dropped behind the sofa. I agreed to it happening on a rug in front but I think it is mixing up two different kinds of plays. This is supposed to a sophisticated kind of Noël Coward/Somerset Maugham/Oscar Wilde play and they don't grope in such an obvious way.'

How could I take Queen Elizabeth the Queen Mother to see that or Mrs Thatcher?

He took it very well and he agreed.

At lunch time Allan was talking about the possibility, supposing it happened, that we got into London almost immediately after the Margate season, if we got a big star. Then we would change the title back again to *Knowing the Wrong People*. The only reason we ever went to *The Division Belle*, which I never liked because it is rather a cheapened kind of title, was because the idiotic manager didn't like the title *Knowing the Wrong People* and wanted *The Division Belle*. Though in fact Allan actually thought of the title. He is very good on titles.

Saturday 7 October
Went to lunch at Eythrope in Buckinghamshire where Dorothy Rothschild used to live who left Jacob £90 million at least, over and above the one-sixth of Château Lafite she had already given him years ago and about which he had previously said nothing to anyone, thinking it not politic.

Jacob said that he used to go and see her once a week for thirty years. That certainly paid off. She had other relations, some closer than he, but she left the lot to him.

The lunch was absolutely marvellous, cooked by a chef who used to work for old Bert Marlborough.[2] The first course was a fantastic cheese pancake. The second was the best cooked and most delicious venison I had ever had. The third was a wonderful-looking pastry cream thing. I had a tiny bit and asked for some cheese as well so that I could finish my claret with it.

We had 1914 Château Lafite followed by a 1949 Lafite. The first had not been decanted quite properly and there was a little sediment in the bottom. The second seemed to have been decanted better. Actually they were served the wrong way round because the older should come after the younger. Jacob was very excited about it. He fetched Michael Broadbent's famous book[3] in which he puts down what wines tasted like when he tried them over the years and he was lyrical about the 1914 Lafite. So was I.

As we walked round the stables, I said to Serena, 'How do you like all this?' She put her arm through mine and said, 'I like the horses but I am not sure about the three footmen and the chef.' She prefers the lovely lunches we used to have on a Sunday when we lived near Stowell. The lunches were in the kitchen at Stowell, a big handsome one. (Of course Jacob and Serena also used the proper dining-room as well.)

Serena still spends most of her time at Stowell looking after the farm there, a big one. She also is looking after the five thousand acre farm around Waddesdon and the Pavilion [at Eythrope].

She does it through a very good estate manager and she is very sharp herself.

I told Jacob I was glad he had gone seriously back into business because he had been wasting his talents, fiddling about with the National Gallery and pretending to know about architecture, when his real function is making money like the rest of the Rothschilds – and he has a gift for it.

Sunday 8 October
Allan Davis came round.

He was despondent. He wanted to get rid of [the maid] Maud's part altogether. I said, 'You are being ridiculous. How on earth could you have a situation with people living at the high level they do and not having permanent staff of some kind, even just a housekeeper, in

---

2. (1897–1972); 10th Duke of Marlborough.
3. *The Great Vintage Book*, published 1980.

their London flat? And she is essential, anyway, for taking the coat to
the cleaners which Philip made a mess of. She has to be there when the
note [from Philip's mistress] is taken out of the pocket.'

Monday 9 October
Spoke to Margaret. She was a bit down about the consistently bad
opinion polls. I said, 'Don't worry about them and don't let them try
and do what they did in the general election, trying to obscure you.
You are the greatest asset the Tory Party has got. Please remember
that. And everybody respects you and even if they don't like you, they
know that you are the best person to run the country.'

She said, 'But they say I am arrogant. "Arrogance", they keep
saying. I am the least arrogant person there is.' I said, 'I know that.
But that is how newspapers represent you. You have got a strong
personality and of course people react always to you but basically they
know that you are strong and that is what is needed in a dangerous
world.'

I spoke to Lee Menzies. He is very bullish about the play. He said
it is a *good* play with heavy emphasis. He said we need a star to come
to London. Kenneth More would have been perfect but he is dead.

When I spoke to Margaret, I couldn't get her to begin with because
she was still under the hair dryer and I had to wait nearly an hour.
The first thing she said to me was, 'How is the play going?'

How extraordinary that with all her preoccupations, trying to
prepare her speech, the pound again plunging today, the interest rates
having gone up on Thursday, all the opinion polls going against her,
all the worries she has, the first thing she does is to ask me how my
play is getting on. Who says that woman is not considerate and
thoughtful of others?

Wednesday 11 October
Allan Davis rings in a great state of excitement. What did I think of
the *Daily Telegraph* this morning? I said I hadn't looked at it.

He said, 'There is a rave review by Charles Osborne.' I read it and
then rang him back and teased him a bit and he got very upset. I said,
'I don't call that a rave review. The fellow says that my dialogue is
"hardly sparkling".'

However, he is right, it is a good review and he thinks it will help
to get us a good star in London.

Kenneth Baker rang. He was returning my call of yesterday. I congratulated him on his fighting speech at the Tory Conference at Blackpool yesterday. I said, 'You have got to go on like mad exposing their Policy Review and what it really means from the Labour Party. There is one thing to console us and that is if the economy is really bad, there is a strong feeling in the opinion polls always that the Conservatives are much better at handling any economic crisis than Labour.'

I also said to him that Julian Lewis wants a job of some sort at the Conservative Party headquarters.

'Julian Lewis', I said to him, 'is the fellow who did that poll about nuclear disarmament and wrote a letter [about it] to the *Times*; in your letter to the *Times* the day before yesterday you picked up what he had said and what his poll had said.'[4]

In the Lords this afternoon Roy Jenkins stopped me in the corridor. He was very impressed by the review in the *Daily Telegraph* about my play, particularly the bit about it being well crafted.

In the morning Ali Forbes had rung mainly about the review in the *Telegraph*. He went into a long and rambling conversation about how he had stopped over in France to talk to the girl who was married twice to Cyril Connolly[5] and once to George Weidenfeld. She showed him an album of pictures and said, 'Could these be done as an album of my pictures like some people do?' And she said she thought on the cover ought to be this picture and she pointed out a man lying on a bed and all you could see was an enormous cock, erect. She said, 'Whose is that, do you think?' So he said, 'I have no idea. I am not a bugger and I don't recognize cocks.'

It was Barbara Skelton, the girl who used to be the mistress of King Farouk (she always fell for fat men like Cyril Connolly, George Weidenfeld and King Farouk), who is the owner of the album of photographs. Her latest volume is already with the publishers. It's obviously very hot stuff and George is going to be very upset.

---

4. Julian Lewis was research director and director, Coalition for Peace Through Security, 1981–5; director, Policy Research Associates, from 1985; deputy director, Conservative Research Department, 1990–6; MP for New Forest since 1997.

5. Author, editor and literary critic; m 2 (1950–6) Barbara, née Skelton, who then m (1956–61) Weidenfeld as his second wife; Connolly was cited in the Weidenfeld divorce case but they did not remarry; she married 3 (1966–8) Professor Derek Jackson (1906–82), his fifth wife; her memoirs *Tears Before Bedtime* and *Weep No More* were published in 1987 and 1989.

They have just announced an awful give-in on the community charge, spending £1,300 million quite unnecessarily. Norman Lamont told me that Malcolm Rifkind, Secretary for Scotland, said, 'Why do you want to do this? You will have to do the same for Scotland and we don't need it there at all. The poll tax is going very well there.'

Thursday 12 October
At 9.45 a meeting with J. J. Warr and Stanley Jackson of the RCA plus Brian McDonnell. They came to Cavendish Avenue. We had a good two hours agreeing the approach to the Home Secretary and placating him, at least on one point, by accepting a part of the Lloyds Merchant Bank recommendation that the RCA should own, or stand in the place of the Home Office with regards to the Tote.

Then off to Margate with Mrs Wood.[6]

There was a bigger house than usual for a matinee, though still not very large. The audience was attentive and laughed a reasonable amount.

Friday 13 October
Rupert rang. He had just arrived from Australia after a twenty-four hour flight.

We talked about Lawson and the pound and he asked me what Alan Walters had said. I said I had spoken to him yesterday but – this is highly confidential – he thinks that we cannot hold the pound up. It is absurd. It is damaging our exports and it is going to cause a recession and a slump and unemployment and it is all a great mistake. I said I was going to write that in the *News of the World*. He was very pleased.

At 10.30 I had to be at the Royal Free Hospital. They fitted on some gadget and many wires and I had to carry a box with a tape in it. It is to see what my heart and pulse do over a twenty-four hour period. I was kept waiting for twenty minutes and then had to go to another department to get a proof from them that I would pay the bill. I said, 'But they know me already.' However, they insisted on it.

Eventually quite a nice coloured girl did the fitting on for me and she said she was sorry they had kept me waiting. I said, 'It is all right. It is just that I happen to be very busy.' She said, 'We have to treat

---

6. Miranda Wood, former secretary to WW, who had also worked for George Orwell, typing the manuscript of *1984* and his essay 'Such, Such Were the Joys'.

everybody the same way whether you are a Lord or not.' I said, 'That isn't quite the point. I am so busy that I would have had to have gone if something hadn't been done quickly.' She asked me what I did and I told her and about all the work I had to do and the articles I had to write so she was mollified and I shook her hand.

In the afternoon I watched Mrs Thatcher making her speech [at the Conservative Conference]. She was magnificent.

They went on cheering for ten minutes or more and Willie Whitelaw couldn't stop them. He was the President in charge of the chair at the time. He rang a bell but still they went on shouting, 'Ten more years, ten more years, ten more years,' and then they sang as well, 'Happy birthday to you.'

She said she had worked until three in the morning on that speech, polishing it and getting it right. She had also put it on the autocue and rehearsed it several times.

She thanked me very much for the roses. She said they had just arrived and she was having them put in water and they looked lovely. She said they were sent down from Number 10 Downing Street. I sent her twenty-four roses with a birthday message telling her, 'They are choppy waters but you will get through fine as you always do.'

Saturday 14 October
Allan Davis on again. Had I seen Ned Sherrin's review in his column in the *Times*?

I looked at it later and all the man had said was that he had enjoyed my play and made some foolish joke about it being the first play of a seventy-one-year-old life peer: 'No end-of-the-peer stuff this.' He said we had rave reviews in the local papers.

Alexander Hesketh is now Minister of State at the Department of the Environment. He is large and cheerful, rather too fat, as I keep telling him.

I told him I thought he did very well in presenting his statement about the community charge.

I said it was only because of him that I didn't get up and denounce it.

He said he completely agreed with me. He said he felt like resigning.

Another trip to Margate to see *The Division Belle*. There was a pretty good audience though it was not totally full.

Sunday 15 October

I had to spend some time in the morning getting ready for the article I have to do tomorrow for the *Times* a year after – actually it is thirteen months after – Mrs Thatcher's Bruges speech. I have so much to do it nearly drives me crazy.

Allan said discouragingly that Peter Saunders had said about the Charles Osborne review that it was a 'kind' notice. He meant that he didn't really mean much of what he said and that he didn't really think the play was all that good. He is so despairing, Allan.

I understand his position. It must be his last fling at trying to get a major play on from scratch and if it doesn't come off, he will have wasted a lot of his time over the last two or three years with me and he probably hasn't got the energy to take up something else new.

I told Rupert that I was intending to go to Hong Kong and write for the *Times* and the *News of the World*. Although some of the expenses would be paid by the Hong Kong government, they wouldn't be enough to cover Verushka and myself. He said, 'Fine. News International will pay the rest.'

I now think it is unlikely that *The Division Belle* will ever get to London. I think Allan has lost a bit of his drive. Too many of the actors who read the play a year or so ago didn't like it and won't believe it is a new and different one. Lee Menzies is only keen if we get a big star and he is not doing much about getting one himself.

Monday 16 October

Dinner with Alan Hare. He had 1976 Forts de Latour followed by 1964 Château Latour itself. The first was extremely good. It is from the vines in the same vineyard, the young ones. They will become Château Latour themselves in due course. This lot tasted nearly ready to be so.

Also present was Lord Iveagh.[7] Alan had said to me nervously as I arrived, 'Please don't ask him about Ernest Saunders and interrogate him, as you sometimes do me, about why the family are not more supportive about this man.'

I promised not to. I had no intention of doing so, actually, but it is true I had ribbed one of the Guinnesses recently about it – I think it was young Lennox-Boyd whose mother was a Guinness.[8]

---

7. (1937–92); 3rd Earl of Iveagh; president, Guinness, 1986–92.
8. On 18 June 1989.

Tuesday 17 October
Went to dinner at a large party for Robin Day and his book given by Weidenfeld. The food was indescribably awful. The wine was a little better than it sometimes is.

Susan Crosland[9] was there. She wears very well and was looking quite pretty. I grasped her by the neck from behind and she said how did I know she didn't have a bad neck? I said, 'Well you haven't. I know you very well.' I am rather fond of her but she writes the most fearful anti-Thatcher tripe in the *Sunday Times*.

George said he thought the book would sell twenty-five thousand copies – that's the amount that has gone out already. Provided there are not too many returned, he will make a bit of money. It has also been serialized in a Sunday newspaper and he must have got quite a lot for that. Robin several times said to me what a generous review I had written about his book and I said, 'Not at all. It was accurate and I like you very much.'

George said, 'I have known Woodrow longer than anybody else in this room. We once shared a house together.' Our relationship has been up and down but I still like him very much.

Wednesday 18 October
Bernard Levin at Margate.

I sat behind him, two or three rows. He watched intently without his concentration wandering throughout, though he shifted in his seat once or twice, more probably because the seat was not quite comfortable.

In the interval I asked him what he would like to drink and he said pink champagne. I said, 'There isn't any here,' and he said, 'What about that bottle over there?' There was a bottle of pink champagne standing on ice, the only one in the theatre, so I bought it for him. It cost £16.50. He only wanted half a glass from it.

Fortunately, three people from the *News of the World* were there, led by Ron Pell [WW's sub-editor]. He had a motor bike crash helmet on. I had expected him to be a big man from his voice on the telephone but he was quite small, with a tiny, Puckish face. I gave the pink champagne to him and his two friends, the chief sub-editor and another sub-editor.

After the play was over I went to say goodbye to the cast. I said I

9. Author and journalist; widow of Anthony Crosland, Labour politician.

hoped to see them all again and thanked them all for what they had done.

Bernard said of the play, 'It is not Shakespeare and it is not Ibsen. But it is very entertaining and funny. Audiences are unpredictable but I can see no reason why it shouldn't run well in London. You must try to put it on in the West End. I will come to the first night.'

'If you were writing a review of the play, what would you say?' I asked him. 'I wouldn't write the headline because I never do that,' he said, 'but whoever did would make it "Entertaining Trifle" and that would be a quote from something I had said in the review.' That he regarded as highly commendatory.

Bernard Levin was very keen to talk about the political situation. He thinks that whereas Margaret seemed beyond mortal a couple of years ago and we could never imagine her being beaten, or even eighteen months ago, she does seem mortal now and we can imagine her being beaten.

He was very gloomy.

I said, 'You don't write much about politics now.' He said he had got tired of the scene. Maybe that is what the trouble is with Bernard. He no longer has that crusading spirit and that intense interest in justice and fairness and supporting Mrs Thatcher, though he does of course still support her very strongly.

Thursday 19 October
Robbie rang from Cornwall. Very bad news. Devenish Brewery have pulled out [of the arrangements for Cornish Spring Water]. They find they couldn't buy the bottles any cheaper than we could and they had relied on being able to buy them much cheaper as they are such a big firm.

However, they are willing to help with the marketing and all the rest of it.

Friday 20 October
Dr Pounder rang up. The tape which I wore for twenty-four hours had been processed. There is nothing wrong with my heart. My blood test showed there was nothing wrong with my liver or my kidneys or anything else.

I said, 'What are we to do?' and he said, 'Absolutely nothing. There is nothing wrong with you. Carry on as before.' I said, 'What about my getting tired?' and he said, 'Well maybe you do too much.' I suddenly felt better and wrote my article in a fairly brisk manner.

However, Dr Pounder wants me to see the surgeon he named so that he could judge whether I should have an operation to remove my hernia.

We went to stay the night at Isabel Derby's [Stanley House, Newmarket]. I am always pleased to see her but I thought it was a long way to go. I would have preferred to have gone up in the morning to see our Tote Cesarewitch race.

After the ladies had gone from the dining-room, John [Derby] started talking rot about Mrs Thatcher and that she ought to go, that she was no good and never had been and so forth. The others were prepared to listen deferentially to him but I wasn't. I launched a tremendous attack on him.

I like him though he is silly.

Saturday 21 and Sunday 22 October

We had a fairly jolly lunch in the Tote room. I met the new Chief Executive at the Jockey Club, Christopher Haines and his wife who had never been racing before, at least not much. He seemed well clued up and business-like. She is attractive. She has four children. Tall, with an interesting face. She told me she does no other work than look after her family.

It is very sad for John Derby, and I think for Isabel, to see their stables, which one sees out of the windows at the house just a few yards away, now occupied by Arabs. John was complaining about the Arab owners and said, 'Of course you can't do anything about them now, if you haven't got £100 million to compete with them,' meaning of course that he hadn't.

He hasn't done much with his life. He thinks he ought to have been in the government but I don't suppose anybody, except for a much earlier Tory Prime Minister, would have ever put him there. But he is amiable and not without some common sense. He is not the sort of person admired by Mrs Thatcher who requires of ancient aristocrats that they should be outstandingly good before they overcome the stigma of being aristocrats.

It was the last night on Saturday of the season at Margate. I kept wanting to ring them up which I did just before dinner. They had what they called a good house coming for the last night but I was sad I couldn't be there.

Wednesday 25 October
Rang Margaret at 8.25 a.m.

She was pretty annoyed about the ludicrous stories of the disagreement between herself and John Major when it was decided to add to
the Commonwealth conference communiqué explaining why Britain
disagreed on certain points and where they disagreed.

The reports said that Britain had tightened up over South African
sanctions.

This was quite untrue so they had to correct the situation and state
the position plainly.

She was irritated by the new row about Alan Walters who is supposed to have undermined the Chancellor of the Exchequer by saying
that he was dead against going into the Exchange Rate Mechanism of
the EMS and the Prime Minister agreed with him. She said the article
in some obscure American journal was written in early 1988. At that
time he wasn't even working at Number 10 Downing Street as her
economics adviser. How could she have stopped him writing something
then?

George Walker of Brent Walker came to lunch. He is the brother
of a great heavyweight boxing champion. He told me that he, too, had
been a boxer.[10]

Though he had been in prison for grievous bodily harm, and I was
told he had been fairly hot early on, I took to him immediately and
thought he was very jolly. I had heard from Nicholas [Banszky] that
he had bought Smith-Haut-Lafitte so I found a bottle of 1962 Smith-
Haut-Lafitte in my cellar and gave it to him as a compliment.

I think we can do some business with him. He is starting this
Hackney racecourse and I said I would back it because it is near
London and there is nothing near there.

He admired the house greatly. These people don't realize that it
isn't mine and is only on a short lease. They probably think I am a
millionaire like they are but that is totally untrue.

I then went on to the Jockey Club to discuss the joint approach of
the racing industry to the Home Office. They seemed to think that the
Home Secretary was not going to do anything in a hurry.

It was then on to the Barbican. This time it was the official opening

---

10. Amateur Boxing Champion, GB, 1951; at this time he had a controlling interest
    in Brent Walker, Mecca and William Hill.

of the Hungarian month [Britain Salutes Hungary] by the Duke of Kent who is patron.

There were some very attractive pictures in the art exhibition. There was a great photograph of the old Lord Rothermere with Verushka's great uncle.[11]

We went down to listen to the concert by the Hungarian orchestra from Budapest. I am not good on highbrow music. I managed to sleep quite a lot through the first part but the noise was pretty loud as they were playing all kinds of Hungarian things, Bartók included.

I talked to Imrey Pozsgay. I wished him good luck and said how brave he had been in initiating all these political reforms.

I had been told by quite a lot of people now that he has no chance or very little chance of winning [the presidency] because he is tarred with the brush of having been Minister of Culture in a Communist government.

One rather touching thing. In the menu the chicken volaille was called Volaille Verushka. That was arranged by Henry Wrong, the administrator at the Barbican – he is just about to leave – as a tribute to Verushka. . .

Thursday 26 October

I watched Margaret in the House answering questions. There was supposed to be a great scene about to develop on the Alan Walters issue and on the communiqué issued after the Commonwealth conference. It all turned out to be an anti-climax. She brushed aside the supposed [reaction] of the Chancellor over Walters by saying that advisers advise but the government Ministers decide, which is what happens, and there is complete agreement in the government about the interest rates and about when might be a suitable time to join the ERM.

Suddenly at ten past six or thereabouts Charlie Wilson rings. Would I immediately write an article within the next two hours about the Cabinet changes. I said, 'What has happened?' and he said that Nigel Lawson had resigned.

I said, 'No, I could not possibly do it because I would have to think about it.' The next thing I heard, when we went to the Hungarian party at the Hungarian Embassy, was that Alan Walters had resigned, too. Nigel had resigned because he couldn't bear being interfered with any more by Walters. I wondered whether Alan Walters knew that

---

11. Minister of Justice in the Horthy Regency. See 18 November 1989.

Nigel had resigned before he decided to resign, which would have made it seem rather unnecessary.

At The Other Club I heard that Douglas Hurd had become Foreign Secretary, so he is out of my hair at the Home Office, and the new Home Secretary is Waddington, who I am not sure if I know at all. He was Chief Whip and an amiable enough fellow I think. Maybe that will help us in our wish to get what we want done for the Tote.

Suddenly I get an urgent message from a Savoy Hotel attendant, would I please go and speak immediately to Brian Walden on the telephone. Everybody said, 'Is that a call from Downing Street? Do they want you to be Foreign Secretary or whatever?' and there was a lot of laughter.

But it was Brian wanting me to ring Mrs Thatcher in the morning and say to her the questions he would like to ask because he would like to have an idea of what the answers were beforehand so that he could phrase them in the most helpful way. He is due to interview her on Saturday morning for putting out on Sunday.

What Brian wanted to know was why everything seemed all right with Nigel a few days ago, and he accepted the fact that Walters was only an adviser, and then it wasn't all right on Thursday, and why she had not just got rid of Walters quietly beforehand. I said, 'She would never have done that. She is much too loyal. In any case, why shouldn't she have an adviser?'

I said, 'Write down exactly what it is you want to know and I shall speak to you in the morning. But I have to go now. I am exhausted.'

He thinks it is the greatest crisis she has ever had. I said, 'It may not turn out to be so. It's a lancing of the boil and Lawson is not all that popular in the City. He is not popular with the backbenchers of the Tory Party. He is a loner and maybe it will all work out. What I had been frightened of, and on my way to the Savoy I felt quite sick in the stomach, was that the Cabinet might suddenly gang up on her also and try to force her to resign. But please note that it is unlike when Thorneycroft resigned in a situation which Macmillan called "a little local difficulty" [because] the other Treasury Ministers went with him.[12] There is no sign of any of the Treasury Ministers going now.

12. Thorneycroft resigned as Chancellor of the Exchequer in 1958 because he wanted more cuts in public expenditure than the rest of the Cabinet; the junior Treasury ministers who resigned with him were Nigel Birch and Enoch Powell.

Hurd has quite happily taken the Foreign Office and Major[13] has a lot of experience as the Treasury's Chief Secretary before. Maybe it will all turn out for the best.'

He also wanted to know if she knew, when she was answering questions in the House, that Nigel had already resigned because he alleged he saw her about three times during the day and he said he was going to resign.

On return to 19 Cavendish Avenue I found that Chips Keswick and Norman Lamont had rung.

Norman said he was disturbed and shaken. Nigel was wrong to have resigned and he had tried to persuade him not to. He thought it was a great mistake and could do great harm.

Friday 27 October
Spoke to Margaret at about a quarter to eight. She came burbling to the telephone, full of life.

She said she had tried to persuade Nigel not to go and I said, 'I think the news is all good. You have lanced the boil which couldn't go on. I am sure Major will do extremely well.'

We talked about Douglas Hurd briefly and I said I was always worried about him. She said she was, too, but he has been a very loyal member of the team.

She says she doesn't think he will rock the boat and of course it was his great ambition to be Foreign Secretary.

She remarked that everyone likes to reach their zenith and it is a good thing when they do; certainly Douglas has now reached his zenith.

I gave her Brian's questions.

I said, 'If you don't want to answer these questions I understand. I told Brian you might tell me to go to hell.' She was quite shocked and said, 'I would never do that.' I said, 'But you might not want me to pass them on to him.'

So the answer to the first question was that she could not have resolved the situation. It would have made no difference if Alan Walters had resigned earlier. There was an irritation going on for a long time from Nigel and the press would have gone on saying there were differences between Number 10 and Number 11, even if Walters had gone before.

The second question was why, since Lawson was happy on Tuesday

---

13. Appointed Chancellor of the Exchequer.

on the very issue re Alan Walters, did he resign on Thursday. Her answer was, 'I don't know. I have no idea. I wasn't here. I was still abroad.[14] I don't know why he did it or why he changed his mind so quickly.'

The third question was why did Walters resign. She said because he was so fed up of being mauled about and battered by the press and the media and by politicians that he just wanted to get away from it all because he couldn't give good advice in such an atmosphere.

And this was not for transmission to Brian: 'Could we not get some great firm in the City to give him a consultancy post so that he could come over here from time to time? Then he could see John Major or even me so we could hear his latest thinking.' I said I would make some enquiries into it.

I rang Brian with the answers to his questions and he was delighted. But I didn't tell him the extra bits, only the actual answers to his questions.

Saturday 28 October
Norman Lamont rings and tells me how long he had tried to persuade Nigel not to resign but to no avail. He says there was some question about when the resignation should be issued.

Nigel said to Norman, 'I don't want to have a row with her now. We have never had one yet.' So he let the resignation go out when she wanted it. Norman and I thought Nigel's comment very funny in the circumstances.

Sunday 29 October
I saw, when I got home [from lunch at the Weinstocks'], the Brian Walden interview with Margaret.

He was far from helpful. He was obnoxious. I was furious. He went on and on and on asking her why she didn't sack Walters and didn't she realize she could have kept her Chancellor if she had sacked her private adviser, etc. etc. The questioning was outrageously impertinent to a Prime Minister. She bore it very well, though after he had asked her the same question about ten times she rebuked him for going on asking the same question.

What a strange idea that a Prime Minister has to obey the dictates

---

14. In Kuala Lumpur, 18–24 October, at the Commonwealth Heads of Government Meeting.

of one of her Cabinet Ministers because he wishes her to sack a private adviser! I have never heard such damn nonsense. What would Churchill have said if he had been told to sack Lindemann, 'the Prof.', or a member of his Cabinet would resign instead? All Prime Ministers have to have advisers. Chancellors of the Exchequer have them, too.

Brian then accused her of being dictatorial and autocratic and said she appeared to people to be going off her trolley. I was amazed at Brian, who had pretended he was going to be helpful, carrying on in this extraordinary way to damage her as much as he possibly could.

Later that evening I rang her and told her I was extremely annoyed. I said, 'I don't know why he had to go on and on and on wasting a long interview when more constructive things could have been talked about.' She said, 'That is exactly what I said to him at the end of the interview.'

I think Brian Walden is running out of ideas. If he were really clued up on English politics and what is really happening, he would have concentrated much more on the things which matter about the economy, the interest rates and inflation and why did the government get themselves into such a mess over inflation. That would have been pertinent questioning.

I told her she looked very pretty and she was very calm and I thought the sympathy would go to her for an interview like that.

We discussed Howe's overtly disloyal remarks about the Exchange Rate Mechanism over the weekend, which were quite unnecessary other than to say that he was really the person who ought to be Prime Minister and that they were going to keep her under control. She said, 'It's what he wants. He wants to do the job but I don't think he is capable of it.'

I asked her if she thought anybody was going to stand against her, because that was what Norman Lamont had said to me was a possibility on Saturday. That is in the November [Conservative leadership] election after the Queen's speech. She said, 'We will have to see.' I said, 'If anybody does, they would be crazy. I see Heseltine says he certainly is not going to.'

I am going to write an article tomorrow for Tuesday's *Times* trying to put all this hate stuff against her right.

Monday 30 October
Rupert rang three times. He was alarmed and worried about Margaret's position. I reassured him. I told him I had spoken to her and she is in

quite good shape. I said, 'Have you read my article in the *News of the World*?' He hadn't by then so I said, 'Well read it and tell me what you think of it.'

He rang again and said, 'Yes, it's fine.' I told him what I was writing for the *Times* tomorrow and he was delighted. He said, 'I have been saying to them over the week-end, the *Times* used to be the Thunderer a hundred years ago so why have you abandoned the tradition?'

The third time he rang he said had I read the *Sunday Times* leader and I said, 'Yes. It was absolutely splendid and Margaret was delighted,' to which he replied, 'They ought to have printed it on the front page.'

Rupert was very sweet. He apologized for interrupting me and I said, 'It's all right, I am only writing for your newspaper,' and he laughed.

Tuesday 31 October
Put in a call to Margaret but she was not available at her normal flat number. I expect she was getting herself ready for the day. That was at half past seven.

I rang Kenneth Baker and said, 'You have really got to get your Cabinet Ministers out supporting Margaret and saying what a good leader she is. It's about time you did it. And they have got to stop going on about the ERM because it is totally irrelevant.'

He said they had hundreds of messages of support for her at the Conservative Central Office yesterday.

The night before I had hand-written a little letter to Douglas Hurd and told him that they should stop sticking pins into each other. They didn't have to say on the hour every hour what the conditions are agreed by the Cabinet for joining the Exchange Rate Mechanism. I told him he would be a brilliant Foreign Secretary and generally congratulated him, beginning with the hymn 'God Moves in a Mysterious Way His Wonders to Perform'.

When Margaret rang back she said what a marvellous article I had written this morning [in the *Times*].

She was immediately concerned about the front page story in the *Times* saying that Hurd admitted that Howe had cleared his speech with him and Major on the question of the Exchange Rate Mechanism. She said, 'This is dreadful. Major is only just there, and Hurd. What are they doing?' She is obviously deeply worried that there is some kind of a plot.

I told her that Hurd had been very good on the television last night, on *Panorama*, and he had spoken in a sensible way about the Exchange Rate Mechanism, indicating there was no hurry and it was something of an irrelevance. He said that he had no difficulty ever from the Home Office in dealing with the Prime Minister and discussions were always very good and went smoothly.

I said about Geoffrey Howe that he is deliberately stirring it up. She loved what I said about him in my article.[15]

I said, 'The support for you is perfectly all right so don't worry,' but she is worried.

After I had spoken to her I rang Douglas Hurd and congratulated him on his *Panorama* performance.

Then I said, 'Is it true what they said on the front page of the *Times*, that Howe had cleared his speech with you over the week-end?' He said, 'He rang me up and told me the bit he was going to say about the conditions of the Cabinet for joining the ERM and asked if they were right because he was going to use them in a speech,' and he had said they were correct. He had no idea he was trying to cause trouble.

I said to him that I still think a lot of people can't cope with her because she is a woman and he said, 'I think that is right,' and he gave as an example Francis Pym who could never understand why she argued with him as he never thought it was the place of a woman to argue with a man.

Then he said, 'Of course you and I, Woodrow, we know how to argue with women. We have strong-willed wives and we argue with them so we think nothing of arguing with women. But some of these old fashioned people think women shouldn't argue at all.'

The reason I mentioned this to Douglas was because Margaret had said to me, 'If Brian Walden had been interviewing a male Prime Minister, he would never have said, "You are very domineering." ' She said, 'You expect a male Prime Minister to be domineering but if a woman is strong, they immediately say she is domineering – there is something wrong about it.'

The truth of the matter is, as Douglas said to me, you have to do your homework, and as he said on *Panorama*, 'You have to know

---

15. WW said, 'Sir Geoffrey is still bitter at losing the two agreeable residences he had as Foreign Secretary and is making a forlorn bid to be prime minister himself. If his careless talk continues, Dorneywood will be at risk.'

what your answers are going to be. You have got to make a good case with her.' That is, of course, exactly how it should be.

When I had finished talking to Douglas, I rang her again to explain to her what he had said and that I didn't think he intended any harm.

I didn't tell her that Douglas Hurd had said to me she is marvellous about all family matters and personal things and very considerate but she has one drawback: she can be very 'insensitive about other people's convinced beliefs in political matters. She just brushes them on one side or dismisses them or squashes them and that is what upsets some people.' Probably Geoffrey Howe. Myself, I do not think it could have upset Nigel Lawson, particularly as he said to Norman Lamont at the end, 'I have never had a row with her and I don't want one now,' over the timing of his resignation statement.

Watching the debate, I thought how the oratory and stature of the MPs had declined. When I think of somebody like Stafford Cripps as Chancellor of the Exchequer, or Hugh Gaitskell or even Hugh Dalton or Denis Healey, it is pathetic to see Major making pedestrian dough of it. The best you could say about him was that he sounded solid and careful. Maybe that will make him a better Chancellor of the Exchequer, but where was the life, where was the spirit?

Even Nigel Lawson's resignation speech, which some were hailing as a great speech, which it certainly wasn't, was not a patch on Nye Bevan's resignation speech.[16]

16. In 1951, over the imposition of NHS charges.

Wednesday 1 November

Spoke to Margaret. I told her I thought Lawson behaved like a shit in his speech and anyway what ridiculous nonsense, saying that you had interfered with him for six and a half years, which is the implication. I said, 'Is he therefore giving you credit for all the success he claims for himself? You can't run a government on the lines he stipulates. It was a rotten speech and it must have gone down very badly.' She said, 'No. Some of them were saying what a very good speech it was.'

She is worried that Lawson is going to go on making a nuisance of himself.

I asked about the Bank of England being an independent authority on fixing the exchange rates and the interest rates, [an idea] which Nigel Lawson suddenly sprang upon the House. She said it was discussed privately but even Treasury officials knew nothing about it. I said, 'Do you think it is a good idea?' She said, 'Not under our present arrangements. Leigh-Pemberton[1] would hardly be tough enough to run a privatized Bank and determine what happens with our money nationally. We would have to have somebody very powerful indeed and I don't see one around.'

She was surprised at Nigel breaking that particular confidentiality over the talks of the possibility of an independent Bank of England.

I attended the [House of Commons] All Party Racing Committee. Stoker Hartington was good. He won unanimous support for the racing interests cum Tote proposals. They are all unanimously against selling the betting shops and they are all in favour of taking the Tote away from the Home Office in the manner described.

There was a somewhat boring dinner at the Andrew Knight's. It was his birthday. I took six bottles of 1985 claret, quite good but not fantastic, as a present.

They do not know how to give a dinner party. We had two fish

---

1. Robin (Robert) Leigh-Pemberton, Governor, Bank of England, 1983–93; life peer 1993.

courses, one after the other, accompanied by a 1977 La Mission-Haut-Brion. It does not improve it to have it with fish, not that I am a great stickler on these matters, but it was light white fish. The year was poor for La Mission-Haut-Brion. He is a multi-millionaire now after his exploits with Black at the *Telegraph* so he could have done better than that.

Of the other guests, only Arnold Weinstock and Netta lifted the heart a bit. And also Bob Gavron[2] who runs and owns the St Ives printing works. He is the son-in-law of Tosco Fyvel and Mary Fyvel. Tosco, who died some years ago, was the great expert on and friend of George Orwell.[3] I was delighted to hear that Mary, though eighty, is full of vim and vigour.

He said after I went out of the printing business they had no competition other than Maxwell and they had made a fortune. It was a pity Banbury collapsed as it did, otherwise I could be very rich by now.

Thursday 2 November

I had a mildly quiet time for a little and was able to compose my thoughts for a bit for the article tomorrow, to review the stricken battlefield at Westminster from the newspapers and consider what I would write. Then came a telephone call.

It was from Rupert. Had I heard the rumour sweeping Fleet Street that Cecil Parkinson is about to resign because he has been engaged in insider trading and he has to go? I nearly fell over with shock. I was quite shaky. I said, 'But this is a terrible thing.' He said, 'It will make it look as though the government is disintegrating. Her position will be very insecure.'

He asked if I could find out something about it. So I rang Norman Lamont but he was in a Cabinet meeting. I decided to ring Bernard Ingham.

'It had all begun from the front page of the *Scotsman*, a paper I don't look at first,' Bernard said. There was a suggestion that a Cabinet Minister had been involved in a syndicate which was doing insider trading and it wasn't necessarily the case that the Cabinet Minister

2. Chairman, St Ives plc, 1964–93; proprietor, Carcanet Press, since 1983; chairman and proprietor, Folio Society, since 1982; m 1 (1955) Hannah Fyvel (d 1965), m 2 (1967–87) Nicolette Coates, m 3 (1989) Katherine Gardiner, née Macnair; life peer, 1999.

3. He succeeded Orwell as literary editor of *Tribune*.

knew about it. This got put out by the Press Association and on *Sky News* and Cecil Parkinson's name had been bandied about.

However, Cecil at once put out a solicitor's statement saying one, that he had never done any such trading; two, that when he became a Minister, as was the normal practice, he gave all his funds for shares to a stockbroker to deal with at his discretion and he didn't know what deals he made; three, that he wasn't going to resign; four, that if anybody printed any allegation that he was connected with insider trading, he would sue them.

I then rang Rupert.

'I am sure it is all right,' I said. 'He is absolutely honest, you know, and he would never do a thing like that.' Rupert said, 'But he lied to his wife,' I said, 'People often do that and it is quite a different matter, behaving dishonourably in financial matters.' He agreed with that.

In between these conversations Brian McDonnell rang. Mr Wheeler MP,[4] who is a Tory, was announcing that the Home Affairs Select Committee, of which he is Chairman, was proposing to conduct an investigation into the administration of the Tote.

My first reaction was what absolute hell, what with discussions with the Ministry and the racing interests, and we have just had all this Lloyds Bank thing. So I rang Mr Wheeler and said, 'Do you really have to do this? You know we are not a nationalized industry.' He said, 'I know that but you do come within the territory of the Home Office.' I said, 'But it is such a bloody nuisance. It wastes so much time and we are just trying to carry out these delicate negotiations with the Home Office.' He said, 'This may well help. Why don't you turn it to your advantage?'

He said he didn't know anything about the Tote until members of his committee demanded to investigate it. He thought it was the name for a ladies' handbag.

The more I thought about it, the more I thought it could be turned to our advantage.

Friday 3 November

Spoke to Margaret early this morning. I wanted to give her reassurance which might have been needed. But she was in quite a fighting mood again.

---

4. John Wheeler, MP 1983–97; chairman, Home Affairs Select Committee, 1979–92, All Party Penal Affairs Group, 1986–93; knight 1990.

She was cross though with Douglas Hurd, to whom the BBC gave a second item on the news, saying that he wouldn't have said some of the things that she said in the Bruges speech and that we must be in the centre of the Common Market, not standing outside throwing stones at it.

But I had always warned her about Douglas.

John Major she thought was perfect yesterday. 'A safe pair of hands,' she said. That is one of her favourite expressions for a reliable Minister.

I looked at Geoffrey in the gallery yesterday when he was dealing with business questions. He really is a sly looking dog, a sort of friendly Newfoundland but hiding a lot of bitterness beneath the exterior.

Of course if there is any real attempt to dethrone her, Willie Whitelaw would be a very key figure. I don't think any of them would dare to move unless he sanctioned it.

Major seems sound enough and I hope to God he is.

Sunday 5 November

Quite a large chunk from my *News of the World* article on BBC [Radio] 4 after the news on *What the Papers Say*. Unusual. They quoted my bit about the French bishops turning over Joan of Arc to the English to be burned because they couldn't bear it that it was a woman who had revived their country.

The night before I had spoken to Alexander Hesketh about the plot to have a stalking horse to stand against Mrs Thatcher. An obscure candidate. Then a number of senior people would put in blank ballot papers, which they can, to reduce the amount of support for her in order to try and destabilize her. These people in the Tory Party are cracked. They are committing suicide and wrecking themselves.

Watched Brian Walden interview Lawson. Brian behaved disgracefully. He sent patball questions to Lawson and delightedly agreed whenever Lawson said Mrs Thatcher knew perfectly well why he resigned and all she had to do was to sack Walters by Christmas to keep him.

Rupert rang, much concerned as to what was happening among the Tories.

He said he thought it was a great mistake for her to say that after the next election she would be handing over before the following election.

At about ten to ten I rang [Margaret].

When I asked her why she had said this about retiring after the next election, she said it was because, and there was a note of weariness in her voice, when she had said previously, years ago, about going on and on, she thought that had done a lot of damage. She wanted to make it clear she wasn't going to go on and on.

I said, 'I wonder why Tebbit said what he did.' She said, 'I know. I was disappointed about that.' He wrote in the *Evening Standard* about her style of government and that she had to alter it, etc. These people have no gratitude for what she has done for them.

I asked her if she knew about the plot to have a stalking horse candidate against her.

She said again, in rather a resigned voice, 'I wouldn't be surprised.' The poor girl has had such a bashing and has been so badly betrayed. I feel terrible.

Ken Baker [rang].

He is obviously anxious to know that I am supporting her and that I know he is not playing a double game. Certainly his *Sunday Express* article was thoroughly outspoken and a hundred per cent in support of her.

When I had finished talking to him, I rang Margaret again and told her about the conversation, saying, 'I think he is genuine.'

Again she said, 'Anyway you and I will go on fighting,' and I said, 'Yes. Certainly.'

Tuesday 7 November
Number 10 rang.

She said she was going to say, on the question of her giving up after the next election, that she had worked it out at about six years but if there was a popular demand for her to stay, she would stay on. I said, 'I think that is an excellent formula.' She is also going to say about Lawson, as she will be asked about him again, that she still finds it incomprehensible that a Chancellor who has been there for six years would resign on so trivial a matter as an adviser.

I said I was appalled by what the *Independent* had said, calling her a liar, but I think she is going to carry it off quite well.

Rang Rupert.

He said, 'Please tell Alan Walters to do nothing until he has had lunch with me next week at Wapping. I am going to give him a major consultancy. It is very important.'

Wednesday 8 November

I had to get up early to go to breakfast with Lord Weidenfeld on the Chelsea Embankment. He had the Israeli Minister of Justice there. There was a very large gathering, several tables. I sat at the same table with Michael Heseltine who looked at me sourly and didn't even smile.

The Minister of Justice said they won't talk to the PLO [Palestine Liberation Organization] because they don't deal with terrorists. But as their state was built on terrorism against the British, God knows why they take that view. Arafat keeps on saying they want to talk about setting up a Palestinian state quite independent of Israel and the Arab states themselves. He should be tested.

Dinner given by the Racecourse Holdings Trust as a farewell to the end of Tommy Wallis' twenty-five years.[5]

I have always liked him very much. A jolly fellow. Full of tips which sometimes work at great odds but more often don't.

I felt what jolly decent and nice friendly people the racing world are. Some of them may not be brilliant but they have very good hearts.

On my left sat Miles Gosling who said that there had been wonderful co-operation with the Tote in Cheltenham where he was Chairman. He is now going to be Chairman of RHT.

Thursday 9 November

Allan Davis rang to say that Tony Britton did not want to do the play. He found the love scenes 'distasteful' – he's over sixty. He is now in touch with Anton Rodgers, or Rodgers' agent, and Allan said he would be much better.

I hope we are not going to fail after all this trouble. We could go for [a star to play] the woman, but he never will. I think it is because he is queer and basically anti-women. He will not recognize that hers is the most significant part. He wants to build up the part of the man more and more.

Caroline [Banszky] has now been made a director of Rothschild's.

She is Finance Director which is pretty good for a girl of her age. She is very bright. Their combined income must be around £200,000 plus.

On to David Beaufort.

David was talking when we got there about the value of Francis Bacon pictures which are now selling at five and a half million dollars

---

5. Managing director, the Racecourse Holdings Trust (subsidiary of the Jockey Club owning and operating its racecourses), 1975–89.

each. He has quite a few which he bought ages ago. He has also got a number of Lucian Freud pictures which are now worth half a million each, if not more.

He has made millions since he has been at the Marlborough Art Gallery soon after the War. Jolly good luck to him. He's worked hard and learned his trade.

Alan Walters arrived.

He said he has got a great scheme which he explained. It is that you take the whole matter of inflation out of the hands of government by having reserve bills which are always exchanged at par and only for cash.

The system is automatic and doesn't require government intervention. It is all done by private enterprise arbitrage.

He said he would really like to say something publicly about the Lawson situation because the *Independent* had lied about it and the *Financial Times* had lied about it. She always told the truth.

He had refused to go on the Brian Walden programme. He said Lawson was not telling the truth either.

Alan Walters said he would like to get taxation down to fifteen per cent all round but cut out expense allowances. We also agreed that there should be no corporate taxation at all (because the recipients of the dividends pay taxes), as in Hong Kong.

Afterwards I drove Alan back to Berkeley Square. I said, 'Please don't make any decision about what you want to do about an economic consultancy in England until you have seen Rupert next Wednesday. He has got some suitable offer I think he wants to make to you.' He said he was afraid of getting involved in the political side of things and I said, 'I think he may have in mind a consultancy with all his interests world-wide.'

I also said that she is very anxious to be able to see him from time to time and he said he is going to see her. And I said that also she would like him to talk to Major so he said yes, he would like to do that, too.

I then popped down to the Lords. She seemed to be in complete control at Question Time [in the Commons].

She looked very neat in her tailored black and white check suit and very fresh, amazing after flying to America on Tuesday evening and back again, in ample time for Question Time on Thursday, after making a major speech about the environment to the United Nations.

Saturday 11 to Sunday 12 November
To stay with the Trees at Donhead St Mary.

A new word has come in, 'Oxfammed'. Anne Tree said that Archie Stirling had gone off with a daughter of Vanessa Redgrave and Diana Rigg (Mrs Stirling) retaliated.[6] She took all his clothes to the Oxfam shop so he had none left. I thought, 'Shall I now get on to Diana Rigg and ask her, as she has apparently abandoned or thrown out Archie, her rich husband, whether she will now do my play?'

(On Monday morning I rang Diana Rigg. She was very friendly but said she can't do it because she has got other work in tow.)

Ned Ryan,[7] who used to be associated with the name of Princess Margaret, told a story of how recently he went to a dinner given by Lord Weidenfeld which Joan Collins [actress and author] was to attend. He was rung up by George to say would he pick Joan Collins up because she didn't like to arrive by herself.

She said, 'I do like to have a walker,' which is an American term for a man who accompanies women on their shopping expeditions and other outings when they haven't got a husband or boyfriend present. He thought that was a bit rum. When he took her back again, the car stopped a few doors away from the house where she was staying because some cars were parked in front of it. So he got out of the car and started to take her to the front door. 'Oh no, don't bother. You're not staying for breakfast,' she said.

Monday 13 November
(Unfortunately the tape on which I made my first description of this lunch has disappeared. Therefore, unusually, this is being written on November 20th and not November 13th, which accounts for the somewhat scrappy nature of it.)

Early comes a message from Marshall of Goring[8] that he will not be coming to the Skadden Arps lunch [at the House of Lords]. He is in the throes of his resignation after the cancellation of nuclear power being [transferred to] the private sector.

John Wakeham, Secretary for Energy, couldn't stay for long but he stayed long enough to explain that the costs of nuclear power had not

6. Archibald Stirling and Diana Rigg, the actress, married in 1982, divorced 1993.

7. Irish property owner and antiques dealer.

8. Chairman, Central Electricity Generating Board (CEGB), 1982–9, World Association of Nuclear Operators, 1989–93.

really been revealed until they were pushing on to privatization and having to assess how much shareholders would have to pay out to finance it. He said that actually nuclear power, when run properly in Britain, should be making a profit and is now.

However, it was best to disentangle the whole shooting match from the shareholders and make the general taxpayer stay as the owner, carrying the enormous costs of decommissioning and also making a profit on its own account.

John Wakeham was in a very perky mood. He is short and jolly and sturdy. He looks like a very good rugby scrum half. He has a round youthful face with curly black hair. He was full of pleasant bounce and confidence.

When the question of a reunified East and West Germany being all-powerful came up, Sir Kit McMahon, Chairman of Midland Bank, thought that they would not be able to dislodge London as one of the great financial centres.

Alexander Hesketh was very lively. He and I are still extremely worried about the silly conspirators in the Tory Party trying to desta-bilize Margaret.

Tuesday 14 November
Took Joe Flom for a rapid, brief tour of the Lords and the Royal Gallery [before the second lunch WW arranged]. He is a charming little man. I like him exceedingly. He is tiny but his grey head is brimming with intelligence.

Sir Peter Walters (Chairman of BP) told me that he had followed a lot of my career because he was born in Aston.[9]

He, too, had watched on TV the 6–2 [Aston Villa] victory over Everton with enthusiasm and delight.

I asked Norman Lamont did we have more investment in America than they have here, to which he said yes, we have much more there than the Americans have in Britain. I said, 'So what the hell is all this fuss about over Ford taking over Jaguar?'

Hector Laing[10] had been making a long spiel about the awfulness of great British firms being owned by Americans. I said, 'Why, so long as the research and development goes on here, the goods are made

---

9. WW was MP for the Aston division of Birmingham, 1945–55.
10. Chairman, United Biscuits, 1972–90; a director, Bank of England, 1973–91; life peer 1991.

here by British people, what difference does it make? You go to the Westbury Hotel in New York you don't find Americans refusing to book in or eat there because it is owned by Trusthouse Forte.'

This reminded Norman Lamont of an occasion when, shortly after Hector Laing had been made a director of the Bank of England, he addressed a group of Tory MPs and said, 'The days of unfettered capitalism are over,' at which point Enoch Powell[11] got up and shouted, 'Stick to your biscuits,' and walked out of the room.

David Stevens told me he understood that the *Mail* was about to run (via Rothermere) Michael Heseltine as the alternative candidate or the leader who should take the place of Margaret. I said, 'They would be very foolish if they did.' But such is the state of nerves and self-generated dislike of the press to Mrs Thatcher that this could possibly be true. David Stevens also told me that Conrad Black was going to come out against Mrs Thatcher. I somewhat doubt this, though apparently there are some rumours to that effect in the *Telegraph* building itself. Of course the more people who fight against her, the more determined she will be to defeat them, which she will.

Afterwards Joe Flom said what an interesting lunch it was and what interesting people. The conversation was totally different from yesterday. I said, 'You have probably made some useful contacts because most of them have got interests in America.' He said he thought that could be helpful.

Dinner with 'Baby' Steinberg[12] (she must be around eighty, small, slight, heavily face-lifted and made up, but bright and quick like a bird) and her husband who has had a stroke but he still dodders around the place. The flat is an exact replica of the one below which belongs to Leonard Wolfson. The family own the whole block in Portland Place. Like Leonard below him, he has got lots of valuable pictures but nothing like the quality or the range of Leonard's.

On my right sat a Lady Weston.[13] Her husband is in the Foreign Office. She was married in 1967, I think, and had her honeymoon in the Mandarin Hotel in Hong Kong. They then went to Peking and the

---

11. (1912–98); Conservative and Ulster Unionist politician and classical scholar; dismissed from Edward Heath's shadow cabinet in 1968 for his 'rivers of blood' speech about what he saw as the consequences of immigration.

12. Aunt of Leonard Wolfson, sister of his father, Sir Isaac; m (1938) Jack Steinberg, chairman, Horrockses Fashions, Butte Knit, 1966–78.

13. Margaret Sally Ehlers m (1967) John Weston, diplomat, knight 1992.

Cultural Revolution began. Ten thousand young Revolutionary Guard people descended on the Embassy with petrol cans and burned it down.

Then they brought their axes out and hacked their way into the place where the men and their wives had taken refuge. She said they stripped the women and took off a lot of their clothes – and then she got embarrassed and said, 'The vital ones you know, the knickers, and sexually abused us. We were in a state of terror for months because we weren't allowed out. But the government (George Brown was Foreign Secretary then) told us it was wiser not to make any commotion about it because it would merely make matters worse. Chou-en-Lai was so ashamed of the behaviour burning down the British Embassy that he sent the army to fight with the Red Guards and drive them off, which they did after a pitched battle. We always feel we owed our lives to Chou-en-Lai. One day, when the thirty year rule is over, I will write exactly what happened, how the women were treated by these people and how we were terrorized and sexually insulted and abused.'

I said, '1997 wouldn't be a very good moment to do it just when the take-over of Hong Kong took place.'

Asa Briggs[14] was there and I told him I was trying to get an honour for A. L. Rowse. He said he thought he should have one: 'One of his merits is that he thought Shakespeare actually wrote Shakespeare.'

Wednesday 15 November
Spoke to Margaret.

I think she is feeling very forlorn of support.

We don't quite agree about the pace of events in Germany. I think the German reunification is going to happen inevitably and very fast, and I think she believes it can somehow be held up. But in general we are on the same line.

On the question of whether there would be a challenger against her for the leadership after the Queen's speech she said, 'There is nothing we can do about it. If there is one, there will be one.' I said, 'I think you will win it easily,' and she said, 'I think so. The support from the constituencies is extremely strong. They don't agree with the MPs who are rocking the boat.' I said, 'A lot of them are people who are retiring anyway and on their way out trying to put a spanner in the works.

14. Historian; Provost, Worcester College, Oxford, 1976–91; Chancellor, Open University, 1978–94; life peer 1976.

And there was an appalling bogus survey of MPs in the *Independent* yesterday.'

She broke in to say, 'The *Independent* is a misnomer – it is not independent at all. It is dedicated to trying to destroy me. If they want an alternative who is the alternative? They can't vote for Sir Geoffrey Howe. He's an old bumbler. And John Major isn't ready yet.' Obviously John Major is her real candidate as her successor when the time comes.

Saturday 18 November
In the evening we went to the Lehár concert at the Barbican. The last time we shall be going in the Britain Salutes Hungary month.

Verushka made the video tape work which showed Esmond Rothermere, the son of the then Lord Rothermere (he was Esmond Harmsworth at the time). There was quite a long passage with her great uncle Emile. He was leader among the group promoting the idea that Esmond should become King of Hungary because his father had used the *Daily Mail* to great effect, trying to right the wrongs to Hungary in the Treaty of Trianon, 1919.[15]

He was a remarkable looking man, her great uncle, Minister of Justice in the Horthy government. Wonderful moustache and a fine voice, though as he spoke in Hungarian I couldn't understand any of it.

Sunday 19 November
Rupert rang from Australia from an aeroplane.

I told him about David Stevens being distressed at persecution from *Today* over Elizabeth Ampthill whom they claim he is going to marry and whom he hasn't seen for eight months. She is the ex-wife of his co-director, Geoffrey Ampthill, on the United Newspapers, *Daily Express*, etc.

Rupert broke in and said, 'David Montgomery[16] is a bastard for doing that and I'll put a stop to it.'

I spoke to Margaret and asked her how the Paris meeting went last night.

She said Kohl began by speaking for forty minutes, assuring

---

15. The Rothermere (Harmsworth) family owned the *Daily Mail*; Esmond (1898–1978) was 2nd Viscount Rothermere, chairman of the *Daily Mail* and Associated Newspapers; his father, 1st Viscount Rothermere (1868–1940), Air Minister, 1917–18, wrote *My Campaign for Hungary* (1939).

16. At this time editor of *Today*.

everybody he was a good European and he was not going to press for reunification.

She said, 'We can't have these borders altered,' so I said to her, 'It is going to happen because people are going to decide for themselves,' to which she replied, 'There is a four power situation. They can prevent it. They have a status in it.' I said, 'I don't see how they can.' She said, 'We mustn't upset the Warsaw Pact and disturb Gorbachev.' I said, 'I agree with that but it is not as easy as you may think to hold back these tides of emotion once they start.'

I told her that Asa Briggs, the Provost of Worcester, would back an honour for A. L. Rowse so should he write in? She said, 'Yes, to me. But it won't be this time round. It has to go through the Maecenas Committee.'[17]

Tuesday 21 November
Repair to the Jockey Club for 10.30 meeting.

We made a few alterations to the final proposal that I had made last night. On the whole minor. Then we went back to Cavendish Avenue. There John Heaton and Brian McDonnell both said they were very worried because they thought the RCA, from the way J. J. Warr was talking, were anxious to move in and take the whole thing over.

I said, 'I think I can manage it,' and they said, 'You can, but we wouldn't be able to when you have gone.' I said, 'I have got to go some time so we will have to make it certain that I am there when they appoint my successor so that I can see he is in my mould.' They thought that was a fairly good safeguard. I was touched by their dependence on me as though I were their father.

I rang Lord Goodman and said that we wanted him to draw up the Trust Deed and that we had agreed with the Jockey Club that we would pay for that.

Willie Whitelaw told me that he was making a speech tomorrow (Wednesday) at the Parliamentary Press Gallery Luncheon at which he was going to break his silence. He was going to tell the Tories that they were on course to win the next election under Margaret Thatcher's leadership which is essential. The only thing that could stop it would be if they all played the fool and tried to destabilize her.

---

17. Maecenas, Roman statesman, was a famed patron of the arts and the poets Vergil and Horace; hence the Downing Street committee responsible for honours is sometimes called the Maecenas Committee.

I saw some snippets of the first televising of the Commons.

I can't imagine this televising of Parliament being a tremendous draw.

Wednesday 22 November
Highland Park Whisky and the *Spectator* Parliamentarian of the Year awards at the Savoy Hotel. I found myself at a fairly jolly table, next to John Biffen.

He thought the Tory Party were making fools of themselves. When I asked him did he think they would put up a candidate against her, he said he thought that was possible but it was a foolish thing to do because this is not the right moment. If you really want to wound her or attack her properly, it should wait another year – after the awful year next year (1990) is going to be. But now she could easily deflect it. He didn't seem to have any great animosity towards her.

One of the winners of the award was John Prescott[18] who is a tough, brutal spokesman on transport. He was very much a thorn in Kinnock's side who demoted him by sending him to Transport. When he accepted the award, he said that everybody knows that these things are really a matter of team effort and you can't do it by yourself. You have to have help. He went on, 'I was very much helped by Paul Channon.' Everybody laughed. Paul Channon was inept as Minister of Transport. Prescott said he had been described by the judges as not a rapier like Cook last year who won the award for Debater of the Year. He said, 'I am the kick them in the balls type.'

There was a new award called 'Wit of the Year'. It was won by Neil Hamilton[19] who used to come to talk to me and enlist my support when he was bringing a libel action against the BBC. He and another Tory were pilloried as pro Nazi, pro fascist, in a *Panorama* programme, quite unjustifiably.

He said when he was rung up to be told he had got an award he thought it was for 'Twit of the Year' not 'Wit of the Year' as it was officially described. He said if he had been 'Twit of the Year' it would have been far more difficult to win because there would have been far

---

18. Labour politician; Deputy Prime Minister and Secretary of State for the Environment, Transport and the Regions since 1997.

19. Conservative MP who lost his Tatton seat to Martin Bell in the 1997 general election; the BBC libel case which Hamilton won preceded the allegations of 'sleaze' which were a central issue in the 1997 election campaign.

more to choose from but perhaps that award could be won during the next week or so. He meant whoever it was who stood against Margaret Thatcher in the leadership election in the Tory Party. He said, 'As Dr Spooner would say, there are many shining wits in the Commons.' (Whining shits.)

John Smith won the Parliamentarian of the Year Award and said that he owed it to Alan Walters. He couldn't have done it without him. He meant that he teased Lawson on the Tuesday so much about Alan Walters that he resigned on the Thursday. That was absolutely true.

Back in the Lords Tony Royle (Lord Fanshawe) told me he had had lunch in the House of Commons members' dining-room with a few MPs. Sir Anthony Meyer[20] is definitely going to put up against Margaret but he has to get a first and second proposer first. Tory MPs are badly rattled.

On the way back from the Lords I gave Roy a lift. I said would he support A. L. Rowse for a knighthood and he said yes. I said, 'That will count a lot as [you are] Chancellor of Oxford.' He said, 'I wouldn't support him for the OM or anything like that as he has been very awkward and prickly and he is not a very sound scholar in some ways.'

A dinner given by Henry Wrong, a farewell to his administration at the Barbican.

Among the guests was Vere Rothermere.[21]

During dinner he said, 'Why should I support her? She has treated me very badly.' I said, 'How?' He said, 'In 1979 she took away my television licence because I was a newspaper proprietor. So I was no longer allowed to have shares in a television station. Then she refused to let me set up my company headquarters in Holland where I could have saved a great deal of money. But she has been supporting people like Robert Maxwell who is allowed to have his business headquarters and all his money in Liechtenstein avoiding tax. She supports Rupert, but she doesn't support me at all.'

I said, 'But she opened your new *Daily Mail* building.' He said, 'Yes that was all right but I didn't talk to her then and I don't get a chance to talk to her. I get invited to Downing Street when everybody else is but I don't get a real talk with her.' I said, 'Vere, are you in need of

---

20. Conservative MP, 1964–6 and 1970–92; 3rd baronet.
21. (1925–98); 3rd Viscount Rothermere; chairman, Associated Newspapers (*Daily Mail*, *Mail on Sunday* etc.), from 1970.

love and affection?' and he said, 'Yes,' and he would like to have an intimate talk with her. I said, 'I will see if I can arrange that.'

I said, 'Meanwhile you are not to veer, to make a pun, away from her.'

His gift in being a newspaper proprietor is he finds some good people and then doesn't interfere with them.

He was telling me also about his enormous publishing interests in America and the fantastic new system they have developed for providing free schools' television for schools throughout America. The only thing they get back is the permission to sell advertising time with suitable advertisements.

Like all these newspaper proprietors, Black, etc., he thinks he wields total power and could bring her down if he wanted to, and he claims that he put her into power in the first place. So many people claim that, they could fill a telephone book.

Thursday 23 November

Rang Margaret at about ten to eight. She was having her hair done. She rang back at about twenty-five past eight. She said she was off to America to see President Bush at lunch time.

I told her about Vere Rothermere and said we ought to do something about it.

She said it was a good idea but did I think we should do it now. I said, 'No, we can wait for the moment. I think it is all right for the moment.'

Then I asked her about putting right her statement that she might retire after the next election. I said, 'They were at it again on the *Today* programme this morning, saying you were a lame duck even if you did beat off the leadership challenge now.' She said, 'I have put it right in an interview I gave to the *Times* yesterday evening. It was a long one. I expect it will be in tomorrow. I used the formula we had discussed before.'

I got so worried for her that I almost thought of cancelling the trip to Hong Kong.

On the *World at One* [Radio 4] Geoffrey Howe made a very good supporting statement for her saying it would be madness to get rid of her because she has done wonderful things, it is a great team and he agreed with her about Europe, although they tried to pretend he didn't. He said he had felt upset at the time of his ceasing to be Foreign

Secretary and lots of people in other countries had too, but he had an important job to do and that particular matter was now all over.

I thought of what Biffen said, that there was no need to have a leadership election now. They could have a look at it again in a year's time and there would still be nearly two years left. I thought to myself, 'Humph, I hope John Biffen is not going to start that sort of thing.'

I went round to the Commons and saw Lennox-Boyd, Margaret's PPS. We discussed the state of the wicket which he thought was pretty bumpy.

I told him that I thought Howe did very well on the *World at One*. He said, 'The truth of the matter is that he adores her. You know what they disagreed about, as you are in close contact with her, but he really does adore her and she ought to pat him on the back and give him some affection from time to time.' (It is amazing how many people want affection from her, including Vere Rothermere.)

Friday 24 November
Set out for Hong Kong on a British Airways aeroplane. There is a new gadget which is a personal video for each first class passenger; mine doesn't work but Verushka's does.

During WW's ten-day visit to Hong Kong he gathered ammunition for his campaign to win more passports for the citizens of Hong Kong in the event of China failing to keep her promises after the 1997 takeover. He also informed himself, by talks with numerous officials and contacts, about the general economic and social situation.

Finally, on Sunday 3 December, WW went to the racecourses at Shah Tin and Macao. His seven-page memorandum to the Tote concentrated on their use of computer terminals for on- and off-course betting centres.

On his last day, with the help of 'an excellent shorthand typist', he completed his Times *article for publication on Tuesday 5 December. He praised Sir David Wilson as 'unusually able, with a shrewd appreciation of how to put the Hong Kong people's views successfully without unnecessarily ruffling Peking sensibilities'. He warned of the danger of corruption ('virulent in all Communist countries') engulfing Hong Kong and considered it naïve to suppose that freedom would remain intact. He believed at the very least the government should offer passports to 200,000 families (around 750,000 people). The only serious obstacle to repression after 1997 was 'the knowledge in Peking that the human capital essential to Hong Kong's success will leave if life becomes intolerable'. He had ended his* News of the World *article of 3 December: 'My advice to Hong Kongers without passports is to leave before July 1997.'*

Tuesday 5 December

The *Times* atrociously cut and mangled my article from Hong Kong.

Their cuts were such that they actually got things wrong in the facts which is infuriating because it makes it look to people who really understand about Hong Kong as though I didn't know what I was talking about. However, the thrust of the article remained.

Went down to the Lords.

There was much agog about the election contest for the leadership. Geoffrey Ampthill thought that about sixty or seventy would abstain or vote against Mrs Thatcher but I said I thought it could be higher. Chips Keswick rang and he is making a book. I bought at fifty-five, meaning that the total number of abstentions and votes against would be higher than fifty-five. In the event it turned out to be sixty, so I suppose I won £12 at £2 a point. I was delighted not to win more.[1]

About nine I rang Margaret. I thought she would be too busy to talk to me. She had been to the Palace for the usual Thursday talk to the Queen. I don't know why this farce goes on. It wastes her time and the Queen has nothing to do with politics anyway.

I told her I was delighted with the result.

Three people didn't turn up to vote at all, including Michael Heseltine. As it was a secret ballot, the two required sponsors of Meyer refused to announce who they were.

What a wretched crew those Tories are! They have got wet rot and always have had.

I told her I had been talking to Rupert and she said how marvellous the *Times* leading article had been in Tuesday morning's paper.

After I had spoken to Margaret I rang Rupert. He said, 'Of course I don't really have any control over the *Times*.'

But then he went on, 'Of course there were several telephone calls

---

1. There were 314 votes for Mrs Thatcher, 33 for Sir Anthony Meyer and 27 abstentions.

during yesterday in which I suggested what they should write in the leading article and it came out very well.'

Thursday 7 December
Rang Margaret but first she was having her hair done. She is going off to the Strasbourg Summit this evening.

She said her technique in answering Kinnock, who goes over the top, is to do it very calmly. She is thinking, of course, of the television and she is quite right.

We then moved on to the question of passports and she said she had a great deal of difficulty with her backbenchers on the question of passports for Hong Kong. Some of them say they have got Indians in their constituencies who have been waiting ten years to have their families rejoin them. I said, 'Yes that is all very well but India wanted to be independent. They are not persecuted there. We are handing Hong Kong over because we have to.'

On the whole she is sympathetic. She told me to get in touch with David Waddington, the Home Secretary, and talk to him about it and I must do that.

Twenty-third wedding anniversary. Went to Claridge's for a little lunch.

The lunch wasn't bad. We both had lobster of different kinds. It was relatively cheap, £61, and a glass of champagne.

In the evening Ernest Saunders. He is the wretched man who has now been waiting three years under arrest on various charges. The trial begins in February and is expected to last a year. He wants me to say in the *News of the World* how can this be a fair trial? All the mud has been slung. In secret proceedings the Judge decided there will be two trials so he will be tried twice. He said that the two trials were divided between the Jews – people like Ronson and Lyons and himself who is an Austrian Jew – and the gentiles in the other trial with him again.

I said I would look into it.

The man has been ruined whether he is guilty or not. I think his offences would not have been offences a few years ago.

Ernest Saunders is not an attractive man but it is difficult not to feel sorry for him.

Saturday 9 December
I had a nice message on a Christmas card from Arnold Goodman: 'With appreciation for an interesting man in a world largely composed of bores.'

Sunday 10 December
It augurs badly for my poor Hong Kongers. Just talked to Douglas Hurd.

Waddington has now reduced the number of people he is going to allow passports to, which has to be very secret, from when Douglas was Home Secretary just recently. I told him I was seeing Waddington on Tuesday of next week and would that be too late. He said, 'No. Keep up the good work. Write away about it. Nothing will be decided yet.'

He said about Margaret at the Strasbourg Summit, 'She was not combative. She was very sensible. She was very firm and it was not at all a bad conference. It was quite different from what the press and media make out.'

At around five I spoke to Margaret.

She said it was quite wrong to say that she was isolated. She didn't agree with the social charter but then none of the others do really when they see the directives and know what it is all about.

She remains stubborn about the pace of the German reunification. She still thinks it can be held up but I doubt it.

Monday 11 December
Dinner at the French Embassy. A medium sized one, three tables with about ten people on each.

There was some excellent Léoville-Poyferré 1981.

Nigel Lawson and his wife Thérèse. I was nervous of them because of the rude things I had written about Nigel over his resignation, which he must have read. To my amazement he was extremely friendly and so was she.

When I was alone with him I said, 'How would you like to be the editor of the *Times*?' I said, 'Charlie Wilson is very good technically,' and he interrupted me and said, 'Yes but he lacks authority.' I said, 'Exactly.' He said, 'I don't want to go back to journalism. After all that is what I used to do before, with the *Spectator* and the financial journals.' I said, 'Yes but this is rather a different kind of thing. It is a newspaper with an incomparable influence, if it is run properly. It would give you a wholly different position from an ordinary journalist.' He began to think about it and said, 'Well it could be attractive.' I said, 'You shouldn't do it unless you were offered about £250,000 a year so you could make some real money.' Then I said, 'Of course I am not authorized to make any offer to you,' and he said he understood that. But I shall speak to Rupert about it.

I think he is curiously loyal to Margaret and would not rubbish her and would support her re-election. But I think at the same time he might put some fire into the paper and make it more interesting.

Peter Carrington was there. Very disturbing. He said Margaret had been there for too long, ten years was too long and she was becoming quite impossible and out of touch. He was amazed at the venom and dislike for her he meets everywhere.

He said that she wouldn't win the next election and she ought to go. I was upset. He has always been a doubtful customer, from the beginning, but he did come round to her and at one time supported her very loyally.

I said I thought Geoffrey Howe had now come round and was being very loyal to her and admired her deeply. He said, 'That is absolutely untrue. What he is saying to me every time I see him, recently as well, is that he hates her and that she has been horrible and he wishes she would go.' I said, 'A lot of that no doubt is Elspeth [Howe's wife],' and he said, 'Yes, but it is not just Elspeth.'

I said, 'I think it will all turn on the mortgage interest rate and the hash that Nigel made of inflation. If they can get that right, she will be OK.' He said he didn't think that would be enough as the Labour Party were looking quite a credible party now.

There was trouble about my mother-in-law, poor soul.[2]

The doctor had said she may have cracked her pelvis but it will get better. I said, 'Well that is fine,' but I really don't know what should be done. I have had her for twenty-four years now, including a year before we were actually married. I like her but she is an intolerable burden. I have longed always to make that top room into an additional library or work place where I could work without being got at and have more books and put my books around properly.

---

2. Ilona, Verushka's mother, usually referred to as 'Nadje' (the Hungarian for 'grandmother') by WW, lived with the Wyatts.

Tuesday 12 December
The Archers' party in their flat overlooking the river. There was the usual shepherd's pie and Krug champagne but I also had a piece of mince tart which was good. Mary Archer was looking very pretty in a green dress. She is much smarter than she ever used to be. She was despairing of her book – the serious one – but was still keen on writing about Rupert Brooke.[3] She is on various committees which keep her occupied, such as the one at Lloyd's, and also on the board of Anglia Television.

I am rather fond of her. She has no hair at all on her face, at least that is visible. She says she does less work than Jeffrey now that she is not a don. He works madly all the time.

She is really quite beautiful in a classical way. She has small soft hands and clear eyes and an oval face. Behind it she can be tough. Her skin is clear and pale.

Lee Menzies was there. He said they are very keen to do the play at Leatherhead.

I spoke to John Major and told him I thought he was doing very well on the television and in his speeches in the Commons.

I said, 'You will get into a greater flow of oration later. You are learning.' He said, 'Yes. I don't dare risk it at the moment because what I am saying is so important it could be misunderstood and cause trouble.'

Wednesday 13 December
The Downing Street lunch in honour of Nemeth, the present Prime Minister of Hungary, was as per usual. 1979 Château Léoville-Las-Cases. An excellent wine but badly wasted glasses, half full and hardly touched, at considerable cost to the taxpayer.

When we got there Willie Whitelaw was in the entrance. He had obviously been to see Mrs Thatcher and he was looking for Cecilia. I was very glad about that because I had told her she must see him from time to time.

She takes much more notice of the things I say to her than I sometimes realize. I find out by accident.

Downing Street looked very festive. A great Christmas tree and Margaret was in smiling mood. She made a nice speech about Hungary

---

3. *Rupert Brooke and the Old Vicarage, Grantchester* was published in 1989; The Old Vicarage at Grantchester near Cambridge was now the Archers' house.

off the cuff. Mr Nemeth, the Prime Minister, made a longish speech which wasn't too bad. I fear that Mr Pozsgay is not going to become President. That is what the Foreign Secretary of Hungary told me before lunch.

That's what happens when you let democracy out of the bag. It doesn't always go the way you would like.

Chips Keswick came to dinner. He brought me twelve bottles of Louis Roederer 1979 champagne. It was a very good year. He is extremely generous. I gave him a 1949 Ayala. It was marvellous, like nectar he said. We also had a bottle of Rauzan-Gassies 1920.

Chips was very downbeat about my prospects with the Tote. He kept saying, 'You must try and get your salary up and get a better pension.' So I said, 'I only get two-thirds of what I am getting now, which is £76,000, and then Verushka gets two-thirds of that when I die.' He said, 'It is not enough. You should get at least £100,000. You can't expect to go on after May 1991 because you will be too old.'[4] I said, 'I don't feel too old and MacGregor was head of British Coal at that age.' He said, 'Yes but that's the way it goes. I have got to retire when I am sixty from Hambros.' He is only fifty-one.

I felt very sad and depressed.

We were talking about the Jockey Club at one moment. He said it seemed to be trying to get into a more modern outlook. I said, 'Yes, I think Stoker Hartington will do very well. I like him.' Then I suddenly realized the gaffe I had made. Chips said he used to like him but he didn't now and didn't see him any more.

Chips said Henry Keswick would like to be in the Lords and would be very good at it. I said, 'I am greatly impressed by him. Since I have got to know him better during the last year I think he has got a lot of sense and great talent.'

I am not sure that Margaret will put him in the Lords but somebody else may one day. Henry is a year and a half or so older than Chips.

My mother-in-law fell out of bed again last night. It is getting very serious. I went up there at ten to seven to put her legs back into bed and found her with the light on. She doesn't know what she is doing.

I am sunk in depression now. When I went to bed I couldn't sleep because I kept thinking how little I had done. I have got nowhere in politics. I am just a journalist who sometimes writes goodish stuff but

---

4. WW remained chairman of the Tote until 1997, the year of his death, when he was seventy-nine.

sometimes not. The people I live among think it is terrible that I should write for the *News of the World*. They are stupid.

I don't really think I have got a talent for writing plays. At least it is not proven yet. I looked at the one I had started, the new one, and I felt that it is not much good really. I am not sure they are not right when they say my method is old fashioned. Allan keeps wanting me to go and see new plays but I don't think there is much point in it.

I haven't got the capacity to write another book, or the time. Everything seems a fearful strain. My livelihood is highly precarious and I so often feel tired because I haven't had enough sleep. I went to bed for about twenty minutes yesterday afternoon after lunch and felt curiously that it quite refreshed me but I was not in any balanced state.

Someone asked me how many copies my autobiography sold and I said, 'I can't remember.' He said, 'I am sure you must know,' so I said, 'Oh about ten thousand. It was a mistake perhaps to have had four chunks of serialization in the *Sunday Times* because everybody thought they had read it.' But the truth of the matter was that it wasn't good enough.

Thursday 14 December
The Other Club.

I sat next to Marmaduke Hussey who wanted to sit next to me particularly.

He said that the Tory government complains much less to the BBC than Wilson and Callaghan who were always trying to twist their arms.

Fitzroy MacLean[5] was on my other side. He agreed with me that it is quite ridiculous for them to talk about four power agreement before Germany can be reunified, the Helsinki Agreement and that kind of thing, because they will just do it and faster than we think.

Opposite us was Leon Brittan.

He believes very much that we have got to go into the ERM and he thinks it will happen even by July next year.

Fitzroy, who is a pretty keen observer of the Russian scene, having been there in 1938 in the Embassy, speaking perfect Russian and going back there a lot, thinks Gorbachev will survive but it is very difficult for him.

Roy [Jenkins] said that when he was in Brussels and kept his diary,

---

5. Conservative MP, 1941–74; commanded British mission to Yugoslav Partisans, 1943–5; writer and journalist; 1st baronet, created 1957.

which he did during that period when he was President of the Commission, he used to write it up a week later and sometimes a fortnight later.

Friday 15 December
Dreadful news in the papers. Tory 1922 Committee in full cry against passports for Hong Kong; even the number of about fifty thousand families they think is far too many.

Margaret said she didn't expect an announcement [about them] to be made this side of Christmas.

She doesn't seem to mind how often I ring her. It is amazing. She actually wants me to do battle the best I can to get more of these passports.

I am not so despondent. It is all a matter of the state of my body which affects my head. Also the house is quiet at the moment. That changed when Nadje went to hospital. It is cruel to say so but I wish she could stay there. Her saturnine nature broods at the top of the house sending out bad vibes as far as I am concerned. But I am fond of her. A poor old lady of nearly ninety, the commotion she makes, the disturbance and the shouts when she and her daughter argue, are all very disturbing. The older I get the more I need quiet around me to concentrate.

Saturday 16 December
Spoke to Douglas Hurd. He said the figure of [Hong Kong] passports is not going to be very high. I said, 'A hundred and fifty thousand?' and he said, 'I won't give you the exact number but a bit higher than that.' I said, 'Is it too late for me to see Waddington?' because he had just said to me that the announcement was going to be made on Wednesday. He said, 'No, anything you can do to stiffen him up the better. Won't you be talking to the Prime Minister before then?' I said, 'Yes. I shall probably be talking to her tonight.' He said, 'Well do what you can with her. She has been wobbling about a bit on it.'

Spoke to Norman Lamont. He is very lukewarm about the Hong Kong people, not at all interested. He said nothing had been discussed at Cabinet meetings. It had been done by a Cabinet committee. Very little is discussed at Cabinet these days. He doesn't believe in Cabinet government anyway. It is impossible.

He is also extremely gloomy about inflation. He thinks it is going to be very difficult to get it down below five per cent by 1992, if at all.

I said, 'Do you think we won't get it right by the next election?' He said he thought it was highly unlikely and he thought the Tories would lose the next election. Good gracious.

Spoke to Margaret.

I said, 'It is too late for me now, I imagine, to see Waddington. It is going to be announced on Wednesday and I am not seeing him till Wednesday.' 'No,' she said, 'I should ring him and say you have seen it in the papers that it is going to be announced on Wednesday and can he see you before.' She wants me to put pressure on him still to get the package higher, if I can, but it is very difficult. He is in a blue funk about the backbenchers and in any case he is not the sort of person who would favour passports for Hong Kong.

Tuesday 19 December
At the Levy Board Ian Trethowan[6] was looking a bit groggy. He is still going along on his crutches. When we went in to lunch, I asked him whether he was in pain and was he making a good recovery. He said he was in a bit of pain but it is not too bad.

As we got near to his office his secretary said, 'Would you speak to Sir Ian?' I went in and he said, 'You are very kind. I have told one or two friends but don't broadcast it. I have actually got motor neurosis.' It appears this is a complaint which is wasting him away and he can't co-ordinate properly – like the young man who sits in an armchair doing better work than Einstein, that's the one at Cambridge [Stephen Hawking]. I said, 'Surely there is some cure?' and he said, 'No, there is no cure whatever. You just go on getting worse.' I felt very sad for him.

At the lunch I sat next to Richard Fries who is from the Home Office dealing with racing affairs. I asked him when we were going to get some kind of movement and he said, 'The Treasury is interested about the exclusive licence and any money there might be in it for them and so is the Department of Trade and Industry.' I asked him whether there was still any steam behind the betting shop sale idea and he said he didn't think so. He personally is against it. I asked him how my proposal was being received which at least admits some item

---

6. (1922–90); Director General, BBC, 1977–82; chairman, Horserace Betting Levy Board, from 1982; knight 1980.*

partly from the Lloyds Merchant Bank proposal, namely the Race-course Association's greater participation. He said it was being taken very seriously. I said of course this was a matter not very high on their agenda but it is important for us.

I then went to the Lords and asked my question about passports for Hong Kong. It was pretty well received but of course they wouldn't give me an answer because there is a statement coming shortly, that is tomorrow.

Saw Waddington.

He was only going to see me for fifteen minutes. Instead we talked for half an hour. He was quite receptive. I spouted away with all my points and he said, 'What am I to say to the Labour Party?' I said, 'Keep telling them that these are not fat cats. They are middling people who have made a lot of sacrifices and will do to get their families educated abroad and get residential qualifications. The rich ones are all right. They can manage anyway but it is the middling ones who are so vital to the economy.' He said, 'But they will say what about the poor people?' and I said, 'They will be no trouble. The handover will make no difference to them.'

I think we are going to get a few more passports now. It will be two hundred and twenty-five thousand, which is not a lot but it is better than the hundred and fifty thousand they were talking about.

Dinner party at Cavendish Avenue. People kept getting smitten by 'flu. We had to substitute Rosemary Lamont and Lady Hesketh. Instead came at the last moment Diane Lever and Clarissa Avon[7] at very short notice. Clarissa was highly amused and said, 'I see someone unexpectedly got 'flu.' I said, 'I hope you didn't mind being asked at the last moment.' She said, 'I never do. Not at all if I have got nothing else to do. I enjoy it.'

The wine was superb. 1958 Léoville-Poyferré. Michael Broadbent says that is a very fine year for Léoville-Poyferré but it should now be drunk up. He wrote that in 1980 and it was still jolly good in 1989. The fillet of beef was dreadfully over cooked. It had gone black, despite my telling Teresa [the cook] not to do that and to leave at least some of it fairly red which is how most people like it.

Alexander Hesketh ate and drank mightily, asking for a second helping of the crab mousse which was the first course, and finishing

---

7. Widow of 1st Earl of Avon (Sir Anthony Eden, Prime Minister, 1955–7) and niece of Sir Winston Churchill.*

off all the bottles that remained of the claret after dinner. He also had a large glass of old brandy and one of Tokay 1963. It was a muscatel dark Tokay. Norman Lamont was very cagey in front of the others about the prospects of inflation.

George Weidenfeld asked Petronella to write a biography of Charles Dilke, the man who had two in a bed in Victorian times and was driven out of Parliament.[8] He always asks everybody to write a book.

Norman Lamont stayed after I had gone to bed, talking about romance to Petronella and Verushka. He said that I had said that frenzied passion died out after seven years and he is always looking for romance which lasts.

What an extraordinary man he is, always restless in his pants.

Wednesday 20 December
Petronella told me that Andrew Knight is going to be the new Chairman of News International.

I had a terrible hassle with the bloody *Times* newspaper. This young man Jim McCue[9] who was at Eastbourne [WW's school] and whose interest I promoted at the *Times*, he rewrites my articles; he doesn't understand them and then he says it is 'house style'.

Thursday 21 December
Had very little sleep last night. Was woken up by the central heating being so high. I was rattled about my ridiculous row with the *Times*.

I begin to think I am coming to an end at the *Times* and maybe my writing isn't as good as it used to be.

I was also a bit hurt that Rupert didn't ring me. He was here. He told me nothing about the Andrew Knight situation. I had thought he might have consulted me over whether I thought it was a good idea.

Allan rang from Spain where he had gone for his holiday.

He has now heard from Gerald Harper who definitely wants to do the play.

We are to meet on January 4th at Cavendish Avenue. Allan wants the butler to be very much in evidence, calling me 'My Lord'. This makes me laugh.

---

8. (1843–1911); he withdrew from public life after being cited in divorce proceedings in 1885–6, returned to the Commons in 1892 but never regained a position of influence.
9. Deputy editor, obituaries, in 1999.

I have received pictures of the actor. He is very good-looking. He is quite well known though I don't know much about him.

Genevra and Antonella and their parents[10] come to dinner. It is the official Christmas dinner for their family because we are leaving tomorrow night for Cornwall. They are rather sweet children. They were delighted with my performing seals and other things I gave them. They were much bolder than last year about the party poppers which explode and crackers which made a bang and had indoor fireworks in them.

I gave Nicholas a 1945 Chambertin. The cork came out easier than the 1920 Rauzan-Gassies which I gave to Chips Keswick. The Chambertin was superb. Nicholas, who loves Burgundy and knows a great deal about it, says he has never had a better one.

Saturday 23 December
Arrived in Redruth to find it pouring with rain.

The news keeps going up and down about Romania. Yesterday morning it seemed the whole battle had been won completely against the vile Ceauşescu. By the evening it seemed that the secret police and the military force were gaining the upper hand. Thousands were being killed. It is very tragic. I can think of nothing else but this at the moment. It was in a Hungarian town where the revolt began. The Hungarians have always been the bravest of the lot in Eastern Europe.

Monday 25 December
Christmas Day and Petronella, Robbie and myself go to Cury Church. I look at the Wyatt window in which my father and others of his family are commemorated and our whacking great crest and motto.

We looked at the area on Goonhilly Downs where the windmills might be put. There is plenty of wind there. It is next to Telstar, built on our land confiscated by the government for the purpose at a rock bottom price. There could be something in this project.

On Boxing Day John St Levan and his wife came for a kind of supper. They had had a most extraordinary Christmas. They were unable to get off St Michael's Mount.

The clergyman couldn't get over for the Christmas Day service in the chapel. When they came on Tuesday evening they had to leave at ten to make sure they would be able to cross again back to the Mount.

---

10. Nicholas Banszky, Verushka's son by a previous marriage, and his wife Caroline.*

I like being with my roots again. It is a long time since I spent a Christmas in Cornwall, maybe not since I was eighteen or younger.

Friday 29 December
Gingo (Count Sanminiatelli) arrives to stay a few days. Anna Lu has gone to Morocco with some friends to go into the desert.

Sunday 31 December
Spoke to Mrs Thatcher. She was worried about the Tory revolt on Hong Kong. I said, 'I am sure you will get a majority. Most of your Tories will subside. Labour won't be united. A number of them will actually vote for the government and a few will abstain.'

In the evening, a very cold one, we went to Andrew Knight's and Sabiha's. I took lots of fireworks, outdoor and indoor, crackers and sparklers and things which went pop and showered presents round the table. That was for the two girls, Amaryllis and Afsaneh. They are aged about twelve to fourteen.

I asked Andrew Knight about his new job with News International and he asked me if I had spoken to Rupert. I said, 'Not for about three weeks.' He said he thought perhaps I would know what it was. I said, 'He hasn't discussed it with me at all.' He said it was to be Chairman of News International in England. He would oversee all the papers editorially and administratively. I thought to myself that it was not going to be very popular with Kelvin MacKenzie,[11] Charlie Wilson and Andrew Neil. He is quite able, Andrew, but not as able, I think, as he is cracked up to be. He doesn't start until March. Rupert is trying to avoid so much jet travelling backwards and forwards which I have continually recommended him to stop because it is wearing him out.

In the night I felt quite ill. My throat was extremely sore and rough. I took about six double indigestion tablets but they didn't seem to do much good. In the morning, after I had woken up once or twice in the night and gone to pee, I felt dreadful.

---

11. Editor of the *Sun* at this time.

1990

Wednesday 3 January

Board meeting at Tote. David Montagu wanted to see me privately before the meeting began. His father, Lord Swaythling, is ninety-one and may now die any minute. He is very ill. He wants to keep his name, David Montagu, because Rothmans is an international company and the business is done internationally.

What should he do?

I said, 'You have no problem at all. You just use your name as you wish, as I do Woodrow Wyatt for my articles and for any business purposes.'

There was a bit of a commotion yesterday. I had woken up in the night trembling and shivering and had to add more blankets and a dressing-gown. When I got out of bed, I practically fell over. I took my temperature and it was over 100.

I felt a bit strange all day but better in the evening. I had lost my temper once or twice and shouted down the house which Gingo overheard. According to Verushka, he said how sorry he was for her having such a difficult husband. I don't actually believe he said that and if he did, he said it to butter her up. Anyway he seems quite contented. He goes tomorrow morning early. Meanwhile, I am having trouble finding clothes, many of which are in the bedroom he is using.

Rupert rings up from Los Angeles: 'Did you see that I have gone into retirement?'

'If it means that you are not going to be jetting backwards and forwards from America so much, it is a very good thing,' I replied.

'It does mean that. Andrew Knight will be in charge,' he said. 'He will be in charge of all the newspapers, even the editors insofar as they are not restrained by the agreements over the editorial policy of the *Times* and the *Sunday Times*.' I said, 'What about Sky Television?' He said he couldn't take that over yet because he would have quite enough to do with the newspapers.

Rupert has actually lost a lot of money in England compared with the year before. His profits are down to £20 million, not even allowing for the amounts that they have put into Sky Television so far.

He said he had been talking to Andrew Knight for over a year secretly. He had to wait for his options promised him by Black in his *Telegraph* company to mature and that was why he hung on, though he was getting pretty fed up with Black. I said, 'Black is a megalomaniac who thinks he can make and destroy a Conservative government.' Rupert said, 'He is not as good as he thinks he is.'

He asked me what I thought about Andrew Knight and I said, 'The first thing that impressed me was [the way] he saved the RAC under difficult circumstances. Some extraordinary property deal was going to be made. They are all still grateful to him in that place, not only for organizing a committee to throw out the existing committee, but for making the place pay, which it does very well now. He is able in that kind of a way.'

Rupert said, 'I am not sure I know him.' I said, 'Maybe I don't either, though I have known him a good many years. He stayed with us in Italy once.'[1]

'Maybe there is nothing more to know. He seems a little enigmatic. He is very cool.' I said, 'I don't think he gets rattled easily.'

I mentioned Nigel Lawson's conversation with me. He said, 'I don't think it is a very good idea now (that is, his being editor of the *Times*), as we are going to have Alan Walters as our economics correspondent.'

Thursday 4 January
Bad news. I ring Allan Davis. He had been eight hours at the Gibraltar airport and only got in at half past three in the morning. The first letter he opened was from Gerald Harper. It said that after careful thought he had decided not to play the character of the leading part after all because it was flawed and he had been given an opportunity to play the lead in *The Dresser* – that is a play in which the leading actor [the dresser] is on the stage all the time and dominates it[2] – and was going to Australia on a tour.

I think Allan is too old now. He hasn't got the drive. If he hadn't gone away on this holiday, we might have seen Gerald Harper earlier and struck while the iron was hot. I have left a message on Gerald

---

1. In August 1986; see Vol. 1, p. 187.
2. The play by Ronald Harwood is set in the dressing-room of an actor playing Lear (based on Donald Wolfit).

Harper's answering machine saying I would still like him to come and have a drink, as I would like to ask his advice about the play.

Friday 5 January
Norman Lamont came to lunch.

I said, 'It is all the same in the end. You know that all this passion, marital or anything else, doesn't last for more than six years at the outside. Somerset Maugham wrote a play in which he says it only lasts for five years.'[3]

Sunday 7 January
Sunday night, dinner at the Michelin garage restaurant [Bibendum] near South Kensington tube station. It was a very good dinner given by the Stelzers. I drank too much.

Irwin Stelzer and Cita don't like Andrew Knight, the Chairman Rupert has chosen for his non-Sky affairs in England. They don't think he will get on well with Andrew Neil and the other editors because he is too supercilious, or he seems to be; he also has no sense of humour and he takes himself immensely seriously; he has little lightness of touch; but he may be quite a decent fellow. That was the gist of it.

Monday 8 January
I got to the hospital (St John & St Elizabeth) at half past seven a.m. and then I was hustled off to get ready. The operation [for a hernia] was to be at half past eight. I was rather startled to hear it would be so quick and was slightly unnerved.

I was fairly woozy most of the rest of the day. The pain was considerable at times but they gave me a number of injections to relieve it. By the evening, I had the last one at about six thirty, there was no more pain, at least not much, just some discomfort.

Tuesday 9 January
Mr Lewis, the surgeon, told me the hernia was worse than he thought by looking at it from the outside. It was bigger and a piece of bladder had got caught in it. I wanted to get out of the hospital straight away but he said I must stay an extra day.

During the morning Andrew Knight had rung up because I had

---

3. *The Constant Wife*, which WW had recently borrowed from the London Library.

rung him on Sunday evening to talk about the extraordinary public row between him and Conrad Black.

Sabiha insisted on coming to see me and she brought me masses of tulips.

Sabiha said she was going to write me a long letter about the situation. I said, 'Well I can't do anything about it.' She said, 'No, but it will relieve me. I will get it off my mind.'

Wednesday 10 January

Desperate attempts to go to the loo properly. Suppositories applied. Nothing happened. Haven't been to the loo since Sunday afternoon. I was told that I couldn't go out of the hospital till I had got my bowels moving. An application was made to Mr Lewis, the surgeon, who allowed me to go home after lunch provided I took sets of suppositories and so forth with me. All very uncomfortable.

Before lunch Sabiha comes to see me again. It sounded a bit tiring. She brought her letter in which she had put what she thought about the Black affair.

Not a terribly intelligent letter but she is an enthusiastic Indian.

She fights for her husband which is highly commendable. She is a nice girl. She brought about three dozen quails' eggs, an enormous quantity of prosciutto, some Pakistani bread and two kiwi fruits. Also some apple juice which was quite nice.

Andrew Knight insisted on coming to see me which he did at about a quarter past four when I had got back to Cavendish Avenue. He was trying to find out my views about the papers he is to take over.

Mrs Tamborero came in at one point with a couple of faxes. One of them was from Irwin Stelzer. He had sent me an article from the *Independent* of today in which it discussed the Knight situation. He [Knight] said, 'Why did he send you that? He's in New York,' so I said, 'Perhaps he thought I hadn't seen the *Independent*, being in hospital, and I might be interested.' He became a bit suspicious. He wandered around the room and sat in my chair and started muddling about with the papers on the table which I thought strange.

Obviously he is looking for my support at the moment.

Thursday 11 January

Gerald Harper comes with Allan Davis. He is tall, quite good-looking, the right age for Philip, good voice, animated, etc.

He thought I must put in a lot of good jokes about current politics

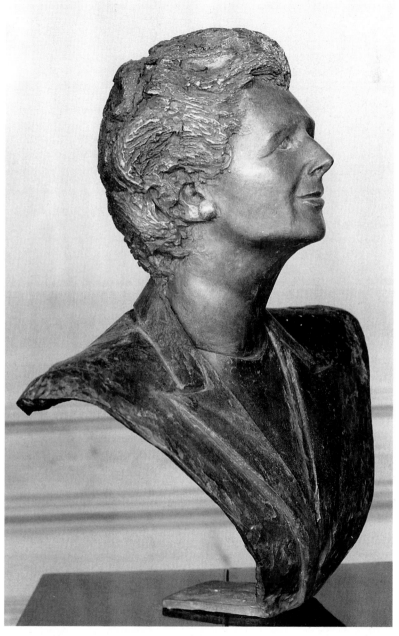

Bronze portrait bust of Margaret Thatcher by Marcelle Quinton. It was unveiled by Mrs Thatcher in 1990 at her former Oxford College, Somerville.

Left: Margaret Thatcher
makes her final speech outside
10 Downing Street, accompanied by
her husband Denis, before leaving
for Buckingham Palace.

Below: Margaret Thatcher, flanked
by Verushka and Woodrow Wyatt,
with her grandson outside Claridge's
where the Thatchers held a party to
celebrate their 40th wedding
anniversary.

Right: Home Secretary David
Waddington at the Conservative Party
Conference in Bournemouth in 1990.

Below right: Geoffrey and
Elspeth Howe.

Left: Cecil and Ann Parkinson.

Below: Nicholas Ridley at his home in Gloucestershire.

Right: William Whitelaw arrives at Westminster Hospital to visit victims of the Carlton Club bomb attack.

Below right: John Major outside his headquarters during the leadership campaign in November 1990, with Norman Lamont on the left.

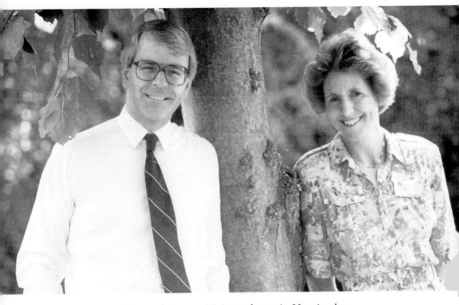

John and Norma Major at home in Huntingdon.

Verushka Wyatt with Home Secretary
Kenneth Baker at the Tote Luncheon, 1991.

Norman and Rosemary Lamont outside Number 11 Downing Street
on the way to deliver his first Budget speech.

Rupert Murdoch, watched by Andrew Neil, executive chairman of Sky TV,
launching Britain's first satellite TV network at the studios in Isleworth.

Rupert Murdoch with his wife
Anna and daughter Elisabeth.

Andrew Neil with Pamella Bordes.

Simon Jenkins, when deputy chairman of English Heritage,
addressing protesters at the site of the Elizabethan Rose Theatre.

and politicians. Philip should be a bit jealous of Heseltine's good looks and say what he thinks about his colleagues.

He said, 'You have got to be really nasty about these Tory politicians and politicians generally.' I said, 'I won't have any friends left.' He said, 'Well that's too bad. You have got to do it.'

He said he would certainly consider it if he were not going to Australia. But in any case I think the play would be improved by the sort of thing he is talking about.

Friday 12 January
A message that the Home Secretary wants to see me at half past two (later changed to eleven) on Tuesday. I won't have had my stitches out by then. I hope it won't be too sore and that I will be in good enough shape.

Sunday 14 January
Poor Nadje had a temperature again. She is now very wobbly and weak and only weighs 8 stone. She used to weigh more than me, not long ago. She went back into the hospital because we can't cope with her, poor woman. She is having to pee every ten minutes. It's totally humiliating, old age, with the collapse of one's extremities. I suppose she ought to go into a home if she comes out again and is not in good repair.

I can't afford a night nurse and there is no room for one anyway here. The servants are getting restless about carting things up and down and so is the au pair girl. Also, she will smoke in bed and she falls asleep so she could burn herself and the house down. I think the poor old soul is losing the will to live, even though she has got a marvellous hearing aid now so she can have the television as loud as she likes without disturbing anyone because it goes straight into her own ear and nowhere else.

I spoke to Margaret. She talked about being on the Wogan show.

I apologized to her for not having seen it. 'I was a bit disoriented last week. I had a hernia operation on Monday morning.' She said, 'Good gracious, you never told me.'

She was astonished when I told her that I had removed myself from the hospital on Wednesday afternoon and had been at work since, though I was a bit woozy to begin with. She said, 'You must remember you have still got stitches in you and you must be careful.'

My mother's birthday. I always think of her a bit on this day. She was a good woman who did her utmost for her family. She never got over my father's death when I was thirteen. It was in 1932. They had been married in 1914, just before the war. That was the sum of her great happiness.

Unfortunately, we were never on the same wavelength. She could not understand what I was up to joining the Labour Party and annoying her rich brother, Arthur, who had paid for me to go to Oxford. He cut me out of his will so I would have been quite rich if I hadn't joined the Labour Party. She read little and understood nothing of my activities. Our relationship was very limited, which was sad.

Had dinner with Rupert at [his flat in] St James's. Anna was there looking younger and prettier and slimmer than I had seen her for a very long time. I told her so. She said she had got slimmer from being at her father's side. He is dying from lung cancer in Australia. He died the day after the Melbourne Cup. He was keen on betting and they each put a bet on, he of only 50p or thereabouts.

Andrew Knight and Sabiha were there.

I said [to Rupert], 'For goodness' sake don't fall for this ridiculous code of conduct you appear to have agreed to for the *Sun* and the *News of the World*, along with other newspapers, not to pay for stories which intrude on privacy and might be scurrilous. This is what the people want. It is only the élitists who don't want the people to know what goes on in high places because they know it already. They think the ordinary people, including the middle classes, are not capable of understanding the tittle-tattle without being put into a deep state of shock and disillusionment – though they themselves, who wish to curb and censor newspapers, are not at all disturbed by knowing who is sleeping with whom and what is going on with somebody's marriage and all that kind of thing.'

'And when people say how can I write for the *News of the World*, I say it is because it has got the largest congregation. Didn't Christ go among the publicans and sinners? I am really a preacher. You are descended from your grandfather who was a Scottish man of the manse and preached away. Remember your own belief that what you say in the *News of the World* and *Sun* about naughty goings-on are part of a morality play: "Look what happens to you if you misbehave." '

I think at the moment Andrew Knight is a trifle bewildered by it all. He has never read the *Sun* and the *News of the World*. We have some criticisms which we share about sloppy reporting, even in the *Sunday Times* and the *Times*.

I told Rupert that she said he deserves to succeed with Sky and he replied, 'I hope then that she will let that Broadcasting Bill go through without amending it to try and make me dispose of my interests.'

We had some made-up dish presumably bought outside and heated up for a first course. It was quite nice. It was followed by the usual chicken. Afterwards Verushka said, 'Rupert must like chicken. We always have it.' I said, 'Perhaps it's because they can't cook anything else.' It was simple roast chicken with a bit of seasoning and gravy. It was good enough but as Dr Johnson used to say, 'Not the sort of dinner you would invite a man to.'

Tuesday 16 January
To the Home Secretary.

He obviously didn't know much about the Tote proposals and asked me to take him through them. I don't think he had read the paper properly.

It was a rather desultory discussion but he said nothing would be decided without talking to me first.

To Wigan. Mr Richard Fries of the Home Office came. I am trying to indoctrinate him with the notion that we couldn't possibly dispose of the bookmakers and generally get him aware of the way all three parts of the Tote are integrated. I think that was a good exercise. On the train up he seemed to think that our meeting had gone well with the Home Secretary.

I said, 'I was rather surprised I had to go through all the figures as though he had never even read [my paper].' He said, 'I think it is a sort of test Ministers apply to see how you put the case over.'

I think that Fries may be on our side somewhat and it may not go too badly, but I'll keep my fingers crossed.

Thursday 18 January
Geoffrey Ampthill says David [Stevens] does intend to marry the lady from Rome who is of Russian origin and had I been invited to the party at Cliveden on Saturday? So I said no. He replied that he thought he was a bit nervous of showing this lady to his friends so soon after Melissa died and he is a bit touchy on the subject.

Saturday 20 January
Woke feeling I had wrenched my wound in some way. There is a ridge of about four to five inches long where Mr Lewis cut into it. I

am now worried because it seems quite hard. The surgeon had mentioned that I might get another hernia. 'Oh my goodness,' I think to myself.

Spoke to Norman Lamont about the great whipping which had to be done to get all the Tories supporting the government over the community charge all over again. There were some rebels, about thirty-six. One of the potential rebels was Charles Irving.[4] When told this during the discussion on the forthcoming vote, Mrs Thatcher said, 'He owes me one,' meaning she had just given him a knighthood. Then she said to the Chief Whip, 'He is always sending me flowers. Do tell him to stop. I don't want any flowers from him.' Presumably the message got across because instead of sending her flowers he delivered his vote in the right lobby.

Sunday 21 January

I asked Margaret how she had got on with Mitterrand in Paris. She said, 'He is very nice when it is one to one, which is what it was. He agrees to a great deal and then he says something different in public.' I said, 'Is he becoming more friendly because of Germany?' She said she thought he was.

Monday 22 January

Messages from Rupert in Bucharest. Must see the Prime Minister for fifteen minutes. Can I arrange it either on Wednesday or at the weekend? I don't know quite what it is all about.

Tuesday 23 January

Rang Margaret to fix Rupert's interview with her.

I spent a large chunk of the morning and until the middle of the afternoon writing this special article for the *Times* about the banks' failure to go on with the Student Loans Company.[5] During my research I spoke to Jeremy Morse, Chairman of Lloyds, whose bank never agreed to go into the scheme; to John Quinton of Barclays, whose

---

4. (1924–95); Conservative MP, 1974–92; he had received a knighthood in the New Year's Honours.

5. The banks had said that the government's proposals for student loans, announced in November 1989, were unworkable.

bank ratted in front of the students' union before[6] and was unwilling
to continue without Lloyds; and to Kit McMahon, Chairman of the
Midland Bank, who said that the government had handled it badly
initially but he had never thought there was much in it for bankers.

Friday 26 January

Got up early, at seven, to prepare to do my *News of the World* article
of which I had done two tiny items the day before. This was in order
to catch the aeroplane to Paris. Also to make sure of buying cigars in
the duty free shop, big ones which are the only real value there. They
had only a tiny selection, no Montecristo No 2.

I was pretty annoyed but bought some large Punch and others, a
hundred. I was taking a risk that I could get them through on the way
back, at fifty cigars for each person including Verushka. As it happened,
in Paris at the airport on the way back I found some Montecristo No
2 so my haul came to a hundred and twenty-five. Verushka then insisted
on buying two hundred duty free cigarettes. Therefore I was in some
perplexity as to what to say and do if the customs stopped me.

Saturday 27 and Sunday 28 January

I am now writing quicker. My head is working better than it has done
for some years. I think that hernia must have been bothering me more
than I realized for a long time.

The great dinner at Pré Catelan.[7]

The main wine was superb; it was Château Margaux 1981, worth
at least £100 a bottle in this country. It was given by the proprietors
of Château Margaux who had something to do with sponsoring the
whole seventieth anniversary of the Prix d'Amérique event.[8] I calculated
there must have been at least two hundred and fifty bottles for the
four hundred guests. That would be a cost of £25,000.

Then we were off to the great anniversary day for the Prix
d'Amérique at Vincennes. This was another terrific occasion. The
course was magnificent and beautifully arranged with lovely flowers in

---

6. WW is referring to Barclays' withdrawal in November 1986 from operations in
   South Africa after pressure by the National Union of Students (NUS) and a fall
   in the number of accounts opened by students.
7. Restaurant in the Bois de Boulogne.
8. A race for trotting horses pulling sulkies (light, two-wheeled vehicles for a single
   driver pulled by a single horse).

patterns and marching military bands, a band of American Marines and lots of excitement. The favourite won. It was the fourth time it had won and it was now ten years old and about to retire to stud.

They said that after ten years it is very difficult to keep a horse controlled in its trotting.

The trotting horses are very beautiful and their motion, once you get used to it, is extremely pretty. The little chariots are gay and the riders are highly skilful. The mounted trotting is also elegant.

The lunch was pretty good with foie gras, a lot of it. Jean Romanet, the head of the society for the encouragement of racing (flat and steeple-chasing, not trotting), sat next to me.

On my other side sat André Cormier, head of the Pari-Mutuel.

Cormier, Romanet and I discussed the matter of the Pari-Mutuel putting bets into our Derby pools. We reached an agreement, as we were rather jolly, very quickly. We could never have done it formally in an office in the same way. The Pari-Mutuel think they could get five to ten million francs in 1990 into our Derby Day pools, if they promoted it properly which they will do. They wouldn't do it before because they couldn't get Brian [McDonnell] (though I didn't tell Brian this) to agree to a sensible commission for them. On the spot I agreed 6.5 per cent for the first million francs and 10 per cent thereafter. With our modern machinery we should be able to manage it quite easily, if Brian puts some effort into it which I shall encourage him to do.

Tuesday 30 January
I called Margaret. She immediately asked me what I thought about the Justice Taylor report on football. I said I thought he was foolish about the ID cards but on the other hand I thought he was quite good on the other aspects.[9]

She was very argumentative about Hong Kong. I nearly said, 'You have got this man Percy Cradock[10] advising and he doesn't know what the hell he is talking about. He is an old China hand and he hasn't even been in Hong Kong since 1983,' but I thought it was not a good moment to do so.

When I got back [from a dinner] Rupert rang within a few moments.

---

9. The report came out against compulsory identity cards for football supporters.
10. Sir Percy Cradock, British Ambassador to Peking, 1978–83, Prime Minister's Foreign Policy Adviser, 1984–92.

He was full of the Andrew Neil case.[11] He is very cross with him because he committed the *Times* to pay for his legal costs. If they had lost, it would have been at least £200,000 which Rupert would have had to pay – and he never consulted Rupert or asked his permission which he would not have given, Rupert said. Fortunately for Rupert the *Telegraph* had to pay the costs of the crazy libel action.

Rupert thought Andrew Neil was quite dotty to have brought it and he made a fool of himself by reviving the whole bloody thing.

I said, 'But he is of course a brilliant editor,' and Rupert said, 'That is true and the paper is magnificent.'

Allan Davis says that Lee Menzies has now withdrawn. He has too many things to manage. Nick Salmon wants to put the play on at Bromley, if we get Gerald Harper.

I spoke to my agent, Laurence Fitch, and he said that on no account should I put money in of my own. It would be all right to arrange for other people to put something in. He didn't even know that money had been raised, about £11,000, by me for the Margate production. I have never had any accounts on that. Laurence Fitch said they took about £18,000. (It turned out it was £12,000.)

I think Lee Menzies has probably withdrawn because he thinks that Allan isn't up to it any more.

Laurence Fitch says that Allan's agreement with me has now run out and all rights are now reverted to me. He mentioned this to Allan and said he would have to pay some more money to keep the rights. Allan said, 'I am not going to do that,' so this means theoretically I could take it to another manager to promote it. Allan would still get his twelve per cent on the play. I said, 'But that would be a terrible thing to do to him. It would break his heart.' He said, 'Perhaps it would but you have to be serious about it.'

11. Andrew Neil, editor of the *Sunday Times*, sued the *Sunday Telegraph* and Peregrine Worsthorne, its former editor, concerning two articles and a cartoon relating to Neil's relationship with Pamella Bordes, a former House of Commons researcher exposed as a call-girl. Neil claimed that the articles implied that he had known during his four-month affair with Mrs Bordes that she was a call-girl.

Friday 2 February

A Gallup poll in the *Daily Telegraph* showed Labour sixteen points ahead.

I rang Mrs Thatcher. The first thing she said was, 'What about this terrible poll? Thank you so much for ringing. It really is kind of you.' That was before I could get a word out of my mouth. She obviously values my ringing her when things look rough.

I said, 'Don't worry. Underlying it is all right. I have the utmost confidence that you are going to win the next election. I know you are. At the moment you are up against the high interest rates and the mortgage rate. That's one thing. The next thing is this sentimental slop about the ambulancemen.[1] The next is the poll tax.' (I said the 'community charge' because I never call it 'poll tax' to her.) 'Are we allowed to put across in government paid advertisements, on television and in the press, why it is a fair charge?'

She said, 'I am not sure how much of that we could do but we could do some. When the community charge gets going people will begin to see that it is not unfair.'

Call from Mr [Jeffery] Maunsell of Goodman Derrick. Had I read a book about treason by a man called Deacon?[2]

'I want to send you a chapter and the dust sheet by fax. Will you read it and tell me to whom you think the woman described on the dust jacket as the wife of a dead Minister – she is still living – refers?'

The fax duly came and I read it all through. The only person who fitted the bill was Clarissa Avon. Not properly because I don't know about her being a Lesbian, which she [the person in the book] was described as being. She certainly knew Guy Burgess[3] and Pope-

---

1. The ambulance staff strike for better pay and conditions had met wide public support.
2. *The Greatest Treason* by Richard Deacon, published in 1989.
3. (1911–63); diplomat who defected with Donald MacLean (1913–83) to the Soviet Union in 1951.

Hennessy,[4] both homosexuals, and other homosexuals, as indeed I do and did.

The book implies that she married Anthony Eden, who is thinly disguised, in order to be able to give information to the Russians and help them. She was alleged to have tipped off Burgess and MacLean that they were about to be seized and investigated. She was described as being a member of a distinguished family. The dates were absolutely right in the book.

I told Mr Maunsell this and he said, 'Ah, that's right and that is our client.' I said, 'Why didn't she tell me? She came to dinner a few weeks ago.' He said she was very embarrassed about it and didn't want to have anything made public. She would never have brought this libel action if it weren't for the fact that the *Evening Standard* and other papers have been pestering her.

I said, 'It is ridiculous. She is the most patriotic person you could imagine. The only time I ever had any arguments with asperity with her were over Suez[5] which she stoutly defended on the grounds of patriotism and I said it was an act of insanity. Also, she used to ask me before she got married and I hadn't understood why, what it was like to be an MP's wife and what was the constituency work like and how would it be, etc. If I had been more intelligent, I would have realized she was thinking of marrying Anthony Eden but she was very reserved and uncertain about it at the time.'

I told Mr Maunsell that I knew her well after they were married, too, and I had known Eden a very long time, too. They had a most successful and happy marriage. She was always very attractive and never had any difficulty, if she had wanted to, in finding men friends and so forth. So he said would I give evidence and I said certainly.[6]

---

4. (1916–74); James Pope-Hennessy, writer and biographer, who was murdered.

5. The British invasion of Egypt in 1956, when Colonel Nasser nationalized the Suez Canal.

6. WW did not have to appear in court. The publishers, Century Hutchinson, withdrew all allegations and apologized unreservedly for the very serious injury caused to Lady Avon's reputation and feelings. There was no truth in, no evidence for the allegations. They paid substantial compensation and her full legal costs. All copies of the book were recalled and pulped.

Sunday 4 February
To Bowden Park. Arnold in a very jolly mood. A delicious 1964 Haut-Brion.

Netta was very funny about her ninety-seven-year-old father. Every time she sees him now he keeps complaining about her mother saying, 'I know she was having an affair with that doctor. I came in one morning to say I was going out and ask what she was doing and she said she was staying in bed because the doctor was coming to see her.' He thought that was very suspicious.

His wife died recently aged ninety-six or ninety-five. Arnold said, 'Actually, though she was a nice and jolly woman, very pretty when she was young, she might have giggled a bit and had some mild flirtations but she would never have done anything with anybody other than her husband.'

Margaret is in good shape. I told her that I thought we mustn't go nap on Mandela because there are many other people in South Africa besides the ANC.

Then she said, 'They have got the opportunity of a lifetime, no not a lifetime, perhaps one which will never return, to sort it all out. But these people are very silly saying sanctions did it. It wasn't sanctions at all.' I said, 'It was due to you putting the pressure on them but from a friendly angle and them seeing that the world had changed and they had got to do it.' I said I thought de Klerk had been very brave.[7]

Monday 5 February
Early in the morning Gerald Harper rang back from my call over the weekend: 'I have been reading the play again and I am seeing my agent today.' I said, 'I think they have got it all set up at Bromley and waiting to go.'

Later in the afternoon I got a call to ring him. Harper: 'You are speaking to a very angry man. I decided to do the play today. I was then told Bromley was off because they hadn't been told in good enough time.'[8]

I spoke to Nick Salmon at Bromley. He said he had been told that

---

7. President de Klerk had announced on 2 February the unbanning of the ANC; Nelson Mandela was released from prison on 11 February.
8. The Bromley theatre had a deadline of Friday 2 February for the information for its programme; it went to press on Monday 5 February with the reserve play substituted since there had been no news about WW's.

the agent of Gerald Harper had been trying to ring him on Thursday and Friday. He didn't believe it because he never got the message. Allan Davis didn't believe it either.

It looks as if we had the fish within our grasp and from the bungling of the fishermen, the fish is in the water again. Later on Monday night I rang Harper just to keep him sweet and said they were fighting away and I was sure they were going to produce something. He said OK but he hasn't yet signed the contract.

I had a horrible afternoon. My right eye is still hurting fairly badly. I asked to see Arnott's man again and was told Arnott wanted to see me himself. I hung about all the morning waiting to get an appointment and then finally I got desperate and rang his reception again and was told, 'You can come at half past two.'

I got in to see Arnott at twenty-five past four, after waiting in the car and telling him to ring me in the car which he never did. I was rather surly.

At 6.30 the Stable Lads[9] came with Frank Chapman from the electricians' union.[10] Viv Baldwin, the unpaid Treasurer, was very reluctant to do a join up with the electricians. Very foolishly, she thought they should keep their total independence, etc.

I think we can do something for them. I saw a way of helping through the Tote via the sponsorship of their annual football match.

In the end he said he thought it was a good idea to set up a working party.

I think this is their only answer. They are in a deficit. They have only got five hundred and twenty-two paying members and they can't go on like this.

Tuesday 6 February
Dinner with Alan Hare and Jill and no one else except ourselves. I didn't realize that Alan had cancer in the prostate. He has had it for about two years but he said they have kept it steady with hormone injections and he feels perfectly well. He is very slim still. At six foot, one inch, he weighs just over 12 stone, which is hardly more than me at just scraping five foot, eight inches.

---

9. See Vol. 1, p. 406, for WW becoming a trustee of the Stable Lads' Association.
10. Not to be confused with Frank Chapple (life peer 1985), former General Secretary of the EETPU and member of the Tote Board.

We had Les Forts de Latour 1976. It was frightfully good.

Alan had been on a visit to Japan last week. He thinks it is a horrible place. He has been there several times. He said that the Japanese are buying expensive wines like Latour and putting them out in their restaurants at enormous prices The Japanese sommeliers train in France and are really expert. They instruct the Japanese businessmen with their enormous wealth on what they should drink and what they should like.

Alan will be quite glad to give up Château Latour because he finds the journeying around the world rather tiring. I said, 'I can't think why anyone would ever want to give it up.'

Wednesday 7 February
The Tote Board agreed my request that we should give £4,000 a year for three years' sponsorship to the benefit of the Stable Lads' Association. This is good news. It will save them and give them a breathing space to adjust themselves to the electricians, if that is what they finally decide to do.

Friday 9 February
I rang Allan Davis. He said, 'I have been dreading this call. We have lost Leatherhead. I don't know if we are going to be able to arrange a tour. Leatherhead has gone because Ray Cooney has written a farce about an MP having an affair with his secretary and they are putting it in the slot that we wanted and it is being billed as a world première. I think we are finished.'

Laurence Fitch said why don't we try Farnham. I asked him to ring Allan and say that to him.

Fun and games at the BBC. I sent them some questions about the composition of the *Today* programme presenters and producers and how they are politically motivated etc. etc. They got on to Charlie Wilson (that is Birt, the Deputy Director General) saying how could I ask such questions about the *Today* programme BBC people, to which Charlie replied, 'It is the duty of a journalist to investigate and ask questions. It is up to the people to whom he asks the questions whether they answer them or not.' The BBC are very touchy about being investigated themselves though they love investigating everybody else.

Saturday 10 February
Went swimming but not more than four lengths.

Then off to Newbury for the Tote Gold Trophy where we had a large party, with thirty-four sitting down in our entertainment room.

I had Gillian Howard de Walden on my right and Serena Rothschild on my left. I put Howard de Walden[11] next to her to talk about racing. She didn't know who he was and I had to explain he bred his own horses and won the Derby with Slip Anchor [in 1985] which was a horse she had never heard of, so new is she to racing. But he was very kind to her and Serena was jolly and gay, almost *belle laide*, as she used to be years ago.

Prince Michael came for a change. He gave away the prize.

John Howard told me about his prostate operation which he had only just had during the week. I said, 'You must sit down.' This was before lunch. I made him sit down and Gillian was very pleased. We compared notes about our internal conditions.

Gillian Howard was looking very pretty in a blue and red speckled dress. I said, 'I suppose you put it on to match my tie,' at which point John Oaksey[12] said, 'It clashes with it,' to which she agreed. So I said, 'What had better happen? Either I take my tie off or you take your dress off. I would prefer the latter but not when there are so many people about.'

Sunday 11 February
Lunch with Harold Lever and Diane. The other two present were George Soros, the Hungarian Jew who left Hungary in 1947, went to America and made a vast fortune, and his wife. He runs Quantum in which Verushka had shares which she bought at $9,000 and then they rose to $16,000 and then fell again to $7,000. They are now back at $16,000. I wish I had bought some when they were at $7,000.

He is a stocky man. He wore brown trousers and a check coat.

Very agreeable, though anti-Mrs Thatcher to begin with in our conversation, saying she had missed opportunities in Europe, she ought

---

11. (1912–99); 9th Baron; m 2 (1978) Gillian (Viscountess Mountgarret); former senior steward of the Jockey Club; racehorse owner.*
12. 2nd Baron; racing journalist ('Marlborough' on the *Daily Telegraph*, 1957–94) and amateur jockey.

to do the right thing in Europe and she wasn't taking the lead when she could.

In the end he could think of nothing she ought to do except something about the collapse of Comecon which leaves the Eastern European countries with nowhere to sell their goods, most of which are no good anyway.

He said, 'There should be a payments union to let them have a tide-over from us.' I said, 'That is fine but she proposes that they become associate members of the European Common Market.' He said, 'They should become full members straight away.' I said, 'I think you are going altogether too fast.'

He then said, 'She should have taken the lead in Germany.' I said, 'She has very much modified her attitude on that and she knows reunification is inevitable. But you know in England there is a game called cricket. The greatest batsmen like Hobbs and Bradman and the West Indian great cricketers always played the ball very late. You wait to see exactly where the ball is before you make your stroke.'

He had a wife with very pretty legs, a rather handsome girl with blonde hair. It is his second wife. She runs a magazine and owns the biggest antique shop in New York, selling mainly English antiques. I don't know why she bothers with all that money but I suppose she enjoys it. She didn't look Jewish. She had a biggish face but quite pleasing, long and quite wide.

I talked to [Mrs Thatcher] about Nigel [Lawson] having rung me up over the attacks on him for accepting X amount of money.

She said, 'He has a right to earn something and I think it is good that he should feel that we are not against him.'

Also I told her that Nigel refuses to publish anything till after the election because he doesn't want to rock the boat.[13]

She was quite cheerful. 'God bless,' she said once or twice at the end when she rang off finally, after about fifteen minutes bubbling away about the Mandela situation. Like me she had been impressed by his telling the crowd to go away and disperse quietly, 'to show we can control ourselves'.[14]

---

13. His memoirs, *The View From No. 11*, were published in 1992.
14. Mandela's address from City Hall, Cape Town, on his release from prison was televised live.

Tuesday 13 February
At the Centre for Policy Studies.

It was for T. E. Utley's[15] annual memorial prize of £5,000 for the best political journalist under thirty-five. Also present was that tall, bulky, amusing fellow, Ferdinand Mount.[16]

I argued that the [age] limits should be raised from thirty-five to thirty-nine because I had a candidate from the *Sun*, Richard Littlejohn, who writes a political column twice a week. I said, 'I don't suppose you would want him because he is not from the toffee-nosed quality papers.' They didn't want him and they said that they couldn't raise the age limit.

I asked how old Mary Ann Sieghart was and they said she must be under thirty-five so I said, 'Well what about her?'

They said they didn't think she wrote well enough and nor did Peter Stothard[17] who is in America and in any case the prize was really intended for someone who had not been discovered.

They all agreed it might be nice to have a woman.

I said, 'What about Dominic Lawson and Nigella Lawson? She writes about politics sometimes. They are children of Nigel Lawson. Dominic has just been made editor of the *Spectator*.' They ruled them out because they had already been discovered.

Tom Utley looks a little like his father who was blind. Mrs Utley said how her husband had always wanted to be on a jury. He had always written on the form that he was blind though he was willing to do jury service and he always got the reply: 'Your application for release from jury service has been accepted,' which used to infuriate him.

Wednesday 14 February
Abdul Al Ghazzi came to lunch and wants me to be televised by Iraqi television urging that prisoners be exchanged between Iraq and Iran.

I said, 'I will look at the paper you have given me. I don't see any harm in my doing it. I was going to say a word or two once in writing

---

15. (1921–88); political journalist, *Daily Telegraph* 1964–87; obituaries editor, *Times*, 1987–8.
16. Head of Prime Minister's Policy Unit, 1982–3; political columnist, *Daily Telegraph*, 1984–90; editor, *Times Literary Supplement*, since 1991.
17. US editor of the *Times*, 1989–92; he became editor of the *Times* in 1992.

on behalf of Iraq and then they started throwing poison gas at people, not only at Iran's troops but against the Kurds in their own country.'

Abdul has been to Budapest where he is building a great exposition hall. I said, 'How are you going to get your money out?' He said he would get it from the people who exhibit there. I said, 'They won't be paying enough to cover the costs,' and he said, 'No but it will be long-term.'

We had some excellent Léoville-Barton 1962 in a half bottle.

He seems to weigh a 189 pounds and his doctor had told him to drink less.

Thursday 15 February
Dinner party at Cavendish Avenue. We had my last bottle of Ayala Champagne 1949. It was absolutely delicious. Only David Montagu, Micky Suffolk and myself drank it, apart from a little for Linda Suffolk and Petronella. It was a dream, though I am sad I will never have any more. At dinner we drank my only three bottles of Château Latour 1960 left.

Andrew Neil, the editor of the *Sunday Times*, came late but it didn't much matter because we weren't quite ready to go in to dinner. Michael Green was there. He is the principal shareholder in the huge Carlton Communications. He is divorced from Sir Leonard Wolfson's daughter.

Linda sat on my right. She is fairly jolly and fairly pretty, but no genius.

When the ladies had left some riotous conversation began. Andrew Neil vigorously attacked Ken Baker, saying that Mrs Thatcher had got it all wrong about Germany and Eastern Europe, the government were making a mess of everything, and he was violently opposed to the community charge. I said, 'That's because you haven't understood it. You haven't read my articles in the *Times* and the *News of the World*,' to which he replied, 'But we all know that your articles are dictated by Number 10 Downing Street.'

Later I said, 'Far from that being the case I oppose the government on a number of issues, for example Hong Kong. Also I have moved amendments against them in the Lords on the trade union reforms. Moreover, the *News of the World* has more AB readers than the *Sunday Times* because its huge circulation contains more AB readers than your paper does.'

David asked him whether he was going to support the Tory Party at the next election. Andrew said crossly and reluctantly that they would, having weighed it all up and down in the balance. His face always appears bad-tempered and red, waiting to burst into a fight like an angry bantam cock.

At one moment Andrew said that his remark that I got my line from No 10 had evidently got under my skin. I suppose it had but it is perfectly true that she and I think alike on almost everything but when we don't I say so.

Friday 16 February
Kenneth Baker said in the morning would I be sure to mention Labour's reduction of the age of consent for buggery to sixteen.

He said it was terribly important because people didn't like it among the working classes, to which I said, 'Some of my homosexual friends won't like it either if I have a dig at this angle,' though that wouldn't have prevented me. If I think it is so important, I might mention it next week.

I have been talking to Elizabeth Berridge a lot. Graham Moore (Reginald Moore) died last Sunday though she didn't tell me until Wednesday. She wanted me to organize obituaries in the *Telegraph* and the *Times*, etc. The *Telegraph* wanted me to write one but I said I couldn't because I am under contract with News International. However, I pushed away and got the *Times* to do an obituary, quite a nice one, and the *Telegraph* did a nice one.[18]

The death of Reginald Moore stirred ancient memories. I knew him in the war when I was editing *English Story* and he was running *Modern Reading*. I used to stay with them when I could towards the end of the War. He was tall and extremely good-looking and very shy and reserved. He had a quiet face and was not keen on parties and meetings with grand literary people and therefore he has been somewhat underrated. I remember many times when we had drunken parties, making champagne cocktails by mixing cooking brandy with perry, the sparkling cider type drink made out of pears. I also used to play darts with him when he started the darts league in the local pub. He won a cup there and he was much too good for me.

He was a warm-hearted, friendly man and helped sort out the stories for me when I was in India and they were sent in for *English*

---

18. Reginald (his professional name) Moore, novelist, editor and sports writer, died aged seventy-five; the *Times* obituary praised Moore's meticulous editing of *Modern Reading*, and catholic but discriminating taste.

Story. This made Elizabeth Berridge slightly overdo it when talking to the *Telegraph*. She said he stood in for me. When they asked me if that was right I said, 'Well you can say he "midwifed" it while I was abroad.' It was a bit of an exaggeration but I knew it would please her.

Poor Ernest Saunders spoke to me (about what I had written in the *News of the World*[19] about whether he would get a fair trial). I said, 'How is it going?' and he said, 'It's agony.' He has got to face six months of it and he is furious because the jury keep getting dismissed because they can't stay long enough. I said, 'I saw one of the discharged jurors leaving. They looked a fairly rough lot.' He said, 'Yes. I don't think many of them are readers of the *Financial Times*. I don't see how they are going to understand the case at all.'

I asked him about his wife and he said, 'She is still not with us,' by which he presumably means she is in some sort of medical care in Switzerland. He also said she didn't want to have anything to do with the case or to be there while it was happening. He said, 'I am very lonely.'

Sunday 18 February
On Friday Alastair Burnet came to see me. He is the main presenter of ITN news and on the board of ITN from which he is resigning because he doesn't like the behaviour of the big operators.

He is tall, stooping, shy-looking, quite an attractive face though it is pock-marked. He is diffident and nervous in his manner which is strange considering he has done a vast amount of television on the news, interviewing, making programmes and so forth. He brought me a paper against the Broadcasting Act being changed so that the Channel 3 [ITV] nation-wide contractors would be the majority controlling the ITN. It was quite diffuse and much longer than it need have been.

He was nattily dressed and said he was ready to go off to the country.

Margaret said the only thing in the papers today that cheered her up was my article. That was the one that explained that the mortgage interest rates are not so terrible.

She was quite cheerful considering all the clouds gathered over her at the moment.

---

19. On 11 February.

Monday 19 February
Lunch with George Walker.

I said I would like to do a national pool bet with him now because he has got as many betting shops as Ladbroke had when we were trying to do it with them. One, it would be good for racing; they would get some money out of it. Two, it would be good for us, meaning him and the Tote. Three, it would annoy Ladbroke. He laughed and said, 'I think the last reason is the one which is most important to you.'

But he has it on board and they are going to examine it. Also some co-operation in Europe between the Tote and Brent Walker to see what we can do jointly.

I think I must also get him to see Margaret. He is terribly pro her and pro women getting full opportunities.

Gave Irwin Stelzer, Gerry Malone (ex Tory MP) and a nice man from Virginia who is head of the racing commission there and is News International's US lawyer, dinner in the Barry Room after a long discussion about the Broadcasting Bill and who they could ask to their Sky studio in the hope of getting them on their side to prevent any move to make Rupert get rid of newspapers or Sky Television.

Irwin said that he had heard that the Prime Minister had called a meeting with Mellor[20] and others on the subject of the ownership of ITN news. So already she had taken action, as suggested by me after talking to Alastair Burnet.

Tuesday 20 February
Telephone call from Duke Hussey. Very hush-hush. He said my article in the *Times* [about the *Today* programme] had done a great deal of good.

I said, 'Why didn't they on the *Today* programme deal in some depth with the ballot rigging in the TGWU? In the public mind Labour is very much associated with the unions and I think that is why they didn't talk about it on the programme.'

I pointed out to Duke that the scrutineer had resigned, no doubt from pressure from me in my *News of the World* article because I had

---

20. David Mellor was Minister of State, Home Office, 1989–90, Minister for the Arts, 1990.

said he had broken the law, and also from a parliamentary question I had put down yesterday which he probably had seen.[21]

He suggested I rang John Birt in the morning without referring to the conversation with him.

He also said that privately John Birt largely agrees with me but he has to put on a different front to defend the BBC in the *Times* which he did this morning.

Wednesday 21 February

Spoke to John Birt privately. I said, 'I am not going to reveal this conversation,' but I told him what had happened about the TGWU ballot rigging.

He then said to me, 'Of course you do know that my private opinions may be different from those I express publicly when I replied to you.' I said, 'Yes, I understand your difficulties as the Deputy Director General for the BBC.'

He then said, 'I think Brian Redhead, if there were a Labour government, because he is so exuberant, would attack them perhaps as much as he does the present government.' I said, 'Well, that is not quite the point. In the meanwhile he is creating the climate in which there could be a change to Labour. By the time he starts attacking the Labour Ministers they will have won the election which they ought not to have been helped to do by *Today*.'

The *Times* began a huge article today discussing the whole issue with a photograph of me at the top. It began by saying, 'Woodrow Wyatt's now famous attack on *Today*.' This one article has made a tremendous impact.

There was a swiping attack against me in the second leader of the *Independent*. It's probably libellous.[22] I discussed it with the News

---

21. In his 18 February article WW had said that Ron Todd's TGWU had 'admitted ballot rigging' after the Electoral Reform Society had discovered 2,000–3,000 ballot papers, which should have been lodged with the independent scrutineer or the Electoral Reform Society, had been stolen from the TGWU headquarters; the postal ballot for the union's executive was being rerun.

22. Under the heading 'Redheads Under the Bed' the *Independent* said: 'The natural inclination is to dismiss Lord Wyatt's McCarthyism as the feeble expedient of a man with a column to fill, a man moreover who has been known to charge that the BBC and *The Times* were "in the hands of Roman Catholics" and to make attacks on black immigrants to this country so crude that they were censured by the Press Council.'

International lawyer who said did I want to bring a libel action. I talked to Ted Pickering[23] and said I thought I ought to write a letter first which I will do but I haven't time today.

The great lunch for Ted Heath's fortieth year as an MP. It was at the Savoy and there were about four hundred and eighty people there. We all paid £40 a head of which £10 went towards buying him a splendid silver bowl. Robin Day made a very funny speech, much the best of the occasion.

Ted told an extraordinary story about how he became MP for the first time for Bexley with a majority of a hundred and thirty-six which had sunk from a hundred and sixty-one after a recount.

He said in that poll five hundred and eighty-one votes were cast for a Communist candidate. That was four times as much as his majority. If the Communist candidate hadn't stood, he would never have started his political career so he owed everything to the Communist Party. He told the Communist candidate, 'In the next election if you have any trouble finding money for the deposit I'll look after that and you must stand again. It's your right to stand.'

I sat next to the jolly Lew Grade, Lord Grade. He told me he smoked sixteen cigars a day until he had a very complicated operation on his heart and was informed by the doctors that he must cut his cigars down to four. He said, 'Actually I still smoke about six rather big ones. But don't tell my wife.'

He was a great early television tycoon, controlling ITV. There was a story that he was attacked by an MP for putting on too much entertainment and not enough culture, to which he had replied, 'Of course we put on a lot of culture. We always put on a lot of political discussions.' The MP said, 'But that's not culture,' to which Lew Grade replied, 'Well it's certainly not entertainment.'

I told him I had written a play and he wanted to know the title. He said, 'The title is all important.' I said, 'It's *High Profiles*.'[24] He said, 'Good gracious. That's a marvellous title. I shall certainly come and see that play when it comes to London.'

---

23. Editor and newspaper executive, formerly *Daily Express*, IPC, Mirror Group; executive vice-chairman, Times Newspapers, since 1982; knight 1977.
24. This was the title WW finally settled for, under which it was published by Samuel French Ltd.

Norman Stone[25] and the Pejacsevichs came to play bridge which we did in my library. He is an exuberant, jolly fellow. He knew a lot of details about the Hungarian families of both the Pejacsevichs.

He likes talking to old Hungarians with aristocratic families. He wants me to be chairman of an appeal or organization to raise money for ambulances in Transylvania where so many Hungarians are. I said I would certainly do that.

He is very lively but has the fashionably rather silly view that Mrs Thatcher ought to be more welcoming to the Germans and their reunification.

Thursday 22 February
A great deal of shenanigans over my reply to the *Independent* attack on me, including calling me a racist, in yesterday's paper. I kept reading drafts to the lawyer.[26]

Other Club dinner. Norman Tebbit said that if Margaret suddenly threw in her towel or died, he would put his hat in the ring and stand himself.

He then started talking about possible people for Prime Minister. He thought Major looked like a potential one.

He thought William Waldegrave had a very good chance and he would rather take him into a public bar than somebody like Chris Patten or even John Major. He said he had the common touch and was very bright. Robin [Day] said, 'Oh he is much too clever. They don't have people with Firsts like that any more.'

Robin thought Heseltine would make a good Prime Minister but Norman and I said nonsense.

Norman said he might win the election if he became Leader six

---

25. Professor of Modern History, University of Oxford, and Fellow of Worcester College, Oxford, 1984–97; since then Professor of International Relations, Bilkent University, Ankara.

26. In his letter, published 23 February, WW put his remarks about Roman Catholics into the context in which they were made, the Nigerian civil war of 1967–70, when he said the Biafran cause was championed by those susceptible to the advocacy of Roman Catholic priests in the area. On the Press Council ruling, WW said that he had Home Office evidence to support what he had said, and the council's adjudication on 7 September 1986 contained more in his favour than condemnation. He then vigorously rebutted the imputation that he was a racist. See Vol. 1, p. 186 for the Press Council censure.

months before it but afterwards he would be no good and would be thrown out.

Kenneth Baker he ruled out completely, he doesn't like him at all. He said, 'When I was Chairman of the party, I took it as my duty to take the flak from the Prime Minister and shield her from it. But Kenneth Baker seems to think she should take the flak from him.' Not much love lost there.

He said there had been a vote at the beginning of the Falklands War when Margaret had gone all the way round the Cabinet (and they had never known her to do it before or since) asking who was in favour of going ahead with this expedition going to the Falklands and who was not. I said, 'And who was against then?' He said, 'Oh, it's a thirty year rule operating. You can't know for thirty years from 1982.' I said, 'So there was somebody against?' and he said, 'I am not going to say.' But he said if the Prime Minister hadn't been a woman, it might never have gone ahead because a man might have been too hesitant to do it but she gave the military the confidence to go ahead.

Alec Douglas-Home, whom I was sitting next to, thought she wouldn't be standing at the next election because she had been there so long and she must be tired. I said, 'I think you underrate her,' and Norman Tebbit said the same. 'She has got amazing stamina.'

Alec looked a bit broody and doubtful and said, 'I think she might win if she is still there, but I don't think she will be still there by then.'

It was interesting that among these senior Conservatives at The Other Club, namely Alec and Norman and Lord De L'Isle,[27] there was even some query as to whether Mrs Thatcher would last until the next election.

They were talking about a similar situation which afflicted the Tory government after thirteen years in 1964 when everything seemed to be going wrong. They didn't dare say it too loud because Jack Profumo was sitting at the other end of the table, but there was the Profumo scandal and Ministers didn't seem to know what they were doing.

I said to Norman Tebbit, 'This is quite a different situation. You have got the best government you have had for ages.'

Saturday 24 February
Breakfast with Allan after my swim. He gets very touchy whenever I suggest that Verushka should have a hand in advising on the dresses

---

27. (1909–91); 1st Viscount De L'Isle (created 1956); Conservative politician.

for Victoria. 'Not professional,' he says. 'Why not?' I ask. 'Oh it's not the same thing dressing on the stage as dressing outside it.' I said, 'At least she knows where to get the cheapest second-hand clothes which look smart. She was the one who lent the pearl choker for Victoria at Margate because she obviously had to hide her neck, and she was the one who produced the suits which Jane, the secretary, wore.'

Spoke to Jacob about his offer to buy 'The Three Graces' in lieu of death duties on his £92 million inherited estate. Apparently the legal inheritance provisions provide that it can be any work of art, not necessarily one owned by the estate, so if his estate bought it, he could get off death duties. Then he would add a few hundred thousand pounds to it and put it in Waddesdon which is nominally National Trust, though the fund which supports it for the National Trust is controlled by Jacob. I told him I would speak to Margaret because it is a question of the Treasury using their discretion.

Sunday 25 February
I told Margaret a little about the conversation at The Other Club but I said, 'I shouldn't repeat these things.'

I said, 'What is Geoffrey Howe's function supposed to be?' She said, 'He chairs quite a few important committees.' I said, 'But why the devil doesn't he come out and defend government policy?' She said, 'You know what he is like and what he is up to now.'

I told her about Jacob's wheeze to find the death duties from the estate of his aunt who left £92,800,000 when she died in 1988 aged ninety-three.

She had enjoyed her visit to Waddesdon for lunch. So I said to her, 'Will you please give this thing a nudge with the Treasury? It is a matter for the Treasury, this question, and whether they will deal with it this way or not. They can if they want.' She said she certainly would.

We talked a bit about the *Today* programme controversy. She thought that Birt's answer to me in the *Times* had been very feeble and I told her what Duke Hussey and Birt had said to me privately, particularly Duke Hussey. She was amused.

Tuesday 27 February
Long talk with Rupert in his car.

Would Simon Jenkins[28] make a good editor? What did I think of

---

28. At this time a columnist on the *Sunday Times*.

him as a writer? I said, 'He's a very good writer, I usually agree with him. He makes excellent points but sometimes he is a bit quirky.'

I said, 'But if he were made an editor, as you were saying there might be a possibility, the responsibility would doubtless steady him down. He could be good.' Jenkins had been assistant editor of the *Evening Standard* under Charles Wintour. I didn't ask Rupert which paper he was thinking of but possibly it was the *Times*. I don't think it would be *Today*, though David Montgomery has asked me to lunch with him – he's editor of *Today* now.

Rupert said he was driving along the road to the Sky studios out at Isleworth (or somewhere like that) counting the dishes on the houses. The numbers are growing.

I said, 'I don't know why Andrew Neil goes on attacking the community charge in the *Sunday Times*. There is no point in it. It's not going to be changed or removed. It's far too late for that so why doesn't he go to town on attacking Labour's alternative?' Rupert agreed. He sometimes gets irritated with Andrew Neil.

We talked about the cricket. I said I had wasted a lot of time over the weekend watching it when I could have been doing something more useful, and I did the same last night. He said that was exactly what he did when he got home last night (that was in London).

One of the reasons why he is a successful newspaperman is that his range is very wide. Apart from being interested in politics and power and all those machinations and also the kind of stories which appear in the *Sun*, he also is genuinely interested in sport, like ordinary people, and he follows it in much the same way.

I told him I wanted to go to the elections in Hungary because that is where it all began – it was the Hungarians who tested out the Russians first to see how far Gorbachev would let them go.

Rupert said, 'Fine. You go to Hungary and we'll pay for it.' So I shall go on the Friday, March 23rd.

Dinner at the Connaught in a private room given by Shandwick which they told me was the biggest public relations firm (not advertising) in the world. Alun Chalfont is a director or whatever of it. He was giving the dinner for Dame Lydia Dunn [of the Hong Kong legislative council] and various people interested in Hong Kong.

When I spoke I had already drunk a fair amount of champagne and 1978 claret, Pichon-Longueville, which was rather good, and some quite good white wine first.

I was rather vehement and said we had betrayed the Hong Kongers.

Most of them looked rather shocked. Afterwards I said to Lydia Dunn, in front of them all, 'Of course we can't do much more about passports, though I will go on fighting for it and I think the lot of you should have been given them. But we live in "Tebbit" country.'

Thursday 1 March
Dinner with the Wolfsons. The food was appalling.

This was against the background of a magnificent Léoville-Poyferré 1970. Ruth explained to her neighbours and me that she had decanted it according to my rules about an hour and a half before we started to drink it.

She is a remarkable girl, Ruth. She must be over sixty now but remains very handsome, doubtless with the aid of a number of face lifts. At one time I was quite keen on her. That was about twenty years ago.

Leonard is very worried about Mrs Thatcher. He thinks she has gone over the top. He thinks they will never recover. I said, 'Don't be ridiculous. Keep calm.' Like all these Tories he panics so easily.

Sunday 4 March
I was knocked back this evening when I was talking to Margaret. We had been discussing the mood in the country and the anti feeling there is against her in the BBC, ITV and also, I said, among many journalists in the newspapers.

When I said to her that people are very ungrateful and look how they treated Churchill (mind you, they did that because they thought the Conservative Party had made a terrible mess of things socially and economically before the War) she said, 'It's me they don't like. It always has been. I don't expect any gratitude in politics.'

She said, 'I am sure I will be able to win it for the last time. I'll have one great effort at it.' I said, 'Why do you say "for the last time"?' She said, 'Because after that I wouldn't be able to go on for a further term because the press wouldn't let me. They won't take me any more.' I said, 'I wouldn't agree with that. You mustn't talk like that.' She said, 'Well I think that's the case.'

I was very sad. Always when I have said, 'You've got to go on for another ten years until I am dead,' she has laughed and said, 'Yes.' It will change again, the tide will turn in her favour, as I told her it would, because they'll get tired of Thatcher bashing and realize what they'd be losing and the life they have been having.

I spoke to Andrew Knight who had been trying to get hold of me. He thinks whether the arrangement with Rupert works or not depends on Rupert not interfering, as he says he won't, and leaving him to make mistakes without complaining. I said, 'He won't exactly do that you know. He'll certainly interfere if it's a matter of serious policy for the newspapers or a change of editor or something like that.' He said, 'I would expect him to be concerned about that.'

I certainly hope Rupert won't hand it all over to Andrew Knight. There might be some nasty surprises if he does. I don't think Andrew has really got newspapers in his blood at all. He has a certain mechanical, useful approach to the administration of them, though that didn't work when he merged the *Daily Telegraph* and the *Sunday Telegraph* into one seven-day continuous newspaper. He presents himself very well and convincingly but I am not sure that he is up to the category of the figure he offers to the world.

Today in his *Sunday Times* article Brian Walden said I was wrong to encourage Mrs Thatcher to be optimistic in my articles. I should say to her that things were very bad and she should do things to meet the criticisms. His main item was that education should be taken away from local authorities and run by the central government to vastly reduce the community charge. That's a really cuckoo idea because there would be very little parental or local influence on the schools. It would all come straight from Whitehall in the worst form of bureaucracy. I would call that somewhat anti-democratic.

Tuesday 6 March
A jolly Tote Lunch.

On my right was David Waddington, the Home Secretary. On my left was Douglas Hurd. Both very friendly. Douglas said they were nearly late because they had to get away from the Prime Minister. He said they were having a very private discussion and he couldn't tell me what it was about. I said, 'Was it about Hong Kong?' and he laughed and said yes.

We all three thought that in three months or so the community charge rumpus would be forgotten.

Douglas said he was talking to the Duke of Marlborough just before lunch but he didn't dare ask him if he was going to be like the other aristocrats, Henry Bath and the Duke of Westminster, who were going to pay the community charge for all their various employees. I said, 'Well I will ask him.' When Sonny Marlborough rang up about the question of his being a member of the Tote Board, I said, 'Someone was talking to me who didn't dare ask you this question I am going to ask you.' He said, 'Yes. I am going to pay the community charge for all the employees on the estate and including in the house. This business about the butler paying the same as the Duke is nonsensical.'

When I said to Robin Cook at the end of the proceedings, 'Did you see from my speech that I am beginning to rather like you?', he said, 'Thank you very much but please don't put that in your column. It wouldn't do me any good at all.'

Wednesday 7 March

Just before our dinner party began Allan rang up, very dejected. The man who controls a few theatres in London, the last ones suitable for us, had read the play and said he would prefer to do other plays to ours. Allan in total despair.

I was shattered. I felt like crying. All those years of work come to nothing. No doubt it was the bungling of Bromley which was the real undoing. But the way the audiences laughed at Margate, which is not a theatre-going audience, convinced me we have really got a good play which would run well, as Bernard Levin has always said it would, in London.

Conrad Black and his pretty, lively wife, Shirley Black, came to dinner. She has fairish hair and nice legs. She likes to show her thighs a bit. She is chirpy. She regards Canada as her home and one of her children is at boarding school there. She looks about twenty-six but actually she is somewhat over forty, if not more.

On the other side was Mrs Michael Howard. She had been married four times. The first time to Robin Douglas-Home who used to play the piano.[1]

She must be about fiftyish. She has a son of twenty-four. She is still extremely pretty, blondeish with nice legs but a little faded in the face. She is not too keen on politics and the constituency work but she goes

---

1. Sandra, née Paul, m (1975) Michael Howard, Conservative politician, Secretary of State for Employment since January 1990; Robin Douglas-Home was the nephew of the former Prime Minister, Alec Douglas-Home, and brother of Charles Douglas-Home (editor of the *Times*, who died of cancer in 1985); Alan Clark says in *Diaries*, p. 85, that Robin was 'brilliant on the accordion'; he committed suicide.

along. She doesn't like Mrs Thatcher but she respects her greatly. She says she uses her femininity very strongly and takes no notice of the wives because they can do nothing for her. I said, 'I think that is not quite true. She is very concerned about their ills and troubles.'

Conrad Black was in a much less pompous or bombastic mood than usual. He warned against Andrew Knight being allowed to have so much to do with the tabloid papers because he doesn't understand them. He thought he was good at the high quality papers. He also said that though he had done well in many respects, it was simply not true that he was the main reason that they had begun to make real money at the *Telegraph*. He was less bitter about him than he had been and had quite calmed down.

I asked him to see Julian Lewis[2] who is worried that Max Hastings [editor of the *Telegraph*] has stopped the flow of good pro-Tory, anti-Militant and anti-Labour stories which used to go to the paper. He has been told that he is only to send press releases and that is not the way to get good stories developed.

Friday 9 March

David Sieff[3] came to see me.

Brian [McDonnell] explained to him all the finances and at the end he was quite happy and said he would like to join the Tote Board, if the Home Secretary agreed. He is a nice fellow, quite tall with a sort of aquiline, Jewish nose. I told him I wanted him because of his interest in racing, because of his knowledge of customer relations from his experience at Marks & Spencer, which I thought could be valuable to us, and because I like him.

In the evening the Pejacsevichs came for dinner and to play bridge.

Livia, my sister-in-law from Hungary was there. She is a sweet girl. Though younger than Verushka by two years she looks somewhat older having not had such an easy life nor the advantages of aids to beauty. She is a good bridge player.

---

2. Deputy director, Conservative Research Department, 1990–6.
3. The Hon. David Sieff, a director of Marks & Spencer; president, Racehorse Owners Association, 1975–8; member, Jockey Club, from 1977; on the board of Newbury Racecourse from 1988.

Saturday 10 March

Had a very jolly dinner with Rupert at the Stafford Hotel.

It is Rupert's birthday tomorrow. We had a delicious champagne first and then we shared some Château Lafite 1976.

Rupert is still madly in favour of Mrs Thatcher, though his newspaper the next day was carrying a poll of Tory MPs saying over a quarter thought she ought to go. He blamed a lot on the community charge.

I said, 'When you were asking about Simon Jenkins being an editor, what were you thinking of? Surely not *Today* or the *Sunday Times*?' He said, 'No, the *Times* itself.' I said, 'He might be able to do it but what would you do with poor Charlie Wilson? He is very good technically.' He said, 'I would have to give him some other kind of a job.'

I told him he must promote more and more Sky Television through sport. 'Are you going to have a go at buying Wimbledon?' He said not this year but, 'We will get it set up for next year.'[4]

Sunday 11 March

To Chevening where Douglas Hurd has his official country house residence. It was a pleasant day, mild. It is a lovely house. Inigo Jones basically.

I talked to Douglas in the garden. I asked him about all the trouble there is supposed to be in the Cabinet and he said it was absolute nonsense and he knew nothing about it. That was Lamont's point, too. He said they seem to be a very happy Cabinet.

He said he has no disagreements with Margaret on foreign policy. I said, 'One has to nudge her a bit in the right direction, like being more positive about German reunification.' He said that he'd done that and I said that I'd done that and now she is doing it: 'She recognizes that you were right.' He said, 'No, she never recognizes that. She just does it and behaves as though it was her idea all the time.'

Monday 12 March

In the morning I spoke to Margaret. I suggested Trefgarne[5] as Secretary of State for Wales to succeed Peter Walker. She asked about Trefgarne and I said, 'He is not bad. It is nice for the Lords to have a proper

---

4. The Wimbledon Championship is still televised by the BBC.
5. Minister of State, Department of Trade and Industry, 1989–90.

Cabinet Minister there.' She said, 'I don't think not bad is good enough.' Bang goes his little dream. She is probably right. I said, 'What about Garel-Jones?' She said, 'Is he Welsh?' and I said, 'Yes of course he is.' She said she would think about that.

She was in very good heart and said, 'I had another battering this weekend. I am getting used to it.'

Tuesday 13 March
Charlie Wilson has been sacked as editor of the *Times*. I feel very sorry for him. He was a good, pedestrian, lay-out newspaperman. His foreign coverage was not at all bad but, as Rupert and I discussed many times, he hasn't got the intellectual depth to write authoritative leaders. Simon Jenkins is to take his place, as discussed previously with Rupert.

He is well known to Andrew Knight because they had worked together on the *Economist*. I hope he will do it well and give the *Times* a bit of a lift. It needs one.

I was rather amused in one respect because we had thought of using his wife, Gayle Hunnicutt, the pretty American actress, in my play. We tried to get her on the telephone in America several times. That was before Margate. Then Allan had said she was not a very good actress anyway so we were quite relaxed about it. Maybe we should have another try because we would get a good review in the *Times*.

We took Livia, my sister-in-law, to dinner in the Barry Room at the House of Lords. Before we left I went to speak to Alexander Hesketh sitting at the long table where only peers sit. He was on his second bottle of Gevrey-Chambertin and going loud and strong.

He said, 'I have got somebody to buy "The Three Graces" for the nation.' I said, 'Where is it going to be?' and he said, 'In the Scottish National Museum.'

I said, 'That means that Jacob's scheme won't operate.' He said, 'No. It is a great snub for Jacob.'

Wednesday 14 March
I asked Rupert how Charlie Wilson took it. 'Like a gentleman who has just been hit in the stomach,' he replied. I said he had made a very good dignified statement and it sounded as if he was looking forward to his new role in charge of European development, particularly in Eastern Europe.

Went to Cheltenham by myself.

After doing all my rounds in the lovely sunshine – I didn't even need my pullover after a bit, let alone an overcoat – I went up to the Royal Box. Was I expected? They wanted to know at the entrance and I said yes, which certainly wasn't true because I hadn't told them I was coming. There was Queen Elizabeth the Queen Mother who greeted me enthusiastically.

We talked about *Spanish Gold* which I sent her, only a paperback but it's one of the funniest of the George A. Birmingham books.[6] She said she had absolutely adored it. She thinks she read it as a child but she couldn't remember it. She said, 'I enjoyed it so much I gave it to the Queen to take to New Zealand and it helped her through the visit. She adored it.'

Thursday 15 March
After all that drink [at dinner with the Earl and Countess of Suffolk] I woke up feeling pretty grim. We had had Mouton-Rothschild '59 and then Mouton-Rothschild '62 and a Filhot at the end. Fantastic. So was the 1972 Veuve Clicquot. And the port, 1963 Berry Brothers, was extremely good.

In the morning Micky told me that we had drunk nine bottles among seven people plus nearly all the magnum of the '72 champagne. As there were four ladies to three men, and the ladies didn't drink so much, we must have had a colossal amount.

Rosalind Morrison[7] was looking very pretty and sexy. She curled up on the sofa beside me and I could feel the sex coming out of her. She's about fifty, fair, with a very good figure, tall, about three or four inches taller than I am. I said, 'How did you come to marry Charlie?' and she said she just liked him. I said, 'He is a new man now.'

I sat next to Queen Elizabeth the Queen Mother at lunch. Opposite us was Charlie Allsopp, a senior partner or director at Christie's. He is an amusing fellow, young (fifty?) with a bright dark face, tall and slim and his face is neat and narrow with fairly dark hair on top of it. His wife is very pretty, extremely dark, with blue eyes and black hair. I asked if she was Italian which I shouldn't have done because I had

---

6. George A. Birmingham was the pen name of James Owen Hannay (1865–1950), an Irish clergyman. *Spanish Gold* (1908), about a red-haired curate, was the humorous novel which gained him a wide readership.

7. Rosalind, née Lygon, m 1 (1967–83) Gerald Ward, m 2 (1984) the Hon. Sir Charles Morrison (Conservative politician, previously married (1954–84) to the Hon. Sara Morrison); they separated in 1999.

met her several times, but she reminded me of an Italian. Her legs are rather thick below the knee and slightly bow-legged, but you can't have everything.

Queen Elizabeth and I rattled away and Charlie suddenly said, 'What a marvellous double act you both are. You ought to be on television.'

Queen Elizabeth said, 'I don't think we would like that at all. We wouldn't be able to talk like we do now.'

We talked for some time about Mrs Thatcher. 'Can't you get her to be more flexible?' she asked. She is devoted to Mrs Thatcher but fears she is not getting her good points across and that is why she is in trouble. Referring to the community charge, Queen Elizabeth said the British don't like too many changes. They like to be left more or less alone. She shouldn't have done all this legislation in her third term but just let things go on. I said, 'It is very difficult because she is a revolutionary or she is nothing.'

She said, 'I know how compassionate she is. After all, that time when Whitehall had been delaying and objecting, she made them give the war widows an improvement on their pensions and that was a wonderful thing for her to do. I know how good she is with people. When she was at Balmoral recently she came to tea with me in the little house I have there – she always does that. My Andrew (meaning her grandson the Duke of York) was there and he asked all kinds of questions and told her a tremendous amount of details about some naval ship which had been done wrong and should have been done in a different way. She listened very patiently and also she asked a lot of questions. When he had gone, I said to her, "I am so sorry Andrew bothered you so much with all those difficult and perhaps unimportant details," and Mrs Thatcher said, "Oh no. I never hear all these details. It is a great pleasure for me to have them and wonder what I can do about it." '

I told her the story of how I had met Mrs Thatcher and gone to Flood Street to talk to her just after she had become leader of the Tory Party. I had told her I would support her because what she was going to do reminded me of Hugh Gaitskell. I had supported her ever since.

I told her what we had had to drink the night before and she said, 'Good gracious, what a marvellous time you must have had. How wonderful. I am surprised you look so well today.' I said, 'I didn't feel well when I got up. I looked in the mirror and saw these awful bags under my eyes and thought I am going to meet you today and what on earth will you say.' She clapped her hands and laughed.

The race was won by Norton's Coin.

The horse comes from Wales and the owner hadn't even had a bet on it.

He was marvellously shy and bewildered and thrilled. It was a pity, no doubt, that Desert Orchid lost but it was very good for racing that a horse which cost about £200 and which he had bred himself had beaten everybody.

It was a marvellous day for the Tote itself. We took nearly £2 million on the whole day which beat our previous records.

Prince Michael was there in the Royal Box. He had come out into the paddock before the race. Before the prize-giving he said to me, 'Do you think I should come to the prize-giving? There will be a lot of people there, won't there?' I said, 'Just as you like.' He didn't come. He is rather timid.

I think there is not a great deal between the ears, as Andrew Parker-Bowles[8] always said to me. I had said, 'Yes, but he can speak Russian and he is not wholly without brains,' which Andrew didn't believe. Andrew Parker Bowles moves very much in court society and knows it all in and out.

Because of Petronella holding me up before I went, trying to write some of her Peterborough column in the Royal Box which I disapproved of (and I had said to her that I wanted to vet what she was going to say about conversations with Royalty because she must not repeat them; one is not allowed to say anything about them at all), we got started rather late. Instead of going home to Cavendish Avenue I went straight to The Other Club.

Duke Hussey was there.

He said, 'I am very grateful to you for having written that [about the *Today* programme]. It has certainly done much good and has helped us a lot. Checkland is no good at all. I thought he was going to be but he isn't. I told you it will take ten years and I have only been there four.' Michael Checkland is the Director General and John Birt is the Deputy Director General of the BBC.

Nicholas Soames said, 'A new doctrine was laid down at the 1922

---

8. Former Army officer, divorced from Camilla, née Shand, the Prince of Wales's friend, in 1995.

Committee today. It was, 'You must put loyalty above principle.' I replied, 'That sounds like a very good principle to me.'

I gave Arnold Weinstock a lift to Grosvenor Square which was a nuisance.

I had wanted to dictate something about The Other Club in private.

I normally like to do it within an hour or so of things happening and sometimes quicker.

Friday 16 March
Rupert rang from his car.

He wanted to know how she was reacting from the terrible polls, even worse ones today, and to the poll which said that Labour were twenty-one per cent ahead of the Tories in the by-election at Mid Staffordshire which was a safe seat with a Tory majority of fourteen thousand.

I told him that BSB [British Satellite Broadcasting] have asked me to be on their panel of commentators in the Robin Day programme which they are setting up for a twelve week period. I said, 'Would you have any objection?' 'No, not at all,' he said, 'they have got plenty of money. Relieve them of as much of it as you can.'

At five o'clock Allan Davis came with two of the men who have got a management business for the theatre. They wanted me to find or raise £30,000 so they could take a ten week tour of *High Profiles* to various parts of the country. Then, if it caught on, it might be able to get to London.

The more I think about it the more disinclined I am to try and raise money from friends when it will probably never even come to London. It was different when I got my first three to put up £10,500. There was a fair chance of it coming to London.

Julian Lewis has thanked me for putting him in touch with Conrad Black. It is all now going swimmingly. He is having dinner with the man at the *Telegraph* to whom he is to supply stories and who will develop them.

Sunday 18 March
'How are you?' Margaret cried cheerfully. I said, 'I am fine but how are you?' She answered, 'Whistling to keep my spirits up.' I said, 'You don't have to do that, darling. It is going to be all right in the long run. I am convinced of it. It is just a terrible patch at the moment.'

She said she was furious with the newspapers again this morning when they said that she was getting the 1922 Committee to alter the rules about any leadership challenge. She said, 'It is nothing to do with me. They want to devise new rules themselves. They are quite sensible.' Then she said, 'No one likes Heseltine. No Department he has ever been in liked him.' I said, 'If he did stand against you in this famous leadership contest, he wouldn't win it. They would never support him.'

I said I think we have to resign ourselves to losing Mid Staffordshire. But remember Orpington.[9] It will all reverse itself eventually.

I really love that girl. She has fought so valiantly. It would be terrible to lose after all the marvellous things she has done to improve the economy which is far stronger than it ever was.

Tuesday 20 March

In this morning's papers there is great indignation about an attack on the Royal Family issued on Iraq television. Princess Diana was accused of being a playgirl before marrying the Prince of Wales. That is nonsense. But Sarah Ferguson had an affair with Paddy McNally. He is very rich and spent a lot of money on her because she never had a penny. They used to have parties with drug taking and she was actually photographed rolling joints.

The accusation that Princess Anne had affairs and actually had one with an equerry at Buckingham Palace is also true. I am surprised they didn't include her [alleged] affair with the security officer.

It is perfectly true that the morals of the Royal Family in a conventional sense are pretty low. Maybe Diana has the odd affair now. I imagine she does, poor child. It must be hell living with that stiff, introspective man.

John and Diana Wilton came to dinner. The drawing-room door was open when I came downstairs and Verushka said to me before I had even seen them inside, 'Isabel Derby is dead.' I screamed at the top of my voice, 'Oh no. No.' I couldn't believe it. It is an unbearable thought.

She had only just come back from Dominica where they had been on holiday. Two heart attacks. The second was a massive one which finished her off. She had been smoking far too much.

Derby was completely broken up when it happened.

She is to be buried at Knowsley.

---

9. Eric Lubbock won Orpington for the Liberal Party in a sensational by-election victory in 1962, but the Conservatives won it back in 1970.

I was stunned and shaken all the evening. Isabel, with her love of dirty stories, asking if I had got any new ones. Elegant walk, slightly haughty attitude to most people. Her pungent comments and her sense of humour. Her generous heart. Her naughty attacks on Jews as well as Arabs. They were so mischievously done that I laughed rather than told her not to be anti-semitic. Her contempt for the Royal Family, 'those Germans'. Her always walking with me down to the paddock before the start of the Derby while her husband walked with the Queen. I would say to her, 'Who is that man walking with the Queen?' She said, 'Oh you mean that man with those Germans.'

She was quite a saucy girl in her earlier days when she was very lovely. Her great affair was with the younger Max Aitken, Beaver-brook's son. I said, 'He was a rather simple minded fellow,' and Diana said, 'But he was extremely handsome and charming,' which is true. I dare say the sex worked very well.

Dear, darling Isabel with my ignorance of horses and our going into the paddocks together and standing at the outside rather more often than going inside. She would laugh at my descriptions of the horses. I don't think I ever want to go to the Derby again. She was full of laughter and we had such funny times when she would bring a little house party over to Newmarket for the 2,000 Guineas into the Tote entertainment room, and for the Tote Cesarewitch. I shall never feel the same again about Epsom or Newmarket. There will be a great emptiness. I felt, 'What is the point of my trying to improve the world by my articles in the *News of the World* and the *Times* when the people I love die? They won't be there.'

Wednesday 21 March
Spoke to Margaret.

We talked of John Major and I said, 'He will make a good successor for you one day when I allow you to go, if I ever do.' She laughed and said, 'Yes. He is the one I have in mind.'

Then came the news from Caroline [Banszky] at Rothschild's that Victor died last night. It was very sudden. He had sent his chauffeur home for the evening and was sitting at home in London at his desk and he went out like a light.

I rang Jacob. He said he was going to be buried in the City, in the tomb he had just discovered, after many researches, of the original N. M. Rothschild who had started the whole damn thing. I said I was very fond of him, though, 'I would get cross with him when he was unfair to you and behaved badly.' Jacob said, 'He was very fond of you. He often said so. You were one of the few people who made him really laugh. He always looked forward to seeing you.' I shall have to write a letter to Tess. I remember a typical Victor gesture when Verushka at dinner said she couldn't find her cigarette lighter and he sent her a hundred for Christmas.

I went to that haven of peace and tranquillity, the chamber of the House of Lords. Alec Home moved a debate on foreign affairs. Graceful compliments to Michael Stewart's incisive mind who died the other day.[10] I never found his mind incisive. I always thought he was an indifferent Minister and not much good as Foreign Secretary. His only capacity was to learn a brief from the civil servants which I found him doing when I took his place as Under Secretary of War in 1951. I would always have been a far better minister than him but the way the cookie crumbled, with Hugh Gaitskell dying and Wilson succeeding, I never had the chance.

Thursday 22 March
Setbacks and gloom. Isabel and Victor gone add to the depression.

Went down to the Lords and sat in the chamber for a little while before going to the meeting on the Broadcasting Bill. Willie Whitelaw and Alec Home were sitting a few feet away from where I sat on the crossbenches. They were deep in conversation. I caught a few words here and there: 'very depressing' etc. They were obviously talking about the troubles in the Conservative Party. As they seemed to be agreeing, I had the feeling that Willie Whitelaw might not stay faithful to Margaret whom *au fond* he has never really liked. That's because Alec said to me at The Other Club that it was time that she went, as I have noted before in this manuscript.[11] When these old battleaxes in the Tory Party start muttering together at such a senior level, there can be real trouble.

Spoke to Margaret. I said, 'Oddly enough, I thought the Mid Staffordshire by-election could have been worse.'

She said, 'How strange you should say that. That was what I was thinking. The number of pledged votes we had, and we did a very thorough canvass, was much less than we actually got in the end.'

It was in fact a swing of some twenty-one per cent against the

---

10. (1906–90); Labour politician, Foreign Secretary, 1965–6 and 1968–70; life peer 1979.
11. On 22 February 1990.

Tories. But of course, as I said to her, in 1933 in the famous Fulham by-election there was just as big a swing against the Tories and they won the 1935 election by a hundred and thirty-three seats.

I said, 'That is the British people all over. They vote only with their pockets. You could have a revolution in Lithuania every day of the week but they wouldn't take any notice. They'd simply be saying they have another tuppence to pay on the community charge.'

Friday 23 March *In Hungary*
The building where I went to see the *Magyar Hirlap* editor, Peter Nemeth, was like an old Italian palace. Beautiful ceilings, fantastic courtyards with a marvellous elaborate fountain and well sculptured figures standing in the middle.

The editor was neat and small and Jewish, with a keen, interesting, dark face and sparkling eyes. He thought there was a little anti-semitism in the Democratic Forum but not much. He wants the Democratic Forum and the Alliance of Free Democrats to get enough support in the elections to be the basis of a coalition government.[12]

They are very lucky in Budapest because they have had no money to rebuild and tear down all the lovely old buildings.

Now they are going to get some money, so with a lick of paint and some refacing of many of the buildings it will look again one of the most beautiful cities in the West, if not the most beautiful with its marvellous situation on the Danube, rising on both sides from it.

Saturday 24 March
A jolly lunch with the editor-in-chief and Rupert Murdoch's partner (fifty per cent each) in *Reform*, the magazine which sells over four hundred thousand a week. His name is Peter Toke.

He is very plump with a round face, looking rather like Pozsgay. He ate prodigiously.

Highly animated, lively, adventurous and a true entrepreneur.

This chap, Toke, is well in with all the political parties and the government. He has made an enormous success of his newspaper.

He brought with him a very pretty secretary, tallish, curly hair and a possibly natural blonde. She had hazel eyes. She had a neat waist

---

12. They emerged as the front runners for the second round of the elections on 8 April.

but a biggish bottom, it seemed, but she was wearing trousers. Maybe it is not as big when she takes the trousers off.

He kept putting his arm on her shoulder, etc. She blushed deeply when I was asking her about the nudes in *Reform*. We had been talking about Anna Murdoch's dislike of them when she had been in Budapest. I said to the editor, 'Are you taking any notice of Anna?' and he said, 'No.' The girl said, 'Hungarian men like to look at nice girls,' and I replied, 'All men do.'

Last year three hundred newspapers started. Half went bankrupt. His is very unlikely to do so and it will make a lot of money for Rupert.

Wednesday 28 March
I am disturbed by the state of the strength of the anti-Rupert feeling over the Broadcasting Bill. I am worried that in the Lords it might be possible that the government is defeated by an amendment requiring people with newspaper ownership not to be allowed to own satellite television stations, even though they may be broadcasting from outside the country. It would be retrospective legislation. Certainly Labour would do that if they came in.

The inaugural programme of the newly devised Robin Day programme for BSB.

The idea is for three people to state a view on a topic they are interested in and be questioned by Robin about it. Then the others barge in and argue with Robin and with the chap who led off the particular item. There is no live studio audience.

I was first offered £150 and I said that was pretty small. As a result the fees went up to £200 a time, which is not much after forty per cent tax – £120 for several hours.

The other two were Nicko Henderson, who used to be Ambassador in America, Bonn and goodness knows where else,[13] and Anthony Howard, lately assistant editor of the *Observer*.[14]

It was like the old days when I used to do *Panorama* and other programmes for the BBC.

---

13. Sir Nicholas Henderson, diplomat.*
14. Deputy editor, *Observer*, 1981–8; at this time BBC TV reporter on *Panorama* and *Newsnight*; obituaries editor, *Times*, 1993–9.

Thursday 29 March
Dinner with the Stelzers at the Connaught Hotel.

Rupert and Anna came, having just got off the Concorde, Anna looking very youthful and bright and very friendly. Rupert immediately got me into a corner to discuss urgently the advertisements he intends to put into the papers to attack the BSB people.

I said, 'I agree with part of your newspaper campaign but you have got to get the nuances right.' Photographs of the BSB Board – 'These are the men who couldn't get it up' – are funny but the wrong nuance.

Saturday 31 March
Went to see Rupert at 5.30 to talk about Sky Television.

I had to get out of the car Verushka was driving because there was an enormous blockage in the road. One could hear the police sirens and ambulances and just faintly see them rushing up and down. When I got to Piccadilly, the traffic was not moving. I crossed the road and found myself among a number of scruffy-looking people but not unduly violent in appearance or manner. Some were carrying anti-poll tax placards. They looked stupid and bovine and had no doubt come up to enjoy themselves in the free buses provided by the anti-poll tax demonstrators.

When I got to Rupert's flat I found Anna there alone. She had been sun-bathing and sleeping on her balcony. Then Rupert rang to say he was going to be late because he couldn't get through the traffic from Wapping. I talked to Anna for some time, about three-quarters of an hour. She was looking very pretty even though she hadn't done herself up to receive visitors, as she said. She wears very well with her fair skin and her blue eyes from Estonia.

Rupert eventually arrived. On television were scenes of utmost violence in Trafalgar Square by the anti-poll tax demonstrators. About three and a half thousand, either from the Socialist Workers Party or from various brands of anarchists and militants, had come to make trouble. Looting of shops had begun and the whole of the centre of the Piccadilly area and up Shaftesbury Avenue was full of youths smashing shop windows and goodness knows what else. It won't do Labour any good.

We talked a long time about how to combat the attempts of BSB to make Rupert divest himself of all but twenty per cent of ownership of Sky Television on the grounds that he controls thirty-six per cent of the newspaper circulation in the country.

I said, 'Your line should be that you broke up the monopoly at Wapping of newspapers in trade union power and enabled new newspapers to come. You are now doing the same with the satellite programmes. You own three satellite stations. There will be forty-two in the end and the more the merrier. There is no reason why anybody should be afraid of that, whether you are the proprietor of newspapers or not.'

While we were talking he rang the *News of the World* several times and started giving them directions as to how to deal with the Trafalgar Square riots on the front page and things they ought to put in.

He did not sound as if he was exactly 'hands off' when he was talking to the acting editor of the *News of the World* today.

I told him I was fairly confident that he would be all right when the Bill came to the Lords because it is now backed by the government. 'Margaret is very keen on preserving your position. She knows how much she depends on your support. Likewise you depend on hers in this matter. She is not worried about the little stations and what they do because there will be so many of them. The concern is what the big five do, BBC1 and 2, Channel 3 and 4 and now the new Channel 5.'

I said, 'Margaret will never stand down as long as she thinks she will win a leadership contest by one vote. She is a conviction politician.'

Rupert needs to get about two and a half million with the ability to watch Sky before it turns the corner and begins to make profit. I am beginning to think he may succeed but I had grave doubts when he started the enterprise.

Sunday 1 April

Told Margaret I thought she had made a very good speech at her Cheltenham Conservative Conference on Saturday and that Rupert was ecstatic about it.

'Were the jokes all yours?' She said, 'No. A couple came from (Sir) Ronald Millar (the playwright) and another from John O'Sullivan. We were working on that speech till three a.m. on Saturday morning.' 'It was well worth it,' I replied, 'and you looked very striking and handsome and well in command and very effective.' She said, 'I thought I had to try and put a stop to all these rumours about a challenge to the leadership.'

She was exercised about the violence in Trafalgar Square on Saturday evening.

I said, 'We have been very unlucky at getting the difficulties about the community charge, which we always knew would happen, mixed up with the high interest rates and mortgage rates. The two at once is a lot to take. But you mustn't be squeamish about making concessions or readjustments in the next year. It has to be done because your winning the next election is the most important thing of all.' She agreed.

We had a bit of an argument about Lithuania. I said, 'I think it is terrible that we are not giving the Lithuanians the support they want.' She started off again about the Helsinki Agreement which had recognized the frontiers. I said, 'Yes but it didn't recognize the theft and rape of the Baltic states by Stalin.' She immediately burst in with, 'It makes it very difficult for Gorbachev. These things take time. He must go slowly.'

I said, 'I don't think it matters if the Soviet Union does break up. It is their problem, not ours.' She said, 'I think we have to be very careful. There would be anarchy and we have to give him what support we can.' It was clear we could not agree on this matter.

I said, 'Whatever you do, don't appoint the Archbishop of York

(Habgood) to succeed Runcie [as Archbishop of Canterbury].' She said, 'He said he doesn't want to be considered.'

I said, 'It used to be said that the Church of England was the Tory Party at prayer. Now it is the Labour Party at propaganda.' She said, 'Oh, what a wonderful phrase.' She is obviously going to trade on that one and use it.

Monday 2 April

To dinner with Marie-Louise de Zulueta, Philip's widow.[1]

Arnold Weinstock was there with Netta.

Lady Aldington[2] said to me, 'Couldn't you write an article about giving up gracefully as Prime Minister?' I said, 'Certainly not. She will not give up and I will advise her not to.'

Arnold was at his most disloyal, attacking her, saying she had been there far too long and that she must go otherwise there will be a Labour government; in any case he wouldn't mind if there were because this government is so terrible. At this point I had a bet with him of £50 that she will win the next election.

Netta said that in the summer, and Arnold agreed, Willie Whitelaw was going to go to her and say, 'You must go now because your time is up. You are too unpopular.'

Even Toby [Aldington], who declared himself as a loyalist, thinks she ought to go. But he has been out of serious politics for quite a long time.

But there is no doubt about it, there is a lot of feeling against Margaret, simply because she is unpopular over the community charge and with the high interest rates.

Of course Arnold is deeply swayed by Sara Morrison[3] who hates Mrs Thatcher and drips poison in his ear all the time. He is also annoyed with Nicholas Ridley in the Department of Trade and Industry and some junior Minister there who won't do precisely what he wants.

---

1. The Hon. Marie-Louise, née Windlesham, m (1955) Philip de Zulueta (1925–89), diplomat, Private Secretary to Prime Ministers Anthony Eden, Harold Macmillan and Sir Alec Douglas-Home; knight 1963.
2. Araminta Bowman, née MacMichael, m (1947) Toby Low, Conservative politician, chairman, GEC, 1964–8 (deputy chairman, 1968–84), life peer (Lord Aldington) 1962.
3. A director of Weinstock's firm GEC since 1980, she was vice-chairman of the Conservative Party Organization, 1971–5, when Edward Heath was Prime Minister.

There was a bit of talk about George Weidenfeld. Alexander Stockton[4] said his business in America had completely collapsed and they were looking for somebody to buy it. The Getty heiress was told by her husband to stop putting any more money on her plaything. She had already lost £12 million according to Alexander, which was probably an exaggeration. He said George is not doing very well in England either. He uses his publishing business to spend money on advancing his social life. 'Whereas we,' said Alexander, 'use our social lives to advance our publishing business.' I think that was supposed to be funny or smart but it didn't seem to make a lot of sense to me.

Alexander's children are the rich heirs because the trusts were arranged to bypass both Maurice and his son, Alexander, and go straight to the grandchildren, or the great-grandchildren.

Tuesday 3 April
I decided to ring Bernard Ingham to tell him about Alec Home and Willie Whitelaw and what was said about him [Whitelaw] plotting in the summer. I said, 'What do you think I ought to do? I don't feel like upsetting her now.'

Bernard said perhaps I might mention it to her gently. I said, 'What I don't want to have happen is for Willie to ask to see her and she will think it is just going to be a friendly chat – and then he is going to throw a bomb in her face.' He said, 'Of course it is so silly because the strong polling evidence underneath is that she is our strongest asset.'

Wednesday 4 April
Spoke to Alexander Hesketh in the Lords and asked if he had heard any curious plots going on. He wanted to know what I meant. I said, 'I think Alec Home and Whitelaw are up to no good.' So he said he didn't know about that and he would put his spies on. He is sometimes quite good at that.

I was rung in the car by Brian McDonnell. A woman had rung him. She said she was speaking from Clarence House and Queen Elizabeth the Queen Mother wanted to go to a betting shop so where was the nearest Tote betting shop because she wanted to put some bets on for the Grand National.

Then Mr McDonnell had a conversation with Mrs Tamborero

---

4. 2nd Earl of Stockton, grandson of Harold Macmillan.*

[WW's secretary] and they both concluded it was all very fishy because if that was what the Queen Mother really wanted to do, Martin Gilliat, the Private Secretary, would ring up. So then they rang to check at Clarence House. The answer was they had never heard of her and it was all an absolute hoax. It turned out she was a reporter from the *Today* newspaper.

I then rang up David Montgomery [editor of *Today*].

He went into a lot of apologies. I said, 'Why did she do it?' He said, 'Just to test you.' and I said, 'What on earth do you mean, to test me?' He said, 'We were trying to find out how people bet and are betting for the Grand National.'

I said, 'Well one thing I can assure you, and this is off the record, is that I have been often with Queen Elizabeth the Queen Mother at race meetings, particularly at jump meetings, and she is only interested in how the horses perform, particularly her own horse when she's got a runner, which she likes to see win. But I have never noticed any sign of her putting on a bet or even wanting to or even wanting to know the price they start at.'

He said, 'I won't print anything to embarrass you.' I said, 'Don't print anything to embarrass the Queen Mother either because it really isn't fair or sensible,' so he promised he wouldn't.

At the beginning of the [Tote] board meeting, Priscilla Hastings said she had to go to the memorial service for Robin Hastings who was the heir presumptive to Jack Huntingdon before he died. She was a sort of cousin-in-law to me now, if she wasn't already, because her son, William Hastings Bass, will now be the presumptive heir to Jack.

Prince Michael started getting interested and I said, 'The Earl of Huntingdon is really the King of England. He is the senior male surviving Plantagenet and when he dies my son will be the senior male surviving Plantagenet, but because the title does not go through the female line he will not be the Earl of Huntingdon.'

So everybody got very amused and I said to the Prince, 'Don't worry, Sir. I am not going to start a campaign to put my son on the throne.'[5]

To dinner at 100 Eaton Place with the new Lady Stevens of Ludgate, the Italian lady.[6]

---

5. Pericles' mother Moorea, WW's third wife, is the daughter of the 15th Earl of Huntingdon (Jack), hence the relationship.
6. Lord Stevens m 3 (1990) Meriza Giori.

I said to David Stevens, 'How is your new marriage going? Are you happy?' 'So far,' he said, 'but it is very expensive.' I laughed. He said she wants all kinds of new furniture and things he can't afford and I laughed again.

The American Ambassador, Catto, was there. He is not a very exciting man but we had a fascinating discussion about Mrs Thatcher and President Bush. I said, 'Has the special relationship gone?' He said, 'In a sense that there was a special relationship between Reagan and Mrs Thatcher. She was very experienced and he was inexperienced and didn't have much intellect so she was able to persuade him to follow her line without too much difficulty. But Bush is very experienced and very intelligent and wants to follow his own line.'

He also defended the position of Bush and Mrs Thatcher on Lithuania.

I said, 'By not backing these people (the Baltics) we are behaving just as badly as Chamberlain.' I wonder whether she, Margaret, is not a bit influenced by Bush on this issue because she doesn't want to have a split.

Friday 6 April
Rupert rang from New York.

He said he thought that if Heseltine stood against her, he would win it. I said, 'Nonsense. Not enough Tory MPs would back him.' He said, 'But he is very popular in the country.' I said, 'So is she in the grass roots of the party.'

Sunday 8 April
Reading the *Sunday Times* editorial this morning I see why Rupert rang me up on Friday night. It is full of all that nonsense about bringing Heseltine back to the government, getting rid of Ridley, making Walker Chairman of the Conservative Party, some kind of tripe about the new business rates alienating all Tory sympathizers in the south and so on and so on. Both the *Times* and the *Sunday Times* now have editors who are daft about the community charge and cannot understand it.

Told Margaret that Arnold Weinstock had said at the dinner last Monday that Willie Whitelaw would go to see her some time in the summer and ask her to stand down. I myself thought that, if that was the case, Alec Douglas-Home had something to do with it.

'That would be devastating,' she said. 'It would be terrible. It would be in the newspapers and it would be very difficult to cope with.' Then she thought for a few moments and said, 'I must take some time to think of a pre-emptive strike.'

She said, 'What you say may account for what Norman Tebbit did.' (That was when he said if there was going to be a contest, he would put his hat into the ring.) 'I didn't mind that at all,' she said.

She said, 'It also probably accounts for that front page story in the *Sunday Telegraph* this morning.' That is where it says that Onslow, the Chairman of the 1922 Committee, would see it his duty to go and tell her that more than half the Tory MPs weren't backing her.

I thought maybe I would ask Willie Whitelaw about this story. I could say to him, 'There is a damaging rumour going around. Is there any truth in it?' I told her this and she thought it was a very good idea. But I can't do it until after the House meets again. She said, 'I'll sit on this, but thank you very much for letting me know.'

She is absolutely convinced, and I totally agree with her, that she has by no means finished putting England straight.

It turned out that David Montgomery had been speaking the truth to me when he said to me that it was a test when they rang up the Tote and said they were speaking from Clarence House.

They tested Ladbroke, William Hill and Coral as well.

The Tote came out as best at being courteous and friendly and reliable.

Monday 9 April

In the afternoon when I was at the Tote, Rupert rang in great disturbance. He said, 'My editors are very worried about what is happening in the country. They think the mood is very bad indeed. It is all over the community charge.' I said, 'Your editors of the *Times* and the *Sunday Times* have always been against the community charge.' He said, 'No, it is not them I am talking about. It's Kelvin MacKenzie (the *Sun*). He's a much more grassroots man.' I said, 'I take that far more seriously.'

He said, 'You are living in fairyland. People perceive it as a tax brought in by the government, even if the councils set the community charge. It is not the old rates.' I said, 'But she can't go back to that.' He said, 'But she has got to do something otherwise she will be done for. There are a lot of people in the Tory Party and in Parliament who are now turning against her.'

He was very worked up.

I said, 'They can only get her out with a leadership contest and I
think she would win it.' He said, 'I am not so sure.'

Rupert also said that she should join the Exchange Rate Mechanism
because it would help to keep interest rates down.

He was ringing from New York and is going to ring again in a day
or two.

I said to Rupert that the *Sunday Times* leading article was crazy in
advocating that Peter Walker should be put in charge of the Conservative Central Office to energize it because he couldn't energize an ice
cream.

Tuesday 10 April

Told Margaret what Rupert had said and apologized for always
bringing her depressing news. I said, 'He is making his suggestions
because he thinks it would be very dreadful if you were pushed out.'

I also talked to her about the ERM. She said, 'We are going to do
that when the barriers on transmitting capital are removed.'

She took it all on board without flinching.

Afterwards I rang Rupert and told him how she had reacted.

These people never seem to have the courage to tell her these things
to her face. They expect me to do it.

Paul Fox[7] came to lunch. He ran Yorkshire Television. His great
ambition had been to be Director General of the BBC but this was not
to be. Instead for the last few years he has been head of BBC Television
which he has been enjoying. He is now sixty-five and has another year
to go. He is a tall, hefty, big-tummied, jolly sort of chap with a partly
bald head. Quite aggressive but well contained within his aggression.
Very friendly.

He didn't agree that the satellite programmes would do the same
for the BBC as ITV had done, which was inexplicable to me.

He said yes, they did want to do a BBC world television news
service. I said, 'Whatever for? Sky is doing it for nothing and ITV are
able to do it, too.'

Paul Fox admitted that my article about the *Today* programme in
the *Times* had certainly smartened them up a bit and fired a warning
shot but he thought I had written it with venom.

He said that Brian Redhead is really a very nice man and why does

---

7. At this time managing director, BBC Network Television; knight 1991; see Vol. 1,
pp. 284 and 292, for speculation in 1987 about the director generalship.

it matter about their politics? 'We didn't ask yours when you were in *Panorama*.' I said, 'But everybody knew them.' He said, 'Nobody knew that [Geoffrey] Johnson-Smith was going to be a Tory MP or Chris Chataway or that Robin Day was going to be a political candidate,'[8] to which I replied, 'Grace Wyndham Goldie[9] drilled us into being impartial.'

Mollie Butler, Rab's widow, rang. She wanted to congratulate me on my article in the *Times* today about Hong Kong, pleading with Tebbit not to go ahead with his attack on the government. She said Rab would have been so much with me in this matter.[10]

Wednesday 11 April
Last night I went to one of Lord Harris of High Cross' 'subversive meetings'. It's a campaign against the anti-smoking campaign. The largest importer into Britain of Havana cigars was there. He says he imports a hundred and fifty million a year. Amazing. I didn't know people smoked so many. It seems altogether the average number of cigars smoked a year is about thirty-seven per head of the male adult population. That includes all these little things like Whiffs and Panatellas and stuff which is non-Havana.

When I got to the place I found 'No Smoking' signs at the bottom and in the lift. All was well at the top and there were posters saying, 'Smoke as much as you like.'

Saturday 14 April *At Bonython*
On Saturday Bob and Molly [Wyatt] came to dinner. Bob[11] was full of interesting details about cricket, how the LBW law, the 1935 new law, had ruined it and how the West Indian bowlers intimidate the batsmen. This, he said, would not happen if a simple law he proposed after the famous bodyline tour of 1932–3 in Australia had been adopted. That

---

8. Liberal candidate, Hereford, 1959 general election.
9. Producer of *Panorama*, retired from the BBC 1965, d 1987.
10. R. A. Butler (1902–82), Conservative politician who put the 1944 Education Act on to the statute book; Home Secretary and Chancellor of the Exchequer; when Anthony Eden resigned as Prime Minister, Harold Macmillan rather than Butler succeeded, and Alec Douglas-Home was preferred on Macmillan's resignation; as Home Secretary again, he reluctantly introduced in 1962 the first legislation restricting immigration; m 2 (1959) Mollie Courtauld.
11. WW's famous cricketer cousin, R. E. S. Wyatt (1901–95), who first captained England against Australia in 1930.

was to draw a line down the middle of the pitch and it would be a no-ball if the ball didn't pitch beyond it. This would avoid the aggressive bouncers which maim and hurt everybody.

It was amusing watching some of the cricket live on Sky Television with Bob and to hear his comments as to how they played their strokes and how the English batsmen really weren't up to it. He thought it was a terrible thing that they hadn't played Gower, who was available there, because he is the best player in England.[12]

Sunday 15 April
We all trooped over to St Michael's Mount where there was a large lunch.

I was wrong in thinking that John St Levan is now worried about the Lands End operation of de Savary.[13]

His visitors have now increased in number because of the entertainment provided by Lands End and its new development. They come on afterwards to see St Michael's Mount as part of their trip.

Monday 16 April
Spoke to Margaret at about half past eight in the morning and asked her how the meeting with Bush had gone. She said it had gone very well and they are beginning to realize we are their staunchest ally.

She said the only thing they disagreed about was the Vietnamese Boat People going into Hong Kong. 'But we didn't talk about it very much and tried to put it on one side.' I said, 'They have got a subconscious thing about Vietnam, nothing can be done about it. They don't realize that these people are not political refugees but are looking for a better life, for which I don't blame them, but Hong Kong can't absorb them and we can do nothing with them.'

I said, 'I am very worried about what Gorbachev is up to in Lithuania.' 'We are all very worried about Gorbachev,' she said, 'but Bush and I feel that we cannot do anything which might dislodge him. It would be fatal.'

She went on, 'They have both got themselves into positions from which they can't withdraw – the Lithuanians and Gorbachev. This is a great mistake in politics, to get into a position from which you can't

---

12. David Gower captained England thirty-one times, in 1984–6 and 1989, and played in 117 Test matches, 1978–92.
13. See 28 May 1989.

withdraw.' (I thought to myself, 'We have got into that position over the community charge but I hope we can get it untangled,' but I didn't say that to her.)

We drove over to Fowey. David Treffry[14] had the most wonderful house. There has been a house there for centuries. It was largely rebuilt in 1459 or 1495 (I forget which), when the French came and raided the town and burned half of the house down and much of Fowey. They still had the original Tudor ceiling in one of the rooms, very handsome.

It is just above the town and has fantastic views of the harbour.

A. L. Rowse was there. He is very deaf. He kept shouting that he agreed with me in everything. He thought Mrs Thatcher was very attractive and he would like to rape her.[15] He then went on to say he thought she was anti-homosexual. (He clearly is one, even if it is latent.)

I said, 'I don't think she is particularly anti-homosexuals otherwise she wouldn't have agreed with the legislation affecting homosexuals.' He said, 'I think you're very much a hetero (meaning heterosexual),' and I said, 'Yes, I think I am. This is the only area in which we disagree.'

He is a very argumentative and didactic fellow. He said, 'They are all against me in the academic world because they hate my theories about Shakespeare. They know they are right but they won't have it and I tell them that they are very third rate because they don't understand what I have written about Shakespeare.' He said he had deduced who the Dark Lady in the sonnets is and he knows he is right.[16]

He mentioned a man called Robert Jackson[17] at the Ministry of Education, who is a Fellow of All Souls and was his pupil, and likewise

---

14. (1926–2000); diplomat, HM Overseas Service, 1952–68; International Monetary Fund, 1968–87; his family acquired the manor of Fowey and the house of Place, c. 1300.

15. This may seem an odd sentiment but Rowse did notice and comment enthusiastically on women's looks. He once charmingly said to the editor of these journals, 'I'm not a hetero, as you know, but if I had been, I'd have married a woman with eyes like yours.'

16. He identified her from the Forman papers as Emelia Lanier, daughter of an Italian musician.

17. MEP, 1979–84, MP since 1983, at this time Parliamentary Under-Secretary of State, DES, with responsibility for higher education and science.

a man called Redwood[18] who is also a Fellow of All Souls and a Minister. As we were going, I said to [David] Harris would he support my application for A. L. Rowse to be given a knighthood and write to Number 10. Immediately he said yes. I said, 'I think I shall try to get hold of these two people who were Fellows of All Souls[19] and are Ministers in the government and get them to do the same.'

Wednesday 18 April

I spoke to Robert Jackson.

He told me that he would certainly write a separate letter of his own to the PM (he sent me a copy, long-winded for a Fellow of All Souls) saying he thought it was a very good thing and he spoke as a Fellow of All Souls. He told me also that the Department of Education had put his [Rowse's] name on the list as their sole nominee for the knighthood they are allowed under the heading of arts or culture or whatever. He said it had been resisted by the British Academy who said he was twenty-five years out of date as a historian. I said, 'That is because they don't like what he wrote about Shakespeare's sonnets and his theories. But they considered him a good historian before that and, in any case, it's general literature with his *Cornish Childhood* and *A Cornishman in Oxford* and his poems and so on.'

I spoke to John Redwood who is very chatty. He is at the Department of Trade. He said he would certainly write in and do his duty, as he called it. We talked about the community charge. He said it had been invented by William Waldegrave and Victor Rothschild in their famous Think Tank in which he was [a participant]. He had resisted it saying, 'They won't like a new tax,' but he was overridden.

I spoke to David Howell who is Chairman of the Foreign Affairs Committee in the Commons. He thought that the Bill about Hong Kong immigrants would carry tomorrow night and that Tebbit and his alliance with Labour would fail.[20]

---

18. John Redwood, MP since 1987, at this time Parliamentary Under-Secretary of State for Corporate Affairs, DTI.
19. Rowse was elected a Fellow of All Souls in 1924 at the age of twenty-one.
20. Forty-four Conservatives rebelled but the British Nationality (Hong Kong) Bill was carried, offering British citizenship for up to fifty thousand selected Hong Kong residents, their spouses and children.

Friday 20 April

Rupert in sharp worry. Rees-Mogg has told him that she will be out soon, she will be defeated in a leadership contest and that Heseltine would win.

I told him that Rees-Mogg is notoriously a bad judge of politics, to which he agreed. He thinks that the next two months will be very serious and anything could happen. He is getting reports that the community charge is ruining small shops. Can something be done?

Norman Lamont is very worried. He says it will be a terrible two months and a terrible year. The two months in particular because inflation will go beyond ten per cent and because of the community charge coming into the April figures.

He said the comrades are very jittery. He thinks she may not be able to hold on to her position. He said even if she is challenged by a donkey in October and he gets a hundred votes, she will have to go. I said, 'She won't go and she won't go if she gets a majority of one because she thinks it is so important that she should be there to carry through her programme of plans for Britain.'

Sunday 22 April

Told Margaret I thought it was important to do something about the little shopkeepers who suddenly find themselves paying community charges far higher than the old rates because they are now rated as businesses.

I said, 'I hear disturbing stories of people being jittery.' She said, 'Is there anybody I should know about?' I said, 'I don't think I should actually tell you who they are but they are people who are loyal to you.' (I had in mind particularly Norman Lamont.)

She thought it would not be wise now for me to speak to Willie Whitelaw in case it precipitated him into taking some action he might not otherwise take. She thought it better to leave it alone for the moment.

At one point she said, 'Cheer up, Woodrow.' I said, 'I am not despondent. I am just naturally worried that things are not running as well as they could. I am trying to find out ways in which we could stop the rot. I am still completely confident that you will win the next election but we are just going to have to work harder.'

I told her that 'When people get rattled I tell them that if you won a leadership contest by only one vote, you would go on.' She said, 'Absolutely right. I certainly would.' She said, 'A leadership contest would be extremely divisive and if I lost it, the party would be absolutely divided.' She was in strong mood to tough it out.

Tuesday 24 April

A party given by Henry Wrong at Spencer House. The lease is for a hundred and thirty years at a very low premium on condition that the whole house is completely restored. The Spencers haven't lived in it since 1880. Since then it has been let to all kinds of people on leases, like Consuelo Vanderbilt who married the ninth Duke of Marlborough.

It has a terrace overlooking the garden and the garden overlooks St James's Park, almost rural. I have never seen such fine rooms in a London house. They are now being filled with pictures and furniture, some of it put in by Jacob [Rothschild], some of it even lent by the Queen, some newly bought.

You can have a party there using all the rooms upstairs and downstairs for £15,000. I don't think, however, that that includes the food and drink.

Jacob was wandering around and I said, 'I think you showed me some of this before you started all the restoration.' He said, 'Yes, of course I did. You came to my birthday party here. Don't you remember it?'[21]

I had to rush off to another party given by David Stevens at Ludgate House, the new headquarters of Express Newspapers. I had not been there before. It is, too, in its way, a fine piece of architecture, modern.

David Stevens was still gloomy about the government and its prospects. He said they never do what he tells them and if they did, they would be in no difficulties. So many people say that. But ideas like his are usually ridiculous.

I hoped to get to sleep early but just after eleven o'clock Rupert rang. He was in Los Angeles where he said it was sunny but cool. Again he went banging on about Mrs Thatcher's problems. I told him that they somewhat exaggerated the difficulty of the community charge for small businesses. It is only a fifteen per cent uplift a year spread over five years and it is phased in, so surely they could manage that. I said, 'Many of these shops who say they are closing are probably closing because the supermarkets offer a better and cheaper service and their day is done.'

I told Rupert that the government's stock in a curious way had

21. On 29 April 1986; see Vol. 1, p. 129.

gone up because of the defeat of the rebellion on the Hong Kong issue and also because of Labour's very bad handling of it. I said it may be that the local elections will be bad but not quite as bad as feared.

Wednesday 25 April
Interviewed for the programme *This Week*. They are trying to find out what people think of the suitability of Kinnock as Prime Minister.

I am too innocent at times and do not think carefully enough. When the interview was over they went out filming the part of the house facing Cavendish Close, obviously making it look as magnificent as possible. I also realized they had put a bust behind me in the dining-room, making it look as though it was all very luxurious. This is presumably so that the viewer might say, 'Well he's stinking rich and therefore he would say that Kinnock wouldn't be suitable as Prime Minister.'

The next day I rang Julian Manyon, the reporter, and said, 'Oi, you are not to use any pictures of my house or the interior at all. That's for security reasons. I get death threats (which is true) and the police are always very worried about my house and me being in it.'

I hope they are not going to cut me up but we will have to see.

Thursday 26 April
I was inveigled by Elma Dangerfield,[22] who must be a hundred and two by now, to go and sit on the platform at the European-Atlantic Group. The Russian Ambassador came. There was an enormous audience of about three hundred people packed into Westminster Hall Grand Committee Room.

The Russian Ambassador was so long-winded, probably on purpose, that although he started at six he hadn't finished answering questions at half past seven so I had no chance to tell him what swines the Russians are being to Lithuania in particular.

Sir Antony Buck,[23] Chairman of the Foreign Affairs Committee for the Tory Party, was in the chair. I said, 'Which is your wife? I hear she is very pretty.' He has just got married and he pointed out a girl of

---

22. Founder and honorary director since 1954 of the European-Atlantic Group; also honorary director, the Byron Society.
23. B 1928; MP, 1961–92; chairman, Conservative Parliamentary Defence Committee, 1979–89; m 2 (1990) Bienvenida Perez-Blanco, but this marriage ended, amid much publicity, in 1993; m 3 (1994) Tamaro Norashkaryan; knight 1983.

about thirty who did look rather pretty sitting in the front row. I said, 'Well done.' He is so old that he is retiring from being an MP but maybe she is also wearing him out. He always has looked somewhat battered and woebegone though he has a cheerful look now.

Friday 27 April

Nervous that I might be losing my £25,000 a year from Skadden Arps, I rang Bruce Buck and said, 'You don't give me enough to do.' 'Don't worry,' he said. 'I am very happy with our relationship.' It seems they are very pleased with the contact I have made for them with the Hungarian lawyers who, he told me, have got international connections and are very well thought of. He then asked me if I could get the head of the Monopolies and Mergers Commission to speak at a conference they are organizing.

But I have been slightly embarrassed by NERA[24] from America, the Marshall McLennan people, wanting me to write a great article about business opportunities in the EEC for some great magazine they are launching. If Irwin Stelzer saw that, he would have a fit and I would ruin my relationship with Skadden Arps, no doubt.

Monday 30 April

Had breakfast with Simon Jenkins, the new editor of the *Times*, in the River Room of the Savoy Hotel.

He was extremely friendly and he said my column is fine. I said, 'My trouble is I never quite know how many words I have got.' He apologized for that and said, 'When you want to write something extra in words let them know in good time.'

I said, 'On this question of the leadership, she won't go, you know. Even supposing a hundred people voted against her in a leadership contest in which, for instance, Ian Gilmour might stand. It wouldn't matter a hoot.'

He said that Norman Tebbit might stand and there might be a second round. I said, 'I think it highly unlikely that Norman Tebbit would stand and even if there were a second round, she would win it so you are all wasting your time. She is what Tony Benn calls a conviction politician. She believes passionately that what she is doing

---

24. National Economic Research Associates, of which Stelzer was president, 1961–85. WW renewed his connection with NERA in 1986 after Stelzer had severed his. See Vol. 1, pp. 143, 205.

is right for the country and I can assure you that if she only won a leadership contest by one vote, she would stay.' He said, 'What, even if Denis didn't want her to?' I said, 'I think that is irrelevant.'

He said, 'I am very glad to have your assurance.' I said, 'It comes confidentially. I have it from the mare's mouth.'

He said he thought there ought to be a slight element of uncertainty about where the *Times* stood on backing her, which of course they would do a hundred per cent when it came up to the election itself.

I said, 'I don't like this idea of uncertainty because it gives a drip, drip, drip effect on the credibility of the government if you start attacking it too much.' He said he didn't think he was going to do that but he wanted to make it look as though they were independent.

He said they had dropped Kilroy Silk because he was no good and they had also dropped Jack Straw[25] because he was an MP; they didn't like MPs writing in the paper with a regular column.

I said, 'I used to be an MP and I rather liked doing that,' and he laughed.

He told me that Bernard Ingham had suggested he meet her and I said, 'That is an excellent idea. You should do so.' (I must tell her that it is important to see him.)

He said he had read the history of the *Times* a lot recently and he had noticed that basically the editors had rarely done particularly well. I said, 'You mean people like Dawson[26] who were in favour of appeasement?' He said, 'Yes.' I said, 'What about William Haley?'[27] He said, 'He was moderately successful but he didn't care about the circulation and didn't seem to mind that they had very few readers.' I said, 'That's the point. When people say to me, "Why do you write for the *News of the World*?" the answer is because it has got such a large circulation.'

He is quite small and has a perky and highly intelligent face, not at all bad-looking. Curly hair and a narrow, sharp, dark face.

I went to see Waddington at the Home Office. He thanked me for

---

25. At this time principal Opposition spokesman on education; Home Secretary since 1997.
26. (1874–1944); Geoffrey Dawson, editor, *Times*, 1912–19 and 1923–41.
27. (1901–87); editor, *Times*, 1952–66; knight 1946.

what I had said about him in the *News of the World*. I said, 'I thought
you kept calm and you had to stick it out about Strangeways.'[28]

No doubt he also thought I had probably done it in order to butter
him up before our meeting. But that was not true. It was my considered
view after reflecting on the whole thing.

I told him the Tote Board felt that it would be intolerable if we
have to hang around till after the next election with this threat hanging
over Tote Bookmakers and Wigan which is so involved in it.

I said, 'If we can now stop this, you can say it has been an interesting
inquiry; they have made changes in the management structure; it was
not a waste of money; the complexities of privatizing the Tote are too
difficult.'

I also told him that even under the 'racing solution' there was
always a danger that they would try and extract more money from us
than we ought to give them. I ran down the details of how much we
had been subscribing. I said, 'I don't think that we can be faulted in a
business sense,' and I explained to him about how we had acquired
a £488,000 investment in SIS [Satellite Information Services] which
was already demonstrated as [worth] nearly £6 million.[29]

He said, 'I don't think anybody is querying your ability to run the
business.'

We parted on very good terms and I think something of what I said
will now be considered. My next problem is how to go on being
Chairman of the Board.

---

28. Waddington had refused to send the Army in to quell the Strangeways prison riot,
    despite pressure from the media.
29. See Vol. 1, p. 319 for the Tote's 5 per cent of SIS 'which I secured for them on
    the ground floor'.

Tuesday 1 May
I rang Margaret and told her of my breakfast with Simon Jenkins.

She said she would certainly arrange to see him. I said, 'I want you to stiffen him up.'

Listened to Margaret in the Commons at Question Time. She was in very effective form.

She said there would be 'adjustments' to the community charge. She had picked that word up from me.[1] On Sunday she had said to me, and again this morning, that 'adjustments was a really good word you used. We're not altering it. We're not changing it. We're adjusting it.'

In the Lords, when I asked my question about our letting down, broadly speaking, the Lithuanians and the Baltic states, there was a lot of disagreement with me.

Bob Mellish[2] said, 'It is the only occasion I think when I have heard you in the House when you were wrong and the government was right.' I said, 'I am very surprised at you, Bob. The old Labour Party used to be anti-imperialist. I have always been anti-imperialist. I am sorry you have changed.'

I like the Pejacsevichs. They are a very soothing couple. They play bridge gently.

Wednesday 2 May
Tote Board meeting.

Peter Winfield[3] was being a bit difficult. He thought we ought to appoint some management consultants or some such to tell us whether we are on the right road and managing the place properly with new ideas. I said, 'Who, for instance in the field of technology? Our business

---

1. WW used the word 'readjustments' in these journals on 1 April 1990.
2. Labour politician, Chief Whip, 1969–70, Opposition Chief Whip, 1970–4; life peer 1985.
3. (1927–99) Property developer and member of Lloyd's; member, Tote Board, 1981–92; racehorse owner.

is quite unique. We are pushing ahead the whole time and developing the best and latest technology. I don't know how a management consultant can help us. All they would do is help themselves to a large fee.' I don't know why he says these things; just to be different, I suppose.

Christopher Haines, the new Chief Executive of the Jockey Club, came to lunch.[4]

He is frightfully pleased with himself. He several times has told me he didn't have to take the position of Chief Executive of the Jockey Club because he is so rich. He made a lot of money out of his last business. He thinks he knows how to run every kind of business.

He is probably a potential enemy.

After the lunch was over I went down to the Lords.

I was sitting on the crossbenches not far away from where Willie Whitelaw was sitting on the front bench of the government side reserved for the ex Cabinet Ministers. I looked at him several times and then he saw me. Usually he smiles at me but I couldn't really catch his eye. He obviously didn't want to smile at me or catch my eye which made me feel, 'Oh God, there is probably something brewing against poor Margaret.'

Yesterday she was magnificent in the House of Commons at Question Time. She looked really beautiful. I thought, 'My goodness, I do love you. You are so brave. Everybody is yapping at you and you stand like a goddess defying them.'

She has great dignity and courage.

I had to go to Priscilla Hastings' seventieth birthday party. Her actual birthday was in February but her children got together this splendid birthday party for her at Claridge's.

When I got in, there was Queen Elizabeth the Queen Mother. For the first time she called me Woodrow which was rather sweet. She said, 'I haven't opened your parcel yet.' I had sent her round a book by George Birmingham in the morning, called *The Search Party*. I told her it may remind her of a Prime Minister we know, in quite a pleasant way.

Immediately she said, 'She is having a terrible time. I do feel so sorry for her.' I said, 'She is fighting back.'

---

4. Chairman, James Budgett, sugar and produce merchants, 1984–9; chief executive, Jockey Club, 1989–93.

   Then she remarked on the appalling attack made by Jean Rook in
the *Daily Express* on Prince Philip. It really was a foul attack.

   She had said, amongst other things, that he is utterly useless, sponges
on the Queen and is horrid to everybody; she hopes that at least he is
of some use to the Queen; he is a Greek Princeling and how dare he
lecture people on how to behave in Britain, and all that kind of tripe.

   Queen Elizabeth said to me, 'Why do you think she writes like
that?' I said, 'Because she's a sensational journalist and she has to have
violent opinions.'

   Then we had a little private talk about the reunification of Germany.
She said she thought it was awful the way everybody talks about it
being such a good idea, inevitable.

   Jeremy Tree[5] was there and we talked rather miserably for a bit
about Isabel [Derby]. He had been on holiday with them before she
died. He said she seemed very fit and lively.

   Jeremy said, 'It was very interesting how they [the Derbys] came
together at the end. They had a lot of ups and downs and various bad
patches.' I said, 'But it ended very well because basically they truly
loved each other despite all her cavorting with other people.' He said,
'Yes. They were really like Darby and Joan at the end.'

   Speaking of Jean Rook, Queen Elizabeth said, 'Women can be very
nasty, you know.' I said, 'I suppose that's so.' I wondered if she meant
herself a little bit because she so often says to me, 'I'm not as nice as
you think,' but I don't believe it.

Thursday 3 May
I spoke to David Stevens and told him there was great feeling in Royal
circles about Jean Rook's attack on the Duke of Edinburgh in the
Express and that I thought I would probably reply to it myself. He
said, 'Of course he is very rude and they are no good really, the Royal
Family, except for the Queen.' I said, 'I think you have got that wrong.'
He said that he agreed that Jean Rook had gone over the top and he
would say something to her about it.

   To Chips and Sarah Keswick for dinner. It was the first time I had
been to dinner with them both for years. I haven't seen Sarah for years
either. She reminded me I had promised to give her lunch in the Lords
but have never done so.

   She is still attractive in her dark way, despite the car accident marks

---

   5. Racehorse trainer; brother of Michael Tree.*

on her face, but she has got fatter in her face and in her body. That small, neat, trim, sexy little figure has gone.

We had a fairly merry time, apart from talking about Isabel Derby whom we both lamented. Sarah and Isabel used to call each other 'Frank'. She said she used to speak to her at least twice a week.

On my left at dinner was a Miss [Tessa] Buckmaster, bulky, tall, young, upper class, barely good-looking. She works as some kind of public relations person to Carlton Communications. The main shareholder, Michael Green, who has made millions out of it, sat on her left. They are engaged to be married.[6]

Sarah takes the view, long established by convention but now disregarded, that engaged people should sit next to each other when out at dinner and do so until a year after their marriage. Miss Buckmaster agreed that it was a good idea. She said she was so pleased to be next to him because they do not really see each other in the office.

It is a strange house, badly decorated and in rather poor taste, very small for somebody as rich as Chips.

Friday 4 May

I had told Margaret that the local elections would turn out better than feared. This morning I was proved right, particularly in London where Kinnock's home Labour council, Ealing, was won by the Tories.

On Bradford, which was narrowly lost to Labour, she said, 'They had only held it for eighteen months. Probably Tebbit's remarks about the "cricket test" had done some damage.'[7]

Went to Mansfield College, Oxford, as guest of Dr Martin Holmes, the economist. The first time I had ever been inside. When I was at Oxford it was a theological college.

One tenth of the undergraduates are still United Reformed Church theologians preparing themselves for ordination in this rather weird church.

The dinner in the tiny hall, with its oil paintings of theologians and Church luminaries and principals of the college, was somewhat like that in other Oxford colleges.

Even the left-wing ones seemed to enjoy the formality and the many

---

6. They married in June 1990.
7. Tebbit had suggested that many former immigrants would support the visiting team from their country of origin when it played in England; Bradford has many citizens originating from the Indian subcontinent.

courses, the circulation of the port and going upstairs to have brandy and liqueurs with the coffee, though the coffee was ghastly.

It was very sunny and warm in Oxford. Seeing the girls, the young ones, and the boys with tennis rackets walking about in summer clothes, I felt Oxford was not so much the home of lost causes but of nostalgia.

Saturday 5 May
To Newmarket.

Baroness Trumpington (Jean).

She said Mrs Thatcher had been a great success when she went to Towcester. It was Alexander Hesketh who charmed her into going there. She was delighted to be clapped by the crowds as she went about the place and she even put a bet on.

Debo [Duchess of] Devonshire came to our surprise. I told the Tote to send her an invitation. Andrew [Duke of Devonshire] had said that she probably wouldn't come and then she turned up.

She had come because 'Dad' had his horse running, Lord of the Field, and she wanted to put a bet on it, which she did. I put £2 each way on at 40 to 1 but it was nowhere to be seen.

Debo asked if I had been to the Sandown racing conference. I told her that I had. It was very well organized and Stoker (her son) was doing extremely well.

She said, 'I am told they call him the Gorbachev of racing because he is trying to get his reforms through while keeping the old fashioned, no-change people contented.'

George Walker and his wife arrived almost as lunch was over which is always a nuisance because there are gaps around the table. He had just got back from America and his plane was late.

He was telling everybody to back the Irish Tirol because he said he knew the people who owned it and trained it and they were certain it was going to win.

But it was Pam, the girl in charge of the Credit Office, who had told me to back it.

Pam is an extremely competent girl, pretty. She has very short hair, tallish and blonde and with nice eyes. She has been promoted to be the Area Credit Manager. She gets on very well with the customers and with her staff. I have always wanted women to be promoted on their merits and we do have a great deal of that in the Tote. Women are not held back because they are women or because they are coloured.

Sunday 6 May

Margaret sounded quite relaxed. She was still at Chequers when I spoke to her at about a quarter past five, it being a Bank Holiday tomorrow.

I told her that John Major had talked to the Lords crossbenchers last week. He spoke without notes and it was a great success. He answered the questions very well and a number of them there said how good he was, better than Nigel [Lawson]. She broke in, 'Yes I think he is. He is not so arrogant. He is much more modest and cautious.'

I said, 'When you do finally decide to go, you will have to wait until he is in a position to take over from you.' She said, 'That has always been my intention, as you know.'

On Europe I said, 'One thing people are going to realize is that nobody but you could have fought and got huge EC rebates as well as you have.'

We must have talked for forty minutes. She said, 'You have cheered me up enormously,' and she repeated her signing off, 'God bless you.' On this occasion I must have done two-thirds of the talking because I am anxious for her to grasp the various points – which I am sure she is doing and she will follow them up.

Monday 7 May

I told Margaret to read Keith Joseph's[8] very satisfactory article in the *Times* supporting her and saying she must stay and also to read William Rees-Mogg's article in the *Independent*. From saying on and on previously that she must go, he has now reversed his position and is saying that she will probably win the next election.

I raised with her her visit to Towcester.

I said, 'I still want to try and get you to go to the Derby.' She said, 'I don't think I can do it when the Queen is there. Maybe somewhere not so grand. Newbury is not far away. I would like to go to Newbury.' So I am now going to arrange a good racing day at Newbury to see how she gets on there. I would like her to see the Tote anyway because it is going to come up more now in government circles.

---

8. (1918–94); Conservative politician; MP, 1956–87, Secretary of State for Education and Science, 1981–6; founder, Centre for Policy Studies; Fellow of All Souls College, Oxford; baronet, life peer 1987.

Spent the night and had dinner at Philip Leverhulme's house.[9] There is a butler and an under butler, about four footmen or the equivalent thereof, and valets for the guests. He has four gardeners and two chauffeurs. When I have to give a tip of £30 in the morning, it will work out at about 50p each because in the morning there were at least six women running around the house cleaning everything up.

It is the strangest house out. It was built in Victorian times by his grandfather. About 1880 or so he began it. He never finished it. It is enormous and yet, as he said, there are very few bedrooms for a house of that size. It is a kind of John Betjeman house. The rooms are curiously quite good in their weird mixture of classical columns and arches and Tudor paned windows. In the distance over the Dee you can see the Welsh hills.

One of the amusing aspects of the place was that he had an underground swimming pool at the bottom of the house, heated to ninety degrees where he swims frequently. Upstairs where his grandparents used to sleep there is an outside bathroom on the terrace, obscured from view, but exposed to the elements, only part covered by glass. They would bathe in it every day winter and summer, however cold.

The house parlour maid attending Verushka said the electric heater couldn't be plugged in because 'the electrics are so old'. There was no lining to the curtains so it was light by 6.00 a.m. A strange mixture of immensely valuable furniture, pictures and ancient discomforts.

I asked him if he was lonely and he said he had been after his wife died (she died in 1973) but then he had had a lot to do. He is still Lord Lieutenant of the county. He is still Chairman of Chester Racecourse. He is Chairman of the trust which holds enormous holdings in Unilever.

He probably has at least £200 million, or so he is rated, possibly underestimated, in the latest list of the richest people in Britain.

But there was no champagne, neither at drinks in the sitting-room before dinner nor in the other room which was the second room we had drinks in before we went in to dinner.

---

9. 3rd Viscount Leverhulme, grandson of the 1st Viscount (chairman of Lever Brothers and founder of Port Sunlight); formerly Senior Steward of the Jockey Club; this was his house, Thornton Manor, in the Wirral, Merseyside. WW went on next day to the races at Chester.

Thursday 10 May

Michael Heseltine has written a great article in the *Times* about changes
to the poll tax. He doesn't demand that it should be removed, merely
tampered with – which is after all what Margaret and the government
are trying to sort out now. Some of his suggestions are pretty impractical like having a directly elected mayor.

On Radio 4 this morning he was very much marking down the
excitement in the press and the media again that he is throwing a
challenge to Mrs Thatcher's leadership.

I talked to Margaret.

We discussed the Heseltine article which she had already read. This
was at ten to eight this morning and she kept saying, 'He's accepting
the community charge.'

Michael's main suggestions could not be put in before the next
election.

To Esher Place. Meeting with the Electricity Union. Bill Adams from
the Stable Lads' Association and myself. I am a Trustee and thus a sort
of trade union official. We were trying to arrange the merger between
the Electricians and the Stable Lads. They will join the Professional
Associations section which will make them sound a bit upgraded. Of
course there is going to be a lot of difficulty with the trainers but at
least they now recognize that the Stable Lads is the negotiating union
and they have nothing to do with the Transport and General Workers'
Union.

I remember Esher Place as a child. I passed the church where my
father was buried just outside the entrance to Esher Place. It is a
splendid house for the trade union to have as its training centre and
for weekend breaks.

In the evening to The Other Club. The fiftieth anniversary of
Winston Churchill's becoming Prime Minister. Because he was the
founder of the club in 1911, with F. E. Smith, there was a celebratory
dinner to which Mary Soames, his daughter, was invited. Young
Winston Churchill, the grandson, and Nicholas Soames, the son of
Mary Soames, are members of the club anyway so they were naturally
there. There was a big turnout.

Talked to Willie Whitelaw before the dinner. He was not exactly
equivocal but he said he thought that when people went mad it was
very difficult to do anything about them.

I said, 'I thought things were calming down.' He said, 'Yes but not
absolutely. If she can get by through the summer till the October

possibility of a challenge to the leadership, then she should be all right.' Then I said that if she won a leadership contest by only a majority of one, she would hang on because I wanted him to understand that. He said, 'That would be very bad for the party.' I said, 'Yes but she would. After all, don't forget there are many people passionately in favour of her in the Tory Party, more than those who are against her for one reason or another.'

As we went on with the conversation it was clear that he felt that the events over the last week in Europe and with the local elections had moved in her favour.

I concluded that one way or another Willie was no longer in some plot with Alec Home to go and see her in the summer and tell her to stand down.

I talked to John Smith.

He said, 'I don't know if it has percolated down to people like you yet but we would run a very tough government, not a reckless one as there was before.' I didn't, unfortunately, have enough time to develop this with him.

Francis Pym[10] was sitting opposite us. He was very friendly, surprisingly so. He has now no bitterness at all about being sacked by Margaret. Moreover he spoke of her in very warm terms and said they would be crazy to try and displace her.

He liked the House of Lords. We agreed that it would be impossible to reform it to be an elected chamber as it would then want power.

David Steel sat on my right. He remarked to those opposite and around that one of the pleasures of no longer being Leader of the Liberal Democrats, as they are now called, is that he is no longer subject to such sharp attacks from me in the newspapers any more.

I remarked that Paddy Ashdown was turning out better than I had expected. He seems to be improving and getting more authority in what he says. I added that I was particularly pleased about his line on Hong Kong which is much the same as mine. I said that I thought the Liberal Democrats would do better than their poll ratings when it comes to the general election and thus help to keep Mrs Thatcher in. David Steel assented to that glumly because he doesn't really want Mrs Thatcher back again.

Mary spoke very well, impromptu, better than her father could.

The Savoy Hotel presented magnums of Pol Roger (Winston's

---

10. Foreign Secretary, 1982–3.

favourite champagne) 1982. We had a good Beychevelle 1979 and our own champagne presented by Michael Hartwell before the dinner. The dinner was much longer than usual and cost £20 as it was a special occasion. It is extraordinary how cheaply the Savoy do it.

The name of the nice Maître d'Hôtel des Salons Privés is Frank Mondelli. He always puts out the Churchilliana and the Club paraphernalia and supervises it. He has done it for about forty years.

Sunday 13 May

I told Margaret that Willie Whitelaw was more positive when I saw him on Thursday evening. I said, 'Brian Walden was saying in the *Sunday Times* this morning that you should take Heseltine into the government.' She said, 'He often says barmy things. Heseltine won't work with a team. He doesn't know how to.'

Then I talked to her about the Broadcasting Bill.

I told her that Julian Lewis and I had been drafting amendments. I read one or two of them about the balancing of programmes which are not impartial, having a discussion at the end of them and then announcing when a counter programme would be put on.

She said, 'You should have the code of practice in the law.' I said, 'That might be difficult. Also, it doesn't cover the BBC.' Immediately she said, 'But the Broadcasting Standards Council is referred to in the Act. It does cover the BBC.' I said, 'But it might be difficult to include such a provision in it and make them responsible.' She said, 'You can do anything in Your Lordships' House.'

Now I see a lot of work trying to go through this damned Act again and get it according to how she would think it would work.

When I told her I was sending her the amendments, she said, 'I shall be able to tell you what answers they are going to give.' I thought that was quite funny because the Ministers wouldn't know that we had their answers before we went on to the attack.

Monday 14 May

The dinner at Cavendish Avenue turned out a great success. For the aficionados of champagne oldish and interesting, I used my one bottle of Bollinger 1976.

Andrew Knight and I discussed Simon Jenkins and his attitude to the community charge. I told him that on the Saturday after the local elections he finished with a last sentence in his leader in the *Times*, 'The poll tax must go.' I said, 'This is not a sensible thing for a

Times editor to do. It can be written in a feature article but anyone who knows anything about politics, and the editor of the *Times* should, must realize that the government could not possibly abolish the poll tax before the next election.'

On my left sat Annabel Astor. I showed her the swordstick given to me by her mother, Pandora Jones, at Bruern Abbey when we stayed there at Christmas in 1964. I showed her the inscription, too: 'The coward does it with a kiss, the brave man with a sword.' I said, 'I was very fond of your mother. Everybody was in love with her.'

Pandora was the most beautiful girl, or at least one of the two or three most beautiful girls, I ever knew.

Tuesday 15 May
Had rather a sweet letter from Queen Elizabeth the Queen Mother. But reading it I wondered whether she saw my article in the *News of the World* the Sunday before last in which I stoutly defended Prince Philip. I tried to get hold of Sir Martin Gilliat to ask him if she saw the article. I don't quite know how to deal with her letter because I suppose I should write back.[11]

David Stevens' annual lunch at the Savoy on behalf of United Newspapers.

On the way in I spoke briefly to Robert Maxwell who came up to me and thanked me for my note about his newspaper in which he had a share in Hungary. He said how amusing it was that he and Rupert should be rivals there. He chatted for a bit and said what did I think of the new *European* which he has just brought out. I said, 'It looks very attractive and well done but I don't really agree with much you say about Europe.'

I spoke to Bernard Ingham and said, 'Do get Simon Jenkins to see the Prime Minister soon.' He said, 'It's all right. He saw her last night.'

On the way out I saw him earnestly talking to Simon Jenkins.

---

11. The letter thanked WW for adding yet another volume to her 'Wyatt Library of Entertaining Books' and went on to say, if he had a chance, would he ask Lord Stevens to keep an eye on the really scandalous attacks on her quite innocent family who did their best to serve their country as best they could. The one on her son-in-law did shock everyone by its bad taste. WW wrote back explaining he had spoken to Stevens who 'was a bit shamefaced and agreed that Jean Rook had gone over the top'. He would speak to the editor, too.

Afterwards I went to the Lords and then across to the Commons to hear the Prime Minister. She was in sparkling form.

On the way back the Duke of Norfolk started talking to me. He had been watching, too, and he said, 'Very good repartee. Like the sergeants' mess. She commanded them all very well. I was in the army.'

Later, to the West London Synagogue. There were over a thousand people for Victor's (Lord Rothschild's) memorial service. Margaret had said at Question Time when asked about her appointments for the day, after reciting the usual meetings, that she was attending the memorial service for Lord Rothschild. Victor would have been pleased. It was a public vindication of his patriotism after the accusations rumoured and muttered that he had been some kind of fifth man.

I found the service powerful. It made me think again of the astonishing vitality of the Jewish race. There were bits out of the psalms, though not as well written as in the English James I version.

At one point Victor's favourite jazz music was played, the stuff he used to play at the piano with a cigarette dangling from his mouth.

William Waldegrave made an address.

He hadn't known him nearly as long as I had, although he knew him much more thoroughly in the Think Tank.[12]

Also Leonard Hoffman, who is a judge,[13] made an address. It was good but he didn't know Victor until the Royal Commission on Gambling in 1976.

Lord Swann,[14] who is a distinguished scientist, described Victor's discoveries and research with him about spermatozoa. The whole affair was interesting and moving.

The Jewish religion as portrayed in that synagogue has strong similarities to the Church of England but it is tougher and more realistic. The rabbis who appear on *Thought for the Day* on BBC Radio 4 are always far more sensible and realistic and in favour of the individual than the hoards of clerics who tout Labour propaganda.[15]

---

12. Waldegrave was a member, 1971–3, of the Central Policy Review Staff, Cabinet Office, of which Victor Rothschild was director general, 1971–4.

13. At this time a judge of the High Court, Chancery Division; life peer and Lord of Appeal, 1995.

14. Professor of Natural History, University of Edinburgh, 1952–65; chairman, BBC governors, 1973–80; life peer 1981.

15. Two regulars on *Thought for the Day* at this time were Lionel Blue and the late Hugo Gryn, both then rabbis at the West London Synagogue.

Wednesday 16 May

I had to go to Lord McAlpine of Moffat's[16] memorial service. He was a nice old stick. St Paul's was pretty full. He lived to eighty-three in a jolly, friendly manner, though Arnold always said he was a crook which I don't believe. He did well out of the construction business but he [helped] a lot of charities. He was very good with the apprentice racing school and he was always very friendly to me with his little lunches and his great annual parties at the Intercontinental Hotel. They were extraordinary affairs with lobsters and crab and even caviar and masses of champagne.

Margaret was there. I thought I was spending my life, and so was she, going to memorial services.

Thursday 17 May

Rupert came to the All Party Broadcasting meeting.

Rupert was very nervous. Ian Orr-Ewing,[17] who was in the chair, said his hands were shaking. He was plainly diffident and doesn't put himself over particularly well.

However, the meeting went off pretty well. I think Rupert will have no trouble at all because of all the propaganda he has done and the arrangements I made for them to make sure they were seeing the right people.

I think there will not be much of an attempt to overturn the Commons decision not to make him divest himself either of his television channels or his newspapers.

Saturday 19 May

To Badminton.

It was a delight to see Caroline [Beaufort]. She is looking so much better than she has for some time. She is enjoying being a Duchess, making little speeches, opening things and being active in the whole neighbourhood.

She said she remembered when we first met properly. That was after I followed her in the streets, thinking what a pretty girl she was, in 1959. She recalled the first meeting which was at Arthur Jeffries' house in Venice.

---

16. (1907–90); Edwin McAlpine, partner, Sir Robert McAlpine, from 1928; racehorse breeder, member of the Jockey Club; life peer 1980.

17. (1912–99); Conservative politician; MP, 1950–70; life peer 1971.

She said as we looked around the house and the garden – Jeffries was a picture and antique dealer and had a lot of money in America, a homosexual – she said to me she would like to see the bedrooms. She realized afterwards that it sounded very much like an invitation to a bit more than a flirtation. But when we went up to the bedrooms and I took her hand, she said I behaved very nicely and didn't press her.

Later in the weekend David said in front of his son, Johnny, who is my godson, and Verushka was there, 'Woodrow was very fond of Caroline. I often wondered if they had an affair. Perhaps they did. Perhaps Johnny is really his son.'

For the record, we never had an affair though it came quite close.

That was when Caroline was very distressed about David's behaviour with Antonia Fraser.

I think at that time Caroline thought she might lose David altogether. But they have now settled down pretty well, although he has his permanent mistress.

At dinner we had a very good La Fleur (Pomerol) 1982.

There was Tracy Ward, married to Bunter [Marquess of Worcester, the Beauforts' eldest son], and her little son Robert. I said to Bunter, 'There's a horse running today (that was on Saturday) called Bertie Wooster. It's hot favourite and I put a tiny bit of money on it because the Tote don't want it to win.'[18] Caroline said, 'I hope that when Robert is older and Bunter has succeeded David, they won't call my grandson Bertie Wooster (Worcester).'

Tracy talked a lot of rot about the Green Party.[19] She is absolutely haywire about politics but she was delighted when I said not everything in the Green Party was absurd – keeping people up to the mark on the environment was good pressure. But their political policies are ridiculous.

At lunch I sat next to Daphne Bath (Fielding), Caroline's mother.[20] I think she is about eighty-nine now or perhaps not quite so old. She

---

18. WW had a standing joke with the Tote: if he backed a horse, it was sure not to win.

19. Tracy Worcester, environmentalist, was in 1999 associate director of the International Society of Ecology and Culture and a trustee of Friends of the Earth.

20. The Hon. Mrs Daphne Fielding (1904–97), writer; daughter of 4th Baron, Vivian; m 1 (1926–53) Viscount Weymouth (succeeded as 6th Marquess of Bath in 1946, d 1992), father of Caroline; m 2 (1953–78) Xan Fielding, travel writer.*

is hysterical with her daughter about plots to kill her. I told Caroline that this was quite a common belief by old people, that there were people listening to them, tapping their telephones, spying on them and doing strange things through the walls.

David said about best friends' wives, 'I don't know why you should think that Woodrow mightn't have had an affair with Caroline. Everybody else has affairs with their best friends' wives.'

David remains astonishingly good-looking. He is sixty but he looks much younger.

Sadly, David is now running the fashionable hobby horse that Mrs Thatcher ought to go. He said, 'The Tory Party always get rid of leaders when they are going to lose an election.' I said, 'She is not going to lose the next election.'

I feel sorry that David is taking this view. He has always been nervous and wobbly though; he always is before every election.[21]

Monday 21 May
Dinner at the Gran Paradiso restaurant in Chelsea.

It was supposed to be in honour of Alexander Hesketh's thirteenth wedding anniversary but I couldn't see Clare anywhere, probably because there was such a crowd. How awful – I was very impolite.

Very late Jacob Rothschild came in. I don't know why he bothered to come as it was well after dinner. Alexander obviously had asked him, although he had been delighted at his being unable to buy 'The Three Graces' because he, Alexander, put a spoke in the wheel.

Before dinner I thanked Paul Johnson[22] for the kind remarks he had made about me in his column in the *Spectator*. He said he thought I had done very well and people had forgotten what a marvellous job I did on the Communists in the Electricians Union. He went on to say that he thought Mrs Thatcher was making too many blunders and he had gone off her somewhat. This worried me because he used to be a very passionate supporter. However, he is a very moody, turnabout man.

Marigold [Johnson] and I were recalling how we had met thirty

---

21. See Vol. 1, pp. 353 and 372, for his fears before the 1987 general election.
22. Writer and journalist; editor, *New Statesman*, 1965–70, he had moved from left to right in politics; m (1957) Marigold, née Hunt (Labour candidate, October 1974 general election); their son Daniel was a leader writer on the *Times*, 1990–1, literary editor, 1992–6, an assistant editor since 1996.

years or thirty-five years ago when she was an undergraduate at Oxford at Nicholas Davenport's house.[23] She was a luscious little creature then. I think she has had a fairly hard life with Paul Johnson. She said that he is a very ascetic person who doesn't give a damn what his surroundings are or what he eats or whether it is comfortable or if there is any furniture. He works very hard. She has some lively children including one who is now writing leading articles at the age of twenty-five for the *Times*.

Tuesday 22 May

Margaret looked very smart in a nice green suit, a skirt and coat with brass buttons on it, at Question Time in the Commons. But she wasn't as sparkling as usual and I think she answered the questions badly about the increased burden of taxation since 1979.

Wednesday 23 May

A maddening day. First to the dentist who was going to pull out my tooth, then down to the oculist, Arnott's establishment in the Cromwell Road hospital. They kept me waiting twenty minutes and I had to dash back to the Levy Board and was two minutes late for the meeting. Then I had to go back to the dentist in the afternoon and have my tooth pulled out. He put in a plate which put me in total agony.

Dashed down to the Lords and was in time to see the end of the ceremony to introduce Mrs Brigstocke as a peeress.[24] She looked very handsome and she has a wonderful figure for sixty. The old gentlemen were all gooing over her saying how beautiful she is.

I dread meeting her after Petronella's rough profile of her in the *Sunday Telegraph* which she knows very well she wrote because Petronella even rang her up but she wouldn't speak to her. I still feel Petronella was somewhat ungrateful.

Afterwards, although I was feeling absolutely ghastly with my tooth, because of the pressure from the plate apparently, we went to dinner with the Stelzers at the Connaught Hotel.

I only ate a few potatoes. I did drink a fair amount of the claret (a) because it was so good and (b) because I thought it would numb the pain.

---

23. Nicholas Davenport, economist and writer (1893–1979).
24. Heather Brigstocke, headmistress, Francis Holland School, 1965–74, high mistress, St Paul's Girls' School, 1974–89.

Cita is very excited about the course she is going to do in Oxford in October.

She still says she can't go up in her Rolls-Royce. I said, 'Don't disappoint them. They'll be looking out for that nice bit of exoticism.' She's a very earnest seeker after truth and knowledge which I greatly admire.

I said to Irwin just as we were leaving did he think I could ask for another £5,000 a year from Skadden Arps. He said leave it to him and he would speak to them. I took him a box of Punch 1970 cigars which was a bit of a wrench because I rather value those old cigars. I also gave Cita a copy of the latest *DNB* with my two entries in it.

Friday 25 May

Justus de Goede, the South African Minister from next door in Cavendish Close, came to dinner with his wife.

He is highly intelligent and more optimistic than I expected. He has more confidence than I had in de Klerk being able to work something out which doesn't give the blacks a one man one vote control.

Saturday 26 May

When I rang to speak to Margaret I was put through to Chequers and then again and again asked to 'hold on, she won't be a moment'. I thought she must have some meeting. When she got to the telephone I said, 'I hope I'm not disturbing you,' and she said, 'I was in the garden giving my grandson a glass of orange juice.' She sounded very happy.

I asked her if she had done anything more about the Broadcasting Bill. She said, 'Yes. I spoke to Waddington.'

I said, 'What about Rees-Mogg? Will he accept this addition to his Broadcasting Standards Council?'

We then agreed that I would have to speak to him and see what his reactions are.

I told her that at Question Time, when she was answering the question about her having put a greater tax burden on the taxpayers than there was in 1979, she could have answered it slightly differently, pointing out that the average incomes had gone up so much that it didn't matter a higher proportion of them was going in tax.

After we had talked for a bit I said, 'You must go back into the garden now and give your grandson another glass of orange juice.'

The public has not the slightest idea of what a vulnerable, human

woman she is, all motherly instincts and feminine instincts and charm
as well. And wonderful good looks and liveliness.

Monday 28 May
I spoke to Rees-Mogg and asked him how he would react to my
amendments to make the Broadcasting Standards Council take over
the job of issuing a code on impartiality and receiving complaints from
people who thought it had been breached. He said he would be very
negative. He didn't want, nor did his Council, to get involved in
anything of a political nature because they feared it would detract from
their credibility acting on matters of taste and violence and sexual
indecency.

He suggested trying to work something in around the Complaints
Commission.

Spoke to Shirley Anglesey.[25] She is Chairman of the Complaints
Commission and very much against my idea that she should take on
this role. She is somewhat left-wing, not at all like Henry and myself.

I reported all this to Margaret. We thought that maybe we would
have to have a new little body or just force one of these bodies to take
it on.

Tuesday 29 May
Dinner at Cavendish Avenue. David Montagu and Ninette (Lord and
Lady Swaythling), Richard Ryder and his wife. He is the Economic
Secretary at the Treasury and his wife worked for Mrs Thatcher for
years as her personal secretary and was given the MBE. He has got a
Norfolk seat. Professor Norman Stone. Eva Pejacsevich came because
Anne Tree couldn't. She was hanging around at home because of
Jeremy Tree's stroke. Michael Tree came. He had just had an operation
for glaucoma in his eye. The Quintons.

There was some very nice 1969 Dom Pérignon champagne first, the
oldest I have now got apart from the 1928. While I went to look for
something Norman Stone rudely helped himself to a whacking great
glass of it. He doesn't even appreciate it.

David Montagu was scratchy this evening. He was grumbling about
why don't we have new pools. He knows the answer, just as Peter

25. Née Morgan, m (1948) 7th Marquess of Anglesey (Henry); chairman, Broadcasting
Complaints Commission, 1987–91; chairman, British Council Drama and Dance
Advisory Committee, 1981–91; DBE 1982.

Winfield does. He is just rattled by the criticisms in the *Sporting Life*, *Racing Post* and press from ignorant fools who think we could rattle up new national pools as fast as lightning if we liked to do so.

He was very silly after dinner. He was running down Mrs Thatcher and the community charge and everything else.

Wednesday 30 May

Simon Jenkins came for breakfast. I was very below par which was a pity.

I asked him how his talk with her went and he said it was rather typical, she lectured him for about twenty minutes and then said, 'Have you got anything you would like to say yourself?' and it wasn't till some time on that they really got down to a reasonable conversation. I don't know why she does this.

He then talked a great deal about the need to have a separate representation in Scotland and didn't she realize that it was like Lithuania, they wanted their independence. I said, 'I don't think it's like that at all. They had a referendum before and they didn't want to have a separate country.'

However, we got on quite well.

Addlepated for most of the day from drinking too much and eating too much rich food. In the evening I went to dinner at Christie's dressed in a black tie. It was a large gathering, perhaps sixty to eighty, in honour of Walter Lee Annenberg, the former Ambassador from the US to London [1969–74].

There was a very grand set at the top table with Peter Carrington who was responsible for giving the dinner as Chairman of Christie's.

When we arrived Peter said to me, 'The *vieillesse dorée*. You will know everybody here.' He meant the opposite of *jeunesse dorée*.

He was right. There were few people under the age of seventy and they were mostly loaded with money. I felt almost young.

I had Mrs Peter Cazalet (widow) on my left.[26]

She told me what it was like staying at Birkhall with Queen Elizabeth the Queen Mother in Scotland. She said, 'I am the only person who takes a black friend there.' This was very coy stuff. She was referring to a black dog she had.

Arnold Weinstock was there and so was Willie Whitelaw. He said he wouldn't be in the House on Monday but if he were, he would vote

26. Zara, née Mainwaring, m 2 (1948) Peter Cazalet (1907–73), racehorse trainer.

against the Bill on the war criminals.[27] Arnold said he would just have an amendment saying it shouldn't be retrospective. I said that is the same as voting against.

'I am going to vote for it, for several reasons. One because I like Lord Mackay [Lord Chancellor] who is first class and I am not going to vote against him. Two because I don't think people who have got away with the hideous things they have done should be allowed to go on enjoying a jolly life if they can be found and successfully prosecuted, and they won't be convicted in a British court without clear evidence. Three because I don't like the growing signs of anti-semitism popping up here and there.' Arnold said the War Criminals Bill, if people were brought to trial, would only add to anti-semitism, but I don't think he is right.

---

27. The War Crimes Bill allowed the prosecution within the UK of people resident here who were suspected of war crimes in the Second World War.

Saturday 2 June
To Heveningham Hall for the great concert given by Abdul Al Ghazzi.
It looked magnificent from the roadway. Remnants only of scaffolding
here and there.

Inside we were not allowed to see the completed shell of the library
east wing. He is very reluctant for anybody to see anything.

In fact, there was nothing you could see that was different from
some years ago after the fire, except the orangery has been done up
again.

I was asked to make a speech after Abdul made his little speech to
the guests. I was then told that Abdul was not going to say anything
at all but that I had to get up at the end and make a speech. I was
slightly irritated.

Before the dinner was the concert. This was pure Marx Brothers.
It began half an hour late. The orchestra sat in a marquee.

The audience sat in another marquee some fifty yards away with
some wretched little flower beds in between plus the odd urn. The
orchestra's marquee was on the terrace so it was higher than the
audience.

It was bitterly cold in the audience tent.

When the interval came Verushka went into the house and refused
to come out again, which was reasonable, even though she did have a
shawl. It was an extremely cold night, raining, and we walked through
puddles.

John Gummer, Secretary for Agriculture, was there with his wife.

He was asked because he is the local MP but he had some other
engagement which prevented him from staying for more than a chunk
of the concert.

He was in the middle of the row with the French over their banning
of British beef, quite illegally as far as the European Commission is
concerned. He thought Abdul had done well with the house but I am
not quite so convinced now as I was.

Abdul assured me they are going to get on with putting the library back into its proper condition and John Martin Robinson says that all the Wyatt bookcases are there, stored in the stables, though some of them are badly burned.

Abdul said he was very sorry we weren't staying the night and he took Verushka and myself up to a room where he gave her a present of some kind of a gold-looking necklace. When we got home and examined it for a gold or a silver mark we couldn't find any. It came from a jeweller in Paris. I shouldn't think it is real, just fashion jewellery.

It looked like about a hundred and fifty people sitting down for dinner. This was fabulous. It was about ten courses, all done by Mosimann's of Belgravia.

It was not until nearly twenty to twelve that this fellow Nigel Playfair [Al Ghazzi's assistant] came to me and said would I now make my speech.

It was quite funny with jokes about Hungarians and my customary joke, because there were people who hadn't heard it, that I only know three expressions in Hungarian. *Sarat pak*, which means I love you, *edam*, which means yes, and *nem* which means no, the last being the most important.

I then did a great spiel about Abdul saying how well he had done at the Hall and how he had been unfairly attacked and all the rest of it.

It was just gone twelve by the time I could get away. John Martin Robinson asked for a lift and I said yes he could sit in the front and not make too much noise. I fell asleep. Robbie was misdirected by John Martin Robinson, who is a fearful know-all, and took the wrong road when we reached Ipswich and started going on the A45 up to Norwich, back in the same direction in which we had come.

I wasn't in bed until gone three and I had all this work to do the following day, with my speech for the Lords as well as my article for the *Times* to go over again, and preparation for the Tote Board meeting.

Monday 4 June
Margaret was having her hair done when I first rang at a quarter past eight. She takes much trouble with her appearance. It is foolish of good-looking women not to make sure their good looks and dress are the best that can be contrived.

She said she had read my article in the *News of the World* and said she agreed with it. I was slightly surprised because I had said Gorbachev was deeply unpopular outside parliament; Yeltsin had been elected

President of Russia because although forty per cent of the parliament were Communist nominees, they didn't dare frustrate the will of the ordinary people which is strongly anti-Gorbachev.

We discussed David Owen and the collapse of the SDP.[1] She thought it was unlikely Labour would let him do anything important and that his natural home was the Conservative Party. I said, 'I agree with that.' When I said, 'Maybe now he has finished in politics. He could get a job as a governor of the BBC or Governor of Hong Kong,' she replied, 'But he has never administered anything.' I said, 'I suppose you think that having been at the Ministry of Health and Foreign Secretary is not administration,' and she laughed. She said, 'Why doesn't he go back to being a doctor?' I said, 'Because there is not much glamour in that.'

Later on Rupert rang and said, 'I see she is off to Moscow to prop up Gorbachev.' I said, 'I have been urging her not to go so heavily for Gorbachev now.'

I have been trying to do too much and am in danger of doing nothing properly. I was not very happy with my article in the *Times*. It is very difficult trying to compress such a big subject as bias in broadcasting and what should be done about it into eight hundred and fifty words.

The debate on the War Crimes Bill.

Hailsham and the lawyers, Lord Donaldson, Master of the Rolls, etc. were at their pompous worst, lecturing to us all about the difficulties of trials after forty-five years.

The ridiculous thing is that if you are a Briton who has committed a murder, you can be prosecuted for it seventy years later, if you are still alive.

The Lords must have been quite mad to throw it out, raising the whole question of the status of the second chamber which in any case is under threat from Labour.[2]

---

1. Of the Social Democratic Party MPs, only David Owen, Rosie Barnes and John Cartwright remained Independent SDP members; the others joined the Liberal Democratic Party.
2. The Lords defeated the War Crimes Bill on its second reading by 207 to 74 votes and did so again in 1991, but the government then used the Parliament Act to put it on the statute book.

Tuesday 5 June

When I got up [to speak on the Broadcasting Bill] I said I could not stay and I would be very brief, which I was.[3] But it was not very good. I cut nearly all the prepared speech out, partly because people had used bits of it already.

Everyone was saying last night that I am looking too thin and I mustn't get any thinner. I fear that is right but what can I do? I don't want another hernia and also I feel better when I am thinner. I look scraggy.

Wednesday 6 June

Read what Frank Longford said about me after I had left, complaining that I had fled away from the House because he had warned me what he was going to say and I hadn't got the courage to stay and listen to it. It was quite ridiculous, about my attacking his son-in-law, Harold Pinter.[4] I remembered the son-in-law, Hugh Fraser.

Frank's only reply to my comment about Harold Pinter's vicious and unbalanced attack on American policy in Nicaragua, and on Mrs Thatcher for approving it, was that I wrote in my autobiography I was in love with Mrs Thatcher. Pretty silly, particularly as I had written 'platonically of course'.[5]

A wet and windy day for the Derby. We had lunch upstairs this time with Ian Trethowan and the Levy Board people. It is Ian's last time there and I had never had lunch there before. It also may be my last time for all I know. There may be another chairman at the Tote by this time next year. The lunch was not particularly good, no better than the one in the Jockey Club rooms below but at least you got champagne upstairs.

I sat next to the wife of Sir Timothy Bevan who had been Chairman of Barclays Bank. Though a strong Tory, she is somewhat against Mrs Thatcher. I told her she was an ass, politely.

Downstairs was John Derby. I was surprised he came. He was in the Derby box which they share with the Devonshires. I spoke to him

---

3. WW had a dinner to go to which he later regretted as 'a waste of time'; he also wanted an early night before the Derby next day.

4. The playwright m 2 (1980) Lady Antonia Fraser, writer, eldest daughter of the Earl and Countess of Longford, after her divorce from Sir Hugh Fraser (d 1984), Conservative MP and Oxford friend of WW.

5. *Confessions of an Optimist*, p. 345.

briefly. He was tolerably cheerful. I couldn't bear to go down to the paddock without Isabel before the Derby began.

Upstairs in the Jockey Club rooms was J. J. Warr. He said, 'I have just met a friend of yours on the lawn down below wanting to know when your play is going to come on – Michael Medwin.[6] He is longing to get back into it and he wants to know when it is going to be on.' I said, 'I would like to know that too.'

Rupert rang and thanked me for what I had said in defence of him and Sky Television in the debate on the Broadcasting Bill on Tuesday night. I said, 'I don't think we are in serious trouble but we have got to keep a look out on the amendments being moved by Alexander Macmillan [Earl of Stockton]. I don't know what has got into him. Has he got some financial interest?' He said, 'He seems to spend his entire time at the BSB office, so I am told.'

Thursday 7 June
We found masses of parcels in the hall.

They were from Abdul Al Ghazzi. A magnum of champagne, a large jar of caviar and a box of twenty-five Romeo y Julieta Churchill cigars for me separately and various scents and other presents for Verushka including a very beautiful French silk scarf. He sent a letter saying it was to thank us for coming to his concert and dinner at Heveningham Hall.

Lately I have been thinking a bit unkindly about him and then I felt a trifle ashamed.

Sunday 10 June
We had dinner at Claridge's.

Before we left Andrew Devonshire came in with Selina Hastings[7] and sat at a table next to us. Nobody noticed them but me. When they were all going out I went over and squeezed the back of Selina's neck and asked her how she was and how her father was. She said he was now very senile. I said, 'I promised your mother I would go and see him.' She said, 'I don't think it would do much good. You would

---

6. He played Jack at Margate.

7. Writer, daughter of the 15th Earl of Huntingdon and his second wife, Margaret Lane; half-sister of WW's third wife Moorea and therefore WW's former sister-in-law.

probably waste your journey,' to which I replied that her mother thought that he might be all right.

Selena still looks quite fresh and young with her plumpness and soft skin. She said what did I think of Petronella's radio article in the *Sunday Telegraph* this morning? I said I thought it was very good. She said she thought it was outstandingly good.

Monday 11 June
Lunch at Number 10. There were twelve in all. I sat on Margaret's right.

I said, 'What are you going to do about defence cuts?' She will not be doing too many. I said that now she had told the Soviet Generals that we no longer regard the Soviet Union as an enemy, Labour will seize on that and we will have to do something. 'I want you to undercut Labour,' I said. (Just before lunch I talked to Alan Clark[8] from the Ministry of Defence who urged me to press that on her. He is trying to get large defence cuts. So I did my stuff for him quite manfully.)

Then came a talk about the Broadcasting Bill and impartiality which prompted me into explaining that this is the last chance we had in the Lords of getting it right.

Ken Baker chipped in and said he thought that it hadn't been properly understood in the Home Office.

Opposite me also was our nice Leader of the Lords, Belstead. He will doubtless be circulating information to Ferrers that my amendments have got to be taken seriously.

During lunch she said, 'I have fought three elections against the BBC and I don't want to fight another election against it.'

It was quite a fascinating lunch but there was no talk of long-term strategy and the community charge wasn't mentioned other than by myself to Alan Clark before lunch.

I think people were slightly astonished when I dared to interrupt and contradict Margaret but she didn't seem to mind at all.

At one point Margaret said, 'Here is Woodrow trying to do all he

---

8. (1928–99) Conservative politician, historian and diarist, at this time Minister of State, Ministry of Defence; he does not mention this lunch in his diary but said of WW on 2 March 1986, 'With the exception of Macmillan (and *he* does it on purpose) Woodrow is the only person I know who seems to be more ga-ga than he is.'

can to help us in the Lords and we are trying to stop him. The amendments must get through.'

Thursday 14 June
Prince and Princess Michael of Kent to dinner. She wore long black trousers with a blouse on top. That concealed the thickness of her legs. She is a handsome girl. There were just the four of us. They were very lively. They are off to Hungary in early July and wanted to talk about Hungary and people they might meet. They are going to Russia in October at Gorbachev's special invitation. Gorbachev was struck by his speaking Russian when he met Prince Michael over here recently.

Prince Michael started talking about his programme in Russia and the aeroplane factory he was going to see when Princess Michael broke in rather angrily saying, 'I know nothing about that. Why haven't I been consulted? I don't want to go and see an aircraft factory.' The atmosphere became turgid and tense. I quickly broke in to say, 'It is a very long time ahead and I am sure they will find you something more interesting to do on that day.'

He had said he was very sorry he would not be at the [Tote] board meeting on July 4th for his and my birthday, but they would send a message from the Embassy in Hungary. I felt rather a heel as I have recommended that his term of office on the board should now cease and that his place should be taken by Sonny Marlborough. He was so much more lively and interesting this evening than he ever is at a board meeting, full of chat.

Marie-Christine, the Princess, was very upset that her mother, and also her brother, had never told her that her father had been a Nazi in Germany. The first she heard about it was when it all broke in the newspapers and there was terrible trouble about it.

They said, 'Why did we have to tell you? It was all dead and forgotten.' The fact of the matter was that he was not a Nazi for very long. Much of the German aristocracy went along with Hitler for a bit until they discovered he was ghastly. He soon left them and was then sent with the army to some distant part. Finally he was arrested by the Hitler government.

Saturday 16 June
Had a long talk with Margaret in the morning.

I began after thanking her for the lunch by saying I was so glad Kingsley Amis [the writer] had got a knighthood. She said, 'Yes. At last.' That was the one I got for him and had urged on her for two or three years.

(I rang Kingsley first thing in the morning when I read about it and I said, 'I was really aroused by them giving the knighthood earlier to the Indian writer from Trinidad[9] and I thought you should have one.' I don't think he realized that I actually got him the knighthood, not that that matters.)

I then turned to the question of A. L. Rowse.

She said, 'But they say he has done nothing new for ages.'

I don't think I am going to get him a knighthood, unfortunately.

I said, 'I think I must write something to counteract the foolish things that Simon Jenkins is writing [about the community charge].' She said, 'Has he been doing that?' I said, 'Haven't you noticed it?' She said no. She doesn't really read the newspapers unless somebody draws her attention to something.

Went to the Trooping the Colour.

It turned out that we did have rather special seats in the Royal Household section. There is a great deal of jealousy in the Household as to who get them. A footman at Clarence House was given one and Michael Oswald,[10] whose wife is Lady in Waiting to Queen Elizabeth the Queen Mother, didn't get one – at least he had to make a great fuss before he got one. He was sitting by us.

Michael said he could write a fascinating book about the intrigues and jealousies and dirty tricks played on each other by the courtiers but it would have to be published fifty years later.

The parade was pretty good but on the whole I would have preferred to have seen it on television.

We had deduced the lunch [at Clarence House] would be in the garden. That is mainly because the Queen Mother likes to wear a hat whenever possible because she is getting a little bald on top. We were shown where we were sitting. Rather to my surprise I was sitting on Queen Elizabeth the Queen Mother's left and the Grand Duke of Luxembourg was sitting on her right.

I have never been to Clarence House without sitting either on her left or on her right.

---

9. V. S. Naipaul had received a knighthood in the 1990 New Year's Honours list.
10. Manager, the Royal Studs, Sandringham, 1970–97, director since 1997; m (1958) Lady Angela Cecil, daughter of the 6th Marquess of Exeter, Woman of the Bed-chamber to Queen Elizabeth the Queen Mother, 1983–97.

Princess Margaret was there in the drawing-room before we went out for lunch. She got up and started talking to me and then I sat down beside her for a moment. I never can get on with her when she is in one of her strange moods. She didn't look at all well. I said to her rather fatuously, 'Have you just been to the Trooping the Colour?' and she said, 'Yes. Why do you think I am dressed like this?'

Rather sweetly at one stage Queen Elizabeth told me 'I am going to drink your health,' and she picked up her glass of port and raised it to me.

She thanked me for defending Prince Philip when he couldn't reply himself. That was in reference to the Rook attack on him in the *Daily Express*.

At this point she suddenly said, 'Look at us. We are just ordinary people – look at us around this table – having an ordinary lunch.'

I thought to myself, 'I don't think ordinary people have a luncheon in a huge London garden with about six liveried footmen wearing medals waiting on them, and with the Grand Duke of Luxembourg with his Duchess and various other people like that there.' Also the lunch was extremely good.

I said to her, 'This is more of a feast.' She laughed and said, 'Yes it is, isn't it. Isn't it nice?'

When the cigars came round she said, 'Look at this box.'

She said, 'This is the first thing my grandson (that's Linley) made.' I said, 'It is beautifully carpentered. It fits exactly. A perfect job, perfectly turned.' So she called across to him and said, 'He thinks it is a very well done job,' and I said, 'Yes, it's lovely,' which it certainly was. As we were going, he came up to her and started teasing her a bit. 'Oh,' she said, 'he is my favourite grandson,' and gave him a great embrace. He is a very nice boy.

She agreed with the Lords about the War Crimes Bill. I explained to her why I didn't and my feelings about Jews and about how they had been persecuted. She said, 'But that is long ago,' and I said, 'Not entirely. There are things going on now,' and so we talked about Jews for a bit and she said she liked them very much but they were a separate people and a strange people, keeping to themselves with their own ways.

I said, 'That is not entirely my view. They have assimilated very well in Britain. It is natural for them to keep their own religion, there is nothing wrong with that, and also their sense of identity. They have suffered so much over the last two thousand years and survived but they have only done it by sticking together when they have to.'

She clearly has some reservations about Jews in her old fashioned English way though she would never be a party to treating them badly. I said it is wonderful that we are such a tolerant nation.

When Princess Margaret got up to go she suddenly came across and very politely smiled at me and shook hands and said, 'I hope you haven't been frozen to death,' indicating that she felt she had been. I do feel sorry for that girl. She always seems rather unhappy and her legs were so thin and she was looking gaunt. She has had a very sad life. Her children adore her. Viscount Linley said she has always longed to go on a bus. He had promised he would take her one day. She has never been on one. I can see that the security angle could be somewhat difficult.

In the evening we went to the Garrick Club to the great party given by Milton and Drusilla Shulman[11] in honour of their daughter's engagement to the Earl of Mulgrave, heir to the Marquess of Normanby.

Peregrine Worsthorne was there.

He said he was writing his memoirs.[12]

I said, 'It will sell very well.' He said, 'The trouble is I am very indiscreet.' I said, 'That will be very helpful with your memoirs.'

On the way out I had stopped to say hello to Milton Shulman to thank him. He was talking to Antonia Fraser. Antonia was on his left and she was talking to her other neighbour so I put my hand on her neck and squeezed it and said, 'Hello. I'll have a kiss before I go.' She said, 'You have been attacking my husband in a horrid way.' I said, 'He is quite able to look after himself' (that referred to Harold Pinter). She said, 'I think it was horrid of you.' Then she leant forward and said, 'A kiss is not for free,' and gave me a kiss.

Dru actually still looks very pretty. I was always rather keen on her. She has got a very pretty figure. Fortunately her daughter takes after her rather than after Milton who I suppose is not too bad looking in a florid Jewish way.

---

11. Milton Shulman, the drama critic, m (1956) Drusilla Beyfus (journalist; associate editor, British *Vogue*, 1979–86); their daughter Nicola m 2 (1990) the Earl of Mulgrave who succeeded his father as 5th Marquess of Normanby in 1994.

12. *Tricks of Memory: An Autobiography*, published 1993.

Tuesday 19 June

Lunch with Piers Bengough [at Royal Ascot]. This is the yearly ritual.

Tea with the Queen was the order Piers gave us as we finished lunch.

I did better with Princess Margaret than I did on Saturday. She was wearing an attractive green outfit with a feathery hat. When she got to me I said, 'What a beautiful outfit you have, Ma'am. It suits you very well and you look marvellous.' Actually this was true. She glowed with pleasure and said, 'We try our best.'

On the way out the Queen unusually smiled goodbye. I talked to Prince Philip, who was standing some way apart, saying how pleased I was that Shavian, owned by John Howard de Walden, had won the St James's Palace Stakes. Philip said, 'It makes a change from the Arabs who seem to win everything.' He seemed to be not at all happy about that. I said, 'They have done a great deal for English racing and they have improved the standard of the horses.' He said, 'I don't agree. English horses and English owners can't compete and they have changed the whole nature of racing. It is not a good thing at all.' That is what a great many of the old guard in racing think.

In the evening Allan Davis rang, just back from Canada. He said he had no news from the young men except that they couldn't get Farnham to take it on. I said, 'I think we must consider the play a dead duck now.'

I went to bed feeling that my whole play-writing career had come to a dreary stop. Also feeling how little I have done. The odd not very good book, articles in newspapers, never got anywhere in politics. It would have been something to have written a play which was successful but now there is really nothing. My right eye is not so bad now but it continues to hurt and I feel, oh dear, oh dear, my life which began with some promise tailing off into nothing much at all.

Wednesday 20 June

The Home Secretary to lunch at Ascot with Mrs Waddington. She turned out to be well clued up in politics, vigorous, forceful and intelligent but now plain. When he arrived he was dumbfounded to see Judith Bathurst but very pleased as well. He said to me, 'She used to be a girlfriend of mine years ago when we lived not far apart.' I whispered in his ear, 'That must have been all right.'

I was amused that Mrs Waddington (married 1958) referred to the meeting with Judith Bathurst when sitting next to me. She said, 'David was pole-axed when he saw her.' It must have been the cause of some marital discussion, doubtless heated.

I found him less intelligent than I originally thought he was going to be. For example, he hasn't taken on board at all the reasons why there was concern about lack of due impartiality on the part of the BBC and ITV.

I asked him what he was going to do about the Broadcasting Bill and he said, 'There is a great deal of steam behind it from Number 10.'

I took him on a tour down to the Tote control room. Though I had explained to him a thousand times in his office and in writing the basis on which the Tote operates, he is still asking questions as though he has no idea what it was all about.

I am very fond of the French Ambassador and his wife.[13] He is extremely intelligent and bright, also very rich. He has just now bought himself back from his family their share of an ancestral castle and he has several houses in France already. Hedwige sat next to me. She was looking very attractive in her *belle laide* way. We had a very serious conversation about Anglo-French relations.

When they went, I said to Luc (the French Ambassador), 'Ask her to pass on the gist of our conversation to you. It was unusual at Ascot to have a really thoroughgoing political review with an intelligent Ambassadress on Anglo-French relations instead of simply gossiping about nothing in particular and talking about people's dresses.'

I was amused at how grateful Judith Bathurst was to be invited to the lunch.

She was introducing John Vestey as her fiancé. He has only been her fiancé for about fourteen years, living together in the same house. He is divorced, she is divorced.

We got lavish promises about the use of their boat in Porto Ercole. It is quite a luxury one but I don't want to use it because I don't like that kind of boat. I like the little fishing boats with little sails, lattice canopies and little outboard motors.

Thursday 21 June
Nowhere near such an interesting lunch at Ascot.

Ian Trethowan was at the lunch, poor chap, in his wheelchair.

He says he thinks he will be dead in six months. Very sad. But he

---

13. Luc and Hedwige de La Barre de Nanteuil.

keeps his spirit up remarkably well. He looks frailer all the time but his brain is absolutely as sharp as anything. I admire his courage.

Petronella brought to Ascot a young man called James Delingpole from the *Daily Telegraph*.

I had expected him to write nothing about it but I was astonished to see in the *Sunday Telegraph* (I am writing this on the Sunday following Ascot) a whole long article about having lunch with us in the Tote Room at Ascot. He got some of the flavour right but not quite.

Friday 22 June

I was told by Mrs Bell, the engagement secretary at Number 10, that she cannot find a date for the Prime Minister to have dinner with George Walker and anyway he came the other day and she met him when they had dinner with the President of Egypt. I thought, 'Gosh that is not the same thing at all. Has the atmosphere changed? What is the point of just talking to him briefly at a huge dinner?'

Saturday 23 June

We went to lunch at Chips Keswick's fishing house at Whitchurch on the River Test. It was built in 1920 by the McAlpine family, very small with a lot of galvanized iron. I say very small but there were about six bedrooms and it is spread over quite a lot of land. The lovely 1920s furniture was still there.

One lavatory, if you looked down to the bottom of the pan, you could see a big trout. It has been there for about three years.

He gave us a wonderful Pouilly-Fumé 1935, a very special one. It was delicious. We had a marvellous lunch of smoked cod roe, fresh large prawns from Billingsgate, a lamb which was really marvellous and I shouldn't have eaten it but I did.

There is a two mile stretch of the river, entirely his private property. He does not let it out at all as everybody else does. He is so rich, Chips, that he does not have to. His trout population is stable at about three or four thousand. Poaching is rigorously prevented by his water bailiff. He also mows the sides of the river bank and keeps it perfectly so it is really idyllic.

Sunday 24 June

To Smith's Lawn, Windsor Park, for the polo final sponsored by Rothmans. David Swaythling (Montagu) is Chairman. It was cold with traces of rain and sometimes a real shower.

On my right was Mrs Johann Rupert, wife of the South African major shareholder of Rothmans who really controls the whole thing and an old friend of David's.

She is extraordinarily pretty. I sat next to her last year.[14] I said, 'You had to leave early to catch an aeroplane, I think to South Africa.' She said, 'What a marvellous memory you have.' I said, 'Having sat next to you how could I forget you?'

She was well clued up on the political situation. The government and business are concentrating on building up Mandela and the ANC because they think it is better to have a united black opposition than one which is creating civil wars among itself.

She is moderately optimistic that things will turn out all right but not ravingly so. She said her family had been in South Africa for three hundred years.

Carla [Powell], who is a very jolly, quite flirtatious girl, said that when she was very young she never allowed men to give her presents because she thought it was improper. Now she said she would like them to give her presents but they don't offer. I said, 'I think they must do because you are extremely attractive. You are only just over forty-five and you look much younger, thirty-five-ish.'

The Queen was there to give away the prizes.

I almost said to her how attractive her clothes were today and how nice she was looking but I didn't dare, as I would to her mother, thinking that I might get slapped down if I said the same sort of thing to her. Though maybe I wouldn't. Maybe nobody ever says it to her and she would be pleased.

Tuesday 26 June

Guildhall. A Lord Mayor's lunch in honour of Queen Elizabeth the Queen Mother's ninetieth birthday which is not until August 4th.

Sitting on my right was Dame Lady Donaldson, wife of the Master of the Rolls, Lord Donaldson. She is an ex Lord Mayor.[15] When I asked her if that was very expensive she said, 'No. That is all nonsense.

---

14. See 25 June 1989.
15. Dame Mary Donaldson, Lord Mayor of London, 1983–4.

In fact you get a very good allowance from the City Corporation. You can live well within it. You have got the house and servants and free living for a year. I just shut up my other house in London and it was perfectly all right.'

She was dumpy but nice and very argumentative.

She started saying the Lords ought to be an elected chamber in which proposition she was backed by the City Treasurer on her right. (His name is Mr Harty[16] and he is called the Chamberlain of London but he is actually the City Treasurer in practice.)

They said there was an idea that the Lord Mayor should be elected on a vote throughout London. I said, 'That would be absolutely dotty. We don't want a Chirac of Paris here.'

Dinner at Cliveden.

Max Hastings[17] was there with his rather pretty wife. He is about six foot eight inches and it is very difficult to talk to him because he looks down on everyone.

He says that Petronella is a star.

He says they are putting her on the staff but she has to learn her trade doing run of the mill things before she can be at the top. She is very bright and clever and gets her brains from me, he thinks. I don't know if that is true. He said he believes in nepotism whatever that might mean. I think he means heredity.

Rosita [Marlborough] and I talked most of the time to each other which was rather rude. She said nobody made propositions to her. I said, 'Perhaps you crush them. You are always very sweet about Sonny and don't want to upset him.' She said she thought affairs were probably too much trouble.

She is a beautiful creature and she was looking splendid tonight. She must be over forty by now but I am not quite sure how old she is.

Wednesday 27 June
When I rang, Margaret was having her hair done at a quarter to eight but she rang back at about nine. We had a brisk talk about the Broadcasting Bill, how Waddington was dragging his feet and what I thought it was important to stick out on.

As for the Dublin Summit, she said she thought it had gone rather well. She said, 'Always the Chancellor of West Germany and the

---

16. Bernard Harty, Chamberlain and Banker, Corporation of London, 1983–95.
17. Editor, *Daily Telegraph*, 1986–95; m (1972–94) Patricia, née Edmondson.

President of France cook something up together without consulting anybody else and drop it on the Summit meeting and try and force it through. If it was not for me, all kinds of things would happen which would never be acceptable to anybody.'

There was a Rees-Mogg party, a very big one, on the terrace of the Lords. A daughter of his has got married and all the children etc. were there. We did not stay long. Parties are tiring me out.

Talked to Geoffrey Howe. I cannot understand why he is so friendly considering, as he must know, that I think he has been disloyal to Mrs Thatcher and have said so and been rude to him.

There is a curious story in the press that he is going to be sent as Ambassador to South Africa and be made a Viscount to get him out of Margaret's hair. Speaking of the story he said, 'There is usually a grain of truth in these things.' I said, 'I don't think so. It is probably somebody making some joke and it gets passed on to the next person. By the time it gets to the third person it has become a fact.' He didn't look convinced. I like him but I wish he were not so difficult about Margaret. It is because time is running out for him.

Thursday 28 June

There was a long article in the *Times* by the Director of programmes at Channel 4, Liz Forgan, attacking my amendments and Orr-Ewing's amendments which are really mine on the whole. I asked Simon Jenkins whether I could write a reply and he said, 'Yes. You don't mean another article?' and I said, 'No, not at all. I mean a letter.' He said, 'Can you keep it short?'

In the end it wasn't very short. The difficulty of having to write a joint letter with Orr-Ewing is that I have to get him to pass it and agree it and Julian Lewis to agree it and God knows what else.

The Home Secretary came to lunch at the Levy Board and asked to have a few words with me privately. He wanted to clear what it was I wanted the Home Office to do about the Broadcasting Bill.

He said, 'I understand what you want but I am not promising I am going to do it all. I had a long discussion with the Prime Minister before Cabinet this morning.'

The *Evening Standard* had rung up before I left for the Levy Board meeting which made me late. 'What are your reactions to A. N. Wilson writing in the *Spectator* a detailed account of a conversation he had with the Queen Mother at your house at a private dinner party in

March 1987?'[18] I dictated something as best I could but they did not publish all of it. I am deeply embarrassed. It shows her in an extremely bad light, making unkind comments about Roy Jenkins and Prince Michael and others which of course were intended to be wholly private jokes, as Wilson knew well because he confessed in the article itself that it was gross impropriety and discourteous and embarrassing to his host, which of course was me.

Now I have got to write a letter to her and to the *Spectator* and I have so little time. And there is a dinner party tonight as well. He behaved in the most unspeakable manner. I said to the *Evening Standard*: 'A. N. Wilson describes himself as a young fogey but he does not understand what a gentleman is. Everyone should be warned not to have him in their house or at a private dinner party.'

It was all done to sour up her ninetieth birthday celebrations. What an unutterable shit the man is.

Dinner party at Cavendish Avenue.

The second wine at dinner was 1946 Château Latour.

George Walker said, 'I would never give this at a dinner party. I would sit at home and drink it by myself.'

I thought to myself, 'If you don't give it at a dinner party when some people understand about wine, when do you drink it?' It was probably worth £150 a bottle, not far short. It had a wonderful smell and drank deliciously like velvet nectar. The bottles were slightly different from each other, naturally, as they of course aged differently.

Tim Bell thought things were being mismanaged at Number 10. 'Let's hope the machine which grinds out things to discredit Ministers and others will be stopped or checked.' He referred particularly to the story about Howe being made Ambassador in South Africa. He seemed to know or think that definitely came from Number 10 as a try out.

Tom King[19] immediately said, 'There won't be a leadership contest. That has all gone by the board now,' which I am certain he is right about.

Friday 29 June
Ali Forbes rang up at great length about A. N. Wilson's behaviour at my dinner party. He said he had often been invited to have dinner with Queen Elizabeth the Queen Mother but he always refused as he is

---

18. See Vol. 1, pp. 308–10, for the dinner party.
19. Secretary of State for Defence at this time.

indiscreet and he knows he would let something out and anyway he doesn't think much of her.

Hugh Montgomery Massingberd[20] wrote a longish article in the *Telegraph* about the A. N. Wilson affair. He had the odd dig at me as well, saying I had once referred to Queen Elizabeth as not being all sugar but there was some acid when it was needed. I thought that was a quite harmless remark. I made it to Elizabeth Longford and it appears in her book about Queen Elizabeth.[21]

Saturday 30 June
A sad visit to Lady Place, Sutton Courtenay.

Hugh Sinclair had been determined to try to get to this meeting of the International Nutrition Foundation, which he knew would be his last.

Alas, his dream has gone which he lived for, dedicated his life to, dedicated all his money to, left his entire assets to, cutting out his family. I suppose when sold up it will come to the best part of £4.5 million, if not more.

He had a remarkable career but essentially he was lazy. He loved doing the research, fiddling about with it and going to meetings raising money, but he never or hardly ever wrote anything substantial.

When they took him off to hospital, they found he had a loaded shot gun by his bed. He was ready to repel boarders at all times as there had been several burglaries within the last year or so.

Other guns were found and according to the auctioneers they must be worth at least £4,000. His early experiments at school and at Oxford had concerned firing guns off just behind people to measure their reactions and what happens to their bodies.

I remembered how hurt he had been when I left my file behind and had to ring up and ask him to arrange for it to be posted. He read the notes I had written during the meeting in which I said how filthy everything was and it was amazing how one could have a place researching food in such a dirty condition.[22]

But he was a thoroughly good man, very sincere, brilliant, a discoverer of important things. It was he who persuaded the government

---

20. Journalist (obituaries editor, *Daily Telegraph*, 1986–94) and author of books on the monarchy and heritage issues.
21. *The Queen Mother, a Biography*, 1981.
22. See Vol. 1, pp. 163, 602.

and the world to understand that eating saturated fats to the extent that everybody was doing with dairy produce, fat on meat which was not free range any more, was killing the human race much earlier than it need.

He was a discoverer of the virtues of fish oil to help with multiple sclerosis and other kinds of diseases; and what Eskimos did and ate and why they live so well because they have the right diet.

He himself died at the age of eighty of cancer. So he didn't live a short life. He never married. He said he had two fiancées in a sad little letter he sent: 'I have had over eighty years of a largely wasted but very happy life (apart from the death of two fiancées, relatives and friends) and I have no regrets whatever except that, having spent much of my life trying to get teaching and research into human nutrition properly recognized, I am deeply concerned about the future of the Foundation.'

Hugh Sinclair's last private and confidential note, which was sent to all members of the Council, finished by saying that he had still been hoping to get Jimmy Goldsmith to produce a professorship of human nutrition at the University of Oxford with a Fellowship at Magdalen College.

I felt a terrible heel but I really could not have got Jimmy Goldsmith to put money into something which looked so peculiar. And now I think it is too late unless they get some very go-ahead person in charge to interest him.

The library of course has to be kept open as it is to do with nutrition research and matters relevant to it for the Foundation. There are other very valuable books. I was also fascinated to learn there is a library of erotica he had in a room by itself. Some elderly gentleman (they are all elderly gentlemen on the Council) immediately remarked it could be very valuable.

By coincidence only yesterday was published after his death a booklet called *Sinclair* in a series 'The Founders of Modern Nutrition'.

Sunday 1 July

'You were very kind to me today.' This was Margaret about my *News of the World* article.

I said, 'When I spoke to Geoffrey Howe the other day [about] the story that he was going to be sent as Ambassador to South Africa, he said there was always a grain of truth in a rumour.'

She said, 'The thought never occurred to me and never would. For one thing I don't want a by-election at the moment which there would have to be. That is quite apart from not wanting to send him to South Africa.'

She was in a strong mood. We had a longish talk and she finally said, 'Thank you for ringing, dear.'

Started work on another shot at getting my play more arresting at the beginning. Had been to the Globe Theatre the night before to see Alan Ayckbourn's new play *Man of the Moment*. That was because Allan wanted me to see how he began it. It was an impressive play.

I didn't see a single pretty woman in the whole place nor a sophisticated-looking man. They seemed to enjoy the play a great deal but I thought, 'Gosh, are these the people I am supposed to be writing for?'

Tuesday 3 July

Dinner at the French Embassy in honour of John Major.

I sat next to Mrs Major who turned out to be completely charming. She had been a teacher. She said that constituency work and the coffee mornings was what she disliked the most, which I understood.

I asked her, 'What will you feel like if he becomes Prime Minister?' She said she had not thought about it yet. I said, 'It is a real possibility you know.'

Jeremy Isaacs[1] recommended to Mrs Major that she read my autobiography which he said was very entertaining.

---

1. General Director, Royal Opera House, 1988–97; previously chief executive, Channel 4, 1981–7, and BBC television producer; knight 1996.

He is very left-wing. He said they are cutting the costs of all the scene shifters [at the Royal Opera House]. That battle has been won. It is not possible to get cheap singers because you have to pay the market price.

I said, 'You just said you don't believe in free markets and now you see how they work.' We had such a long talk that I began to like him rather a lot, curiously. Bernard Levin has always liked him so he must be quite a decent chap at heart.

Rang Margaret to point out to her my article in the *Times* this morning about the ending of the Dock Labour Scheme which has brought great prosperity to the old Scheme ports and how Labour had opposed it. Today is the anniversary [of the repeal] and it might be useful to her at Question Time.

Later in the afternoon I went down to the Commons from the Lords and heard her answering questions and there it was, duly planted by some Tory backbencher, a question relating to the ending of the Dock Labour Scheme. She trotted out the facts she had got from my article and finally finished with a triumphant, 'Labour wrong again!'

Wednesday 4 July
My birthday. They were very sweet to me at the Tote Board, drinking my health and giving me a present of a cartoon of myself smoking a cigar with a great Tote behind it. The same morning I received a letter from the Home Secretary wanting to muck about with the structure of the board. Very tiresome.

When I got back before going out to dinner, there was a fantastic satinwood humidor for holding a hundred cigars sent by Abdul Al Ghazzi. It must have cost him a mint. It is the most beautiful object. Then arrived also an egg cutter from Katie Macmillan so I suppose I shall have to write and thank her for it and make some show of making it up after her appalling behaviour.[2]

Thursday 5 July
Peregrine Worsthorne had written a very silly article in the *Daily Telegraph* this morning boasting that he was also at the famous dinner party when A. N. Wilson breached the conventions. He said he didn't recall my telling the guests that they were not supposed to say anything though they realized that it was understood. He said he dined out for

2. See Vol. 1, August 1987, for her disastrous holiday with the Wyatts in Italy.

months on what the Queen Mother had told him and he had talked to people in the Garrick Club about it but he had never said anything to the press. But he didn't see why one should not talk about these things.[3]

There was a strange dinner at Conrad Black's house. It is modern but vaguely classical at Highgate. You have to climb a longish path up a hill to get to the garden gate. It had been decorated by Sally Metcalfe who was also present. I thought it was fairly ordinary though the little library was charmingly done.

We had not gone to the *Spectator* party because I was pretty annoyed with the editor of the *Spectator* and didn't wish to meet A. N. Wilson either. Conrad Black made no reference to the affair of the Queen Mother 'interview', other than to say that he had not read my letter in the *Spectator* yet.

Shirley Black said she had changed her name to Joanna because she did not like the name of Shirley. I said I was sorry because I did like it. She was looking youthful and fresh and had her two little children in the room with her when we arrived. The unfortunates were made to say good night to Lord Wyatt and shake hands with him before they were hustled off by their nanny, looking bewildered.

On my left sat a handsome Jewish lady called Gail Ronson.

Her husband, Gerald Ronson, is standing trial in the famous Ernest Saunders case.

She said that when they had been at some party and Margaret had seen them in the distance, she made a point of going up to him, shaking hands with him and wishing him good fortune. That is one of her most noble characteristics, never letting down a friend.

Saturday 7 July
The great event at Chatsworth.

We were only asked because, when Andrew's horse ran in the 2,000

---

3. Worsthorne concluded: 'According to Woodrow Wyatt, A. N. Wilson's behaviour was ungentlemanly. A gentleman should never divulge private conversations. Up to a point that is undoubtedly true. My rule, however, is slightly different. Anything I feel free to tell my private circle, or talk about at the bar of the Garrick, for example, should be assumed to be publishable in this diary unless there are obvious and overriding arguments against letting readers in on the fun. That, I declare, is conduct perfectly becoming to a journalist and a gentleman – just possibly a professional duty.'

Guineas, Debo came in to lunch in the Tote room and she sat next to me and we had a kind of reconciliation. She has also been saying silly things to people like Jacob that the reason why we had had a breach was that I had made Andrew drunk. On the contrary, I never did anything of the sort.[4]

The house was fabulously decorated. The courtyard was covered with awnings and made into a dance floor. The tent where we had breakfast had lovely stars in the ceiling against a sky which was realistic.

But most spectacular of all was the fireworks display which began at 1.00 a.m. A huge float was pulled round the lake with nymphs and whatnot dancing on it, the Beethoven music crashed out and the fireworks crashed out all around. I thought it must be like something at Versailles given by Louis XIV except that his technology would not have been so good.

The party was in honour of the young Earl of Burlington, son of Stoker Hartington. He has fair hair like a girl's in its huge length, all round his neck and on his shoulders. I cannot see the point of this kind of thing but there were several young men there who ape this style in which the hair looks dirty and unkempt.

During the evening, soon after I arrived, my white waistcoat kept coming undone at the back. I had not done enough tests with it, not having worn it for ages. This was somewhat embarrassing and it inhibited my enjoyment. I could find no way of securing it properly though there was a very nice footman who recognized me and helped me once.

There were about fifteen hundred guests. It must have cost the best part of a quarter of a million pounds, if not more, up to half a million.

Tuesday 10 July
Meeting with the Home Secretary about the board members, etc.

My own position came up. I said I wanted to renew it for another three years.

The Home Secretary said he would like to talk to me privately about that in a week or so. So I think I shall have to get on to Margaret about it.

To the Royal Berkshire Golf Club dinner with some eighty people from the banking world, lenders and borrowers. The lenders had been

---

4. See Vol. 1, pp. 467–9, for WW's version of what happened.

playing a golf match against the borrowers. Chips Keswick in charge as President.

On the way back Chips told me he thought Rupert was in a lot of trouble. He is terribly over-geared and over-borrowed. He said that Hambros Bank called in their loans to him and he was not very pleased. He said, 'But we are bankers. We are not taking risks. But forget I said that.'

I hear quite a lot of comments from people who may or may not know what the state of Rupert's finances are. Chips thought he travelled backwards and forwards too much, jetting all over the world and doing too many things. I said, 'That's why he's put Andrew Knight in charge here. He can't stop. I hope he isn't going to get into serious trouble.' But I don't think he will. I think Sky Channel will work out in the end although it is going to take a couple of years or so for him to start making money on it. Meanwhile, he has borrowed up to the hilt and with bank rates as high as they are it is not very funny.

Wednesday 11 July
This is the day I have to make my major speech on the Broadcasting Bill.

We do pretty well. I get concessions from the government but not as many as I would have liked.

Unexpectedly, I also made a speech about the amendments in which people wanted to divest Rupert of his [satellite] shareholdings.

Thursday 12 July
I slept on the whole very little. The [previous] morning, trying to put my trousers on, I had put one leg into the wrong trouser leg and fell, hitting my side halfway up on the pointed end of my large Lytton Strachey table. (It formerly belonged to Lytton Strachey.)[5] It was very painful. It woke me up several times in the night. Then I was rattling around in my head about things I had forgotten. I was also over-excited having made two speeches in one day and mulling it all over. I got up in the middle of the night and started reading in the library.

Went to lunch at Drue Heinz's. There was an enormous gathering of about sixty, including such people as the Duke of Gloucester and Angus Ogilvy.

---

5. (1880–1932); biographer and essayist, prominent member of the Bloomsbury Group.

Before lunch William Rees-Mogg and Paul Johnson and Andrew Knight were all pontificating away about Nick Ridley's extraordinary interview in today's *Spectator*. He had more or less likened modern Germany taking over the European Commission to the same thing as Hitler [doing so] and he made statements which were wholly out of keeping with Margaret's and the government's line. He had put her into a state of deep embarrassment. I don't know if he will resign or what he is going to do.

I watched her at Question Time in the House of Commons on a television set at the Tote. Nick Ridley is still in Budapest. She defended him stoutly and said she wasn't going to sack him despite Kinnock jeers.

In the morning I had spoken to Ken Baker about how far we had got with the Broadcasting Bill amendments. He thought we had done pretty well and wouldn't get any further for the time being. Then he said, 'What about this thing that Nick Ridley has done? It is terribly damaging. It will split the party at a moment we thought we had got all the quarrelling about the Common Market bridged over and soothed down.' I said, 'Do you think it is as serious as all that?' He said, 'Yes. It is the most serious thing that's happened for a very long time.'

That was what Rees-Mogg was saying, that he will have to go or if he doesn't go, she will have to go. It may be the finish of the whole government.

I said, 'You are talking like Dick Crossman always used to, [saying] that we are standing on the edge of a precipice, one step further and we are all going to be killed. You get over-excited about these things.'

However, it is rather more serious than usual.

It is jolly bad luck on her, particularly as she did so well at the seven power economic summit in Houston, Texas, which she had just come back from this morning.

He was a total ass to say all that stuff to Dominic Lawson, the editor of the *Spectator*, in this long interview. It was tape recorded, which Nick knew, and he knew perfectly well it was all going to be printed, nothing like the A. N. Wilson and Queen Mother situation.

The Other Club dinner. I sat next to Julian Amery who was sitting in the chair.

Alec Douglas-Home was sitting opposite me.

I asked him whether he would have sacked Ridley if he had been Prime Minister. He said certainly. I said, 'She is always very loyal to her friends and I think she could ride the storm.' He looked rather doubtful as he seemed to think it was either him or her, which is a mistaken impression in my view.

Julian said poor Catherine, his wife, is unable to get out of bed sometimes for days. I keep feeling guilty that I have not been to see her. There never seems to be time.

I took Arnold home to Grosvenor Square. Surprisingly he said he agreed with everything Ridley had said about the Germans. I said I thought he would be rather pleased at his discomfiture. He said, 'No, not for that.'

Friday 13 July

I spoke to Margaret just on half past eight. We talked for about twenty minutes about the Ridley affair. I said, 'I don't think he ought to go.' She said she would have to leave it up to him but she hoped he wouldn't have to go.

Then she said, 'Of course what they are really doing is trying to get at me.'

She pointed out that he had seen him as the son of an old friend[6] and Mrs Ridley had cooked his lunch and met him at the station.

She said, 'Of course any Minister should always have his Press Officer present and then the Press Officer can say, "That's off the record. The Minister did not want that to be printed, did you Minister?"'

I asked her about the alleged Number 10 delay in making Sir John Sparrow[7] the new Levy Board Chairman after Sir Ian Trethowan goes. She said, 'I haven't heard anything about it. Nobody has put him forward to me. He was in my Policy Review Unit at Number 10.' She seemed to have no objection to him when I said that everybody seemed to want him. (Ian Trethowan had asked me to raise it with her.) She was able to switch on to such a minor problem amid all her troubles as a matter of course.

---

6. Dominic's father was Nigel Lawson, the former Chancellor of the Exchequer.
7. Director, Morgan Grenfell Group, 1971–88; seconded as head of Central Policy Review Staff, Cabinet Office, 1982 until 1983, when Mrs Thatcher closed the unit; chairman, Morgan Grenfell Asset Management, 1985–8, Universities Super-annuation Board, 1988–96, Horserace Betting Levy Board since 1991; knight 1984.

Rupert rang in the evening from Los Angeles in a great state about Nick Ridley.

Saturday 14 July

Again spoke to Margaret first thing in the morning before going down to Henry Keswick's. I told her about the poll in the *Sun* coming out enormously in favour of Nick Ridley.

On Friday he only got back late at night and she has not seen him yet but she will be talking to him over the week-end.

She was at this point clearly inclined to keep him. Certainly she is not going to ask him to resign and is leaving it to him if he feels he can't face all that he has to do.

The *News of the World* was very agitated about what would happen if he resigned before the deadline came when I could make alterations to my article. I said I could make an alternative, which I did, one which said he never needed to resign.

Carla Powell was staying at the Keswicks waiting for her husband. He was at Number 10 with Margaret. He told Carla that he would ring me if anything happened. This he did a short time before the official announcement was made that Nick Ridley had resigned. There was an exchange of letters. He did not think he could go on with all this furore and being baited by everybody. So she reluctantly let him go.

The notice Charles gave me was enough for me to ring the *News of the World*, Patsy Chapman, the editor, so she knew what had happened and tell her to use my alternative plan.

Henry Keswick's is a lovely house to stay in. We had a beautiful bedroom, or at least Verushka did, looking out across the hills and up a marvellous avenue of trees and across to the swimming pool which is concealed by the work of Clough Williams-Ellis[8] (who was the architect of all the new parts added on to the Queen Anne house). The additions were made under the instructions of Geoffrey Fry, one of the chocolate people, who had been PPS to Baldwin.

Michael Heseltine had nearly bought the house but when Henry mentioned this to him he said he had looked at it very hard but he did not think it was perfect architecturally.

Henry Keswick had only paid £177,000 for it in 1975. It must be

---

8. (1883–1978); perhaps best known for Portmeirion holiday village in north Wales, he included 'sections to Oare House' in his *Who's Who* listing; knight 1972.

worth about £12 million by now, especially as there are about a hundred acres of land around it.

He showed me a lovely foal, black, perfectly formed, called Oare Sparrow (after the name of their house). It has a very good pedigree and he is hoping it will win the Oaks.

Charles Powell arrived in time for dinner and said everybody had been greatly distressed including Margaret about Nick resigning but there did not seem to be any alternative at that stage. Henry said about how he had been at one of these Anglo-American international conferences last night at the house where Ronnie Tree used to live [Ditchley]. Hurd and Carrington were making noises saying that Ridley must go, whereas the French Ambassador, whom he had equally insulted in his quoted remarks saying the French were poodles of the Germans and ought not to be, actually agreed with Nick Ridley.

Henry said that, among the Tory politicians there, the senior ones were obviously behaving in a most destructive way towards Nick Ridley, thinking it was a marvellous chance to get rid of him and have a dig at her at the same time. That confirmed what she said to me.

Then came more messages from Number 10, nothing to do with Nick Ridley, that the *Independent on Sunday* was about to publish a leaked document. It had been written by Charles Powell. It was on a seminar for people like Douglas Hurd, Tom King, Margaret and other leading lights of the Cabinet, at Number 10 with a group of historians including Norman Stone and Hugh Trevor-Roper, all of renown for their knowledge about Germany. They had been thinking about what the long-term strategy and attitude should be to Germany. There was in fact nothing insulting for Germany in it.

On the contrary, it came to the conclusion that Germans were now quite different from what they had been in 1940 or 1945. They were unlikely to start a war and all the rest of it but they certainly were going to be, with East Germany added, far and away the strongest power in Europe and if they tried to push too far in dominating the EEC, we would have to make alliances with other people to check them. It was all very good common sense stuff.

I said to Charles, 'How did they get this document?' but he didn't know and said somebody had leaked it.

Charles Powell works terribly hard. He hardly ever has any time off at all, much to the displeasure of poor Carla who does not see anything like as much of him as she would like to.

I was surprised Drue [Heinz] had also been at the Ditchley conference but she goes everywhere. She loves all that kind of thing and she had given them a lot of money at Ditchley. She gives many things in England a great deal of money. She is really very nice.

I had quite a quarrel with Tess about the Common Market and Margaret Thatcher. She is very anti-Mrs Thatcher though she works for Kenneth Clarke at the Ministry of Health as his political adviser. I suppose she is echoing to some extent Kenneth Clarke's views. She seemed to think we were doing nothing about Europe and were absolutely anti.

She squashes Henry who dotes on her though disagrees with her. She is getting rather fatter, too.

However, she has got a lot of charm and she had decorated the house beautifully with lovely curtains. All the amenities are frightfully good, bathrooms and so on and my dressing-room was enchanting where I slept the night.

Sunday 15 July
Margaret came to lunch.

She was looking very young and wearing a smart red suit and high heels. Everybody had been agitated about what they were going to wear. Carla had said to the women, 'You can't wear trousers. You will have to wear a skirt because she will be wearing a proper skirt or summery dress.'

I said, 'I am going to wear my summer suit and nothing but an open necked and short-sleeved shirt.' Henry did the same and Charles Powell almost did the same. Denis, when he arrived, was wearing a rather smart summer suit with a tie. He was very relieved to see the men were not dressed like that and took off his coat and tie.

Margaret was getting very hot and did not want to sit in the garden very much. She walked around to have a look to begin with and then they said, 'Would you like to sit in the shade and have a drink?' She said yes but after a time on the terrace she said, 'It's very hot here too,' and she came back into the drawing-room. However, we had lunch outside, just the same as we had done the day before, where it was pretty hot but there was some kind of a pergola without any leaves on it.

Nick Ridley was also supposed to have been at that lunch but it was thought advisable for him not to come in view of what had happened.

Ridley rang up and spoke to Carla, who was staying in the house, and sent a special message to me to say how grateful he was for the article I wrote in the *News of the World* this morning. Margaret did not mention it, maybe because she had not seen it yet, or it could have been because I had to put it all in the past tense and said she should never have let him go, that it would diminish her authority, not enhance it, which I fear is true. But the fuss won't last very long. As I said to her, it will all come out all right in the end – it will all blow over.

After lunch Henry was very keen for her to go and see his foal and she walked in the great heat to go to see it, which she did not really like very much. But before then she planted a tree in the walled garden. It was a Chinese tree, it looked like a kind of Chinese oak, and she did it with enormous enthusiasm. There was a lot of earth piled all round the hole and she picked up the spade, dug the loose earth and started ramming it in. Denis said, 'I tell you, when she plants a tree she really plants a tree.'

As she went I gave her a kiss and I had little bugs from the garden on my face. She said, 'I see you don't like the heat any more than I do.'

Some of us went and had another swim and then we all went home, having congratulated Tess on arranging everything so well, which indeed she had done. She was looking much prettier and jollier at lunch time, showing off her legs to some advantage and wearing a skirt. I began to like her much more all over again.

When I came back Allan Davis was asleep in my bed having been to a garden party with his agent in Horsham. He had been let in by the au pair girl. He was a bit exhausted. At half past six we started talking about the play again. He said Lee Menzies is very determined to do it at the moment and thinks he is going to get Windsor.

Monday 16 July
Dinner with Jonathan Aitken.

Jonathan Aitken is convinced that the Tories are going to lose the next election because of the time for a change factor; they have run out of steam and have made too many mistakes and so forth. John Redwood from the Department of Industry, who worked with Nick Ridley, had quite a different view. He thinks that the tides are turning and that the Nick Ridley affair will not lose them votes.

Adam Faith, the pop singer, was there. He politely told me, and it may be true, that he reads my articles every week in the *News of the World*; he is a great fan of mine and always agreed with them. He said he had given up pop singing to go into writing a financial column called 'Faith in the City' in the *Mail on Sunday*.

He wanted to give up singing before he began to sink in the charts.

I enjoyed the evening, particularly meeting John Redwood and talking to him seriously for the first time. Slightly built, he has got a lean, inquisitive, dark face, lively eyes. You can see his brain is enormous; he uses it acutely and sees things clearly. No wet he.

Tuesday 17 July
I went to listen to Margaret, the first time she was answering Questions since the Ridley affair and the leaked document printed by the *Independent on Sunday*.

She was in total command. Her resilience is amazing and her skill at dealing with questions is fantastic.

I wrote in the *News of the World*, in the altered edition, that handing Ridley over to the baying mob would weaken her authority. I fear this may be true. This was very much echoed at dinner last night when a number of them said she is now prisoner of Hurd, Major and Howe.

I do hope I was wrong. She is such a brilliant politician, based on fierce conviction of what she does, that she may manage to maintain her total supremacy.

Thursday 19 July
Went to hear Leon Brittan talk to the Bruges Group. There was all the usual stuff about if Britain does not join all stages of the EMS, including having a single currency and a Central European Bank, we will be left on the sidelines. He proclaimed himself a federalist. He said we had given up our sovereignty to NATO.

When I asked him at the end how he squared saying that with being a member of the Cabinet which defended the Falklands without the permission of NATO, and we would not have taken the blindest notice of NATO if they had refused that permission, and did he hope for a future in which we would not be able to defend the Falklands again without the permission of the European Commission, his reply was as follows: 'NATO was not concerned with the area we defended.'

I like him, however. In many respects he has done very well as Commissioner for competition, etc.

Saturday 21 July

A broiling hot day, over 90°F. Margaret was at Newbury, a great
success. She arrived punctually at half past twelve. She was wearing a
hat and then she took it off and then she put it back on again, saying
to Verushka, 'I don't really like wearing this hat. My hair gets in such
a mess.' She is very conscious of her appearance, as well she should
be. She hates the heat and she was recalling how hot it had been the
previous Sunday at Henry Keswick's.

She sat between Henry Porchester, Chairman of Newbury, and
Stoker Hartington as Senior Steward of the Jockey Club.

They were all anxious to try and corner her. However, the field
opened up, as it were, a bit after lunch. She came with me to the Tote
control room and saw some of the girls as well. I had the heads of
divisions (apart from of Bookmakers who was away anyway on
holiday) all there to answer her questions. She took it all in very fast.

Everybody seemed so surprised at how friendly she is because they
are all misled by the media propaganda describing her as a horrible
old creature.

When she went down to the Silver Ring, they all shouted nice things
to her. I wanted this to happen. I wanted her to have an afternoon
where she could feel quite happy and realize that a lot of people
have considerable affection for her. They are not all anti-poll tax
demonstrators or 'down with Maggie' brigades, interest and mortgage
rates complainers. Though in the Newbury area there must be a hell
of a lot of people affected by high mortgage interest rates.

Arnold Weinstock turned up and was greatly surprised to see
Margaret. He was clearly irritated at this well kept secret. He had a
horse running which duly lost. Margaret kept saying while the race
was on, 'Do let's hope Arnold's horse wins. Otherwise he will be
impossible.'

Then we were off to Castle Hedingham to stay with Diana and
John Wilton.

The food was delicious. The house is very pretty and very well
arranged.

It was almost impossible to sleep. It was not so much the heat,
because the whole atmosphere was cooling off, but the front of the
house is on the road, a busy road with lorries and cars going by all
night.

I had wondered what John had meant at dinner when he said,

'Couldn't you use your influence to get heavy traffic diverted from this road?'

I am always very happy to be with Diana Wilton. She is a very gentle, soothing creature and John is easy to get on with as well as being intelligent. He would be quite happy to sit doing nothing and saying nothing all day except for reading.

When we got back to London I rang Margaret. She said what a happy afternoon it had been and she had enjoyed it enormously.

I said, 'By the way did you have a chance to say anything to David Waddington about my own position?' 'Oh yes,' she said. 'I did.' I said, 'How did he seem to react?' She said, 'Very favourably. And about the age, I said Denis is seventy-five and he is going strong so Woodrow can do the same. He is not seventy-five by any means yet.'

So it sounds as though it is going to be all right with Waddington about my carrying on for another three years from next May when I shall still be only seventy-two. If I last until I am seventy-five, that will be fine and then I will see how I feel at the end of that period, if all goes well.

Monday 23 July

Dinner party at Cavendish Avenue. Drue Heinz, Clarissa Avon, Evangeline Bruce,[9] Roy Jenkins, Charles Allsopp, Ali Forbes, the Pejacsevichs.

I gave them 1967 Château Lafite – three bottles. It was frightfully good. Not a drop was left. Roy enjoyed it greatly. I did it specially for him. I am very fond of Roy and always will be but he is terrible on Mrs Thatcher.

I said, 'In an election now, would you vote Labour?' He said yes. That's because he wants to get her out. He wouldn't even vote for his own curious Liberal SDP party.

He said, 'She's not pompous. But she is getting very fat and looking very heavy,' which (a) I don't agree with and (b) doesn't seem to be a very relevant criticism.

He takes very much the Sir Leon Brittan line on Europe. Before dinner somebody said, 'Monsieur le Président should go in first,' and I asked, 'Are you still called Monsieur le Président?' He said, 'I am on the continent but not in England because we don't do that sort of thing

---

9. Widow of David Bruce (1898–1977; US Ambassador, 1961–9).

when somebody has retired from a post like Ambassador or head of some organization.'

I think Roy would very much like to go on being called in England President of the Commission.

Wednesday 25 July
The new Archbishop of Canterbury has been announced, the Bishop of Bath and Wells, Dr Carey. He has to be better than the ghastly Archbishop of York [Habgood], or the idiotically naïvely left-wing Bishop of Liverpool, the cricketer David Sheppard.[10] From the sound of it he seems quite reasonable being an evangelical and believing in the old doctrines of the Church. I don't think he is a political anti-Mrs Thatcherite.

Ernest Saunders came to ask me for advice.

He said, 'What do you suggest my line should be to counsel?' I said, 'Tell him to make a speech a bit like Marshall-Hall[11] would have done, taking the jury into his confidence and siding with them:

' "If there has been any dishonest handling of money, none of it came his way. Moreover the shareholders got enormous benefits from his activities. He made many millions for them and they saw their share prices go up ten times or more in value. He did it for them. He was their employee and he was a faithful servant to them and I think it is safe to say that he could not have done anything really dishonest, though there may have been unconventional transactions." '

He asked me if I thought the jury would take a lot of notice of the Judge's summing up. I said, 'They are bound to. He is their guide.'[12]

When I shook hands with him and took him to his car he was looking very worried. He said, 'Perhaps the next time you see me you will be visiting me in prison.' I felt very sorry for him. The fellow is shattered.

It will be three and a half years or nearly four years from the time he was first arrested by the time the verdict is given.

---

10. David Sheppard captained the England cricket eleven in 1954.
11. Sir Edward Marshall-Hall QC (1858–1927), celebrated advocate and Conservative MP.
12. WW read Law at Oxford and took his Bar finals but never practised.

But I suppose he was guilty of rather more than unconventionality.[13]
Dinner with Irwin Stelzer.

We had a very good bottle of Dom Pérignon 1975.

The man sitting next to me had previously worked for NERA and was now working for a new firm which is also employing Irwin and Alan Walters in New York.

I realized at once, when my neighbour disclosed that he had been working for NERA, that Irwin would know that I was now working for NERA again. So my best kept secret from him turned out not to be a secret at all in the end. I was slightly relieved because he is still extremely friendly.

I wish I didn't have to do this consultancy work. I find it a bit grubby because one always has to declare an interest if one speaks to anybody about it, or a Minister, or write to them. I wish I was rich enough not to bother but I am not. I wouldn't even be able to have a holiday in Italy this year if I didn't have these consultancy arrangements with Skadden Arps and NERA. I certainly would not be able to live at the standard I do. But it would be nice to be shot of it all and just write plays and my articles. In these consultancy jobs I am a sort of contact man. I have never done it before in my life. I have always been able to paddle my own canoe without having to suck up to anybody.

Saturday 28 July
The Test Match at Lord's, in the box provided by Paul Getty for Bob [Wyatt]. Getty is gentle and nice, anxious to do good, and confused. He is a hypochondriac, apart from having been a victim of drugs for years. That's why his KBE (honorary) was delayed so long. He doesn't know that I gave it a prod with Mrs T and cleared it saying, 'I think he is cured of his drug addiction now.'

He has a large sheep-like-looking face with a big nose and a beard. His face hangs down. He dresses very badly. His feet are enormous and uncertain in their placing or moving. He was wearing big black shoes. At least, he does try to do good. I thanked him for the good things he has done for England. They are many though he got into a muddle during the miners' strike and gave Scargill's Women Against

---

13. He was found guilty of twelve offences. In December 1996 the European Court of Human Rights ruled that his trial had been unfair because of the use of evidence given before the inspectors without the right of silence.

the Strike people money but, when tackled afterwards, gave to the non-striking miners and their families as well.

He now adores cricket. When I asked him if he preferred it to baseball he said yes, baseball was like draughts and cricket like chess with its subtleties.

Robert Runcie was there with his wife. I told Robert that I had written something quite complimentary about him in the *News of the World* for tomorrow morning. He said he didn't get it. I said, 'You should read the *News of the World*.' He said, 'Yes, I remember a bishop once saying to me he read the *News of the World* to find out what his clergy were up to.'

Robert said of his successor, Bishop Carey, 'He is a very good scholar though he doesn't have the academic brain of Habgood who was a Fellow of King's (Cambridge). But people like that live in a rarefied atmosphere, not like Carey who goes to pubs and among sinners. One shouldn't neglect the sinners. I like them.'

I said, 'In that case there's a big one over there: Tony Lambton – you should go and talk to him.' He immediately went and sat beside him and talked for half an hour with great animation and enjoyment.

Tony Lambton was there because he is a friend of Paul Getty's, mildly. Both he and Tony have a weakness, which I share, for attractive women. They both sat next to the wife of Ted Dexter, the famous cricketer, and chatted her up for quite a long time. She is very attractive.

Tony later said to me what enormous charm Runcie has.

He said it was quite a thrill for him to meet my cousin, Leonard Hutton[14] and other famous players from the past whom he read about and admired when he was a boy and when he was young. That was an unusual confession for Tony.

We had quite long talks of a very friendly kind about politics and all the rest. He is looking forward to seeing us in Italy when we go to fetch some of the pictures he still has of mine and he says there is still some of the furniture. The breach now seems to be repaired.

Tony remains constant in his admiration of Mrs Thatcher and believes she will still win despite the treachery of the Tory wets whom he despises.

The day before, Gooch, who is a plodding batsman, made three hundred and thirty-three runs. He came within thirty-three runs of

---

14. (1916–90); captained Yorkshire and England; made over a hundred centuries in first class cricket; knight 1956.

beating Leonard Hutton's record against really good bowling from an Australian Test team. I said to Leonard Hutton, 'He nearly got your record.' 'Too close for comfort,' he replied.

Tony was amused when he asked Bob about Gooch's bowling. He had just put himself on. Bob said, 'He is what I call a friendly bowler. I would like to bat against him all day.'

We were all waiting to see Victoria [Holdsworth], Paul Getty's girlfriend. But she didn't turn up. She is a friend of Tony's through whom he knows Paul Getty.

Monday 30 July
Another visit to Lord's.

Denis Compton[15] said Bob was a much better player and fast bowler than he was. They both became very modest and said no, the other one was. But I think Compton was the better.

Robert Carr (Lord Carr)[16] was also there. We talked at length about poor Ian Gow who was murdered in his car, rather like Airey Neave,[17] this morning. When he got into his car it blew up with some Semtex device.

He himself had the front of his house blown out when he was Home Secretary.

Carr said when he stopped being Home Secretary he said to the police, 'Get it quite clear and make it known that I am not the Home Secretary any more. It is Mr Roy Jenkins now. Don't let them go for the wrong person.'

Tuesday 31 July
Margaret is quite shattered by Ian Gow's murder yesterday. She described how she went down to see Jane Gow and how stricken she was at the thought that anybody could have got into the car.

She said she is now going to cut her stay in Aspen short so as to be back for the funeral which she thought would be quite soon.

She spoke with more emotion that I have heard for a long time and for considerable length.

Poor soul. Ian Gow was her PPS for her first four years as Prime Minister. He was a round-faced, sweet, cheerful man, always ready

---

15. (1918–97); Middlesex and England player; made 123 centuries in first class cricket.
16. Conservative MP, 1950–74; Home Secretary, 1972–4; life peer 1975.
17. Conservative MP, 1953 until 1979 when he was murdered by the IRA.

with a joke, and always had some sensible observation, sometimes both at the same time. He was knowledgeable about political feelings. It was sad, however, that he resigned from the government over the Anglo-Irish Agreement. I pleaded with him a lot at the time to come back again afterwards but he wouldn't budge.[18] She missed and misses him.

---

18. See Vol. 1, p. 120, for WW's approach to Gow.

1–8 August
To Italy.

The house has a beautiful view of the sea from all its windows and terraces, and staircases going down to the sea-water pool just above the sea. But the conditions for me working are hampered and difficult. I have to write and dictate in my bedroom which I am sharing with Verushka.

The holiday has cost a fortune. It worries me that we cannot possibly have another one like this. I owe so many thousands in income tax and I ought to be saving up for it. I don't know how long I shall be going on with the Tote or with any of the other jobs I have got.

I have done my revisions to *High Profiles*. Taken out Maud, with regret, added a few pieces, made a few more jokes and generally tidied it up.

The Wiltons here as usual.

Thursday 9 August
The annual party of Judith, Countess of Bathurst, and her inamorato, John Vestey. Queen Juliana of the Netherlands was there. She looked even more dried up and shrivelled than before and remains intensely boring. Prince Bernhardt was also there. He seems to have got smaller and more aged, strikingly so. He aired his opinion that Bush should have acted a year ago to stop the Iraqis.[1] That seemed quite nonsensical.

There was the usual more or less social set of Porto Ercole there.

Mark Burrell is an interesting man with a bald head, prematurely more or less.[2]

He is high up in BSB.

I asked him whether he thought BSB would ever make any money

---

1. Iraq had invaded Kuwait on 2 August; the US ordered troops to the Gulf on 7 August; the UK said it would send forces on 9 August.
2. Director, Pearson, since 1977 (executive director, 1986–97); director, BSB Holdings, since 1987, BSkyB Group, 1991–4.

and he seemed rather doubtful. He was also doubtful about Sky. He then said, 'There probably isn't room for both of us and there should be a merger.' I said, 'Of course. You should both be attacking the BBC and the ITV together and also presenting your case together to the government instead of scrapping among yourselves.' I said, 'I will raise it with Rupert.'

Friday 10 August
Ring Margaret. Tell her I think she is doing everything absolutely wonderfully well over Iraq and that the BBC overseas broadcasts are nothing like as biased as the ones at home. They have a lot of praise for her including this morning President Bush's compliment to her on her leadership.

I said, 'I kick myself that I didn't say to you Kuwait is about to be invaded by Iraq. But I dare say you knew that all the time.' She said, 'No, we didn't. We didn't think Saddam would do it.'

She was confident though that the blockade of Iraq would work. I said, 'But it didn't work against Rhodesia, the sanctions.' She said, 'No. They were getting stuff through South Africa. But the point about Iraq is that the oil tankers which take the oil away from Saudi Arabian and other ports, now that we have got the United Nations sanctions, won't load up the oil from Iraq.'

I said, 'It has to be a fight to the finish with Saddam. He cannot possibly climb down. He can't allow the Emir to be restored. He would lose so much face. The only thing that can happen is that he gets so hemmed in by the blockade and lack of funds that there will be a revolution within Iraq and he will be deposed.'

She was very bullish about the possibility of squashing Iraq.

She had just been talking to Andreotti (Prime Minister of Italy). He said to her that we ought to keep everything within a United Nations force. He doesn't want to contribute anything to the American and British forces (which have now been added to by Australia). I said, 'That shows you the Common Market is no good when it comes to a joint foreign policy.'

Thank goodness she is running the country and is such a strong leader in the Western world, while Mitterrand, Kohl and Co run around and do nothing. She said the Community ought to be doing more than any of us with troops and aid because they have got much more to lose than we have. We have got our oil and the Americans have got a lot of their oil.

I said, 'I don't think Kuwait can be restored without some form of democracy or a better one than they have got. And that is Saudi Arabia's weakness in the Arab world.'

She then said that Ian Gow's funeral had been very moving and she had read the lesson there.

She is still very upset about that murder.

Tuesday 14 August
Cino Corsini gave his annual party in the arboretum.[3] Queen Juliana was there and so was Prince Bernhardt.

I took the Quintons, who arrived yesterday, to start a little tour of the garden. They were not very keen to go far. I said, 'I must pee.' When we started climbing up from one level to another I said, 'There are some bushes which will do here,' and I was just undoing my flies when Tony Quinton said, 'Look out. The Queen is coming.'

I wonder what she would have thought if she had seen me peeing. Not much I imagine. She's a hardy old soul.

After the arboretum party we had dinner as guests of the Pejacsevichs at the Gamberi Rosso. It was very good. I drank far too much wine. Tony Quinton pontificated quite a lot and made a number of jolly jokes. Somebody was talking of gaffes and he said the worst gaffe he ever heard was Isaiah Berlin's at a party of George Weidenfeld's.

Somebody said to Isaiah, 'What was the worst mistake you think Wilson made?' and he said, 'Oh that terrible lavender-paper honours list.[4] Dreadful people, crooks and a worthless crew,' and then he suddenly realized that George Weidenfeld had appeared in that list and he had no way out to cover up his gaffe.

Marcelle Quinton is a very bright lady. I like her. She is very enterprising. She has got an excellent line in doing sculptures of heads from photographs. She charges an awful lot for them. She did one of Mrs Thatcher. She just saw her once and asked her if she was satisfied with her hair that morning and she said yes and turned one way and another.

---

3. See 8 August 1989 and Vol. 1, p. 617, for this famous garden.
4. The draft of Harold Wilson's 1976 resignation Honours list was written by Marcia Williams (life peer 1974, Lady Falkender), his Political Secretary, on lavender-coloured paper. It included Lord Kagan, manufacturer of the Gannex raincoat Wilson always wore, who was subsequently imprisoned for evading excise duties.

She completed the bust for Somerville College and Mrs Thatcher was delighted with it.[5]

Marcelle is extremely thin and skinny. She doesn't like the sun. She has what you might call a piquant face. She is not pretty but she is lively. She is dark and can be very entertaining as well as sharp in her comments.

I asked her what they all talked about at these famous women's lunches that she and Netta and Verushka and others go to. She said, 'About you, of course.' I said, 'What do you mean, about me?' She said, 'No, men generally and husbands, love affairs.' I said, 'Do you never talk about anything serious?' She said, 'No. It's all gossip. I don't talk about sculptures. That's my work. I relax when I have these women's lunches.'

In the afternoon the *Times* rang, somebody from the arts pages. He wanted to know what I thought about the revival of the play in which Churchill is accused of arranging for the murder of General Sikorski, the leader of the exiled Polish army, in a plane which crashed in Gibraltar [in 1943].[6] He said that the pilot of the aeroplane was now dead. The play had been called off after it began originally for fear of libel action from him.

'Why do you ask me?' I enquired. 'Because you said it was outrageous at the time.' I said, 'Certainly it was. It was in 1968, not long after Churchill had died.' He said, 'Do you think a distance in time makes any difference?' I said, 'Not to the question of the lies told but it may not raise so much indignation now. I still think, however, that it shouldn't be shown.'

When I recounted this story, Tony Quinton said I was quite wrong, it was censorship and it ought to be allowed to be shown so that people could see it for themselves. I said, 'Maybe, but I think traducing someone like Churchill who is obviously unable to answer is pretty disgraceful.'

---

5. See illustration. Marcelle Quinton's other sculptures include Bertrand Russell (1979, in Red Lion Square, London WC1), Iris Murdoch (1974), Harold Lever (1981), George Weidenfeld (1990), Harold Macmillan (in the House of Commons) and Drue Heinz.

6. *Soldiers* by Rolf Hochhuth (1967).

Wednesday 15 August
We played bridge. Marcelle is an aggressive player. She keeps analysing every card everybody plays and tells them when they have done it wrong. She accuses people of cheating and is a very bad loser. I was determined to win the final game of the rubber to win the rubber. I played my cards in what she afterwards called an unusual and brilliant way. She was greatly mortified that she was defeated.

They are only staying until Thursday morning because they have a free trip on Mrs Wrightsman's private aeroplane. (She is the one who pays for so much of the Metropolitan Museum in New York.)[7] They had one out and one back. Originally the Quintons were going to be staying till Saturday. We were effectually prevented from asking anybody [else] to stay that week by their change of plans which they never announced beforehand.

Thursday 23 August
We went to see Tony Lambton. He asked us to be there at half past twelve so we could sort out the pictures. We got there on time and he didn't turn up until nearly one o'clock, having gone into Siena to see the bank. However, he had sorted out the pictures.

Tony was very amiable and friendly but pretty rude about everybody else who had been around the place or he knew. Anne Lambton was there and I again complimented her on her acting. She moves beautifully. Her gestures are fine, she acts extremely well, her voice is excellent.

They both, she and Rose, the other daughter who was staying there, have an amused view of their father and his malice about everybody else. He was attacking Rupert saying he was Jewish, that his mother was a Jewess which is true, and that he is part of an international Jewish conspiracy. The daughters both laughed and said, 'Not all that again.'

Tony doesn't look very well. I think he is probably very unhappy sitting about in Italy most of the time.

Friday 24 August
The new house in the mountains is a cross between James Bond, the Great Gatsby, Blackpool illuminations, discos – it's a nightmare in

---

7. Jayne Wrightsman, widow of Charles Wrightsman, whose fortune was from oil.

short, though it is fascinating to see this place. It was converted from an old house into this monstrosity by a Belgian ex-diplomat.

A bar downstairs is behind a chunk of a Renaissance altar from a church. The stereo music reverberates throughout the house, lights flash on and off if you press a button in the disco area. The sun can be warm but it is frequently cold and very bitterly windy.

The [Banzsky] children, one aged five and the other aged three, scream all day long, fall over, fight. They are allowed at lunch and at dinner where they squabble and dominate the conversation and everybody has to say how much they love them. They are given presents about five times a day.

I like them but it is almost impossible to have a conversation with anybody.

There was a thoroughly nasty letter waiting for me at the top of the mountain from Irwin Stelzer, accusing me of going against Rupert's interests because I am now back on the advisory board of NERA and they have been employed by Sadler (he's a retired civil servant) to do the inquiry into the effects of cross-ownership of newspapers and television. I knew nothing about the inquiry – or that NERA was involved in it.

I ring Dermot Glynn [chief executive] who tells me that it was something he didn't think worth telling me about. It is a perfectly straightforward thing where they are giving advice on questions to ask.

He [has] probably put poison into Rupert's mind against me – all very disturbing. I tried to get Rupert but he was in Los Angeles, coming to England early in September.

I am afraid he is going to try and undermine me with Skadden Arps, on which I considerably depend for their £25,000 a year, with all this income tax coming up.

Meanwhile, I continue with this terrifying, expensive holiday which is almost a complete wash-out apart from finishing my play and modifying the first one.

Poor Jack Huntingdon is still lingering at death's door. I wish I had gone and seen him while he was still *compos mentis* but somehow it never fitted in with the times.

Saturday 25 August
We went to Sismano where Anna Lu [Gingo's wife] has a castle. It was part of her inheritance from her father, the Prince Corsini. It is very beautiful. She has had it for four years and is doing it up.

Gingo spends only a little time there, preferring Perignano, where he is busy growing his wine. He brought us two dozen bottles. The white is reasonable. The red is not very good. However I said they were both very good. He puts 'Produced by Conte San Miniatelli' on the labels and makes it look as grand as he can.

Sunday 2 September
The holiday which was sometimes almost like a nightmare ended yesterday.

This evening I spoke to Margaret. She asked my opinion on why Kinnock asked for a recall of Parliament. I said that he didn't do it earlier because he was in Italy on his holiday. But he must have felt under great pressure, once Steel and the Liberals had asked for a recall of Parliament, to do so from his own side.

She said, 'What is Benn's line going to be?' I said, 'Obviously a very left-wing one, that we shouldn't be supporting feudal monarchs in the Gulf states.'

I warned her that the question of why we didn't know Kuwait was going to be attacked could come up so she ought to have a good answer. She said, 'Mubarak, the President of Egypt, saw the President of Iraq two days before and was quite convinced by his assurance that he was not going to attack Kuwait.'

Tuesday 4 September
I wrote this morning to Margaret Huntingdon. Poor woman. She herself is eighty now and very frail, I gather. I couldn't be at the funeral on Sunday at Ashby de la Zouche but we sent flowers. The *Independent* has asked me to write an obituary of Jack Huntingdon at the suggestion of Moorea, which surprised me. He was a dear, sweet man and I have many happy memories of him. I hope that we can get back his great mural ('The "Mexican" Garden of Eden') which he did for us when we had the house in Italy.

Thursday 6 September
Our projected meeting with the Home Office to go over the amendments [to the Broadcasting Bill] was cancelled because the parliamentary draftsmen hadn't yet had time to prepare them, having just come back from holiday.

I think they are going to be more or less all right despite an idiotic speech made by David Mellor (now Arts Minister) pretending they were not accepting my amendments but outlining the plan for accepting them, broadly so. Mellor likes to show off, keep on side with everybody and make a noise for himself.

Rang Peter Stehrenberger and said, 'This is the time when I ask about my salary for the coming year from News International. I'd like £110,000 – an upgrade from £90,000. My twenty-two-year-old daughter has been offered £40,000 a year and a car. I think my column in the *News of the World*, plus the fortnightly column in the *Times*, plus a lot of book reviews must be at least worth £110k, particularly as I also help in many other ways the interests of Murdoch.' Rupert's coming on Sunday. Peter Stehrenberger said he would speak to him because he's seeing him on Monday morning before he goes on holiday.

I hope Rupert hasn't had poison put into his ears by Irwin.

I've written to him saying what an ass he is to say I could ever do anything against Rupert's interests merely because I'm on the advisory board of NERA which was doing a job for the Sadler inquiry on how a newspaper should behave if they have television interests.

Margaret said she's spoken to Waddington and it will be all right. I hope so or I shall be in Queer Street financially.

Listened to Margaret and Kinnock in the emergency debate on Iraq.

Labour is so far on her side with what she is doing with President Bush and taking a lead world-wide. But there will be trouble if there is an attack on Iraq or even on Kuwait to recapture it without United Nations approval. This could well happen as the waverers in the United Nations get the upper hand. In that case we would have to act because not only must Kuwait be restored to its former state but Hussein must be ousted. He is too dangerous to have around with his installations for making nuclear weapons and all his foul poison gas weapons with missiles to fire them.

Friday 7 September
Verushka and Petronella went to the requiem mass for poor Claudie Worsthorne. Perry was in tears throughout. He's lost without her.

Apparently many people asked why I wasn't there but I had to write my article for the *News of the World*.

Saturday 8 September
Ron Pell of the *News of the World* told me they tried very hard to get Kinnock to do one of the columns in my space while I was away. His

own people tried to get him to do it. But he said he didn't want to be a stand-in for me. Very foolish of him. Edwina Currie, apart from Margaret Thatcher, was the best of the columnists who took my space. Edwina was very lively, to the point, earthy, funny. Maybe in my present state of nervousness I fear I might have to give the column to her permanently.

Norman Lamont rang. He thinks it could well come to war. He doesn't believe that Margaret is going to benefit the Tories in the same way as she did over the Falklands.

He's deep into the spending Departments' claims on the Treasury, trying to resist them as best he can.

I said, 'The Iraq affair is going to push inflation up higher.' He said, 'You can say that again.' I said, 'It may not be quite as bad as you think,' but he is very pessimistic.

Sunday 9 September

Told Rupert what Irwin had been up to with News International/ NERA, saying that I was acting against his interests. He knew nothing about it but he was very quick to say, 'Don't take it seriously. Irwin is very prickly.'

Pru[1] had a son and so he is a grandfather now.

Very briefly I told him that Stehrenberger was going to speak to him about my salary tomorrow. He said, 'We haven't got any money.' I said, 'I know. The advertising's very low. But you'll come through.' He was on the defensive at once so that he wouldn't have to pay me too much extra.

He asked how Margaret was. I said she was in very good spirits. She had to go to Balmoral this weekend. 'How boring for her,' Rupert said.

To lunch at Bowden. Verushka didn't come because she said she wrenched her back dealing with the Hoover yesterday.

Arnold was very friendly and not at all prickly.

Tuesday 11 September

Congratulated Margaret for her performance in the House last week.

I mentioned to her about backing Tokes for the Nobel Prize – the pastor in Timişoara who started the Romanian revolution against

---

1. Murdoch's daughter, by his first marriage, m 2 Alisdair MacLeod.

Ceauşescu.[2] She was interested. I said I would send her a little note about it all, together with suggestions to Charles Powell of things she might want to cover in speeches in Hungary.[3]

Thursday 13 September
Spoke to Margaret at 7.20 a.m. When she came on sounding a tiny bit breathless I said, 'Am I too early?' She laughed and said, 'No, not at all.'

I gave her a résumé of my conversation with Mellor yesterday, with me at Doncaster, opening a stand, talking to him in his office. He had sounded as if most of the amendments were going to be OK but he didn't want to deal with the point about making the BBC comply with the ITC code or have a similar code of their own. I told her that he had said it was one bridge too far and that the BBC charter was coming up in six years' time for renewal, to which I had replied I would be dead by then.

'That's another two elections,' exclaimed Margaret in horror. She said she would try to deal with it.

Saturday 15 September
I urged on Margaret that she should encourage the Hungarian and Czech peoples to join the Common Market and say that would be possible. She said she thought there could be an association quite soon.

Rupert has only agreed to £100,000 a year for me. I think he is very mean about it, particularly because of all the things I do for him outside writing my columns and my book reviews. Also when you compare it with what John Junor gets now, at about £130,000 a year for writing one wretched little column in the *Mail on Sunday*, and a free car with a chauffeur.

Tuesday 18 September
Went to the Levy Board meeting.

I am afraid I have fallen out a little with my new friend, George Walker. I strongly resisted his being allowed to have William Hill betting in a great tent and funfair place in the Silver Ring at Ascot on September 28th and 29th, on the Brent Walker Festival Day of Racing. It breaches all the rules.

---

2. President of Romania, 1967–89.
3. She visited Czechoslovakia and Hungary 17–19 September.

Had lunch with Abdul Al Ghazzi. He thinks there ought to be some compromise about Kuwait although he agrees that Saddam was very wrong to have invaded it. He said he is not an Iraqi himself. He is related to the Kuwaiti royal family and comes from the same tribe as they do.

He had just been in Russia and had long talks with Mr Popov who is the Mayor of Moscow and probably the third most important man in Russia after Gorbachev and Yeltsin. He has complete control in Moscow. He wants to get a lot of business people setting up ventures in Moscow from Britain. I said, 'They may not be very keen. They may not get their money out.' He said he thinks they will. Popov wants to be met by businessmen and perhaps Mrs Thatcher in Britain, to where he is very keen to come. Abdul says he is going to pay his fare. I said, 'That part is not a very good idea. If he comes, he should come either under his own steam or as a guest of some business group in Britain.'

Wednesday 19 September
Went to the Sky Television studios.

I had to do about three to four minutes straight to camera explaining without interruption what the amendments to the Broadcasting Bill really mean and why they don't involve censorship but prevent censorship by those who put on slanted programmes, refusing to allow the opposite views to be put.

Thursday 20 September
Went to Birmingham. I was given lunch by Professor Lightchild, the young Director of Electricity Regulation under the new Electricity Act. His lady Deputy Director, who is very keen on racing, came too. They have decided to reverse their original objection to our wind farm at Bonython on later evidence supplied by us. If I hadn't intervened, they would never have reversed it.

The Home Secretary has agreed to John Sanderson, David Montagu and Peter Winfield[4] going on at the Tote Board but he won't allow Priscilla Hastings or Frank Chapple to continue.

---

4. Senior partner, Healey & Baker, 1975–88; chairman, London Auction Mart, 1980–92; member of Tote Board, 1981–92.

Saturday 22 September
At Allan's instigation I saw *Hidden Laughter* by Simon Gray. A very good play. I sat in the front row by myself at the side where I had Felicity Kendall frequently sitting at a table in the front of the stage almost on top of me. At one point I could see up her bare legs to her tiny strip of knicker between her legs. I couldn't help looking every now and again but I don't think she noticed it. However, later on when I was looking at the other actors and not at her she began to cross her legs a bit and pull her skirt down. She is quite attractive and does have nice legs.

If I could write a play as good as that I would be delighted.

Sunday 23 September
Margaret enjoyed her tour in Eastern Europe.

I asked her if she had seen Tokes, now Bishop Tokes, in the hospital in Hungary. She said no because she had been strongly advised this would cause deep offence to Romania so she had compromised by sending him a card and flowers which the Ambassador would deliver.

I said, 'You may be cross with me on Tuesday morning because I am writing in the *Times* that I think you should lower interest rates by a half per cent next month and then perhaps a little later another half per cent.' This was after she said there was an awful lot of doom and gloom about the place in the economy.

I said, 'Your drive against inflation will still continue even if you bring the interest rate down to fourteen per cent because that's still pretty high.' I said also that I wished all the talk about joining the ERM was over.[5]

Before speaking to Margaret I had spoken to Norman Lamont.

Norman says it is the most hard work he has ever had, dealing with the grounds in which he has to agree, or mostly disagree, with the demands of the spending Ministers. He says it gives a great insight into their characters and of course you can tell from how they deal with it which ones are run by the civil servants and which are putting forward a case genuinely which they believe in.

---

5. WW added a note to the manuscript here saying: 'NB The interest rate came down by one per cent on Friday October 5th. We also signalled entry into the ERM which I was not so keen about.'

Monday 24 September

Had a pretty successful meeting [on the Broadcasting Bill] with the Home Office officials. They are going a long way to meet the amendments but they are still not allowed by Ministers to include the BBC in the instructions the ITC get to draw [up] the code on impartiality. They also won't listen to the notion that there should be some kind of an appeal from the authorities at the BBC and ITC when complainants are fobbed off.

I then had the idea that we might say in the Bill that they should have an internal ombudsman at the IBA and at the BBC, as they do at newspapers nowadays.

I am in the middle of my complaint against the IBA on the *Media Show* programme which was so disgracefully biased against my amendments. I have rejected a request by the *Right to Reply* of Channel 4 to appear on the programme on the grounds that it is now with the IBA and I don't want to cross wires.

Tuesday 25 September

Rang Margaret as promised to tell her what had happened. She said, 'Oh dear. I did send a note down about making the BBC come under the same instructions for a code on impartiality to be drawn up as the ITC had. Perhaps it hasn't filtered down yet.'

Then she had a brainwave: why not put into the Bill an amendment which says that the Home Secretary may by order require the BBC to do the same as our amendments, now accepted by the government?

She was also taken by my notion that there should be an internal ombudsman.

We talked a bit about the economy. I said, 'Do read my article this morning where I explain that the RPI [Retail Price Index] is hopeless as a guide to inflation. That's apart, of course, from saying that Major ought to reduce the interest rate by half a per cent now and half a per cent later in a month's time if all went well.' 'Good, Woodrow, I will dash off and read the *Times* now.' This was at about five to eight.

Immediately after I had put the telephone down Ken Baker, Chairman of the Tory Party, rang.

He said, 'I agree completely with what you say. We must ease it that little bit but don't, for goodness' sake, say I have said so.'

I don't think he likes putting his head above the parapet too much unless it looks pretty safe.

Later on in the morning I talked to John Banham, the Director

General of the CBI [Confederation of British Industry]. It was really to talk to him about Abdul Al Ghazzi's suggestion to bring Mr Popov over from Moscow to talk to British business people. He said, 'It's a very good idea and it could coincide with Douglas Hurd's drive in November to encourage business people to go to Moscow.'

He thought the best thing to do would be for me to write to him about it all and he would say that I had suggested to him some way in which Mr Popov could be invited other than as official guest to the government or by business people.

Chips came to dinner. It was Verushka's birthday. He didn't know. Verushka is not keen on people knowing it's her birthday. However, Janka made a chocolate birthday cake rather prettily decorated with marzipan roses, yellow ones. When Petronella brought it in, we had stuck some non-blowable-out candles on it. Verushka tried to blow them out and of course they burst into flame again. Jolly joke.

Chips is in rumbustious shape.

We talked about some of the people Mrs Thatcher fell under the spell of. I said, 'She has a weakness for raffish characters who make or seem to have made a lot of money.'

He spoke of Jeffrey Sterling[6] and said he is a Jew. He said he is also a very sycophantic man but he has given her a lot of good service, as has the newly knighted Michael Richardson[7] of N. M. Rothschild. He said these people oil away but they do actually deliver some goods for her.

Chips' great ambition is to be Governor of the Bank of England. He said he thought he had fluffed his relationship with Mrs Thatcher when I gave him the opportunity to meet her and she might not think much of him. I said, 'On the contrary. She thinks very highly of you and you've got some very good things through. I will enquire when the next Directors of the Bank of England are being appointed and see whether I can do anything.'[8]

We drank 1937 Château Capbern, a good cru bourgeois.

I got a bit drunk because we had a lovely bottle of Bollinger 1979, a special year, and a lovely bottle of Tonnerre Chablis, Premier Cru.

I told him about Ernest Saunders' son, James, wanting to see me to

---

6. Chairman, P&O Steam Navigation Co., since 1983; at this time chairman, Royal Ballet School, and trustee of other arts organizations; knight 1985; life peer 1991.
7. Vice chairman, N. M. Rothschild & Sons, 1990–4; knight 1990.
8. He was appointed a director of the Bank of England in 1993.

give him advice on his appeal. Chips advised me against seeing him, probably correctly. I said, 'The boy is very loyal to his father.' Chips is convinced the father is a crook. I said, 'Yes but it is quite touching that he is devoted to his father like that. Would you be, Petronella, if I got into disgrace?' Chips piped up, 'I would be, however awful your action was supposed to have been.' So it all ended in happy mutual esteem, assisted no doubt by the wine.

Wednesday 26 September

Lunch with Bill Cash[9] at the Carlton. We had to climb up funny, poky back stairs, very narrow. Finally we got to a dining room which hadn't been affected by the [IRA] bomb blast. Donald Kaberry, [former] Tory MP, was nearly killed and is now making a good recovery. A tough old bird.

Bill Cash is a pretty good egg, very pro Mrs Thatcher. He wants to enlist my support and help in his pro Bruges campaign in the Commons and generally.

I rang James Saunders and said I didn't think there was much point in his coming to see me because it [the appeal] is a technical matter.

I said, 'Give him my regards. You are a very loyal son and you fight very well for him.'

Thursday 27 September

I was alarmed by the *Today* programme on Radio 4. At about twenty past seven there was Mellor blowing off in his usual oily way, saying that the amendments the government would agree to in the Broadcasting Bill wouldn't apply to the BBC.

I was hopping mad. I couldn't get him at his office because he is going to Japan this afternoon. But I got them to give me his home number and I rang him there.

Once again he said he refused to put in anything about the BBC, not even the suggestion which Margaret had made to me about putting a one-liner in the Bill saying that the Home Secretary could have power to apply to the BBC the requirements on drawing up a code for the ITC.

I said, 'But over a hundred of your own Tory backbenchers have signed a motion agreeing with our amendments.'

He said, 'Waddington agrees with me. I cannot advise my colleagues

9. Conservative MP since 1984.

to do what you want about getting the BBC into the Bill. We would be in a very delicate political situation. We would be having a scrap with the broadcasters at exactly the wrong moment and we would probably lose it.'

What he really means is that he doesn't want to damage his reputation and his image with all the broadcasting people. He is thinking in terms of his own future career, no doubt, after Margaret has gone.

Friday 28 September
Told Margaret that Mellor wouldn't advise his colleagues to brawl with BBC.

She said, 'If you do have the BBC in the Bill, won't that mean they'll be attacking us horribly and with enormous bias from then on, including during the next election?' I said I did not believe it. 'I would think many bad things of the BBC but the people at the top are much more honourable than that and they wouldn't allow it simply because the BBC had been brought into line with the ITC as far as the law is concerned with its code of impartiality.'

She said she was leaving for New York tomorrow morning. She would try and get a note down, particularly to see if she could make them reconsider. But clearly she thinks she can't go on overruling Waddington and Mellor.

Adrian Rowbotham came to see me. He is Mrs Tamborero's brother-in-law. He is trying to promote his film business. He has obviously done a lot of very good things but is finding it uphill work in the economic climate at present to get all the work he would like. I suggested British Coal and the Jockey Club and even British Steel.

Saturday 29 September
To Ascot on a wet, overcast day.

We had to arrive by twelve because Princess Michael was going to preside.

When she arrived we all stood around waiting to be presented to her. A bit absurd really. When she got to me she gave me a great kiss and said, 'What a marvellous, beautiful bow tie.' I said, 'You look pretty good yourself.' She did as a matter of fact. She was wearing a pretty white dress and hat. It didn't show a lot of her legs but you saw enough of them to see the whole Junoesque figure in proportion.

Later in the Royal Box or 'Queen's Stand', as it is called when the Queen is there, we had a long talk. I said I was so sorry about Prince

Michael [not having his membership of the Tote Board renewed] and I had been having fearful rows with the Home Secretary for three to four months but I couldn't get my way.

I didn't say actually that I didn't fight very hard to keep Prince Michael – I had a rather sweet letter from him – because he hardly ever attends board meetings; indeed I was quite ready to sacrifice him. She said the money was very important to him. They have got none. Even the secretaries' costs have gone up enormously. She has got to buy a thirty acre field nearby her house and she doesn't know how she is going to raise the money. They mass-produce lambs by making the ewes give birth double the number of times that ewes usually do. They bleat and they are pathetic. The bleating keeps her awake because it is only just by their house, and so on.

I said, 'Maybe I'll speak to George Walker who is a very nice man.'

If he got a directorship there [with Brent Walker], it might be quite a good thing for him. Princess Michael said, 'But it's pubs and betting shops.' I said, 'Yes but he also owns marinas, hotels, property developments and so forth. It's not a great disgrace.' Then she said, 'He has to look after one of the family already,' meaning the Marquess of Milford Haven who is married to George Walker's daughter.

She said, 'Your newspaper was horrid to me last week.' I said, 'I don't read those parts. What was it all about?' She said, 'They tracked me down in America where I was staying with somebody. Actually they got it right but not all the details. Do you think I could sue them for libel?' I said, 'Not if they have got enough of the details right.'

She said that a *News of the World* reporter had rung up Michael pretending to be the man concerned and said, 'I think you ought to know your wife is staying with me.' But Prince Michael is so naïve and innocent that all he said (instead of getting angry, which he would have done if he'd been a European, and shouting at him and saying how disgraceful and she must return here at once) was, 'I never mind what she does when she's abroad. She can do what she likes.' She said didn't I think it was a dirty trick of the *News of the World* to ring up and pretend to be the man concerned? I said, 'Yes I'm afraid it was but I'm really not responsible for what they do.'

Actually I thought that if she didn't misbehave herself, she wouldn't get into trouble, as I have told her several times.

Angela [Oswald] said when they went on their recent annual trip to stay at Balmoral, the Queen suddenly took the Thatchers to have tea with the Oswalds staying at a nearby cottage. Angela took lots of photographs.

She sent the ones in which Mrs Thatcher and Denis were included to her. She got back a sweet letter in her own handwriting, thanking her and telling her how much she had enjoyed the tea. Angela thought that was remarkable considering she has, according to her staff, some five thousand letters a week to deal with, sometimes twelve thousand.

Queen Elizabeth the Queen Mother had twelve thousand letters on her ninetieth birthday. They are still dealing with them because even Queen Elizabeth herself can't answer them all in her own handwriting.

Tuesday 2 October

Saw Michael Day, the Commissioner for Racial Equality. He had been complaining that I had written unfairly about his organization, saying it ought to be wound up. He gave me some reports where they had done some useful work in stopping really foul discrimination against blacks or coloureds in housing. I can't use them this week because I haven't enough space but I will try next week.

Wednesday 3 October

I told the Tote Board that we were going to seek to make a film with Adrian Rowbotham portraying the Tote in a good light. Peter Winfield was very keen on the idea and so was the other board member present, John Sanderson.

Spoke to Margaret. Congratulated her on her trip to the USA.

I said, 'There've been an awful lot of attacks on our amendments even in Tory papers. The *Times* has been terrible but I shall be answering them in an article next Tuesday morning, as well as the other attacks.'

I told her my notes and suggestions on her conference speech would be sent down this morning and if I have any further ideas I will let her know.

Thursday 4 October

I wrote a letter of protest to the Home Office, David Waddington, about the way they are playing the fool with our board membership. Also, they have issued a press statement saying the matter of privatization of the Tote is still under consideration, which has once more raised alarm among our staff, particularly in the bookmaking part.

So far this year, despite all the adverse conditions, in our first six months, our profits are forty per cent higher than last year. Nevertheless, people go on saying that I'm a deadbeat and ought to be removed. I attacked Richard Evans who wrote a silly article to this effect in the

Times. I think my main enemy is Christopher Haines at the Jockey Club.

Arnold rang and said, 'What about this man Michael Blackburn?[1] Why don't you put him up for membership of the Tote Board?' I said, 'I can't put anybody up at the moment because they are playing the bloody fool.' Michael Blackburn is a friend of Peter Winfield who used to be senior partner of Touche Ross, the famous accountants. He is the man that David Swaythling suggested, against my express instructions not to, when we talked to the Home Secretary. David mentioned him as a possible successor to me. I have now decided to meet him and see what he is like. But I would like to get my own position out of the way before pressing for a new board member.

David Sieff is the new member I want.

I had a nice letter from John Patten thanking me for what I wrote about the Hattersley nonsense on the crime figures being due to Margaret Thatcher's materialist policy.[2] Actually I also mentioned John Patten as being the intelligent Minister of State at the Home Office, so doubtless that pleased him quite a lot.

I thought we got on pretty well with Ferrers and the Home Office officials, making the government change its mind about the ITC having to put in rules describing what impartiality is in its code.

Thursday 11 October
The amendments which are to be moved by the government have sparked much trouble from Willie Whitelaw. I had a long talk with him yesterday to persuade him not to vote against the government. We had to agree on a compromise. The ITC are being consulted about the rewording of one part of the instructions and dropping another one which they don't like.

He was very worked up about it all, saying Margaret and he had never agreed about this question of bias and he thought the government should not be involved in it. I said, 'It isn't, because the ITC is going to draw up its own code.'

I have been spending a lot of time giving interviews to BBC news and BBC2 *Newsnight*, which I did last night very late. I got up this

---

1. Chairman, Touche Ross, 1990–2.
2. *News of the World*, 30 September 1990; Roy Hattersley was at this time Opposition spokesman on home affairs as well as Deputy Leader of the Labour Party.

morning to go and do the Radio 4 *Today* programme with Brian Redhead. He was very friendly.

Julian Lewis is always ringing up with some further objection or query and argues with me. However, he did agree I had reached a sensible compromise.

He understands nothing of politics in practice and thinks every procedure can be manipulated and the government can bludgeon anything it likes through. It can't, even in the Commons, and certainly not in the Lords. Julian works very hard but talks and shouts too much, very didactic and German. He's been marvellous in helping with the amendments but is often tiresome. I am a paragon of tact compared with him.

My speech went well. Norris McWhirter[3] listening in the gallery described it as 'a blinder'.

The house was packed. On hearing the government's little amendments to the amendment, Willie said he would support the government. Ferrers wanted to get it all through today but I agreed with Belstead (Leader of the House) that too many crossbenchers, Tories and Opposition were annoyed at the 'discourtesy' of the late amendments to an amendment and we risked the probability of losing the lot. So the small alterations will now be on the third reading, Monday October 22nd.

Friday 12 October

Rang Margaret at about 7.45 p.m. to congratulate her on her splendid conference speech.

She said, 'Jeffrey Archer made perhaps the best speech at the conference from the floor. He was marvellous, telling them all to stop quarrelling and to get behind the leadership.'

Saturday 13 October

A very nasty profile of me in the *Independent* with a huge cartoon of my face.

It was a scissors-and-paste job taken from clippings, many of them quite inaccurate about me, things I was supposed to have said which I didn't and things which were supposed to have happened which never

---

3. Author, publisher; director, Guinness Publications; chairman, Freedom Association, a political pressure group arguing for free enterprise and the rights of individuals, since 1983.

did. The gist of it was based on an alleged remark made by my brother when he was three and a half (which is extremely unlikely), that he wanted to club me to death because I was no use. This was when I had just been born. He never did anything of the kind. The question in the profile was, 'Is Woodrow Wyatt any use?' and the answer we got was no.

I thought to myself as I read it (and I didn't even finish it because it was the usual drivel) that if I'm no use why have they devoted an enormous amount of their main feature page at the side of the leaders to saying so?

The modern style is that if you have a profile of anyone or an interview with anyone, you always have to say how awful he or she is and use all the snide remarks and the tattered, unfriendly comments that you can pick up from anywhere.

The memorial service for Hugh Sinclair [in Oxford] was pleasantly done.

Jerry Kerruish was there.[4] He is a Fellow of Magdalen, where the memorial service was held in the chapel because Hugh Sinclair was a Fellow of Magdalen from 1937 to 1980 and then an Emeritus Fellow from 1980 till he died.

We went together to the President's lodgings, where I once again met Anthony Smith,[5] who is the new President of Magdalen. They appointed him because they thought he would be modern, do new things but more particularly produce a whole lot of money from Paul Getty with whom he had been closely associated. When he was head of the British Film Institute he got Paul Getty to spend a lot of money on a Moving Image Museum.

Heads of colleges and Chancellors now seem to be appointed on the basis that they have got to raise money, not for their academic qualifications and their supervision of academic standards.

The meeting of the Council was a little sad. We were trying to decide what was to be done with the property that Hugh had left.

We want to keep his name going in connection with some

---

4. Canon Kerruish, Oxford friend of WW; see Vol. 1, p. 418, where WW says he ought to have been made a bishop 'but unfortunately he was right-wing and had the disadvantage of believing in God'.

5. Director, British Film Institute, 1979–88; President, Magdalen College, Oxford, since 1988.

scholarships for research and a chair, following the things he wanted to have studied.

Sunday 14 October

I was distressed over the week-end because I completely forgot to ask Robbie [WW's chauffeur] to collect the twenty-five red roses which I had got for Margaret's birthday, which was on Saturday, and they are still lingering at the shop. That is the first time I have ever failed to let her have red roses on her birthday.

Nelson Lankford of the Virginia Historical Society rang me by appointment. He is writing a book about David Bruce, the wonderful American Ambassador who was in London between 1961 and 1969.

I talked to him often about wine and non-political matters as well as about politics.

He was unusual for a US Ambassador in that he had joined the diplomatic service, unlike the patronage Ambassadors we usually have here because they supported the President of the day in his election campaign and in other ways. They know nothing. David Bruce, however, was able to influence policy in Washington and in London.

Women loved him and he was very fond of them but not for sexual affairs. When he died, I wrote to Evangeline [his widow] a letter in which I said among other things, 'Not even Henry James could have described his talents, manners and virtues adequately. Such exquisite charm was born not only from his very considerable mind but also from great sincerity and love of people.'

Monday 15 October

Got the flowers off to Margaret. I rang Amanda Ponsonby and explained why they hadn't come on Saturday for her birthday. She seemed to be rather touched that I had taken so much trouble to resurrect the situation. I got some fresh ones from the flower shop.

The marathon of the Broadcasting Bill continues. More conversations with Ian Orr-Ewing, Julian Lewis and particularly with Alun Chalfont who has at last returned.

Wrote a letter to the *Times* in answer to Liz Forgan's, the Director of Programmes at Channel 4, attack on me last Friday saying I should have made my complaint about the *Media Show* to Channel 4 and exercise the *Right to Reply* and so forth. Fortunately, I've had a letter from the Chairman of the IBA in which he said, *inter alia*, that the programme was biased and it did not properly deal with the issue concerned and they had told Channel 4 that.

Verushka is going to Newmarket with Princess Michael on Thursday. She had said she didn't want to go alone and would very much like Verushka to go with her. Verushka very decently said yes. Princess Michael describes herself as a Hungarian now so no doubt she wants an unofficial Hungarian 'lady-in-waiting'.

Tuesday 16 October
Spoke to Margaret to tell her how we were getting on with the Broadcasting Bill amendments.

She immediately began by saying, 'Thank you very much for the lovely flowers.' I said, 'They should have arrived on Saturday.' She said, 'No, it was wonderful because the ones I got for my birthday on Saturday are now all dying off and yours are so lovely and fresh.'

I explained where we had got to and she said, 'It has all been worthwhile then?' I said, 'Very much so. Even though we haven't got the BBC in, they are bound to be influenced by it.'

The bookmakers are fighting desperately to pull the Levy back which would be a tremendous crash, bang, wallop to racing finances.

When I was in France the other day [6–7 October], the Pari Mutuel said racing is getting £200 million this year alone from the Pari Mutuel which makes us look silly internationally. We can't attract the best horses because the prize money is so dim. The Jockey Club were delighted I had said that.

I rang George Walker who is in deep trouble. It looks as though the whole of his business may go up the spout because bankers and others who would now be supporting him, if they thought he was a true gentleman and one of them, are turning against him, remembering he was a boxer who once went to prison.

I told him that I was supporting him and if there was anything I could do to help, I would be delighted to do so.

Thursday 18 October
Robbie [Lyle] comes to tea with his inamorata, Tessa Mayhew. She is a pleasant girl, not good-looking but not unattractive. Darkish, tall, slim, with funny little gaps in her upper teeth, straggly dark brown hair. I tell her she will have to control Robbie if his substance is not to disappear.

She has a house in Islington and she's a partner in Herbert Smith, the solicitors. She is thirty-seven.[6]

Then I had to dash off to the Vintners' Hall for the Saintsbury Club[7] dinner, wearing a dinner jacket. I took Neil Zarach[8] whose family came from Russia a hundred years ago.

When I got home Pericles had been calling. I rang him back. He told me what he had told Verushka, about being put in jail by his wife for picking her up and putting her outside the front door. They are now irrevocably heading for divorce which is an excellent thing, as I told him. I never thought it would last with her being fifty and he only twenty-six. They had the usual quarrels about money.

Then followed a call from Rupert from Australia. He wanted to thank me for the messages of support I had sent him and I said, 'I love you and I am sure it is going to be fine; you will work it all out.' He was clearly deeply grateful. People in difficulties are usually neglected by their so-called friends who want to stay clear of all the trouble. I told him that Margaret was supporting him and he was very pleased about that and would I thank her.

Friday 19 October
Spoke to Margaret after the defeat of the Conservative candidate at Eastbourne.[9] I said, 'Labour has come out of it very badly, within three votes of losing its deposit.' She said, 'We had a great scrap at Question Time yesterday.' I said, 'Yes but I'm not sure it was wise to call Kinnock a crypto Communist.'

I told her about Rupert and she said, 'I would very much like to give him lunch the next time he's here.'

I got it arranged one way and another so he can see her on Monday October 29th at twelve o'clock.

---

6. Her father was Christopher Mayhew (1915–97): Labour MP, 1945–74, Minister of Defence (RN), 1964–6; then a Liberal MP, July–September 1974; m (1949) Cicely Ludlam; life peer 1981.

7. Founded in 1931 by a small group headed by André Simon in honour of George Saintsbury, literary historian and wine connoisseur (1845–1933); its membership consisted of twenty-one 'men of wine' and twenty-five 'men of letters'.

8. Entrepreneur; his wife, Eva, was born in Hungary.

9. The Liberal Democrats won the seat in the by-election caused by Ian Gow's murder.

Saturday 20 October

To Newmarket for the Tote Cesarewitch. Quite a nice party in our entertainment room.

There was Sir Michael Sandberg who used to be Chairman of the Hong Kong and Shanghai Bank and the Royal Hong Kong Jockey Club.[10]

He is now representing in part the International Totalisator Systems which supplies us with equipment so I can get on to him when I want something done. He is a nice fellow, short, rubicund and energetic. We talked a lot about Hong Kong.

On the other side Diana Wilton talked to John Howard de Walden a lot. She hadn't really talked to him before and she didn't realize how intelligent and fascinating he is.

He is very keen to do a little piece in our Tote film.

The film makers were out and about from early morning till the end of the racing.

They had a crew of twelve, which I thought was an enormous amount, though Adrian Rowbotham said he had to have that because of the union rules. I made my little speech before I presented the prize to the elegant winning owner, the Spanish Marquesa de Moratalla who had £4,000 each way on her horse Trainglot at 16 to 1.

I said, 'I am happy on behalf of the Tote – the biggest sponsor in British racing and all our profits go back to racing – to present this trophy to the winning owner.'

That's all I shall say throughout the whole film. I hope it will be good. They certainly seem to know what they are doing.

We arrived back at the Wiltons at something like twenty past seven.

I wore my jolly slippers with the Baron's coronet on them.

John said, 'Where did they come from?' I said, 'Trickers. They were quite cheap, £65.'

He said, 'Do they have ones for Earls?' I said, 'Yes I think they do.' So he said he was going to buy some.

Then Diana said, 'What about those slippers I gave you which Miki Nevill (Lady Rupert Nevill)[11] did the top for but to my design? You

---

10. Chairman, Hong Kong and Shanghai Banking Corp., 1977–86; chairman, Board of Stewards, Royal Hong Kong Jockey Club, 1981–6; director, International Totalisator Systems Inc.; knight 1986, life peer 1997.

11. Chairman, Regional Arts Board for Kent, Surrey and Sussex, 1972–89; née Wallop, daughter of 9th Earl of Portsmouth; m (1944) Lord Rupert Nevill.

can't wear them. Perhaps they fit Woodrow.' They were brought down and they do fit. They were made about twenty years ago and he had hardly worn them because they were too tight for him. I said, 'I thought you had small feet and hands like Churchill.' He said, 'Yes but apparently not as small as yours.' I am now the proud possessor of these lovely slippers with velvet tops with beautiful patterns on them plus WW because Diana had repeated twice his initial of W, so they suit me very well.

Monday 22 October
'Oh, wherefore come ye forth in triumph from the north?' (Macaulay on Naseby.) We won the amendment by a hundred and fifty-five to a hundred and sixteen, a majority of thirty-nine, very good for the Lords on such an issue as impartiality in broadcasting. Alun Chalfont made an excellent speech; so did John Boyd-Carpenter who pointed out that if we didn't carry the amendment, it would be a signal to the broadcasters they need take no notice whatever of impartiality in future.

I spoke without notes and I was told it was the best speech I had made throughout the committee stage or even on second reading on the issue.

In organizing the campaign Ian Orr-Ewing was splendid, though he didn't speak very well in the debate, and of course Julian Lewis did sterling work even though he can be maddening at times.

Tuesday 23 October
Thanked Margaret for her help in getting the Home Office and government to push the amendment to the Broadcasting Bill through more or less unchanged. She said she only gave a little help. It was all due to me. So we dealt with that subject on the basis of mutual congratulation, her having said it couldn't have been done without me and my saying it couldn't have been done without her, which was true. I think it will make a difference; otherwise the broadcasters wouldn't have been so angry about it again this morning.

Wednesday 24 October
Not exactly nervous but anxious about the outcome of my interview with Waddington on my appointment at the Tote. I was in an outrage-

ously irritable and unfair mood. Because Flavio and Teresa are no longer here, no one has cleaned my shoes since July.[12]

Preparing for the interview with Waddington, I was trying to make myself vaguely look younger by wearing a tight enough collared shirt. It is difficult for me as I have got a lot thinner and it makes me look older. I chose a smaller bow which is better than a big one, now my face is not so round. Verushka applied a little make-up to make my face look browner and younger.

Waddington said he intended to reappoint me though he wasn't sure about the length yet. My reappointment would be without any prejudice to my further reappointment at the end of any term I was given. I pressed him hard for three years, citing people like Lord King who is seventy-three, the same as me, and head of British Airways; Charles Forte, eighty-one, still Chairman of Trusthouse Forte; the Chairman of Nissan was made Chairman at seventy-three and is now seventy-eight. He said, 'They are not government appointments.' I said, 'John King's was.'

I nearly mentioned Ian MacGregor being appointed head of the Coal Board at the age of seventy-one and staying for four years but then I thought this might not be a good idea because he could have said, 'He was seventy-five when he went so, if we give you two years, you'll be seventy-five then.'

It was a very amiable meeting. I told him I was very fit and my brain was as good as ever but I don't think he had any doubt of that since I wrestled with his officials over the Broadcasting Bill amendments.

Soon after I got back to Cavendish Avenue Richard Evans rang up from the *Times*. He was the fellow who wrote some disagreeable things about me in the *Times* not long ago. He said, 'I have now heard from unimpeachable sources that you are going to be reappointed for three years.'

I said, 'I know nothing about my appointment,' which was quite true in a sense because I don't know what the final details are. I said, 'Please say nothing about it and don't quote from me. I don't want to make any comment and I wish you weren't writing the story.' He said, 'I am going to write the story and I want to know your achievements to answer your critics, of which there are some in the racing world. I was told that it was suggested to Number 10 that there should be a

---

12. Manuel and Rebecca replaced Flavio and Teresa in 1991.

new face and you can imagine what the Prime Minister had to say to that.' I made no comment.

I arranged for him to ring me at the Tote after the first race at Ascot when I can get the details together. He rang and I produced them on a non-attributable basis.

I hope he gives me a fair crack with his four hundred and fifty words.

I rang Richard Fries, the civil servant who was present at my interview with the Home Secretary, and warned him what had happened and told him what I had said.

Thursday 25 October
That bloody man Richard Evans, this new man they have got on racing in the *Times*, did cut me up rather badly. He used only a snippet of what I explained to him about the achievements of the Tote since I have been there. Otherwise it was tittle-tattle. He said that a senior personal aide of Mrs Thatcher didn't want me to go on being Chairman, officials in Whitehall and at the Home Office didn't, but she was sweeping it all on one side, the implication being because I write articles favourable to her in the newspapers. He omitted to say, of course, that one of them is the *Times* in which he was writing all this nasty stuff.

I spoke to her and I felt bound to tell her what was in the *Times* but before I got to that she was quite bullish about what Waddington might do. I told her what he had said about it being without prejudice to my going on later but that I wanted the full three years so would she say something to him about it. She said she would. She said, 'I will see what I can do.'

In response to the *Times* piece she said, 'They're trying to make out it's a show of favouritism from me.' She was clearly worried because it was not the sort of attack she wants on her. I had always been afraid there was far too much talk, and a lot of it comes from her, of my association with her.

I said, 'I have got some enemies.' She said, 'Anybody who does things well always has enemies.'

The trouble is that some Jockey Club people, having utterly failed to make the best of their commercial advantages – for example, they failed to get in on the act on SIS, which they could have done, and the Tote got five per cent – think, 'What can we squeeze? Why, the Tote: it could provide much more money for racing, if it was run properly.'

It is a bloody disgrace. They never supported our having betting shops. We had ten years in which we weren't allowed to start betting shops in the high street. And then they say why haven't we got more betting shops? How can I get more betting shops if they have already been established, ten thousand of them, mostly owned by the big chains?

I wrote a letter immediately by hand to Waddington saying I forgot to mention that Quintin Hogg was eighty and doing very well as Lord Chancellor – and that was a government appointment.

The Other Club was somewhat depleted. There was a great dinner at the Victoria & Albert Museum given by the Italians for the Italian President.

William Douglas-Home[13] took the chair and kindly invited me to sit next to him.

Opposite me was sitting Robert Carr, a former Home Secretary and rather wet.

Robert Carr said, 'She [Mrs Thatcher] is not really a Tory.' I said, 'Precisely. That is why I support her. But if you threw her out, unless I was satisfied you had got somebody who was carrying on with her objectives, I would start attacking the Tory Party very strongly.'

Andrew [Devonshire] wanted to make a bet that there would be no war in the Gulf before January 1991. Nobody would take him up on it.

Friday 26 October
Poor old George Walker is under terrific pressure and it looks as though he is collapsing. Today his shares dropped to 19p at one stage. I paid 392p for them. Nicholas [Banszky] says I mustn't buy any more because it would look like insider trading.

But I would like to buy some cheap ones to even off the price and I think he will get through.

Dinner with Irwin Stelzer at Harry's Bar.

Andrew Neil was there, very lively and argumentative and very friendly. I liked him much better than I usually do. He said he is a hundred per cent for Mrs Thatcher. I said, 'That's not how you write. Two out of three of your leading articles are OK but the third is horrid.' He said, 'That's necessary. Doesn't anybody tell her things she ought to know and doesn't want to hear?' I said, 'I think there is no

---

13. (1912–92); playwright brother of the former Prime Minister, Sir Alec Douglas-Home (Lord Home).

shortage of people telling her what she doesn't like and she tries to deal with it. We don't all just butter her up and tell her we think everything's OK when it's not.'

He said he had only been invited once to have lunch with her or talk to her privately in a reasonable way and that was years ago. She had been furious with him over the story about the Queen disliking her because she wasn't in favour of the Commonwealth and because she went on refusing to have sanctions against South Africa when they all wanted them.

He said that when Brian Walden spoke to her about it privately, she first of all denied the Queen was against her and then finally looked up and said very sadly, 'Yes, it is so.'

I thought, 'I don't think they are against her now. Certainly Queen Elizabeth the Queen Mother isn't; in fact she is very pro her.'

Andrew Neil doesn't agree. He said the Queen would vote Social Democrat or Liberal Democrat. Certainly I think Prince Charles would.

My tummy is in a state of disorder. I had some rather nice tagliatelli at Harry's Bar with lovely white truffle plentifully spread over the top as it was shaved off by the waiter. It didn't seem to do me any great harm but my tummy is still gurgling.

Irwin is now very friendly again.

He's pretty worried about Rupert's situation. We both think he has so much resilience that he'll get through somehow.

Sunday 28 October
Spoke to Rupert.

He said he was pretty tired and exhausted. He has been here wrestling with BSB. He wants to do a deal with them by which they stop fighting each other and BSB comes on to the Sky satellite.

At the moment they are losing well over £1 million a day (that is BSB) and they are going to lose £900 million before they have the slightest chance of making a profit, whereas Sky only look like losing £200 million which is a hell of a difference.

All was going quite well but Blakenham, who is Chairman of the *Financial Times* and part of the Pearson family, is very much against Rupert.

They thought they had reached an agreement at some moment and then Blakenham broke it up.

When he sees Margaret tomorrow he wants to talk to her about this BSB business and how he is trying to get something done.

I asked Rupert whether he thought that Bush was going to stand firm and take out Saddam with force because he looked very wobbly. He said, 'If it had been Reagan, he would have gone in on the first day. But with Bush it's different. I think there's a sixty–forty chance he may be all right but Baker, the Secretary of State (equivalent to our Foreign Secretary), is very anti-force and he keeps getting at him and so do the others. They are frightened of this peace movement.'

I spoke to Margaret half an hour after she got back from the Rome Summit where she had had a rough time.[14]

She said, 'Did it come over well?' I said, 'Yes. I saw you on television and I heard you on the six o'clock news in detail. Gerald Kaufman[15] was attacking you, saying you had been isolated because you are so rude and aggressive to everybody and that is not the right way to set about it.'

She said, 'They were very rude to me.' I said, 'I don't see what you could have done other than say you disagreed. If you say you disagree, it's rude, and if you say you agree, it's polite but impossible.'

I told her I had had a long talk with Andrew Neil who is a bit hurt that he hadn't been asked to lunch at Chequers or Downing Street or to have a talk with her for years.

I said, 'Basically he is really on your side and I think it would be worth humouring him a bit. He is a real Thatcherite prototype because he came from a very humble beginning. He fought his way through good school and university and he did very well at an early age. He is just your sort of person even though he is chippy.'

Monday 29 October
Rupert rang from his car.

He said on the matter he was talking to me about yesterday, namely BSB, did I think it was right for him to raise it with her? If anything happened, he doesn't want it suddenly to be taken up by some Department of Trade Minister [who might] ban the solutions to the problems on the grounds that it is a merger. I said, 'Yes of course you must.'

He is worried about the so-called isolation of Margaret at the summit. I said, 'No. She's right. What they should have got on with

---

14. The EEC leaders had agreed a timetable for monetary union which Mrs Thatcher denounced.
15. Opposition front bench spokesman on foreign and Commonwealth affairs at this time.

was the nitty gritty of the farmers' subsidies. What they are trying to create is a fortress. They call us Little Englanders but they want to make it into a Little Europe excluded from external trade.'

Christopher Mayhew rang. 'Is Lord Wyatt there?' I said, 'Yes,' and he said, 'This is a distant relative of yours.' He was talking about his daughter's engagement to Robbie Lyle. He said, 'He's very rich, isn't he?' I said, 'No, he's not at all. He's got some land which could be worth £2 million but he has got no income. I have explained this to your daughter and I have told her to come to me if she has any difficulties with his extravagance.'

He said Robbie had given him five of the largest cigars he had ever seen. I said, 'That was typical of him.' He said he had made a very good impression. I said, 'I'm sure he has. He has got a good deal of charm. I am very fond of him and always have been.'

Lunch at Green's in Duke Street, St James's, with Charles Anson[16] and Robin Janvrin.[17] Anson has taken over from Janvrin as Press Secretary [to the Queen] and Janvrin has gone up to be Assistant Private Secretary. We went over the course of the Royals. I said again that it doesn't matter having a few bad hats, in fact they are important in the mix.

I saw Alun Chalfont with Ian Orr-Ewing and Julian Lewis about the drawing up of the ITC code. Alun is doing it pretty well.

Alun said that the Home Office people and the IBA people are trying to get him out of being Deputy Chairman. They say he can continue as Chairman of the Radio Authority but not as Deputy Chairman of the ITC. He will go before he is able to make sure that the rats don't get at the code after January 1st.

I said I would take some action.

In the evening we went to Kensington Palace for dinner with Prince and Princess Michael. The dinner itself was very good. It included venison, beautifully cooked, which I like very much. The wine was also excellent and so was the champagne.

The Hungarian Ambassador and his wife were there. She sat on my left. A homely, plump creature plus earnest-looking rimless spectacles, but with more intelligence and culture than I had previously realized.

---

16. Former diplomat; press secretary to the Queen, 1990–7.
17. Press secretary to the Queen, 1987–90; assistant private secretary, 1990–5; deputy private secretary, 1996–9; succeeded Sir Robert Fellowes as private secretary, 1999; knight 1998.

Prince Michael drank a toast to Hungary and the Hungarian Ambassador, to which the Hungarian Ambassador replied in a charming, simple manner. Everyone in the room had a touch of Hungarian in them (sometimes completely Hungarian, like Mark and Eva Pejacsevich), apart from myself.

When I tried to go Princess Michael said, 'No you can't go. I haven't talked to you,' and she made me sit down beside her on the sofa.

She was looking very beautiful tonight. She said, 'You must have another drink. You're not drinking anything.' I said, 'I am quite happy only to drink from your eyes,' which pleased her a lot and made one or two people laugh who heard it.

She wanted to belabour me for the umpteenth time about how her horse had come third at Newmarket and did I think it was a good horse and what was it going to do next year. I said, 'Take the advice of Barry Hills [trainer], he knows. And don't try and get into races which are too grand for it. Stick to ones it can actually win and it will make you a lot of prize money and be more valuable as a dam.'

Then she started on about Mrs Thatcher who she said had gone miles down in her estimation; she didn't like her any more, she had let her down. This was because they had wanted to go to Moscow and Russia; Mrs Thatcher had said to Princess Michael, when she wrote to her, that there was no reason why they shouldn't go. Then the Foreign Office got into the act and said they couldn't go because he looked too much like the last Tsar and it would be upstaging the Queen's visit. So Mrs Thatcher had let the FO cancel the trip. That was as far as the official part of it, staying at the Embassy, was concerned.

Princess Michael said, 'I am still going to go. I don't care what they say. They won't put us on the Civil List. We've got no money so we are going to do some business there and try to make some money. So I shall just defy them.' Whether or not Michael goes along with that I don't know. He would be unwise to do so, but he may do it.

She looked around the room and said, 'You see, look at this house. It's a tiny house. It's far too small for someone in the Royal Family.' I said, 'But you have made it very pretty.' She said, 'That's different.'

Wednesday 31 October

I spoke to Margaret early in the morning and told her about Alun Chalfont. She said, 'I am seeing Waddington today. We must deal with [this] straight away.'

I told her that Simon Jenkins was shortly coming to have breakfast with me. She said he wrote a wonderful leading article on Monday. It wasn't only the thoughts in it, it was such beautiful language.

She was in sparkling condition, full of fight, as she always is when she's up against it.

I duly told Simon Jenkins what she had said and he was delighted, as well he might have been.

The breakfast was fairly chaotic. We have all these girls in the house who can't speak English. I didn't get a fish knife and fork for haddock, the plates were cold, it didn't come up at the time I said it should because they didn't put it in to boil the moment he arrived, there was no spoon for the marmalade, and I had to have tea when I wanted coffee because there wasn't enough coffee in the coffee pot.

It was all a bit like *Dad's Army*, slightly off-putting when I was trying to concentrate on talking to him, but quite funny in its way.

Just before Simon Jenkins arrived Rupert rang. He said he had a very good meeting with Mrs Thatcher who was in splendid form, and he talked about the BSB business. He said, 'But I do hope she realizes how serious all this business recession is. Our advertising is virtually non-existent.' I said, 'Is it making it more difficult for you financially?' He said, 'Yes it is.' I said, 'Oh dear. Are you going to get through all right?' He said, 'I hope so. The big banks are all right. It's the little banks which are running away.' Poor Rupert is very worried.

The shares I bought yesterday in Brent Walker at 65p or 66p are already down to 51p so everything I do is a disaster.

Went to lunch at the Savoy Grill with Paul Zetter[18] and Sir Neil Macfarlane who used to be Minister for Sport.[19] On the way in I met Robert Maxwell who greeted me with an outstretched hand saying, 'How are you, My Lord?'

Later I noticed that the guest he was waiting for was Andrew Neil, editor of the *Sunday Times*. I was greatly amused.

As I went in, there was Auberon Waugh sitting by himself, eating some nuts and obviously waiting for a guest. I said to him, 'I hope I haven't kept you waiting, Bron.' He gave a great start, thinking that perhaps by mistake he had asked me for lunch.

It turned out to be Charles Moore he was waiting for.

---

18. Chairman, Zetters Group, since 1972.
19. Conservative MP, 1974–92; Parliamentary Under-Secretary for Sport, 1981–5; knight 1988.

He then said, 'Are you having lunch with Bob Maxwell?' and I replied, 'No. I haven't got a long enough spoon.'

Macfarlane was dead against everything Margaret was doing.

He is really rather bitter because he doesn't like having been sacked as Minister of Sport, at which he was not particularly good. That's the trouble with governments which have been in a long time. There are so many people who lose their jobs as Ministers or think they ought to have been given jobs and haven't been.

Paul Zetter wants to do a pool with us, reconstructing old races with different names. It could be a possibility but he said it would need a £200,000 promotion and he was willing to put up half.

He was certain it would get £5 million revenue a year. It might do, I don't know. It's worth exploring.

Zetters has five per cent of the football pools market as against Vernons with twenty per cent and Littlewoods with seventy-five per cent. It is still an enormous amount they have. He said the reason they didn't do better was because Littlewoods got in first. His father didn't establish Zetters until about 1933 and Littlewoods were established in 1923. He said, 'I have never forgiven my father for the ten year wait.' They were Jews from the Continent, I think originally from Russia and then from Germany. He is a very nice man.

Thursday 1 November

I nearly rang Margaret this morning but I can't keep pestering her on my position. I think I'll ring her tomorrow morning after she has seen Waddington about it today because it is getting rather embarrassing.

Went to the farewell party given by Bob Maxwell in honour of Monty Court who is retiring from the *Sporting Life* editorship.

Suddenly he said, 'His Lordship has to make a speech. He's been given no notice but he's used to this sort of thing.'

I went on about Monty Court being the best editor I had known and I was glad to hear that *Sporting Life* wasn't now losing money.

At about this point Maxwell announced that Geoffrey Howe had resigned. My immediate reaction was, 'And a very good thing, too, but no doubt it makes the government look a bit untidy.' He couldn't go on saying different things from the Prime Minister over the single currency and the Central Bank and all the rest of it in Europe.

Friday 2 November

Margaret said that when Geoffrey Howe came to see her at six o'clock she had a party for the Lord's Taverners (that's the MCC cricket supporters) going on. So she had to leave that and listen to Geoffrey Howe about his resignation. She said she hadn't even had time to think what next to do.

I said, 'You don't really need a Deputy Prime Minister, do you?' She said, 'No. That was just invented for Geoffrey.'

I said, 'He's been sulking away for so long. He's never forgiven you about not being Foreign Secretary any more and nor has Elspeth.'

I said, 'It will all be forgotten in a few weeks. I am sure there won't be a leadership contest.' She said she didn't suppose there would be but she wasn't certain.

About Lord Chalfont wanting to go on being Deputy Chairman of the television side of the ITC and give up the radio, she said, 'I spoke to Waddington and he is now going to ask to see Alun Chalfont. He'll suggest two ITC deputy chairmen. The Home Office has already invited someone else to succeed Alun. Waddington didn't know anything about it.' I said, 'That's the trouble. They just put things in front of him and he signs them.'

I asked her about my position and she said, 'They've been saying you ought to have only one year as you are only a part-time chairman.' I said, 'How ridiculous.' But she said she thinks it will now be two and I will be hearing about it soon.

She is obviously a bit beleaguered in the sense that she doesn't like to impose her will so much.

She agreed with me when I said that Ken Baker had been very good on the television last night and on the radio this morning about the Howe situation. When I had suggested making him Leader of the House she said, 'Oh no, he must stay as Chairman of the Party.' Obviously she trusts him and thinks he's doing a good and loyal job, contrary to what the media say about her thinking he's no good.

When I spoke to Norman Lamont, he said he thought it was all rather serious and John Major had been shattered. I said, 'But he's all right, isn't he?' (meaning loyal to Margaret). He said, 'Yes, I think so.'

I said, 'I thought you all got on rather well in the Cabinet and were on the right track dealing with single currency and the Central Bank.' He said, 'They don't discuss it in the Cabinet at all. They are really rather like *Spitting Image*,[1] Cabinet meetings.' I said, 'You're not serious?' He said, 'Yes.' I said, 'Why are you all so bloody wet?' He said, 'In fact it doesn't amount to very much. The real things are done elsewhere.' I said, 'That's natural. It's much more like a meeting of non-executive directors, the Cabinet.' He said when he's at a Cabinet meeting he's just thinking about his work and how to advance what he is trying to do.

Lamont thinks that Hurd really doesn't altogether agree with Mrs Thatcher's policy but he thinks that John Major does. The Tories are certainly reeling all over the place at the moment.

Sunday 4 November
Talked to Norman Lamont. He was gloomier than usual, thinks there could be a real problem and there could be a challenge to the leadership. I said, 'She won't go, even if she only has a majority of one.' He

---

1. Satirical television programme which parodied current affairs and politicians, using puppets.

said he thought that wasn't very democratic. I said, 'Why not?' He sounded a bit wobbly and said, 'She is not sensitive to different opinions. She squashes them altogether. She is not skilful at handling people.'

He said he had a sharp exchange with her not long ago. She wanted to get something spent which he, in his role as Chief Secretary to the Treasury, was trying to prevent. 'I hate you,' she said, 'when you put on that face,' meaning when he was looking mulish and stubborn about it. Then she went on, 'If you'd been in my government in 1979, we'd never have got anywhere,' at which point Norman had said, 'But I was in your government in 1979.'[2] I said, 'Did she withdraw?' He said, 'No.' However, he thinks all will be well if Major and Douglas Hurd and she stick together.

Norman Lamont would be in favour of a referendum on the issue of the single currency and a Central European Bank. He said the Cabinet never discuss these issues.

Nicholas Soames rang up in a rambling, worried way.

He thought there might be a leadership challenge and that lots of people were very rattled.

Rupert rang up to say they had concluded their Sky-BSB deal at a quarter past three in the morning. He said that when I spoke to Mrs Thatcher, would I try and say to her that there should be no reference to the Monopolies Commission or any other body on the merger because there is no law about it [satellite ownership] as there is with newspapers.

He was furious with the *Sunday Times* leading article which said she ought to go and that she was a liability to the Tories. Would I tell her that he didn't agree with it?

Eventually I got her at about twenty to eleven.

She said, 'I do admire Rupert so much. He identifies his problem and he sorts it out. He is wonderful. He is also a very sweet person. I am very fond of him.'

She was genuinely a little concerned about the rumpus following Howe's resignation. I said I had noticed all the leading Tories, including Major and Hurd, were rallying.

---

2. He was Under-Secretary of State, Department of Energy, 1979–81.

Monday 5 November

Michael Trend[3] and his wife Jill came to dinner. She is small, blondeish, quite attractive, friendly, with a cheeky little face. I was greatly relieved. Previously Michael Trend's choice of women has been bizarre. I hadn't seen him for a long time, certainly not since his wedding which was some four years ago.

He said that she was very useful at his selection conference at Windsor where he was adopted as Conservative candidate. He beat Michael Antrim who had been a Minister in a Tory government. When they asked what a wife should do to help in a constituency he had said, 'As much as she can but I'm afraid mine can't stand up at the moment because she's pregnant.' All the women applauded like mad. There were more women than men at the selection conference so he thinks that's what won it for him.

He has been worried a bit in his constituency in the last few days by the number of them who he had thought were very steady and strong and are now saying they thought it was time she should go.

He said Charles Moore is going to take over as editor [of the *Telegraph*] from Max Hastings. I said, 'That's very tolerant of Conrad Black because he was pretty vile to him in the columns of the *Spectator* when he was the editor.'[4] He said he thought Conrad Black was a decent fellow and highly intelligent.

He is one of Nicholas' friends [Nicholas Banszky] from Westminster and Oxford.

It was great fun to see him again. I had always regarded him as a larky sort of fellow.

He brought fireworks, a box of them. We set them off one by one in the garden after dinner.

Afterwards we went up to the top sitting-room where he played the piano and Petronella sang some of my favourite songs. I said, 'You must come more often. It is very difficult to persuade her to sing.'

---

3. The Hon. Michael Trend; home editor, *Spectator*, 1986–90, then chief leader writer, *Daily Telegraph*; Conservative MP, Windsor, since 1992; m (1987) Jill, née Kershaw.
4. The *Spectator* had published in November 1985 an authoritative analysis by the Canadian writer John Ralston Saul of the aims, talents and business operations of 'the Canadian ideologue who wants the *Daily Telegraph*'. Charles Moore became deputy editor of the *Daily Telegraph* in 1990; editor, *Sunday Telegraph*, 1992–5; succeeded Max Hastings as editor, *Daily Telegraph*, in 1995.

Tuesday 6 November

Rupert is off to America tonight and he is coming back next week to go on seeing this thing through. It has made an enormous difference to his position financially with the banks, etc., and his shares have gone up by twenty-five per cent.

Mr Michael Blackburn came for a drink. I think he is after my job eventually as Tote Chairman. He seems an agreeable enough fellow, rather rough.

Off to dinner at the Andrew Knights.

Andrew said that Chips had behaved very badly over withdrawing the Hambros loan from Rupert when he was in difficulties. I said, 'I suppose he thought he had a duty to his shareholders.' He said, 'Well it is not the action of a friend. I know he is a friend of yours, but he is a fair-weather friend.' I hope Rupert is mainly through his difficulties after the merger with BSB but he still faces a terrific loss of cash from the cutting off of advertising caused by the recession. *Today* is losing £10 million a year and so is the *Times*.

Andrew Knight is a strange fish. There's no real life in him. He's more like a death's head. His approach is clinical but inhuman. I hope he is able to do for Rupert what Rupert needs from him. Typically, as he changed his job he changed his outlook and approach. Once he hated and despised the *Sun* and the *News of the World* and all their works; now he defends and approves of them. He's a real Vicar of Bray.

It's extraordinary how they live. Some sort of au pair girl brought the supper around, very late. Yet they have £11 million. Their house is more hideous looking every time I see it.

Wednesday 7 November

Christopher Mayhew and Cicely, his wife, came to dinner with Robbie and his fiancée, Tessa Mayhew. Petronella was also there. I knew Christopher at Oxford over fifty years ago. He was a leading light in the Labour Club which I joined, as well as joining the Liberal and Conservative Clubs to find out what wares they all had to offer. He was a somewhat self-important President of the Union. He is three years older than me.

He wanted to know why I didn't retire but kept writing my columns, running the Tote and pushing forward changes in legislation in the Lords. I said, 'I have to do it to prevent myself losing the use of my brain and getting addled. Anyway, I enjoy it, though I am very lazy.' Of course, which I didn't mention, I need the money badly.

Christopher was a scholar at Haileybury as well as an exhibitioner at Oxford. He is quite bright. I said to him, 'You got into the government early because you were at Haileybury and Attlee, an old Haileyburian, wanted to advance Haileyburians, as Baldwin used to advance old Harrovians.' Christopher said no, it was despite his being at Haileybury that he agreed to Ernie Bevin's request to have him as Under Secretary of State at the Foreign Office.

When we were both Labour MPs after the War we did a number of things together. One was to have our forces not so far east of Suez. Events in Kuwait may have proved us wrong but politically it was impossible for Arab rulers to continue to be propped by us – they'd have been overthrown. Christopher always took the credit for any progress we made, though he was by no means always responsible for it. That used to irritate me.

But he is a jolly fellow.

Friday 9 November

Started speaking to Margaret at about ten minutes to eight and was still talking to her at ten past. She said she was going to the BBC for lunch today. 'You didn't hear that,' she said. I suppose it was for security reasons she said that. She said, 'They still think I listen to the *Today* programme every day but I don't.' People at LBC [London Broadcasting Company] had said, 'Why don't you try listening to our programme?' She had been doing that and finds it less irritating with its less bias.

She now gets up at six in the morning or a bit before and listens to the news then. She says she doesn't work so late into the night now. She finds herself much fresher and able to get on with her boxes and so forth at six or six-thirty in the morning than after a day's work.

She said, 'Geoffrey Howe is eking out his time, smouldering away.' She then said he is going to make a speech, saying there were great differences between her and him on Europe, during the debate on the Queen's Speech. I said, 'I think it is extremely unlikely that he will stand against you,' and she agreed. I said, 'Heseltine probably won't because he would be thrashed and that would be his last chance. He may wish to bide his time.'

I asked her whether John Major and Douglas Hurd were steady and sound and she said yes. She clearly didn't have any worries on that score. But she seemed not to worry very much about a challenger anyway, except that it is irritating and undermining. I think she has a marvellous mechanism for switching off worries of that kind and getting on with her work.

Saturday 10 November

Weirdly, the BBC keep ringing me up and asking me to appear in a programme. Yesterday it was to be on a news programme talking about Lithuania.

It must be because I have been attacking them so much on bias and I told Duke Hussey that I was blacklisted by the BBC. Maybe he hopes that I will say to Margaret that he ought to be given another term as Chairman.

Monday 12 November

I spoke to Margaret.

She was anxious to talk about the leadership thing.[5]

She said she had hoped for something better yesterday from the *Sunday Times* than Andrew Neil's attacks on her again. I said, 'Rupert rang me from Australia and he was very upset about it,' but this doesn't cut much ice with her at the moment because she is wondering why the hell he doesn't do something about it.

She made a very good point, namely that when she stood against Heath they were in opposition and had lost an election. Now she is the Prime Minister and nobody should stand against a Prime Minister in office in the midst of delicate negotiations.

I said, 'Maybe it would be a good idea if Heseltine does stand against you and thus get rid of the thing because he would be soundly defeated.' She said, 'Maybe but it might make even more divisions.' I said, 'I am sure you would win all right.' She said, 'Yes. We must keep battling on.' She said that several times, 'Yes, Woodrow, we must keep battling on.'

Richard Needham, the Irish Earl of Kilmorey and a Northern Ireland Minister, made a ridiculous remark on his car telephone to his wife. He said, 'I wish the old cow would resign,' meaning Margaret. This was somehow picked up by some paramilitary organization in

---

5. November 15th had been announced as the date for nominations for the Conservative Party leadership contest, with the first ballot to take place on November 20th. Michael Heseltine formally signified his candidature on November 14th.

Northern Ireland and leaked to the press. He just added fuel to the interminable speculation about the leadership contest which is running daily in the BBC, ITV and the press.

Went to Wigan. Peter Lloyd, the Minister of State at the Home Office responsible for the Tote, came too. He was greatly impressed by everything he saw, as indeed he might be.

He said he didn't think more than a hundred would vote for Heseltine if he stood. We discussed the difficulties of the government which over eleven years has collected a lot of dissatisfied people who had been either sacked or never given a job. He is staunch for Mrs Thatcher. It was his birthday and I made sure to give him a cake with candles on it saying Happy Birthday.

He is not a high flyer but quite sound. He asked a lot of questions, many of them very sensible.

Margaret made a rollicking, fighting speech at the Lord Mayor's dinner at the Mansion House. She received a lot of applause when she said she was still at the crease though the bowling was hostile and she was going to knock it all around the ground because that was her style.

Geoffrey Howe made a dreadful speech in the Commons saying there were all kinds of differences of opinion between himself and Mrs Thatcher which he had concealed out of loyalty for years, that it wasn't just a matter of style, etc. etc. Norman Tebbit on the television directly afterwards said it was all a lot of rubbish and so did Kenneth Clarke (Secretary for Health) but when I went to the Lords, before I went to the T. E. Utley memorial dinner for the judges of the winner of the annual prize, I saw Tony Royle (Lord Fanshawe) who had been in the smoking-room of the House of Commons. He said that the centre of the party, meaning the Tory MPs in the smoking-room, were absolutely shattered and shocked by what Geoffrey Howe had said and that half of them had turned against Mrs Thatcher so it was going to be a near-run affair if Heseltine were to stand.

When I got to the Utley party, there was Ferdinand Mount who is quite a good judge and used to work in Margaret's policy unit at Number 10. He was not at all certain that she would win and nor were some of the others there. And yet this is the place where she has her photographs all over the walls, the Centre for Policy Studies where we had the supper, I having missed the lecture.

Ferdinand Mount said, 'Of course the Tories always do this at the end of a long period of power. They fell apart at the end of their thirteen years from 1951.' If Heseltine wins that contest, I shall certainly be thinking seriously about telling my readers to vote Labour. Kinnock can hardly be worse than Heseltine.

Heseltine was in Germany today saying we wish to go step by step and cautiously, and not rush into single currencies and so forth, identical with what she says. Geoffrey Howe was saying the same sort of thing so what the hell are they all talking about? There is no real split at all, only that they don't like being run by a woman and they are getting battle fatigue.

Wednesday 14 November

When I rang this morning she said, 'How nice to hear a friendly voice.' I said, 'It always will be.'

She then went on to tell me that it wasn't true that Howe and Lawson had threatened to resign if she hadn't agreed to setting out the terms for joining the Exchange Rate Mechanism at the Madrid Summit. 'We did not agree to giving a date for it and they had accepted that.' She said the timing was dependent on certain conditions being fulfilled abroad in Europe and internally on inflation in Britain. There was complete agreement between the three of them on that and no question of resignation by either of them.

I told her that Heseltine had been ringing everybody around, including Julian Amery. He had said would he vote for him and Julian had said, 'I'm not saying who I'm voting for,' though of course he is going to vote for her.

She said, 'They don't seem to understand that this is just for the leadership of the party, not for being Prime Minister.' I said, 'I think it would be unwise to say that now. Wait until the contest is over and if it goes wrong.'

I said, 'I wouldn't go into the tea room now to talk to all your backbenchers because it would look bad. At the moment you will have to stay aloof.' She thought that was correct as well.

I spoke to Norman Lamont and he is deeply worried. He thinks she should just win but it might not be by enough to stop a second ballot.

Chips Keswick rang up to say how outraged he was at what I had recorded in my *Times* article about treacherous Tory MPs. I said, 'Why don't you write a letter to the *Times*?' and he said he would. He then told me what he would write, very short, and I said, 'That would do fine. Sign it Chairman of Hambros Bank.' I had told him that early this morning she had said that a lot of her difficulties came from business people supporting Heseltine on narrow, self-seeking, short-term positions.

Talking to Julian Lewis, who is at the Conservative Central Office, I said, 'Why don't you get the Conservative chairmen from the constituencies to get up and say it's monstrous to try to destabilize her and that the party activists were very much in favour of her in most places?'

Later Julian rang to say he had an idea, and did I think it was a good one, of young candidates writing in or announcing that they are completely behind her and the Tory MPs shouldn't rock the boat. I said, 'Excellent.'

Rupert rang and wanted to know the form. I told him I thought she probably wouldn't get driven to a second ballot but even if she did, she would stay if she won it; that the waverers in the centre had had a shock from Howe because they don't understand the way things are conducted at a higher level, but I thought the impact would wear off and then rebound in her favour when they saw how treacherous and disloyal it was of him.

In the tea room at the Lords, Lord Rees, a somewhat dowdy ex Tory Minister whom she foolishly made a peer,[6] said to me that she is finished, that she has been shot so full of lead she can't recover. Christopher Mayhew said all his Tory friends said she was going to lose in the first round. Bill Cash, the Tory MP who is a good egg, I met in the members' lobby just outside the Commons chamber, said he is telling the Whips to search out the people who didn't vote in the contest a year ago but were not people who cohered together, to get them into line to vote for Margaret. He was struggling very hard on that. I thought to myself that the Whips officially were not supposed to do anything about it, but that's another matter.

At tea time Andrew Davidson[7] said that she would get by all right. Dinner party at Cavendish Avenue.

Henry and Tessa are very keen on Mrs Thatcher winning. Tessa also told me that Kenneth Clarke, whose political adviser she is, was also mad keen on her winning. Later she told me that education is in a hell of a mess. No Secretary of State stayed long enough to make an

---

6. Peter Rees, Conservative MP, 1970–87, Chief Secretary to the Treasury, 1983–5; life peer 1987.

7. 2nd Viscount Davidson, Deputy Chief Government Whip, House of Lords, 1986–91.

impression. They were simply not interested. The whole thing was in the hands of the civil servants who are all very left-wing on the subject and thoroughly complacent.

Thursday 15 November

I told her [Margaret] that Ken Baker had told me the Conservative Central Office is taking a neutral stance and won't help to get support from the local constituency parties to make sure that their MPs support her and she was furious. She said, 'It's my office. They're working for the Prime Minister and the Leader of the party.'

I spoke to Rupert and told him I thought the *Times* was being somewhat wobbly. I said, 'The trouble is that Simon Jenkins has got that community charge as a bee in his bonnet.' He said, 'Don't worry, it will be quite all right on the day, you will see.'

Then I said, 'The *Today* newspaper is running Heseltine as their favoured candidate.' 'I know,' he said, 'David Montgomery is being a pain in the arse. But surely it doesn't matter?' I said, 'It doesn't help.'

I saw Willie Whitelaw and said how glad I was he had made a statement in support of Margaret. He said, 'I didn't want to seem to be interfering from the House of Lords but the whole thing is so absolutely ghastly and they are behaving so abominably that I thought I must say something. I particularly wanted to get rid of this nonsense that I would go to see her to tell her to step down, which I have no intention of doing. She ought to win. She must win. But I am very worried that she is not going to win by enough. I don't know what her friends and advisers are telling her.'

I said, 'Of course everybody is lying like mad. People say they will vote for Heseltine to him and that they will vote for Margaret to her campaigners.'

Willie said he thought it might go to a second ballot and that it would then be a very serious matter because then one might have to go and advise her to stand down.

I pointed out to him that in the Labour Party rules, if the Leader is Prime Minister he can only be challenged if it is suggested by a majority at a party conference on a card vote. I said, 'You can imagine what would happen to that in a Tory Party conference.'

Then he said, 'Whatever happens we can't have her humbled. But then she is wise enough to know that.'

I think Willie is on the level and sincerely wants Margaret to win

and to win well. He was making very complimentary remarks about
her courage and the need for her to stay.

Norman St John-Stevas described it [Howe's resignation speech] as
treachery. He [Norman] lost his job in the Cabinet[8] for making too
many frivolous jokes about her, including 'the Blessed Margaret' crack,
but he wasn't perhaps quite up to leading the House. I was delighted
that he showed no malice or bitterness but fervent support for her in
her hour of trouble.

It worried me about Willie saying that perhaps there might come a
time when perhaps he should go and speak to her and to advise her
to go.

I spoke to Rupert about Andrew Neil. He said Andrew Knight was
trying to persuade him not to support Heseltine and to write much
more measured articles, lowering the venom against Margaret. Rupert
says that he can't sack him now (but there are other reasons why he
would like to) because if he did there would be a great outcry about
censorship and it would rebound badly on Margaret. 'Anyway,' he
remarked, 'the way I was allowed to buy the *Sunday Times* precluded
me from interfering with the editor.'

To dinner at the French Embassy.

I asked Hedwige about going to stay in Luc's family château, miles
away from Paris. She said she wasn't looking forward to it.

She prefers Paris.

Luc himself is going to be in charge of a Pearson-backed daily paper
in Paris which is profitable, with a hundred thousand circulation, a lot
for Paris.

Arnold was there and so was Netta.

I said, 'Arnold, you are surely not going to back Heseltine?' He
said, 'Yes. It is time for her to go. She is not doing the country any
good. Heseltine would be much better.' I said, 'Arnold, you have had
enormous help from her.' He said, 'No, never.' I said, 'How can you
say that? After all she gave you a peerage,' to which he promptly
replied, 'Anybody else would have done.' I went on, 'And she has been
fantastic in getting you export orders and defence orders. You know
that very well.' He said, 'Well, yes, she has once or twice.' I said, 'All
I can say to you, Arnold, is *Et tu, Brute!* I am deeply shocked. I don't
think I can speak to you,' and I went away.

---

8. He was Chancellor of the Duchy of Lancaster, Leader of the House of Commons
   and Minister for the Arts, 1979–81.

We got home at just about twelve and I started ringing Irwin Stelzer to see if he could bring some pressure on Andrew Neil not to be so bloody daft. However, Irwin didn't think it was all that important. I said, 'It certainly is. He might swing a few of those Tory MPs and we want a big majority.' He was in New York and he said he would ring on Friday to say what he had been able to do.

Friday 16 November
Spoke to Rupert who said it was difficult for Andrew Knight to budge Andrew Neil, even though he said several times how distressed Rupert would be.

He said, 'But we are all being rather absurd. The electorate consists of three hundred and seventy-two people. There's Andrew Neil rewriting and rewriting and polishing his leader and it might only affect one of the three hundred and seventy-two electors.' So I said, 'Many of them read it and he might turn some of them the other way.'

I think there will be a terrible bust-up with Andrew Neil soon. I said I would do my best to explain the position to her when I spoke to her.

I have been asked to appear on *Question Time* on BBC1, Robin Day's old programme, next Thursday.

Arnold is slightly ashamed of himself. He rang up in the middle of my writing my article to say he had had a letter from Hanson wanting a hundred businessmen to sign a letter to the *Times* saying these prominent businessmen all believe Margaret should be completely supported. Then Arnold said to me, 'How can I do that? It is interfering in a private affair, the election of a Tory leader.' I said, 'It is hardly private. It affects the entire nation. But I can't talk to you any more about it at the moment because I am writing my article,' so he rang off in rather a shamefaced manner.

I spoke to Margaret five minutes after she returned from Northern Ireland. She said she had just walked in and I asked if she had had a good day. She said, 'Splendid,' and I think she was glad to get away. I warned her about the *Sunday Times* and how we were all trying to get him to tone it down, and about Rupert's difficulties in sacking him though he may do it later.

I said about Andrew Neil that I couldn't understand his position: 'He says he is a Thatcherite but in fact Heseltine is a corporate *dirigiste* – the exact opposite of Thatcherism.'

I told her that I had talked to Willie Whitelaw yesterday and he had come out and said that she should be backed.

She remarked, 'He didn't get much publicity for it.' I said, 'No,' and she said, 'That's because the BBC, the ITV and the press are all against me.'

I mentioned that Waddington had now written formally to me about the two years.

She said she is going to London tomorrow morning from Chequers to work on her speech for Paris. She will be in conference in Paris on Tuesday when the result of the ballot is known. I thought how dreadful for her if they bring her a note saying she has lost or will have to go to a second round.

Darling Margaret. She said again that if they defeat her in the leadership, she will fight on as Prime Minister until she is defeated in the Commons. I said, 'That is a last resort. You shouldn't speak about it now.' The dear darling doesn't deserve this treachery from the cowardly mob of Tory MPs who can't see what she has done for them and that she is their only hope of keeping their seats. If she goes, the party will be split from top to bottom for years and Labour will be let in to continue the decline of the 1970s.

Saturday 17 November
Rupert rang on his way to the airport.

When I asked Rupert how his affairs were getting on, he said, 'I don't have any.'

I said, 'I didn't mean that kind of an affair. I meant your financial affairs.' He said he would know completely in about three weeks' time. Some of the smaller banks in the USA might go bust and then he would still be in difficulty because it affects about ten per cent of his money. But he has been working very hard at it and it sounds as though he will be all right.

If he hadn't had so much preoccupation with Sky and saving his own giant empire which was in acute trouble, I think he would have paid more attention to what Andrew Neil was up to in the *Sunday Times*. I hope Andrew Neil will be for the chop after all this.

Rupert says the *Times* will be OK on Monday and that even tomorrow in the *Sunday Times* there are articles of equal length on the opposite page to Andrew Neil's treacherous one.

There was worry about Douglas Hurd because yesterday he said, when pressed by some television interviewer, that he supported her completely, not just for this day or till Thursday, and he is one of her sponsors. When they asked what happens if she doesn't get a big enough majority on the first round and so avoid a second round, he said, 'I will not stand against her as long as she is standing.' It seemed a perfectly respectable thing to say but it was boosted by the press today and on the BBC, even the *Times* fell for it, as him saying that he was biding his time and was ready to step in, as though he were trying to undermine her, which is the opposite of the truth.

Incredibly, this mad system, and complicated one, was wished upon the Tories by Humphry Berkeley[9] who, a year after he had invented it and sold it to the Tory Party, joined the Labour Party. He then went over to the SDP and two years ago he rejoined Labour. He really made mugs of the Tory Party.

The final undoing of poor Bruce Anderson, who was sacked by the ghastly Max Hastings from the *Sunday Telegraph*, was his repeating in last Sunday's Mandrake [column in the *Sunday Telegraph*] some gossip from a journalist's conversation with Prince Charles at High-grove, reporting that Prince Charles greatly dislikes Andrew Knight.

Anderson should not have repeated the story because it was told to him by a journalist from the *Telegraph* on a totally confidential basis.

Sunday 18 November

Bernard Ingham said that the soundings from MPs seemed as though there would be a reasonable majority of more than two hundred but you can't tell because they all lie so much. I said, 'I want to tell you again, for goodness' sake get her on to that television on Monday during your conference in Paris. First of all it would show her doing her natural job as Prime Minister effectively and it will impress any wavering Tory MPs.'

He said, 'But supposing they ask her questions about home affairs?' I said, 'It doesn't matter. She's so good at answering questions. She can deal with everything and turn it to her own advantage.'

I believe I have just about persuaded him. He is a very good man. He adores Margaret and is just fearful that he might put her in a position in which she makes a mistake or is caught out.

Later I told Margaret that I felt more optimistic this morning.

She said, 'I've just been told that the Jonathan Dimbleby interview

---

9. (1926–94); Conservative MP, 1959–66; joined Labour Party 1970; joined SDP, 1981; rejoined Labour, December 1988; social reformer and writer.

on the BBC (*On the Record*) was terrible, that he let Heseltine say anything he wanted.'

Then she said, 'He lied when he said he had told me five weeks before that he was going to resign over Westland if he didn't get his way or wasn't allowed to put it to the Cabinet. It wasn't true.' I said, 'That doesn't matter. People won't remember little bits like that. He was very evasive and he didn't sound at all convincing about why he flounced out of the Cabinet over Westland.'

She thanked me very much. I called her 'darling' several times. As we talked the note in her voice which had begun depressed and worried had become more and more confident and cheerful. I hope I have done her some good in that respect because the aura which comes out of her has an effect.

I do wish Margaret had listened to me when I asked her some weeks ago to see Andrew Neil.

When I wanted her to have a dinner at my house with Vere Rothermere she never got beyond commenting, 'He sees me at Number 10 and elsewhere,' and didn't take on board the fact that he felt that was all in public and what he needed was a bit of nursing and a bit of love. She is foolish at times not doing a few obvious things to get people on her side, instead of which she alienates them.

Alexander Hesketh rang. Pretty alarmed. He had just been doing a tour of the Midlands. He said that the younger generation particularly don't want her any more, all this business of 'going on and on and on' worries them a lot. They prefer Heseltine.

He said the only thing that can save her or get her a decent majority is to announce she is going to get rid of the poll tax because they are all against it and everybody would rejoice. I said, 'How could she do that? She has gone to Paris now.'

He said, 'She could just send a message to Christopher Patten telling him to announce it at half past two tomorrow afternoon.' I said, 'I don't see how you could possibly do that. It would look like panic and she won't go back on it because she believes in it. And what would Christopher Patten say?' He said, 'He would be delighted. He hates defending it.'

Monday 19 November
To Parliament. Had a longish talk with nice John Smith, the Labour shadow Chancellor of the Exchequer. He says his information is Heseltine will get a hundred and thirty, she will get two hundred and there

will be thirty abstentions. This would be enough to prevent her having to stand in a second round.

John Smith says they have got the [Labour] party under real control centrally. They won't allow anybody to stand at a by-election other than the one selected by head office. I said, 'Who would have thought five years ago that the Tories would have lost grip of their party and you would have complete grip of your own?'

He agreed I was right in saying that he, John Smith, would have just about the same policy on the Common Market as the present government and Mrs Thatcher. He doesn't want a single currency, certainly not without years of explanation and caution and finding out what it all meant. Nor did he want a Central European Bank without political control. He said, 'But I am not saying that very loud at the moment.'

John Smith is looking much better and slimmer than he has been for ages, or at least since his recovery from his heart attack. I like him a lot. He is amusing, fairly cynical, but a decent guy at heart. He has a round face, not quite so round now, but still pleasing and reassuring.

Arnold was very keen to tell me that all the charges against his head people at Marconi had not only been withdrawn by the prosecution because they said they couldn't sustain them as there was no real evidence for them, but the Judge had ordered that the Crown pay all the expenses of the defence. I said, 'That's marvellous, wonderful. You must be delighted.' As usual Arnold said, 'Who is going to give me back my four years of worry and the loss of business I had and the damage caused by GEC's reputation being wrongfully smirched? Why should I have to go through all this?'

Tuesday 20 November

Norman Lamont said that Heseltine even canvassed him for his vote. He's a friend of Heseltine's.

He's been canvassing everybody, he said, 'like a child molester hanging around the lavatories and waiting to pounce on people'.

Norman says that a lot of the Cabinet are against her and that she has only got three real friends including himself. He said, 'Anyway, when this is over she must be told who her friends are. She lives in cloud-cuckoo-land.'

I told Norman that if she loses the election today, she won't go. She is still the Prime Minister and she will ask for a vote of confidence from the House of Commons. If she loses it, she will ask for a general election. He said, 'Good Lord, do you really think that she would do that?' I said, 'Yes.' He said, 'Well that's really good.'

By four votes Margaret failed to get a clear fifteen per cent majority over Heseltine who got a hundred and fifty-two votes to her two hundred and four. The whole thing is utter madness. She immediately announced that she would go on to the second round.

Douglas Hurd can't possibly oppose her because he swore that he won't stand against her. Heseltine said he will stand against her.

She only has to get a clear majority this time and if people don't bugger about with it, I think she ought to do it. But some people say no, that a lot of people who voted for her will now vote for Heseltine. I hope to God it isn't true.

Talked to Rupert who said Simon [the *Times*] would be fine in the morning. Even *Today*, David Montgomery, would be much better and Kelvin MacKenzie [the *Sun*] would be fine as well.

Dinner at the Montagus. Emma Soames said her brother was very evasive about which way he voted. I said, 'Tell him I will never speak to him again if he doesn't vote for Mrs Thatcher in the second round.'

I had a lively conversation with Conrad Black. I said, 'I hope you are not going to sack Bruce Anderson. He is quite remarkable as a journalist.'

He said, 'It was his insubordination. He was told not to print this thing about Andrew Knight which the Prince of Wales had said, and he disobeyed.'

He said he had jollied up the leader in the *Daily Telegraph* for tomorrow and they were very stoutly behind her.

Once again Conrad Black asked me to write for him. I said, 'I can't do that. I'm under contract for Rupert. It's very kind of you to suggest it but I couldn't possibly leave Rupert. Do you think Rupert is going to come through his troubles?' He said, 'Yes, certainly. I think he is a great man.' I said, 'He has got a great admiration for you too,' so he was pleased about that.

Hedwige [wife of the French Ambassador] said Heseltine went to the Embassy for dinner and he sat next to her. He preened himself and his hair all the time. Then he said to her 'Do you know that I have got millions of pounds? I am very rich, many millions.' She said, 'Why do you think he told me that? Was he proposing to make a proposition to me? Maybe I have got more money than he has.'

Wednesday 21 November

Tried to get hold of her but couldn't. I spoke to Willie Whitelaw who promised me that he was not going to go and tell her to quit but that he would only go and see her as a friend, if she wanted to see him. Then he said, 'Of course we don't want her to be humiliated.' I said, 'I don't think she would mind about that.'

He said, 'Of course it is a matter for the Whips.'

Then I said, 'Fortunately, knowing her nature, she might easily decide on a dissolution and ask for a general election.' He said, 'Goodness, don't let's say that. It would turn hundreds against us in the parliamentary party.' I said, 'I don't know what she'll do, but she has hinted it.' This wasn't quite true – she's been much more definite than that to me.

I then rang Baker and said much the same to him.

He wasn't exactly hedging his bets but it sounded a little bit like that.

At lunch time on the radio Quintin Hogg [Lord Hailsham] came out loudly in support of Margaret.

I watched her make a statement about her Paris meetings. She was looking very smart. When I rang her in the morning and wanted to speak to her I was told she was having her hair done. That was at about a quarter to eight, Paris time. She was wearing a kind of gold jacket and black skirt and beautiful shoes. Her legs were looking marvellous.

Foul gloom among nearly all I saw.

I am unable to get through to her and can only send messages via people like Charles Powell and John Whittingdale, her Political Secretary at Number 10, telling her to go on fighting.

Susan Crosland[10] came to dinner with us in the Barry Room. Though she is politically pro Labour, she is passionately in favour of Margaret and thinks the whole thing is appalling and she hopes she wins.

She is still an attractive girl. She has got over Tony's death now at last. I told her that the reason why she was able to spread the money from her sex novel over three years was because Tony and I had

---

10. Author and journalist; widow of Anthony Crosland (1918–77), Labour politician and writer, author of *The Future of Socialism*; he was Minister of State for Economic Affairs, 1964–5, when WW was a Labour MP.

reached that agreement when he was Chief Secretary to the Treasury in the Commons with a Labour government years ago.

Last night Alistair Horne[11] referred to the letter I had had from Professor J. B. Haldane in which he said that Harold Macmillan was expelled for buggery from Eton and had never been back to the school again. He said he decided not to use it in his book about Macmillan by agreement with me when I sent him a copy of that letter. But he said that some people have got wind of the situation and were asking him about it, was he a homosexual. I said, 'Tell [them] you know nothing about it and don't quote that letter.'[12]

Thursday 22 November

The fateful day. Twenty-seven years ago John Kennedy, President of the United States, was assassinated. She was assassinated this day. When I rang her in the morning, they said she was too busy to speak to me and that she wasn't speaking to anybody. I couldn't even get hold of Denis Thatcher who they said wasn't taking any calls. I couldn't speak to Charles Powell, I couldn't speak to dear Bernard Ingham. They were all getting ready for a Cabinet meeting at nine o'clock.

I spoke to Norman just before eight.

He said, 'It's no good, Woodrow. She is going to be terribly badly beaten by Heseltine. We can't possibly have Heseltine as Prime Minister. I would support her to the end and I have told her that I will fight for her and go down with her, but it's no good.' I said, 'You are all wrong. Opinion would swing her way this weekend when people realize the enormity of what they are doing. It's only about the ruddy mortgage interest rates and possibly a grumble about the poll tax. The economy is coming right and she would survive it and then have just as good a majority as before.' But they are all scared stiff, even the Cabinet.

At about half past nine the announcement came that she had resigned. That fearful crew, the Tory Party, had let her down. She was reported as saying her Cabinet hadn't got any balls yesterday and she was quite right.

I haven't yet found out why she didn't fight on, as I would have wished her to do. Even if she was beaten, it wouldn't have mattered.

---

11. Historian and biographer of Harold Macmillan.
12. The suggestion that Macmillan had never been back to Eton was refuted in the press after publication of Vol. 1; the letter is referred to in Vol. 1, p. 146.

A little later in the morning I spoke to John Major.

The *Question Time* programme on which I was to appear had been cancelled, as far as I was concerned, because they were revamping it on BBC1 tonight. So I wanted to tell John Major that they wanted one of the candidates and could he get in fast.

He was very touched and said, 'But I can't you know. I will tell you privately why not. I have this fearful dental problem. I have just had an awful operation on my teeth and I really can't speak properly. It would look very bad on television. But I am not saying that is the reason to anybody else.'

I said, 'Anyway, for what it is worth, I'm backing you.' He said, 'It's worth a great deal.' I said, 'I believe you are the only one who understands what she was trying to do, believes in what she was trying to do and will be able and anxious to carry on with her radical revolution.'

At home I watched her make her last speech as Prime Minister in the Commons, defending her government on a vote of no confidence from the Opposition. She was brilliant and funny, with a lovely blue suit and a sparkling diamond brooch.

She was magnanimous, saying she was sure her party would win, whoever the Leader was, at the next election, and she would be behind the Leader (not at all like the sulking Heath who sat throughout the speech, sullen on the government benches further down in the same row). She trounced the Opposition and she gave a magnificent defence of her record and her government's record, her reasons for her actions in Europe and the meaning of a slide into a European federal union.

The Tory benches were cheering her, the foulest of the assassins were cheering her. There was a sense sweeping over the Tory benches of deep shame over what they had done to this marvellous woman, and obviously a feeling of deep regret and the knowledge that they would live to rue the day. I was crying through most of her speech so it was just as well I wasn't in the gallery for the Lords because it would have looked very odd.

I must tell her that she must not give up her seat in the Commons but wait and see what happens. If Heseltine becomes the Prime Minister, I believe they will lose the next election and they will want her back. She is only sixty-five and she will have had a rest.

Then it was off to The Other Club. Tom King was there. He is one of the nominators for Douglas Hurd. I said, 'I must tell you honestly, Tom, that I prefer Major to Douglas, though I like Douglas very much.

I give half a point to him, one to Major and nil to Heseltine, and if you elect Heseltine, I will never be able to ask people to vote Tory again.'

I said about Douglas, 'He's very good but I have a suspicion of people who are brought up in the civil service (which of course Douglas was) and I think he would be too willing to compromise.'

Tom King said, 'Who would Major make Chancellor of the Exchequer?' I said, 'What does that matter? He could be his own. But why not Norman Lamont? He is very good.' Paul Channon immediately said, 'He is very good and he would make an excellent Chancellor of the Exchequer,' so that obstacle was removed.

The betting book was then brought out and I bet everyone who wanted to take me that with Heseltine Prime Minister and Leader of the Tory Party, he would lose the election. I bet a bottle of good claret. There were several takers. Arnold Weinstock was one, Nico Henderson was another, William Rees-Mogg was another; I think Tom King was one too.

We all agreed that it had been a most shameful episode in Tory Party history.

We talked about how it all went wrong.

Of course all agreed that the real thing that did for her was Geoffrey Howe in his vile, disloyal speech.

We were thinking of new members. I said, 'Why not have Peter Kellner?' because we wanted more on the left and he writes very good stuff in the *Independent*. He used to write for the *Times* and the *New Statesman*. But they decided he wasn't clubbable. So I suggested Gordon Brown of the Labour Party because he is very civilized and intelligent and they thought that was not a bad idea. Then somebody else suggested a fellow called Blair.[13] I said, 'I had suggested Charles Moore. What about him?' But he didn't get enough votes.

I talked quite a lot with Paul Channon, telling him how I had been reading his father's diaries again.

I said, 'You must have masses of stuff not yet published which I suppose you can't use for libel reasons.' He said, 'Yes, there could be quite a lot of that, and upsetting people who are still alive,' which I suppose he didn't want to do.

He said, 'You know a lot of it is very boring. It just goes on telling

---

13. Both Tony Blair and Gordon Brown were suggested on a similar occasion in October 1988. See Vol. 1, p. 653.

you that he didn't feel very well this morning and he didn't want to shave or whatever it might be, trivial matters like that.'

I said, 'I knew him a little.' He said he knew that. Obviously I am mentioned somewhere in these diaries but perhaps not in a very flattering light.

Actually I think my diary, although his is very high society with Kings and Queens and so forth, in parts is better than his. It touches more levels and a wider interest.

I suddenly decided I rather liked Paul Channon. I hadn't been sure before.

There was surprise at The Other Club at the failure of the *Times* to give her whole-hearted supported this morning. I too was surprised. I noticed also that Rupert didn't ring all day today, which he usually does when there is something happening.

Only the *Telegraph* was still starkly battling for her.

At The Other Club most thought the tide was flowing in Major's way.

Then there was a discussion and it was said that a regicide isn't usually the person who inherits the crown, meaning that Heseltine was the regicide.

The whole of Eastern Europe is astounded and bereft because they knew she fought for them and but for her stand, which included deploying cruise missiles and being strong in the face of Russia, they would never have got their freedom. She was the first person to recognize Gorbachev as a person you could do business with.

They are stunned in America. Only the bureaucrats in Brussels are delighted because they know that if Heseltine wins, he will be a push-over and British interests will be surrendered in order that he may be personally popular with the continental leaders. This may not be so much so with Major.

How I wish Margaret had consulted me about her campaign managers and the style of the campaign earlier and properly.

I had less influence on this campaign than I had on her general election campaign when I made them display her more prominently on the television.

My brave darling, my heart bled for her.

Friday 23 November
Spoke to my darling Margaret for about twenty minutes. She said that on Wednesday evening the Cabinet had all come into her room one by

one to be asked by her where they stood and what they thought. They told her that they thought she hadn't a hope and they wanted to protect her from being humiliated and that she should go, and if she didn't go, Heseltine would be elected Prime Minister. 'They sold me down the river.'

One of the things she said she had to put up with, wearing a smile, after her speech yesterday, was large numbers of Tory MPs coming up to her to shake her hand and congratulate her on her speech when she knew they had voted against her.

She said when she was faced with this tremendous weight of evidence that she was going to be defeated, she thought she had to think of the Conservative Party. I broke in, 'I don't give a damn for the Conservative Party, only for the country.' She said she thought it might have been bad for the country, too.

She said, 'The trouble is it's all anonymous, secret balloting.' I said, 'Yes, even Caesar was able to say, "*Et tu, Brute!*" as his assassin stuck the dagger in.' She said, 'I only needed three extra people to vote for me and I would have won with a majority plus fifteen per cent.' I said, 'The *Sunday Times* and others swayed the balance there. You would have got it otherwise.'

I said, 'Why didn't your big guns fire?' She said, 'I think they didn't want to have it treated as an election between equals, suggesting that Heseltine was really my equal in being the challenger.'

I said, 'Damn fools. You weren't enough in evidence.' She said, 'That was what I was advised against, not to go round the tea rooms, etc. making it look as though I was on the same level as Heseltine.'[14]

She said that Douglas Hurd was hinting he might stand if she were removed. I said, 'I warned you several times he was not a friend of yours.' She said, 'I know, and he's a very cold man. He was sitting next to me in Paris. I did a good speech and was congratulated on it as being the best speech by the other world leaders there. But Douglas just picked up his papers and walked away from me at the end of my speech without saying a word. He is not the sort of person you could turn round to as one would to a friend and say, "Was that all right?" '

I said, 'I know you want Major to win and so do I.' She said, 'It may be inverted snobbishness but I don't want old style, old Etonian

---

14. WW himself had advised against this on 14 November but had asked Bernard Ingham on 18 November to make sure she appeared on television in Paris in her role as Prime Minister.

Tories of the old school to succeed me and go back to the old complacent, consensus ways. John Major is someone who has fought his
way up from the bottom and is far more in tune with the skilled and
ambitious and worthwhile working classes than Douglas Hurd is.' I
said, 'Also John Major would be determined to continue your achievements and take them further.'

When I was saying to her how magnificent she was in her speech,
so gracious, I started to sob. She was practically consoling me.

I said, 'What are you doing this weekend?' She said, 'Packing all
my stuff up here and at Chequers and arranging for the removal.
Alistair McAlpine is lending me a small house near here to store
all my files and papers. I haven't got a big enough house.' She was
contemplating moving out of the fairly small house at Dulwich to a
bigger and more central one. She said, 'I have to earn some money.' I
said, 'You can do that easily with your memoirs.'

I said, 'I will go on ringing you, if that's all right.' She said, 'Yes,
they will still be putting you through to wherever I am. Please do.'

In a way I suppose I have always been in love with her, not physic-
ally. It's her noble spirit and clear mind and sense of duty and patriotism, her clarity of purpose and intention and her strength. How
could they throw all that away after she had done so much for them
and had so much still to do for them? I think at heart the Tory
Party and the British just want to go on declining gently because they
are idle and their will has gone. They don't mind drifting deeper and
deeper into a welfare state system and mentality, avoiding struggle to
create wealth and modern industries and services.

They are so feeble that they didn't know how to value her. They
deserve a Socialist government and a continued descent from our once
great glory.

I was asked earlier this week if I would give an interview for
Panorama about Mrs Thatcher.

It was all arranged but when I rang, to make sure they were coming,
they asked me a lot of questions, wanting me to say what Mrs Thatcher
had been telling me about the crisis as it developed. I said, 'I am not
going to reveal private conversations with the Prime Minister to you.
I didn't realize it was going to be a gossip column.' He said, 'No. It's
history. It's a very important historical event.' I said, 'It's not for me,
not at this moment anyway.'

Norman Lamont said the Major camp was gaining momentum and
lots of people who had voted for Heseltine in the first round were

switching to him because they wanted to make an act of contrition to Margaret by backing Major.

Talked to Conrad Black whom I am beginning to like better all the while. I said I thought he was wrong to come out for Hurd in the *Daily Telegraph*. He said the *Sunday Telegraph* would be coming out for Major.

Saturday 24 November

Yesterday I was feeling annoyed with Bernard Levin because I didn't think he had supported her enough. This morning I got this letter: 'Dear Woodrow, You, at any rate, have nothing to reproach yourself for. Your loyalty, courage and determination never faltered for a moment, right to the last. And you were right to the last. The pygmies have got Gulliver, and I hope it chokes them. Be glad for what she achieved, and be proud for what you did. All my love, Bernard.'

At Newbury.

Talked to Queen Elizabeth the Queen Mother whom I almost literally bumped into as she was getting out of her car. I said, 'May I come and have some tea with you or talk to you a little later?' She said, 'How are you?' I said, 'Very sad,' and she said, 'So are we.'

She said they think it is desperately unfair and an appalling way to do things. She says they would like Mrs Thatcher, if she were willing, to come and stay again at Balmoral. They admire her, they think she was wonderful and she did so much for Britain, not only at home but in the world at large.

Queen Elizabeth said, 'What will Bush do without her?' I said, 'I think he may slide and be unable to gather the resolution or support from the rest of the world to deal with Saddam Hussein.'

I mentioned to her the story which had been put about that the Queen had disliked Mrs Thatcher because of her attitude towards the Commonwealth and not agreeing that the sanctions should be put on to South Africa. She said it was pure invention.

I explained to her that one of Mrs Thatcher's worries about a single currency and the creeping federalism was that they would be a threat to the Queen.

Our sovereignty would be diminished and so would the effect of the Queen being the head of our state and the symbolism which goes with it. It wasn't just rhetoric. The Queen Mother said, 'She (Margaret) is very patriotic and I think more women are more patriotic than most men.'

She could see I was badly shaken and she, too, was really moved.

Back in London I asked the editor of the *News of the World* what news they had and I was told that Major was drawing ahead of Heseltine with Hurd trailing. The editor, Patsy Chapman, then said, 'We got a frightfully boring piece from Major about a classless society which was in all the papers this morning. But what we would really like would be a human story about his own background and what it was like at home, and his upbringing. Can you do anything about it?' I rang their campaign headquarters and talked to Richard Ryder.

Rupert rang latish at night and we had a long talk. He said he was in favour of Major and I said I would be able to keep contact with Major all right. I said, 'I have been doing so all day with his camp.'

I told Rupert that Simon Jenkins was seeing Major, whom he had never met before, at eleven on Sunday morning. I had arranged this.

I had told Richard Ryder to get Major to make the odd joke. I said, 'We don't want him wandering around and looking like an undertaker,' which Ryder thought was quite funny.

Sunday 25 November
I rang Simon Jenkins and put to him the better claims of Major.

I told him what Rupert had said, that Rupert is in favour of Major, to which Simon replied, 'Rupert doesn't know anything about it in this political scene now. He just takes on the views of the last person he has spoken to.' I didn't think it was quite like that but he was fairly adamant. Simon said he was reserving his position and he would think about it hard.

I reported to Richard Ryder what Simon Jenkins had said.

I got a message from both ends, one from the Major camp and one from Simon Jenkins, that the meeting with John Major had gone very well.

I was able to tell the Major camp that Rees-Mogg was coming out in favour of Major in the *Independent* tomorrow morning. He was at lunch at Bowden with his jolly wife, Gillian.

Tony Lambton rang up. He said he was very sorry for me. I said I was more sorry for her and worried about what was going to happen with the Major campaign. He said, 'I am very sorry for you because now you have lost your great influence.' I don't think that's of any great importance. I didn't tell him that if Major wins, I think I shall have quite a lot of influence still, over both him and Norman Lamont.

Monday 26 November

Spoke to Margaret for about twenty minutes. Despite her harrowing time at Chequers yesterday, saying goodbye to a place she loved, she seemed vigorous and cheerful. I told her I had a nice message for her and then told her what Queen Elizabeth the Queen Mother had said.

I said to her, 'I don't think you should become a Countess for the time being. Wait and see what happens. You wouldn't have to go into the Commons, if it's Heseltine who wins. You could just opt out for a time and maybe they would ask you back again.'

She said she didn't intend to ask for a peerage until the next election because when you stand for Parliament, in her view, you make a sort of contract with the electorate that you are going to stay there until the next parliamentary election at least. She said she didn't want to be a hereditary Countess: 'We haven't got the means.' I said, 'But Attlee was and he didn't have the means, much less than you.'

She said she was worried even about the expenses of maintaining an office. 'It costs a lot, as you know.' She remarked that Heseltine had become some kind of a cult figure, going around and saying what wonderful things he had done for Merseyside. 'He is giving the impression that he somehow cared about the unemployment there and did a great deal, when actually nothing happened at all from his mission to do something about it.'

She reverted again to the last hour or so. 'The staunchest ones even came and said they couldn't support me, one after another.' I said, 'Norman Lamont wanted to back you and said he would go down with you.' She said, 'Even he was one of the ones who said I should stand down.' I said, 'What about Major?' She said, 'He was very stout.'

She said that she was hurt that William Waldegrave came out against her and others whom she had built up and promoted because she thought they were good and loyal to her.

I said, 'I always told you that Hurd was against you and others too, but I didn't like to tell you too often because it was only undermining you.' She said, 'It seemed as though I could really trust practically nobody.'

I said to her, 'Would you like me to go on ringing you up? In 1975, when we talked at Flood Street, I then appointed myself as an unofficial member of your staff and I would like to go on being that, unless you get bored with me and want to sack me. Do you remember that, when you told me what you were going to do and what your ideas were, I said, "If you are going to do all that, I will back you as best I can"?

And you did stick to what you said you were going to do and I have been backing you as best I can ever since.' She said, 'Please go on ringing me up.' She said she had had a longish talk with Simon Jenkins about John Major.

Simon Jenkins told me that he was going to come out in his leader tomorrow morning supporting Major, though he had a few criticisms. He thought he was being over-confident. He didn't like him having people in his office when he was interviewing a serious person like himself, the editor of the *Times*, as though he couldn't be trusted to get it down right. But when I told Norman Lamont this, he said, 'It was not a minder for guarding against Simon Jenkins. It was in order to stop our man saying things he ought not to say at this moment.'

I am continually in touch with the Major camp and they now think he could just win it on the first ballot but I am not quite certain.

Tuesday 27 November

I saw that Mrs Thatcher said at her farewell party last night at Conservative Central Office, when asked what she was going to do in politics now, 'Be a back-seat driver.' I was very alarmed. I rang her and said, 'This is going to cause some trouble.' She said it was typical of the BBC, 'faithless to the last', to play it up. I said, 'Yes but it may rebound on Major a bit.' She said, 'But it was only a chance remark.'

I said, 'Rupert rang and asked me to say that before you consider giving your memoirs to anybody, will you let him come and see you first, as he has the largest publishing house in the world.' She said she would. I was thinking that would give her enough money for her offices and so on straight away.

Norman Fowler[15] has come out for Heseltine, as indeed has Peter Walker, not that he matters much. It is slightly worrying about Norman Fowler but he did say that if she had stayed in the race, he would have gone on voting for her to the end.

The *Times* had a splendid leading article; a very reasonable, careful assessment of the candidates, saying that Major was the man. So Simon Jenkins did me proud.

Allan Davis says there is no hope now of doing the original *High Profiles* play and why didn't I write a play about Mrs Thatcher herself.

---

15. Conservative politician; MP since 1974, at this time Secretary of State for Employment; knight 1990.

I have thought about it a little but I don't know if it would be any good.

Went to hear her do her last Question Time. She said to me this morning she wasn't going to do another one on Thursday because she doesn't like making all these last appearances.

It was one of her best Question Time performances and when little Rosie Barnes, the SDP lady, quite a pretty girl, got up and first of all paid her a tribute and then said, 'As the third ballot in this leadership contest is done by a form of proportional representation with a single transferable vote, would she not, as one of her last acts, recommend this for the ordinary parliamentary elections in England?' She replied, 'In the circumstances I think I prefer first past the post,' to great laughter. If that had been the rule, she would be there now.

She looked very smart and dignified, with very sheer black nylon stockings and pretty black shoes and a black skirt with a dark blue jacket which I suppose is appropriate for a Tory Prime Minister, but with white edgings and trimmings. I knew her heart was bursting though no one could have guessed it.

I rang Rupert when I got back and told him that Major had got a hundred and eighty-five votes, two short of a complete majority, but that the other two had conceded defeat. Instead of a real third round, because in this crazy system there has to be a third round, they would vote for Major and advise their followers to do the same. I was glad to see Michael Heseltine on TV, standing at his front door looking very dejected, with his wife, Anne, who looked absolutely shattered. I felt sorry for her because she is quite a nice girl and she has a great deal to put up with, being married to that swine.

Poor Douglas only got enough votes in third place not to be completely disgraced.

Douglas looked a bit disappointed but he bore it well.

Then the party authorities announced that there would be no third ballot so John Major goes to see the Queen tomorrow to become Prime Minister. Fantastic. But it is still deeply unjust.

Dear Margaret was cheated. It will be an eternal shame for the Tory Party and a deep and dreadful loss.

I then went to the College of Arms where John Martin Robinson had a party for his book about Stowe.

He is some sort of a Herald now.[16] He doesn't get paid for it but it is a nice title and he wears a lovely costume.

He is delighted the way Heveningham Hall is going.

Everything has been smoothed out happily with the curious people, relatives of Abdul and so forth, who have been looking after the reinstatement of the house.

Jennifer Jenkins was there. She is Chairman of the National Trust who are publishing John Martin Robinson's book.

Before I left home I spoke to Rupert about the result and said how relieved I was that Heseltine hadn't won because I was then released from my pledge to tell my readers to vote for Mr Kinnock if the swine Heseltine were elected Prime Minister.

Wednesday 28 November

Spoke to her as Prime Minister at Number 10 for the last time this morning at around 8.00 a.m. She sounded brisk and vigorous and warm and friendly. She was delighted that John Major had won without a further ballot.

She is confident he is going to carry on in her direction.

She said somebody had lent her a small flat in Albany[17] where she can be at nights when she comes up from Dulwich. We chatted on as though she hadn't got to be at the Palace by 9.45 to hand in her seal of office, and then she suddenly said, 'Oh hello, John,' and then to me, 'Woodrow, we're desperately busy. I'll talk to you later.' It was obviously John Major who had come into the room. There is a connecting door between Number 11 and Number 10.

I am feeling less sad because she is so full of fight and will still do great things in the world. At least we have stopped this terrible man Heseltine and avoided a spongy compromise in the middle with dear Douglas Hurd.

It is true that John Major is a hard worker, which is good because in today's politics in England detail is all important for a Prime Minister. But I doubt if he will ever have the total dedication and superhuman energy that Margaret has. We must wait and see.

Frank Longford came up to me and said, 'I appreciate your sorrow, Woodrow. It is like losing a wife.' I thought that charming of him.

Spoke to Norman [appointed Chancellor of the Exchequer] before

---

16. Maltravers Herald of Arms Extraordinary; the book was *Temples of Delight*.
17. Albany Chambers, Piccadilly.

our dinner party. I said, 'Hooray, hooray, hooray. At least one good thing has come out of it all.' I said I didn't like his sidekick, now made Chief Secretary and in the Cabinet, David Mellor.

I told him I thought Major had shown a great sense of humour in making Heseltine Secretary for the Environment. Heseltine, having campaigned on the wonderful things he was going to do with the community charge, will now be stuck in the position of having to produce something.

The dinner party was quite jolly.

It was for the retiring Tote Board members, except that David Montagu and Ninette couldn't come.

Princess Michael kept putting her hand on mine. She had on a fairly low cut dress and she turned to me, pushing her breasts slightly at me, 'so you can see my bosoms'. They are rather full, round and pretty, and she has a very smooth skin. I was talking to her about the sort of diet I have and she said why did I have it? 'Are you not well?' I said, 'On the contrary. I have a low cholesterol count, low blood pressure and the doctors say I have the heart of a boy of eighteen.' She said, 'You can be my toy boy then. How lovely. Do all the other bits work all right?' I said, 'Yes, not too badly.'

I said I thought the Queen Mother liked her. She said, 'No, she doesn't. We have several times asked her to come to dinner with us and she has always refused.' Marie Christine thinks she has been very badly treated. The others, like Princess Anne and Princess Margaret, have countless affairs and nobody complains about it. But whenever she does anything, there is all hell to pay because she is a foreigner.

But she had noticed in Jean Rook's column in the *Express* this morning the comment that Princess Diana must be very happy and sexually fulfilled, not put quite like that but that was what it meant, otherwise her face wouldn't look so much as though she was in love. Jean Rook said this proved that the Prince of Wales and she must have a wonderfully happy marriage and a very satisfying sex life. We both laughed because of course they have no sex at all together, as far as we know, and there is some other young man involved. Marie Christine said it was the one she had been visiting when she arrived at six in the morning at Kensington Palace having been caught speeding. She said it must be awful for Diana to have such a doleful life with the grim and gloomy Prince Charles.

Winfield didn't drink anything. He is hobbling around with a stick. I find him increasingly unpleasant. When I said to him, 'I hear that some board member, as reported by Richard Evans of the *Times*, was not in favour of my continuing,' he said he didn't know that but I think he is the traitor. He is bloody lucky to have been kept on by my recommendation.

Princess Michael and I were talking about the dreadful Fergie, Duchess of York. I said, 'When I talked to her I thought she was immensely stupid.' She said, 'She's not. She's very sharp and clever and she has made very great friends with the Queen. She's with her always. They go to the theatre together. They go to all kinds of things together. She has certainly inserted herself there extremely cleverly.' Naturally Princess Michael dislikes her intensely.

Thursday 29 November
In the morning I rang Margaret to say hello to her in her new house at Dulwich.

She said she was coming down with a bump. In Downing Street she had so many people to do things for her. When flowers arrived they would make notes to say who they had come from and she would send a little note back, and she could arrange for things to be typed. Now she hasn't got anything like that and flowers are being sent to her by the hundreds, if not thousands, of bunches. She has thirty thousand letters to answer from people who wrote to her saying how sad and angry they were that she was no longer Leader.

But she is not looking backwards.

I said, 'You'll get plenty of money from the memoirs. We're not talking in hundreds of thousands but well above that.' She said, 'I feel I would need someone to help me. I must think about it all.' I said, 'Rupert's got an idea about that.' So she said, 'Who?' and I said, 'John O'Sullivan. He knows you well. He admires you greatly and he can help you write it.' She said, 'What a wonderful idea. That would be marvellous.'[18]

She said she has an office in the Commons, which is the least they can do, and she also has her Political Secretary, John Whittingdale, helping her for a bit.

I went down to the Commons to try and get in for John Major's first Questions.

---

18. In her acknowledgements to her book *The Downing Street Years*, she says: 'John O'Sullivan came skiing in occasionally, tuned up the arguments, pared the prose and pushed forward the narrative.'

She was there, sitting right at the back benches, not in any way intruding herself. I suppose she wanted to see how her protégé got on but she is so brave and noble, that girl, that she would show no rancour, no bitterness. She was received with huge applause when she arrived at the chamber from the Tory benches. I suppose they are still ashamed of themselves.

Later Norman Lamont said she had to be dissuaded from sitting three benches directly behind John, in full view of the TV cameras, looking like the back-seat driver.

I rang Rupert and said, 'You know you have got to give her a lot of money. She needs it. She has got less money than I thought.'

He wanted to think about what sort of book it should be.

I asked him how he was getting on with his financial affairs and he said it was still a bit hairy. He has got another ten days to go through before it is absolutely OK, but he thinks it will be.

I thought to myself, 'It would be awful if he signs her up and then goes bust,' but I suppose the publishing would carry on. I am also wondering whether I shouldn't recommend her to have an agent. An agent would collect at least ten per cent but might protect her better and see that she got a really good deal. In the ordinary course of events I suppose I ought to be getting some commission but of course I would never suggest it and Rupert, who is curiously mean about these things, would never even think of giving me something for having got him the memoirs in the first place.

Winfield and the other board members were saying how generous I had been to give the dinner. This made me feel very guilty about having to ask the Tote to pay for at least part of it. I think the whole thing including the wine and the brandy and the Tokay and the port and the champagne and so forth must have come to about £700.

After talking to Brian he says he insists that I put in the bill. I thanked him for the flowers he sent Verushka. He said, 'Supposing they had gone to a restaurant in a private room, it would have cost an enormous amount of money.'

There was a great dinner at the National Portrait Gallery given by Henry Keswick and Jayne Wrightsman.

On my left sat Virginia Fraser, the wife of Simon Fraser (the Master of Lovat).[19] She is very pretty.

---

19. Virginia, née Grose, m 1 (1972) the Hon. Simon Fraser, Master of Lovat (1939–94); m 2 (1999) Frank Johnson, journalist.

She said his uncle, Hugh Fraser, adored me and often told stories and jokes about the times we had together, including the time when we went round a gallery in Florence. I kept looking at pictures and saying, 'I think that one's a fake, you know. It's not right.' In front of a crowd of spectators he said, 'My friend is a great art expert. He is worried about the provenance of a number of pictures in this gallery.' I stood in front of a Titian and said, 'No, that's not Titian. And that's very doubtfully So-and-so's.' Great consternation was caused in the crowd and among the officials who began to gather, looking rather angry.

She remembered my article in the *Times* about Hugh [on his death], 'Farewell Bonny Gentleman'.

The house of the Tory candidate, Alan Duncan,[20] used for the [Major] campaign headquarters was in Gayfere Street, Westminster. Alan Duncan is a great friend of John Wakeham and also a friend of a Tory MP called William Hague who is PPS to Norman Lamont and has a room in Duncan's house. They just marched in and took over Duncan's house while he was out and began the campaign – William Hague said he was sure he wouldn't mind.[21]

---

20. Conservative MP since 1992; Parliamentary Political Secretary to William Hague since 1997.
21. William Hague, Leader of the Conservative Party and the Opposition since 1997, had been elected an MP in 1989 and now became Lamont's PPS.

Saturday 1 December
Another attack on me by Richard Evans in the *Times*. Yesterday he referred to me as seventy-two and now he refers to 'the septuagenarian', making it clear I am too old to do the job. Why didn't the Tote try to buy William Hill? My executives had to alert me to the fact that it could be coming up for sale.

These are all lies.

I have known all the time that they are never going to sell their betting shops, that is Brent Walker and their William Hill betting shops, not even if there is a break-up of the whole affair. In any case where would we get £600 million to £700 million from and get enough profit out of those betting shops, which are not well run, to cover the interest charges?

At Sandown I talked with George Walker who was laughing about the nonsensical rubbish written in the press about the Jockey Club buying his betting shops and then the Tote buying them.

I told him I was very pleased he had got through his troubles, at least for the time being. He had got another bank to fill in the space at the last minute.

Sunday 2 December
Margaret is very anxious to do some lectures in America, quickly if possible before the end of December, while she can still attract a great deal of money. She has been talking to Ronald Reagan about it and he has helped to produce some very good offers. I told her that Rupert and I thought she ought to have an agent and I suggested one name to her, Hilary Rubinstein of A. P. Watt.[1]

I said, 'Of course the disadvantage is that you have to pay them ten per cent but with a book of your enormous potential this might be worth it – all the world-wide possibilities. Rupert is very anxious that

---

1. Managing director, A. P. Watt literary agents, 1965–92, Hilary Rubinstein Books Literary Agents, since 1992.

you shouldn't just take a price from him out of friendship but see if you get other offers which are better which he might have to match.'

She said, 'What I like about Rupert's suggestion is John O'Sullivan whom I could do it with very well.' So I arranged that I would get Rupert to ring her on Monday to arrange a meeting.

She said her intention is to do three things at the moment: these lectures to earn money. Then she wants to get her foundation going, the Margaret Thatcher Foundation. A trust is being set up. It is to make sure that the principles and the philosophy of what she was trying to do live on and help Eastern Europe and elsewhere. The third is the book.

She said, 'I am not going to the House for Questions any more. But I shall be going into the Commons twice next week because they have got a three-line whip, ironically enough on the community charge.' I said, 'You don't have to do that.' She said, 'Yes, I must, to show I am a loyal member of the party.'

Several times she said, 'I have got to do a positive job and do positive things. I intend to go on having influence.'

She said, 'I don't like it when they seem to be trying to distance themselves from me. On the community charge we all agreed to make the refinements to make it more acceptable all round. Now they seem to be talking about abolishing it. Also, I don't like the way it is suggested that somehow they will be different on Europe. That has been coming over from John Major.' I said, 'I think he is only trying to rephrase it slightly to keep everybody united. I don't think he means anything different in substance.'

She said, 'I have spent eleven and a half years making decisions. I have enjoyed it. Now I miss the decisions and I am not even able to say whether they are doing things right or wrong because I don't know how the problems are being presented.'

When we were talking about how the Cabinet let her down I said, 'I know that Arnold Weinstock has written to you to ask you to go and stay at Bowden. But for about a year he has been saying you ought to go and he wants Heseltine to succeed you. I had some furious rows with him about it.'

I nearly didn't say anything about Arnold because I thought it might upset her a bit more. I refrained from it while she was still Prime Minister but now I think it important for her not to be living under illusions. Now that I have told her that, maybe he would be a good person to get a subscription out of for the Foundation.

Tuesday 4 December
Had a meeting with Adrian Rowbotham over the composition of the film.

We went to the curious club, the Academy Club, attached to the *Literary Review* which Auberon Waugh has. We waited nearly an hour for our food though it was all supposed to be ready.

Bron came in, who is in a sense the proprietor, ordered something and had it immediately. After a bit I threw a piece of bread at him which hit him just over his ear, a very good shot. He then came up to me and said he hadn't noticed I was there. He saw that we got our food quicker.

He was at school[2] with Adrian and Bron once said he was the only man that he had kissed. That was because they were in a school play, *The Importance of Being Earnest*, and Adrian was playing Gwendolen, the heroine, and Bron Waugh played the hero who kisses her.

Went to the Lords for a meeting of our little committee to try and make sure the ITC obey the Act of Parliament properly. There are still a great many defects in the ITC code – oh for Mrs Thatcher to force them to do what they are told. The Home Office are wobbling.

Had a rather jolly dinner party. William and Annabel Astor were there. So were John Patten and his pretty wife, Louise.

Robin Harris[3] was there, the old stalwart from Margaret's Policy Unit at Number 10 who has now been given the sack. Piers Bengough and his wife Bridget. Charles Moore and his wife, Caroline, too.

William Astor is at the Ministry of the Environment as a junior Minister, as well as being on the front bench as a whip in the Lords. He said Heseltine tells them they have to be in by 9.15 every morning and report to him to chat over the issues of the day. What actually happens is that they go in there and Heseltine does all the talking, gives them their instructions and there is no discussion of any kind. I said, 'It sounds just like what Mrs Thatcher was supposed to be in her Cabinet meetings, but never was.' He agreed that Heseltine is a ghastly person but he thinks he may do quite a good job of fiddling about with the community charge.

Piers Bengough came fresh from the committee which he had been presiding over for nearly two years which has now disqualified Aliysa,

---

2. Downside. Bron played Jack who kisses Gwendolen at the end of the play when she discovers his name is in fact Earnest.
3. Director, Conservative Research Department, 1985–8, Prime Minister's Policy Unit, 1989–90; assistant to Margaret Thatcher since 1990.

which won the 1989 Oaks, for alleged doping. The Aga may take it to the courts. Meanwhile he says he is going to take all his ninety horses in Britain overseas to be trained which is a great blow to the English racing industry. Already there are fewer horses in training than there have been for years. When Piers told the Queen about this, instead of saying, 'How awful,' she said, 'I don't blame him. I would have done the same.' But they should have given him the benefit of the doubt because it was pretty obvious that the forensic tests were not very sound.

During dinner John Patten was sitting next to Annabel Astor who was on my left. He said he had read somewhere that everybody, once every two or three minutes, had thoughts about sex but he wasn't sure that he did. I said, 'I used to but I don't have them once every three minutes now, perhaps only about once an hour when I look at a pretty girl and think how nice it would be to go to bed with her, like you Annabel, for instance.' I then said, 'Why don't they say this about women? Women have plenty of thoughts about sex. As for men, they call them dirty old men when they grow older but they are just the same as they ever were.'

Wednesday 5 December
Rupert is still very worried about his financial affairs. He hopes to get everything finished by the end of the week but he may not and will have to come back again later.

Dinner party at Leonard Wolfson's. Very boring people. The food was really disgusting. But there were at least quail eggs before dinner which I could dip in some pepper. There was some Château Mouton Rothschild 1970 which was extremely good.

It must have been worth £200 or £300 a bottle.

Leonard was in a very foolish mood. He and Ruth had wanted Heseltine to win.

She had got it all wrong about Europe and the economy, and business people all wanted Heseltine. I nearly lost my temper.

Thursday 6 December
Rang Margaret. Got her in the end at College Street.[4]

She was not at Albany at all now because of the difficulties with the security.

---

4. Alistair McAlpine had lent her this house.

She immediately began by saying, 'What a wonderful article you wrote in the *Times* on Tuesday. I must thank you.' I said, 'It was nothing at all. It was just what I think.' She said, 'It gave me an enormous lift. My spirits were getting a bit low, as you might realize, and I thought it was a wonderful thing. I am going to have it put in one of those iron frame things and hang it up. I want to see it always.'[5]

She said George Weidenfeld had approached her [to publish her book]. I said, 'I have known him for many years. His business is shaky. In any case it is always difficult getting money out of him and he doesn't give a very good bargain. If Rupert can't come up with all you want, you can go somewhere else [when] you have got an agent.' She said, 'I would prefer to do it with Rupert because he has been so wonderful and supportive of me, even if I do it for a little less.'

After that I had a long talk with Hilary Rubinstein.

I said, 'Write to her and tell her the target you are aiming for is around the £5 million mark. Give her all the details.' He said, 'Isn't it rather impertinent to tell her about tax deductions?' I said, 'No. She loves all those details.'

Friday 7 December

Rupert is horrified that Sarah Hogg[6] has been put in charge of the Policy Unit at Number 10. She talks nineteen to the dozen and is very silly and rather wet. Not at all on Thatcher lines. Rupert thought it was a bad omen.

I can't stop being sad about Margaret. I wake up at nights and think the whole world has changed and that the most appalling things could happen. England has been betrayed. I get a lot of letters, from my articles, supporting her now and only one or two saying good riddance.

---

5. WW argued that, 'So far, the shock of Mrs Thatcher's shabby deposition has not fully percolated into voters' minds. When it does, there could be a strong backlash against the party responsible for removing the most innovative and successful prime minister since 1832 while in full vigour.' He ended by warning that Mrs Thatcher would not stay silent if the tenets of Thatcherism were dismantled.

6. Former economics journalist; head of Prime Minister's Policy Unit, 1990–5; daughter of John Boyd-Carpenter (Conservative politician, life peer 1972); m (1968) Douglas Hogg (Conservative politician, elder son of Lord Hailsham); life peer 1995.

Saturday 8 December

I congratulated Norman Lamont on the excellent, tough line he had taken at the European meeting on the single currency.

Then he said, 'Do you think I should go and see her? I would hate her to think there was some plot, which had the backing of the Cabinet and which got her out, because that wasn't true. Bruce Anderson wrote a bloody silly thing for the *Spectator* saying the Major campaign had all been planned for the Wednesday and that simply was not the case.'

He said, 'It was not planned beforehand because we had no idea what she was going to do. We would have done nothing disloyal and did nothing at all until she had made up her mind. There would have been no such campaign if she had decided to go on standing.'

I said, 'You will have to watch out for Bruce Anderson – of course it was a great coup for him to be seen running your campaign with you.' Norman said, 'He wasn't. He just turned up there.' I said, 'But he was photographed standing behind Major. No doubt that was for publicity purposes for himself.' He said that was so. I said, 'You mean you didn't want to throw him out because he could be useful and many hands on deck was a good idea.' He said, 'That was about it but we didn't invite him to come and join our campaign and he was never officially a part of it.'

Dinner with Rupert at Santini's in Ebury Street where George Moore once lived.[7] It is a new but exceedingly fashionable restaurant, Italian.

He said he had been talking last night to Andrew Neil and Andrew Knight.

I said, 'What is going to happen to Andrew Neil?' 'He's looking for another job,' said Rupert. I said, 'Good.'

He then told us that Andrew Knight and Sabiha are in marriage crisis. Sabiha has a boyfriend called Foster who is an architect.[8] Andrew travels abroad a lot and can't spend all that much time with her. Rupert has asked them all to come to Aspen for the Christmas holidays, the two children as well. I said, 'But they have asked us for the New Year's Eve traditional dinner and fireworks.' It seems they may seriously be about to split up which greatly upsets him, Andrew. He is a curious, withdrawn man.

I asked Rupert whether he was doing all he wanted and Rupert

---

7. (1852–1933); Anglo–Irish novelist; his *Conversations in Ebury Street* was published in 1924.

8. Norman Foster, internationally famed architect; knight 1990, OM 1997.

said, 'Yes, he is doing it perfectly.' I said, 'He's a good number two.' Rupert said, 'He doesn't have all that much of an original mind but he certainly works out the details extremely well,' and that he was a great asset to him. I was delighted to hear this.

We talked about Bush getting ready to surrender over Iraq and Kuwait. I said, 'Margaret could have stopped him but Major can't.'

Sunday 9 December
Rupert had said he had never met Lamont and I said I would try and arrange for him to have lunch with us all today at the Stafford Hotel.

I said to Norman, 'Rupert is a good friend to people he likes and it is worth meeting him.' So there was a jolly Sunday lunch at the Stafford Hotel in a big alcove where nobody could overhear us.

Norman was anxious to explain that it was totally untrue they had done any planning for Major's campaign before Margaret had said she would not carry on to the next round on the early morning of Thursday. They then rushed out and organized it. He said they were extremely annoyed with Bruce Anderson.

But it was true that a number of people had said to Norman that they would support Major if he was running in a second ballot and Margaret wasn't there.

Norman said at times they kept trying to reduce the number of people pushing around in the house in Gayfere Street but John Major kept saying, 'Don't do that. They might be offended if you turn them all out. Let's have pretend meetings with them.' The real meetings were going on upstairs.

Of course the reason why John Major didn't troop in when the rest of the Cabinet did, one by one, to see Margaret was that he was recovering from his mouth operation, on his wisdom tooth, and he wasn't even there. Obviously, as he was in hospital for the relevant two or three days, he could have had no part in planning a campaign prior to her announcing that she wasn't going to carry on.

Norman is looking for an economics adviser. I suggested Patrick Minford and one or two others.

I then asked whether he and Rosemary would like to come and stay with us in Italy in August. He said it would be a lovely idea. I think it could be rather fun. I like Rosemary. She is a jolly girl.

Spoke to Margaret.

She told John Major he had made a great mistake in putting Heseltine in his Cabinet: 'You should never put someone in your Cabinet who will try to oust you to become Prime Minister.'

I said I thought it was lovely her getting the Order of Merit and also the baronetcy for Denis.

I told her Norman Lamont would like to see her. 'He wants to explain to you that they did not have any disloyalty before the time when you definitely said you were not going to stand.'

She said, 'They were all hysterical, it was extraordinary. They had no courage at all. Norman Lamont gave the same advice not to stand. He might have said he would go on supporting me but he wasn't going to go out campaigning for me. I have been wronged. Only one member of the Cabinet would have gone out campaigning for me.'

She said there was a dinner at Garel-Jones' house on the Wednesday night. I said, 'Norman Lamont wasn't there.' She said no, but she thinks one or two members of the Cabinet were there and they were arranging what to do. It was all aimed at defeating Heseltine. I think she is a bit low again now, poor girl.

Monday 10 December
Norman Lamont told me I had got something completely wrong about the announcement of Margaret's not standing for the second round. It was on the Wednesday evening that she asked the Cabinet Ministers to come and see her and they trooped in one by one and gave their opinions. It was not on the Thursday morning. Thursday morning was a very early but ordinary Cabinet meeting. Norman said no campaigning was done by John Major's people until after she announced she wasn't going to stand in the second round and would be resigning as Prime Minister.

I said, 'What about this dinner party at Garel-Jones', who is her enemy or certainly no friend of hers?' He said, 'There wasn't a dinner party.' It was after the result was announced that he saw Garel-Jones and one or two other people did, too, in the corridor and he said, 'Come and have a drink' because he lives close by in Westminster, and they did, discussing what had happened. But there was no plot at all. Kenneth Clarke, one of her most devoted supporters, was there also. There was no starting of the campaign to back Major or anybody else that evening.

I said, 'You had better go and speak to her. She would be willing to see you.' He said, 'What do I have to say?' I said, 'You had better explain exactly what happened and try and convince her. But none of you was willing to campaign for her.' He said, 'That is not true. I myself told her that I would campaign for her if she decided to go on.'

Tuesday 11 December

Rupert had seen Margaret. She was very tired from a cold or 'flu. He said it was very sad, her little house in Westminster lent by the McAlpines. There was just a girl at a switchboard and one secretary and a policeman outside.

On the memoirs, she still hasn't quite made up her mind what sort of book and what is to be done but she said that she wouldn't take an advance on anything she hadn't written yet. Rupert thought to himself that it was the first author he had heard of who wouldn't do that.

Talked at length to Ken Baker [Home Secretary] first thing in the morning. I said it had been agreed with Margaret, David Waddington and myself that Alun Chalfont would continue as Deputy Chairman of ITC and do the radio authority as well. Ken said it hadn't been agreed, at least according to what he was told, and he had already written to someone to offer him the job of Deputy Chairman of ITC. I said, 'Oh my goodness, there is going to be real trouble.' He said no, the man he has written to is very robust.

Then he said would I have lunch with him *à deux*. He wants to talk to me about lots of things but he obviously doesn't want any officials present.

The Parkinsons, the Norwichs, Susan Crosland, the Swaythlings, Simon Jenkins and John Derby came to dinner. Petronella should have been there, too, but had a temperature and couldn't come down. Cecil Parkinson wanted to go up and see her but he was not allowed to.

Cecil Parkinson said that on that Thursday morning, her last Cabinet meeting, she was dressed in black. When she began to read out her statement that the Cabinet had advised that she would not win if she stood again, she was crying and couldn't go on reading her statement. The Cabinet sat there with their heads hanging in shame. They couldn't look at her. He, Cecil, said, 'Why doesn't the Lord Chancellor read the statement?' That was to give her a little time to recover herself but she went on and when she got to the passage saying that it was evident that the Cabinet wanted her to resign because she wasn't going to win, he shouted out, 'Rubbish,' and thereafter he resigned before Major could form his government.

Cecil is certain that John Major does not believe in her radical revolution. I said, 'Would he not privatize British Rail and Coal and the Post Office?' He said no. I said, 'Norman Lamont says he would.' He said, 'I don't believe it. The radical revolution has gone.'

He said, 'It's no good telling her that people like Bush are going to ring her up. She has got to realize that she is now nobody and no one is going to take any notice of her.'

Wednesday 12 December
Very amusing. The *Sporting Life* naughtily carried an interview with me a day early and without checking, as they had promised, that I approved of the wording of the interview. I didn't get a chance so they made some mistakes and they left in some rather more violent and slip-shod attacks on the Jockey Club than I otherwise would have allowed. I was a bit alarmed to begin with but Geoffrey Webster and John Heaton (Marketing and Public Relations Director, and solicitor, of the Tote respectively) thought it was marvellous and about time we answered back. Brian McDonnell of course was nervous, taking a rather civil servant view, but the general impression in the Tote was hooray.

In the Lords, Waddington was making his maiden speech as Leader of the House. John Major came and sat on the steps to the throne to listen to him. That was rather decent of him. He was there for about forty minutes. He still looks rather grey, the unknown Prime Minister, but there may be a lot to him. We have to wait and see.

Denis Howell[9] rang up and said would I look at the plans that Alan Meale[10] had got – he is a Labour MP – for getting a commission set up to run racing and just remove the Jockey Club altogether.

It would be very funny if the Jockey Club were removed. It is really rather ridiculous nowadays. It seems to be so out of touch in many respects, despite Stoker Hartington, and particularly because of that ass Christopher Haines, the Chief Executive.

Margaret was at the Jeffrey Archer party. Contrary to what Cecil had been saying about her looking twenty years older, she looked in rather good health this evening.

Jeffrey Archer was in his usual ebullient form. He had a four-feet-high model of W. G. Grace in the hall. He fancies himself as a cricketer but I don't think he can play for toffee. But I do find myself quite liking him. He did a very graceful thing. During some part of the

---

9. Labour politician; Minister for Sport, 1964–9 and 1974–9; Opposition spokesman on sport until 1992; former Football League referee; life peer 1992.
10. Labour MP since 1987; member, Select Committee on Home Affairs, 1989–92; chairman, Parliamentary Beer Club, since 1994; PPS to John Prescott, Deputy Prime Minister, 1997–9.

proceedings he made an announcement that something was coming in for Margaret. It was a marvellous Christmas cake looking like a box in which you receive decorations and on the top there was an exact but enlarged replica of the Order of Merit.

Thursday 13 December
The wretched squirt, Christopher Haines, Chief Executive of the Jockey Club, came to see me at Putney [the Tote headquarters]. He pretended he had never said anything about making £18 million profit immediately out of the Tote if he ran it. He pretended he never made any attack on me. I think he is much chastened by my attack on the Jockey Club in yesterday's *Sporting Life* and today's *Racing Post*. Having talked to Brian and myself for about an hour or more, he said he had learned a lot and understood it better now. I think he dare not be an outright enemy any more.

Dinner with David and Sally Metcalfe.

On my right was Annunziata Asquith.[11] I hadn't seen her for a couple of years or so.

She said she had never got married because she never met any man she felt it was worth sacrificing her aloneness for.

I asked her whether she ever wanted children and she said, 'No not really.' She said she thought she didn't have a mother instinct in a conventional sense.

She is forty-two. She is fair and very pretty still with lovely legs We talked about Harriet Crawley with whom she is in partnership with her art gallery and decorating business. She said, 'Harriet never knows what she wants to be. She sits and discusses with me for hours what she should do, should she write a novel, should she stand for Parliament in England, should she try being a member of the European Parliament?'[12]

Evelyn de Rothschild greeted me there with great friendliness.

---

11. Lady Annunziata Asquith, writer and journalist, daughter of the 2nd Earl of Oxford and Asquith, granddaughter of Raymond Asquith. See Vol. 1, pp. 18 and 134, for her friendship and business associations with the Crawley family.
12. Harriet Crawley's novels include *The God-daughter* (1975) which WW said (Vol. 1, p. 212) was 'about her association with Victor [Rothschild] and her dismay when he tried to make it non-platonic'; she stood as Conservative candidate in the 1987 general election against Ken Livingstone at Brent and as a Pro-Euro Conservative candidate in the 1999 European election.

He said, 'You never take me seriously. I am not as stupid as you think I am. I'd like to help with the Tote. I think we could devise a scheme in which you could sell off your betting shops in part, get an equity base with them and then even venture to buy things like William Hill by rights issues and that kind of activity.' He said, 'You never ask my advice. You only go to people like Hambros. I suppose it is because of your relationship with Jacob that you have never really liked me.' I said, 'But I do like you, Evelyn.'

I must obviously follow up his suggestion on the Tote. I dare say it will turn out to be pie in the sky again, but it might not be so I must have a go.

Friday 14 December
Spoke to Anthony Montague Brown[13] who told me that when Winston resigned from being Prime Minister he was continually sending for him from the Foreign Office. He had been number three on Winston's secretarial staff at Number 10. He requested him to go out and join Max Beaverbrook and himself at Cap d'Antibes; Beaverbrook supplied the tickets.

After a while the FO thought it was too much of a good thing and wanted the position to be regularized so Macmillan said to Montague Brown that he should be seconded to be Winston's Secretary. He said, 'But of course we won't forget you and it will only last for a few years in the nature of things as he is so old.' Anthony Montague Brown said they certainly forgot him at the Foreign Office after the few years stretched to ten until Winston died. Winston paid his salary, the basic one, to the Treasury but none of the allowances for being abroad and the other perks you get for being at the Foreign Office which he never received the whole time he worked for Winston.

I reported the gist of this conversation to Margaret and said, 'I'm afraid it means you won't get one free from the civil service so it's not much good pursuing Robin Butler as we thought.'

I felt very sad about this. It is the most difficult thing for her to be cast down into nearly nothingness after eleven and a half years.

Before I rang Margaret I had spoken to Norman who told me he had seen her the day before for a couple of hours. She remained unconvinced there was no plot against her though he thought he had

---

13. Diplomat; seconded as Private Secretary to Sir Winston Churchill as Prime Minister, 1952–5; continued as his Private Secretary, 1955–65, until his death.

persuaded her they had not started the campaign for John Major until after she decided to resign.

She refers to Heseltine as 'that bastard', poor girl.

I thought it was very game of Norman to face her and try to assure her he had been loyal to her but she wasn't going to believe him. Cecil Parkinson has obviously been saying to her that Norman betrayed her, though he used to be a great friend of Norman's. I think that could well be out of jealousy more than out of accuracy because Cecil Parkinson would have liked to have been Chancellor of the Exchequer. For a long time Norman was somewhat junior to him and now he is way above him, particularly as he has now left the Cabinet.

When I told Margaret I had spoken to Norman, instead of talking about the plot and the intrigue she immediately carved into saying, 'I don't know whether they are going to carry on with my policy. I think Norman is in favour of the line against the single currency and the European Bank but I am not sure that the others are. I think John Major has only got three Cabinet Ministers, apart from Norman, who agree with him on Europe. They are all beginning to waver. And what on earth was William Waldegrave doing saying he didn't believe in producing a market atmosphere in the National Health Service?'

Sunday 16 December
Talked to Margaret after getting Denis on the telephone who sounded a bit rough. Margaret, too, was tinny. This was around six in the evening at Dulwich. I think she is hating it there. I told her that John O'Sullivan was coming over specially to talk to her about the shape of what she was going to write and that Rupert hopes she would begin with a short book.

Rupert is nervous that she just wants to start the great opus and it would be terribly boring and take ages to get to the exciting stuff.

We got some quite good replies to the advertisement in the *Financial Times* about the sale on a royalty basis of Cornish Spring Water.

Robbie [Lyle] thinks that the National Trust won't come up with anything like the amount we want [for the sale of land]. I said, 'Don't be in too much of a hurry about that. Is Tessa staying there? She seems to be a very sensible girl.' He said, 'It takes a lawyer to tackle a lawyer,' meaning she hopes to make them backtrack on all the death duties he has been paying based on Cousin Molly's will in 1949 which ought to be out of time. I said, 'I think she is very good news and I am delighted about it.'

Monday 17 December

Dinner at 19 Cavendish Avenue. Lord and Lady Stevens, Lord and
Lady Hanson, Henry and Tessa Keswick, Chips Keswick, Petronella,
Norman and Rosemary Lamont. We had the standard dinner for these
days: fish tureen, veal, and pancakes stuffed with walnuts and chocolate
sauce. The claret was Château Lafite 1967.

Lord Hanson, who I suppose is one of the richest men in the world
let alone in England, has no real concept of wine at all and was amazed
to find how delicious this was. I had to explain to him how it was
done to get to the glass in perfection.

Norman said to me that he had, during his two hours with
Margaret, kept calling her 'Prime Minister' and why don't we do this
in England as they do with Presidents in America?

He told her he would like to see her frequently and she said she
would come and see him at the Treasury which he thought, and I agree
with him, would not be a good idea.

Norman said Margaret went into the ERM only because people
like Major, Hurd and Lawson forced her to do it and we are now on
a slippery slope.

He said he thought we could rely on Major. I said, 'Then why
doesn't he tell the truth as Mrs Thatcher would have done? What is
the point of the Uriah Heep approach to Europe if he intends to stand
by her policies on it?'

James Hanson said Mrs Thatcher must get down to organizing
her future. It was no good talking about this foundation which he
disapproved of. I asked why and he said, 'She is trying to raise £10
million or so from business people like myself and it wouldn't go into
the Tory Party funds now that they have to raise the money for the
next election. We won't pay twice.'

It was very much, 'The King is dead, long live the King.'

Norman had to go and vote on the capital punishment debate but
he came back later, not having stayed for the division on treason. It is
still treason to have an affair with Princess Diana, for example, and it
is punishable by death.

Talking to James Hanson, I said that if Mrs Thatcher wanted to
make Jeffrey Archer a peer, why shouldn't she? He may have done
some irregular actions in his past but he is a jolly fellow, he had been
good to her, he had been a great support to the Tory Party and there
were far worse people than him in the Lords.

Friday 21 December
Allan Davis told me that he still believes in me as a playwright. Lee
Menzies said we were snookered on my first play by Margaret going.
I asked him if he would like to see the second one and he said he
would. Allan Davis says he doesn't even want to read it because I had
mentioned there was a ghost in it and he said, 'You can't have a play
with ghosts in it.' I said, 'J. M. Barrie did.'[14] I think Allan feels that I
am very old fashioned. Maybe I am but maybe people might like an
old-fashioned play.

Sunday 23 to Wednesday 26 December *In Cornwall, at Bonython*
We are having some quite jolly games of bridge with Christopher
[Mayhew] and his son, James, a pleasant fellow who lives in France.
The first night they won easily because I was exhausted after the night
train journey and we had very bad cards, Verushka and I. The second
night I was much rested and my brain was working. Verushka and I
then won. As we began to win, Christopher started humming so I said,
'Stop that, Christopher. You are trying to put me off.' 'Oh dear, was I
humming?' he said. I said, 'Yes, because you are losing and you are
trying to stop my concentrating.' Engagingly, he admitted it.

I am very relieved that Tessa has arrived because I think she can
take on the responsibilities and I hope save Bonython.

On Saturday night came the local choir singers and the Constantine
band. Peter Long, the vicar, conducted the service in a somewhat
aggressive way. He called for peace in the Gulf and made a number of
other left-wing utterances. However the carols were good. The Cornish
pasties were excellent, hot, all eaten outside with the mulled claret. It
was cold and windy with a touch of rain and I later found I had caught
'flu.

We had to have our Christmas dinner at lunch time because of the
hordes of children.

It was a pretty appalling Christmas.

Thursday 27 December
Returned to London in a poor state. First of all my briefcase and bag
containing books, etc., were left on the platform. They wouldn't give
us time to load the train with the luggage. The door we were supposed
to be getting on the train at was just off the platform because it was

---

14. Perhaps WW was thinking of *Mary Rose*.

such a long train. Verushka yelled and pointed to the bags and briefcase but the guard refused to do anything about it and off we went with me in a panic thinking, 'Gosh my tapes are in it, my secret manuscript and so forth. As well as £200.'

After a lot of commotion we arranged that the bags and briefcase would be sent on to the lost property office at Paddington. They eventually arrived at eight o'clock in the evening.

After supper, still feeling tired and jaded, I rang Margaret at Dulwich. She answered the telephone herself, poor dear.

When I asked her how she was she said, 'I am at times up and at times down and this is one of the down times.' She talked about the world at large, saying that the position of Gorbachev is extremely worrying, although she thought he should still be backed. I said, 'I am not sure there is anything left to back there. Russia is going to split up.'

Andrew Knight was nearly killed in a skiing accident at Aspen so Sabiha and the children went out there. He said after the accident he saw everything quite differently and he felt that life was worth living after all. But I don't think there is any reconciliation.

Allan Davis has written a silly letter to investors telling them their money in my play was lost, ending it with the information that Leighton Productions had been generous enough to accept the scenery in lieu of storage charges.

Friday 28 December
Cita and Irwin Stelzer gave a dinner in a private room at the Connaught.

The claret was excellent and lavishly supplied. It was Pichon-Longueville, Comtesse de la Lande. It is next door to Château Latour. It has a similar taste to it but not quite so good. Even the distance of a few yards makes a difference in the soil and it is only a yard or so between the vineyards.

At the end a fat lady, quite pleasant, the Director of Corporate Relations at News International, called Jane Reed, was put to sit next to me. She thanked me for all the help I had given behind the scenes to Sky Television, making sure it hadn't been referred to the Monopolies and Mergers Commission and that it was not made subject to the amendments moved trying to make Rupert divest himself of Sky the moment it started to make a profit.

We talked about the merger between Sky and BSB. I said, 'I think

I had a little hand in that because I was sowing the idea to Burrell of the Pearson family and a director of BSB when I was in Italy.'[15]

Sunday 30 December
I spoke to Patrick Minford. Norman Lamont said he had been unable to ask him to be his economic adviser because the morning he was going to ring him, he read that he had said that no one but a madman would have gone into the ERM and got themselves into such a muddle as the government had. He thought that would send the wrong signal, if it was then announced that he had become his economic adviser. I told Patrick this but said, 'You are not to know it when he speaks to you. He still wants to talk to you.'

Monday 31 December
A geriatric supper at Arnold Goodman's flat in Portland Place.

Arnold Goodman is a dear, sweet man, full of kindness but in politics of muddle-headedness, too. He always took a strong anti-Thatcher line, being I suppose with his heart somewhere in the Labour Party. But his brain on other matters remains good though the poor fellow can't walk about very easily. He doesn't drink and the wine was execrable. The food was cold cuts.

---

15. See 9 August 1990.

1991

Tuesday 1 January
Irwin Stelzer said my article in the *Times* today about Kinnock and Major was far too kind to Major. I thought it was a pretty cool look at him because I had said that his pretending to be a new government was clever but not wholly admirable morally.

Wednesday 2 January
Had a charming letter from Queen Elizabeth [the Queen Mother] about my sending the David Cecil anthology of his friends' memories of him.[1]

She writes these letters in her own handwriting and writes out the full address on the envelopes herself. Her letters always arrive by registered post. This one came from Sandringham.

Irwin Stelzer and Cita came to dinner plus Frank Johnson[2] and Miriam Gross[3] with whom he is no longer living.

Plus Peregrine Worsthorne, whom I saluted as Sir Peregrine. He is very pleased about his new knighthood.

Perry was in good shouting form.

His great thesis was that you had to have a classical education in order to be a good Prime Minister or a politician. You couldn't be concerned with industry or trade which should be left to lower people without culture.

Irwin was much affronted by this and said it did not apply in America. 'On the contrary,' said Peregrine, 'people like Jefferson and Washington and even Calvin Coolidge had been great classical scholars

---

1. Lord David Cecil (1912–86) was Goldsmiths' Professor of English Literature at Oxford, 1948–67; *David Cecil: A Portrait by his Friends*, collected and introduced by Hannah Cranbourne, was published in 1990.
2. Associate editor, *Sunday Telegraph*, 1988–93; deputy editor, 1994–5; editor, *Spectator*, 1995–9.
3. Arts editor, *Daily* and *Sunday Telegraph*, 1986–91; literary and associate editor, *Sunday Telegraph*, since 1991; m 1 (1965–88) John Gross, writer, editor and critic; m 2 (1993) Sir Geoffrey Owen, former editor, *Financial Times*.

looking down on the industrialists and the people who merely wanted money.'

Around this point Frank Johnson referred to Americans as a lesser breed, which wasn't precisely tactful. Peregrine said that economists were no good, that they always got it wrong and were wholly unreliable, which likewise was not pleasing to Irwin's ears.

The conversation arose about whether Jewish politicians had been allowed a real chance in England. Everybody said, 'Of course, Disraeli.' Irwin said, 'But he wasn't a Jew. He changed his faith.' I said, 'But he was of the Jewish race.' Irwin said, 'What do you mean by the Jewish race? There is no such thing.'

I said, 'In that case why are the Jews so keen on going back to Israel if it is only a matter of religion and not of race?'

I am very fond of Irwin. He is very clever and argues well but he is completely illogical.

Frank said he had been asked to lunch by the Chancellor of the Exchequer which he thought was rather grand. He then realized it was Norman Lamont who he thinks is not at all grand. I said, 'I like him. He was very loyal to Mrs Thatcher really.' He said, 'Oh no he wasn't. I had lunch with Cecil Parkinson and Mrs Thatcher and it was quite clear he was organizing that campaign for Major before she decided to resign.'

I don't think that is true myself.

Frank said, 'What do you think the true position of the Thatcherites should be? Should we drink to our sovereign over the water?' I said, 'Be suspicious and watch carefully that Major doesn't slide.'

Thursday 3 January

I had wondered whether John Major would answer my letter. Today one arrived. It began typed, with 'Dear Woodrow' and 'Yours sincerely John M' in handwriting; then written underneath it in his handwriting: 'Do keep in touch. It will always be lovely to hear from you. I read so much that is said to be my view – and isn't – it will always be nice to talk to someone I can speak to frankly. We must keep the revolution on the rails.'

He has probably noticed what I have been saying and may be a bit hurt. Maybe I am misjudging him. It is a bit early to say. I must arrange to see him. Perhaps I had better not ring him up as I used to ring Margaret. Perhaps I should establish a reasonable relationship with him because he is obviously anxious to assure me that he is not going to depart from Margaret's principles. He, of course, is the only one in the clear over her deposition because he was in hospital having his excruciating wisdom tooth operation at the relevant time.

This evening Petronella said that Peregrine is having an affair with Lucinda Lambton.[4] I said, 'She's very nice, eccentric and amusing. But she looks rather like a Charles Addams character, not at all attractive.'

Lucinda, who was married to Roy Harrod's son, is forty-seven and Perry is sixty-seven.

Sunday 6 January

Margaret answered her telephone at Dulwich. She had had quite a restful New Year in Switzerland and she is wondering when to make her re-entry into the political scene with an important speech, which she is not going to do in the Commons. She has to think of the right venue and the right subject. She was irritated by the absurd publicity given to her for agreeing to be the Honorary President of the Bruges Group, suggesting she was going to attack John Major, which she has no intention of doing.

Monday 7 January

Went to an excruciatingly boring dinner given by Peter Winfield as Master of the Worshipful Company of Feltmakers.

I was the last main speaker.

I was particularly pleased with the great response I got when I explained why I wasn't a Tory and had only ever been in the Labour Party which didn't treat their leaders in such a shabby way as Mrs Thatcher had been treated.

I gave a little homily, jokingly, to Sir Jeffrey Sterling, just made a life peer, and mentioned what had been said to Disraeli about what it was like being in the Lords: ' "I am dead, but I am in the Elysian fields." That, for the benefit of those among you who didn't have a classical education, is in Greek poetry the happy land or paradise.'

I teased David Montagu [Lord Swaythling] and Peter Winfield by thanking them for their always great loyal support to me on the Tote Board.

---

4. Photographer, writer and broadcaster; eldest daughter of Viscount (Tony) Lambton and Bindy; m 1 (1965) Henry Mark Harrod; m 2 (1986) Sir Edmund Fairfax-Lucy; WW refers to her engagement to Peregrine Worsthorne a few days later and they married in May 1991.

What second rate people these all are, who get themselves dressed up with chains and funny hats as masters of livery companies, assistant masters, High Sheriffs of London and God knows what! It is the most utterly bourgeois affair; all having great pretensions, putting on airs because they think they have become distinguished, flattering each other.

Wednesday 9 January
Went to the Basil Hotel for the launch party for the great new radio authority which will control all radio in Britain apart from the BBC. Alun Chalfont is the Chairman. We had a talk about the ITC code. He is still on the ITC Board, though not Deputy Chairman.

I think we have done about the best we can now on that ITC code. I can't spend a great deal more of my life on the subject.

Saturday 12 January
To Dorneywood.[5]

Off we go to Ascot.

Of course Peter Winfield, always anxious to push himself forward and show how important he is, was lurking about and had been all day in the Tote entertainment room so he could speak to the Home Secretary whom he pretended to be a great friend of. It turned out that Ken Baker, who is very good at remembering people, did just remember him but not with much enthusiasm. I arranged that Winfield sat at another table, as Ken Baker's table was already full of other people, which I had contrived for it to be so that Winfield couldn't sit at it as well. So he sat with his face red and self-important at another table, arranging all his bets. He is a very lucky better. He won about £1,000 that afternoon with a dual forecast and so forth. He has a great deal of money from his estate agency business, Healey & Baker, and drives around with a chauffeur and a great Rolls Royce. I was a fool to get him renewed.

Before dinner Ken and I had a brief talk while the guests were arriving. He said I was not to bother at all about all the attacks on me, including the one in the paper this morning saying how appalling it was that I had a pension and didn't contribute to it in the same way as other people did. This is basically untrue in any case and it had all been approved by the Home Office.

---

5. The new Home Secretary, Kenneth Baker, now had Dorneywood.

At dinner was Sir Leslie Porter, who used to be the head of Tesco and still owns a large number of shares in it as it is a semi family firm, and his wife Lady Porter, now made a Dame, who is Chairman of Westminster City Council. I had a long talk to Leslie Porter before dinner about Tesco's wines. He said he was going to send me some of them. He is a jolly little chap, like a sort of elf, small, smaller than his wife.

Lady Porter sat on my right. She thanked me for all I had done to help the Westminster Conservative campaign in my articles in the *News of the World*. That was last year when they triumphantly held the fort despite the poll tax, or perhaps because of the poll tax – they had got the lowest one apart from Wandsworth in London.

She is quite a tough lady but quite pleasant. She talked about her daughter in Israel. I was trying to establish with her what it meant to be Jewish. Nobody who is Jewish seems to understand it, whether they are Jewish by race or Jewish by religion or both or neither. But they still feel Jewish. However, she talked on the subject much more sensibly than Irwin Stelzer.

During the weekend I was told that Heseltine had actually been offered the Home Office but had decided he wanted to go to the Environment. I would have been in a real pickle if he had been made Home Secretary with a supervisory function over the Tote, after all my attacks on him and denouncing of him.

Talking about Ruth Wolfson, everybody was astounded that after forty-one years of marriage she could go off with Jarvis Astaire whom I call a masher, a man with some money but no substance.[6] She said she just got bored with Leonard who never talked to her and he didn't want to go out in the evenings and was interested only in books and politics. Now she is reported as being happier than she has ever been in her life. She is sixty-two. She is apparently having glorious sex and a most remarkable rejuvenation.

Poor old Leonard is completely shattered.

She's gone to live in the Berkeley Hotel. I said why not with him, Astaire, but she doesn't want to do that openly. She just spends all the time she can with him. I don't think they are actually going to get married.

---

6. At this time he was deputy chairman, Wembley Stadium, and chairman, Viewsport; board member, British Greyhound Racing, from 1991; president, Royal Free Hospital and Medical School Appeal Trust, from 1991.

During the talk at Dorneywood people said that Margaret had been making mistakes towards the end, such as implying in the House that the hard ecu would be no good, although this was the line which Major had been trying to peddle to avoid going into the single currency.[7] It is true that she did become a little brittle and said some rather incautious things, upsetting people unnecessarily.

I told Ken Baker that I had written rather rudely about the government's education record in the *News of the World*. He said, 'Oh dear, why have you done that?' and started lecturing me about how marvellous he had been as Secretary for Education during the three years he was doing it. I had forgotten he had been there so long.

Tuesday 15 January
Levy Board meeting. The horrible Haines was there.

Just before lunch I said to him, 'I see you have been thinking it is a Jockey Club responsibility to find out who owns the Tote. I can tell you. It's been known a long time. The government does not own it. Its assets are vested for the time being in the members of the Tote Board who dispose of them in any way they like or not, as the case may be. That's why it was never on to say that the Tote should sell its betting shops. That could only happen if there were legislation.'

He thinks I am after him and he's right.

Wednesday 16 January
My trip to Cornwall was cancelled. Aly Aziz,[8] who we hope will put money into Cornish Spring Water, felt he did not want to go down by aeroplane.

I think also he was nervous about the possibility of war breaking out in the Gulf.

Instead we had lunch in his office. There was quite a constructive conversation and I think something may conceivably come of it. Perhaps one of the many ventures I get involved in which never come to anything could succeed. My life is littered with failed projects.

---

7. In *The Downing Street Years*, pp. 720–1, Mrs Thatcher describes a minute Major sent her on 9 April 1990 saying he had found 'little support for our alternative approach – a "hard" ecu circulating alongside existing currencies, managed by a European Monetary Fund'. She did not agree with either his analysis of further options or his conclusions.
8. Chairman, the Dashwood Group.

Thursday 17 January

I somewhat overslept.

When I came into my library it was already ten to eight and I was astonished to hear that we had been bombing Iraq most of the night.

I rang Margaret at about ten past eight.

She thought Major was doing fantastically well, keeping up the right position. I said, 'It's all due to you really. You were in America on August 2nd. You were able to stiffen Bush and get him organized in what he had to do, get the coalition going, and you backed him thoroughly ever since. Without that we would not have got to the stage of really attacking Iraq.' She did not demur.

She thought it was high time we did it.

She said, 'Of course when a war begins (she was obviously thinking of the Falklands), politicians must stand back and let the professional people get on with it. That's obviously what John is doing.'

I felt so sad for her. She ought to have been Boadicea leading her troops again, this time in a much bigger fight even though we are only junior partners with the Americans.

I was wondering whether to take up Major's suggestion that he would like to have the occasional frank talk with me when he could say what he really thought. Maybe I shall. But he doesn't really need a man to talk to him as Margaret did. It was because of the female–male relationship that I could talk to her and she talked to me frankly. The same applied to one or two others like Cecil Parkinson. If you are a male Prime Minister, you have lots of male cronies who go over things with you in total frankness. If you have a female friend who is bright enough, you can do the same. Asquith used to when he was Prime Minister and doubtless Lloyd George did as well. A male Prime Minister has less need to look outside his own immediate circle of colleagues in the government or his party for frank talking and advice and exchanges of ideas.

All seems well so far but at tea time Ian Orr-Ewing and myself, and one or two others who were in the last war, agreed we did not believe the stories that the entire Iraqi air force would be brought down so soon.

Alexander Hesketh came and sat down opposite me in the tea room. He is getting fatter. He ordered a plateful of sandwiches and some crumpets and then said, 'To hell with it. I shall have a chocolate éclair as well.' I do wish he would listen to me about his diet.

We went to Rocco Forte's for his surprise dinner for his birthday. He genuinely knew nothing about it when he got home.

There was a jeroboam of Moët & Chandon 1976 champagne.

We sat down next to Michael Caine [the actor] and opposite his wife, who looked very pretty, dark, from Guyana, but she said practically nothing.[9] Michael Caine and I had an immensely jolly conversation. He asked whether I had ever been to Langan's [Brasserie]. I said, 'Yes, once. It's a terrible place, full of noise and the food wasn't all that good and there seemed to be photographers lurking around the place.' He then said he owned it.

I said, 'I thought it was owned by a man [Peter Langan] who committed suicide by burning himself to death.' He said in fact he wasn't trying to commit suicide but to set fire to his wife. Having poured petrol all over the place, he set light to himself. He said he was a very difficult man. I said, 'He sounds it.'

Aliai Forte, Rocco's wife, was looking very pretty. She has lovely skin and a round, blonde, angelic face. She is maturing very well and becoming quite a real person. I like her more every time I see her. I also liked the feel of her shoulders and her face when I kissed her and I thought, 'What a pity one is getting so old.'

That afternoon when I saw David Stevens he said, 'Is your friend Murdoch going bust? It doesn't look as though he will survive.' He was very pleased about that. I said, 'I am sure he will get by,' so he changed his tune and said, 'Yes I suppose he will. I have got great admiration for him.'

The knives are always out for somebody who looks as though they may be on the ropes or near there, but I am confident that Rupert will bounce back and arrange his affairs OK. It would be rather serious for me if he doesn't.

I sent a note to Kenneth Baker, as he asked. I told him that there was no financial crisis in racing. They just don't like the idea of being affected by the recession like everybody else. I said they all quarrel like mad and what we really need is a racehorse authority, as suggested in the Royal Commission's report. We had also suggested in our submission to the Home Affairs Committee that one Jockey Club member would be quite enough on the Levy Board.

---

9. Michael Caine m 2 (1973) Shakira Baksh.

Monday 21 January

I am feeling a bit despondent; my play-writing has obviously been no good and I have wasted all my time. Though they won't make me resign from the Tote, the attacks are not exactly cheering and they continue the whole time. I feel that a lot of purpose has gone out of my life now that Margaret is not PM and I can't give her advice and suggestions which might have some effect.

Duke Hussey rang to say that he completely agreed with what I had written about the BBC keeping its reputation as the anti-British Broadcasting Corporation with its *Panorama* programme the previous Monday [on the Gulf War]. I had written that in the *News of the World*. He said that the producer of the programme had been told that if he did it again or anything like it, he would be fired and that was it.

He said he is gradually getting control. I thought, 'It's a long time, "gradually",' but I told him that I thought the reporting was not at all bad now. Even Brian Redhead seemed to be impartial to the point of actually being more or less on our side. He said he had stopped all the nonsense about not calling British troops 'our troops'.

Tuesday 22 January

In the Lords Baroness (Sally) Oppenheim came up to me and said, 'Have you heard from our unfortunate friend?' To begin with I thought she meant Margaret but then I said, 'Which one?' and it was Leonard Wolfson she was talking about.

She suggested I should ring Leonard but I got Verushka to do so while I was in the room with her and she asked him to dinner. He was very pleased and said he hadn't realized how many friends he had got.

There seems to be general agreement among the ladies, who discuss this matter interminably, that Ruth Wolfson had it all too easy. She had no problems with her children, no problems with her husband, no problems with money and she just got bored with not enough to do.

I have always found her quite entertaining. She can be serious on some subjects, particularly wine and art which she took a course in. Leonard said could he bring a lady with him to dinner, to which we of course said yes.

Thursday 24 January

Talked to Norman Lamont.

I asked him what he was doing about making sure that the other countries helped with our defence costs.

I thought it was very strange that such action would not have been so vigorously taken, getting more money from Saudi Arabia, Germany, Japan etc., if I had not prodded him. But that is how government works. In the old days I would have told Margaret and she would have acted on it. Now I have to do it through Norman and others.

To The Other Club. Arnold Goodman was congratulated on his performance on *Desert Island Discs*. I was asked by Robin Day whether I had been on it. 'No,' I said. He said, 'That's one of your great failures.'

Fitzroy Maclean said he had been on *This is Your Life* and explained how he had been tricked into going on it.

He was told by his publisher, who was then Mark Bonham-Carter at Collins, that it would be a very good thing if he went on a chat show on the day concerned because it would help his next book. Then he rang his wife from Scotland and said, 'I can't come down for that. I'm not going to be bothered to go,' so she got on to Queen Elizabeth the Queen Mother and said if there was any way to persuade him to come, it would be if she were to invite him to lunch, so she did. So then Fitzroy rang and said, 'Isn't it marvellous, Queen Elizabeth the Queen Mother has invited us to lunch so I will come down to London after all and do that chat show.'

Everybody at the lunch knew about it but him. Queen Elizabeth was 'in on' the programme with everybody else at Clarence House but keeping it secret. It was very sporting of Queen Elizabeth, but she loves that kind of thing. When he got to the studio, he couldn't understand why Douglas Fairbanks Jnr was there because he did not seem a very literary person to have a discussion with about books. Then suddenly they slammed it down on him and said, 'This is your life' and away they went.

Lord Goodman said he chose opera mainly for *Desert Island Discs*. Somebody who had heard it said the interview was very good – that was Robin Day. He said he couldn't bear the opera but he liked the interview.

I sat next to Norman Tebbit and opposite Denis Thatcher and Duke Hussey.

Denis said rather gloomily, 'I suppose they will be regarded as the disastrous Thatcher years.' I said, 'Of course they won't. They were the most triumphant years. She lifted England to new heights which it would never have reached. She stopped the genteel decline.'

The wine was fabulous. It was Château Latour 1975. It had been given by Mary Soames after the dinner she came to.

I made my gift of a dozen Château Ségur 1984. It looked rather miserable by comparison.

Just as he was going, Denis said to me, 'My dearly beloved says that she looks forward and loves talking to you on the telephone more than anyone else.' I was very touched and said, 'You know I adore her.'

Friday 25 January
The Ritz Hotel, Paris. We had a very pretty little suite on the sixth floor overlooking the courtyard. It was with two bathrooms, a charming sitting room and a bedroom with a vast bed, all elegantly furnished. They had used old bound copies of the *Agricultural Review* and *Punch*, beautifully bound, to decorate some of the shelf space as well as the pretty busts and ornaments.

The Ritz seems to be suffering from a lack of Arabs and the whole of Paris is almost denuded of tourists, foreign and French [because of the Gulf War]. The French are far more panicky than anybody in Britain.

We met Luc and Hedwige.

Luc said France wasn't keen on the Gulf War because they felt it was nothing to do with them. He agreed with me that it was a lot to do with them. It was a fight for the world to make sure that Saddam didn't get a stranglehold on oil prices and up the prices two or three times to the wreckage of industry everywhere and the developing countries as well.

Luc said there is actually a majority of opinion on the right in France but the Socialists get away with it because Mitterrand has managed so well to organize the Communist element behind him without making any concessions to them. He has also greatly moderated his policies. I said, 'What about people like Le Pen?' He said, 'They're there because we've got four million Muslims and they play on that. Giscard and Chirac are unwilling to let either of the others take the lead so they squabble away on the right and are disunited.'

Hedwige was looking very jolly and very attractive in her *jolie laide* way and Luc is enjoying himself running this newspaper for the Pearson Group. He is also writing about art. He would rather be in London as Ambassador though he is finding compensations.

Saturday 26 January

Had a most useful talk with Cormier, head of the PMU. He hates Ladbroke even more than we do. We will work together with regards to the inquiry by the EC into betting which is being conducted by Coopers & Lybrand, and also with regard to the Home Affairs Committee of the House of Commons.

Off to the great dinner before the Prix d'Amérique. Our spiffing driver whizzed us there in about twelve minutes, amazing, from the Hotel Ritz.

I found myself between the wife of Jacques Chartier, who is the head of the trotting in France, and on my other side a quite pretty lady, half German, half Corsican. I tried to talk to them in French and made a few jokes and compliments but they didn't make any attempt at all to speak English or to understand what I was talking about.

I thought to myself how rude these middle class French people are. If they had been in a similar position in England, every effort would have been made to make them feel at ease. I felt as though I were a Chinese, regarded as inferior by Westerners and not worth the bother of taking any trouble with.

Monday 28 January

In a desperate hurry to write my article for the *Times* because I had to be at the Dashwood Group in the City by two o'clock to continue discussions with Aly Aziz about possibly coming into Cornish Spring Water.

It transpired that they had wanted me to write about how different it would have been if Mrs Thatcher had been in charge now instead of John Major. Fortunately I never got this message.

I said, 'It is too late now. I have already finished my article. But maybe I will do that in a fortnight.' But actually I thought to myself that I don't want to go into this particular game.

At the meeting with Aziz things went pretty well. There seems to be some hope of saving Cornish Spring Water and getting some money out of it, too. Robbie has said he would let me have half the royalties.

Off to see Margaret at 93 Eaton Terrace, lent to her by the widow of the last Henry Ford. It is a charming flat on the ground floor but with a kind of staircase going down, a duplex.

We began by talking about the famous memoirs.

I said, 'Have you thought more about having an agent?'

She said, 'I want to deal direct with Rupert because I trust him. I don't really want to have an agent.'

She said she wanted someone to help her. I said, 'Have you not got John O'Sullivan?' She said, 'Yes, but he is in America, though he can help. But I want Robin Harris.' I said, 'Yes but he can't write like John O'Sullivan.' She said, 'But he can do all the research, put it together with me, and help me shape it and write it.' Harris was the fellow in her Policy Unit who left when Major came in.[10]

She said she was going to America on Friday for Reagan's birthday party on February 6th when he will be eighty. She said she is going to be given the Congressional Order of Freedom. She is delighted.

She said she would make a speech while she was there and probably deal with the Gulf War.

She said she got briefings from John Major. I said, 'I hope he asks your advice,' and she said they do talk about the Gulf. She was very anxious to point out that she chose the commander of the British forces in the Gulf against the wishes of the defence chiefs. But she thought he was an excellent man, very sound with a lot of dash and a real professional.[11]

I said, 'John Major's doing quite well at the moment.' She 'Yes. He inherited a Rolls-Royce machine from me. But they don't understand that they have to make decisions quickly. They are not on the ball. They are not fast enough, none of them. I would read these papers late at night and get up early in the morning, as you know, at six o'clock, and I was making decisions and keeping up with events. But I think they are not doing it.'

She said, 'If I do leave the Commons, I would want to go to the Lords. I couldn't not be connected with the Houses of Parliament.' I said, 'I understand that completely.'

At about this time Denis turned up and asked me if I would like a drink, my having had only one small cup of tea and not liking to ask for another. I said no thank you. He immediately had a whisky and

---

10. Assistant to Mrs Thatcher since then and warmly thanked in her acknowledgements in *The Downing Street Years* as 'my indispensable Sherpa in the enterprise of writing this book'.

11. In *The Downing Street Years*, pp. 825–6, Lady Thatcher says that against her reluctant Defence Secretary, Tom King, she backed Sir Peter de la Billière: 'I wanted a fighting general.'

was surprised I wouldn't have one. I said it was too early for me. Then she had a whisky, both of them quite strong.

From there I went down to see Catherine Amery at No 112 Eaton Square, having bought £14 of flowers at a barrow in Belgrave Square. I was taken up to the third floor and there was poor Catherine with her face blotched in a hideous way and her fingers and her hands mottled and blemished. Her stomach was very swollen and she smelled a bit of pee and there was a sort of commode there.

She was smoking away like mad. I said, 'I am sure you are not allowed to do that,' and she said, 'It doesn't matter now.' She was smoking forty cigarettes a day. Poor soul. I told her I had been talking to Mrs Thatcher and she was quite interested but she always thought that Mrs Thatcher was someone who thought nothing of her father, which was true.

Then we went on to a dinner with Lord Stevens. I said, 'You should let Norman Tebbit write in the *Express*. He said he had been pushed out because he attacked journalists.' He said, 'I don't think that was the reason.' I said, 'I think he did the *Sunday Express* column quite well.' He said, 'But nowhere near as well as John Junor.'

He said he would look into it.

Cecil Parkinson was there. I said, 'Have you fallen out with Norman Lamont? I thought he was a great friend of yours.' He said, 'Why do you say that?' I said, 'I heard some sort of rumour that you had over what happened to Margaret.' He said, 'Well, not really, but we were very close. We think alike on everything.'

Then he said very confidentially, 'On the Wednesday morning, after the first result on the Tuesday evening, Norman talked to me a lot and said she was not going to win the next round and so we have got to organize a campaign to ring people up to support Major. If he told you he did nothing until after the Thursday Cabinet meeting, he was not telling you the truth. He was organizing it beforehand.' If Cecil was telling the truth, and I think he may have been, Norman was not telling the truth to me. But perhaps both are interpreting the truth differently.

Soros, the Hungarian financier, was there with his wife. He said that the enormous amount of money he had put into Hungary in his foundation works in such a way that the moment he dies it finishes. He said that all these self-perpetuating charities are no good at all. They all become corrupt and inefficient.

He is quite nice, that man. I said, 'What do you think will happen with the stock markets now?' He said, 'I think the war will be quite good for them. If it is won successfully, there will be a kind of euphoria and it won't break out till later, the dreadful state that the world's economy is in.'

This house, which is next door to Rocco's house, was incredibly ugly. It has the same rooms as Rocco's house but it is all badly furnished, the pictures are fearful and it looks really vulgar. Meriza Stevens said she had tried to make it look like a house in the country. I thought she had made it look like a boarding house in the country pretty well.

Wednesday 30 January
Leonard Wolfson could not bring his temporary lady friend to dinner because she was ill. Diane Lever came instead.

I gave her a little tour of the house. She had never seen my library before nor had she ever been upstairs to where we have the television in the sitting-room. We bumped into my mother-in-law struggling with her hand supports to get into the bathroom. I showed her Petronella's room, a nightmare of untidiness. Diane said the house was lovely.

I showed her my first editions, the Graham Greenes, and the Wyatt drawings and she was very appreciative, so naturally I thought what a sweet girl she is. Poor Harold hasn't been out of the house now for a very long time. When I rang up the other day to go and see him he was too ill.

We talked freely with Leonard about Ruth's disappearance. He said he wouldn't have her back now even if she wanted to come. He had been quite shattered originally when she left him this note saying she wanted to leave him and she had gone because she was bored.

Leonard said he hadn't realized how many widows there were around, many of them attractive. I said, 'It's because you are so rich. They are all making a beeline for you.' Diane said, 'No nice woman would ever make a first approach,' and Leonard said, 'I'm not finding that at the moment.'

Thursday 31 January
Got up at half past six, with a violent cold and sore throat last night, to get to the airport to meet Aly Aziz to catch the plane to Newquay, Cornwall, for the great inspection of the Spring Water operation from the ground. I felt like death.

The visit went off pretty well. Stuart-Smith, Aziz's henchman, had paid one visit already. Aly Aziz asked many questions of a pertinent nature while his son, who travels with him always, said nothing as usual.

Our side would only keep twenty-five per cent of the company but there would be substantial royalties of which Robbie has promised me half. If anything materializes and the company develops, there should be something for Verushka after I am dead. She is going to need a lot of money, the way she spends.

Friday 1 February
Rupert appears to be out of trouble, at least for two or three years. This is a comfort. I don't think he will get rid of me as long as I can go on writing reasonable columns both for the *Times* and the *News of the World*.

I went on Wednesday to the first open session of the [House of Commons] Home Affairs Committee on the levy. There were three officials from the Home Office, headed by Richard Fries. My God, how feeble and footling and low level they are. Fries mumbled away and couldn't explain the relationship between the Home Secretary and the determination of the levy. Yet he is the ass who has been trying to get me out, I think, and trying to rely on the absurd report from Lloyds Merchant Bank.

It seems that the Home Affairs Committee is determined to examine the Tote during this session. They are particularly interested in such juicy items as my pension.

Sunday 3 February
I had a longish talk with Norman Lamont. I said, 'I told you in the *News of the World* this morning to borrow up to £8,000 million and have lower, not higher, taxes. And I said you have got to get the interest rate down pretty quick.' He said, 'My God, I wish I could.'

I said, 'Maybe you should have an election in the summer.' He said he was against that because he thought it might rebound. I said, 'You may find it even tougher later on.' I think Major at the moment is not in the mind to have a khaki election in case it went badly and anyway it would look as though he was trying to cash in on the war.

I said, 'Your best chance of beating the other side is that if we are still in economic crisis, everybody will say that Labour will make it even worse so we had better stick to the bloody Tories.'

He said he is very anxious not to go down in history as having let her down because he didn't, even though it doesn't matter to him now because he is Chancellor of the Exchequer and she is finished.

Monday 4 February
Went to a housewarming party given by Charles and Caroline Moore. The house was in Thornhill Square, N1, somewhere north-east of King's Cross. The square is immensely pretty but it has long been a slum area and is now being gentrified. The little house was charming, with its ceiling decorations and cornices and so forth.

The wine was execrable. I drank nothing, not even tomato juice because I couldn't find any.

Enoch Powell was there, very heavily saying 'My Lord' to me. He is a bit of an ass: he could have gone to the Lords himself, if he hadn't been so absurd about not wanting anything but a hereditary peerage – which wouldn't matter to him anyway because he only had two daughters to pass the title on to, so he wouldn't have been able to do that anyway.

He sees nothing but woe for the future and our relations with the Common Market and Germany and so on.

Tuesday 5 February
Neil and Eva Zarach came to dinner.

Eva is a pretty little thing, lively, a very keen businesswoman. I think she does it much better than he does. She has now got a splendid business with caviar, Chinese caviar from their shore of the Caspian Sea.

Thursday 7 February
We had quite a good [Tote] board meeting. Now things are moving back our way a bit David Montagu and Peter Winfield are much calmer; no more nonsense from them and they are actually quite co-operative. They are cowards at heart, both of them.

The IRA from a van parked outside the Horseguards entrance to Whitehall fired three mortar bombs at No 10 Downing Street. They all missed except one which landed in the garden and broke a lot of windows. Major is now called a hero for saying, 'Gentlemen, I think we had better go somewhere else and start the meeting.' He had just begun a War Cabinet meeting. I don't think that is particularly heroic, rather normal. However, he is a decent chap.

I have written to him asking for a knighthood for my cousin Bob and another for A. L. Rowse. I have also suggested going to see him because I have things I would like to talk to him about which I don't like to put on paper.

Friday 8 February

I was cheered by the Jack Logan column in the *Sporting Life* this morning. He referred to George Wigg: 'Soon after he had been appointed Chairman of the Levy Board he said that he felt like Santa Claus who comes bearing gifts and is hit on the head with a sledge-hammer. Woodrow must feel the same when he considers the millions the Tote has given to racing under his chairmanship. No wonder their reaction to Portman Square is the same. Why is it that the Jockey Club has failed to come to terms with two such warm-hearted characters? Perhaps Harold Macmillan was near the mark when he said that human nature finds it harder to forgive a benefit than an injury.'

Saturday 9 February

I was amused at last Wednesday's Home Affairs Committee hearing to see Stoker Hartington wearing white socks. When Tony Lambton commented on his new son-in-law (about to be), Peregrine Worsthorne, he said, 'He wears white socks. He's not one of us.' Does that mean that Stoker Hartington is not one of us?

On Saturday evening we had dinner with Arnold at Santini's in Ebury Street.

Arnold said he doesn't mind if there is a Labour government. I said, 'You don't mind because you think it is easier to get contracts out of them.'

I said, 'Are you doing well out of this war?' He said everything they produced is working excellently well, including the laser which they could put on any old aircraft to guide the bombs from the bombers straight on to the target.

Sunday 10 February

I asked Alexander Hesketh if he wanted to be Chief Whip. He said he thought there was no alternative. If Bertie Denham was going and if he was asked by Number 10, what could he say? I said, 'You will have to spend a great deal more time sitting in the Lords.' He said, 'But the advantage is that when there are holidays and you haven't got a ministerial job in a Department, you don't have to do any work. And that applies to the daytime, too. For example, I wouldn't have to be going back to London today and go through three boxes by Monday lunch time if I were Chief Whip.'

I talked to Ken Baker. I asked him whether he thought they were keeping up the radical revolution. He was hesitant and said, 'Well, in some ways.' I said, 'I agree with this opting out of schools.' He said, 'That was my idea.'

Went to lunch with Diane Lever and Harold Lever. He seems a bit better but he had to lie down pretty soon after lunch. The occasion was meant to be for Leonard Wolfson to meet a lady who looks about sixty but is very elegant and very rich.

He took no interest in the lady whatsoever.

Just before lunch he told Diana he now thought he had found the woman to replace Ruth. She looked very like her, was an old friend of Ruth's and he hoped it was going to go well. He has started divorce proceedings against Ruth. She didn't want him to do so. He is a little hard and curious, Leonard, though pleasant and kind no doubt in other ways. All people are a mixture.

On my right sat Marigold Johnson.

Tina Brown, now the editor of *Vanity Fair* in America,[1] has been a terrific success increasing the circulation from about two hundred thousand to around three hundred thousand and making pots of money for the owners. Marigold said she first met her at our house at dinner when Tina came with her husband, Harry Evans, who was then the editor of the *Sunday Times*. He came on his motor bike. He used to ride about on this dangerous instrument. Mrs Thatcher was there and when the last course was over and the coffee had been drunk, the ladies had to go into another room and Mrs Thatcher stayed talking to the men.

I said, 'That was perfectly proper.' Marigold said, 'Yes but Tina Brown was furious.' She was not used to how things were done at that level of society. She said to her, as they went into the other room, that it was absolutely appalling and she had never known such a thing could happen and should she register her disgust by leaving at once? So Marigold had said, 'Don't be so silly.' I had always thought it was Marigold who had leaked this story to *Private Eye* but it seems it wasn't. It was obviously Tina Brown.

I remember how she [Tina Brown] came to lunch with me once round about that time and gave me a kiss in the hall, very sexy, and

---

1. Editor, *Tatler*, 1979–83; editor-in-chief, *Vanity Fair*, 1984–92; editor, *New Yorker*, 1992–8; since 1998 starting *Talk*, a magazine for the film company Miramax; m (1981), his second marriage, Harold Evans (editor, *Sunday Times*, 1969–81, *Times*, 1981–2; founding editor, Condé-Nast *Traveler* magazine, 1986–90; at this time president, Random House Publishing).

tried to be a little bit seductive. She had wanted me to tell her the names of the people who came to our dinner parties and I refused, although we had some general conversation. She was doing some kind of an interview with me. She was working for the *Tatler* at the time. She has done incredibly well. She is a hard little nut although there is some softness about her. She is certainly very pretty and she looks very pretty still.

Poor Harry Evans never got on well in America. He edited some travel magazine which didn't get very far and he is now Chairman of Random House, the publishing firm which is doing Rupert Murdoch's memoirs. She is thirty-four now but she must have been about twenty-seven or less when I first met her. Marigold said she had met her mother who was very tough and immensely ambitious. Her daughter seems to have inherited both those attributes, as well as a good deal of talent.

I think Paul was slightly horrid to Harold Lever, I hope unintentionally, when Harold was claiming something he had done during a Labour government in preventing Wedgwood Benn[2] getting his way by having trade union leaders put on the operating boards of BP. When he had finished his long and rambling story which was extremely boring, Paul said, 'Of course we all know that you have saved the country several times and are the most important person in the nation.' Poor Harold was a little hipped. Paul said, 'I didn't mean exactly that.'

When I told Paul Johnson truthfully that I think his articles are a very high standard, they are the first I turn to in the *Spectator* and I read all his columns in the *Daily Mail*, he turned to Verushka and said, 'Woodrow is getting kinder as he grows older.'

He is very talented. Marigold said he makes much more money out of his books than out of his articles.

I told Marigold about Pericles. She was fascinated and said he must be rather a splendid person. I said, 'I think he is.'

---

2. Tony Benn, left-wing Labour politician, advocate of unilateral nuclear disarmament, extended public ownership and constitutional reform, on which issues he has challenged successive Labour leaderships; son of 1st Viscount Stansgate, a Labour peer, he disclaimed his peerage for life in 1963 and shortened his name from Anthony Wedgwood Benn; Postmaster-General, 1964–6; Minister of Technology, 1966–70; Secretary of State for Industry and Minister for Post and Telecommunications, 1974–5; Secretary of State for Energy, 1975–9; MP for Chesterfield since 1984.

I said, 'We never told him not to marry.' She said, 'No, they never do what you say,' at which point Paul Johnson said his children did, and she said, 'When?' He was rather discomforted by that.

Paul Johnson told a story that it wasn't Nigel Lawson who broke up [his first] marriage but Vanessa Lawson.[3] She had fallen in love with Henry Fairlie.

Henry, who was always a drunk and a hopeless case, eventually went to America where he died not long ago. He was a brilliant journalist, brilliant at dissecting politics, but he never came to anything for lack of staying power. Henry Fairlie had told her that he was in love with her. She had reciprocated and he said they would elope: 'So meet me at the Ritz bar at six o'clock tomorrow and we will go off together.' Vanessa left a note on the chimneypiece for Nigel.

She went to the Ritz bar and waited and he didn't come.

So she dashed back to the house and took the note away from the chimneypiece just in time before Nigel got in. It then turned out that Henry Fairlie had simply forgotten all about it. That was before she went off with Freddie Ayer.

When I said to Marigold that Vanessa always reminded me of Queen Nephertiti and she was so beautiful, Marigold said that was exactly what Paul Johnson always called her, which he did a few moments later. She was of the Salmon family who owned Lyons.

Paul has a son [Daniel] working on the *Times* who writes occasional leaders and other things under his own name. He says Simon Jenkins is very nice but no good as an editor and he hasn't improved the paper anything like as much as necessary. I asked Paul if he agreed and he said, 'Yes. Simon has got no personality and no strength of character. He's a wet. He'll never make anything of the *Times*.'

Verushka came back from seeing Nicholas [Banszky] this evening and said that George Walker has now gone bust.

So I will have lost all my money on my shares, about £4,000 or so, and there will be renewed clamour about why the Tote doesn't buy William Hill.

---

3. Nigel Lawson m 1 (1955–80) Vanessa, née Salmon; she m 2 (1983) Sir Freddie Ayer, philosopher; she died in 1985.*

Monday 11 February

Dinner with Countess Karolyi who is a National Health Service doctor. We had thought it would be rather a tedious dinner with poor food. How wrong we were. At 42 Drayton Gardens you do very well indeed.

There are two thousand patients in her practice.

I asked her how many hours she worked. I said I thought most doctors were pretty bad and spent most of their time playing golf.

She said, 'I do as little as possible. I only work a very few hours because I am an aristocrat and I don't propose to work hard.'

Nevertheless, she kept on arguing with me about Margaret Thatcher, saying she was no good. I said, 'Do you actually vote Labour?' She said no but she wouldn't mind: 'Margaret Thatcher has been so bad for the Health Service.' I said, 'She actually improved it, making people like you work a bit harder.'

Countess Karolyi comes from a very grand aristocratic family in Hungary.[4]

Deirdre, married to Johnnie Grantley, was there.[5]

She is the oldest child of Billy Listowel. She said she was having dinner with him tomorrow night so I said, 'Give him my regards. We nod at each other in the Lords.' She said, 'He nearly left the Labour Party and would have done, if they hadn't become less run by the lunatic left.' He used to be Secretary for India under Attlee. He was cut out of his father's will because he became a Socialist. I said, 'I was disinherited twice for being a Socialist.' (Three times actually. My cousin Molly of Bonython; my uncle Sir Arthur Morgan who would otherwise have made me his principal heir above his Communist daughter; and my mother.)

Wednesday 13 February

On my way back to the Lords I was pursued by Robert Rhodes James.[6] He was the man who was thoroughly drunk the other day and attacked me in the lobby outside the Commons saying what was I going to do

---

4. WW says elsewhere that Countess Boritshka Karolyi's mother was 'a Princess Windischgratz'.

5. Lady Deirdre Hare, daughter of 5th Earl of Listowel (1906–97, former Labour minister), m (1955) 7th Baron Grantley (1923–95).

6. (1933–99); historian, writer, Conservative politician; MP, 1976–92, having been a House of Commons clerk, 1955–64; knight 1991.

now that Mrs Thatcher had gone and I had lost my leader and my love and a jolly good thing too.

This time he was complaining about Petronella having written in 'Peterborough' something wholly inaccurate about him in connection with Israel, having rung him up, and the only thing she got right was his name. I said, 'Well, that was something.'

I said, 'I am not responsible for my daughter.' He said, 'No. I have got four daughters, too.' I said, 'Mine is rather a bright girl.' To which he replied, 'You could have fooled me.'

He is an amazing fellow, very talented. He edited the Chips Channon diaries, a Fellow of All Souls, and all the rest of it. Bitter and twisted because Margaret never gave him any promotion, he having attacked her policies regularly.

Arnold and Netta came to dinner.

We discussed the Jockey Club and the evidence they gave this afternoon at the Home Affairs Select Committee which I had listened to. The Jockey Club are completely inept. They brazenly demanded two and a half times the levy they are getting now with a levy rate of two and a half per cent.

He said, 'They're not business-like.' He had been interested to begin with but they had totally ignored his 'Blue Book' in which he had advocated greater rewards for the efficient racecourses and tapering off the rewards for the less efficient ones, which might have involved shutting a few racecourses but it would have smartened them all up.

Of course the Jockey Club remains self-elected and it perpetuates at the top people who are not up to much like nice Ailwyn Fairhaven[7] and Rupert Manton.[8]

We had quite a jolly dinner. I produced another bottle of Gazin 1960. Arnold liked it and was unusually complimentary for a change.

Thursday 14 February
Had to get up at twenty past seven to be ready to receive a telephone call from the BBC, Radio Manchester, to talk about my statement that the Tote was ideally placed from the marvellous complex we have at Wigan to run any national lottery which might emerge.

Having done that, I had to rush through my glances at the news-papers and listening to the news in order to be at the Dorchester Hotel

---

7. 3rd Baron Fairhaven, senior steward of the Jockey Club, 1985–9.
8. 3rd Baron Manton, senior steward of the Jockey Club, 1982–5.

at 10.00 a.m. to meet Professor Aganbegyan. Abdul Al Ghazzi was already waiting for me and the Russian Professor came down a few moments later. He was quite heavily built, not tall, squat and broad-shouldered, dark with a lively intelligent face. He spoke in an animated manner in quite good English.

I then went down to Goodman Derrick to see Diana Rawstron [solicitor] about the will and the arrangements with Ian Chapman and his publishing firm.

She is a very jolly lady. She is Scandinavian. She has a slight accent that way.[9] She has nice blonde hair and face, quite pretty, quite a good figure, slightly large with big well-proportioned legs. She has understood now that it is diaries and she is quite excited about it and says she is longing to see them.

In the morning when I was talking to Aganbegyan and Abdul, suddenly Field Marshal Lord Bramall came up to me and said, 'How nice to see you here, Woodrow.' I introduced him to the Russian and to Abdul and he said, 'I am managing this hotel now.'

When he had gone, I told Professor Aganbegyan that until a year or so ago he had been Chief of Staff and head of all the armed forces in Britain but he is now running the Dorchester Hotel. He was rather surprised because this couldn't possibly happen in Russia.

The menu at the great dinner, at which I was described as joint host with Abdul Al Ghazzi, was beautifully printed. On the front there was a lovely coloured picture of Heveningham Hall. On the back was my description of how it had been built and James Wyatt's connection, and how Abdul had saved it for the nation when it was in a very bad state in 1981.

The turnout was very good, about thirty-six people: prominent businessmen like Professor Roland Smith, Chairman of British Aero-space; Lord Haslam, until January 31st Chairman of British Coal; Alan Lewis who has a big firm of cosmetics and has or is trying to get interests in Russia, and also heads a section in the CBI which is trying to advance trade with Eastern Europe. There was Sir Patrick Sheehy, Chairman of BAT; Sir Robert Wade-Gery, Executive Director of Bar-clays de Zoete; a lot of economists including Patrick Minford and two of the ones who had written the letter in the *Times* on Wednesday saying the government should leave the Exchange Rate Mechanism altogether.

---

9. Diana Rawstron comes from Yorkshire.

Also present was Monsieur Robert Mitterrand, elder brother of President Mitterrand, who looked very like him and is very charming. He is a friend of Abdul in business, I dare say.

The professors and so forth from business schools were pretty elevated. There was also Sir Christopher Hogg, Chairman of Courtaulds, and Lord Hesketh, the Minister of State for Industry at the Department of Trade and Industry.

I made all the arrangements and invited the people apart from a few Abdul brought like Sir Ian Gilmour MP and Sir Denis Walters MP, both on his governing board.

Professor Aganbegyan handled it well.

He didn't pretend everything was all right or that they were getting on famously with moving to a market economy. On the contrary, he said the bureaucracy is still very politicized and it is very difficult to get things done.

Aganbegyan said he thought that Gorbachev would survive.

He also thought the dialogue between him and Yeltsin was healthy, produced ideas and criticisms, and got things moving more. But they are in a fearful position.

Everybody is so used to the food subsidies that now the shortages are terrible. They find it very hard to face the transition between a very low level subsistence and a much higher standard of living which can only be got through pain and energy and reshaping and reconstruction.

A great deal of the stuff we said to him very politely and firmly I am sure he will take back to Moscow and try and get something done about it. He is a great personal friend of Gorbachev and has been one of his main advisers on the economy. He of course admires Mrs Thatcher and wants to get her sort of free economy across if he can.

Unfortunately, he said they have no training or understanding of businesses or factories. He told us that one of the best things we could do would be to find places for them in Britain where they can learn.

Not to be too conceited, I think in fact very few people could have got that gathering together and managed it so well that everybody there felt they had had a most interesting and valuable occasion as well as a jolly good dinner.

Saturday 16 February
Talked to Norman Lamont who said he would very much like to see Rupert for lunch. He felt the *Times* under Simon Jenkins' editorship

was going very much anti-government and making contradictory statements.

I said, 'Why don't you speak to Simon about it?' He said, 'Because he is an old friend and I don't like to.'

Monday 18 February

I woke up with a violent headache. I couldn't think straight. This was a pity as it was the day in which I had to make my speech in the Lords debate on racing.

I was the only person there not kow-towing to the establishment Jockey Club line, apart from Lord Plummer, a former Levy Board Chairman, and Willie Whitelaw.

Henry Porchester, sitting in front of me, when I said that the Jockey Club could have had a Tote monopoly in 1928 (when the Tote was set up), if it hadn't been for their desire to make special prices with the bookmakers on their own horses, kept nodding his head in agreement with me. Nobody challenged this.

Andrew Devonshire also startled the Jockey Club by saying, in contradiction to his son (the Senior Steward), that owners shouldn't ask the government for more prize money. They should be in it for fun, like owning a yacht.

Tuesday 19 February

In the evening I had to address the All Party Parliamentary Racing Committee. All the same faces were there again. There was Sir John Wheeler,[10] Chairman of the Home Affairs Committee, and a number of their members. There were all the people from the Lords, some members of the Jockey Club. I began by saying this was like [in] *Guys and Dolls*, the oldest established permanent floating crap game in New York, with all the same characters turning up.

Nicholas Soames was particularly nasty. That was because he had not been asked to the Annual Tote Luncheon because he knew that I thought he behaved appallingly in voting against Margaret while pretending he wasn't. He even asked me was I attacking the Jockey Club because they didn't want me reappointed? I said, 'On the contrary. I was assured by the Senior Steward that they did want me reappointed

---

10. Conservative MP, 1979–97; chairman, Home Affairs Select Committee, 1987–92; knight 1990.

and there was no question of them being against me officially. As for other elements of the Jockey Club, that's another matter.'

I made a ten minute speech in which I defended the Tote's record. But I was asked a lot of questions, most of which were reasonably hostile though some were quite friendly. Nicholas Soames laughed sneeringly when I said it is not generally realized that we are not in any way required by the legislation governing the Tote to help racing; we do it voluntarily. I said, 'I don't know why you're laughing, Nicholas. I suppose you would never help anybody voluntarily,' which made everybody laugh.

Wednesday 20 February
Levy Board meeting and strategy review. The man, Christopher Haines, who is one of the Jockey Club representatives on the Levy Board though he is not a member of the Jockey Club, and Christopher Sporborg[11] were there.

Haines looked very subdued. I think he now realizes what an idiot he had made of himself and of the Jockey Club with all their preposterous demands,

When I went down to the Lords, Baroness Trumpington came up to me. She had been at the All Party Parliamentary Racing Committee meeting the night before. She said, 'You were a brave boy last night. I admired you a great deal for your courage and the way you dealt with the questions.'

Thursday 21 February
Talked to Margaret and asked her what she felt about the situation with regards to Saddam Hussein's equivocal delays via the Russians. Their Foreign Minister is going to Moscow this evening to give an answer from Baghdad as to what they mean by their conditions for withdrawal from Kuwait.

She thought Gorbachev might be doing it for internal reasons, to take everybody's mind off their own internal situation in the Baltic states.

She said she thought that the Russians had been playing a double game all the time and so had France. They are both big suppliers of equipment for the military in Iraq.

---

11. Deputy chairman, Hambros, since 1990; joined Tote Board, 1993; Jockey Club finance steward since 1995.

We both agreed that John Major was still doing pretty well over the Gulf War and Bush was being unexpectedly tough.

I asked her whether she had seen Lord Harris' article about the social market in the *Sunday Telegraph* and she said yes. I said, 'It was terrific and I totally agree with it. I think this business of talking about social markets is just a fudge, trying to pretend to be left-wing.' She said, 'I moved the Labour Party miles to the right and now they seem to be wanting to move it back to the old consensus Labour Party.'

On the social market I said, 'This is being used by people like Chris Patten and I really have no regard for him at all. I think he is terribly wet and all things to all men, trying to appear as a great left-wing figure.' She said she absolutely agreed.[12]

We discussed the proposed new substitute for the community charge produced by Heseltine.

She said she thought it was quite mad to have two taxes, one a variation of the old rates and the other a community charge paid by everybody.

She said she is going to break her silence in America when she goes there, on March 8th, to receive this Medal of Freedom, the highest of all that Congress can give any foreigner. I said, 'Are you going to talk about English politics there?' In a rather doubtful way she said, 'No. I am going to talk about the whole principle of enterprise and the social market doesn't mean that at all. It just means spending more than we can afford and dressing it up as some phrase used by the Socialists.' I said, 'Have you spoken to John Major about it?' She said, 'No I haven't but I am going to make this speech and I am not going to be silent any more.'

She sounded very vigorous and quite jolly. Then she said, 'I can't go on talking any more because I am just having a hairdo.'

I think she is going to be giving John quite a lot of bother before long.

The Other Club.

---

12. In the *Sunday Telegraph* of 17 February, Lord (Ralph) Harris of High Cross (founder president of the Institute of Economic Affairs, life peer 1979) began his article by saying that Mr Lamont attached more importance to the 'market' half of the phrase and Mr Patten to the 'social', and went on to challenge Chris Patten's version of the social market: 'His wing of the post-Thatcher Conservative Party have always wanted a larger role for government.'

The first person I saw was Robin Day and I sat next to him He said, 'Your daughter is heavily under attack for the profile on Christopher Patten.[13] It was a bit bitchy, actually.' I said, 'First of all, it's an editorial affair. The person who writes most of the profile does it under the instructions of the editor, having been told what angle he wants. The editor then rewrites bits, as happened in this case, and alters sentences and attitudes, just the same as when you write a leading article in a newspaper. It's the editorial function. That was exactly the position of Petronella. In any case, I am not responsible for what my daughter writes. I have enough difficulty being responsible for myself.' Robin accepted that as a reasonable explanation.

The fat boy, Nicholas Soames, was there but he sat down a few places away from me on the other side of the table. I threw a piece of bread at him which hit him on the side of the head. He laughed and said, 'You were absolutely brilliant last night. We couldn't lay a glove on you. You mastered everybody.' So I thought that was quite pleasant of him.

He then said he was going to stay with Queen Elizabeth the Queen Mother at Cheltenham and he would see me at Cheltenham. I said, 'I hope you don't shout at her as much as you do me.' I wonder what he says to her about me because I know how fond she is of me. I call him the fat boy now because that is what he is and looks like. He talks a great deal of nonsense these days.

Saturday 23 February
Talked to Margaret. We were both delighted that the Russian moves had not delayed the preparation for the ground attack against the Iraqis.

Went to Kempton Park Tote Placepot Hurdle. Quite a valuable race. There were only seven runners which was disappointing. The owners complain there is not enough prize money and yet they can't be bothered to run in an important race like that.

---

13. In the same issue of the *Sunday Telegraph*, 17 February, the anonymous profile called Patten, who had been appointed Chairman of the Conservative Party by Major, 'a Consensus Man, a darling of the Tory left'. It continued, 'Beneath the amiable, donnish façade is insincerity and indecision,' and alleged there was a nagging worry at Central Office that when the election campaign began his heart would not be in it.

John McCririck[14] talked to invited guests in the Hampton Suite where we were entertaining about eighty to a hundred customers from our betting shops. Those were people who bet a lot with us and are known to the managers and to Joe Scanlon who is Managing Director of Tote Bookmakers. I like John McCririck a lot these days. He wears extraordinary clothes, a sort of weird shawl or coat and a peculiar hat. His vivacity on *Channel 4 Racing* has done an enormous amount to promote racing and to bring people out of the betting shops to the courses who otherwise would not have come.

Sunday 24 February
The ground war [in the Gulf] has started. The Queen, astonishingly to me, made a short broadcast to the nation. Probably because of recent criticisms of the Royal Family.

I had a note from Norman to say he was going to consider very seriously Chips' claims to be a director of the Bank of England which I had sent him.

One reason why Norman Lamont, John Major and Chris Patten are getting more excited about the newspapers than Margaret, sending messages around from 10 Downing Street, is that she never used to read the newspapers, only little summaries edited by Bernard Ingham which she glanced through. She mainly listened to the BBC Radio 4 or LBC. Often she was quite oblivious of attacks on her in the press unless somebody pointed one out to her.

When I returned the pretty napkin to Diane Lever which I had absent-mindedly stuffed into my trouser pocket when we had lunch there with Leonard Wolfson, she said, 'You're in good company. Michael Foot[15] and Isaiah Berlin have both done the same when having lunch or dinner here.' So I rank among the absent minded. I bumped into Michael Foot the other day. He was very friendly. He said, 'You are still alive I see,' and I said, 'Yes and so are you. Remarkable.'

Tuesday 26 February
Spoke to Margaret. I said, 'I hope they go on to Basra.' She agreed.

---

14. Racing journalist, famous on television for his fast talk and bookie-style hand signals.
15. Labour politician and writer; Leader of the Opposition, 1980–3; b 1913.

I had a very interesting letter from Ken Baker marked 'in confidence'. Clearly he agrees with me about racing.[16] On the telephone this morning he said he heard I had flayed about in the Lords to good effect. He is clearly on our side. I said, 'But what about David Sieff? You haven't put him on the board yet.' He said he is talking to him, whatever that means.

We agreed, Ken and I, that we must go on to Basra. He added that we should destroy Saddam and create a new government in Iraq. I said, 'That wouldn't be a good idea because puppet governments are never satisfactory. We have to get his own people to throw him out.' He said, 'If we had a number of prominent Iraqis setting up a government that could do the trick.'

I had a great wrangle with the *Times* about my piece on the attacks on the Queen not paying income tax and so forth. I had to agree to some cuts.[17]

Wednesday 27 February
John Wilton has embarked on using the Barry Room for dinner, with us as his guests.

It was a gossipy kind of dinner. John says that Tony [Lambton] won't go to the wedding or the party his daughter Lucinda is giving for it when she marries Perry Worsthorne.[18] Lucy and her father never got on but she got on all right with her mother, Bindy, who will be there.

I commiserated with John on the birth of a son to the Duke of Westminster whose fortune, though not his title, only the Marquess part, would have been inherited by John if the Duke had been killed in a motor car or an aeroplane or some such manner before having a son.

---

16. The short letter thanked WW for his helpful papers on racing's financial crisis (sent 16 January) and the Tote's performance over the past five years (handed to him earlier). They were in full agreement about the need for racing to put its own house in order and did not see the Tote as a means of protecting the industry from the realities of life.

17. WW argued in the *Times* on 27 February that the nation had 'a remarkably good bargain' when the cost of the Civil List was compared with the revenues the Queen ceded from the Crown estates and other expenses she paid.

18. But see 11 May for the wedding, which Lambton did attend.

Thursday 28 February

Cease-fire announced after the collapse of the Iraqis. Margaret is delighted.

I said I thought we should have gone on to Basra because the Iraqis are so self-deluding that they believe Saddam's claim that he really won a victory.

Later she went to the House of Commons. John Major paid a graceful and charming tribute to Margaret as the initiator of Saddam's downfall. She, seeming nervous, dressed in red and rather tense, in turn paid a handsome tribute to his cool leadership and that of President Bush.

The *Times* published a letter today from Andrew Neil, indignant about my assault on the *Sunday Times*' attacks on the Queen and the Royal Family in Wednesday's *Times*. Andrew said I was 'discombobulated' by fawning on the Queen.[19]

Spoke to Charles Anson. He had told me yesterday that everyone from the top to the bottom had been delighted with my *Times* article (meaning the Queen herself at the top). He wanted to know if I was doing the same in the *News of the World*.

At the Lords, Frank Longford said, 'Elizabeth (his wife) thought it was tremendous and absolutely right. It was the first article she had read of yours for a very long time with which she completely agreed.' 'Oh dear,' I said, 'perhaps there was something wrong with it after all.' Elizabeth has written two well researched books, *The Queen Mother: A Biography* and *Elizabeth R*. Because she knows what she is talking about she agreed with me, though she's Labour like Frank.

In the Lords I was going past the peers' lavatory when I bumped into Leonard Wolfson. He was with a tall girl, very slim, with a figure exactly like Ruth Wolfson's and a face not dissimilar, but younger and prettier. When he introduced me to her – her name was Estelle Jackson – Leonard popped into the lavatory and left me talking to her by the ticker tape.

She was very well dressed and had a beautiful diamond brooch on. I assume she is pretty comfortably off and not just after Leonard's

---

19. WW faxed Neil to say he could not find 'discombobulated' in his dictionary but presumed it indicated praise. Neil replied that, on the contrary, 'to discombobulate' was a US jocularity meaning 'to throw into confusion'.

money, though she might like to be called Lady Wolfson. Clearly she is the one that Leonard intends to marry when the divorce comes through and I think he will be very lucky. What an ass Ruth has been.

Friday 1 March
I spent over three-quarters of an hour talking to John Major. I congratulated him on the splendid way he had been conducting our part in the Gulf War. I also said I found his tribute to Margaret in the Commons yesterday very touching and characteristic of him. He said quickly, 'I made the same tribute to her in the Cabinet meeting in the morning.'

I explained briefly to him my relations with Margaret since I first talked to her for two hours about her intentions when she became leader 'of your party' in 1975. I told her, 'If you stick to that I'll back you.' I told him I had some input into the 1979 Conservative manifesto. She stuck to what she told me and I stuck to her.

I said, 'I used to speak to her at least once a week and sometimes twice or more if she was in difficulties. I would make suggestions to her on how to deal with them. I have been talking to her more since she stopped being Prime Minister because I feel very protective about her. Four times out of five she says during our conversations, "We must support John." ' Instantly he said, 'That's very nice of her. I am very grateful.'

Tea was brought in for me to the little sitting-room where Margaret used often to sit. He sat in a high padded armchair and I sat opposite him. He said, 'I have often sat where you are and argued with Margaret.' I said, 'She never minded arguments. She longed to persuade people. Often I found when she said she disagreed with me she would actually go and do the thing I had suggested.' He said, 'Exactly the same happened to me. Then she would behave as though it had been her idea in the first place.' 'Same here,' I said. 'And I would sometimes remind her that it had been my idea in the first place.'

He talked of the misconception of the world about her and how kind she was to everyone personally. I said, 'She had to put on a tough persona because she was a woman leading a party which could never get over its dislike of being led by a woman – at least the old style Tories of whom there were many.'

I said, 'You know she's going to America next week and she's going to make a speech. I asked her what it was going to be about and she said about the principles of Thatcherism and how they must be maintained. I then said to her, "Are you sure you are not going to say critical things about the government while you're abroad? It's not the custom." She replied she would not do that.

'But she is worried about a number of things. And it is important not to hurt her feelings by making it seem that the government doesn't believe in what she has stood for.'

John said, 'There's a great deal of rubbish talked about this. It makes me very cross. I am carrying on with exactly the thrust and intentions of all she did when she was Prime Minister. But I have a different style from her and it would not be in my nature to be as confrontational as she is.'

The more I looked at him, the more I thought what an engaging and intelligent face he has. I like his tall, neat, trim figure and the modestly confident way he holds himself. In the beginning he had asked me if I wanted to be alone and not have Andrew Turnbull, his Principal Private Secretary, present. I said I was sure I could rely on his confidentiality.

I said, 'I never repeated what Margaret said to me and I will not repeat what you say to me. But that didn't stop her from saying to people that when talking to me I had said this, that and the other. I had wished she wouldn't do it because it was bad for my reputation for everyone to know I had such a close relationship. It made me look as though I was in her pocket, which could take away some of the effect of my support for her. Sometimes she would get cross with me because I had attacked something she or her government had done and I always said to her, "If I don't do that when I think it is right, and I never do it when I don't think it is right, all those readers of the *News of the World* won't take me seriously when I advise them to vote for her or her government." '

I had already explained to him that I was not a Tory, which he knew anyway.

We discussed the community charge and what I saw as an apparent move to put back the rates in some form and have a service charge as well.

I concluded from what he said that nothing will be done about alterations to the community charge which I, or even Margaret, would be likely to disapprove of. Improvements might be suggested before the election but they couldn't possibly be put into action before it.

I said I, as well as she, was concerned over the talk about the social market economy which suggested that, after Margaret and her government moving Labour a hundred miles to the right, the government now wanted to move back again towards Labour and a consensus policy. He said, 'Absolutely not.' I said, 'That is what Chris Patten has implied with his talk of the "social market economy" and he is Chairman of the Conservative Party.'

John said, 'He only said it once and there have been acres of stuff written about it since. It's no different from what Margaret used to say to me when I was sitting where you are. She would say we have got to have a market economy which is effective so that we can do all the social services that are necessary.'

I said, 'She will say what she feels, if she thinks you are not sticking to the true faith, but she won't undermine you. If she is in the Lords, she will speak as a respected elder statesman without harming you or your party, at least not much.'

Early in our conversation he said that I had been very critical of the ERM and had attacked the government on it.

He said, 'I think the ERM's going to prove a great success, keeping us with a downward pressure on inflation.' I said, 'This is what Norman tells me all the time and I have said I don't agree with devaluation. Maybe I shall be eventually a convert to the ERM and if I am, I shall say so. But I am very glad that you are not a convert to the idea of a single currency and a Central European Bank.'

He confirmed that absolutely, saying he would never go into a single currency or a Central European Bank.

There was talk about the election date. I said, 'I believe everyone would accept it if you decided to have an election in early June, on the grounds that since 1979 each Tory government has never run more than four years and so this is normal practice.'

He was very frank. He said he agreed with me and was glad to hear my views. I shall now not be surprised if that isn't exactly what happens, an election in the first half of June.

As I got up to go he said, 'How is Bob?' and turned to Andrew Turnbull and said, 'Do you know who Bob is?' and he made a motion as with a cricket bat.

Before I finally left John said he would like me to come and talk to him again. I said, 'I don't think it is a good idea for me to be seen here unless it is for some formal lunch or dinner. I think it would be better if I rang you occasionally when I have some feeling that something is going wrong or a suggestion to put to you. Would that be all right?' He said it would be fine.

Saturday 2 March
I told Margaret the gist, but by no means all, of my conversation with John Major. I told her he is devoted to her and gave the most emphatic reassurances that he is sticking to her principles concerning everything he was doing, whether it was health, education, privatization, the lot.

Margaret said, 'He's a very decent fellow.'

Sunday 3 March
Spoke to Norman Lamont. I told him that I had seen Major but he was not to say so and that I felt quite happy now that he is not doing any backsliding.

Norman talked about the irreconcilables in the Tory Party. I said, 'There are bound to be some of them. Don't forget that in your Budget it'll be OK for you, with the recession and the war in the background, to do a little borrowing if you want to, after paying off so much of the National Debt. I wouldn't call that over-spending.' He said, 'But she does.'

The government are still obviously pretty frightened of Margaret. It looks as though I shall have to be building a bridge between them.

Tuesday 5 March
At the party after the memorial service for Sir Ian Trethowan,[1] I had a long talk with one of our chief critics, Lord Zetland.[2] He didn't mind my jokes at all. I had made two or three at his expense [at the Tote lunch earlier].

I said, 'I don't mind your saying we ought to be allowed to do the various things you suggest and that the law ought to be changed. What I object to is your saying we could do them if we weren't so uncommercial.'

When I talked to Robert Runcie (who gave the blessing and read

---

1. He had died on 12 December 1990, almost exactly a year after he had told WW the seriousness of his illness – see 19 December 1989.
2. 4th Marquess of Zetland; director, Redcar and Catterick Racecourses; member of the Jockey Club, steward, 1992–4.

some of the prayers) he said, 'Now that I am no longer Archbishop I can whole-heartedly back the Sunday Sports Bill, go racing and urge that betting shops should be opened on Sundays.' He's a very nice man. He was chatting up a rather pretty woman as he has a keen eye for feminine beauty. I must remember to ask him to go racing with us.

I was standing by Patricia Rawlings, the girl who is a Strasbourg European MP.[3] I touched the back of her neck as she was talking to the American Ambassador and she turned so I said, 'Go on talking to that handsome young man.' The Ambassador said, 'How marvellous. I haven't been called that for a very long time – young, I mean.'

We then went to a party at the Savoy for the investiture, as it was described, of Sir Tim Bell, knighted that day by the Queen. He said that he couldn't reconcile himself to the new administration because of Margaret. I said, 'Every time I speak to her she says we must support John.' Of course Tim is out of it all now and they won't give him the job of public relations for the Tory Party again.

Wednesday 6 March
Before the [Tote Board] meeting began David Montagu [Swaythling] asked to talk to me privately. He has some kind of malignant cancer in his blood. It is very confidential and he doesn't want me to say a word to anybody. He thinks he will be all right as they said you can live on for years with it but he is going to need a lot of medication. He also says that at the moment he gets very tired in the afternoons and he is getting very tired altogether. He looked very white and not at all well.

When I looked at the two of them [Swaythling and Winfield] in the board meeting when they were discussing my having a successor appointed, I thought, 'I could well see both of you out.'

The trouble is that they want somebody like this man Blackburn who is a friend of Peter Winfield's from Touche Ross, an accountant, a horse owner and a drinking companion. I certainly don't want three accountants on the board – Brian [McDonnell] plus Phillips, who is coming to be a financial director with a seat on the board, plus this fellow.

Afterwards I said to Brian, 'Racing is a very snobbish world. This fellow Blackburn wouldn't be socially acceptable.'

---

3. Conservative MEP, 1989–94; life peer 1994.

Thursday 7 March

Went to the National Portrait Gallery where John Bratby[4] has an exhibition. This was the preview. There were a number of weirdies about the place drinking unappetizing-looking wine and nibbling unattractive-looking bits of snacks.

Soon I bumped into Ken Baker and asked him what he was doing there. He said, 'Getting some culture.' We discussed Bratby briefly and then I asked him what he was doing about making David Sieff a member of our board. He said, 'I am talking to him next week.'

As we looked at the picture of John Braine, the man who wrote *Room at the Top*, I told them how when I was on *Panorama* I interviewed him just before his book was published. I saw where he worked. He demonstrated how he wrote lying in bed with his head back on the pillow, holding a large notebook above his head and writing away upside down. I told them that when I said on the *Panorama* programme that there was a lot of sex in John Braine's *Room at the Top*, the publishers told me afterwards that the next day sales soared – sex was not so common in books then.

John Bratby was looking very old and deaf, and his hair was very white and sparse, tied up in a knot at the back. He has got enormously fat. Yet he is just over ten years younger than me. His present wife, Patti, was there. She said that when I came to be painted by John Bratby at their house in Hastings, I brought my own wine with me and it was a very good idea because they had enjoyed it.[5]

I still have the portrait in the top sitting-room which he did and which was on the front cover of *Confessions of an Optimist*. But Verushka doesn't like it so perhaps I should give it to the National Portrait Gallery.

Andrew Neil in his letter to the *Times* reproached me for referring in a manner he thought more worthy of the *News of the World* to his

---

4. (1928–92); painter and writer; m 2 (1977) Patti Prime.
5. In a letter dated 21 January 1983, quoted in *Bull: The Biography* by Howard Wright (1995), Phil Bull, the betting expert and founder of Timeform, wrote to John Bratby, in response to Bratby's querying what he thought of Woodrow, that he was a political maverick, low on logic and high on self-display: 'He should have been an actor.'

scurrilous affair with Pamella Bordes. I sent him a fax message and got the attached reply. I am sorry he was upset.[6]

Friday 8 March
Just as Brian McDonnell was going home a fax arrived from Richard Fries, the civil servant dealing with Tote affairs.

Fries said he was about to send to the Home Affairs Committee a potted version of the Lloyds Merchant Bank report and he had agreed the text with Lloyds Merchant Bank.

This was in breach of our agreement with the Home Secretary at the time and also it is quite unnecessary to send it so soon because the Tote is not going to be investigated by the Home Affairs Committee until May 21st. He has done it as one of his last acts before going to be in charge of immigration.

Their inquiry into privatization began in September 1988, for goodness' sake, and the whole thing is totally irrelevant now anyway. It sounds as though I shall have to ring Kenneth Baker at home, if I can get him over the weekend, to have this nonsense halted.

Saturday 9 March
The great wedding between Tessa [Mayhew] and Robbie [Lyle] in the St Stephen's Crypt Chapel followed by a tremendous reception in the Lords dining-room upstairs.

Christopher [Mayhew] paid for the reception replete with champagne and quite good things to eat, plus a cake made free for Robbie by the Roux Brothers from the Gavroche. As Robbie has no parents we stood in the line with Christopher and Cecily Mayhew to receive all the guests. There were about two hundred and they took ages to go by.

Tessa looked attractive. She is not a bad-looking girl. She had a pretty silk cream-yellow dress and the bridesmaids were dressed similarly but in cheaper material.

At the dinner after the wedding Simon Weinstock, when I said I

6. In his *Times* article of 27 February about the Queen paying tax, WW had upbraided Neil for attacking the 'extra-marital fling' of Lord Althorp, brother of Princess Diana ('Such prudery was rum coming from the editor of *The Sunday Times*, whose exploits with Pamella Bordes were well aired in court'). Neil thanked WW for his fax but said he was perennially puzzled by those who professed support in private but could not resist personal jibes in public.

had had a bit of a breach with Arnold his father over Mrs Thatcher, said, 'I thought it was over the Jockey Club.' I said, 'No. Don't take that seriously. Why is your father fussed about that?' To which he replied, 'I suppose now he has joined it, he feels himself a part of it and has to defend it.' I said, 'What absolute nonsense. He should agree with everything I said.' The breach was about Arnold's disloyalty to Mrs Thatcher.

Sunday 10 March
Urged Norman Lamont to push for an early June election while the going is good and to take no notice of the Ribble Valley setback which was only about the poll tax, a sort of protest vote.[7]

He said it was his advice to John Major to say at the leadership contest that he would get rid of or transform the poll tax because the others were going to say the same and he wouldn't have got the job of Prime Minister if he hadn't followed suit or taken the lead in it.

Monday 11 March
Abdul Al Ghazzi's secretary told me she had not liked to disturb me over the weekend but she had some bad news for me. I thought she meant that Abdul wasn't coming to lunch on Wednesday as agreed. No. It was that he had had a terrible stroke and a brain haemorrhage exploded, with high blood pressure going to three hundred, and was now dead. I was stunned. She said they were all stunned too.

I thought, oh gosh, he was only fifty-four, but he did over-eat and over-drink and he travelled a lot and he was very fat for his size, but perhaps not excessively so compared with others.

He was a dear friend, just like Emil Bustani, much the same sort of character.[8] He was generous, outgoing, kind, loyal, everything you could desire, as well as of high intelligence with great knowledge and enterprise. He built his enormous business up over years. I don't know how much money he had but it must be a terrific amount.

In the afternoon I went to see the brother and the secretary and others of the entourage at the house facing Park Lane just by Green Street. They were all desolated.

They said they are taking him to where his tribe was. The chiefs of

---

7. On 7 March the Conservatives lost the by-election, caused by David Waddington's peerage, to the Liberal Democrats by a 25 per cent swing.

8. Emil Bustani was a Lebanese politician, killed in an aeroplane accident in 1963.

it (and he is one) are related to the royal family of Iraq. It is near Basra. They have to go through Jordan by road and they must go on the terrible pitted roads to Baghdad and on to where the family vaults are. The youngest brother is not allowed to leave Baghdad where he is at the moment.

It seems they have the money to carry on with Heveningham and at his offices just off Park Lane (that beautiful house which is Grade One) but obviously they won't be able to go on expanding the business with the imagination and flair that he had. The library at Heveningham is just about ready and now he will never see it completed. He was so proud of what he had done and justly so.

I told the mourning Arab relations and men of affairs that I had been ashamed of my countrymen for the way they had vilified him and even called him an agent of Saddam Hussein, saying that Heveningham had belonged to Saddam, and how the xenophobic people of Suffolk had abused him and vandalized his property.

Tuesday 12 March

Panic before the dinner party. Mrs Black (Joanna) could not come. She was sick with some 'flu or some disorder. Annunziata Asquith was tried but she had to go to a Benjamin Britten opera, *The Turn of the Screw*, and said the screw would be turning when she thought what she was missing. We then tried Robin Day to ask if he had got somebody he could bring with him, which he duly did.

Claire Hesketh [wife of Alexander Hesketh] asked me why I called Pericles 'Pericles'. I said, 'Because some people, as in the case of your husband, are called after a murderous, orgiastic, drunken tyrant. I thought I would call my son after the founder of modern democracy as a better example.'[9]

David Airlie[10] took me on one side and thanked me for what I had written about the Queen's finances in the *Times* and in the *News of the World*.

There were some attacks made at this stage on Robert Maxwell. Everybody agreed that he was a crook, including the Airlies, but in some ways likeable. I said, 'I don't think he's very likeable.' Conrad said he couldn't possibly do any deal with him, he was so dishonest

---

9. The democracy of fifth century BC Athens was, of course, not completely 'modern' as it excluded women and slaves.

10. 13th Earl of Airlie, Lord Chamberlain of the Queen's Household, 1984–97.

and devious and wriggled out of things and gave you false information. 'Not at all like Rupert,' he said, 'who's absolutely straight.'

Mrs Murdoch was somewhat discussed for not having helped him in England and her dislike of the English because she thought they didn't recognize her properly. The other day she was caught by that ghastly man, Francis Wheen, who always cuts me up in the *Independent on Sunday*, and he made a right guy of the poor girl, over her new novel.[11]

I like Conrad Black more and more. I had thought he was overweening at one time but he is becoming less bombastic and aggressive the more confident he gets, as is often the way. I think I must mention to Major to give him a peerage. That would bind him very strongly because I think he has loyalty in his make-up quite keenly.[12]

Wednesday 13 March
Went to stay with Micky Suffolk at Malmesbury.[13]

It is a friendly house. Linda Suffolk is blonde and pretty and slimmish, cheerful and sprightly. They have two enchanting girls though he has other children, including an heir, by previous marriages. The girls are just gone four and seven.

Micky is the chef when he wants to do something serious for a meal. He is a very good cook. There was an excellent soup accompanied by Vouvray 1959.

Thursday 14 March
Left early to be at the racecourse [Cheltenham] by ten o'clock so I could do my rounds. Verushka was to follow later, to be delivered at the Royal Box for lunch with Queen Elizabeth the Queen Mother.

Queen Elizabeth was wearing a delightful red and blue patterned

---

11. Francis Wheen, journalist (diarist, *Independent on Sunday*, 1990–1; columnist, the *Guardian*, since 1994; regular contributor to *Private Eye*). Anna Murdoch's third novel was *Coming to Terms*, following *In Her Own Image* (1985) and *Family Business* (1988).

12. William Hague, Leader of the Conservative Party, nominated Conrad Black for his list of working peers published in June 1999. However, Black, who holds dual Canadian and British citizenship, was barred from taking the peerage under a 1919 Canadian law forbidding Canadian nationals from accepting titles from foreign governments.

13. 21st Earl of Suffolk and Berkshire; m 3 (1983) Linda Viscountess Bridport, née Paravicini.

dress, very effective and it suited her very well, and a very nice matching hat. I told her she looked wonderful. She said, 'Do you like it? I was rather nervous about it.'

I also complimented her on her brooch.

She said, 'Oh it was given me by the King,' meaning George VI. I said, 'What good taste he had. Everything you have worn that you have told me was given you by him has been really lovely and has suited you perfectly.' She said, 'I think men are much better at choosing things for women than they are themselves.' I said, 'Yes but only if they are interested in women,' and she laughed.

Queen Elizabeth had seen the Tote film and read my speech.

She said, 'Of course you only make these attacks on the Jockey Club to be provocative. You like to stir it up.' I said, 'No, they began it.'

Of course the Queen and she love the Jockey Club people because it is all rather a hereditary affair and they are all grandees, or a lot of them are, of the aristocracy. But against my strictures on the Jockey Club she obviously knew how pleased the Queen had been about my putting the record straight over the £1.85 million a day she was supposed to have as an income and supporting the monarchy in a vigorous way.

We talked [with Charlie Allsopp of Christie's] about how Michael Broadbent, the great wine expert at Christie's, used to come on his bicycle to Cavendish Avenue when one of the famous 'drink-tank' lunches, including Lord Rothschild [Victor], Michael Tree, David Somerset, etc., would be at our house instead of the alternative at Christie's. I said how he brought decanted bottles in his little basket in front of his bicycle, wearing his high winged collar.

The Gold Cup race was very nearly won by a French horse, owned and trained in France, called The Fellow. Queen Elizabeth kept saying, 'I'm so glad the Frenchman didn't win. I like the French, of course, but I don't want them to win these races.' Actually, she doesn't really like the French very much at all.

In the paddock before the race I presented André Cormier to her and told her that he was the head of the French PMU. Afterwards I said I thought it was a good bit of Anglo-French relations and she said, 'Yes, you are quite right.' I was also thinking it might spur Cormier on to get these PMU bets into our Derby pool which he has been promising to try to do, though he says the government won't let him

478   1991

yet and that he has had a lot of difficulty in getting PMU bets into the Belgian system.

As she went to go, I said to her, 'Would you like to come to dinner again?' She said she would love to. I said, 'We won't ask A. N. Wilson this time,' and she laughed a lot.

Up in our own sponsors' box I had a long talk with Alan Meale, a member of the Select Committee on Racing. He is Labour but very friendly. He is going to supply us with the questions the day before the Tote is examined at the end of May. He thinks that Wheeler, the Chairman, is hostile to me and one other, a Tory MP called Gale,[14] but on the whole he thinks they tend to be friendly. And he certainly is.

Back at Charlton Park, Micky [Suffolk] was getting ready to do his cooking. He asked everybody how they would like their steak. It was really fillet of beef and was sliced. Like a very good cook he produced the slices everybody had asked for done in their different ways.

Rosalind, the wife of Charles Morrison, the MP for Devizes, now resigning, and Chairman of the All Party Racing Committee,[15] arrived before dinner and before everybody else was down. I said to her, 'Where is Charlie?' She said, 'Up in London running the country.' I said, 'It would be better for the country if he were down here and not making a mess of the country.' I am rather fond of her. She is quite beautiful in a blonde way, with a lovely figure and intelligent, smiling face. God knows what she can see in him.

Irrational noble impulses overcome me. They make me feel I must make friends and see the good in people like Christopher Haines or Nicholas Soames, approach them and be friendly and kind to them. I get rushes of emotional feeling that I should be Christian and forgive my enemies and turn the other cheek. Fortunately, these feelings don't always last too long. When carried away by such emotions I am liable to be dangerously accommodating and give my position away to those I should be more cautious with.

Tuesday 19 March
Telephoned Norman to wish him luck with his Budget. Said I was going to Michael Howard's to have dinner with Mrs Thatcher. 'She'll hate it,' he said, meaning the Budget.

---

14. Roger Gale, Conservative MP since 1983; former BBC journalist.
15. Not to be confused with the Home Affairs Select Committee currently investigating racing and possible privatization of the Tote.

A nice little house. Sandra Howard was looking pretty.

When we arrived Denis and Margaret were already there. I sat on the sofa with her. She prattled away about her trip round America and how wonderful it had been when she got the Congressional Medal of Freedom. They had stayed the night in the White House. She had slept in the Churchill Room. They had breakfast alone with the Bushes.

She gave some lectures which I think she was well paid for (£27,000 a shot).

Nick Ridley and his pretty little wife arrived. So did Mr and Mrs Carew Pole.[16] I had met them before, not very interesting. His father was Lord Lieutenant of Cornwall and he will be a baronet when his father dies. They have got a large property just inside Cornwall. They are an old Cornish family, rather grand. He knew my brother quite well and said how nice he was. He was telling Margaret how he had been High Sheriff of Cornwall and how he had been very brave with his Parkinson's disease.

He said he was on the planning committee and knew about our wind farm. I said, 'You should support it,' and I gave him a lecture about the locals who wanted it.

Sandra rushed in and out in between cooking the dinner. There was soufflé with a fish flavour in it, not at all bad, nor was the curled up lamb. There was some excellent 1982 cru bourgeois Les Ormes-de-Pez, but I drank too much of it.

Margaret drank whisky pretty heftily before dinner, as did Denis. She was getting a bit tight. She looked well but a bit overblown.

She was indignant about the ending of mortgage relief up to the full tax rate, but stopping at the standard rate of twenty-five per cent and of course still attached to the maximum £30,000.

'Hurting our own people,' she said and repeated it several times. I said I always thought mortgage relief was wrong in any case. I think that because it distorts the housing market with an unwarranted subsidy which costs goodness knows how many billion a year. That didn't go down all that well, though she was, as ever, very friendly to me.

---

16. Richard Carew Pole; he succeeded his father as 13th baronet, 1993; High Sheriff of Cornwall, 1979; director, South West Electricity Board, 1981–90; councillor, Cornwall County Council, 1973–93, chairman, planning and employment committee, 1980–4, chairman, finance commission, 1985–9, chairman, property committee, 1989–93; member, Countryside Commission, 1991–6.

The real difficulty is that on Thursday the Cabinet are going to endorse a property tax. This reduction of the community charge is only going to last one year. Michael Howard said he had been alone in the Cabinet in resisting this property tax.[17]

At times Mrs Thatcher was making carping and critical remarks. She said that Norman had praised Nigel Lawson and whatever for. I said, 'He didn't really praise him. He said he was glad to have worked with him and for him and he admired him, as you did at one time. But you seem to have missed out the bit, or not heard it, where he praised at great length all the achievements of the last ten years of your government.'

Reluctantly she said, 'Well yes, he did do that.'

A little later she said, 'We must go up and watch the "Norman Conquest", and see him on the television.'

It was about a quarter to eleven by the time it came on. She sat down and said, 'Could I see the television?' and I said, 'Yes, fine, at a different angle from yours,' and when it began she pretended to be asleep. Denis actually was fast asleep.

When it ended she said, 'That was a very good presentation.' I said, 'You know he is devoted to you and admires you greatly and believes in all you did.' She said, 'But he was plotting against me.' I said, 'No. We have been through all that. He wasn't plotting against you.' I said, 'You must be fair, darling.'

There were some comments on John Major being exhausted, 'wiped out' was Bush's comment when he met John in America. But he has a bad throat, etc. I said, 'Of course it is a contrast with you who never got tired.'

I jollied her along as best I could without going back on her which of course I never would do. When I was going Michael Howard thanked me for trying to keep her in line. I seem to be keeping the Tory Party together now, bridging the gap between the Prime Minister and the Cabinet and Margaret. She has a lot of supporters.

Denis was very friendly and jolly and talked about golf. He was pretty drunk; so was I by the time we had finished.

I said to Michael Howard, 'Do you think that if they lose this election there is any possibility of her coming back?' He said, 'No, none whatever. They would never have her back now, even if they

---

17. The government was moving towards a tax based on (i) the value of a property and (ii) the number of adults living in the property.

were completely defeated or even if John Major would suddenly die.' That's from somebody who is one of her strongest supporters.

Michael Howard didn't agree with my view that they should have a June election before Major's popularity came down and before it was realized how serious the underlying recession had been and unemployment went on going up. He said, 'Unemployment never matters.'

Thursday 21 March

There was a better atmosphere at the Levy Board. The Jockey Board representatives, Haines and Christopher Sporborg, were delighted that I supported the Jockey Club very strongly about the care that has to be taken in the cuts not to destroy country racecourses or evening meetings or Bank Holiday meetings. These are very profitable for the racecourses concerned, even though they may not add much to the levy.

[Later] I was delivered a letter by hand from David Swaythling enclosing a letter he had sent to the Home Secretary asking that Peter Winfield and he could have a separate interview with him in order to explain that the Home Secretary was wrong not to put David Sieff on the Tote Board. I was pretty livid. First of all, I had been talking to the Home Secretary several times about David Sieff. He saw him last week and said he would let him know the outcome very shortly. Secondly, it showed complete lack of confidence in me. I think what they are really up to is to try to get this bloody accountant from Touche Ross on the board.

There is something very strange about the alliance between Peter Winfield and David Swaythling.

At The Other Club. Ted Heath decided to come. He looks extraordinarily gross with an enormous stomach hanging over his trousers. Someone had told him that Callaghan had resigned from the Club because I had become a member of it.[18] He said, 'How sensible of him.' When I went to sit next to Robin Day one away from Ted, where there was an empty seat, Robin said, 'Why don't you sit next to Ted?' and I turned to Ted and said, 'Because you wouldn't like me to sit next to you, would you?' He said, 'No, I wouldn't.'

But later I started talking to him across Dickson Mabon[19] who sat between us and after Dickson Mabon had gone I said, 'I am still very

---

18. See Vol. 1, p. 651 – Callaghan resigned in protest against the remarks WW had made about him in a review of his memoirs.

19. Labour MP, 1955–81; SDP MP, 1981–3.

fond of you, Ted.' He said, 'You have written some horrible things in the newspapers, very dangerous stuff.' I said, 'Yes but you have done some pretty strange things, too. How are you getting on with your memoirs?'[20] He said, 'Because I can't produce a certificate to say I am ill, as Attlee and Wilson apparently did, I have to go to all the various Ministries where records are kept and they won't come to me as they would if I pretended to be ill.'

We began to get on better and better. I said, 'You seem to be enjoying yourself now. You seem to be very happy with what is going on.' He chortled and said, 'Yes. Of course, to have her defeated makes me feel very good.'

Robin [Day] said he thought I should recognize the changed mood because my columns were going to look very much out of date if I didn't adapt to it: 'If you keep on supporting Mrs Thatcher, who is now dead and gone, and all those kinds of things in the *News of the World* and the *Times*, they will probably get somebody else to write them.' This was frank and may be helpful.

I said, 'Don't worry. But I don't think John Major is drifting away from Thatcherite principles, as you seem to think.'

When we were talking about an independent bank, Gordon Richardson[21] said he had always wanted the Bank of England to be independent. I said, 'What difference would it have made?' He said he would have had control in everything as Governor, of his own reserves, instead of the Treasury having control over them.

Arnold Weinstock was very jolly. There was no sign of any annoyance about the Jockey Club and my attacks on them; he seemed to think I was quite right. I told him I had put out the olive branch.

Saturday 23 March

Today's headline story on the *Sun*'s front page, plus picture, is of Grey Gowrie, the former Arts Minister, now head of Sotheby's in London. He was going into a sauna establishment and massage where the ladies give hand relief for £10 and full intercourse for £100. He had been watched by the *Sun* going in a number of times, having been tipped off by an employee of Sotheby's. Andrew Knight had wanted to suppress the story when he discovered it was about to be printed. He spoke to Rupert who happened to be in London and he said, 'You

---

20. Published 1998.
21. Governor, Bank of England, 1973–83; life peer 1983.

can't take it out now. If you had stopped it earlier it might have been all right but now it looks like some kind of censorship and favouritism.'

Rupert asked me did I think Grey Gowrie was the sort of person who could cope with this type of revelation. I said, 'I am sure he is. It is also quite reasonable to say that it is in the public interest to print such an item because I suppose they are entitled to know how the great and the good carry on.' Grey had said he could not live on his Ministerial salary of £33,000 in the centre of London so he left the government and got £200,000 plus from Sotheby's.

I find it very strange that people can go into these massage centres, like the Duchess of York's father, Ferguson, and Grey Gowrie. Grey is very attractive and charming and full of life and has a beautiful wife. I wouldn't have supposed he had to pay for such seedy pleasures but you never know what anybody does or will do.

Rupert said they had two other entertaining and sensational revelations for the *News of the World* tomorrow. I said, 'I don't mind this kind of thing. I find it amusing. I wouldn't like to be a victim though I can't help laughing at those who are.'

Rupert said the *News of the World* and the *Sun* are buoyant with advertising because they have got a different type of advertising from the *Times* and the *Sunday Times* where the advertising for high spenders is very much down, and the *Sunday Times* is very weak at this time itself. He is moving *Today* into Wapping. I said, 'Isn't it making a loss?' He said, 'It's making a contribution to overheads.' I said, 'But the *Times* is making a thumping loss.' He said, 'That is true. But now we have built Wapping in such a way that we have got to take these newspapers in there to reduce the overheads, even if they're not doing very well.'

I told him that I had recently had dinner with Margaret and she seemed to be all over the shop now with her book. 'I thought you were going to publish it and she wanted you to do it because she felt she owed so much to you. Now she is apparently putting out tenders to publishers and agents, whereas she had not wanted one originally.' He said, 'Yes, it's Mark Thatcher, the son, who has taken charge of her affairs and she is doing everything he tells her.'

Rupert said, 'He has even got a Maxwell publisher (Macmillan of New York) on the list. When people talked about getting three to four million for her memoirs, Mark replied he could get more than double that, eight to ten million.' To which Rupert commented, 'Good luck to him if he can but I don't think he will.'

It is amazing how besotted Margaret is with Mark.

I said to Rupert, 'I am worried about her.' Rupert said, 'It is no good pushing away as though she is expecting to come back and trying to work it so she will. Her only chance of ever coming back is to do nothing about it whatever.'

Norman Lamont rings. He has been doing the Brian Walden programme this morning.

He said that the entire fifty minutes was spent on the accusation that they were not maintaining the Thatcherite policies. He had tried to explain that they are evolving as they go along and everything has to be flexible.

Norman said, 'I don't regard you, Woodrow, as a journalist, but I have come to the conclusion I don't trust any journalists.' I said, 'You are quite right. I am not like that because I am a commentator. I am interested in policies, not in revealing confidences or stirring up trouble between people. And I never attack my friends, you may have noticed. I never attack Roy Jenkins who is a great friend of mine though there have been quite a lot of things I could have attacked him about.'

What I should have said and I must remember to tell him next time is that I am really still a politician and a preacher. I just want people to do the things I think they ought to do for the good of the country and I am not an ordinary political journalist.

I said to Norman, 'Stop worrying about these things. They're not important.'

Wednesday 27 March

Willie Whitelaw said earnestly to me, 'We must get Margaret to go to the Lords. I saw her today and she said she doesn't want to leave the House of Commons to Ted,' to which his reply was, 'Where has that got him?'

Dinner with Julian Amery. It was his birthday. He was seventy-two. We were asked only on Sunday. Catherine was upstairs in bed, looking very ill, poor girl.

I have known that house since before the War when I used to go there when old Leo Amery, his father, was alive.[22] He was a short, energetic little man who had been pushed by Winston into the swimming pool at Harrow. Winston was under the impression that he must

---

22. (1873–1955); Conservative politician and minister (Unionist MP, 1911–45); author; Fellow of All Souls College, Oxford.

have been younger than him because he was so small. But then it emerged he was a school prefect so Winston got into a great deal of trouble because Leo Amery was much his senior.

The house is redolent of decay. Once it had some remarkable Persian pictures acquired by Leo which Julian had to sell. They were replaced by much inferior Persian pictures. The round dining-room table is badly scratched and scored.

Julian lives with as much pomp as he can manage. There was a butler – I don't know if he is permanently there or not – and the odd servant. He gave us some very good Crystal champagne and some excellent Burgundy. Dinner was the standard one of smoked salmon followed by baked ham with some kind of cherry jam sauce. Then came shop-made ice cream in a tub.

The conversation was more amusing after dinner upstairs, alone with Catherine gossiping about her sister-in-law, Katie [Macmillan], and Alexander [Stockton], Katie's son.

Now he is off with Lady Mancroft's daughter by her first marriage, who previously married Peter Sellers and various other people.[23]

Thursday 28 March
Talked to Norman. The usual concern about what Margaret thinks and what she is going to do.

Spoke to Margaret. She described Nigel Lawson's speech as 'completely selfish, thinking only of himself', and said he had no business to undermine John Major in that way.[24] Anyway, he was to blame for the troubles over the inflation. But she thought it was foolish of John Major to rebuke Nigel Lawson and quarrel with him openly in the House of Commons. She would not have done that. She would simply have ignored it.

I said to her, 'I do think you ought to leave the Commons, even if you didn't move into the Lords. You can make a speech or a statement, anywhere you want. Choose your platform. It will have much more effect than in the House of Commons where you have to stand up from the back benches which I think is demeaning.'

She said she was tugged towards staying in the Commons because

---

23. Miranda, née Quarry, daughter of Lady Mancroft by her first marriage, m (1970–4) Peter Sellers, the actor (1925–80) as his third wife.
24. Lawson had called the new proposals for the community charge 'son of poll tax'.

there were all those people who support her there who keep saying, 'We've only got you to rely on to stop them backsliding.'

I think she is wavering.

In the evening I rang Simon Jenkins up and complained about the extraordinary article in the *Times*, with the headline 'Mystery Fuels Rumour that Heveningham Hall is Owned by Saddam'. I said, 'You are fuelling the rumour. It is absolutely ridiculous. You might as well say there is a mystery about who owns News International.'

I took him through the article and Simon Jenkins had the grace to say that I was right.

Sunday 31 March
The Duchess of York is having an affair with a young man, Wyatt, the rich son of a rich American family. He is the one who, with his mother, got into the Royal Box at Ascot because they thought they were inviting Verushka and myself.

The Duchess of York was there on that occasion and no doubt took the opportunity to get friendly with him.

Monday 1 April
In the evening came the BBC Radio 4 fifteen minute programme on the finances of racing. It was a shoddy piece of work. I had been greatly deceived by the producer who said there would not be personal attacks on me. Out of my twenty minute interview they put about two minutes, wholly unrepresentative of what I had said, while the yapping cur and running dog of the Jockey Club, Richard Evans, was allowed to repeat the lies about the Home Office not wanting me to be reappointed and that it was the last act of Mrs Thatcher, just as she knew she was not going to win the second round, to have me reappointed.

Fortunately, I have proof in letters from the Home Office that it had all been arranged in the summer, long before anybody thought there would be a challenge to Mrs Thatcher's leadership.

Wednesday 3 April
The Tote Board meeting. I completely squashed David Swaythling and Peter Winfield. I said I would not put up with nonsensical talk about my appointing a deputy chairman. I said my health is very good and I looked pointedly at both of them who look on the verge of dying.

The meeting was a bit acerbic to start with. However, it came on to an even keel later.

We now, at last, have got David Sieff put on the board. I told them that.

I had already told them it was not necessarily the case that I would be giving up in two years' time. It depended on how things developed.

Thursday 4 April
Had a long talk with Margaret. Yesterday she made an indignant pronouncement that the government was doing nothing, and nor was America, to help the Kurd refugees by sending mercy missions with food and medical equipment.

She said somebody from Number 10 was going round this morning to talk about what they were going to do now. It took her to galvanize Major who is on holiday.

She said sadly, 'Please keep ringing and drop in whenever you feel like it.'

I felt as though a knife had gone into my heart.

Fascinating visit to the Marx Memorial Library in Clerkenwell Green. The library is in a house built in 1737. It is very beautiful in its way.

Once the English Heritage helped the Marx Memorial Library but it refuses to do so now on the grounds they have no money left after helping cathedrals. The poor dears are facing a bill of £28,000 to repair the roof.

The lady who runs the building is obviously a Communist but very charming.[1] She showed me the room where Lenin sat and edited *Iskra*.[2] They have also got the first edition of *Das Kapital* and copies of various books by Karl Marx. Karl Marx actually worked in that house which belonged to a friend of his.

The purpose of my visit was to take part in a Channel 4 programme on Jack Huntingdon's life and paintings.[3] In that Marx Memorial Library in 1935, when he was Viscount Hastings, he painted a remarkable mural showing the revolution, as it were, against the status quo. It is a humorous picture in some ways though it is intended as a serious proposition showing the overthrow of the old order. He painted himself as one of the figures in it, in the tradition of classical painters.

The Marx Memorial Library has now got a genuine function. As the librarian explained to me, students of all kinds, whether they were pro- or anti-Communism, could find tracts there which are nowhere else in existence, not even in the British Museum – all the Chartist material, all the trials of the Chartists, the pamphlets which were issued.

I promised her I would see what I could do with Edward Montagu[4] to activate the English Heritage scene again. 'After all,' I said, 'he was

---

1. Tish Newland, librarian of the Marx Memorial Library since 1989.

2. *Iskra* (*The Spark*) was an illegal Marxist newspaper. Lenin arranged for its publication and distribution before he left Russia in 1900.

3. The 15th Earl of Huntingdon was a pupil of Diego Rivera; he exhibited in Paris, London, Chicago and San Francisco.

4. 3rd Baron Montagu of Beaulieu; chairman, Historic Buildings and Monuments Commission, 1983–92.

a great friend of Jack Huntingdon and he lived near him at Beaulieu.' I gave them ten quid on the spot and in return I got a few postcards including one showing the mural of Jack Huntingdon.

The television programme contractor, Channel 4, is paying them a fee which is enabling them to restore Jack's mural which at the moment is hidden behind a lot of bookcases. I thought it was my duty to do what I could in Jack's memory, to speak about him and say how good an artist he was and how splendid a fellow.

As he grew older, he was far from the left-wing, near Communist he was in 1935.

Friday 5 April
Went to see Margaret at Eaton Square. It was half past six and unusually for me I had two fairly large gin and tonics. She had some strong whiskies. I began to get a little drunk and she was getting a trifle high.

She is becoming more worried about John Major and whether he has enough guts and drive.

She said, 'We should say to the Iraqis, "We won't have a real cease-fire and a peace until you hand over Saddam Hussein to be tried for his war crimes." '

She said nothing was being done about the contracts in Kuwait for its reconstruction. The Americans were very clever and paid in advance for two years' oil supplies from Kuwait, though they are not ready to produce it yet, and they are securing all the contracts.

We talked about various members of the Cabinet. She likes Tom King and thinks he is quite a stout fellow, though I reminded her we had a lot of difficulty with him over the union reforms when he was Secretary for Employment.

She thinks Ken Clarke is good, though he was against her, wanting Major. She much admired the way he faced up to the ambulancemen and now at the Education Department, stoutly leading the reforms in education and with the teachers. She said it was crazy to put David Waddington into the Lords and cause the Ribble Valley by-election.

'Do you think', she asked, 'that Heseltine is finished?' I said, 'Not quite, but he is getting himself very snarled up.'

I asked, 'But why did you give Michael Heseltine the job of Secretary of the Environment in the first place, if you thought he was no good?'

She said, 'I didn't think he was no good. He has that Welsh gift of selling things and he has a certain appeal. I thought he was good at business so he would be good there, but I thought in the end that he only really made his money out of property deals. From the very beginning I knew how impossible he was with his staff and how disdainful he was of ordinary people.'

I said Major was terrified of her and so was the government. I said, 'That is a very good thing because as long as they are terrified of you they will do the right thing.'

Saturday 6 to Sunday 7 April
To Oare House, near Pewsey [Henry Keswick's]. It rained and the house was bitterly cold.

Alastair Goodlad,[5] Deputy Chief Whip, was there, suspicious of me as being a die-hard Thatcherite. He told Henry Keswick [that] Julian Amery was leading a little group to egg on 'the Queen over the water'. I think that is very unlikely but I must check with Julian.

Only forty-eight, Goodlad is very large, round-faced and fair with an enormous stomach. I told his wife he should cut down on eating and drinking or he would blow up. This was relayed to him and he wasn't very pleased. I advocated far less saturated fats or he would have a heart attack. His wife was charming.

In the tack room there was a photograph of Mrs Thatcher and Tessa Keswick standing side by side looking into the box where the foal, Oare Sparrow, was last summer. It was a day full of flies and heat. In the foreground of the picture was the back of myself wearing my white straw hat.[6]

Algy Cluff was there.[7]

He made a fortune, that is to say about a million pounds, years ago for Tony Lambton. He put money into Cluff Oil, as it was then. It is worth about two and a half million now I suppose. I never have the luck to get in on an investment on the ground floor of something like that.

Cluff is tall, fair, with a narrow, almost anxious face. Not bad-looking, a tiny bit precious. He told me he took enormous quantities

---

5. Conservative MP since 1974; Deputy Government Chief Whip, 1990–2; Chief Whip, 1995–7; knight 1997.

6. See 15 July 1990.

7. Chairman and chief executive, Cluff Mining; chairman, the *Spectator*, since 1985, proprietor, 1981–5; a director, Centre for Policy Studies; m (1993) Blondel, née Hodge.

of sleeping pills because he could not sleep but now he is trying to give them up; he gets more nervous and jumpy as a result. He is enormously rich. He is unmarried. He is just fifty.

He is a sort of junior Lonrho now, with very little oil but a lot of gold in Africa and elsewhere. At one time he owned the *Spectator*. He is still the Chairman of it.

The food is good at Oare House. At lunch time on Saturday there was a fantastically good Irish stew but alas! with the fat and potatoes and all the rest. There was a pleasant Burgundy. At dinner there was a grouse apiece plus some excellent Lynch-Bages 1971.

When I held it up to the light Henry said, 'Why are you looking at it?' and I said, 'Because I just wanted to see the colour,' which was a very good, strong colour. It had a lovely velvety taste but it would have been still better if it had been decanted properly. I suspect he waves the bottles about when he brings them upstairs.

Tessa is still working as political adviser for Kenneth Clarke. I said that Mrs Thatcher thought very highly of him though he plotted against her. She said he did nothing of the sort. He was absolutely backing her to the end. He then supported Douglas Hurd and not Major.

I said I would like to get to know him a bit because I think he has a great future and could even be Prime Minister, if Major falls down on the job. He is only a couple of years or so older than Major.

I am beginning to think that Ken Baker isn't up to all that much, judging by the way he has handled the Tote's affairs and the way he dithers and doddles over everything that comes up.

When I was talking to Cluff and he was asking me why I left the Labour Party, I said, 'I made a break with them after Hugh Gaitskell had gone and they were going on this ridiculous nationalizations deal. I was miles ahead of my time. At one point in 1963 I was advocating a Lib-Lab pact which the Liberals would have accepted. It would have curbed the Labour Party in its dotty nationalization scheme and made them more sensible. I had always been aiming for a point when in fact both sides could completely accept the private enterprise ethos and they could just argue about how much more money you may spend on education, or health, or what foreign policy, but not throw the baby out with the bathwater whenever Labour takes over in an election.'

Tuesday 9 April
Had a satisfactory meeting with Alan Hall [lawyer] and the wind farm people.

Carew Pole, the dirty dog, at the county council meeting was the main protester against the planning for our wind farm, so he played a dirty trick on me. My conversation with him obviously did no good at all; in fact it had the opposite effect.

There is trouble with Aly Aziz. He wanted to cut the royalties to 1p per three litres and keep it at that for seven years. I made him start at 1p and move over to 2p, as before, when we got to five years. So I have done Robbie a pretty good turn.

It was a day in which I did not have very much to do so I decided to go and see our new shops, fourteen of them, in the Northampton area. I was rather pleased with all the new staff we have got there and how they are getting on.

I had rung Aidan Crawley[8] and said I would call in on him if that was OK.

He is living in a house which is in the Doomsday Book, extremely ancient, built in the marvellous Northampton stone which gets harder and stronger as the years go by, not like the Cotswold stone which flakes and crumbles. He said his sitting-room was only 1780.

He is eighty-three tomorrow. He has a very charming garden and does it himself, the mowing and all the rest. He doesn't like to come to London at all now if he can avoid it, though he might come up for the cricket when the West Indies are here.

He looks after himself, cooks for himself. He wanted me to come and have lunch with him. He thinks Major is a very good egg and very courageous but he never liked Mrs Thatcher and thought she ought to go. I had arguments with him about that before.

I was very pleased to see him. I was glad he said he was quite happy there, not lonely, watches the television if he wants to, writes, reads. He finds it difficult to walk about of course, since that awful motor smash in which Virginia got killed when he was driving, though of course she was dying anyway. I had not seen before a very nice drawing by her of Augustus John. He said it was at Chester Square but probably not in a prominent position.

---

8. (1908–93); politician, journalist, writer; Labour MP and minister, 1945–51; Conservative MP, 1962–7; chairman, London Weekend Television, 1967–71; president, MCC, 1973; m (1945) Virginia Cowles, journalist, who died in a motor accident in 1983; see Vol. 1, p. 622 for the death of his two sons in an aeroplane accident in 1988.

Of course poor old Aidan has had a very tragic life, with his two sons being killed in an aeroplane accident.

Aidan was very proud of them. They were so good-looking. Now he has only his daughter Harriet.

Thursday 11 April

Margaret said she had a fascinating time in America.

The Plaza Hotel was only a third full. That is the state tourism has got into. I told her I used to go there when Beaverbrook had a flat at the top of it in 1952. His mistress's panties were hanging in the bathroom but I didn't tell her that, nor of Beaverbrook's embarrassment when I went to pee and saw them.

Saturday 13 April

Just before I left for Ascot Norman Lamont telephoned in a great state. He had found that the *News of the World* are running a story about him. The suggestion is that he has made £15,000 a year by letting his house to some tenants, furnished. There is a clause which says he can get his house back when he requires it, which is perfectly normal and after all, they may lose the election or he may lose his job as Chancellor, etc.

We discussed whether I should ring Patsy Chapman but we thought on the whole to leave it alone. I said, 'If it is anything outrageous, I will answer it in the *News of the World* next week anyway.' He said it is getting absolutely impossible the way the press chase every Minister in the government. The other day one of his Ministerial colleagues had his house visited by a press man and when his wife opened the door he said, 'Oh, we didn't know you were here. We thought you'd left your husband.'

He, Norman, had been told that they had a picture of him going into a brothel but he thought they may have got him confused with Lord Gowrie.

On getting back [from Ascot], I hadn't been in long when Norman rang again. He said, 'It is very serious. The story apparently is on the front page of tomorrow's *News of the World* and it says that I have let my house to a porn queen.' I said, 'Have you?' He said, 'I have not the slightest idea. I have never met the tenant. We had references from the solicitors and the agents and the Abbey National Building Society and he was held to be very respectable. In the story it is going to be alleged that the woman told Rosemary [Mrs Lamont] that she was a therapist.' I said, 'What does that mean? It doesn't sound very desperate.'

I said, 'Get them to ring at once the legal department, the lawyer on duty at the *News of the World*, the libel lawyer, and say that if there is the slightest suggestion that you have done anything improper or that you knew that the person the house was being let to was an undesirable character and didn't care because you wanted the money etc., you will bring a hefty action against them for libel. And don't forget that if you got £100,000 from them, owing to the beneficence of Chancellors of the Exchequer, you pay no income tax or tax of any sort on damages for libel.'

He was still very upset and kept on saying, 'It is terrible, I can't get on with my work and I worry about it. I have got all these meetings and so forth to go to.'

During the week I was thinking about Graham Greene and the fact that nowhere in the obituaries and the very full write-ups of his love life was mentioned Catherine Walston, Harry Walston's wife.[9] She was a Roman Catholic and kept a resident priest in their Queen Anne house near Cambridge with a huge, three thousand acre, very profitable estate attached. When Graham Greene came to stay, which was often, they would make love and then go to the priest, get absolution and start all over again, having promised they wouldn't sin in that manner further.

Sunday 14 April
I got up early and examined the *News of the World*. There is a terrific splash on the front page with a picture of this repulsive looking woman who is the tart. She was shown with whips and all the rest. She had offered a *News of the World* reporter her services, anything he liked, bondage, she tied up, he tied up. He had gone round to see her and as usual 'made his excuses and left', having paid for the entertainment which he said he declined.

It was fortunate I had told Norman to get a lawyer to ring the libel

---

9. Catherine, née Crompton (1916–78), an American though her father was English, m (1935) Harry Walston (1912–91, life peer 1961, Labour minister in House of Lords, joined the SDP in 1981). Her long affair with the novelist was described, after WW made this entry in his journal, in Vol. 2, published 1994, of Norman Sherry's *The Life of Graham Greene* and Michael Shelden's 1994 *Graham Greene: The Man Within*.

Conrad Black, chairman of the
Telegraph newspapers.

Robin Day, when presenter of
Question Time.

Bernard Levin, journalist and author.

Brian Walden, former Labour MP,
television presenter and journalist.

A. N. Wilson, author.

Anouska Hempel (Lady Weinberg).

Bruce Montague, who played the MP Philip in Wyatt's play *The Division Belle* at Margate in 1989.

Caroline Blakiston, who played Philip's wife Victoria in Wyatt's play, seen here in Channel 4's comedy, *Brass*.

Leonard and Ruth Wolfson.

The Duke and Duchess of Marlborough.

Left: Lady (Serena) Rothschild.

Below left: Sir Peregrine Worsthorne with his wife Lucinda Lambton, after he was knighted by the Queen at Buckingham Palace in 1991.

Below right: Sir Charles Powell, former private secretary to Margaret Thatcher, and his wife Carla after he received his knighthood on the same day.

Opposite: Woodrow Wyatt shows Margaret Thatcher the Tote Control Room during her visit to Newbury in 1990.

Opposite below: The Queen Mother at Ascot in July, 1990.

Left: 'Stoker' Hartington, Senior
Steward of the Jockey Club.

Below: Wyatt entertains Douglas
Hurd (*right*) and Kenneth Baker (*left*)
at the 1991 Tote Luncheon.

Right: Pyrrhic Dance, the horse in
which Woodrow Wyatt had a share.

Below right: The Marx Memorial
Library in Clerkenwell.

Bonython in Cornwall, the house of Woodrow Wyatt's brother Major Robert Lyle and his nephew Robert Lyle.

lawyer at the *News of the World*. He used Carter Ruck, the famous, expensive libel lawyer. The story began with the *News of the World* saying there is no suggestion of any kind that Norman Lamont knowingly let the house to people who were going to use it in this manner and he had no idea who they were and what they would get up to.

There was a repeat of the story on the front page of the *Sunday Times*, oddly enough. They also emphasized that Norman knew nothing whatever about it.

When I spoke to Norman I said, 'That's come out very well. You look like the victim, innocent of anything. Calm down.'

I told him that I wanted to keep myself in reserve in case anything awful happened that we would have to get Rupert to deal with. He said, 'Do you think there is any likelihood of that?' in a nervous voice. I said, 'None at all. I have heard nothing whatever for ages.'

I think he feels he has had a narrow squeak because of his own curious behaviour, getting the black eyes publicized very heavily, when he had a fight with Olga Polizzi's friend outside her house.[10]

Monday 15 April
Talked to Andrew Turnbull, Major's Private Secretary, the chief one these days.

I said would he please tell Major that it is very important to keep some element of the accountability of the community charge left in, whatever final suggestions are made.

Turnbull was very forthcoming and said that what they are proposing is a banded property tax on the value of the house in which you live plus the two head counts for a flat rate tax with two people assumed to be living in the house, and you got one payment back if there was only one person living in the house. I said, 'That's not really accountability.' He said, 'No, but can you think of how we could attach accountability to it? It is very difficult.'

I had a message from Margaret saying that as I was seeing her tonight and it was really only journalists coming to lunch on Wednesday, and I can see her any time I like and I don't count as a journalist, and they were overbooked anyway, would I mind not coming to lunch? I said I was delighted not to.

Norman is now worried that he can't accept any rent because he would be living on immoral earnings. I said, 'Surely your solicitors can

---

10. See Vol. 1, p. 18.

deal with that. Put it into escrow until the matter is sorted out.' He said they are worried now that they can't get these people out.

I arrived at Julian Amery's and found that President Iliescu of Romania was already there; so were his Foreign Minister and the Romanian Ambassador in London, who acted as interpreter.

Margaret then sailed in looking rather attractive with a lovely diamond brooch and green dress. She was full of vim and cheerfulness and took over the conversation pretty well.

Robert Cranborne[11] said he had just come back from Moscow where he had been talking to all the malcontents who wanted to get rid of Gorbachev. Margaret was shocked and said, 'Who would they put in his place?' He said, 'There are plenty of people there who can be put in his place.'

Before we went down Julian was earnestly telling me that Margaret must leave the Commons.

I said, 'I am so glad you are giving her that advice.' I had been told quite differently by Norman Lamont that he was egging her on to stay in the Commons and make a bloody nuisance of herself to John Major.

Iliescu made quite a good defence of what was going on in Romania. He defined it as really democratic though he admitted that the opposition parties weren't able to get on to the television. I questioned him closely about the anti-Hungarian attacks by Romanians in Transylvania. He said they were very beastly to the Romanians when they were top dog. I said, 'I dare say but they never stopped them teaching their own language in schools as your predecessor, Ceauşescu, did.'

Margaret held forth at great length about how awful it was that we had not gone on to depose Saddam Hussein.

She made it clear that she did not think Major had been doing very well.

Later Robert said, 'How can she say these things? They will go straight back to Bucharest and they will be used against Major and Bush.' I said, 'No, I don't think so. They are not very important.'

When we discussed the Kurds and the difficulty of finding self-governing territories for them on a contiguous basis after they had been divided up among other nations with our help and the French help at the end of the 1914–18 war, she said, 'The British are always at their worst when giving away other people's territories.' I thought

---

11. Viscount Cranborne; Conservative MP, 1979–87; Leader of the House of Lords, 1994–7; shadow Leader, House of Lords, 1997–8.

that was a very good remark, the best of the evening, and so did Robert.

I fear that I began to like Mr Iliescu. He had some charm. He is short, swarthy, with a lively, roundish face. Very much on the ball.

When Margaret had gone Robert said he was surprised how friendly she had been. I said, 'Yes, and you were always beastly to her.' He said, 'No I wasn't.' I said, 'Of course you were. When you went to have dinner at their flat at Number 10 and she started opening tins you said, "Why can't you open a tin of caviar? I am sure Denis would like it." You were sneering at her and made her feel that you were very grand and she shouldn't be cooking now she was Prime Minister as that wasn't the way a Prime Minister should live, implying that the great Salisbury, your ancestor, would never have lived like that.' Robert was rather shamefaced and said, 'I suppose you are right.'

Had a friendly letter from John Major this morning in reply to my one suggesting he goes for an election in early June. I had another one marked heavily 'in confidence' saying he was going to keep in mind for the appropriate moment offering a peerage to Conrad Black.

Tuesday 16 April
Dinner at 19 Cavendish Avenue for Douglas Hurd (the Foreign Secretary) and Judy, Micky and Linda Suffolk, Max Hastings and his wife Patricia, Henry and Tessa Keswick, Lord Weidenfeld, Petronella and us.

They were offered with the pudding what Micky always calls a pudding wine, a sweet white wine. This was Graves Royal 1947. That, too, was delicious and quite a lot of it was drunk, even by me, with the lemon soufflé. Then followed, only basically for Micky, the remains of a 1906 Tokay which had been specially bottled from the Hapsburg vineyard in Hungary and put in the cellars, and labelled as such, of the Hapsburgs in Vienna. It was miraculous how well it tasted, as though it had been born yesterday.

Douglas thanked me for my note about David Owen and the possibility of his being Governor of Hong Kong.

I said, 'Of course he would want to make sure of his remit.' He said, 'I know. He might want to be too independent, "a loose cannon".'

Wednesday 17 April
Meeting at the Home Office with Ken Baker to talk about Tote affairs.

He is not going to announce anything on the Tote's future until the next session. We agreed for various reasons that privatization was off.

I told him I wanted Tote Bookmakers to be able to bet like everybody else on non-sporting events. He said, 'Would that require legislation?' I said, 'No, only an affirmative resolution,' and Rawsthorne, the civil servant now responsible for racing, who was sitting there, agreed.

After a while he asked the two officials to go and we settled down to a private chat. He reiterated that I was absolutely in control of the Tote without any possibility or expectation of interference from the government or the Home Office. He also didn't like this business of the 'colleagues', as he called them, interfering with Tote affairs.

The more I talked to Ken the more I felt he is really a very good egg. He remains totally loyal to Margaret and what she tried to do, while being totally loyal to his party and doing everything he can to make sure they will win.

I was also pleased that the new man who has taken Richard Fries' place seemed much more reliable, intelligent and streetwise than the silly Fries who was always against the Tote and me.

Thursday 18 April

Spoke to Margaret.

I said, 'Have you made up your mind what you are going to do?' She said, 'No. And I am certainly not going to tell *them*. I keep saying I will wait until after the May elections before I make up my mind whether I am going to stand at Finchley [her parliamentary constituency] or not.'

She then said, 'I am the only woman in the country who hasn't got freedom of speech, except for privately among friends. They all complain if I make any comment at all.'

Duke Hussey has been reappointed for five years as Chairman of the BBC. At dinner on Tuesday, when somebody asked Douglas about the BBC and I said they were still very biased, Douglas was rather tight-lipped about it. It evidently was he who persuaded Major to reappoint him. This is a mistake. He has been far too wet and weak the whole time. Margaret would not have done that.

Listened to the entire debate on the committee stage of the Criminal Justice Bill about whether mandatory life sentences for murder should be changed to the discretion of the judge.

During the debate, beside me on the Conservative front row reserved for great government dignitaries of the past, side by side were sitting

Boyd-Carpenter and Quintin Hogg [Lord Hailsham]. They were fiercely disagreeing. I said to them 'There's a division among the parents-in-law,' and they laughed, the reason being that Sarah Hogg is John Boyd-Carpenter's daughter, married to the young Hogg, Quintin's son who is now Minister of State in the Foreign Office.

They are not very rich, the two fathers, and their clothes sometimes betray it. Quintin Hogg's left boot, which he wears well over his ankles, possibly because he had an injury once, with the shoelaces going up all the way, had a great crack over the toecap and you could see his sock right the way round under the boot. John Boyd-Carpenter's shoes also looked fearfully battered though there were no actual holes in them.

Friday 19 April
To the Marx Memorial Library. I am getting rather fond of that place. In the audience for the unveiling of Jack's mural were a number of ancient dedicated Communists, 'old believers'. The librarian is a pleasant, plump lady, around fortyish I would say. She had put on a nice pinkish patterned dress and had done herself up to be as smart as she could but she is not a sophisticated person. I like her.

I said, 'I know this is a very impertinent question but are you a Communist yourself?' She said, 'Yes I am.' I said, 'Good gracious. A nice girl like you? What sort of a Communist? A Ken Gill sort?'[12] She said, 'I am more inclined to his version.' That means she is a dedicated, almost Stalinist, believer.

The three daughters of Jack were there.[13] Moorea was looking rather older and extraordinarily more like an Italian, taking after her mother, every day.

She looks very little like her father, whereas Harriet, now about forty, who lives rather a curious life with somebody in Oxford, and who is the widow of Charles Shackleton, Eddie's son, has a tiny-featured face, prettyish. She is fair. She looks very like Jack. Selina, on the other hand, doesn't look much like Jack but like Margaret [Lane], her mother, when younger, plump but merry and friendly.

Moorea was extremely friendly and chatted about Pericles.

---

12. General Secretary, Manufacturing, Science, Finance Union, 1989–92; president, TUC, 1985–6; chairman, *Morning Star*, from 1984.
13. Moorea (m 1 (1957–66) Woodrow Wyatt; m 2 (1967) Brinsley Black), Hunting-don's daughter by his first wife, Cristina, née Casati; Harriet and Selina, daughters by his second wife, Margaret Lane, the writer.

Saturday 20 April

Norman rings. Had I seen the cartoon of him in the *Sun*? I said, 'No.'
He said, 'It's terrible. It shows me naked on a table being whipped by
this girl who has got into my house as a tenant.' He thinks it is
absolutely libellous and what should he do. He was consulting his
lawyers, the Carter Ruck firm.

I rang Rupert and mentioned it to him. He said, 'He will have to
be very careful how he settles the proceedings against the *Sun*. They
will think he has something to hide and go on digging.' He had seen
the cartoon and thought it was just a silly joke; in fact he thought it
was mildly funny.

Rupert was far more interested in what was going on in the country.
He thinks Norman is not a good Chancellor because he has put two
and a half per cent on VAT which he says is a blow to retailers and
will stop people buying.

Sometimes I have slight tinges of disloyalty to Margaret and think
she behaves a little bit as she first did when I knew her originally in
Parliament eleven years ago, being rather bossy and aggressive. She is
complaining to everybody, 'I am gagged.'

If she had been more polite to people like Geoffrey Howe, and even
despite the poll tax, she would have kept her job. But there is something
magnificent about her courage and her galvanizing energy, making
them all do things they didn't want to, the privatization of nationalized
industries and the reform of the trade unions and taxes, and how she
changed the whole attitude of the nation to make it prosper and
important in the world again.

But she can be petty and is unfair, I think, to Major. I have been
having some not exactly spats but arguments with her, trying to persuade her to be more supportive of him. I dare say Elizabeth I was like
that. When you get to know these domineering, remarkable women at
close quarters, and are involved in their courts, really they are all the
same, having great bursts of generosity and kindness and consideration
and understanding but when anything that even hints of disloyalty or
what they suspect as disloyalty [arises], they are prone to listening to
suggestions that someone has been disloyal, though the imparter of
that information or misinformation just wants to do So-and-so down.
Capriciousness is the mark of these genius women.

Sunday 21 April

Margaret: had I read the attack on the front page of the *Sunday Times*? I said I had glanced at it, 'Something to do with Mark, wasn't it? But I have read all that stuff before.' She said, 'But it was terrible. It is bad enough when they attack me but now they are attacking my family and saying terrible things – that he is upsetting all my friends, interfering and spoiling the book. How can Rupert do this to me?'

She talked very freely of the lunch she gave [for selected journalists], in which Irwin Stelzer was included. I said, 'How did he come to be there?' She said, 'I heard he was a lively person.' I said, 'I have known him for years. He is very intelligent and a great fan of yours.'

I don't know what kind of impression he made but he flew over specially from America just to go to that lunch.

I told Rupert what she had said about the attack on Mark and he said, 'It's what all her friends are saying and they gave all this information to the *Sunday Times*.' I said, 'It's a bit old hat.' He said, 'It may be but it is true and none of her friends dare tell her what a dreadful mess Mark is making of her affairs.' I said, 'I certainly don't dare tell her. There's no mileage in it. She would just get angry and I would lose contact with her altogether. She dotes on him.'

After a bit I said, 'Do you think you might ring her up, if you are going to be here until tomorrow evening?' He said, 'I was just thinking about it. Perhaps I could but I will have to prepare very carefully what I say to her.' I said, 'Yes, and rehearse it in front of the mirror.' He laughed.

I also told Rupert the state that Norman was in, anxious about these cartoons.

The trouble is newspapers will bring anybody down just for the hell of it these days, however important they may be for the country and however good a job they are doing. They think it shows their power, titillates their readers and helps to sell their newspapers.

Wednesday 24 April

Spoke to Andrew Turnbull, John Major's Private Secretary, and suggested the Prime Minister should see Rupert when he is next in England on 7–8 May.

I said I wondered whether they couldn't be a bit gentler with Margaret and consult her a bit more.

Andrew Turnbull said that on the alteration of the community charge to a council tax, she was informed yesterday. Portillo, number

two Minister in the Department of the Environment, went to talk to
her about it. He said she was incandescent but at least they did
tell her about it in advance.

Friday 26 April
Had been dreading ringing Margaret. I knew she would denounce the
new council tax, wondering what I would be saying about it in
the *News of the World*.

I was right. When I spoke to her at half past eight in the morning
she was in full flight on the council tax. Four million would be exempt
so the accountability would be gone. Four million would be free to
vote Labour, which they will do as they did before in local elections.
The valuation of houses is far too complicated, 'many of our own
people will be hit'. Rows over the bands because many will be indignant
with those just alongside when their properties are valued higher. There
will be many more complaints than before. It is much less fair now
than the community charge.

She then banged on that the most important subject for the general
election would be Europe as well as the economy, but Europe in
particular: 'On Europe they'll sell us down the river.' When I demurred
she said, 'Yes, you'll see.'

She still hasn't made up her mind about going to the Lords or
staying in the Commons.

I feel so sad for her. She really has nothing to do. She is not getting
on with that book because she really does not know how to and that
boy, Mark, has fouled everything up with people who might help her
write it and publishers and all the rest of it. Michael Richardson of N.
M. Rothschild says to everyone that they really haven't got any money.
But I find that hard to believe, that Denis didn't really make any
money at business, or very little.

Saturday 27 April
To Sandown.

At lunch Queen Elizabeth [the Queen Mother] was opposite me.

She feels very deeply for Margaret and fully appreciates the wonderful things she did for the country.

When I told Queen Elizabeth that the headline for my piece about
Prince Charles' speech, which was focusing on Shakespeare, was 'Prince
Charles Ain't Half Bard' she trilled with delight. I said it was typical
News of the World.

I told her that all was made up between myself and Stoker Hartington and his man, Christopher Haines. They had been to lunch with me and we were now joining in sensible things which could actually be followed through. She was very pleased.

I said that even Mark Zetland is improving now and beginning to understand more what it is all about.

He was there at the lunch.

He referred to himself as Zany Zetland. I said, 'How did you know that I had dubbed you Zany Zetland?' He said he had been told but he wasn't in the least put out. He said he was going to dub me 'Wily Woodrow', which sounds more friendly than antagonistic.

There is much talk these days about Petronella's profiles and articles. She has been doing some excellent profiles in a new slot arranged for her in 'Peterborough' and she has her own artist to draw the pictures of the victims. They are extraordinarily good though her style has not yet fully matured. The one on Nicholas Soames was much liked by Evelyn, making a guy of him. She has an amazing grasp of politics in general – her Lucian Freud profile was highly amusing though it infuriated Bindy Lambton.

Monday 29 April
Set out [for Hexham Racecourse] in the driving rain from Putney with Robbie [chauffeur].

Arrived at Hadrian's Wall a little after four.

I had never seen it before and was determined to see this miraculous part of my history before I died.

We trudged the half mile up and down hills and slippery walks to Housesteads Roman Fort.

One can only marvel at these extraordinary Romans who managed to create comfort and elegance while carrying out their duties – that is of course for the commanders though the auxiliaries didn't do badly, as witness their running water latrines and the reasonable-sized barracks.

At Hexham I was the guest of honour, never having been to this racecourse before. It is spectacularly beautiful, even in the mist and rain, with magnificent views across the hills.

Despite or because of my being the honoured guest they belaboured me with requests for money to help them build the new part of the new stand and to sponsor the longest steeplechase in the country, a four mile race. And despite my being told there would be dinner, all I got was a few anchovy eggs, not very agreeable, and all there was to drink was some nasty-looking wine or whisky. So I had a large whisky and ginger ale and felt a bit warmer.

Tuesday 30 April
Board meeting at Wigan. It went surprisingly well. Peter Winfield and David Swaythling now seem in full retreat. At the next meeting David Sieff will be there. He was appointed from May 1st. He has been busy firing goodness knows how many people at M&S headquarters in Baker Street. This set up some alarm among the girls and staff at Wigan, wondering whether he had been brought in to do the same at Wigan.

Thursday 2 May

A great garden party in St James's Square to celebrate the hundred and fiftieth birthday of the London Library founded by Thomas Carlisle. He was irritated at having to wait for books in the Reading Room at the British Museum.

Ken Baker was there, so was Norman Lamont. We all chatted a bit. Norman whispered to me that he hoped his troubles with the *News of the World* were over but he was not sure. The maid taken on by the vicious perverts and sex-providing couple, a Brazilian, had been deported that afternoon, with the *News of the World* paying her fare.

It was bitterly cold. Queen Elizabeth the Queen Mother trooped around the tents – at least we had some cover. I did not realize she was coming by in the tent we were in until I saw Martin Gilliat [her private secretary]. He is very tall and she is very small. She wore no hat and her hair looked rather thin. She looks better with a hat on. She wore a very flimsy, chiffony dress and she had put on her shoulders what looked like an old horse rug but I assume it must have been superior to that. When she saw me she smiled with great pleasure and came over to me. 'You have a very restrained tie on today,' she remarked. 'Yes, I'm in London, Ma'am.'

When I was talking to Margaret, Sir Terence Heiser, Permanent Secretary to the Department of the Environment, came in. She turned away from him and said, 'I am not speaking to you.' She meant because of the way they had mucked up her community charge. She then proceeded to talk to him and argue with him for the next fifteen minutes.

The civil servants and Ministers are still terrified of her and talk to her as though she were still the Prime Minister.

I had not been back long when Norman Lamont was ringing again saying that the *News of the World* were going to do a big thing again about the people in his house and the Brazilian girl. He thought that the *News of the World* were linking themselves with criminals and this was terrible. He was going to see if they couldn't be sued and prosecuted and he was going to talk to the Secretary to the Cabinet in the morning. I said, 'Do try and take it more lightly.'

He said, 'What are they trying to do to me? Are they trying to get me to resign? I am fed up with it all and if that is what they want, I'll leave the government.' I said, 'You can't do that. You've got to think of your duty to your country and to John Major. You're a good Chancellor of the Exchequer and you're doing well. So calm down. But I will try and get Rupert,' which I did desperately but I found out he was in Russia.

Norman said the *News of the World* sent a minder down with this Brazilian girl. She was saying she had a lot of stuff she could reveal which would discredit him and so on but he couldn't think what on earth it could be.

Friday 3 May

Before finishing off my article, which I had nearly completed the day before because of Bob's ninetieth birthday lunch at the Berkeley Hotel, I thought I would ring Patsy Chapman.

She said, 'He has got to get them [the tenants] out.' I said, 'Yes but it is so difficult to get the evidence. You know what courts are like.' She said, 'Our solicitors have offered to hand over all the evidence we've got to help him so that his solicitors can build up their case strongly.'

I reported this to Norman and he said the solicitors of the other side had offered to hand over the evidence but only on condition that he didn't sue them for libel. I said, 'So far they haven't libelled you so why can't you say that if they will let you have the evidence, you won't sue them for libel over anything they have said so far.'

I had to be very careful how I talked to Patsy in case she thought I was using my position to exert influence on the *News of the World*'s freedom of action. But she did warm and get kinder as I talked.

Then it was off to the Berkeley Hotel.

The place was stiff with old England captains, Test players and people like E. W. Swanton, the noted writer on cricket. Tim Rice[1] was the organizer and he paid for some of the guests to come at £100 a time. It was under the auspices of the Lord's Taverners and Bob was made an honorary member for life of the Lord's Taverners.

I made a little speech about Bob.

---

1. His lyrics for musicals include *Cricket*, 1986.

I recounted how I lived in his reflected glory very successfully as a schoolboy. When I was twelve he was made a captain in the last Test at the Oval in 1930 against the Australians. The newspapers had roundly attacked him and the selectors for removing A. P. F. Chapman who was a bit of a drunk but a brilliant slip fielder and a brilliant batsman, when on form, in a flashy way. 'Even the *Times*', I said, 'wrote a leading article attacking Bob. When he went out to bat, to make a great partnership with Herbert Sutcliffe, the crowd felt he had been badly treated and they stood and applauded him all the way to the wicket. There were tears in his eyes which was strange for Bob. I had greatly resented the attacks made upon him, as a twelve-year-old boy, and I thought it was wonderful that the crowd did that.'

I said, 'I owe to him my ambition to become famous as he did. But I am afraid I only became infamous in many respects.'

I also said how I always admired his courage and determination, his mastery of the art of cricket, his skill and his modesty 'which is unusual in a Wyatt. I have never been accused of modesty.'

The lunch went on with speeches. Bob's was good at the beginning but he went on far too long about all the LBW [leg before wicket] rules.

Telegrams were read out. One was from Harold Larwood who lives in Australia. He is eighty-seven. He said he thought (wrongly) he might have been selected for England before Bob but Bob was certainly the oldest surviving Test captain. Another telegram came from Bradman, perhaps the greatest batsman of all times apart from Jack Hobbs, saying how much he had admired Bob as a cricketer and as a person and how difficult he was to get out. There was always relief when they got him dismissed in a Test Match. He also referred to his amazing wicket-taking capacity. Sometimes he would open the bowling for England.

There was a letter from John Major, quite a long one, very complimentary to Bob, saying how he greatly wished he had been able to come to the lunch but he had important official engagements of long standing so was unable to.

Saturday 4 May
2,000 Guineas Day.

John Howard de Walden said, 'You didn't use very much of me in that film about the Tote, only the bit where I said how good you were.'

I said, 'That was the bit I wanted you to say. We didn't have very much space for anything more.'

Kenneth Rose[2] had come by train. When I met him at the garden party for the London Library on Thursday evening, he said I had not asked him to go racing lately so I asked him to come.

He was trying to find out who this person was and who that person was, because of course he is the great snob diarist as Albany.

We had a very jolly conversation about George V whose biography, which was a great success, he wrote with quite a lot of co-operation from the Palace.

I said, 'They were helpful weren't they?' and he said, 'Yes, about almost everything, but they fussed a bit about some things.' I said, 'You mean where you say that George V stopped the Tsar, his first cousin, from coming to England when Lloyd George had arranged for the cruiser to be standing by at Leningrad and he could easily have been taken off? King George V stopped it because he was told the Tsar would be very unpopular in England. The dockers were making a very revolutionary noise and he might lose his throne.'

He said they asked for a final proof.

What came back was in her writing at the top of the pages, 'Let him publish. E.R.'

At Castle Hedingham [with the Earl and Countess of Wilton] we promptly began to play bridge before dinner. Margaret Anne Du Cane, Viscountess Stuart, had been invited specially for the purpose of making a four as John doesn't play.

She is now completely separated or divorced from her husband whose father[3] was once in love with Queen Elizabeth the Queen Mother, and by all accounts was reciprocated in this affection – this was before she was engaged to the Duke of York.

I always feel very relaxed seeing John and Diana; they are no effort and revel in amusing gossip. The food is good, so is the plentiful wine and champagne.

2. Historian; *Sunday Telegraph* diarist 'Albany' from the start of the newspaper in 1961 until 1997.
3. 1st Viscount Stuart of Findhorn (1897–1971), Secretary of State for Scotland, 1951–7; m (1923) Lady Rachel Cavendish (d 1977), daughter of the 9th Duke of Devonshire. Margaret Anne, née Du Cane, m (1979) 2nd Viscount Stuart.

Sunday 5 May

The treat I had been looking forward to. Lunch with Paul Channon, the son of Chips Channon the great diarist.

Paul told me that his father never read again the pages he had written in his diary, they were just left in manuscript, unedited, untouched, ungone over, even the elementary mistakes once they had been written. They had all been typed since his death. There were stacks of them held in a secure place, millions of words. Often he didn't write them for months at a time and sometimes for years at a time.

It is odd that this seemingly frivolous man suffered from acute snobbishness and longing to be in the abodes of ancient title. Surprisingly for America, from which he came, he should have had a perceptive eye and understanding of human nature and a willingness to be honest about himself in his diaries, never pretending he hadn't made the bloomers he did – for instance, hating the removal of Chamberlain to whom he was devoted and hating his successor, Winston, with whom he was later reconciled.

I sat next to Ingrid who used to be married to Jonathan Guinness and about whom I had said when she left him for Paul, 'She is the girl who thinks that more than one Guinness is good for you.'[4]

Paul is nervous, jumpy, a bit jittery. He has a red blotch towards the top of his right cheek nearly under his right eye. He is a jangly sort of person. As a Minister he did fairly well but made bad public relations mistakes. He was supported by Margaret, loyally. I wrote in support of him when I felt he was unfairly under attack. In the downstairs loo by the front door there was a large letter from Margaret to his constituency chairman in Southend when she couldn't come to the annual dinner. It was full of praise for Paul.

Poor Rachel Willoughby de Broke has died of cancer. I wanted to go and see her but she didn't want anyone to go and see her because she wanted to be remembered as she was before being ravaged by the disease.[5] She was a great beauty in her day and a sweet woman, kind and intelligent. But she and her husband got through a lot of money with reckless betting.

---

4. Ingrid, née Wyndham, m 1 (1951–62) Jonathan Guinness, m 2 (1963) Paul Channon, whose mother was a Guinness.

5. See Vol. 1, p. 23, for her beauty.

Monday 6 May

Rupert rang, just back from Moscow, full of his adventures.

I told him why I wanted to get hold of him in Moscow, to try and prevent the *News of the World* cutting Norman up again.

'Oh they're far too sensitive,' said Rupert. I am not sure he is right. It seems very much overdone to me.

Later that evening Norman said that they were digging away to make a connection between Norman and the two vice dealers, even saying he was at Cambridge with the man. He was at Cambridge with the man in the sense that he was in the same university at the same time but he never met him.

I told Rupert I was sure that Major would raise this with him and I wanted him not to fall foul of Major. The intervention, which I think I did rather tactfully, with Patsy Chapman has at least had some effect. Rupert either does not know what his people get up to or doesn't care. I fear it is the latter. He is still very worried about his newspapers and the drop in advertising and he is doubtless anxious to keep their circulation up.

I have never known a period in which you have to have so tough a skin to be in politics.

Wednesday 8 May

Rupert's version of his meeting with John Major is that he is paranoiac about the press. He told him not to take so much notice of it and laugh off things like Norman.

Major told Rupert that his options were almost closed on the June election. His backbenchers would think he was mad if he went for it, but he has obviously got an inclination to do so.

Rupert said that they didn't pay to get the Brazilian girl out of the country.

Rupert said, 'We only paid her £3,000 for her story and it was the police who arrested her and deported her as an illegal immigrant. It was nothing to do with us.'

Thursday 9 May

Talked to Margaret.

They are just moving their things out of Eaton Square, ready to go to Chester Square.

She was eager to know what Rupert had made of Gorbachev. I told her that he is talking about growing chaos and he thinks that America is now becoming antagonistic to them, just like in the Cold War days. She said, 'How silly of him. Why on earth would they do that? It couldn't possibly be true. It would be very much against the West's and America's interests.'

She sounded quite chirpy and said, 'God bless you,' when we had finished talking, just in her old style. I am desperately worried about her. I feel that Mark has mucked up her chance of a quick, high-priced sale for her memoirs.

To The Other Club.

Norman Tebbit is afraid that we are drifting into a federal state of Europe with a single currency and a single bank. I said, 'I don't agree.' He said, 'But Major won't say that we will never do it. It's a question of when the conditions are met.' I said, 'But they never will be met.'

I asked Tom King why on earth we were cutting our defences at the moment when we know we may be expected to deal with situations far away which we haven't forecast and when we don't know what the hell is happening in Russia.

He is fighting away as Secretary for Defence but I think he is not strong enough.

Charles Powell said to me he doesn't propose to go on with the foreign service. A new Ambassador has just been appointed to America and he doesn't want to go to Bonn, so he is going to try to make some money while the going is good.

Friday 10 May
Michael Snapes of Coral rang up. He began to speak and I said, 'You've rung up about the fact that Coral may be for sale.' He said, 'You're psychic among your many other gifts.' I said, 'I just saw it on the ticker tape.' He said, 'Would you be interested?' I said, 'It's a question of the money.' He said, 'We think we might be able to devise something.'

I think they have in mind some scheme by which maybe we can buy it gradually out of the profits or have a half share or whatever. I said to him, 'I hope this doesn't make any difference to our co-operation over developing these devices for the Coral and Tote betting shops?'[6] He said, 'No, it makes no difference at all.' It is a marvellous dream that I could get hold of Coral.

---

6. The technology to link Coral as well as Tote betting shops with the Tote pools on course.

Saturday 11 May

Arrived at about ten past four at Lucinda Lambton's funny little house for the wedding reception (in a vast tent in the garden).[7]

Paul Johnson was just finishing a speech as I arrived.

Perry Worsthorne then launched into his which I couldn't hear much of except the word 'passion'.

He made an oblique reference to his no longer editing the comment pages of the *Sunday Telegraph* and going on a sabbatical in September to write his memoirs. There had been indignation among his friends, particularly at the *Telegraph*, that they should have chosen just before his wedding to make the announcement of his 'resignation'. Charles Moore assured me that he had in fact written in his own resignation and they had been quite surprised. He would continue writing the leading articles once a week or thereabouts.

The guests were a cavalcade of my past and present.

Cynthia Judah, who was once married to Robert Kee,[8] greeted me warmly. I hadn't seen her for some years.

I had been mildly keen on Cynthia once, before she settled down with Robert Kee. Her marriage inevitably broke up. It came together again and broke up again.

Miriam Gross introduced her daughter, much the same age as Petronella. She writes music for songs but has no lyricist. I recalled Harry Parr-Davies who wrote things like 'Wish Me Luck When You Wave Me Goodbye' for Gracie Fields[9] and for whom I had written a song. It began, 'Is it still the fashion to entertain a passion which stays with you by night and by day' etc. It is still with Boosey & Hawkes but it never got off the ground though Harry thought it was rather good. Miriam was looking prettier than I had seen her for a long time, wearing a nice hat and suit. It reminded me of how she looked years ago when we used to meet with Michael Astor.

I saw A. N. Wilson lurking about, looking at me and obviously trying to make up his mind to come and talk to me but I avoided him because I didn't feel like forgiving him for his appalling behaviour when he wrote up in an article what Queen Elizabeth the Queen

---

7. In Buckinghamshire, after her marriage to Peregrine Worsthorne.
8. Writer and broadcaster; m 2 (1960–89) Cynthia, née Judah, m 3 (1990) Catherine, née Trevelyan.
9. She sang it in the 1939 film *Shipyard Sally*; Parr-Davies died in 1955.

Mother had said when he came to dinner with us and rubbished her considerably.

Tony Lambton I spotted at one end of the marquee, just after I had said to Alistair Horne that he wasn't coming because he didn't think that Perry was 'one of us' because he wore white socks. I went over and spoke to him and said I was surprised he was there.

Petronella looked very pretty. Two people said she looks like me which never pleases her. Her face is reminiscent of mine but considerably more attractive.

I put a little note in the Victorian chamber pot decorated with flowers and roses which we gave to Lucinda (she is an expert, on the television and in books, on loos), wishing them an exciting marriage and saying that the chamber pot could be used for plants or its original purpose.

I decided to look through the entire house. It has a strange hall decorated with Gothic pictures and dark wallpaper. The rooms are all tiny. One or two of them look out straight on to a lovely green hill, rather close. There were several four poster beds but too small for both the large and fat Peregrine and the even larger and fatter Lucinda to romp together in without damaging themselves or the bed. The little bathroom upstairs had a pretty old fashioned metal shield around the shower.

It is an old vicarage. I would find it pleasant.

Then it was on to the village of Turville, much closer to Oxford. We took George [Weidenfeld]. Just before we arrived Petronella wanted some cigarettes so we stopped by a pub. George said, 'Let's have a glass of cider,' so we went into the little pub. George was at once very happy because he likes anything like a café where you sit and talk to each other at a table. At about twenty past seven I said, 'We must go,' because we were first of all calling on the Quintons to be shown his library before we went over to the Hornes, just opposite, where we were having dinner.

George seemed reluctant to move. He was recounting all his adventures. He said he had very much disliked Barbara Skelton but she had been included at the last minute in a party to go to the opera. She was then married to Cyril Connolly. After the opera was over, on the way to where they were having dinner, she wanted to call in briefly to her flat to pick something up so George went with her and then she brushed against him and he seized her and kissed her. He never liked her. He only married her because she made him. It was all lust. 'From desire to divorce in only twenty-two months.'

He had been afraid she would cut him up badly in her autobiography but on the whole she had been fairly mild. I said, 'I never was able to have a conversation with her at all. I found her very metallic and strange.' He said, 'Yes but she was very attractive to many people including King Farouk when she was a secretary at the British Embassy. The British Embassy sent her back to England because they thought it was an unsatisfactory arrangement to have a secretary who was the mistress of the King at the same time.'[10]

I begin to like him very much again as I used to when I first met him in 1944.

The Quintons' house is very pretty with a wood full of bluebells, a hundred and fifty to two hundred yards away at the back. In what had been intended as stables, but never got properly converted into them, he had built himself an enormous library. He must have had five thousand books in it;[11] lots of philosophy because that is what his occupation was. He is very proud of a long shelf of P. G. Wodehouse. I said, 'Are they first editions?' He said, 'I don't think so. I don't care if they are or not. I don't mind about first editions.' I pulled out one or two. There were some early ones which were first editions, without their wrappers, but none of the noted ones were first editions.

He had a number of books by A. L. Rowse whom he admires as a writer but says is a very difficult person, always complaining that everybody is a fool and an idiot and idiots never understand. I said I had recommended him for an honour but it had been turned down by Margaret because somebody pointed out to her a book he had written about his contemporaries which was very unpleasant. Tony said, 'There's nothing in that particularly but I expect it was Isaiah Berlin who stopped it because he hates A. L. Rowse.' I said I thought not and I would now try it again. Tony thought he shouldn't be given a knighthood, that the CH might be appropriate.[12]

Before we left for the Hornes we went through the kitchen into a smallish room in which Marcelle does her sculptures. She had done

10. See note, 11 October 1989, for Barbara Skelton's relationships with Connolly and Weidenfeld. Weidenfeld's memoirs *Remembering My Good Friends* were published in 1994.
11. Twenty thousand in fact.
12. Rowse was made a Companion of Honour in 1997.

one of Margaret Thatcher which was unveiled in the week when Margaret went to Somerville.

There was one almost finished of some conductor whom I had never heard of.[13] We looked at it. George said, 'That must be the very best thing you've ever done, or certainly one of the very best. You've got him perfectly, it's wonderful.' She lapped it up and didn't think it was flattery but merely an accurate testimony to her skills as a sculptor.

The Horne house is another old vicarage and it was directly on the other side of the road from the Quintons. Again, pretty with a nice garden.

Alistair Horne also had an outdoor library but it is not as big as Tony's and more cosy. Tony's wife has a lot of money which has made life more comfortable than if they had to live on what he has earned and his pension from being the head of Trinity College, Oxford, and anything he might have acquired as head of the British Library.

Sheelin [Horne] has blue eyes and fair hair, longish.

She had an Irish father and a French mother. She is very attractive though now a trifle overblown. Previously she was married to the son of Lord Eccles whom she found unbearably pompous.

In the car George was telling us how he was going to put lots of things into his memoirs such as the wife swapping set of the 1960s.

I knew all those [people].

George said that they would have either formal dinner parties with black tie or 'come in cowboy costume'. He made it all sound very funny and certainly libellous for any survivors.

George is working away on rather good lines to get Jews reconciled to Germany. He wants to get the Germans to put money into Israel.

Sunday 12 May

Norman has become very friendly with the head of the Bundesbank, Pöhl, who thinks a single currency probably wouldn't work anyway and that the British would have no need to join it. Lamont thinks the same and that it doesn't matter if the others have one and we don't come in.

They sat at their great meeting the other day and Herr Pöhl said

---

13. The conductor was Lorin Maazel, Pittsburgh Symphony Orchestra; Marcelle Quinton had also sculpted Weidenfeld, in 1990; see the photograph in this volume of her portrait of Margaret Thatcher which is at Somerville College, Oxford, where Thatcher read Chemistry, 1943–6.

to Norman, 'There's not one Finance Minister from the European Community now sitting around this table who believes in a single currency. It is only Kohl and Mitterrand.'

I said John Major is doing well. But he ought not to talk a lot of Fabian wet-sounding rubbish about a Citizen's Charter. I can't understand what it is and I am sure that the readers of the *News of the World* won't either.

Tuesday 14 May

Went to the lunch given by David Stevens at the Savoy. Bumped into Kenneth Baker and briefly told him what was going on [about Coral], saying it is perfectly legal, doesn't require legislation. We are allowed to dispose of and acquire assets as we wish and that is all that would happen.

Dinner at Cavendish Avenue. Mr and Mrs Andrew Knight, David Metcalfe, the Ryders, Chips Keswick, Lady Annabel Goldsmith, William Shawcross and Olga Polizzi. He is her live-in lover. They hope to get married and I think they may.[14] She has had diabetes lately and looks rather thin, poor girl.

I told Annabel to give my love to Jane [Rayne], her sister. I said, 'We were all in love with her at one time.' She said she had never met anybody who wasn't.

The first time the Knights had been since the commotion when she was leaving him and was living with Foster, the architect. I think he is still around.

Andrew said that of course Lloyd George and Eden would have been in a very difficult position if the newspapers had published scandals about their lives. I said, 'This is the real difference today. Then the privileged few knew all about these scandals and kept them to themselves so it didn't matter. Now on a democratic basis the public wants to hear about them too. I am not quite sure that it matters as much as people think it does because they either take it with a pinch of salt or snarl and say, "We always knew politicians were like that anyway, just like other people." '

During the discussion about harassment by the press Andrew Knight said we were wrong about one thing, the *Sun* saying about the Prince of Wales being with his girlfriend when his wife was not well and there was a picture in the paper. Chips said, 'He was with my wife at the

---

14. They married in 1993.

time and they were both comforting a friend of theirs who had cancer. When the newspaperman came round in the middle of the bloody night with a photographer, I put him in the dustbin and said, "Now get out." I could have been sued for assault but I don't give a damn.'

They had been ringing Chips up asking what his relations with his wife were and all that kind of thing which he refused to answer. Of course Chips is very much living a different life from his wife because although in a sense they share the same house, they don't share much the same friends or go to the same places.

They didn't go till after 12.50 so by the time I got into bed it was just about one o'clock. Then I read the book by Julian Critchley[15] called *Hung Parliament* which is extremely entertaining. I am reviewing it for the *Evening Standard*.

Thursday 16 May
Lunch at the Levy Board. Ken Baker came.

He is a very smooth operator, Ken. He talks a lot while giving nothing away. His message to the racing world, boiled down, was: 'You get nothing from the government and if you need any more money you had better get it out of your own endeavours.'

Saturday 18 May
Allan Davis came at 11.30. We will call the play now *High Profiles '90*. He said, 'Don't spend too much time on rejigging it. I am not going to spend too much of mine because my time is getting increasingly valuable as I grow older and so is yours.'

He thinks Gerald Harper may still be willing to do it.

I tried to get hold of Andrew Turnbull at Number 10. It is not like the old days – he wasn't there. I then asked to speak to Major. They rang back and said he wouldn't be in until after half past ten and then they would ask him if he would like to ring me. He never did.

I wanted to tell him that he must get Lord McColl[16] into the Ministry of Health team. He is the only person capable of putting across the new hospital reforms. He argues the daylights out of Ennals in the Lords who was Labour's last Secretary for Health.

---

15. Conservative MP, 1959–64, 1970–97; knight 1995.
16. Professor of Surgery, Guy's Hospital, since 1971; PPS to the Prime Minister and Deputy Speaker, House of Lords, 1994–7; Opposition spokesman on health since 1997; life peer 1989.

John Major had gone to the cup final this afternoon. If Margaret had still been Prime Minister, I would have got a call back from her immediately because she would know it was important.

Sunday 19 May

To Bowden Park. The weather was milder but there was still a wind. Talked to Arnold at length about the Coral adventure. He was unsympathetic until I told him the advice I had been getting from Simon [his son], whereupon he began to change his tune and said, 'It might well be possible,' and talked of six and a half per cent convertibles and being very careful to get exact warranties and indemnities when you buy part of a business.

Arnold gave us some 1966 Château Figeac. It was a splendid wine, first growth of St Emilion, and the year is fine. He was fussing about when it had been opened and said it wasn't quite right but I said, 'Nonsense, it is absolutely perfect. There is not a single speck of dregs in it. It has been beautifully decanted and it is exactly as it should be.'

During lunch there was some talk about attitudes towards Jews and so on. I said, 'The greatest love of my life was Jewish, perhaps not the greatest, and also my second wife was Jewish. So I don't think you could accuse me of being anti-semitic, even subconsciously. It would be a funny way to express it.' Verushka got very annoyed because I had said that somebody was the great love of my life as she thought it was insulting to her. That happened a good fifteen years before I had even met her.

Wednesday 22 May

Up at a quarter past five to catch the aeroplane to Paris to talk to Cormier about the possible participation of the PMU in our Coral venture about which I am getting more hopeful.

We learned a great deal of value to us vis-à-vis our negotiations with Coral who own three hundred shops in Belgium which are in fact worthless to them but they would not be worthless to us.

I got six bottles of the marvellous mouthwash, Eludril, without which my teeth would entirely collapse from rotting old age.

Then it was out to dinner at 11 Downing Street with Norman Lamont.

I think it was Rosemary's first real dinner party at Number 11 where she is now the entranced châtelaine. She is thriving on it and looking very pretty.

The house itself is not as bad as I remember it but it has been much altered since the days when I spent a fair amount of time there with Stafford Cripps.[17] We had dinner at the top in their little private dining-room and private drawing-room etc.

Peter Palumbo, now Lord Palumbo, and his wife came soon after us.

He made enormous sums of money in property development and is now Chairman of the Arts Council.

Palumbo is short with a round face. He is only about fifty. He looks well fed but he is pleasant and civilized. He argued with me that it is necessary to subsidize theatres because that is where we get our great playwrights and actors from and that this is a great tourist attraction.

Norman said that he had, on my advice, told Major that they really must make use of Lord McColl.

It is a very different show from when Mrs Thatcher used to run it. I would have got straight through to her instead of taking three days to get a message through, and she would have done something about it straight away.

Ken Baker is very sympathetic to the Coral acquisition but wonders whether the bookmakers would object. I said, 'Of course they will but there is nothing they can do to stop it. Racing will be behind it.'

I told him what we had discussed with the PMU in Paris in the morning.

Norman is getting rather fat, a bit like Nigel Lawson became but not quite as bad yet. He is very cheerful. He is eating too many grand dinners and drinking too much. Such are the temptations of high office.

Roy Jenkins never lost his lean look when he was Chancellor and I don't think Denis Healey overdid the fleshpots. As for Stafford Cripps, none of them has ever reached his heights of austerity in living. That was because of his health.

I wonder sometimes whether Norman isn't anxious to delay the election till next year, not just because he thinks the economy would be better and more favourable to the Tories being elected, which I doubt, but because he fears that maybe Labour would win a June election or even an October election and his stay at the Treasury would have been extremely brief.

---

17. As a young Labour MP, WW was personal assistant to Cripps on the Cabinet Mission to India, 1946; Cripps followed Hugh Dalton as Chancellor of the Exchequer, 1947–50.

Friday 24 to Monday 27 May

Euston Station is badly arranged. The porter has to carry your luggage up the steps. There were no trolleys to be found. He had already been given £5 and he disappeared for some time. We were both getting agitated so Verushka went off to look for a trolley and I turned round slightly to talk to a policeman. As I did so, without either the policeman or myself noticing, somebody swiped my briefcase.

I hadn't even locked it with the code numbers. I lost all my credit cards, three wonderful Romeo y Julieta Churchill cigars, my monocular [eye glass], various cufflinks including the silver button ones that Petronella gave me for Christmas, and a large chunk of this manuscript, making me fearful of what would happen if it got into the wrong hands and was given to a newspaper – or even to the security people who might tell Major and Co. They would regard it as a great security risk because some of what I write in it would come under the Official Secrets Act quite easily, as well as making them very nervous talking to me. Above all there was my telephone book which I have had for forty-five years with a lot of private telephone numbers in it, the owners of which would not be best pleased to have available to a mischievous press and public.

It also had details in it of our attempts to get hold of Coral.

Holker Hall is large and comfortable.

The first bit was built a couple of hundred years or more ago on to a very old house. There was a large addition in Victorian times which is not at all bad. Hugh Cavendish[18] keeps the house open to the public and there are all kinds of entertainments in the park like archery and a motor museum.

The new gardens, double ones side by side, were made within the last four years and are very pretty. There is a waterfall, similar in appearance and manner to the one at Chatsworth but nothing like so big. Hugh Cavendish is a relation of the Cavendishes of Chatsworth.

He also owns the Cartmel racecourses a mile or so away.

Three aunts live in houses around the place on the Holker Hall estate, all provided by Hugh Cavendish who is very kind hearted.

One of the aunts, Diana, now aged eighty, was married first to Bob Boothby but it didn't last very long though she remained good friends

---

18. Chairman, Holker Estate Group, since 1971; a government whip, House of Lords, 1990–2; m (1970) Grania Caulfeild; life peer 1990.

with him until he died. She then married a good painter in 1942 who died four years later.[19]

She didn't marry again until 1971 when she married 6th Viscount Gage, father of Camilla Gage who is married to the judge, Sir Edward Cazalet.

Her parents had been very much against her knowing all these bohemian people like Cyril Connolly and Tom Driberg and Peter Quennell[20] but she had enjoyed it. It was a break from the conventional life she had been brought up with.

Also there was Hugh's sister Susan who had another little house provided by him. It directly overlooks the sands and the sea. She wrote for *Harpers & Queen*.

[After] an early marriage when she was about nineteen, later she married Quentin Crewe.[21] That lasted for some twelve years. I have often wondered how Quentin Crewe made love because he is permanently crippled in a wheelchair and has got some form of wasting disease which she said is now getting slightly worse, after being stable for a long time. They have a rather pretty daughter called Charity to prove that it could be done.

On the Saturday I went down to Haydock to give away the Tote sponsorship prize and came back in time to see the last two races at Cartmel where there was a crowd of over ten thousand, with a fun fair in the middle.

The new Earl of Huntingdon, with Robin Hood among his Christian names, was there.[22] He is the Queen's trainer.

He told me that he said to the Queen, 'You know they say I am really the King and you should be training my horses; you would

---

19. Diana, daughter of Lord Richard Cavendish (1871–1946, brother of the 9th Duke of Devonshire), m 1 (1935–7) Robert Boothby (1900–86, life peer 1958, politician remembered for his long liaison with Lady Dorothy Macmillan, wife of the Prime Minister Harold Macmillan and a Cavendish, daughter of the 9th Duke of Devonshire); m 2 (1942) the painter Campbell-Gray; m 3 (1971) 6th Baron Gage (d 1982).

20. (1905–93); writer; married five times; knight 1992.

21. (1926–98); writer and journalist; m 3 (1970–83) Susan, née Cavendish (editor, *House and Garden*, 1994).

22. William Hastings Bass, racehorse trainer, son of Priscilla Hastings (member of the Jockey Club and Tote Board) and Captain Peter Hastings Bass (d 1964); succeeded his cousin the 15th Earl (Jack) who had only daughters.

probably do it better than I do,' but she didn't think that was very funny.[23]

On Monday all seemed set fair and then half an hour before our race at Cartmel a deluge began and a storm, such as had never been seen before at that time of the year at Cartmel, came bursting over the hills.

In the tent was John Golding who had been driven out of the leadership of his union (the National Communications Union) because the *News of the World* had printed some story they had got from an enemy in his very left union about his being in a brothel. His wife was there too, Llin Golding, who took his seat as an MP. Also Bill Jordan, President of the AEU.

Llin is the daughter of Ness Edwards, once a Labour Minister. She is quite pretty but indignant at not being asked to the Annual Tote Luncheon though she is an assiduous attender at the All Party Racing Committee. I said I would do something about it.[24]

At one point the sound couldn't be heard on the internal broadcasting television at the racecourse. I said to Bill, 'Surely as an engineer you could fix it?' He said, 'I could but I am not going to because I would get into trouble with Hammond.' He's the General Secretary of the Electrician's Union.

I ate enormous breakfasts. For my third breakfast on the Bank Holiday Monday I had scrambled eggs, bacon and mushrooms to start with. I then advanced to having smoked haddock with a poached egg on top.

Tuesday 28 May
Went to the reception given by Sir Geoffrey and Lady Leigh to mark his knighthood in the Lancaster Room at the Savoy. There was a huge attendance. Lashings of champagne and food, smoked salmon ad lib plus all kinds of cold cuts.

It was paid for by his company, London Properties. I think it is crazy to celebrate a knighthood. We had met them at Dorneywood

---

23. A claim to the throne via the Plantagenet line, but WW usually argued that his son, Pericles, would be the claimant from the Huntingdon line.
24. John Golding was MP for Newcastle-under-Lyme, 1969–86, and General Secretary, National Communications Union, 1986–8; his wife Llinos won the seat in the 1986 by-election after his resignation.

when we were staying with Kenneth Baker who turned up later looking very pleased with himself and friendly.

At the party Alexander Stockton came up and said that Catherine [Amery] had died on Sunday which shook me rigid. I remember that beautiful girl from 1949, perhaps the most beautiful girl in London, full of gaiety, night-clubbing and all that kind of jolly thing. Her last years were in agony because she had drunk too much earlier and she smoked too much. One way and another she was covered with sores and had also her back broken from collapsed vertebrae.

When I got back home I rang Julian. It was Monday morning when it had happened. He had gone to be with her at nine o'clock and went to fetch her a cup of tea which she had asked for. When he came back she was dead. All the family had been there with her in the last few days. Poor girl.

I find it difficult to write to Julian because on the whole they hadn't got on very well for many years. Of course she was difficult but Julian was difficult, too. I don't know what will happen now to Julian because it was her share of the Macmillan Trust and the income from it which kept No 112 Eaton Square going. Perhaps there is an arrangement for it to continue. Julian sounded very low, as well he might, poor fellow, because they had been through a great deal together.

Wednesday 29 May

The Sanminiatellis arrived nearly an hour late last night. I wanted to see myself in the programme on television about the Marx Memorial Library and the uncovering of Jack Huntingdon's mural. So I went upstairs and had my dinner by myself, which may have seemed rude but as nobody seems to know how to use the video any more. I had to do that or miss it altogether.

It is a hell of a nuisance their being here in some ways. I can't find anything. I have to sleep in my little bedroom and take all my clothes up and look for them and shave upstairs in that squalid little bathroom, lose my toothpaste, can't find the razor. But they are very nice and they are deeply touched, according to Verushka, that she gave up her big bedroom for them with the bathroom attached and I had been inconvenienced.

Alistair Horne and his wife came to dinner, Rocco and Aliai Forte and so did Jake Radnor and his wife. She was born in Chile and spent much of her life in Argentina. Gingo spent a lot of his early life there so they had a lot to talk about. Rocco and his wife were able to talk in Italian.

I told Alistair Horne, the biographer of Macmillan, that Catherine Amery had died on Monday morning.

I said, 'She was his favourite daughter.' He said, 'No, I don't think she was. I think Sarah was. They seemed to go up and down at times.'

Friday 31 May
The funeral of Catherine Amery in St Paul's Church by Wilton Crescent. It was unbearably sad.

Alan Hare said to me mournfully, 'Another one gone.'

Later I spoke to Margaret and I told her where I had been. She hadn't known that Catherine had died last Monday and I explained how little there had been in the newspapers to tell her so. She would have gone if she had known and was rather upset I hadn't thought to tell her. She said how she had been to see Catherine the night we had dinner there with the President of Romania. She thought she looked dreadful. 'It was drink, I suppose?' she said. I said, 'Yes, it was partly the Cavendish curse.' But in the end she kept breaking her bones and when her second vertebra went, the agony was unbearable. She said, 'She must have had . . .' and she gave the name which I can't pronounce – osteoporosis.

We discussed Julian at some length. She said he had great talent and gifts as a writer. I said he had been a good Minister of State at the Foreign Office at one time and she said, 'But he was in the clouds.' I said, 'Yes he was concerned with the "great game". I several times asked Eden to make him a Minister which he did in the end but for a long time he said he wouldn't because he wrote him such extraordinary, far fetched memoranda.'

He was always wanting to plot schemes from the old empire days like taking over Albania or the Yemen. Margaret liked him a lot.

Saturday 1 June

After visiting a betting shop in Salisbury, on to [the Radnors' at] Longford Castle.

Jake has some terrible disease in his back. As a child of two or three he had to wear braces and do dreadful exercises. He has never been able to walk properly and hobbles about somewhat with a stick but very gamely.

He is a very shrewd businessman and has done magnificently with his very large estate, trout farm, quarries and new developments.

Jill, his third wife, is enchanting.

A picnic on the top of a great hill on the estate. From it you could see the Isle of Wight in one direction, just. Dorset to the right. Straight ahead is Trafalgar House, given by the nation to Lord Nelson's family.

The hill we were sitting on the top of, Jake has put into strict conservation because it has got lovely wild flowers on it. We looked for orchids, little blue ones, and found a number.

Sunday 2 June

Yesterday a plot was unearthed. Convicts, while they were in jail, had planned to raid the National Gallery and also Jake's house. Just as they were about to start the raid, their car was clamped for parking where it shouldn't have. The police became suspicious, examined the contents of the car and found a list of paintings at Longford Castle with details of their plan to raid other famous collections. They are under arrest.

Jake is very worried about the security and the insurance, as well he may be.

The Pleydell-Bouverie (Radnor) family are Huguenots and came to England about 1690. They made a lot of money from trade across the seas and that is why there is a ship on their coat of arms and a ship stands in the centre above the front of the house, carved in stone.

Tuesday 4 June

Dinner party. I got out a Château Lafite 1973, a magnum, which Jacob and Serena Rothschild gave me for my birthday eight years ago. I also gave them that delicious Pavillon Blanc. But the dinner party was a collapse.

First of all, it had been built around the Conrad Blacks because that was the date they chose and then they said they couldn't come because Mrs Black, Joanne as she calls herself now, hadn't told him that she had arranged a birthday party for her brother and his wife. They said they would come in later at 10.15 but they never did. Irwin Stelzer had been asked for the sole purpose of meeting Conrad Black and had flown over from America. Cita wasn't there though she had been expected so at the last moment we had to get Susan Crosland who very decently came. Michael Howard, the Secretary for Employment, left a message through his secretary on Monday morning to say he couldn't come because he had to make a speech on Wednesday and he had to work hard on it on Tuesday to get it right.

So all we were left with was Irwin and the Quintons and Nicholas Lloyd and his wife. It was a terrible waste of a marvellous dinner except that it was quite amusing.

I congratulated Lady Lloyd, as she now is, on how well she is doing with the *Sunday Express*, making it really lively.

The pair of them (she is professionally Eve Pollard) are the most remarkable man and wife team in Fleet Street. She has become enormously fat and she is very jolly.

Irwin said he thinks they should bring down interest rates with a big bang and so does Roy Jenkins; doing it at half a percentage point at a time is like trying to cross the Sahara Desert half an inch at the time.

Friday 7 June

Richard Evans, the running dog of the Jockey Club element who think they ought to be able to get more money out of the Tote and keep attacking us for inefficiency, used some stolen documents in his *Times* article. They were management accounts for the end of March 1991. He endeavoured to show that our turnover had gone up but our profits had gone down through mismanagement. As often happens with stolen documents, the recipient doesn't understand them fully, particularly if he is only a racing correspondent who doesn't understand finance.

The documents were stolen from the Tote and supplied to the *Times*.

Not so very many years ago the *Times* was a gentlemen's newspaper and would have returned a stolen document to the owner. Now they just call it a leak, as though they were not participating in the theft by being the receiver of stolen goods. That is a euphemism which Fowler in his *Modern English Usage* would have poured contempt on.

Saturday 8 June

Richard Evans at it again. This time he has documents from what was supposed to be a locked file in a locked cabinet at the Tote. It contained a letter from David Montagu [Lord Swaythling] in which he said how delighted he was that I had managed to get the Lloyds Merchant Bank's ridiculous report suppressed and he made very uncomplimentary remarks about the people who conducted the report.

Later in the evening Rupert rang and said how was I. I said, 'I am extremely annoyed at the *Times*' use of stolen documents.' He said, 'Ah. You're as bad as John Major. You worry about what the press says. You don't want to take any notice of them.'

I said, 'This is particularly related to trying to get me forced out of the Tote by the Select Committee on Home Affairs in the Commons – the meeting is on Monday. The standards of the *Times* have fallen. This man has been running a vendetta against me for months.'

Rupert was pretty unconcerned on the whole but I think he took some notice. I said I thought it was a bit rough that at one end of the paper I was portrayed as a respectable authority with my column and at the other end I was shown to be more or less a crook. I said, 'I feel very hurt after all the efforts I have made behind the scenes and with government to do what I can to support Sky Television and your affairs generally.' I think he took the point though he feels he can't interfere. That's what he always feels.

Later that night Andrew Knight rang.

We discussed the issue at some length and then he said he would look into it.

Monday 10 June

There was a call from William Waldegrave saying would I ring him at this time or that time. He wanted to speak to me urgently. But I couldn't possibly because I was so busy preparing the answers to the possible questions from the Select Committee. It was obviously about my article and the photograph of him they had put in the *News of the World* with the word underneath, 'Failed'. I hadn't said that. I only meant he had failed to get his hospital reforms across, not that he had failed as a Minister. But I am beginning to wonder about that too.

The meeting with the Select Committee was hilarious.

I was able to establish that Richard Evans didn't understand that they were management figures, not financial figures, and that there were development costs of £640,000 which would have shown a very big increase in profits over the year.

I was asked by the committee did I agree with the letter that David Montagu had written and I said, 'Yes, completely. I had only been restrained by my executives and my colleagues on the board from putting into our submission to the inquiry into the Tote much the same sort of language. But now it has been done for me by the *Times*.' Everybody laughed.

Ashby, this twerp, a Tory barrister from West Leicestershire,[1] then read out the letter in which it was suggested that we had prevented the Lloyds Merchant Bank people from seeing the people they wanted at the Tote. I told them it was quite untrue. They saw every single person they wanted to and we showed them the board minutes (he had raised that, too) – that was in spite of the fact that we had been reluctant because they related to the conduct of people.

But the element of truth in it was that we did for a very short time, and then we let them see the board minutes and we let them interview anybody they liked.

We had a triumph with the Select Committee. My own people were thrilled with my conduct of our case and my defence and it was quite clear that the Chairman was on our side. He came up to me at the end and said he thought it was totally irrelevant and unimportant, this argument about the Lloyds Merchant Bank report, because it was totally out of date.

Ashby asked a question about entertaining. I said it was minimal, the most expensive item was about £7,000 for the Tote Annual Lunch which 'could be counted as help to racing', and everybody laughed. Sir John Wheeler said, 'I hope you had good port there, Taylor's 1981.'

Tuesday 11 June
The press was extremely good, the *Guardian*, the *Independent* and the *Telegraph*, about my session with the committee. The only one which was really bad was of course Richard Evans in the *Times*.

---

1. David Ashby, MP, 1983–97.

I gave Patsy Chapman lunch at the House of Lords. She is forty-three. She is a jolly little girl.

I said, 'What about the morality of stealing documents?'

She said what I should do is to write to the *Times* asking them how much they paid their source for the documents they used which were the property of the Tote, with a copy to the Press Complaints Commission and a copy to the ombudsman of the *Times*.

She said, 'If they have to admit they paid, of course it is absolutely against the code.'

She doesn't like the *Times* because they are always writing lofty stuff about the *News of the World* and its methods.

I said, 'Will you be sitting on the Press Complaints Commission if the case against the *Times* is heard?' She said she would be and would take great pleasure in getting them censured, if it was appropriate, but 'don't say I said so'.

A little later in the afternoon I spoke to Alan Meale.

He said that Wheeler is very keen to go to the House of Lords. He said some of the others are of the freebie type, always going on trips abroad, and that Ashby himself is a great lover of publicity. He also likes little trips abroad.

Wednesday 12 June
Things may be hotting up a bit about our attempt to buy Coral. The trouble is that they want the bids in by July 12th. The Home Affairs Select Committee won't have reported by then so the bankers and potential investors may not be willing to promise us the cash until they hear the results of that. If the committee were to recommend the selling of Tote Bookmakers and/or Tote Credit, they could put us into difficulties. I don't think they will but I have got to try to get them to speed up their report.

Andrew Parker Bowles lives in the basement flat of Hugh Cavendish's London house.

His wife, Camilla Parker Bowles, is the one whose name was often associated with the Prince of Wales and still is.

Thursday 13 June
To 11 Downing Street for the Lamont cocktail party. Rosemary Lamont was looking very attractive in a white dress which suits her with her blonde hair and blonde complexion. She revels in it all.

Talked to George Weidenfeld. I asked if he had any suggestions for someone to come to lunch with the Queen Mother. He said, 'Yes, Andrew Roberts[2] who has written a marvellous book about Halifax.'

He wants to show me his memoirs before they go to the printers to see whether he has gone too far with comments about living people and would lose all his friendships or whether he could go a little further.

Norma Major was looking rather smart in a nice apricot coloured suit. I told her not to worry about people saying she was drab and dowdy because it simply isn't true.

Norman introduced Petronella to the Prime Minister saying, 'She often rings me up and asks me to ring back because she wants to know something.' Major said, 'Do you ring her back?' Norman said, 'Always,' at which point Major pulled out a piece of paper and carefully wrote on it, 'Chancellor too accommodating,' and showed it to them both. He really does have rather a good sense of humour.

I took Arnold [Weinstock] and Ian [Gilmour] to The Other Club. I sat opposite Peter Shore who was the chairman for the evening and on his right was John Smith. On my left was Jack Cunningham. He is shadow Leader of the House.

Norman Tebbit loves arguing with me about immigrants.

I said to Norman, 'I think they all assimilate in the end. They usually do over a period. But we don't want any more for obvious reasons.'

He said he didn't agree because some of them insist on sticking to their own culture, like the Muslims in Bradford and so forth, and they are extremely dangerous.

At which point a general conversation began with Jack Cunningham, Peter Shore and John Smith who was saying, roughly, that a Labour government wouldn't be as awful for Norman Tebbit and people like him as he thought. He flared up and said, 'No. They've been voting against the Prevention of Terrorism Act, they've been encouraging the IRA. That's why my wife is crippled for life. That's why I am in a terrible situation, had to leave active politics and earn money to be able to have attendants for her and all the things she needs. These people (leering at them) would add to my taxation not only with the fifty per cent tax but with the nine per cent on national

---

2. Historian and journalist; *The Holy Fox: A Biography of Lord Halifax* was published 1991.

insurance. I wouldn't be able to afford to keep my wife in some comfort any more. It's difficult enough as it is. I hate them. They're awful.'

Peter Shore didn't say very much (previously he had been agreeing with me about the Common Market). The others got very excited and said it was unforgivable to talk in such insulting terms to fellow members at The Other Club. 'There's nothing in the rules of the Club to forbid such arguments,' Norman retorted.

The rule actually states, as I reminded them, 'Nothing in the rules or intercourse of the Club shall interfere with the rancour or asperity of party politics.' They said he was going well beyond that, he was making personal insults to them and it was intolerable. At one point I thought John Smith was going to go and that Jack Cunningham might.

I calmed everybody down. I said, 'Oh well. It's understandable.' Then everybody said they felt very deeply for Norman and what had happened to him and his wife and perhaps he didn't realize what good will there was to him on the Labour side on that, but he still replied, 'But you've encouraged terrorism and the IRA.'

Then came up the question of new members of the Club. It had been agreed that there were far too many members from the right and we must get it balanced again. I was saying, 'If people on the left feel outnumbered so heavily they won't come here,' and the Labour people agreed with me. I said, 'I would like to have Gordon Brown and Robin Cook,'[3] at which point the Labour people said, 'We don't want Robin Cook, he's difficult and you can't rely on him.' They obviously think he's a bloody nuisance. Norman Tebbit said, 'You can't have him because he's got a beard.'

It was agreed that Tony Blair and Gordon Brown should be the two to go for, so I have sent in my form accordingly.

Later that evening I was thinking that our system, by which you only have two parties, Labour and Conservative, as real contenders, and you have Ministers in the Commons, unlike the American system where the Ministers are not party politicians in Congress, entrenches ideology. It means that the Labour Party in opposition is always having to talk about its dislike of private enterprise and make strictures upon

---

3. Robin Cook was at this time chief Opposition spokesman on health and social security; WW knew Cook because of his interest in racing – he attended the 1990 Tote Annual Lunch; until he became Foreign Secretary in 1997 Cook wrote a tipsters' column in the *Glasgow Herald*.

it whereas it wouldn't have to if their leaders didn't have to keep on side with their own party.

Friday 14 June
Apparently the company (Samuel French) who bought the publication rights of my play when it was called *The Division Belle* now want to publish it and get royalties from amateur groups to perform it. They want to do it in November or December. I have spoken to Allan Davis about it as I don't quite know what version to put in.

I went to dinner, as promised, with Raymond Blackburn[4] and his wife Tessa (who had asked me if I would do so at the wedding party for Lucinda and Peregrine Worsthorne) in a little house in Chiswick.

He has now got eight children, three by his first wife and five by this lady, Tessa Blackburn, who is a very pleasant woman and mothers him and protects him and preserved him and made something of him. Raymond said did I realize at the time that he was suffering from alcoholism. I said, 'Yes of course I did. Don't you remember, John Freeman and myself in particular were trying to stop you going into the chamber when you were drunk? You got very angry with us.'

I didn't obviously mention the fearful business when he went to prison for fraud. That was when Eddie Shackleton, in my view, let him down by giving evidence against him in court so he was struck off. But he still takes an enormous interest in the law and writes backwards and forwards to the Lord Chief Justice today and Lord Denning[5] and all the rest of it. Poor chap. He did have some little businesses which have done reasonably well and he didn't seem too poor.

Tuesday 18 June
The racing press and the *Times*, Richard Evans of course, picked up some of the nasty attacks on me and the Tote made in the Select Committee inquiry yesterday. There were queries about my pension and about my car which they hadn't dared put to me face to face.

I think we must now say we shall have to reconsider our policy of helping racing. That's because the ghastly squirt, Haines, from the

---

4. (1915–91); left-wing politician, journalist and solicitor; Labour MP, 1945–50, Independent MP, 1950–1; m 3 (1959) Tessa Hume; he published *I am an Alcoholic* in 1959.

5. (1899–1999); Master of the Rolls, 1962–82.

Jockey Club, supported by Kenneth Young,[6] who used to run Extel, both had the cheek to say the Tote was hopelessly inefficient and didn't give any real contribution to racing at all; it was only for commercial reasons when we gave sponsorship or put up buildings.

We shall have to say we are considering our sponsorship programme and instead of half a million a year we will make it in proportion to Ladbroke's with regard to their size and our size. That would bring it down to £20,000 [or] £30,000 a year, so racing would lose half a million pounds' worth of sponsorship immediately. Also, as every racecourse must provide facilities for the Tote, all we shall do is only pay the ground rent and not give them any payments on our turnover which represent over fifty per cent of our net profits.

Lunch up in Piers Bengough's room on the first day of Royal Ascot. John Wakeham[7] was there. He is very worried about the Tories being on the verge of losing the next election though they have still got a year to go. Would I put over to him or direct to the Prime Minister any ideas I have got? I said, 'Certainly. But I don't get the same kind of quick reception and understanding as I used to get from Margaret.'

He is a very nice chap, John Wakeham. I sat next to his wife at the lunch. She said he is really only leaving the Commons because he still has a lot of pain and trouble from the Brighton bomb explosion when he was badly injured and his wife was killed. This was his new wife, a very charming girl.

Wednesday 19 June
Lunch party in the Tote entertainment room at Ascot.

We had golden caviar which came via Eva Zarach who has a concession from the Chinese for this lovely caviar. It is just as good as the Russian at half the price.

The whole lunch was very good and well arranged by Verushka who does these things brilliantly.

Ken Baker came in with Mary Baker. He, too, was very gloomy about the Tory prospects.

I think Baker is friendly and I don't think he is going to do anything unpleasant to the Tote as a result of the Select Committee's report.

---

6. Deputy chairman, the Post Office, 1990–2; chairman, Girobank, 1989–90.
7. Secretary of State for Energy at this time, also responsible for development of presentation of government policies; member of Tote Board since 1997; m 2 (1985) Alison, née Ward; life peer 1992.

One day there may be this mythical supreme authority in racing which would require legislation.[8] No doubt the Tote could come under that, as it does now under the Home Office. But there could never be any interference allowed in the day-to-day running because the racing industry would simply try to milk the Tote and never allow it to develop in the long term.

During the afternoon Sir Nevil Macready,[9] Chairman of the Horse-racing Advisory Council (HAC), responsible for the joint evidence of the HAC and the Jockey Club against the Tote, came in with his wife. I gave them some champagne. Then he said perhaps it was a bit of a nerve for him to come in. I said, 'I wouldn't say that exactly but I thought your behaviour was disgraceful.'

He crept off with his tail between his legs.

Though the attendance was fifteen per cent down, the Tote's take yesterday was only five per cent down which was remarkable. So much for the nasty critics who say we don't sell properly on the courses.

On Wednesday afternoon Peter Lloyd[10] gave evidence at the Select Committee. He did us very well and said it was entirely up to us what we did about buying Coral and that it was nothing to do with the Home Office.

Thursday 20 June
The last lunch of the Royal Ascot week.

I told Sir John Sparrow, Chairman of the Levy Board, what I was thinking of doing in relation to our contribution to racing. I said we wouldn't actually carry it out but we could threaten to do it and they would get very alarmed.

Friday 21 June
Up at the crack of dawn to leave by car in the pouring rain to Wigan.

The first thing which went wrong was that Sir John Wheeler, the Chairman of the Select Committee, missed the train. The Clerk to the Committee, Paul Silk, rang from the train to tell us that. I spoke

---

8. In April 1999 the idea of a trust run by racing was rumoured to be 'a New Labour-type solution' for privatizing the Tote.

9. 3rd baronet; managing director, Mobil Oil Co., 1975–85; chairman, Crafts Council, 1984–91, Horseracing Advisory Council, 1986–93; trustee, Victoria and Albert Museum, 1985–95; m (1949) Mary, née Fergusson.

10. At this time Parliamentary Under-Secretary, Home Office; knight 1995.

to Sir John Wheeler, having tracked him down. He said he got caught up in the underground by some dislocated service and arrived at the barrier at Euston and they wouldn't let him through, though he still could have got on the train. When Alan Meale and John Greenway, the two MPs, arrived they laughed and said he is always missing trains.

The visit passed off extremely well. The 1963 Graham's port I had laid on which had been carefully decanted was drunk happily by the others. So was the Château Palmer 1976.

Saturday 22 June

At Ascot, where I had to go because we had sponsored a seventh race and Verushka presented the prize, I said to Piers Bengough, the Queen's representative, that as his representatives from the Jockey Club and the HAC said we didn't make a genuine contribution to racing, we only did it for commercial reasons (and that applied to our sponsorship, our payments to racecourses and our contributions to new buildings), the board was now going to reconsider its policy.

He was absolutely shaken.

I said, 'Maybe it won't happen but you will jolly well have to disassociate yourself from all this rubbish.' He said he hadn't really been following it. Nobody had consulted him on those statements and he is a member of the Jockey Club as well as being in charge of Ascot racecourse.

Sunday 23 June

We left for the polo in Windsor Great Park, the Guards Polo Club. It was David Montagu's great day because he is Chairman of Rothmans and they pay for it all; it goes to charity and so forth. It was excruciatingly wet and during lunch it was announced that no polo could possibly be played, about which I was very pleased and the others didn't seem to mind.

Talked to Margaret who said she felt very battered. She thought she had been misrepresented in America and had never known such a barrage of untruthfulness and falsehood being leaked out from Number 10 and everywhere else.

She said, 'They keep talking about being at the heart of Europe but we are not at the heart of Europe, we're on the edge of Europe.'

Then we discussed whether she was going to make a speech [in the House of Commons debate on Europe] on Wednesday or not.

She said, 'Don't worry, Woodrow, I would be very dignified.'

I talked to Norman after that and I said she was thinking of making a speech. He said, 'Oh my goodness.'

He said, 'It's very silly, all that talk about the ERM, because it was under her that we went into it.' I said, 'But she says she was pushed into it.' He said, 'She would never have taken that excuse from anybody else, being pushed into something they didn't want.'

Oh dear, oh dear, it's rough out there. She is being somewhat difficult at the moment. If I say so in public, I shall lose any influence I have got with her.

Monday 24 June

We have sent out our blockbuster to all the racecourses, saying that as the Jockey Club and the Horseracing Advisory Council think we don't make any non-commercial contributions to help racing, the Tote Board would review the whole policy of help to racing on July 2nd at our board meeting.

I talked to Willie Whitelaw and said I was trying to persuade Margaret not to speak on Wednesday.

I said, 'Why don't you speak to her? I think she might take some notice of you. Tell her she would come out of it very badly, which I am sure she would.'

Tuesday 25 June

Decided to ring Margaret to make a last plea that she shouldn't speak in the debate in the Commons.

She said, 'I think you're a good parliamentarian and I shall take your advice. It is quite a relief as a matter of fact because I won't have to prepare a speech. But I was only going to speak very briefly.'

I relayed that to Norman Lamont via his Private Secretary.

I said I would speak to Andrew Turnbull.

I said, 'You can let the Prime Minister know that the danger appears to have passed. I can't guarantee she won't change her mind though I don't think she will.'

Peter Carrington is appalled at the defence cuts, as I am.

He told me that when he was Foreign Secretary he had asked on how many occasions since the last war British troops had been called out to deal with an emergency and to put down trouble and on how many occasions had the trouble requiring the sending of British troops been expected. The answer was forty-two times and only two had been anticipated.

Wednesday 26 June
Had lunch with Bruce Buck at the Berkeley Hotel. He gave me the
dismaying news that Skadden Arps business is twenty per cent down
and he wants to cut my retainer fee. He suggested something like to
half, but not immediately. It will be quite a serious blow. He wants me
to try to get Skadden Arps the job of being the lawyers for the flotation
of British Coal when it happens. He also wants me to help them in
Hungary which I will do if I can.

Having told me that she wouldn't be speaking in the Commons
debate on Europe she did. I saw it all on television before we left for
Cliveden. She seemed nervous, her hands were shaking a bit to begin
with. That was because she didn't have the dispatch box to rest her
papers on and had to deal with them by hand with no physical support,
standing on the back benches. She looked magnificent in a suit which
had a jacket at the top in cherry red and a beautiful brooch. Actually
she did no harm to her reputation. On the contrary she had nearly all
the Tory MPs cheering her. She utterly discomforted the Labour
benches who had nothing to offer as an alternative to the Major policy
which she roundly supported, though she set out a set of guidelines
which might not be quite in tune with him. It was a terrific performance.

As we set out to Cliveden it was again raining. Once a year by the
dinner they give they [William Astor and family] partly reclaim their
own house which is used as a hotel.

We took Rosemary Lamont because obviously Norman couldn't go
as he had to be around the place as well as voting at the end of the
debate in the Commons.

She racketed away, gossiping her head off and describing all kinds
of things at Number 11. She was looking pretty in her white dress.
She has blossomed enormously.

Forgotten is the trouble at her house which they had let to a man
who turned out to be associated with a prostitute.

On my left sat Vivien Duffield[11] who is very friendly these days.
She says she never intends to get married to Jocelyn Stevens[12] as it

---

11. Daughter of Sir Charles Clore, chairman of the Clore Foundation since his death
    in 1978; deputy chairman, Royal Opera House Trust, since 1988.
12. Grandson of Sir Edward Hulton; former journalist and deputy chairman, Express
    Newspapers; rector and vice-provost, Royal College of Art, 1984–92; deputy
    chairman, ITC, 1991–6; chairman, English Heritage, from 1992; knight 1996.

would raise complications about the way her father's money was left to her and why should they get married? They get on very well together and they have always agreed that if ever either of them were to throw the other out, they would shove off without any complications. She is no beauty but she can have charm when she tries, which she was doing this evening.

On my right sat Rosita Marlborough. We had a very merry conversation. 'Can you get it up?' she asked. I replied, 'Would you like to find out?' We talked about being different people according to whom we spoke to.

I had wanted to go at eleven but we didn't get away till twelve. The dinner went on a long time. It was extremely good. There was Echézeaux to drink as well as very old Krug champagne beforehand.

Thursday 27 June

I was not capable of thinking straight when Nicholas Wrigley of Rothschild's came to lunch at the Tote. I was not at all dynamic. Tom Phillips is struggling a bit to produce the figures on which we must base our bid for Coral's. Nicholas Wrigley said, 'I must have these figures urgently at Rothschild's.' I said, 'That means burning some midnight oil.' Heaton, McDonnell and Phillips were rather distressed. I said, 'It has got to be done.' None of these people really work hard enough.

Went to Michael Howard's party in their little house in Walpole Street, off the King's Road.

I was astonished that Zany Zetland was there.

He said he didn't agree with what the Jockey Club and HAC representatives said about the Tote's contribution to racing being of no value. I said, 'You had better write a letter to that effect. Otherwise you will get no help from us at Redcar. You may even lose our sponsorship.'[13]

I am not sure I trust him but maybe he can be saved from the burning.

I made one person happy – Valerie Grove who writes interviews. I said to her, 'When I see one of your interviews, I start at the beginning and go right on to the end because I enjoy them so much. They are very well done.' She is the wife of the editor of the *Sunday Telegraph*.

---

13. Zetland was a director of Redcar.

She is quite good-looking in a heavyish, dark way with hair popping around her face.[14]

She said she had just been interviewing Lord Alexander who is now Chairman of the NatWest Bank. She said she was frightened of him. When I said, 'Why?' she said, 'Because he is so big.' I said, 'Did you tell him?' and she said, 'Yes. He also made a very good defence of their policy of high interest for small businesses.' I said, 'He would because he is very able as an advocate. Whether he can run a bank or not is quite another matter. Getting a verdict in favour of Jeffrey Archer in his great libel case is somewhat different from organizing a huge business in banking which has gone wrong.'[15]

Then it was off to David and Sally Metcalfe's. Once again Rosita Marlborough was there.

She said, 'Do you think you have achieved much?' I said, 'No, nothing really.' She said, 'Did you want to be Prime Minister?' I said, 'Of course. That was the reason for going into the Commons. But I joined the wrong party at the time for various reasons; otherwise I might have made it.' She said, 'Why do people want to achieve things?' I said, 'Were it not better done, as others use, / To sport with Amaryllis in the shade, / Or with the tangles of Neaera's hair? / Fame is the spur that the clear spirit doth raise / (That last infirmity of noble mind) / To scorn delights, and live laborious days.'[16]

The house is beautifully arranged. On the whole they have very rich people there, exceedingly so, mega rich.

How I get in I cannot conceive because I have no money at all and I don't think anybody thinks I've got much, apart from seeing Verushka's dresses which are clearly very expensive.

Bindy Lambton was there, wearing the most astonishing looking Victorian dress of broderie anglaise and an extraordinary headgear of white material of a flimsy kind which trailed on the ground behind her. She was obviously getting rather drunk. I said I was going home, which I intended to do, at something just past eleven. When I got downstairs I found the jolly chap who is a banker and calls himself Prince Rupert Lowenstein struggling with Bindy in the hall. She was

14. Valerie Grove, journalist; columnist, *Sunday Times* 1987–91, *Times*, since 1992; m 2 (1975) Trevor Grove, editor, *Sunday Telegraph*, 1989–92.
15. Robert Alexander QC became chairman, National Westminster Bank, in 1989; life peer 1988.
16. Milton, *Lycidas*, 1.64 ff.

sitting in a chair and had got stuck there somehow. Would I take her home? I said I was sending the car back for Verushka but with the best show of enthusiasm I could muster I said yes.

Robbie was away because his knee is swollen up and he can't walk. I had a fresh-faced driver who looks a bit like Michael Trend. We got her with great difficulty into the car. She wanted the windows open and she started being sick, or tried to be, out of the window. Then she said to me, 'I am going to die tonight. I know I won't live through the night. And you will be able to record, as people do in their diaries, that you were with me on the last night of my life before I died, very drunk.' I said, 'You are certainly very drunk but it is not the last night of your life.'

She lives just beyond the Town Hall in the King's Road in those beautiful 16th century houses.

'Will you take me in?' she asked. We went through the garden gate and I found the right hole for the key (there were two holes and I didn't know which one to use in the front door). Then I got her inside and said, 'Are you going to be all right now? Are you alone here?' She said, 'I don't want to wake anybody up now.'

'Do you want me to help you upstairs?' I asked, dreading the answer yes. Fortunately she said no, she could manage.

So that was the end of a bizarre car drive and I didn't get into bed until 1 instead of the 12 I had hoped.

Friday 28 June
Margaret announced her decision not to stand at the next election.

When I spoke to her I said I thought she had been right to make her speech in the Commons and when she followed her instincts she always was.

She said, 'I changed my mind because I felt I couldn't face myself if I didn't make the speech. I had something to say and people would have said I had flunked it – and I didn't like the idea of that.'

I said I thought she also made the right decision about not standing again.

Saturday 29 June
Julian Lewis rang. He lives opposite the Conservative Party headquarters in Finchley and works hard for them at election time.

He wants to get on a shortlist and asked if I would talk to Mrs Thatcher about it. I said, 'I certainly will at the right opportunity. She knows you believe entirely in her outlook and don't want any back-sliding.' I also said to him, 'Of course it's an advantage your being Jewish because there are a lot of Jews in Finchley,' and he thought that could be so.

In the evening Norman Lamont rang.

I said, 'Margaret did you no harm at all in the House, on the contrary she did you a lot of good. Are you pleased that she has announced she is not going to stand again after the next election?' To my surprise he said, 'No. She's needed there. There are a number of people like Chris Patten and others who are very wet and Liberal Democrat minded. She needs to be there to help stop them from breaking her achievements and not carrying them through.'

I said, 'Why didn't you say that to me before?' He said, 'Because it would have been disloyal to Major who is very relieved she's said she's going.'

I said, 'You should have told me. It's a great pity because I would have not given her the advice I did which was to leave the Commons.'

We talked a bit about the party at Cliveden which he had missed. He said, 'Were there a lot of attractive people there?' I said, 'Do you mean beautiful girls?' and he said, 'Yes.'

Norman's eye never ceases to rove. Even if he's not there, he does it in his imagination.

Tuesday 2 July
Tote Board meeting. David Sieff, I think, will be most helpful in making the savings which we must have.

In the evening there was a dinner at 19 Cavendish Avenue. Mary Rothermere arrived late, having just jetted over from America and then overslept. Despite her many silly ways and her enormous bossiness, which doesn't affect me because she's in no position to boss me, I like her very much.

I said, 'You must be a marvellous mother and very keen on children, very maternal, because you have had seven.' She said, 'Not at all. We just never got the birth control right, neither I nor my first husband. In those days it was all rather defective. You either forgot to put in a cap or didn't get it adjusted right and all the other measures were ineffective.' Though she said she did like her children, she would never have had seven intentionally.

I had planned what I thought was quite a special treat: the Pavillon Blanc 1983 (the white wine of Château Margaux) to be followed by a 1967 Château Margaux, and then two bottles of 1960 Château Margaux because that was all I had left.

Arnold Weinstock soon started complaining about the white wine and said it was corked. I said, 'You don't understand what great white wine is. You've never had it before.' Then David Montagu started saying much the same and they were sending their glasses up to me. I got rather annoyed.

Netta [Weinstock] was sitting on my left and she said, 'Would you say that to someone in their house if their wine was corked or would you just drink it and say nothing?' I said, 'I would do the latter,' but to tell the truth I might not if it was Arnold, and perhaps not if it was David Montagu because he doesn't know much about wine at all and he pretends he does and he is much more easily hurt. After a bit I did reluctantly agree to myself that it had a slightly musty taste, the first bottle, but I thought it was still very good and lovely.

Poor Andrew Knight was subjected to something of a tirade from me about the stolen documents used by Richard Evans in the *Times*. He said that the Tote was seething with discontent and Richard Evans says he can get any documents he likes from it.

I said, 'Your opinions are perfectly OK and you can say whatever you want to say, just as C. P. Scott used to say, but the facts are sacred, as he said.[1] You don't present them objectively, you don't present both sides of the case.'

He said he understood the point and that it was his fault that Richard Evans went on to racing. He had been media correspondent and he suggested he be given something else to do: he was given racing.

Saturday 6 July

To the Coral Eclipse at Sandown. Peter Sherlock, the Bass director concerned with the sale of Coral, was at my table. Mike Snapes was there, Managing Director of Coral.

I had some discussion with Peter Sherlock.

He sees the future very much going our way with big Tote pools and that is why he still wants to go on with sharing the costs with us of the device we're developing.

Of course, once we got their shops added to ours there would be huge pools all the time.

He asked me whether I thought the horseracing authority which had been recommended by the Select Committee would ever come into being. I said, 'It's most unlikely. Also they will not privatize the Tote,' and I explained the difficulties that if it were privatized, the exclusive licence to run pools on horseracing would go to the highest bidder such as Ladbroke who would skin the racing industry, once they had inserted themselves, and bugger the whole thing up.

I also had a £150 bet with Coral, which I don't have to pay tax on because I had put it on at the course, for the Tories to get the most seats at the next election. That was at 5 to 6 on. I said, 'You are giving money away,' and they laughed. 'Are you so sure?' I said, 'Yes. Major will win by about thirty to forty seats whenever the election is.'[2]

---

1. C. P. Scott (1846–1932), editor, *Manchester Guardian*, 1872–1929, said in 1926, 'Comment is free but facts are sacred.'
2. The overall Conservative majority in April 1992 was twenty-one.

Monday 8 July
The lunch with Sir John Wheeler, Chairman of the Select Committee
inquiring into the Tote. He has been Chairman of the Home Affairs
Committee for twelve years so he knows more about the operations
of the Home Office than anybody else alive.

He said he thought there would be nothing in the report which
would be likely to put off anybody in the City. The report praises the
Tote's achievements. There may be one or two little minor criticisms
but they are nothing for me to worry about.

He was very sorry he couldn't come to Wigan but he got a very
enthusiastic appraisal from the two MPs who came, plus Paul Silk who
is Secretary to the Committee.

I told him about the bottle of Taylor's port I had for him at Wigan
but that I couldn't now give it to him until after the report was
completely finished.

I said, 'I don't want any suggestion of impropriety so when your
report is out it will arrive whatever the report may say.' I said, 'It was
only meant to be a friendly little gesture, the same as had been received
by the other members of the Committee who came to Wigan when
they were presented with their Tote umbrellas.'

I rather like John Wheeler at close quarters. He is intelligent. He
would have made a good Minister.

Tuesday 9 July
Rebecca [the cook] reported that the water had ceased to flow in the
kitchen. This was true. I rang the London Water Board emergency
service and threatened them with execution, or thereabouts, if they
didn't get it on immediately. Maybe they would have to send tankers
because the Queen Mother was coming to lunch and I couldn't say to
her that owing to the incompetence of the London Water Board we
couldn't have any lunch.

It turned out there was some leak in Wellington Road and Lord's
cricket ground.

Fortunately, my threats to ring the Chairman, Sir Roy Watts, at the
London Water Board, alarmed them sufficiently to get the action
required in time.

I was still dealing with the press release for the publication of the
Tote Annual Report. This is very tricky this year.

Then I saw there were no flowers on the table. It looked bare
without them.

I went and cut some roses and we had a very pretty assembly of them in a coloured, flowery, china holder in front of the Queen Mother but not so high that it prevented her seeing and talking to the people opposite her.

The guests to entertain her were George Weidenfeld; Dr John Casey of Gonville and Caius [Cambridge] who has written an interesting book of a scholarly nature but is supposed to have a good sense of humour;[3] Andrew Roberts, the young biographer of Lord Halifax in a book called *The Holy Fox* – the Queen Mother knew Halifax well; Alistair Horne and Alan Ross.[4]

The lunch was the same as the successful one Rebecca produced for the last dinner.

Rebecca complained there was not enough to provide all the servants, the security man who comes with the Queen Mother, Mrs Racz [Verushka's mother] and everybody else with exactly the same. Verushka quite rightly said she couldn't afford it, and that doesn't happen anywhere. It certainly doesn't at Chatsworth or at Bowden or any other grand house we go to like Micky Suffolk's.

Andrew Roberts arrived far too early and he was put in the drawing-room while I resumed the pouring out of the 1961 port and the opening of the Mouton Rothschild, the white wine and so forth with José who arrived just after half past eleven. Only he can do it with me really, Manuel [Rebecca's husband] being utterly hopeless and incompetent. The table wasn't even laid properly, minus the gold-plated silver goblets, minus the glasses for the brandy and the port. As I was just getting everything ready there were still calls from the Tote about what the exact wording should be of our press release to accompany our accounts and other details.

Queen Elizabeth arrived at about four minutes past one.

Afterwards two of the men said she looks much younger in real life than she does in her pictures. They were amazed that she didn't show the slightest sign of losing her memory or grip on everything which is happening today and her total recollection of the past. I said, 'She will still be going strong when she is a hundred and I am well dead.'

3. In the notes WW sent the Queen Mother beforehand about the guests, he said *Pagan Virtue*, published in 1990, 'contains interesting thoughts on such subjects as the nature of courage and fear'.

4. Poet, cricketer, journalist; editor, *London Magazine*, since 1961; born in Calcutta, his mother was the daughter of an Indian Army officer.

I told Queen Elizabeth that I had just been finishing a book review of the Boothby book by Robert Rhodes James and thought it was very good but that Alistair Horne told me that he had finished his for the *Daily Telegraph* and thought it was rotten. We had a fierce argument. She said, 'He was a lovely man. He was a bounder but not a cad. He was very amusing.'

She enjoyed the frank discussion about his relations with Dorothy Macmillan, Churchill and all the rest of it. I said, 'The press knew all about it,' and she said, 'We all knew about it.' I said, 'But of course in those days it was different. People hadn't decided to make public all these scandals.' She said, 'Now they think of nothing but nastiness whether it's about the Prince of Wales or anybody else.' I said, 'It's because there's growing democracy and a feeling that in the old days a privileged circle only knew about these things so why shouldn't the grown-up, modern democrats know about them too.'

At one point there was quite a strong discussion about the Queen paying income tax. Queen Elizabeth was very frank about it. I said, 'I do my best to defend the Queen. I know what the real position is.' She said, 'When we bought Sandringham (George VI and she), we had to borrow the money to pay for it.'

She feels Rupert Murdoch is a Republican. I said, 'That is true up to a point, but not really. I keep him under some restraint.' She said, 'But not much.' I said, 'I do. Why do you think I am able to write in solid defence of the Queen and the monarchy in the *Times* and the *News of the World*? Nobody has ever tried to stop me doing that. I think I am a bit of an expert on the Queen's finances and the nonsense about her having this vast personal wealth. If they had it, why was the Duke of Windsor not even able to sell Fort Belvedere, had no money at all and lived at a lower standard than ex King Farouk of Egypt?' She agreed and said, 'Of course he hadn't got a penny.'

George Weidenfeld, as I hoped because I had put him on her left, got on very well with her but he didn't shine as much as usual.

Alan Ross was curiously shy. He talked about owning jumpers (horses) to her. He said two horses had collapsed on him and died and he didn't want any more for the moment. I said, 'He's a poet and a cricketer and has written beautifully about India where his mother was the daughter of a great official.' So we talked about India for a bit.

I had not realized that Queen Elizabeth had never been to India. She said how much Queen Victoria had adored India. Queen Victoria had all these Indian servants and there was a special island near Frogmore,[5] in the lake there, where the Indian servants of Queen Victoria are buried. Her husband, George VI, had four ADCs who were Maharajahs and they were splendid.

She said they would have gone to a durbah in India, her husband and herself, but it had to be cancelled because of the War.

I said, 'We understood the Indians because we had a caste system so we understood them having one, although we don't really understand our own caste system.'

She liked my cocktail pretty well, the dry martini with bitters and the curly piece of lemon. I put that in for decoration but it got in the way when she was trying to drink it out of the glass I always give it to her in. I said, 'Well let's throw it away.' She liked the white wine but what she really adored today was the Mouton Rothschild 1967. She wanted to go on drinking that and she didn't want any of the Tokay 1924 and she didn't want any of the port 1961. She asked for more claret.

We shifted people around a bit so that she got talking to everybody and then I said to her, 'Would you like to go next door or would you prefer to sit here?' She said, 'Oh I'd prefer to go next door, it's such a pretty room.' She liked to see the greenery when she looked out of the window, or so she said. 'I've never been here before in daylight.' I said, 'I'm afraid it shows how dilapidated the house is,' and she laughed.

She said she was quite busy later on today as she had to go to a Canadian Association meeting. She said, 'Do you know, although they came in first in the War and fought for us, there is no memorial to the Canadians in England?' I found that extraordinary as she did. All the other Commonwealth countries, pretty well, have one.

She said, 'I am very keen on the Commonwealth. They're all like us.' I said, 'Not quite, you know. There are a few non-white ones which have very little like us.' It is the Queen and her delight to be the Head of the Commonwealth, making them feel they still have a great reach over the chunks of the world which used to be the British Empire.

She didn't leave until a quarter past three.

At the National Gallery there was a preview of the Sainsbury Wing. At least it was supposed to be a preview but there was such a throng of people you could hardly see anything. I managed to stand back and look at the architecture leading from one room to another.

---

5. Mausoleum in the home park near Windsor Castle where Queen Victoria and Prince Albert are buried.

It is magnificent and the colour against which the pictures are shown is very well chosen. The pictures are hung so that you can really see them, which you couldn't before very well.

Leonard Wolfson and his new girlfriend were there. I asked when they were going to get married. Leonard said, 'I wouldn't say that to a journalist,' but she said, 'He's not that kind of a journalist.' Perhaps she was anxious to know the answer herself. I said, 'No. I'm just popping the question on behalf of her.'

Wednesday 10 July
Some letters have come in from the guests of yesterday.

Queen Elizabeth was particularly taken with young Andrew Roberts, as indeed I was. He is short and blond, eager and bright as a button, extremely knowledgeable, with a charming smile. Dr Casey was tall with a bald head, somewhat severe, but he managed pretty well and was not entirely humourless. Alan Ross is still good-looking, tall and slim with curly dark hair and quick movements, as befits an athlete.

Thursday 11 July
I had to be at Lime Grove by nine o'clock. This was to do some filming for the great Lime Grove programme going out on August 26th. The studios and the rabbit warren of offices are to be closed. The bit we did was about *Panorama* in the early days. I had a discussion which went very well and amusingly with Christopher Chataway[6] and Charles Wheeler[7] who was a producer at one time on *Panorama*.

At lunch time there was the Drue Heinz annual grand party with about a hundred people in her rather handsome town house in Hay's Mews.

I saw Duke Hussey who came bumbling over to me to say he was glad I had written to John Birt congratulating him on his eventually becoming Director-General of the BBC in 1993.

He said he couldn't have got John Birt into the job at all if he hadn't delayed the handover date.

The lunch was extraordinary for the hottest day of the summer, the temperature now having suddenly reached ninety after all the cold and

---

6. Olympic athlete and television journalist before he became a Conservative MP and industrialist; knight 1995.
7. Journalist and broadcaster since 1940.

the rain. The first course was smoked sea trout wrapped in melon with some nasty horseradish sauce, followed by an enormous hot game pie with quails' eggs. Naturally I splashed an egg out of my plate on to my coat and irretrievably stained it. I tried to get it off with fizzy water without success.

Just before that either my neighbour or myself had knocked over a glass of champagne which shot on to my neighbour on the left, Miki Nevill (Lady Rupert Nevill) whom I always rather like. I said, 'Don't worry it's only champagne.' She said, a trifle crossly, 'But it's made me wet.' I said, 'That's fine because it'll cool you down.' We had just been talking about sweating and she had said she hardly dare kiss anybody because she would stick to them.

The last course was a chocolate concoction with fruit in it. Grey Gowrie's wife, a nice German girl said, 'Don't eat it,' and we had a jolly talk about the right sort of food to eat.

She must be about forty-seven or forty-eight now. She has no children. Gowrie had children by a previous marriage and is now a grandfather and doesn't want any more children. I thought she was sweet and pretty with her blonde hair and blue eyes.

It must have been very wounding for her to have had all that in the newspapers about her husband going to a massage parlour. Her name is Adelheid Gräfin von der Schulenburg, a very grand aristocratic Prussian lady indeed but charming and simple.

I was talking to a dark, fifty-year-oldish lady, an American, who had been working closely on Ronald Reagan's public relations.

She asked me who the tallish, grey-haired man was a little way away. I said, 'That's Stephen Spender, a poet who is also ambidextrous between boys and girls.' The next moment he came up and pretended he had overheard what I was saying about him. Actually I had also been saying he was a very good poet but perhaps not as good as he thought he was. He said, 'Woodrow, you wicked old devil.' I said, 'I'm not as old as you and I don't think I'm as wicked.'

Then it was on to Ruth Wolfson's birthday party in Lyall Mews, Belgravia, given by her paramour, Jarvis Astaire, in his fairly splendid, rearranged and beautifully decorated house with a little courtyard. Not as grand as Drue Heinz's but not at all bad. There was a band playing in the corner and he had put a tent roof over the courtyard. There were little things to eat. He is very Labour and has been a supporter of the Labour Party for a long time. Everyone was muttering behind their hands, as they always do, that he was the only person on the lavender writing paper list which Marcia Falkender arranged for Wilson's resignation honours who didn't get the knighthood he was down for.

Quite a lot of people were there who were Leonard's friends. He would have been horrified probably. As Arnold said to me on Tuesday night: 'Leonard will never forgive you if you go to that party.' There was Ruth, an ardent anti-Socialist, frolicking away with Labour supporters, having entirely changed her views because of Jarvis Astaire.

Friday 12 July
The *Evening Standard* rang. 'We understand you hosted (ghastly word) a lunch for the Queen Mother at your home' (rather than house, of course). I said, 'I have heard nothing about it.'

Of course I had told a lie saying I knew nothing about it but what I meant was I knew nothing about it that I would repeat to the press.

I rang all who had been there. I said, 'For God's sake don't say anything about having lunch with her or anything about the lunch because I don't want a repetition of the A. N. Wilson affair.'

We all agreed that if questioned, they would say it was a private party and they had nothing to say about it, and to repeat, 'I have nothing to say about it,' again and again until the person from the press who rang up gave up.

I was much amused that Chris Patten is mad keen to get my support in my articles in the *News of the World*. I was sent a mass of stuff he had written to Gerald Kaufman[8] over Labour's ambivalence on retaining nuclear weapons.

So long as I go on writing those columns the Tory government is going to be very polite to me.

Yesterday Robert Rowlands, who conducted the interview with me at the *Panorama* programme, gave me a video in which there was a profile made about me on *Panorama* in 1965. It was when I was opposing the nationalization of steel and the Labour government had a majority of three. I looked at the video. It was ghastly. My face was fat, almost bloated. I said foolish things about agreeing with the nationalization of single products like electricity and coal. (I no longer do of course.) They showed me at Banbury with the newspapers I

8. At this time shadow Foreign Secretary.

then owned, talking boastfully about my ambition to own a national newspaper. I thought, 'How terrible, what a failure I have been. It all came to naught.'

On the other hand I think my brain might have improved over the last twenty-six years. I have certainly grown more sensible and know a great deal more than I did then and I hope I am wiser.

After initial depression at seeing this video because of what I had failed to do and my deterioration since, I began to think that perhaps the autumn of my life was not so awful.

Verushka said how much younger I looked then: 'It suited you to be fat and round-faced and now you take these pills.' One is to retard the Parkinson's syndrome (which is not the same as Parkinson's disease but slightly akin to it) and then the pain in my right eye causes endless trouble and needs drops in it all the time.

Saturday 13 July

To Lord's and the box Paul Getty provides for Bob [Wyatt] at the more important cricket matches and tests. It was the final of the Benson & Hedges Cup between Lancashire and Worcestershire.

I said to Anne [Lambton], 'Denis [Compton] used to have beautiful black hair.' He said, 'Yes, I made a lot of money out of Brylcreem and their posters.'

When Colin Cowdrey came in I congratulated him on how well he had conducted the South African affair. Last week they managed to get South Africa into the cricket fold again. He said he had a lot of help from John Major. It was quite difficult persuading all the Commonwealth countries. In the end even India came round. So did the African National Congress because so many of their own followers were upset at never being able to compete in the Olympic Games or at cricket or rugger and other sports with international teams.

It was also the week in which President Bush lifted sanctions against South Africa. Of course, these things wouldn't have happened if it hadn't been for Margaret because tough sanctions, which the others all wanted and which she held out against, would have ruined the country completely. There would have been worse fighting and internecine strife than there is at the moment – and apartheid wouldn't have been on the way out.

Sunday 14 July
Went back to Lord's.

Worcestershire won and they didn't require more than forty-one overs to do the job in. So I won my bet with Denis Compton.

It was rather unfortunate that, as the individual members of the losers and the winners were being presented with their medals, the Lancashire fast bowler Wasim Akram was booed by a section of the crowd. One or two of the elderly MCC gentlemen were very shocked and called it racist. I wasn't quite sure if it was because Akram had bowled some very nasty bouncers (he was the fast bowler against Worcestershire) but I dare say in deepest Worcestershire they do not like 'the nignogs' very much, as they would call them.

However, when D'Oliveira, the half and half, who was once prevented from going to South Africa with an English team because of apartheid, came to get his medal there was a very big cheer. There was also a good cheer for de Freitas, the half and half fast bowler who is also quite a good batsman, when he came to get his medal, a losing one for Lancashire. It would be very sad if the crowd began to be racist against coloured members of teams other than their own.[9]

Thursday 18 July
Jolly evening at The Other Club. Quintin Hogg is a sweet, dear man. He is convinced that when he dies he is going to be judged by somebody who has suffered, meaning Jesus Christ who suffered for mankind, and he is going to be judged very harshly because he has behaved so badly.

I said, 'You mean sins of pride.' He said, 'Yes, I had those too.' I said, 'All you wanted to do was be Prime Minister which is a perfectly reasonable ambition.'

Robin Day wished he hadn't ever given up *Question Time*.

I tried to encourage him and said, 'Maybe the BBC will ask you to come back again. This fellow Sissons, as everybody knows, is no good at all doing your programme.'

Roy [Jenkins] was sitting opposite me. He has sent me a proof copy of his memoirs.

He said, 'I talk about you a lot in the 1950s and when the Bevan split happened.' I said, 'You've always been a marvellous developer of your own character, a person conscious of his defects who has improved himself and decided to overcome them. I think you have

---

9. WW wrote to this effect in the *Times* of 16 July 1991.

been a tremendous example of what one can do with oneself, if one examines oneself honestly. I have always loved you.'

Suddenly I felt how good people are, Robin on my left, Roy opposite and Quintin on my right.

It seems that Margaret is now only going to get £1 million for her memoirs when I could have got three to four million if only she had listened to me. I had it all organized with Rupert and a perfectly good agent.

What a foolish girl she is. She's so besotted with that fellow Mark, her son.

Friday 19 July
Took George Gluck (the Hungarian-born, Canadian American with a Canadian wife, posted by Skadden Arps to Budapest) to see the Hungarian Ambassador.

The meeting with the Ambassador went extremely well. He offered to help him get interest from British businessmen and go to seminars where he can talk to their representatives. I have told him I will do all I can to help him. I must write to Bruce Buck to say what I am doing and try to avert the fifty per cent cut in my pay.

Trouble with Brian McDonnell. He has heard about the cuts I am making [at the Tote] and the savings achieved. He was supposed to be getting on with it but never did. He is very indignant that I was doing it while he was away. I said, 'They have got to be done. You know you promised the Select Committee there would be a £500,000 saving this year and we certainly aren't on course for anything like it. You know what David Sieff said at the Board meeting about the cuts.'

Saturday 20 July
Verushka bought a silver pepper pot for £57 to give the Archers for their silver wedding.

When we got there Mary said, 'You shouldn't have brought any gifts. We said no gifts.' I said I didn't know anything about that but we left it there and she seemed quite pleased.

There were about two hundred people there [at The Old Vicarage, Granchester]; a huge marquee had been erected.

There was a beautiful menu with a picture of Jeffrey and Mary getting married. She looked exceedingly pretty, as she still does. She has one of the most beautiful, unblemished backs I have ever seen. Her face is pretty good, too. She has dark hair. She was wearing a very lovely dress. Only a few years ago, before this trouble with the libel action over the tart he sent money to at a railway station to get her out of the country, she was rather down and depressed with Jeffrey's curious activities. But not now. She has him exactly where she wants him, under her thumb.

I was put to sit at a table with Margaret and Denis Thatcher and Cecil Parkinson and his wife, Anne, to whom I sat next. On the other side was Virginia Bell, Tim Bell's wife.

Jeffrey, with great tact, had put John Major at another table among some show business people.

Jeffrey himself sat at a different table with his wife so that neither John nor Margaret would be offended that one had been given the priority over the other.

I had spoken to Margaret on Friday.

When I said how strange the Summit was without her, she said she had been feeling it very keenly because she had arranged the Summit, what was going to happen and that Gorbachev should come to it, which he did in the end. She said the Summit didn't achieve anything and it was wrong to say the economy was improving.

Poor girl, she was very bitter.

Virginia Bottomley asked to be introduced to me. She is a junior Minister at the Department of Health. She said a great honour had been accorded to her in that the *News of the World* had asked her to write my column for one week in August. She asked me how she should do it. We sat and talked earnestly about that for a bit. She is supposed to be very pretty and she has not got a bad face. She still looks fairly young and cheerful. Apparently Tory MPs lust after her greatly but I can't think why. She has got very big feet and she is too tall. She wears flat shoes and doesn't dress particularly well but she is agreeable.

Robert Rhodes James was thrilled at my review of his book on Boothby and thought it was very generous and kind. I said, 'Although you were cross with me,' and he said, 'No, it was really with your daughter.'[10] I said, 'No, you were cross with me. You said it was a good thing that Mrs Thatcher had been got rid of and now what would I do with no one at the top to deal with. But all that doesn't make any difference to me when I review a book. I reviewed Julian Critchley's

---

10. See 13 February 1991.

book very favourably, too. I thought it was good and I only go on what I read in the book.'

Robert Rhodes James had shown the whole thing to Catherine Amery and obviously she didn't like it but agreed it was absolutely fair and true what he said about her mother [Lady Dorothy Macmillan].

Some Shakespearean actors did three scenes from Shakespeare which took a fairly long time. First was the *Romeo and Juliet* scene from the balcony, 'A rose by any other name would smell as sweet.' Next came an extract from *Henry V* and his rough wooing of the daughter of the French King.

The final extract was from *The Taming of the Shrew* when Kate has been tamed, so to speak, and makes a speech to all women saying they should obey their husbands and 'place your hands below your husband's foot', which she then proceeded to do. Mrs Thatcher did not look at all pleased, as well she might not. When that episode finished she decided to go with Denis but maybe it was not that which prompted it, just the general feeling that she was not the great figure she had been and people at the party were more interested in sucking up to John Major than they were to her.

When she had gone Mary Archer said to me it was quite relief in a way because the cabaret they were having, which is now performing at the Ambassadors Theatre, contained a jokey reference to Mrs Thatcher in one of the songs.

Mary herself sang a very good song about 'Who Wants to be a Name at Lloyd's?', based on 'Who Wants to be a Millionaire?'. She is representing a lot of the aggrieved Lloyd's members who feel they have been done out of their money by the incompetence of Lloyd's themselves.

One song in the cabaret went pretty near the knuckle when it talked about spotted backs. Mary had claimed in the court that the tart had said that Jeffrey had lots of spots on his back and she knew he hadn't any at all.

They were up on the platform together for a while and cut a great twenty-fifth anniversary cake together and danced together for the first dance. It was all rather sweet. I think basically Jeffrey Archer is a decent fellow but he lives too often beyond the bounds of probability.

After the Shakespearean interludes and the cabaret John Major came briefly up to my table and started talking to me, saying he was meeting Bob [Wyatt] at Edgbaston on Thursday. Then the party broke up fairly quickly but he had obviously come looking for me. I do rather like him and I think he's doing pretty well on the whole. But it is a fearful balancing act for me. If I praise him, she doesn't like it.

I saw Margaret's pleasure when I told her it was perfectly possible, after my talks with Patric Dickinson, the Richmond Herald, for her to be first of all made a life Baroness and at the same time made a life Countess. There was nothing to stop it happening and there was precedent for it.

We left at about a quarter to two in the morning.

When I was saying goodbye to Mary I said, 'You have always been in my heart,' and she looked at me rather sweetly and said to Verushka jokingly, 'You are very understanding about it.' Earlier Jeffrey said in quite a serious voice, when I was sitting just behind where they were standing, 'There's your boyfriend Woodrow. Go and sit with him.'

Monday 22 July

The pace on our attempt to buy Coral is hotting up.

CIN [Coal Industry Nominees], the very big venture investment people, are willing to fund us with the £70 million, on certain terms, of course. The bank are willing to bankroll us with £100 million for seven years and roll it over. The whole affair looks very good if Coral are prepared to accept our offer. I was there at Rothschild the other day when it was said, 'You never know whether they have really got anybody else interested in it or not.'

There is a lot of talk going around in the upper echelons of society about the low level friends John Major has. At the Archer party he himself chose a table consisting of people like Tim Rice, Sarah Brightman, David Frost and his wife and other people in the entertainment world or on the fringe of it. His parties at Downing Street appear to be stiff with them.

Wednesday 24 July

I rang Andrew Turnbull with instructions for the Prime Minister on how to write my column: to put in a cricket joke or so, write about his Citizen's Charter, do at least four or five subjects, don't talk down but 'speak as though he is talking to you'. I said to keep sentences short, only two to a paragraph and words of one syllable if possible.[11]

Got a pre-release copy of the report on the Tote. It is not at all bad.

---

11. Margaret Thatcher had written the column in the *News of the World* for one of the weeks WW was on holiday in August 1990.

I have made a press statement picking out the bits which say how wrong all the criticism of us had been from the HAC and the Jockey Club and thanking the Committee for recognizing our achievements; for not wanting us to have our betting shops sold, and our credit business; for encouraging our expansion in the high streets and for praising our technology and the vision we have of the future; and for pointing out we had the skills and the determination to make Tote betting far more of a rival to bookmakers' betting with our new gadgets.

Went to the press conference held by Sir John Wheeler.

He made a special little thing at the end of the press conference, saying how honoured they had been with my presence and, 'His Lordship attended nearly every meeting the committee had, on the bookmakers and on the Tote and on the Levy Board. No one can doubt his involvement and enthusiasm.' I managed to say thank you very politely. I had thought I might praise him a bit but then I didn't think it was quite suitable because it might look like a put-up job.

Richard Evans who writes for the *Times* was there. He had already told Geoffrey Webster, whom he had met at Bath, that he considered the Tote report was 'a damp squib'. What he meant was that it didn't support his attacks on me.

Thursday 25 July
Lunch at Clarence House.

Unfortunately, we couldn't have lunch in the garden under the trees.

The dining-room looked very pretty. It is not exactly a palace, Clarence House, but more like a large country house, comfortable and lived in and with its large garden, which she says is not as nice or pretty as ours (goodness knows why she says that).

You don't hear any of the noise from traffic. The windows seem to be kept pretty well shut all the time. I had noticed that before.

The drawing-room has some nice pictures in it, one by Augustus John of her and one by James Gunn.

I told Queen Elizabeth I had left for her birthday the book about Bob Boothby and one about the last Sultan of Turkey whom she met several times before the War and remembered. 'Ah, he's my librarian, you know,' she said, turning to somebody standing by her. 'He always provides me with interesting books to read.'

Before lunch Margaret Thatcher, Queen Elizabeth and I were talking together.

Queen Elizabeth was saying how awful it was that Saddam Hussein was still there. I turned to her and said, 'If this lady (pointing at Margaret) had still been there, Bush would never have given up so soon, she'd have made him go on to Baghdad, we wouldn't have left the place till Saddam Hussein had been removed.' The Queen Mother said sadly, 'I know. It was the wrong time,' meaning it was the wrong time for Margaret to have gone.

I had Margaret on my right. After she had been talking for some time to her neighbour, Nico Henderson, I said, 'Don't you love me any more? You're not talking to me.' She said, 'Oh yes, yes. We were just talking about something to do with the United Nations.'

She is not very easy to tease. She almost took it seriously. I do think she is not quite so pleased with me as usual because I do say kind words about John Major to try and soften her asperity towards what he is doing.

Talking to the Earl of Cadogan, a relation of Ian Gilmour, I said, 'Ian let Margaret down. He doesn't know it but it was only because of me that he got into the government at all. I said she ought to have him. Then he behaved very badly towards her, was speaking against her and wasn't loyal at all. I have fallen out with him. I used to be very friendly with Ian and we had lots of silly jokes but that has ceased. Caroline in a way is worse than Ian.' He said, 'Yes, the women often are.'

Margaret ate everything. She had two enormous helpings of the first thing which was a kind of salmon mousse topped with lots of shrimps and then more shrimps in a sauce to go with it. She had an enormous helping of the second course and two large helpings of the pudding. Then she started eating cheese which I didn't have. She drank quite a lot too.

Friday 26 July

I was interrupted in the middle of [doing] my article by getting a letter from the Home Secretary, passing on the information that Peter Lilley, the Secretary for Trade and Industry, is on the warpath. He's a mad ideologue who thinks if the government has anything to do with any organization, they should never be allowed to merge with or acquire anything in private enterprise because they are using government money to do it. He wants the Monopolies Commission to examine the Tote's acquisition or anything we do with Coral on the ground that it breaches competition laws.

Of course it is all absolute rubbish because we have never had any money from the government and we have got complete power to do what we are doing. The new entity combining our bookmakers and theirs, and our credit business and theirs, would be on a hands-off relationship with the Tote Board and the Tote Cash division. The new entity would get no favoured treatment from us.

I had a long talk with Graham Atkinson of the Office of Fair Trading and had to explain the whole thing to him because he is the man who has to give the advice.

I don't see how it could raise a monopoly query in the high streets because we would still have less than eleven per cent of the whole and Ladbroke and William Hill would have about twenty-five per cent and nearly twenty per cent.

I had also spoken to Ken Baker about the recommended pay increases for the board at eight and a half per cent, the same as the staff. He said it was too much and it should be six and a half per cent. I couldn't be bothered to argue with him at the time but later I rang him back and said, 'What about seven per cent?' and he accepted that.

I don't get my increase until August. I am most concerned actually to try and get it to £100,000 before I leave the job so that I can make a clean £66,000 pension on retirement and Verushka would get two-thirds of that which should be £44,000. But it isn't index-linked as it is for civil servants.

Sunday 28 July
Quite pleased with my article for the *Times* on the foolish reductions in the armed forces. Decided to send a copy to each Cabinet Minister to read on his holiday.

Monday 29 July
Wonderfully hot on arrival [in Italy]. We had a quiet dinner with Gingo and Anna Lu [Sanminiatelli]. I had to deal with telephone calls intermittently to do with the ludicrous situation created by Peter Lilley, Secretary for Industry.

Anna Lu has been bringing some beautiful things from one of the palaces in Florence.[12]

---

12. In March 1999 Princesses Anna Lucrezia (Anna Lu), Lucrezia, Cristina and Nerina Corsini and Prince Filippo Corsini were acquitted of charges of illegally disposing of about a fifth of their art collection housed in the Palazzo Corsini in Florence.

She put out the very best china for us, all museum pieces. Gingo says this is not sane because they can get broken. But she replied, 'They will probably be broken after I am dead so why not enjoy them now?'

Thursday 1 August
Arrived at Villa Safir.

John and Diana Wilton arrived. They bring the usual news of staying at the Cetinale as well as a letter from Tony [Lambton] plus some wine which he described as a present of goodwill.

Saturday 3 August
Henry and Tessa Keswick arrived. He brought me a box of Montecristo No 1 and my favourite cigars in some respect, Ramon Allones, squat and thick. They were clearly astonished by the elegant house, well equipped with bathrooms, bedrooms, big sitting-room, wonderful view over the sea and the swimming pool likewise.

Henry had three boiled eggs for breakfast every morning he was here. I said he must stop eating and drinking so much or he will blow up and have a stroke and die.

Sunday 4 August
Carla Powell had made splendid commotions to organize a boat trip for Henry Keswick. Her son works for him in Jardine Matheson's in Hong Kong.

It is a large boat with a crew, cabins etc.

At about a quarter to two hot, fresh anchovies arrived. Henry and I think this must be the lunch as we had been drinking wine. I ate seventeen of them, delicious. Then after an interval of a quarter of an hour, the table on the deck at the stern is enlarged and laid with knives and forks and plates and glasses for the real lunch which was four courses.

This day I made a first attempt to start my new play.

Monday 5 August
Great friends of the Keswicks, and particularly of Tessa, are Anna Lu's brother, successor to her father the Prince Corsini, Filippo and his wife.

He is not much like Anna Lu to look at and nowhere near so lively, as I tactfully but not very successfully pointed out to his jumping-about little wife, full of fun and jokes. I said, 'You're more like Anna Lu than your husband is,' to which the Princess replied, 'I am a cousin of hers, too.'

Friday 9 August
The Pejacsevichs arrive so we got the bridge set up. It is lovely to see them. I find them soothing except for when Mark starts being dogmatic about politics of which he has not a glimmering.

I fear that the Coral thing is off. Bass have withdrawn Coral from the sale because they said no offer was good enough. They wanted something well over £200 million and we were not prepared to go beyond £170 million. All may not be lost. Peter Sherlock is still anxious to press ahead with a joint venture in the development of the terminals in our and his betting shops to link them directly with our pools on course, particularly for jackpot and placepot and exotic bets. I think this may really come off and it will give us an outlet of eleven hundred shops, including our own and Coral's, immediately.

Saturday 10 August
The Queen Juliana party plus Prince Bernhardt, given by the Vesteys. Prince Bernhardt fastens on me for some reason. He asked me how old I am and was having a bet on it. I said, 'How old did you think?' He said, 'About seventy.' I said, 'I am seventy-three. How old are you?' He said he was eighty and his daughter, the present Queen, had given him a marvellous party for his birthday recently. She had flown in some fantastic band of musicians and so forth from Mexico. He said she is supposed to be going on a state visit to Japan but her husband won't be able to go. He is in a state of terrible melancholy and manic depressiveness and is in hospital again (that is Klaus, the German).

I suggested he ought to see Giovanni Ricci[1] who is perhaps the best neurologist in Europe. He was very interested and kept shaking my hand and said, 'Thank you very much, thank you very much.'

Monday 12 August
The Wiltons leave.

I was sorry to see them go but one bedroom was required for

---

1. Father of Aliai, Rocco Forte's wife.

the Lamont boy and his sister and another for Petronella, while the Pejacsevichs were still in the other one.

I have now written 5,924 words of the play.

I had to send a cab to fetch Norman from the airport because Verushka had fetched Petronella in the car the day before and did not want to drive backwards and forwards to Rome in the heat. It cost me three hundred thousand lire (£150 more or less). They made no offer to pay for it because of course they are very poor with only his £55,000 salary as Chancellor of the Exchequer on which tax has to be paid and with two children at fee-paying schools. He now has to dress a bit better and entertain often at their own expense when it is not government hospitality. She has a little money I think, but not much.

Norman had met Valentine Pavlov – he is the Prime Minister of the Soviet Union – and he said looked like a real thug, a Billy Bunter thug, with a horrible fat face. I said, 'You mean he looks a bit like you?' He said, 'No, much worse.'

Pavlov said to Norman the West did nothing to help Gorbachev: 'You see the man drowning and instead of throwing him a rope you send him a swimming manual instruction.' I thought that very funny. He was referring to the West saying you have to learn how to make private enterprise work before we give you any cash.

Tuesday 13 August
Took the Lamonts to the Vesteys for dinner. Lamont was much taken with Judith, Lady Bathurst, the mistress of Vestey whom he won't marry, much to her annoyance, having deserted her husband.

She is still fluffily pretty and engaging in a kittenish way, small and slight. I wasn't surprised that Norman, always on the alert for some feminine attraction, was taken by her.

Wednesday 14 August
A new figure has come into our lives called Roberto Scio.

He owns the Pellicano, the best hotel in Porto Ercole by far, a remarkable place which he designed beautifully, with the gardens down to the sea and the swimming pool just before you get to the sea, a dance floor and wonderful food.

He has another hotel near Rome and another property in Bophuthatswana. He was amazed to meet an Englishman who understood what that was all about.[2] I said, 'They should have had diplomatic recognition from us. I tried to get it for them. I gave up.'

Norman told me that Major is now considering November [for the general election] because the private polls in the Tory Party are rather better than the public opinion polls which show no gap now between Labour and the Tories.

Friday 16 August
Frank Johnson arrives.

He was a bit surly because, as the house was so crowded, he had to sleep on the sofa in the big drawing-room. It is about thirty yards long. I think he thought he was being treated as a social inferior; but who was to be turned out for him? I wasn't going to leave my bed. He was lucky to be there. He has got an enormous chip on his shoulder because he left school when he was sixteen and is the son of an East End pastry cook. But he is very clever and can be very attractive.

Monday 19 August
Went down to swim, as I always do, naked, between eight and half past. Mark was doing the same with me. Women were told if they wanted to swim naked, they could do it at half past eight or half past seven but to look out for us, if they didn't want to see naked men, and not to come when we were swimming.

I listen to the wireless from England as I swim. The momentous news came. An emergency committee of eight had put Gorbachev under house arrest and taken control because the country was slipping into an ungovernable state. The Communist hard-liners were established and the clock was to be put back and never put forward again.

I went past Norman's window on my way to breakfast, he was just waking up, and shouted, 'Gorbachev's gone. He is in prison. *Now* what about your defence policies?'

I spoke to Margaret on the telephone. She said, 'Now we will realize how good Gorbachev was and how difficult it had been for him to organize these compromises and to persuade them all to come along.' I said, 'The real truth of the matter is he was never going to get anywhere after his first great perestroika moves until he abandoned Communism and insisted on trying to run a modern, free enterprise country.'

---

2. WW visited Bophuthatswana in 1986. See Vol. 1, p. 93.

As the day wore on it was apparent that there was some sort of vigorous opposition in touch with the foreign press and making announcements.

There were signs that not all the troops were on the emergency committee's side.

We went to the annual Arboretum party which Gino Corsini gave once again. Queen Juliana and Prince Bernhardt were there. Gino had been told that Norman Lamont was very important but he couldn't remember what he did or why. So he said to Prince Bernhardt, 'There is a very important man who the Wyatts have brought over. His name is LeMond. He is the man who won the Tour de France.'

Gino took him up to Prince Bernhardt and introduced him. He was very polite and almost deferential to this great bicyclist, though he must have been surprised at his shape.

When Prince Bernhardt discovered who he really was he said, 'Just another politician' and completely lost interest in Norman.

Wednesday 21 August

Yeltsin prevented them taking over the parliament. All day there were signs that the coup was collapsing. Gorbachev returns to Moscow. His statement sounded very dodgy. I think there is something fishy. Why did the conspirators fly back to see Gorbachev after the coup collapsed? Why did they go back to the Crimea and want to see him? Perhaps it was because there was agreement between them that if the plot succeeded, Gorbachev would have returned to power.

Norman handsomely congratulated me on my prediction that great good would come of it and it wouldn't last, the coup: 'Very prescient of you.' He was having conversations with Major and I said, 'Now tell him to recognize the Baltic states but still be cagey about aid, even though the coup has failed, until they have a proper structure.'

I said to Norman, 'We're still wrong on that defence policy. Keep your powder dry. Don't think that the world is now settling down to peacefulness because the coup has failed. All kinds of things might happen inside Russia and outside it.'

Norman said what do I think of Chips Keswick? I said, 'Extremely good. He would like to be on the Board of Directors of the Bank of England.' He said, 'Yes, I think he will be. Robin Leigh-Pemberton[3] likes him very much.'

---

3. Governor, Bank of England, 1983–93; life peer 1993.

Did I think Chips would like a knighthood? I said, 'Yes.' He said he would recommend it. I think Henry [Keswick] would like a knighthood, too.

On the night before the Lamonts went, the 21st, we had a very jolly game in which one side has to chose titles of books and films to act for the other side to guess. Even Frank Johnson joined in quite merrily. My team, at my instigation, set Norman to do *The Satanic Verses*, so with his somewhat chubby body he stood and tried to place horns on his head and imitate a tail with his hands at the back, which he did rather well. But they couldn't get it for a long time.

I had to do *No Sex, Please, We're British* which was slightly embarrassing with a thirteen-year-old girl there [Sophie Lamont]. I did my best rolling around on the floor and grunting. That was guessed and there was much applause.

Thursday 22 August
Olga Polizzi arrived in the afternoon on a Forte plane.

Speaking of Major, Olga said he was a strange man, very gauche. She said, 'He had never met my father and he came up to him and said, "Hello Charlie." My father is very old fashioned and was highly indignant at being called not only by his Christian name by a man he had never met before but also by being called Charlie, which he loathes.'

Major had been making level-headed statements up till now but after he had a quarter of an hour's conversation with Gorbachev on his return to Moscow he said, 'Why is everybody saying that Gorbachev is finished? I had a very good conversation with him and he seems in full control, full of vigour and confidence.' That showed that Major hadn't realized what had happened and that from now on Yeltsin will be the boss. Gorbachev is brushed aside and might even disappear himself.

Major is also missing the bus on quick recognition of the Baltic states. He is hanging about instead of getting on with it fast to reap the benefits.

Sunday 25 August
Olga went for a nine mile walk round the valley with Roberto. I said, 'You must be mad.'

She did look quite exhausted when she finished but she is very fit, swims a lot and says she often walks from where she lives in Chelsea to Trusthouse Forte in Holborn.

When I told Margaret that Norman was staying and he was very staunch against a single currency etc., she said, 'He's the strongest of them all,' which surprised me. I told Norman and he was very pleased. He said he is still devoted to her though she thought he wasn't. He said should he go and speak to her about his trip to Russia and tell her what everybody was saying in Moscow? I said, 'Of course. She'd love it.'

Monday 26 August
Gingo comes to stay but Anna Lu can't come because she has to look after all the grandchildren.

He said the death duties when the old Prince [Corsini] died were the largest ever in Italy, at over £200 million. Now the property is divided up into three sections among the eldest son (the new Prince and head of the family) who has seven parts, and the children who got two parts each, being four sisters in all. They had agreed everything very amicably. Anna Lu has got her castle in Umbria and a large chunk of one of the palaces in Florence with many of the great pictures.

Tuesday 27 August
I have been delighted the last few days that the Baltic states are getting recognition immediately. Even Bush is now moving towards it, though he has been very slow and so was Major to begin with.

Olga leaves in a scatty state and the driver who was taking her in a taxi to Rome (we were thankful we did not have to pay for it) was getting more and more worried that she would ever catch the plane. When she did go, she left an enormous cape behind, beautifully coloured and embroidered, which she was going to wear at a ball in Venice and which we have now got to take back.

Wednesday 28 August
Gingo leaves before lunch. I didn't have such a good day yesterday with my play but I had a super one today and finished it, that is the first draft.

It was pretty obvious that Frank Johnson only came for the exact number of days that Norman Lamont was going to be here because he wanted to squeeze as much out of him as he could.

Mark Pejacsevich was arranging for Norman to go to talk to his bank, Flemings, so Frank wasn't the only person there to use Norman for his own purposes. It's understandable.

Sunday 1 September
Back from Italy.

I spoke to Allan Davis. He has got a new play starting and is not interested in mine, I don't think. I rather hope not, in a way. He is seventy-eight on September 2nd.

Monday 2 September
We went to the surprise birthday party of Cecil Parkinson, his sixtieth. This was at Brocket Hall belonging to the somewhat bogus Lord Brocket who calls himself Lord Brocket of Brocket Hall.[1] The title was only created in 1933 and he is already the third one. He married an American model who, I think, must have supposed he was a great aristocrat.

But the house is remarkable. It once belonged to Lord Melbourne.[2] Caroline Lamb, his mistress, is reputed after a dinner in his honour of men guests to have jumped naked out of a great cake which was carried in. The next owner was Lord Palmerston[3] who was reputed to have had sexual intercourse with a lady on the billiard table.

Cecil had no idea that this huge [lunch] party had been arranged, with about two hundred people in a great marquee, champagne flowing etc.

The Speaker of the House of Commons, Weatherill, made a speech which was pretty tedious. But he did say that when Iain Macleod[4] first

---

1. Lord Brocket inherited Brocket Hall in Hertfordshire, but little money, when he was fifteen; he borrowed money to make it a successful conference centre. A classic car collector, in 1995 he was sentenced to five years in prison, of which he served two and a half, for a £4.5m insurance fraud involving the alleged theft of his valuable collection of cars; m (1982–95) Isabell, née Lorenzo, of Long Island, NY.
2. Prime Minister between 1834 and 1841.
3. He formed his first administration in 1855.
4. (1913–70); Conservative minister who died shortly after his appointment by Heath as Chancellor of the Exchequer.

saw him in the House of Commons when he became a Member, he asked him what subjects he was going to choose to speak on. He said, 'I wouldn't like to speak on anything unless I have a thorough understanding of the subject.' Iain Macleod replied, 'Then we won't be hearing much from you.'

Petronella had a delightful article in the *Sunday Telegraph*. Someone had written a letter about a man being sent to prison for thirty days for sexual harassment for pinching a lady's bottom. The *Sunday Telegraph* asked her to test the situation the other way round to see how men would react if women pinched their bottoms. So she stood outside the Reform Club for about an hour and a half and proceeded to pinch men's bottoms. She had a brilliant photographer and one man they photographed was jumping up in the air and looking very startled. Another picture was of Petronella with her notebook roaring with laughter. She did look extraordinarily pretty. The man was quite a good sport, too.

Dinner given by the Anglo-Hong Kong Trust who are all very rich. Algie Cluff is the President.

Charles Moore said, 'Democracy is bound to come to China very fast now that Russian Communism has gone.' I said, 'Nonsense. It's the only Communist country in the world where if there were real free elections, the rulers would get ninety per cent of the votes.'

He was very surprised when my neighbour, the Hon. Nellie Fong, a member of the Hong Kong Legislative Council, agreed with me completely that China won't change for years. But she thinks they will allow a little bit of freedom in Hong Kong.

Saturday 7 September
The final of the NatWest Trophy between Hampshire and Surrey. I went to the Paul Getty box at Lord's.

Auberon Waugh was due to come at lunch time.

He hopes to interest Paul Getty in the *Literary Review*.

Eventually he turned up just halfway through lunch, wearing a Panama hat and the same kind of beige-coloured summer suit as I was wearing.

Paul Getty arrived with Victoria Holdsworth, his girlfriend.[5] I duly introduced him to Auberon Waugh and tried to get them to sit together but they seemed shy. It was a long time before I got them actually

5. They married in 1994.

talking and then not very much because Bron had to go to catch his train to Somerset. He said, 'I'll write to him and I'll say something about the *Literary Review*.' I said, 'Yes, I should do that. You've made a contact now.'

When Paul Getty came in I was fascinated to see how the immensely wealthy alert people enormously. Everyone was trying to get his attention, trying to speak to him and say nice things to him, perhaps in the hope he might be touched one day. He is a pleasant fellow. We had a long chat about politics.

Victoria Holdsworth is exceptionally pretty. With a cat-like face and a friendly caress on the arm she is like an affectionate cat. I noticed her apply that to Paul. She has a clear complexion and an unlined face. She told me she would be fifty this year. I was amazed but I dare say she has been helped by the cosmetic surgeons.

Wednesday 11 September
Brooks' Club for launch of Roy's autobiography.

For the second time today I talked to Saumarez Smith of the Heywood Hill bookshop.

Smith is worried about the Net Book Agreement being smashed by a campaign to get rid of it. The new owner of Hatchards, T. A. Maher,[6] is advertising the sale of best sellers at cut prices before Christmas. When Maher wrote to me in favour of smashing the Net Book Agreement I had replied to him, what would happen to shops like Heywood Hill's? No answer.

I bumped into A. N. Wilson who eagerly wanted to talk to me. I merely said, 'Hello, nice to see you,' and moved on as quickly as I could.

Philip Ziegler[7] told me that he had all the official papers to write Harold Wilson's biography. Solly Zuckerman[8] said, 'What is an official biography?' He said, 'It is certainly, as far as I am concerned, one in

---

6. Terry Maher, at this time chairman, Pentos, Dillons Bookstores, Athena International and Ryman.

7. Historian, biographer and editor; he wrote the life (1985) and edited the diaries (1988, 1989) of Lord Louis Mountbatten; his life of Wilson was published in 1993; as editor-in-chief at William Collins he was WW's editor for *Confessions of an Optimist*.

8. (1904–93); Lord Zuckerman OM, Chief Scientific Adviser to HM Government, 1964–71; president, Zoological Society of London, 1977–84; life peer 1971.

which I get the official papers and all the documents I can lay hands on from the family or the estate and then write exactly as I please without any censorship.'

I said it will be a dreadfully dull book. He said, 'No, you can't believe that. You know very well how adroit a politician he was and the guile he used.'

In his graceful, well phrased speech, Roy said people sometimes asked him if he were retiring. He said they have done that several times when he has changed his job. His reply was that when Harold Macmillan was Chancellor of Oxford University when he was ninety and he had a speech to make at Oxford in which the Vice Chancellor was present, he said he found it a sad occasion because it was the last time (and everyone in the audience thought he was just about to announce his retirement) he would be on the same platform with the Vice Chancellor, 'because I understand, Vice Chancellor, that you are retiring this year'.

Rupert rang from Los Angeles. He advised against waiting for a May election. I explained why I disagreed. I said I was seeing John Major tomorrow and I would pass on his views but I still disagreed and he should read my article in the *News of the World*. He said he had.

I said, 'BSkyB is going well too, isn't it?' He said, 'Yes. We have got two million dishes out now and even the *Financial Times* says it should be in profit by the end of 1992 or certainly by the beginning of 1993.'

But of course Pick[9] previously, when I fixed my trip to Hungary for October 13th, said that the debt burden is still very heavy and will remain so.

Saturday 14 September
Met Arnold at the train at ten o'clock for Doncaster where we were going to see the St Leger. Arnold had said it was quite unnecessary to get the seat reservations which I had wanted. He was proved wrong. After some hassle we did find seats, plus Simon [Weinstock], but not all together at the same table.

I had told Arnold to use his old age pensioner's rail card and he secured one for the purpose. I was flattered when the ticket collector came round and demanded to see my rail card to prove

---

9. Sir Edward (Ted) Pickering, executive vice-chairman, Times Newspapers.

I was entitled to travel at the cheap rate, as though he thought me under sixty. Arnold had forgotten to bring his rail card so he had to pay the supplement. I said, 'I don't know how you run that business, GEC, you're so incompetent getting on to a railway train.'

Arnold has forty-five horses in training costing more than a million a year and the winnings now are not anything like that.

Later on in the evening I said, 'Why on earth do you do this?'

He said, 'It's a hobby.' I said, 'You mean you don't want to do stamp collecting, or play golf or fish or shoot?' He said, 'Exactly. It relaxes me.' I said, 'I suppose my hobby in a way is writing in the *Times* and the *News of the World*. Also I need the income but I would do it for nothing if necessary, or very little, because I like to give my views on politics.'

Arnold was impressed by all our equipment in the control room. I talked to him about the kind of help GEC might give to our people in dedicated lines [for] the arrangement with Coral by which they are going to put our device in all their betting shops so bets will go straight into the pool.

The race: Saddlers' Hall [Weinstock's horse] was running well and easily within himself as they came towards the final bend.

Then Toulon accelerated, right from the back, as Troy [Weinstock's winning horse in 1979] once did in the Derby.

If the race had been one and three-quarter miles long instead of adding an extra hundred and thirty-two yards, Saddlers' Hall might just have done it.

Arnold's second prize was £65,000.

I was quite ecstatic. I get a very enthusiastic feeling, almost like the owner, when Arnold's horse wins a big race [prize].

Monday 16 September
I had been due to see Major on Thursday afternoon and couldn't because he was still stuck in Paris. Norman said that wasn't the real reason. The real reason was that Norma Major is ill and very low and in a depressed state, though she has not said anything to the press, and he had to go and be with her.

Norman said if they went on until May, he is pretty certain they would have inflation down to three and a half per cent or thereabouts by then.

I went to Spink[10] who had some drawings, architectural ones, by Samuel Wyatt. There was a pair, which they sold me, of two octagonal lodges, designs for, very beautifully done. They were only £380. Some buildings he had planned, much bigger drawings for farm buildings, were £600.

I stopped on the way to the Tote at the China Reject shop which is extremely good value and looked at a breakfast set with two cups and saucers and plates. A tea set for Verushka cost £73 but they were Royal Grafton and beautiful.

Tuesday 17 September
Talked to Ken Baker at the Home Office. He was by himself in his office and said, 'I thought we would talk without officials present.' I handed him our comments on the recommendations and conclusions of the House of Commons Select Committee on the Tote. He glanced at them briefly.

He said, 'I am going to do a Fabius and rely on masterly inaction.'[11] I said, 'Do you mean like General Kutuzov[12] who retreated in front of Napoleon and then defeated him?' He said, 'Precisely. I am not going to make any announcement about the future of the Tote other than to say that it is under consideration.'

On the question of the Horserace Advisory Council he said, 'I see that you are sympathetic to the idea that they should take the Home Office's place, if that was thought right.' I said, 'Yes but I would only agree if they were absolutely at arm's length in relation to the Tote, exactly as the Home Office is.'

He said, 'I think it may even be dangerous for you to think of it being transferred to a horseracing authority. The moment that is done, the Department of Trade and Industry and the EC competition people will say it's in effect a privatization and they'll want the whole thing to be up for grabs.'

I said, 'Do you mean Ladbroke would be allowed to tender for the best racecourses, like Ascot and Newmarket, to run a Tote?' He said, 'Yes. The whole thing would go for six – the Tote monopoly licence.'

---

10. London numismatic and fine art dealers.
11. Fabius was a Roman general (d 203 BC), called *cunctator* (delayer) because of his successful delaying tactics in the war against Hannibal.
12. (1745–1813); Russian soldier, Prince of Smolensk, he fought Napoleon in 1812 at Borodino and then defeated Davout and Ney at Smolensk.

I said, 'Do you mean our exclusive licence?' and we both laughed. It was a very shrewd point and I think we had better calm down on that one.

We agreed not to press putting through an order in the House which would allow us to bet like any other bookmakers on Miss World, politics, the next pope, landing on the moon etc. He said, 'Don't do it because even though it would only be a trifle of legislation, people would say why are you bringing forth only this tiny bit of legislation and why not the whole of the Tote? It would stir things up. Let's let sleeping dogs lie.'

This also included the idea which comes from the Jockey Club and half-baked people like Zany Zetland that there should be greater outlets for the Tote (which would also mean, of course, bookmakers) in places like cafés, shops, post offices and even pubs. He said, 'You would just raise a hornets' nest. Leave it alone.'

I told him about our new device which could do lotteries as well. I said, 'If there is a lottery, I should be very keen that the Tote should bid to manage it because we are well equipped to do so with our integrity and these wonderful machines which can do any lottery you like.'

I then mentioned to him my talk with Norman concerning the possibility of dropping half a per cent of the betting tax and giving the £30 million it would save to racing. I said I thought that doing this would in fact increase the revenue. I said, 'Of course it's on the precedent of what he's done with the football pools.' Ken said, 'I'm very hostile to the whole of what he did about the football pools. I think it is quite wrong to use public money on things like that and you can't say it isn't public money when you reduce a tax and apply what you would have collected in tax to something quite different. I would also be opposed to the suggestion you are now making. Racing has got to find its own money in its own way.'

I told him about our arrangement with Coral to have our new device which we are developing put in their betting shops.

I complimented Ken on his forward-looking prison programme in which they are going to have civilized conditions.

I said I always thought that the worst thing about punishment in prison is deprivation of liberty. He said, 'Yes, you don't need to add degradation to that.' I said, 'Absolutely right. It just makes people more bitter and turns them worse when they come out.'

Prince Michael is in a great state about the gates in honour of

Queen Elizabeth the Queen Mother in Hyde Park. He had wanted to have some splendid new design with the lion and the unicorn balanced on the top. The Queen Mother had agreed to it and then went back on it, having been got at by people like St John-Stevas.[13]

After a bit I said, 'I will talk to Martin Gilliat and ask his advice. But I am not going to dare speak to her.' (He had said, 'You're such a good friend of hers you might be able to influence her.')

He was off to Holland. He has already tried to get me to tell him what to say in a speech to bankers in Zurich. I said, 'I hope the notes I sent you of Andrew Neil's speech in the USA were of help to you.' He said he thought they might be. I said, 'Why don't you develop that theme?' I am bloody well not going to write his speech for him as well.

Wednesday 18 September
Dinner at Cavendish Avenue. Tim Bell, Mark and Arabella Lennox-Boyd, Charles and Caroline Moore, Bernard Levin, George Weidenfeld, Carla Powell, Petronella, Verushka and me. To those who looked as though they could appreciate it I gave Krug 1962 before dinner.

Petronella is full of joy. From the end of October she will be writing Mandrake in the *Sunday Telegraph* and contributing other things under her own name.

Carla Powell sat on my left. On her left was George Weidenfeld.

He explained his technique [with women]. He said, 'The first thing is you have to get the girl ready to go to bed with you and I do it by asking her to explain and describe her life and her interests. But I've done it so often that I don't actually listen. Sometimes they will say, "But you're not listening," and I say, "Oh yes, I've been listening all the time but I was just thinking about something you said at the beginning," and go back on that a bit.' They get so flattered by his great interest, though he is not even listening, that the next stage is quite easy.

He told us something he put in his memoirs about a very aristocratic lady at a ball many years ago. There was a marquee and so forth in the garden. They went off into the bushes and had a piece of tempestuous sex. The girl said, as they got up and she smoothed down her clothes and put on her knickers again, 'Now I've had my first Jew.'

George is a very brilliant publisher but he doesn't read the books. He smells them and feels them and quickly glances through and says,

---

13. At this time Lord St John of Fawsley was chairman, Royal Fine Art Commission.

'This one is no good,' or 'This one is going to be very good.' He has hardly ever read a book he has published, certainly not all the way through. George admitted that was absolutely true and said he wanted me to write him another book, of reflections and thoughts. I said, 'But you published one, *To the Point*, and it's out of print and now I sell them at £5 a time from the remaindered stock to Heywood Hill.' He said, 'I mean a fuller one than that,' and then he told Carla how I had written my autobiography when I was thirty-two, *Into the Dangerous World*.[14] He remembered quite a lot of it.

When the ladies left, a fierce argument broke out about Croatia. Bernard Levin said, 'We don't want to take any notice of it. We can't be concerned with their quarrels.' I said, 'You mean they are only a lot of foreigners and we don't mind how many they kill of each other.'

Tim Bell agreed that we should recognize Croatia and give it an international status.

Mark Lennox-Boyd, being at the Foreign Office, was shooting the Foreign Office line, saying you can't recognize a country unless it is in full control of its area. I said, 'Rubbish. We recognized the exiled Polish government when they hadn't got anything They had been completely overrun by the Russians and the Germans. We recognized the Free French government under de Gaulle as being the proper government of France and they weren't even in the country.'

I had a talk with Caroline Moore. She is a brilliant girl, once a don at Peterhouse [Cambridge]. She used to invent those fantastically difficult Christmas competitions for the *Spectator*. She is now quite content being a mother of twins and doing no work at all except the odd review. I asked, 'How can you waste your talents like this? You can hire a nanny.' She said, 'I think it's my duty to look after my children and bring them up. Maybe after a few years I will go back to work.' I said, 'But what's all this women's lib about and fighting for

---

14. In his foreword to this book, published by Weidenfeld in 1952, WW says: 'Although there is much about myself in this book it is not intended as an autobiography; rather it is an attempt to mirror the times in which my generation has grown up through the medium of myself, the only constant, if changing, factor known to me throughout them.' WW wrote the book when an Opposition MP, after Labour's defeat in the 1951 election. He sketches his childhood and Oxford literary ventures. Then, after a vivid chapter on his experiences as a young officer in Normandy at the end of the war, he writes about his career in politics. The book includes witticisms but almost no gossip.

women's rights if you don't exercise your talents?' She said, 'I don't care. I'm not a feminist.' She is rather a beautiful girl.

The party broke up at about ten to twelve. I was pretty half seas over because I had drunk some of the port I had produced at the Queen Mother's lunch, and so did the others, as well as everything else.

Before the dinner I went to Adrian Rowbotham's fiftieth birthday party at the Groucho Club in Soho.

Jilly Cooper was there. She told me how grateful she was for a very kind review I had written about a book of hers years ago. I said, 'I had forgotten. It couldn't have been one of your sex books.'

I was somewhat disappointed in her appearance though of course she is getting on a bit now.

She has this strange gap in her teeth. She was pleasant enough and when I went she said she would like to have lunch with me. I said, 'Oh yes,' and thought no more about it.

Thursday 19 September

Alastair Aird[15] rang in response to my call to Martin Gilliat seeking advice for Prince Michael.

Alastair said the Queen Mother did not approve at all of the design. He was there when it all happened. She didn't like the look of it and didn't think they should be mucking about with the lion and the unicorn. The lion should be on the ground and not up in the air and it should be facing the unicorn as usual in the Royal Arms.

He said Prince Michael should write to him and then he'd see if it would be a good idea for him to go and see her.

I said, 'You had better prepare the ground or sound it first.'

With that we agreed that we like Prince Michael very much but he is a great enthusiast and he can get a bit carried away.

Saturday 21 September

Allan Davis and I adjusted *The Division Belle* as best we could to a more or less modern version. He arrived at a quarter to eleven and he was still there at half past four.

He glanced at my new play, *Is She Past It?* He thought it was a wonderful title. He says, 'It begins very well. You go right into

---

15. Comptroller to the Queen Mother since 1974; knight 1984.

it. You've learned something.' Then he said, 'This reminds me of something Caroline Blakiston said about your play: "It's very good but he's written it with his head and his balls and not his heart." This I think you have written with your heart.'

Tuesday 24 September
Lunch with the Al Ghazzi brothers. The elder of the two I had not met before. He is the head of the tribe now which has about thirty thousand people in it, a bit scattered, well south of Baghdad. He was very interesting about the custom by which he still acts as a judge in disputes between various members of the tribe.

Saddam Hussein asked him to provide money after the war but he refused. But he hasn't been molested as a result. They are still having great difficulties in getting the Swiss end sorted out though they have more hope on it now, that is to release the money so that they can get back Heveningham Hall from the receiver.

They are both very much against Saddam Hussein.

The two brothers hope that I may be able to urge the government to let the use of Heveningham Hall to be changed so that it can then be sold at a proper price.

They think it would be worth a lot of money for a hotel for conference people or whatever. But we will have to see what happens.

Wednesday 25 September
Dinner party at Cavendish Avenue.

There was nobody, apart from Henry Anglesey and myself, really bashing away at the Château Latour 1968 which was recorded in the famous blind tasting of the great Sommeliers of France in 1982 as the ninth best out of thirteen of the Latour vintages from 1958 to 1970.

Henry was in a very skittish mood. He was talking about his now dead brother-in-law, Raimund von Hofmannsthal,[16] who was married to his now dead sister, Liz Paget. He said he remembered sitting with him once with a girl between them, and Raimund, always on the look out for pretty girls, said, 'You have the most kissable lips.' She was very flattered and pleased. He said he always made remarks like that about girls when he wanted to seduce them. Frank Johnson was horri-

---

16. Son of the Austrian playwright, poet and librettist Hugo von Hofmannsthal.

fied and said he wouldn't tell anybody they even looked pretty until he had been out with them at least ten times.

Shirley [Anglesey] was a bit annoyed with me – she sat on my right – because I kept saying she was very left-wing and a supporter of Kinnock, which of course was going it a bit, though she always disagreed with Henry and myself about Mrs Thatcher. I said, 'Are you going to vote for Major this time?' She said she might but she was really going for the Liberal Democrats. I said, 'There you are, you are sloppy left-wing.'

She is still the Chairman of the Broadcasting Complaints Commission. I said, 'You are very loath to crack down on the left-wing propaganda stuff when it comes your way.' She complained our amendments to the Broadcasting Bill, which had introduced a lot of checks on bias, were very difficult to understand.

I showed Henry my slippers which I was wearing with my coronet on them and I said, 'I am only a life peer and I can't wear mine after I am dead but you can wear yours after you are dead.' He said, 'John Betjeman always said that however awful a hereditary peer was, he was always nicer than a life peer.'

William Shawcross said he had almost finished his book on Rupert. When I was asked by Diana Wilton why Rupert was so anti-establishment and anti the Royal Family and his papers were, I said, 'It was like this. Rupert's father was Sir Keith Murdoch and owned a newspaper himself, as well as being a journalist in Australia. They were very much establishment figures there. The mother was a dame and chairman of all kinds of things like the National Museum. But during the First World War he came over, deciding to write reports about the Anzac troops, mainly Australians, in Gallipoli.

'He was horrified at the way they were being treated and put, he thought, as cannon fodder ahead of the British troops. He made a great outcry, wrote in the *Times* about it and went to see Lloyd George and got the whole situation altered. But that is how they began to feel anti the British imperial idea, because they felt they were just being used. And the throne is very much the centre of that.

'Then when Rupert left Oxford and his father wanted him to go back to Australia, he said he wouldn't because he wanted to stay in Europe for a couple of years. By the time he got back his father was dead. He bitterly regretted not having seen his father again before he died. That is no doubt part of the reason why he still keeps up the element of the anti-imperialist establishment, in his honour so to speak.

'Then when he did buy the *News of the World* in England, and Anna came to England with him, she thought they would be able to meet what passed as "society" in England. But they were rejected by it because everybody turned up their noses at the *News of the World*, so Anna wanted to go back and live in New York. All these things made a kind of feeling that way.

'But actually Rupert is extremely pro-English, even though he became an American in order to own a television station and a newspaper in the same town in America. He is far more interested in English politics than he is in American or anybody else's.

'I love him dearly but I think he has not been paying quite enough attention to what his newspapers have been saying lately.'

Friday 27 September
Talked to Margaret after her return from Washington.

She thinks the attitude on Croatia has been weak.

She was told that John Major had said that Serbia and Croatia were like two ferrets fighting in a sack. She said, 'What a dreadful thing to say! It isn't the truth at all. The Croats are democrats and the others are Communist.' It is very odd how, even if we haven't been talking to each other for some time, we nearly always come to the same conclusions on issues.[17]

I told Norman after I spoke to her that she would like to see him.

I said, 'Ring her now,' and gave him her private number which he hadn't got.

Sunday 29 September
Talked to Margaret again.

She is much opposed to the Bush unilateral disarmament of nuclear weapons. I said, 'I hear they are even talking about us not having a Trident.' She said, 'Good Lord, we must have that. They don't seem to understand the situation at all. I'll bet that Bush didn't consult them, just made a telephone call before it was announced.'

She thought they had no option but to postpone the election till May or the spring.

---

17. WW's article in the *Times* of 24 September had called for an armed force, under the auspices of the UN or the EC, to save Croatia.

Monday 30 September

Talked to John Major at Number 10. I advised him to go for an election in May when he would be fairly certain of a decent majority.

When I came in I said, 'I've got a few notes here, aide mémoire, in case I forget something. They won't take me more than five hours.' He answered that he was already running late and had had to give up two speeches he was supposed to have made, one to some newspaper press fund, in order to see me. I said, 'I am only joking,' but I think he realized that and perhaps he was joking back.

I said, 'Though Labour are managing to make themselves look more moderate and think they have got away with that, you can say that in their moderate guise they now plan to do only moderate harm. That is the sort of thing which Winston would have said.' He said, 'Did he say that? How frightfully good.' I said, 'No, he didn't. I just invented it.' He said, 'Can I use it? Can I plagiarize it from you?' I said, 'Yes. That's why I said it to you, so you can use it, if you want to.'

We talked about Margaret and I told him that she is passionate for him to win and how distressed she had been at the beginning of the week when the polls seemed to be going badly.

I told him she was concerned about the move towards federalism and the single currency.

John said, 'I am playing the negotiations very long and that is my objective, to stick it out as long as I can. The longer it is strung out, the longer it will take for any of the things we don't want to happen.'

I said, 'How often do you see her?' He said, 'I haven't been able to see her for a long time because she has been away so often.' I said, 'I think it would be a good idea to see her again and keep her in your confidence. Where do you see her when you do see her?' He said, 'I go and see her at her house.' I said, 'That's very decent of you.' He said, 'Oh no, I think it is very right for me to do that and not ask her to come here. We fence around, not really getting on to the points about which we disagree. We have rather stilted conversations.'

I said, 'She is very anxious you shouldn't, what she calls "fight on their ground". I don't quite know what she means.' He said, 'I know what she means. She means all about pensions and welfare and so on.'

Then I said she hates the Brussels politburo, unelected and initiating issues.

He said, 'We're stopping it. We are going to have a European parliament with more power over them.' I said, 'I don't think that is going to do much good.' He said, 'It's better than we have got now, with Delors doing it all by himself.'

He made it clear that he's still keener to go in November than wait till May because there were too many risks in May. I said, 'You want a good solid lead, you know, before you do it. I think you would win but you might not get much of a majority. I don't think it would be a hung parliament.'

I said, 'If you had a flotation of BT privatized shares before Christmas, it would be marvellous and it would go down very well.' He said he thought it would and he thought Norman was handling that issue very well, too. I said, 'You're going to win anyway. It's really whether you scrape by or whether you get a better majority.'

I said, 'I hope you noticed the Gallup poll on September 6th which showed that seventy per cent said they didn't want any cuts in defence. I think you are making a great mistake to make these cuts.' He said, 'It would save £2 billion.' I said, 'Over a period, not at once.' He said, 'That's true but we are spending more proportionally than any other nation on defence.' I said, 'That doesn't matter. We have a particular role with our professional defence forces.'

I said, 'Margaret is worried you are going to give up Trident.' He said, 'No that's absolutely safe. This afternoon, just before you came, I had the American Ambassador here and he assured us that they were not going to stop the supply of Trident to us, whatever the Russians may say about it.'

John thanked me for the support I gave him. I said, 'I have to attack you sometimes when I think you're wrong. Otherwise it's not taken seriously when I say how good you are. Margaret didn't always understand that. It's strange about Margaret and myself because we think in exactly the same way when we are apart. We both thought how badly we were behaving over Croatia. She was ringing up the Foreign Office.' He said, 'I know. She made a tremendous fuss.'

Then I said it had been reported to her that he had said, 'It's only two ferrets fighting in a sack.' I said, 'I thought it was unlike you to say that.' 'You're quite right,' he said. 'What happened was this. Some people from the Foreign Office were here discussing it and someone from the Foreign Office said that those people would fight each other very viciously and I said, "You mean like ferrets in a sack." ' I said, 'Some unkind person made sure it went to her.' However, he wouldn't be drawn into discussing it with me about whether we should do more about Croatia.

By the time I left I think he more or less agreed with me that he should wait till May.

When talking about Margaret he asked me how much I kept in touch with her and I said, 'Frequently. I have spoken to her twice last week for example and I rang her from Italy.' He said, 'Good, because she is very lonely and it is very important for her that her old friends should keep in touch with her and not desert her. I hope you will go on doing that.' I said I would certainly. He said how fond of her he was himself. But it was quite funny how he spoke of their conversations being somewhat stilted.

As I went out Jeffrey Archer was coming in. How strange they are, Margaret and he, to see so much of Jeffrey Archer who is a real rogue though quite amusing. I was always terrified he would get her into trouble and I hope he won't get John Major into trouble.

Tuesday 1 October

Aly Aziz and his wife and son by his first marriage came to dinner.

Robbie and Tessa Lyle were there too.

Aziz's wife is charming and rather attractive. They got married in 1976. She is Spanish basically and comes from Costa Rica. They seem to be enormously rich. They have a house in the Boltons with a swimming pool at the bottom of the house. They have a house in Monaco and they jet all around the world on his business trips.

However, my main interest was in seeing that everything is OK with Cornish Spring Water. They will go into profit I am sure under him but there is trouble about the angles of the boreholes and getting enough pressure for the new boreholes. I think something can be done about it. He has spent quite a lot of money on it already. The royalties should mount and maybe there should be as much as £4,000 to £5,000 this year of which I am supposed to get twenty-five per cent.

In the afternoon Brian [McDonnell] and I went to the Jockey Club. Peace has now broken out and they kept apologizing for their appalling behaviour earlier, trying to excuse themselves.

We then got down to how to get more money into the levy from the bookmakers and also how to deal with the Secretary of State and the Treasury.

There had been a furious argument about the price of the product at the Levy Board. I said, 'The bookmakers have got the price of their product, too. Racing can't exist without them.'

I told the Jockey Club not to be so much on the defensive. It's a great institution and it does the things it's best at extremely well: the licensing of racecourses and making sure they behave properly, the licensing of trainers and jockeys and making sure they behave properly, the integrity of racing as far as photo finishes and stewards' inquiries and all the rest of it are concerned, maintaining respect for the racecourses where people can bring betting complaints. All these things are very important. And the fixture list, they are learning to do that more effectively, though they should be more flexible now to meet the book-makers halfway.

I said, 'Don't worry too much about democratizing yourselves, although it would be best if you were seen to have a system for the Senior Steward and the other stewards arriving at the top.'

They explained that they did have a voting system on that and people were very carefully examined first. They had to have served on a committee at the Jockey Club and have shown that they were really interested in racing and understood it well enough before they were eligible to be voted for as a steward.

Thursday 3 October

Norman told me the decision to wait till the spring had been taken by John Major on Sunday. I had no influence on him at my talk with him on Monday. But I think my influence could have come earlier through the *News of the World* articles I had written and the views I had given him before about waiting till 'The Darling Buds of May'.[1]

I heard quite a good joke. President Carter, President Nixon and President Jack Kennedy were all in a ship sailing on a cruise when suddenly there was an awful explosion and the order was given to abandon ship and to get into the lifeboats. President Carter cried out, 'Women and children first.' President Nixon cried out, 'Fuck the women and children,' and President Kennedy cried, 'Is there time?'

Tuesday 8 October

To Gresgarth Hall. Mark Lennox-Boyd and his wife Arabella. It is a very charming house. Parts of the back are 13th century, the side is an elevation put on in 1810 from samples from architectural books of neo-Gothic windows with a neo-Gothic appearance, almost like church windows but extremely pretty. I slept in what they now call the River Suite where Verushka would have been, too, if she had been able to come. There was a very comfortable large bed and another bedroom next door and a lavatory and bathroom and shower and everything also en suite, telephone supplied.

---

1. WW ended his *News of the World* article on 8 September, 'If Mr Major keeps the good judgment he's evolving, he'll wait for The Darling Buds of May.'

The gardens had been planned, and are still developing, by Arabella who is one of the world's greatest experts on gardens now.[2]

They cleared a piece of the woods over on the other side of the river (it is surrounded by rivers) so there is a marvellous prospect with a nice little Chinese type bridge to cross over.

Inside the house was decorated beautifully. They only bought it when he became the MP for Morecambe and they now intend to live there indefinitely.

At dinner Margaret was there. Just before dinner we watched a part of the Tory Party Conference on the news. She kept muttering and complaining all the time that they were selling the pass on Europe, that they were not doing the right things about going forward and so on.

She thinks almost none of them in the government is any good. I said, 'You can't possibly think that, Margaret, because you appointed them to your Cabinet yourself.' She said, 'I don't think they are what they used to be.' She said she thought Major was full of vanity and doesn't want to disagree with anybody; he just wants to be liked and he will sell us out to Europe.

I said, 'You're being very unreasonable. He was your chosen heir.' She said, 'Yes but I think he has deceived me.' I said, 'I don't think he has at all. How often do you see him?' She said, 'Not very often.' I said, 'How do you get on when you do see him?' She said, 'All right in a way but he's vague.' I said, 'Do you state your disagreements?' She said, 'He doesn't like that. He fades away when you do that because he doesn't want to disagree with anybody.'

She was denouncing our joining the Exchange Rate Mechanism, the stage we are in now, and I said, 'But it was under your government,' and she said, 'Yes but I was pushed into it by Howe and Lawson at the Madrid conference because they said they would resign if I didn't. I said, "It is extraordinary how the two of you can come and say a thing like that to me." They said, "We are going to resign if you don't give a date when we're going into the ERM." '

I said, 'But it's not turned out too badly, that part.' She said, 'We should never have gone into it at all.'

She said, 'If they do go too far at this Maastricht conference in December, I shall vote against it, and I shall vote against anything

---

2. She won a gold medal and the overall Best Garden Award at the 1998 Chelsea Flower Show.

which looks as though we are sliding down the path into a federal Europe or to a Central European Bank or a single currency.' I said, 'What, even if it is just before an election?' She said, 'Yes. I can't help it. There ought to be a referendum.' I said, 'It would be very difficult to define the terms.' She said, 'Oh no. You can do that. People ought to be knowing what it is all about. There ought to be a referendum. They had a referendum about going into the Common Market and this is much more important.'

She was in fairly strident form, pulling them all to pieces.

We had a very jolly conversation during dinner when I was disagreeing with her and saying, 'No. You contradicted yourself. You didn't say that before.' She took it all extremely well and every now and again she said, 'Now you listen, Woodrow, you listen.' I said, 'I am listening and have been listening,' and then I made her listen to me. The others were amazed at the way I talked to her because they are all still frightened of her.

Margaret eats very heartily. She had two helpings of the very rich pudding which was a sort of tart with cream all over it. I didn't have any of it because I thought I might be ill. She drank a good deal of whisky before dinner. She was a little high at one point and that was why she was getting more excited.

She said she was dreading tomorrow because she was going to the party conference [in Blackpool] to the platform. I said, 'Don't dread it. It's going to be spectacular. You'll get an ovation which will last about ten minutes at least and that will be a message to the platform not to betray your ideals and your philosophy.'

Wednesday 9 October
When I woke up it was twenty past eight so I had to hurry up to get downstairs for breakfast. There was Margaret already eating her breakfast, a nice large one.

After I had been for a walk round the garden with Arabella we went back in and Margaret was just about to go. She had changed and she said to me, 'I am wearing my Tory true blue outfit now,' and she looked stunning. She had her best jewellery on. She said, 'I'm not going to make a speech. I'll just go there.'

We watched her on the television. I don't know how long the ovation went on for but it was very difficult to stop them.

Afterwards I explained to Mark Lennox-Boyd that I had made the arrangements for John Major to see her.

I said, 'I am trying to act as some kind of bridge. I love her, you know. I adore her. I think she is absolutely wonderful. She should never have been got rid of.'

Earlier Margaret had said that the most terrible thing which John Major did was to go back on the community charge. She said, 'That was letting me down. He had always been for it.' I said, 'He felt he couldn't win the leadership contest if he stuck to it.' She said, 'He's got no principles. Of course he could have done. That's the act of a weak man, not of a strong one. We should have fought it through and he would have won the leadership contest just the same.'

She said, 'No leader should ever want to be loved. He should do the right thing whether people like it or not.'

Mrs Archie Hamilton[3] was very nice, tall like her husband. Highly intelligent. She said her mother, who had got a very good degree, had now turned against education for women. I asked, 'Why? Because she thinks it stops them looking after their homes?' She said, 'No, because she thinks things are so weighted against women that it's not sensible for them to try to compete.' I said, 'I think that's absurd. Women are more and more growing to the stage where they can cope with a job and take time off to have babies and return to the job and employ a nanny.'

Archie Hamilton, son of a peer, said, 'That's not a nice thing, to be brought up by nannies.' I said, 'That's extraordinary. You were brought up by a nanny, weren't you?' He said 'Yes.' 'What do you think is wrong then? You seem to be all right. It's not like having a surrogate mother.' (Though it was in a way with me with Miss Winterbon because my mother was always so busy trying to run the school she didn't have much time for me, at least not as much as she would have liked – she had plenty in the holidays, of course, but then we didn't really get on, perhaps because I regarded Miss Winterbon as my mother by that time.)

I was glad that Margaret was full of praise for Ken Baker. She said how loyal he had been to her and how good he was. She was going to stay to hear his speech at the conference but she wasn't going to listen to Rifkind who really ought to have been in the Labour Party. She would also listen to Michael Howard who has been stalwart for her.

---

3. Anne, née Napier, m (1968) the Hon. Archibald Hamilton, younger son of the 3rd Baron Hamilton, Conservative MP since 1978, at this time Minister of State (Armed Forces), Ministry of Defence, knight 1994.

Friday 11 October

In Budapest. Drove with the Pejacsevichs and Mark's friend, Imre Zichy, to the Glucks.[4]

Mrs Gluck is a charming lady who is a lawyer herself. She has two children, one is about eight, the boy, and the other, a girl, about five. She abandoned her work recently to come to Hungary with them and look after them so the family can be together.

She is shortish, a little plumpish and dark with quite a pretty face. They are very Jewish and had a great star of David in brass over the chimneypiece, so they don't make any bones about it and like you to know that they are Jewish. Him I find agreeable and very hard-working, conscientious, determined to get on.

I am trying to help him and Skadden Arps in Hungary. The idea of Mark Pejacsevich going there was that they should meet to try and do some mutual work because Mark is working quite high up in Flemings Merchant Bank, though he is not a director. Mark is an aristocrat. When he came to England he weighed in at once and got any job he could until he could finally work his way up. That was in 1946.

Imre Zichy comes from an enormously rich, aristocratic Hungarian family. They had great estates in Hungary and in Austria. Of course they lost everything in Hungary. Fortunately, his grandfather had money overseas, quite a lot of it, and he developed a business which is extremely profitable, spraying buildings to resist fire. He wants to start a little business in Hungary to help the remainder of his family who stayed in Hungary and never got out.

Saturday 12 October

We had lunch with Peter Toke who runs the *Reform* weekly. He owns about twenty-five per cent of it and Rupert [Murdoch] owns fifty per cent.

There was very nice fellow with him, a Canadian Hungarian, sent over specially by News International to see what the hell was going on and put it right.

The daily paper they have got is terribly over-manned and still has the old Communist outlook, giving favours to people by the stories they write about them and then in return they get gifts. He thinks the daily can be made to make money but he is not so sure about

---

4. See 19 July 1991, when WW took George Gluck to meet the Hungarian Ambassador in London.

the weekly. He was very helpful to me with all kinds of information which I was trying to get about what is going on in Hungary.

Poor Toke was very subdued.

He is thinner and he didn't have his pretty secretary[5] because the supervisor from Murdoch and his wife were present.

Sunday 13 October
I decided I must go out into the country to talk to a less rarefied type of Hungarian than those in offices and Ministers. Livia, my sister-in-law, drove me out in her tiny little East European, Communist-made car. We had lunch in a restaurant, third class, where we had been once before. We talked to the people at the bar and those eating their lunch. I was rather elated because I felt the youth of Hungary are going to be its saviour. They are not infected by the Communist disease from the last forty-three years. They are determined to fight for a new world and are very ambitious.[6]

Tuesday 15 October
To the Berkeley Hotel, the annual dinner of the Hong Kong Trade Development Council.

This year the main speaker was the Governor of Hong Kong, Sir David Wilson.

Henry Keswick was one of the luminaries there who thinks David Wilson ought to be thrown out and he may well be. He has a weak face, poor chap, but he may be no worse than anybody else in the run-up to the handover in 1997.

MPs had to leave early to vote on the defence cuts. The government, unfortunately, won easily.

Wednesday 16 October
Conrad Black gave a great dinner at Harry's Bar which he had taken over completely for the evening.

On my right was Marcelle Quinton.

When I asked her how much one of her sculptures cost she wouldn't tell me but she said the reason why she was there was because Conrad Black had ordered a bust of Cardinal Newman, long since dead. She

5. See WW's last visit, on 23–24 March 1990.

6. WW used this material in his *News of the World* article of 20 October, and he wrote about the new Hungarian enterprise culture in the *Times* of 22 October.

said he was the only person who ever tried to negotiate a price with her. He had asked if he had two, would it be cheaper, and she had said no, so he had to pay the full price for one, which I think annoyed him but not enough to prevent him asking her to the dinner.

Verushka sat between Sir Ronald Grierson and a Canadian tycoon on Conrad Black's board. Ronnie said she didn't seem a day older than when he first met her. That was when we went to a party over twenty-five years ago, held at Lord Bearsted's magnificent country house. It was the night that Heather Bearsted told him she was leaving him the next morning and going off with Ronnie Grierson, who was present at the party, and was going to marry him. It seemed a bit rough on him the night he'd spent a fortune on a magnificent party for her.[7]

Beforehand I introduced Alistair McAlpine, who was the last Treasurer of the Tory Party, to John Smith. I said, 'They are having to call him back to raise more money for the Tory Party to fight you at the next election.'

I said, 'Of course Labour would have a much better chance of winning if you were the leader and not Neil Kinnock.' He didn't demur but said Kinnock had greatly improved in stature. I said, 'But he has clearly got no brain power or application to detail.' He said, 'He has got a better education than John Major.' I said, 'Yes, but John Major has improved himself enormously,' which he agreed to.

In the Lords in the afternoon Lord Carver made a most extraordinary speech. He was a former Chief of the General Staff. I thought we were very lucky there hadn't been a war when he was there.[8]

Carver doesn't want any nuclear weapons at all. He agreed with all the cuts and thinks they should even go further. My friend, Edwin Bramall, the most recent of the Chiefs of General Staff to enter the Lords, was horrified.

Friday 18 October
A lunch for Jo Flom of Skadden Arps at 19 Cavendish Avenue.

Michael Howard was my principal guest to entertain Jo.

The other guests were Michael Bett, the Deputy Chairman of British Telecom; Simon Osborne, the British Rail Board solicitor; Lord

---

7. Heather, née Firmston-Williams, (d 1993), m 1 (1947–66) 3rd Viscount Bearsted, m 2 (1966) Ronald Grierson (vice-chairman, GEC, 1969–91; chairman, GEC International, since 1992; knight 1990).
8. Field Marshall Michael Carver, Chief of the General Staff, 1971–3; life peer 1977.

Rockley, the Vice Chairman of Kleinwort Benson; James Ogilvy (Angus Ogilvy's brother) from a company called Foreign Colonial Management; and Sir Robert Wade-Gery, an executive director of Barclays de Zoete.

Sir Robert[9] shook me before he went. We had been discussing the government's attitude towards Europe and Michael Howard had said that we were not going into the single currency and the Central Bank and a federal Europe etc. Sir Robert said to me, 'They'll have to do that. We have got to do that.' I said, 'You don't mean that?' He said, 'Yes. I can't understand all this business about not realizing that England is going to have to disappear into a federal government. With the way things are going there is nothing we can do about it.' I thought, 'Good heavens, if somebody like that feels this way it's the end of everything.'

Later we had dinner with Irwin and Cita Stelzer at the Connaught. As usual they produced the Calon-Ségur 1961. The Connaught have now learned to decant it properly. It was very beautiful wine. The dinner was in honour of Jo Flom and his wife. His wife is enormous, about twice his size, overpowering this tiny, brainy man. She turned out to have plenty of brains as well.

They have been touring around the Skadden Arps empire. I have been anxious to do all I can for Skadden Arps for fear of losing a chunk of my £25,000 a year from them. Times are hard for this great firm of corporate lawyers as well as for others.

Irwin and Cita were extremely friendly. Also there was a charming man, Simon Hornblower, who at my instigation encouraged Cita to proceed with a classical education.

He happened to be at Harvard when I was trying to find the right person for her. He is a fellow of Oriel [Oxford College]. He talked about the James Wyatt building of the library and how it was the most beautiful thing in Oriel.

Simon Hornblower is a slightly puzzled-looking academic, a trifle out of place at the Connaught Hotel in that he wore country clothes of a sporting kind. I liked him a lot. He was jolly interesting and has just produced a great commentary on Thucydides which has taken him years to do.

---

9. Deputy Secretary of the Cabinet, 1979–82; High Commissioner to India, 1982–7; knight 1983.

Saturday 19 October

Off to Newmarket for the Tote Cesarewitch and to stay with John Derby. It was bitingly cold; the wind tore through my overcoat and my ultra-warm vest.

Verushka had been urged to democratize the seating arrangements by Geoffrey Webster. He said that some of the journalists had complained they had been put on lesser tables, below the salt as it were, apart from the grandees. So at my table as well as the wife of Sir John Sparrow, Chairman of the Levy Board, and Priscilla Hastings who was also staying at John Derby's, was the editor of *Pacemaker* and the editor of *Sporting Life*. The editor of *Pacemaker* arrived forty minutes late, well after the lunch was nearly finished, which wasn't quite his fault because he had some trouble with a parent who had a car accident. He was very charming and civilized. The editor of the *Sporting Life* never turned up at all and sent no word of apology.

On Sunday morning I walked round the gardens thinking how much jollier it would have been if Isabel had been there. In the drawing-room I could hardly bear it the night before because I remembered her so well standing in front of the fireplace making her jokes, turning her quick face and warming her bottom. Fortunately, we were not put to sleep in her bedroom as Diana Wilton had been.

Monday 21 October

Rupert and Anna Murdoch came to dinner; so did Norman and Rosemary Lamont, Mark and Anouska Weinberg, Jacob and Serena Rothschild and Angus Ogilvy. The wine was 1985 Pavillon Blanc, the Château Margaux white wine, absolutely superb. Previously I gave those who like old champagne some Krug 1964.

Then we had Haut-Brion 1967 for the red wine.

Everybody was lapping it up except for Angus Ogilvy[10] who had intended to come by cab but couldn't get one so had driven his own car. He was terrified of driving back to Richmond Park and being stopped by the police and breathalysed.

Norman got on very well with Rupert. I had wanted them to meet because I want Rupert to support Norman; in particular if he gets into any scrapes, to have them suppressed in the *News of the World* and the *Sun*. Anna very much liked Rosemary and they got on well together.

---

10. The Hon. Sir Angus Ogilvy (knight 1989) m (1963) Princess Alexandra; they live in Richmond Park.

Rosemary first of all had not wanted to come because she was so
frightened of Rupert and all the business about the Olga black eyes
and the stuff about the tart and her house in the *News of the World*.

I warned Norman about Margaret voting against them if the Maastricht thing goes too far. He said, 'It's not going to go too far.'

They [the Murdochs] are going to Estonia. Her father was an
Estonian and she was going to have a look at his country, having been
born in Scotland and having a Scottish mother. I think she had been to
Estonia once or twice. She had on a very elegant suit with pink facings.
I told her how beautiful she was looking and that she never aged at
all which did not displease her.

Jacob told everybody that I was the best man and only witness to
their wedding at the registry office in Devizes. I said, 'Yes, I had quite
a lot to do with promoting your marriage.' He said that was quite right
but I am not sure he knew exactly what I was referring to.

It has gone very well. He needed her money from her father[11]
to begin with and now he has got a huge vast fortune.

Even after death duties what his aunt left him must be worth at
least £80 million, apart from the money he has made himself.

Wednesday 23 October

NERA meeting plus lunch. NERA is owned by Marsh & McLennan,
the biggest firm of insurance brokers, and God knows what else, in the
world. The President Ian Smith came, the top man. He was very quiet
and highly intelligent with a lean, narrow face and a sharp interested
nose, very short cropped grey hair, frizzy on the top. He had read my
article on Hungary and said I was very optimistic. I said, 'Yes but I
am quite right.'

I saw Peter Carrington at the Lords.

I asked Peter why he got involved and he said because the Dutch
asked him.

He is suddenly looking grey and shrivelled and much older. I think
it has been very hectic for him acting as the European Community
mediator, trying to find a solution for Yugoslavia.

Thursday 24 October

Saintsbury Club. Took Micky Suffolk.

I was trying to get Micky into the Club.

---

11. Sir Philip Dunn, the son of the Canadian steel magnate, Sir James Dunn.

He has got masses of first class wine. He would give us some and would be a good ballasting against the trade.[12] We need more civilized, jokey men of the world.

Micky and I were talking about not remembering people's names.

He said not long ago he was somewhere with his wife, Linda, and a girl came up to him and said, 'Hello, how are you?' He couldn't remember her. Then she said to him, 'Would you remember me if I took my clothes off?' He blushed deeply to the roots of his hair because he had had an affair with her some years before. (She had said that to him in an aside while Linda was not listening.)

The wine was pretty good tonight. The Château Pape-Clément 1962 was terrific.

A couple of places up on my left was a man called Eric Shorter who used to work for the *Daily Telegraph*.[13] He said how much he admires Petronella and how well she writes. I said, 'She is now going to take over the "Mandrake" column,' and he was very impressed. I said, 'She writes far better than I ever did and is much funnier.' He said, 'How nice for her to have a father who supports her.' I said, 'I recognize her quality.'

Saturday 26 October
Oare House is very lovely.

Henry [Keswick] is very proud of his gardening. He showed us some melon seeds which came from Blenheim. He said they are very good and they will be planting them soon. Around the gardens everywhere are beautifully trimmed yew hedges in splendid formations designed by Clough Williams-Ellis who designed all the extras to the house, namely the wings on either side, which he did in lovely red brick matching the middle of the house, the original 18th century house.

There was the oak planted last year by Margaret growing well with lovely yellowish foliage. He pointed across the field to an oak planted by Stanley Baldwin. This was when Geoffrey Fry was his Private Secretary, when he was Prime Minister.

Fry owned Oare House and Baldwin used to stay there. Baldwin's

12. The club was founded in 1931 for twenty-five men of wine and twenty-five men of letters.
13. Drama critic and arts writer.

oak was doing very well. Henry said the two oaks will be able to look at each other in forty years' time.

Alan and Jill Hare were staying. So was Jessica Douglas-Home[14] who used to be the girlfriend of Roger Scruton.[15]

Her new boyfriend appears to be a man called Rodney Leach, aged fifty-six.

I used to play tennis with him and Jacob Rothschild years ago, which he well remembered.[16] He is now acting as Chief Executive for Jardine Matheson where Henry, the oldest [Keswick] brother, is running the show as Chairman for the family and I suppose the public shareholders, such as they are. They have floated their insurance company to the public.

At lunch we had an argument about Gorbachev and Yeltsin. I found Rodney Leach extremely intelligent; he had a double First at Oxford. He agreed with me in particular about the coup being a put-up job by Gorbachev and his pals and if it had succeeded he would have gone on running the USSR in the hard-line way. But he didn't, so he disowned them all.

We each had a grouse for dinner and there was 1973 Château Latour (in magnums) in honour of Alan Hare.

Alan said Rupert always used to be very kind to him when he was in charge of the *Financial Times* as Managing Director. He had told Michael [Blakenham] not to get paranoiac about Rupert having some Pearson shares. I said all he really wanted was to have a joint newspaper in New York based on the *Financial Times*. He said Rupert's buying shares in Pearson made Michael decide to sell Château Latour in a panic, which was a great pity.

Sunday 27 October

I had an enormous breakfast. I always do at Henry's. He eats enough for seven people, as he was doing in Italy when he stayed with us.

I am rather pleased about him being so happy. He used not to be so contented before he married Tessa six years ago. Now I think he has got everything and he enjoys it and uses it well. He is an extremely

---

14. Widow of Charles Douglas-Home (1937–85, editor of the *Times*); m 2 (1993) Rodney Leach.
15. Philosopher; at this time Professor of Aesthetics, Birkbeck College, London University, and editor, *Salisbury Review*.
16. He worked for N. M. Rothschild & Sons, 1963–76.

generous person and I found the whole house happy and comfortable, except that Robbie had forgotten to take my talking machine out of the car so I could neither do my manuscript nor answer the readers' letters I had with me.

Monday 28 October
Talked to Norman who is very upset at the *Sunday Times*, Andrew Neil, writing a horrible leading article saying the Tory government was no good and that Norman should go and be succeeded by Michael Heseltine.

He said, 'Why did Rupert do that? He was so friendly at the dinner party on Monday.' I said, 'I don't expect he knew anything about it. He never does.'

I also spoke to Margaret who is getting very heated, not unnaturally, about the way things seem to be drifting.

I said, 'I am very glad you are banging on about Croatia, and so am I.' She said, 'I am "banging on",' in a very funny voice as though I shouldn't refer to her great activities as banging on but it was only meant to be friendly.

When Rupert spoke to me, he rang from a car in Paris.

He said he hadn't read the article.

He said, 'Tell Norman not to fuss so much. I wish we had the power in our newspapers that they think we have, but don't tell him that. We haven't got the power at all.' He pooh-poohed the idea that it could affect the poll rating by two per cent.

Tuesday 29 October
Lunch with little Patsy Chapman. She was very sweet and brought me a bottle of 1975 Dow's port. I looked it up in the catalogue of Berry Brothers and they are selling it for £23, so that was a nice little present. She had rung Mrs Tamborero before and asked could she pay for the lunch. She said it was not allowed at the House of Lords. But including the tip the lunch was only £30 so I got practically all of it back with the bottle of port. That is the weird way in which my mind calculates these matters.

She told me she had met Peter Mandelson[17] at the Tory Party Conference. He arrived as a correspondent for the *People* at the *News*

17. Director of Campaigns and Communications, Labour Party, 1985–90; industrial consultant, SRU Group, 1990–2; Labour MP since 1992.

of the World/Sun party. He attacked her and said, 'When are you going to pension off your dreadful Woodrow Wyatt?' To which she said, 'You are being ageist.' I said, 'If he wants me pensioned off, it sounds very much as though they are afraid of what I write. Anyway, I won't even get a pension.'

She is a pretty little thing. We talked about various subjects I get interested in like the National Health Service. She is certain that is the great key to the battle between Tory and Labour.

Another meeting at five-thirty, in a part of London University, of the organization Transylvania Aid Direct. We have got our charitable status. I am the Chairman. Verushka came too and was extremely useful. We appointed her as Chairman of the sub-committee to raise money. We need at least twelve buses at £1,000 each or slightly less to organize children so they are able to go to the schools they need to go to.

Wednesday 30 October

Beginning at 10.30 at Cavendish Avenue there was another long and complicated meeting with Peter Sherlock of Bass, lawyers from both sides, Brian McDonnell and John Heaton, nine of us in all, desperately trying to thrash out a quick agreement. We got some excellent concessions from Bass.

Richard Evans has heard about this agreement coming up. We don't know how he heard about it and find it very puzzling. Brian said when he met Alan Meale (Labour MP) recently he said, 'I think this deal you are doing with Coral is a very good idea.' So we were all rather puzzled and we all want to get it out pretty quick.

Twenty-two people were invited to dinner by the Stevens, packed into the dining-room too tightly.

On my left was Debbie Owen[18] whom I was pleased to see and talk to. Although it had been a blow to her losing the Jeffrey Archer connection as his agent, she has not suffered. The argument was that he wanted to reduce the amount of commission from ten per cent to a lower figure. She said, 'No, that is the price and it always has been.' He said, 'Yes, but I know how to do it all myself now. You've taught me.'

I said I didn't have an agent: 'I did have one once but they never do anything I can't do. I negotiate direct with Rupert Murdoch on

---

18. Literary agent; m (1968) David Owen, Labour and SDP politician.

what I get paid by News International. Occasionally I write some extra articles if I have got time for one publication or another. But I handled the negotiations for my book [*Confessions of an Optimist*] and got quite a lot of money for it, and the serialization and got quite a lot of money for that. So I don't really need an agent. But I do for plays because I don't know my way around that world.'

David Owen ridiculed the *Sunday Times* nonsense about his being Secretary for Health in a Conservative government. He said, 'I would never join them for the same reasons as you never would, Woodrow.' I talked to him about the Hong Kong governership a bit and he said he was not so keen on it now anyway. I told him what Douglas Hurd had said about him being a loose cannon and he laughed and said maybe that was true because he would certainly want his own way.

Time wears on. Debbie is not attractive as she used to be because she is obviously not taking all the measures that women can take now.

Monday 4 November

Princess Esra Jah gave a reception for Princess Michael of Kent at her strange house on Campden Hill. She is the ex wife of the Nizam of Hyderabad.

The champagne was good and so were the little things to eat – real caviar on rounds of bread of which I ate about six.

A lot of the usual people were there: David Metcalfe, Anouska and Mark Weinberg, various publishers and reviewing types because the party was in order to promote Princess Michael's book.

Marie-Christine [Princess Michael] was full of affection, giving me a great hug. I told her that her book was excellent and very good stuff for people who know a little bit about history and would like to know some more.

She is hoping I am going to review it in the *News of the World*. I think I will make a mention of it.[1]

Prince Michael was standing a little forlorn in the middle of the large drawing-room.

I asked him whether he had read his wife's book. He said not yet but he was taking it with him on his foreign travels which he was going on the next day. He said, 'She is having a tremendously tiring time with all these television interviews and interviews with people in the newspapers.' So I commented, 'And you're going to get the hell out of it.' He laughed.

He told me that owing to my intervention he is now getting a little progress with his famous memorial gates for Queen Elizabeth the Queen Mother. There will be a lunch at which he is the host. People like Roy Strong will be there and the conversation will be brought round to how wonderful it would be if the original design were carried through.

---

1. The book was *Cupid and the King: Five Royal Paramours*; WW recommended it as 'a jolly Christmas present' in the *News of the World* on 17 November.

Marie-Christine is a bouncy, jolly girl. She was beautifully dressed in some sort of black outfit.

She exudes sex. I hope her book is a great success. It was suggested that she didn't write much of it but even if she didn't, the ideas were hers and the drive.

The place was full of exceedingly rich people whom Marie-Christine loves to be surrounded by, hoping some of the money will drop off into her lap. The ultra rich Indian Princess is undoubtedly a genuine friend.

Tuesday 5 November
I was asked by the Royal Free to go to a lunch at the Skinners' Hall because they were going to start a fund-raising appeal for building up the deteriorating hospital and adding two storeys to it.

I like the Royal Free people a great deal. I chose the Royal Free to write about in last week's *News of the World*, explaining what a trust hospital does and why it had been such a success at the Royal Free.

My direct host was Roy Pounder and I sat on his left. Next to him was a man from Glaxo who recommended against producing Branigen in England. I asked why and he said, 'We don't think it is a sound product.' I said, 'In that case why do you manufacture it in Italy?' He said, 'It's only done under our name.' I said, 'Do you mean to say that Glaxo are willing to have produced things under their own name without being satisfied with the product?'

He hummed and hawed and Roy Pounder said, 'Lord Wyatt has been telling us about this drug for some time. We are having it investigated and trying to test it.' So the man from Glaxo said, 'That's why Sir Paul (Girolami, Chairman of Glaxo) got on to me wanting to know what was going on, because Lord Wyatt had spoken to him about Branigen.'

I went to the Dulwich Picture Gallery. I said as I went in, 'Do I pay 50p instead of £1.50 as I am an old age pensioner?' They said yes, so I gave them a £5 note and out of the change I gave them £1 and said, 'This is my contribution to the gallery.' They thought that was very funny. Then I wandered around the place looking at all the splendid pictures.

When I came to come out they stopped me and said would I sign their special visitors' book. I said, 'Why, what's that for?' They said, 'Because you are a VIP.' I said, 'No I'm not.' They said, 'Yes we think you count as one. We've recognized you. We'll give you a separate page to yourself, just like Margaret Thatcher had.'

This was the area which she bought a retirement house to live in. It is very beautiful with wonderful old houses with nice gardens and the green of Dulwich College which I drove around.

I was musing on how extraordinary it was that P. G. Wodehouse and Hartley Shawcross were both Alleynians, as old boys are called there after the founder Alleyn. Hartley Shawcross was Attorney General when P. G. Wodehouse wanted to come back after the War, having been in Paris and Germany. Shawcross said in the House he could not give an assurance that Wodehouse would not be prosecuted if he came to England.[2] So the poor old boy was driven by another fellow old boy to go and live in America.

I then went on to our new betting shop at Tooting Bec which is doing magnificently well. It only cost us £55,000 to fit it out. There is a new licence – they hadn't given a new one for a betting shop in that area for thirty years. They are taking business away from William Hill and it is running already at £14,000 a week. If you had to buy a shop with that level of turnover, you would pay at least quarter of a million for it so it was a very good deal.

On to David Rees, my curious bookseller who sells me first editions. We had a merry chat about my first editions of *Goodbye to All That* by Robert Graves. Originally I had a very good copy and a nice dust cover, a first edition but without the famous poem by Siegfried Sassoon which was removed after a hundred copies.[3] He had just sold me a Siegfried Sassoon edition not in very good condition, not as good as mine, for £225 and I am going to give him another £35 when the dust wrapper is found.

I also bought a first edition of Raymond Chandler's *Spanish*

---

2. The comic novelist (1881–1975) was living at Le Touquet in France at the outbreak of the Second World War. He was interned by the Germans in 1940 and taken to Germany, from where he foolishly made a number of broadcasts to America, for which he was paid. Although these were innocuous in themselves, they understandably created a furore in Britain. After the war he settled in America and became an American citizen but was knighted in 1975.

3. Graves had included a private 'letter-poem' Sassoon had sent him containing comments on mutual friends like Lady Ottoline Morrell. Miranda Seymour says in her book *Robert Graves: Life on the Edge* (1995), 'The comments were harmless but Sassoon felt his confidence had been betrayed.'

[*Blood*],[4] in good condition but it only cost £25 because quite a lot had been printed. He also was at Dulwich.

When I got back into the car Robbie [WW's chauffeur] told me that Robert Maxwell had just died. He is said to have fallen out of his yacht near Tenerife.

But I think it is highly likely that he actually committed suicide because his empire was in the most chaotic mess and he was in real trouble. He had to sell Pergamon Press which was the foundation of his fortunes based at Headington Hall [in Oxford]. Maybe it was his last fling to go on that yacht. He was a man of astonishing bravery and perhaps he thought, 'I am just going to remove myself now.'

Wednesday 6 November
Everyone is talking about Maxwell. I don't think he did commit suicide.[5] He was a fighter and if he expected to face fraud charges, he would back himself to get lawyers to defend him successfully. Even if he was utterly bust, he would have money hidden away somewhere.

Even if there was something to do with being a spy for Israel, why would he care? He was Jewish and in later years devoted to Israel, after earlier denying he was Jewish. He had enormous courage. Though he was a crook and a bully he did have some successes as well as crashing failures.

The annual dinner given by the Tony Quintons at the Garrick Club for about thirty people or maybe a few more.

I, alas, had to sit next to the wife of the Earl of Onslow, of American origin. We hated each other on sight. She sneered at the *News of the World* and I sneered at her for sneering at it.

John Julius Norwich was there with his wife who is very pleasant. At the end I said to John Julius Norwich that I was very sorry about the profile of him [in the *Sunday Telegraph*], which I had never read. When I asked Petronella what it said – and I don't know how much of it was dictated to her by her editor – Petronella said she had said he wasn't a very good historian. In a self-deprecating way he laughed and said, 'I think that is true.'

---

4. Collection, published in 1946, of stories which had originally appeared in the pulp magazine *Black Mask*; WW gives the Chandler title as '*Spanish Gold*'; he must have mistakenly recalled the title of the George A. Birmingham novel he discussed with the Queen Mother on 14 March 1990.

5. A change of mind since the previous day.

I said to John Julius, 'I cannot possibly be responsible for what Petronella writes. I was very upset when she did that about you.' He said, 'Don't worry, all is forgotten.' He gave me a great hug and said, 'Anyway, how could anyone hold anything against such a pretty girl?'

The invitation arrived from Margaret and Denis for their fortieth wedding anniversary at Claridge's on December 12th.

Friday 8 November

I am in a fair state of confusion. The fax machine went utterly wrong in the morning. It was jammed. People were trying to send messages to me but they couldn't. The paper was twisted inside. I had to get two secretaries over from the Tote to put it right because Mrs Tamborero had gone to Spain.

Then Pericles banged on my door and I was in no condition to greet him as warmly as I would have liked. Robbie took him back to his mother's with his luggage because he is going to stay there. He then came back for dinner and that was very agreeable. He is much fatter but still a good-looking boy. His hair is short and he doesn't wear a beard any more. He was respectably dressed in the kind of Italian style grey suit which they wear in America.

He has sorted out the financial affairs with the ghastly Maria, as she turned out to be, and now it is all over. He said to me quite honestly he had enjoyed it very much whilst he had been married to her and been with her.

Sunday 10 November

Talked to Norman.

He said he had seen Margaret and talked to her about his trip to Russia where he said their problem was that they had this huge deficit. To which she replied, 'You're not one to talk about that,' meaning he was running a deficit of £20 billion for the coming year which would have been £27 billion but for the proceeds of privatization. He said to me, 'She would have done the same, you know. It's a cycle of economic up and down and you have to do this at some stage.'

Monday 11 November

Went to speak to the City of London School political society, sixth form boys; the adjacent City of London girls' school sent girls as well. One was astonishingly beautiful. She had long, beautifully groomed auburn hair which she kept twirling around her face and pulling back in a seductive manner though I don't know if that was intentional. I couldn't help looking at her.

Edmund Glynn, the son of Dermot Glynn,[6] was chairman of the meeting.

I always like talking to people of that age who are clever.

I gave a fairly hilarious account of why the House of Lords was more representative of democracy than the Commons.

Tuesday 12 November
Dinner party at 19 Cavendish Avenue. Ken and Mary Baker, Algy Cluff, Chips Keswick, Lady Selina Hastings, Lord and Lady Stevens, Lord and Lady Rees-Mogg, Petronella, Verushka and myself.

Andrew Knight and Pericles came in later for coffee as we were finishing the claret in the dining-room. The claret was 1962 Léoville-Poyferré. It was glorious. Unfortunately the corks had broken in the bottle so I had a lot of trouble decanting, particularly as the lunatic Manuel was in charge tonight as José couldn't come in.

Ken talked to me about the levy. I said, 'Give them £41 million. The Jockey Club are going to put in for £50 million. The original offer, the tentative one which was not accepted, was £38.5 by the bookmakers. They can afford £41 million.'

Andrew Knight attacked Chips for not standing by Rupert when he was in trouble. His was the only bank which withdrew their support. He said, 'We gave him six months' notice.'

Chips said he had met Rupert in the street not long ago and Rupert said there were no hard feelings.

He said Rupert had said to him, 'You said I was over-trading and of course I was.'

I chivvied Andrew about being so keen on the Germans and thinking they are no danger to us. Everybody agreed they were and he was in a minority in wanting to be in a federal Europe. Andrew is a swarthy New Zealander with Maori blood so naturally doesn't have emotional feelings against Britain being swallowed by Brussels.

Meriza Stevens and David Stevens were singing the praises of Robert Maxwell. David said that you could ring him up at any time and get good advice from him.

Meriza told me she had been more than once on the yacht off which Maxwell was drowned and she didn't think it was possible to fall off

6. Chief executive of NERA.

it. They had also stayed with him at Headington Hall which they said was very comfortable. His ambition was to overtake Rupert Murdoch.

Algy Cluff said he must have been pretty short of money. He gambled like crazy. He went to Maxim's in Bayswater regularly to gamble as well as to eat and would often lose £100,000 or so a night. He must have lost well over one and a half million recently in gambling.

Wednesday 13 November
Bill Cash lost his chairmanship of the backbench Foreign Affairs Committee of the Tory Party. Norman Fowler replaced him. It was said that Major was very pleased and that the Whips had been instructed to get a massive vote for Fowler as Bill Cash is an anti-federalist.

I took Pericles on a little tour of the Lords. I told the attendant, a charming grey-haired man in the Lords lobby, that I wanted to get him into the House as he was my son. He said, 'Is he your eldest son?' I said, 'Yes. He is my only son.' 'Then he has the right to sit on the steps of the throne,' which Pericles had not wanted really to do, being shy about it.

So Pericles was duly taken around and out at the other end from where I was then sitting and sat on the steps to the throne, making a courtly bow to the throne just before he did. He looked very handsome.

Thursday 14 November
Rang Norman Lamont about the Cash affair and said, 'Was the government really behind that? I thought Bill Cash was very level-headed and sensible about the European Community.' 'I hope not,' said Norman. 'It would be very foolish of the government if they had done.'

Stoker Hartington gave me lunch in the Berkeley. Neither of us drank anything.

We had a constructive discussion on how the Jockey Club should frame its statement to the Home Secretary [on the levy]. He said when he got ready with the draft he would ask me to come in and look at it.

He said it is terrible in the Jockey Club upper reaches; there is still a fearful amount of snobbishness and people who ought to be made stewards are not. He is trying to overcome that.

At one time everybody was very snobbish about Ron Muddle, except for John Howard de Walden who liked him a lot. Stoker said, 'I like him a lot too. He has been very good for racing and made us all think.'

Ron Muddle took the Jockey Club to court for their refusal to allot him fixtures at his new racecourse. All that now seems to be in the past.

I think they now realize that I have a considerable influence with Ken Baker so it doesn't do to antagonize me any more.

Dinner with Countess Karolyi in Drayton Gardens. One guest was Count Bethlen. His family were the virtual rulers of Transylvania for centuries. He was running the estates as head of the family when the Communists took over in Romania. He was in prison for eight years.

He said it was terrible. For three months he had been manacled with an iron chain joining his wrists, connected to a very heavy iron ball so he couldn't walk or move properly.

In the end they let him out, he got to Hungary and was able to escape in some way in 1967.

He is charming, carries no bitterness. In short, he is a saint and shames all of us who have such cosy lives in England and have never have never had to face anything of the kind they have had to in Central Europe or indeed in many other countries.

Saturday 16 November
To Ascot with Pericles. He thought he would like to go with me to a race meeting.

We were expected at 12 in Sir Piers Bengough's entertainment room just behind the members' stand which is the Royal Household stand. To my surprise I found Queen Elizabeth the Queen Mother there.

I talked to her before lunch and for a while when I was sitting next to her. She said, 'Now you must talk to the Duchess.' That was a Dowager Duchess of Westminster who used to own Arkle.[7]

I had a blinding blank of amnesia. I suddenly couldn't remember the name of the chap who used to be Chairman at Cheltenham.

The Duchess said, 'I'll whisper it to you when it's safe.' After a few minutes when he wasn't looking – he was sitting at the same table, opposite us – I said, 'I think it's safe now.' Than she whispered to me, 'I'm afraid I'm a member of CRAFT. Perhaps I shouldn't say this to you, but it stands for "Can't Remember A Fucking Thing".' She, too, had forgotten his name. Later on when we left the lunch table to go and watch a race on television she said, 'I've just remembered it. It's Miles Gosling.'

Queen Elizabeth talked at length to me about the European

---

7. Cheltenham Gold Cup winner 1964, 1965, 1966.

Community. She is terrified of the Germans and said, 'Never trust them, never trust them. They can't be trusted.' I thought that quite amusing as the Royal Family is of German origin.

I told her that relations were now good with the Jockey Club. We were firm friends and I was helping them frame their case with the Levy Board. She was delighted and clapped her hands.

I talked to Piers Bengough about the horse which he withdrew from the sale at £21,000. It was a colt of Sovereign Dancer origin with a very good pedigree. I had been told by Bridget Bengough that John Hills was going to train it and it was going to be leased to people who would pay the expenses for two racing seasons, get the prize money and also half of anything it was sold for above £30,000.

It will cost me £5,000 each racing season. In consequence, I have decided not to put any money into Allan Davis' play.

I would much rather spend that on a horse and get some fun out of it. I am pretty certain his play won't make any money but even if it does, you would have to pay tax on it and it is not a very exciting operation.

Before writing my article on Friday morning I had rung Richard Ryder, the Government Chief Whip.

I said, 'What about the unfortunate Mr Cash who was thrown out of his job as Chairman of the Conservative Foreign Affairs Committee?' He said, 'It wasn't because the government did anything about it. The Whips did nothing at all. It was because some months ago he put down a motion about the Community which he said had the approval of Downing Street and got a hundred signatures but it hadn't had the approval of Downing Street at all. It was rather a tendentious motion, committing the government to things they couldn't be committed to at that stage. That is why he got thrown out. It wasn't a plot at all. It was spontaneous.'

Tuesday 19 November
Reception at the Hungarian Embassy for the President of Hungary.

I asked him where he learned to speak English so well and he said, 'In prison.'

Prison is where many Hungarians imprisoned by the Communists learned a great many things.

Later Evelyn de Rothschild came in. He said he was going to send a demand notice to be paid the money the Tote owed Rothschild's for what they did over Coral. I said, 'Ho, we haven't had a bill yet. All we have had is a letter saying did we agree to the amount of £25,000 you were going to charge us and I was going to tell you on Thursday when we have lunch with you that we did agree.' He wanted to know how well his team performed. He said, 'It's like getting rooms in a hotel. You only know from what people who actually use the hotel rooms disclose whether it is any good or not.' I said, 'I think they are excellent.'

I have written to John Hills [trainer] about my taking a share of the lease in the horse, by Sovereign Dancer. I have chosen the name Pyrrhic Dance, which he said is available, so all is quite fun.

I think Verushka will be pretty annoyed when she hears about it.

Wednesday 20 November

Talked to Margaret before 8.00 a.m. She got back from America last night but she was already well into preparing what she was going to say in the Commons debate on Maastricht this afternoon. She still does not believe the government is doing the right thing.

I said, 'I think you should do it in this way: praise what the government say at its face value – the stand against federal government and not getting involved in the single currency and the Central Bank and so on.'

Later When Margaret spoke she was in high form, sparkling away, commanding the attention of the whole house. There were a lot of noisy interruptions at one point which she dealt with excellently. She followed exactly the line I suggested to her in the morning, praising John Major's stance and saying she was going to back him on it, which obviously took the wind out of the Labour Party's and the Liberal Party's sails.

She also praised Douglas Hurd for doing what she had told him. He was blushing deeply and people were laughing. Eventually Douglas got up and said, 'She has had many Foreign Secretaries in her time. May I on behalf of them all accept her tribute.' That was quite funny but not really at her expense.

She was making a lot of jokes, showing great sense of humour as well as engaging the deep seriousness of the problem, asking for a referendum before we made a final decision on a single currency.

Thursday 21 November

At 9.15 Brian McDonnell and Tom Phillips, our Financial Director, were due at the house to be followed rapidly by Peter Sherlock of Bass and their lawyers. We had another of these eternal arguments and discussions, trying to sort out the nuts and bolts of our agreement.

I was irritated because John Heaton's wife had a baby and he decided to take the whole day off from the morning onwards yesterday to take his wife to the hospital and he took another day off today. I had needed very badly some information for the Levy Board about what happened the last time the bookmakers challenged our sole possession of the tents and marquees for Tote betting and not allowing a proliferation of bookmakers. As a result, I couldn't deal with the situation as well as I would have wished. There is going to be another bloody inquiry into it so that will give us a lot of work unnecessarily.

When I spoke to Brian [later] on the telephone, I said I had been rather annoyed about not having all this stuff which John Heaton should have dug out for me. He said, 'He's asleep now.' I said, 'Good heavens. Did he have the baby or did his wife have it? How many days is he proposing to stay away because his wife has had a baby?' He said, 'We're lucky because nowadays husbands are allowed six days to be away.' I said, 'Whatever for?' He said, 'To look after any children at home.' I said, 'But he has got his mother there. I spoke to her on the telephone and she is looking after the child.' It's incredible. The country's going very soft, aided by the European Community which is telling us how many days people should have off when their wives have babies.

At The Other Club.

Jacob [Rothschild] is very disappointingly in favour of a single currency and was agreeing with the clown Winston Churchill that it was inevitable that we would go into it and that it was all the thing of the future.

Jacob asked, 'Have you seen about my new appointment?' I said, 'No. What's that?' He said, 'I'm Chairman of the National Heritage Memorial Fund.'

I immediately talked to him about my Marx Memorial Library, Jack Huntingdon's mural and how they need £8,000. He said that is the sort of thing they could deal with. So maybe I shall take that up with that curious lady who still remains a Communist and is the librarian.

There was a lot of Churchillian booming without the content tonight. There was Nicholas Soames, a grandson by his mother Mary, and there was young Winston, a grandson direct.[8] They were shouting their heads off with shallow arguments. It's extraordinary how they are a sort of pastiche of part of Winston's appearance, his build and panache, without the brain which made the roar and the noise palatable. These two have got only the push and none of the talent.

Denis Thatcher was there.

He is not going around any more abroad on her tours and her lectures where he says she picks up 'valuable shekels'. He said when he used to go with her when she was Prime Minister he could do things to help the Foreign Office to sell things for Britain but now they wouldn't take any notice of him. Arnold Weinstock and I both said we were not so sure about that.

I met Paddy Ashdown,[9] the new member, for the first time. He looked at me a bit sideways because I always make fun of him in the *News of the World* but he smiled agreeably enough as we shook hands.

Friday 22 November
Rang Norman and congratulated him on his excellent speech winding up the debate [on Europe].

I said, 'I agree with Mrs Thatcher that there should be a referendum before we do anything ghastly or contemplate anything which would change the character of the nation.' He said he agreed, too. I was very pleased because that is not the line John Major has been taking since she made her remarks about a referendum. First he seemed to welcome it and then he back-pedalled, saying it was for Parliament to decide the issue in a parliamentary democracy.

In the afternoon Amanda Smith from French, the theatrical publishing company who are publishing my play (to which we have now decided to give the name of *High Profiles*) came to see me. She seemed highly intelligent and we raced through all the points she had.

Saturday 23 November
Set out to Cornwall with Pericles driving.

The house was very cold.

Tessa said would I tell her what I thought of the new arrangements she had made in the dining-room. They had moved the picture of my

---

8. WW means by the male line, Winston Churchill being the son of Randolph, the great prime minister's only son.

9. Leader of the Liberal Democratic Party, 1989–99.

brother to a side wall and stuck a terribly bad late Victorian picture of the death of Nelson in its place. The other changes of pictures were lamentable.

There may be promising news about the wind farm which could make somebody's fortune when I'm dead.

Wednesday 27 November
Had breakfast at a quarter to seven so that I could be at Battersea Heliport by eight-thirty to catch the Sea King helicopter to Portland to visit the HMS *Polar Circle*, intended or hoped to be the replacement for HMS *Endurance* of Falkland Islands fame.

It is a magnificent vessel, a hundred yards or so long and high, with the most modern bridge in the world according to the Captain, button pressing and no wheels.

Captain Turner is a splendid fellow. We were told all kinds of secrets about what it could carry. I thought that was a trifle unwise because you can never totally rely on MPs.

Their role is to patrol around the Falklands to prevent people pinching the fish and trawling when they shouldn't, and to observe what is going on in the areas we claim in Antarctica and in other people's areas, for example the Argentinian area.

It was pleasant to be back in the military atmosphere. It reminded me of when I was Under Secretary at the War Office.[10] They are very efficient in many respects, those who run our services, and very keen and patriotic. They are pretty distressed about the government's absurd cuts in naval strength.

Thursday 28 November
I listened to Major at Question Time. My God, he is pedestrian and footling. He and Kinnock exchanged puerile third form repartee at the bah-hoo level. Pitiful. Major lacks the magic and the majesty of Margaret and will never have it.

Friday 29 November
Rang Margaret at about half past eight. She got back from Kuwait last night. She bubbled away with excitement from the visit.

We discussed the coming talks at Maastricht.

She said, 'Reporting is terrible. I never said John Major was arrogant

---

10. May–October 1951, the last days of the Attlee Labour government.

as I've been alleged to have done. I only said it would be arrogant not to consult the people in a referendum before we took irrevocable steps.'

I was glad to hear her reverberating with vitality.

To the Garrick Club for the *Times* op-ed party. Dear Philip Howard. It's his last appearance as literary editor. I met his successor, Paul Johnson's son, Daniel, who has many of the gestures and appearance of his father. He is very clever. He got a First at Oxford in History. He wants to know what sort of reviews I would like to write.

In came Simon Jenkins, the editor. He said Paul Johnson's son had been writing a lot of the leaders. I said to Simon, 'Most of your leaders are rather good but I thought she was rather hurt that you attacked her the other day.' He said, 'It is very difficult to be both supporting of John Major and herself at the same time.'

He said, 'At Number 10 they now regard her as the enemy.' 'They must be crazy,' I replied. 'She is on their side and supports what they are trying to do but he is naturally anxious in case we go too far.'

I got them interested in a campaign to get poor A. L. Rowse made a knight before he dies, or given some honour.

When I got there Philip Howard introduced me to Fiona Mac-Carthy, who wrote a biography of Eric Gill which is extremely good.

I told her that there is an exhibition of his drawings and paintings for sale in Jermyn Street next to the shop which sells the cheeses [Paxton & Whitfield]. She is going to go there.

She is now engaged on writing a book about William Morris. If she spends as much time on research on him as she did on Eric Gill, it is going to be very good. She discovered new papers about Eric Gill and a whole horde of letters and hitherto unpublished stuff about William Morris, who also had a very strange sex life, living in a ménage à trois at Kelmscott, the house he loved the best.[11]

I greatly enjoyed talking to all the young sparks.

I don't seem to have any generation gap with them at all. There is possibly a brain gap because their brains, when they got Firsts at Oxford and were Fellows of All Souls, were probably rather better than mine.

---

11. *Eric Gill* was published in 1989, *William Morris: A Life for our Time* in 1994. Morris had two houses called Kelmscott: Kelmscott Manor House, Oxfordshire, acquired in 1871, and Kelmscott House, Upper Mall, Hammersmith, London, acquired in 1878.

Sunday 1 December
Rupert rings from Aspen. He sounds very lively. He is coming to England for one day tomorrow, chasing up banks to get his loans in order the way he wants. 'Not that it's much use coming to England,' he said, 'because the banks are so difficult here. But I shall mainly get it from other countries.'

He said that Norman Lamont was on television at lunch time with Brian Walden.

According to Rupert he had said he might have to raise interest rates again. Rupert thought that was a very silly thing to do because it would be all over the newspapers the next day and would cause a run on the pound.

Monday 2 December
Contrary to what Rupert thought there was no commotion in the press about Norman hinting he might have to raise interest rates again. I had already gathered from Rosemary that he said no more than he always says on these occasions; that he wouldn't rule out anything if it were necessary.

Tuesday 3 December
Continuing my mad extravagance I went again to the Jermyn Street exhibition of Eric Gill engravings. I bought one, rather a nice one of a woman suckling a baby. £70 plus VAT. Crikey.

I found that I hadn't ever read the Eric Gill book by Fiona Mac-Carthy though I had told her I had. I must have read extracts from it in the *Sunday Times* or wherever. I got a paperback copy.

When I had told her about the exhibition – and she hadn't been there according to the proprietors of it – I said I had nearly bought one but I wasn't quite sure. She said, 'Weren't they explicit enough?' She meant in sex terms. They weren't particularly explicit. The ones which were more explicit, with the beautiful curly pubic hairs that Eric Gill puts in some of his drawings, were rather more expensive. One in particular, which was a very triumphant penis attacking a lady, also naked, was very expensive so I couldn't afford that anyway.

Went to Clerkenwell to the Marx Memorial Library to see the Communist lady, fair-haired and gently plump-faced, who runs it. I wanted to pick up my Marx Memorial mugs and also to talk to her about getting some money from the National Heritage Memorial Fund.

I told her how to prepare the case. She will send it to me to make sure she has got it right and then she will write direct to Jacob.

She told me her husband has what the *Birmingham Post* called the most unenviable job in Britain. I said, 'What's that?' She said, 'Circulation and Promotion Manager for the *Morning Star.*'[1]

She was also rather sweet and agreed that they had made a pretty good cock-up of the Soviet Union, considering it ought to have been one of the richest countries in the world.

I said, 'You're an English eccentric, you know, whether you like it or not; you still peddle the lost cause of a failed religion enthusiastically.'

In the *Sun* this morning there was an attack on Norman for looking so awful in his television broadcast on Sunday. That was obviously put in at Rupert's behest. It said he must get on with his job more, etc. On the other hand, maybe it wasn't Rupert because he really likes Norman. I wish they wouldn't put these attacks on Norman in because it embarrasses me as well.

We had a jolly Tote Board meeting in the morning. David Sieff is helpful. He thinks we are making excellent savings. I think we could make a lot of money out of our telemarketing and he agrees with my line rather more than Brian does.

We have got this marvellous job going for about a year from which we are bound to make about a quarter of a million at least, if not more, advertising this wonderful device for videos – just look up the number in the newspaper against the programme you want to record and then point the machine, which costs £69, at the video machine and press the number and it will automatically decide to put itself on at the right time, allowing a little space on either side and even adjust itself if, for example, there is a special news programme making it run late.

David Sieff said he was going to buy one immediately for his wife

---

1. The *Morning Star* is the only UK Communist daily newspaper; Tish Newland m (1979–96) Bob Newland; the Marx Memorial Library received £365,000 for its refurbishment from the Heritage Lottery Fund in 1997.

who can never make the video work. The other day he asked her to put it on for a race at Newmarket and she put it on for a race at Chepstow.

The party given by the Prices, former US Ambassador to England, in the Royal Suite at Claridge's.

I talked to Susan Crosland who remains looking pretty in spite of being around sixty, perhaps a bit more. She said she was meeting Auberon Waugh for dinner tomorrow night.

He said Susan's last book was much better written, much more entertaining and worth reading than any of the Booker Prize nominees.

I said, 'That was very kind of him,' but actually, though I didn't say it, I think that's a lot of rot. Her book was absolute sex piffle. She said it has sold millions and she is writing a third one now. I said, 'Is it even steamier?' She said, 'I suppose so.' She says she finds she can live very well now, far better than just writing articles, on the proceeds of her novels.[2]

She said, 'You and I must be the only two in this room who have ever voted Labour.' I said, 'Would you vote Labour again? I don't think Tony would,' meaning her late husband. She said, 'I don't know. I would do it out of sentiment. I remember you writing when Mrs Thatcher was deposed that you wouldn't vote Tory again and you would advise people to vote Labour at the next election. That was sentiment. It wasn't your head.'

I got embroiled for a long time with Mark Thatcher.

He said he was going to take up residence in Switzerland because there they would never join a political union with Europe or the single currency and therefore, as taxes were all going to be dictated by Brussels, it would be the only place where the taxes were not the Brussels taxes which would be enormous after the single currency came in.

There were a great many evidently rich people there. Poor little 'Baby' Steinberg came in looking very sorrowful, as well she might, and thanked me for going to the memorial service [for her husband]. But I didn't actually go. I felt a heel again for never having written to her. Oh dear, it's too late now, but there are so many things I ought to do and don't find the time and energy for.

---

2. *Dangerous Games* was published in 1991, *Ruling Passions* in 1989, *The Magnates* in 1994.

Wednesday 4 December

Dinner at Amabel Lindsay's.[3] It was timed for eight-thirty. We actually sat down at a quarter past nine. She was very hurt when I wanted to go at half past eleven. I said, 'I am an old man and I need sleep.' She can't understand that. She has got nothing to do and is a rich, merry widow.

There was a pleasant man, John Gross,[4] now theatrical critic for the *Sunday Telegraph*. He used to edit the *Times Literary Supplement* and was married to Miriam Gross. He said he always thought of me as a literary figure. He said when he was a young boy he used to read my collection of *English Story*. He said, 'You don't seem to have done so much about literature since.' I said, 'No. Cyril Connolly used to describe me as "failed literature".' John said, 'He's the one to talk.'

We talked about the plays he likes and dislikes.

He said Pinter gets too fanatically political.

We agreed Alan Ayckbourn was good and Peter Shaffer and even the fellow Hare who wrote the play about Rupert.[5]

On my left was Susanna Johnston.

She is quite a jolly lady, sister of Alexander Chancellor and daughter of the man who had much to do with Reuters.[6] She said, 'My father only saw things in terms of news. He wasn't interested in the feelings or emotions or meanings behind it, just the news.'

I said, 'I think the criminalizing of drugs should be ended. That's the best way to get rid of the peddling and the crime associated with them. Put them on sale at Boots at a very low price. I know your daughter had some trouble with drugs.' She did. She was the girl who

---

3. Widow of the Hon. Patrick Lindsay (d 1986) and daughter of the 9th Earl of Hardwicke.

4. Writer, editor, critic; Fellow, King's College, Cambridge, 1962–5; editor, *Times Literary Supplement*, 1974–81; theatre critic, *Sunday Telegraph*, since 1989; m (1965–88) Miriam, née May, who m 2 (1993) Sir Geoffrey Owen, former editor, *Financial Times*.

5. David Hare and Howard Brenton wrote *Pravda*, in which the pivotal character is a newspaper proprietor.

6. Sir Christopher Chancellor (1904–89; knight 1951) was general manager of Reuters, 1944–59; Alexander Chancellor at this time editor, *Independent Magazine*.

went to prison for being in possession of illegal drugs and having passed them on to the Guinness girl who was found dead at Oxford.[7]

When Amabel saw me smoking my own cigar she said, 'What a pity. I've some cigars which Chips Keswick gave me. He said to keep them in a cool place so they've been in the refrigerator for a few months.' I was absolutely dumbfounded and said, 'Good gracious, they must be in a terrible condition.' She said, 'Oh no. I'll go and get them,' which she did and she handed me one which was frozen stiff. I said, 'I don't think this is smokeable. It's a very good Montecristo.' She said, 'Well take it home and put it in your humidor or somewhere and then tell me how I should keep them.'

Thursday 5 December
Dinner with the Weinbergs in their strange house. The downstairs walls were previously black. Now they have been painted green. The lighting makes me feel as though I were under the sea. There is a heavy ocean-like colour. The floors are slate and slippery, where they are not marble and also slippery.

The back looks out on to a big garden with a swimming pool which is not yet finished. Mark said that Anouska is always altering what the builders do and making then start again.

On my right sat Jane Stevens.[8] She is still a lady-in-waiting to Princess Margaret. I asked her if Princess Margaret is still very unhappy.

She said, 'She is not unhappy. It is quite possible for a woman to live alone, I do, without being unhappy and without being desperate to have a man to marry.'

Anouska, on my left, was very chatty. We talked about what I called, to her surprise, 'her Victorian work ethic'.

I said, 'If you're not running your hotel, Blakes, or your dress business, you are always looking for something to do that's useful. You're not a flibbertigibbet at all as you sometimes appear to be.' She had taken great pains with the dinner which was terrific.

When we arrived Anouska gave us a present. She had heard it was our silver wedding and she thought it was today and not on Saturday.

---

7. Olivia Channon, daughter of Paul and Ingrid (formerly Guinness) Channon died in 1986; Rose Johnston wrote about her prison experience in *Inside Out* (1989).
8. Jane, née Sheffield, m (1956–79) Jocelyn Stevens; see 26 June 1991 for Jocelyn Stevens and Vivien Duffield.

She gave this special dinner for us and the present was two very pretty silver pots on silver trays.

Tim Bell suddenly got up, said it was our silver wedding anniversary and made rather a moving speech which greatly embarrassed me.

I was so surprised by this unexpected speech that when he ended I failed to say anything which was extremely gauche of me.

With the dessert courses there was Tokay, chilled. Verushka didn't want any and the butler said, 'It's specially for you, m'Lady,' as she is Hungarian, so she had to have some.

William Shawcross said that Maxwell, whom he met a number of times and had written to him when trying to prepare his biography on Rupert, was absolutely obsessed with Rupert and that was his downfall. He always wanted to have a bigger publishing empire and be more important in newspapers and have more influence politically than Rupert. So he plunged and plunged and now it seems he even pinched the pension funds of his workers.

Friday 6 December
Hussein Al Ghazzi came to see me about Heveningham Hall. They can't get the money through from Germany till March.

The more the revelations come out about Maxwell the more it seems that he probably did commit suicide. It wasn't just a matter of him being afraid to be put on trial for fraud. He had absolutely blown everything he had got and a great deal more besides.

Saturday 7 December
I talked to Emily Blatch, the Minister in the Environment Department. It is very tricky for Heveningham Hall.

She said, 'Can't Al Ghazzi, the younger brother, get on to the Kuwaiti bank and tell them to hang on a bit or lift the receivership because he is going to get this money?'

I relayed that to Hussein.

I had a dream the other day about Michael Howard. I dreamed he had been blown up and killed by a terrorist bomb in his house. I thought should I warn him that I had a premonition. Then I thought that would sound ridiculous so I haven't done it.

Sunday 8 December
Talked to Norman Lamont to wish him good luck at Maastricht where they are off to this afternoon. I said, 'Are you still standing firm?' He

said, 'Absolutely. There's still the same plan that we would want the opt-out clause on the single currency and the Central European Bank; and Parliament will decide some years later.' I said, 'That's fine because that doesn't raise any question of a referendum now and there will be no real quarrel between John and Margaret.'

Monday 9 December

Though our silver wedding anniversary was on Saturday 7th, we had a party for twenty-four for dinner on December 9th.

Earnest debate with Duncan McEwan of Christie's in the morning who consulted books and references from Michael Broadbent's notes. I said I had four kinds of 1966 (the year of the marriage) claret: Cantemerle, Rauzan-Gassies, Pontet-Canet and Haut-Batailley. Though the Rauzan-Gassies is said to be the best, being a second growth and nearly the top of it, we chose Haut-Batailley which though fifth growth should be much higher.

It was superb. We opened six bottles. Maybe we could have done with slightly less because nearly a complete one wasn't drunk but everybody loved it even though they didn't want red wine to begin with. There was also the magnificent 1986 Pavillon Blanc, the white wine of Château Margaux. We began with a 1947 Moët & Chandon champagne plus a magnum of Moët & Chandon, old but not a vintage year, plus a 1982 Krug which Irwin and Cita Stelzer kindly sent us.

Then we had Tokay Essencia 1967 and a very good 1961 port and of course brandy, etc. and more champagne.

Verushka made everything very beautiful.

The silver on the tables, and we had twenty-four of my crested plate set still left so there were just enough to go round, looked very good. Candles were blazing everywhere.

On my right sat Sonia [Sinclair] to begin with and on my left Diane Lever, the two women whom I had known longest. Sonia said I have curious fits when I don't like her any more, which is not true, so I was very jolly with her and complimented her on remaining so youthful.

Mark Pejacsevich was on my table and he bet me £5 that Petronella wouldn't sing after the food was over. I said, 'I think she will if I ask her,' which I did in my speech and she obliged by singing my favourite 'As Time Goes By' with a beautiful voice. An amazing voice that child has. Everybody was stunned.

I made a little speech in which I referred to everybody in the room and the reason they were there and the time I had known them. Julian

Amery from Oxford; Arnold Weinstock (and Netta) I said had helped me in adversity;[9] David Swaythling I said was a great help and very loyal on the Tote Board (which is not quite true but it is more or less). I said of Nicholas, my step-son, that 'it is amazing that he is now older than his mother and she is now younger than when I married her'.

The wronged and injured Caroline Banszky[10] sweetly brought two silver pigs, one with a blue ribbon and one with a pink one. Julian Amery became very keen on her during the evening as he sat next to her. He is very susceptible. He dotes on Petronella and when he insisted on making a speech he told everybody that he is her godfather.

There were poinsettias on the stairs and flowers everywhere. Robin Day was an angel. He not only brought a huge bunch of flowers but a very expensive silver-backed address book on which he had our initials inscribed. It must have cost him at least £150–£200. I was very worried about it because he really hasn't got any money. The de Gelseys,[11] who are very sweet (I don't know them all that well though Verushka has known them a long time), brought a pepper pot with a silver stand below which is nice but not extravagant considering how rich they are. Netta brought a beautiful silver photograph frame. Dear Chips went out and bought a pot made of silver with silver flowers and little emerald ones as well. Arabella [Lennox-Boyd] sent from Aspreys another huge silver photograph frame on which she had our initials carved and the date 9.12.91 because she didn't realize the anniversary was actually 7.12.91. Diane Lever had sent two lovely silver candlesticks.

When I talked about Arnold having helped me in adversity he apparently put his hands on his head because he was so embarrassed. He hates being praised. He likes to be thought of as a hard-hearted villain which he is far from being. I did say, however, that though he was one of my oldest friends he could be difficult.

When they went I gave all who wanted one of my books or two or three if they wanted them. They all asked me to write things in them. For Tessa Keswick, because Robin Day had been saying how outspoken I had been about sex with various people, in her book I said, 'What a pity I didn't know you earlier.'

---

9. At the time of the collapse of his printing business.
10. The Banszkys were about to divorce.
11. Alexander de Gelsey, born Budapest, m (1969) Romy, née Cairns; Honorary Consul of the Republic of Hungary since 1990.

Wednesday 11 December

Clearly Major has done brilliantly. He conformed exactly with what I laid down in my article in the *Times* on December 3rd. He accomplished more than I thought he possibly could. We are not drifting into federalism.

I spoke to Michael Howard, the Employment Secretary in the Cabinet, at about nine.

I said, 'You, Michael, seem to have won a great victory on the social charter by opting out of it.'

I then rang Andrew Turnbull, Major's Personal Private Secretary. Had a long conversation. He had been up since 4.00 a.m. because though he didn't go to Brussels he had to wait for Major to return which he did just before 4.00 a.m. Then they worked out the statements for today and so on. He is going to send me a special brief saying exactly what the result was.

I then tried to get Margaret but she wouldn't ring back. I kept on getting the message that she was in a meeting.

Norman Lamont and I think she doesn't want to talk to me because she is not yet reconciled to the fact that he, Major, has pulled off a great coup and it wasn't her who did it. In some ways it is possible that he may have got more by his less full frontal methods than she would have done.

I went to the Lords Gallery in the Commons and listened to it all. There was Margaret and she nodded agreement the whole time but didn't say a word. Major got a very good reception. The Labour Party were all over the place.

I said in the Christmas card I had sent round to him, 'I think you have done better than I would ever have dared to expect you could. YOU ARE NOW A STATESMAN. Congratulations on your great triumph.' It seems I have rather committed myself to Major now but I think Margaret would be silly to try to spoil the broth.

Thursday 12 December

Claridge's. Margaret and Denis have their fortieth wedding anniversary celebration.

In the morning I had spoken to Margaret.

She thought that John Major had made a good performance in the House, by which she meant she wasn't so sure about his performance at Maastricht itself.

She said, 'He has agreed to the process towards the single currency. Why couldn't they have opted out of that altogether, the same way as they opted out of the social charter?'

I rang Andrew Turnbull at Number 10 and said, 'This conversation is between me, you and the Prime Minister only,' and I told him roughly what she had said. I said, 'That should be a guide to you. If you let me down, I can be of no further use because she will be very cross if she thinks that I am talking to you as well as to her.'

She is curiously reluctant to discuss these things with me now because she knows that I think she must not put herself in the position of criticizing things she would have done herself.

I left [the party] at nearly twenty to eight to go to The Other Club. When I got to the door there were Margaret and Denis.

She said, 'We're just waiting for the Prime Minister,' in rather a wistful voice.

When I had asked her in the morning if he was coming she had said, 'No, he's got a reception at Number 10. We didn't know the dates were clashing.' I thought to myself, 'That's a very good move on John Major's part, very conciliatory.'

Poor darling Margaret. It is the most appalling thing that has happened to her. I can see her sad, if not bitter, at not being in charge at Maastricht.

But I think she is too shrewd politically to get herself out on a limb in not supporting the government on this. I said, 'You can win the election on this,' and she genuinely does want John Major to win it so her emotions conflict all the time – he does it wrong, he must do it differently but nevertheless he must win the election.

Then it was off to The Other Club.

I ribbed Fitzroy Maclean for backing Serbia against Croatia. He said he now thinks it is half a dozen of one and six of the other. The Serbians have no business to be destroying Dubrovnik and murdering the Croatians.

I said, 'Which do you think are more important, ancient buildings and monuments which civilized people regard as the heritage of man, or the people themselves?' He hesitated a bit. I said, 'My answer is you can always replace the people, and I don't really mind how many of those are killed, provided that their wonderful buildings remain. I would give my life to save St Paul's. People did in the War when they went and defused bombs inside it and were risking their lives. They thought the building was more important than they were.'[12]

Altogether it was quite a riotous, interest-packed day, even including at the Levy Board where Evelyn de Rothschild was the guest at lunch time. He has become very friendly to me and wants me to work on the Levy Board – John Sparrow and Tristram Ricketts – not to sell the United Racecourses, of which he is the Chairman, too soon. That's Epsom, Sandown and Kempton.

On the other hand, Christopher Sporborg was all for getting something done now because he wants the Jockey Club's Racecourse Holdings Trust, who own a number of very well run racecourses, to buy it.

When I said goodbye to Christopher Sporborg I said, 'I want the Jockey Club to have it and I will do what I can to get it negotiated a little later. That's the right place for it to be. It's a total guarantee that racing will always continue in those places.'

Actually Epsom is going to make a bomb. Maybe the policy of letting boxes out for a whole year isn't such a good one. Companies can't afford it any more and they think it looks extravagant today anyway. United Racecourses can make more money, they've discovered, by renting them out on a daily basis. At Epsom itself, after all, the only thing they have got there is the Derby. They are getting a lot of money from Sandown but that is nothing to do with racing. It is used for conferences and exhibitions and they are going to do the same at Epsom. So Evelyn hasn't been running United Racecourses too badly.

Friday 13 December
Spoke to Margaret and thanked her for the lovely party. She said, 'Wasn't it nice?' I said I was so glad John Major came and she said, 'Yes it was very good.'

I said, 'I am going to write in the *News of the World* and in the *Times* next week that I think he did a pretty good job at Maastricht. He was really pushing your views, you know.' She said, 'Yes, I know.'

---

12. Harold Nicolson wrote in the *Spectator* in 1944 that he would be prepared to be 'shot against a wall' if his death could save a Giotto fresco from destruction, and that he 'would not hesitate an instant to protect St Mark's in Venice, even if I was aware that by so doing I should bring death to my sons'. Nigel Nicolson commented (*Sunday Telegraph*, 23 May 1999), 'His sons, who were both with the army in Italy, were not best pleased when they read this.'

This was quite a different mood from yesterday morning when she was saying she had to make up her mind and consider it all.

After a bit she said, 'Woodrow, I have got to run. I've got some milk on the stove.' We both laughed. It is odd that Margaret is still doing her own cooking for breakfast and has to dash from the telephone to stop the milk boiling over.

I rang Andrew Turnbull after I had spoken to Margaret and said, 'Another conversation strictly between you, me and the Prime Minister.' I told him that Margaret had just said to me that she was going to support him now and that she had been delighted that he came to the party.

He immediately told me that in fact that conversation of mine with her yesterday morning had been a catalyst. When I told her what a pity John Major wasn't coming, it was followed, Andrew told me, by an immediate olive branch from the other side saying would he like to come. John said yes he would, so an invitation was sent round by hand. He hadn't ever had an invitation from Margaret before.

Saturday 14 December
Went to Lingfield to open a new restaurant.

When I got there I found that the man who runs it and one of the principal partners owning it was Nigel Kent-Lemon[13] whose father I knew.

He was the man who invented the EM2 quick-firing rifle which was the best in the world and which Churchill abandoned when he became Prime Minister in 1951 because the Americans wanted to standardize on a Belgian rifle which was nowhere near so good. Kent-Lemon said, 'I have got a book, published in Canada, written about my father and all about the whole story of the EM2.' He showed it me and the others at the lunch and there was my speech in the House and the articles I had written in *Reynolds News* about it.

They were all very impressed, particularly at the part where Churchill had congratulated me on my shooting. He said he had noticed that my prejudice against the rifle had not prevented me from making a remarkable score with the Belgian rifle that morning, when

---

13. (1946–98); chartered accountant; consultant to the casino industry; visiting lecturer, Institute for the Study of Gambling and Commercial Gaming at the University of Nevada, Reno; chairman, City Clubs; chairman, Lingfield Racecourse, 1991–98; member, Tote Board, 1998.

some of us had gone down to the range.[14] Winston had been acute enough to get the results and every shot I fired was a bull except for one which was an inner. I still had use of both eyes at that time.

Nigel Kent-Lemon is part owner as well, and also runs, Maxim's, the gaming place where Taki[15] had said that Maxwell had been losing £1 million a night, probably out of the *Mirror* pension funds, and thought nothing of losing £250,000 a time. He had been doing it more and more just before he died because he was getting more and more reckless and desperate. He hoped to win some of the money back because he needed to save himself.

Kent-Lemon said, 'There's not a word of truth in that. He hadn't been in Maxim's for two and a half years. He never owed us any money' (the query in the newspapers was 'Did he ever pay his gambling debts?') 'and he hadn't been in the other gaming clubs, either Crock-ford's or Aspinall's.' I said, 'How do you know?' He said, 'Because we all three of us, the big clubs in London, check with each other who has been in and who have been the big spenders, and he hadn't been in any of those either.'

He said, 'Originally when asked by newspapers for my comment, I said, "I have no comment" because we never comment about cus-tomers.' I said, 'I might use it in the *News of the World*, without involving you personally.'[16]

He had brought down from Maxim's some beautiful bottles of 1983 Léoville-Poyferré.

I told him about these expensive meals that Neil Zarach and Eva, his Hungarian wife, gave us at Crockford's. He said, 'They are not expensive at all. They are all free.' I said, 'Are they free at your place?' He said, 'Yes, of course.' I said, 'You wouldn't make much money out of me because whenever I have been to Crockford's I have stopped when I have either won £50 or lost £50. I wouldn't dare go on gambling because I think it could be addictive.' He said, 'Yes but you usually have in a party people who are going to spend a lot of money.'

Sunday 15 December
Norman Lamont is much concerned about the *Sun* report about his son being in hospital.

---

14. The House of Commons has its own rifle range.
15. *Spectator* columnist.
16. WW did, on 29 December 1991.

Later Rupert rang up. He is in London very briefly. I told him about Norman and he said, 'Tell him not to rise so much. There is nothing serious about it.' I said, 'Why did they persecute him about his son? Photographers were massed there, other newspapers joined in outside the hospital and also they were ringing him up when he was trying to prepare the details for the important conference at Maastricht, demanding a statement from him on the allegations that his son first of all was there for drug abuse and had been suspended from his school and secondly that he was there for alcohol abuse, neither of which statement was true, it being a simple appendicitis. Why does Kelvin MacKenzie do these things, ringing up personally to the Treasury to Norman's private office?'

Rupert replied, 'He's got nothing better to do. He ought to be doing something more important,' but he wasn't at all bothered.

Monday 16 December
Up at 6.00 a.m. to catch an aeroplane to Brussels. Brian McDonnell accompanied me. It is to attend the hearings of the commission on gambling in the Single Market, including lotteries and horseracing.

In the afternoon the discussion in the hearing centred on lotteries.

The representatives of the various interests and governments and associations read their prepared scripts, having already put in papers which said just about the same.

It was like a whole series of trams on different lines but never diverging from the lines on which they were set, determined to ignore what was going on in the other trams.

Before we went out to dinner I had been to see Leon Brittan in his splendid office where he is the Commissioner for Competition.

He said, 'I think the Prime Minister is moving towards the idea that a single currency is inevitable and that it isn't true that you will be affected in your own taxation policy. It's only insofar as interest rates are concerned and meeting the deficit requirements and the inflation requirements.' He thought John Major did very well and that there was a triumph for him, although the outcome was one which also pleased the Germans, the French and the Italians. He said it was his, Leon Brittan's, idea that we should be allowed to preserve all matters of defence and foreign affairs to ourselves if we thought our vital interests were affected.

He agreed that we have a very good chance if we challenge the Community if they try to use Article 118A, the health and safety regulations for workers, as a way of making us vary our pay, hours and conditions of work and everything else.

I asked Leon if he was going to do another stint here and he said he might do. He was supposed to give up at the end of this year. I said, 'You have a very good position to advance here and come back to politics later.' But I don't think he will have a chance actually, myself, to return to politics in Britain because he can't put things across properly, particularly on TV.

Tuesday 17 December

I made my first statement from just a few scribbled headline notes and spoke for about five minutes. It woke the place up.

Then I made three interventions later.

I made a lot of jokes to the discomfort of Ladbroke sitting opposite me. I warned my European friends that the smile on the face of the tiger may be agreeable but it will devour you just the same, if it gets the chance, and you will all be idiots in Europe if you give them, the bookmakers, a chance. Their only interest is to get as much money as they can out of racing for developing hotel chains, buying property in America, anything other than putting money back into racing.

Back to England in time to go to the Jeffrey Archer party. He has become extremely pompous. You are not allowed to smoke in the apartment now because it damages the pictures, according to him.

Jeffrey dragged me off to talk to Margaret but I am not sure she wanted to speak to me. This is because this morning, Tuesday, I had written an article in the *Times* in which I had said that John Major had done her proud at Maastricht, done what she had wanted to do and that she would be supporting him in the election: they would get a majority of around fifty because he has done so well at Maastricht and had the whole party's support.

Her mood changes pretty fast. It was clear when I talked to her that her mood had changed. She was not at all so keen on praising his Maastricht activities. Again she kept repeating that we were sliding on the inevitable way to the single currency.

I still don't think she will vote against but I am not so sure she is going to actually vote for him. Nicholas Ridley, Norman Tebbit and Lord Harris of High Cross stir her up the whole bloody time. It is very silly because they won't embrace the good things Major has done and build on those.

I told Margaret I had had a long talk with Leon Brittan. 'Oh,' she said looking very severe, 'you don't want to trust him.'

It was a fairly boring party. There was the usual shepherd's pie, in which there was too much salt, and the Krug champagne.

I could feel that Margaret was upset because she feels that I have moved away from her, which I haven't, not from the things she says she believes in, in supporting Major.

Wednesday 18 December
To the Jockey Club to talk to Stoker and Christopher Haines. I told them what I had done about opening the way for them to challenge our laws on gambling on the grounds they were anti-competitive.[17] They should get in touch with Leon Brittan and raise what I had discussed with him.

I also told them what I had done about the breeders, the question of the differential between the taxes on breeding, VAT, here and on the Continent.

I told them I thought a lot of their plans for the horseracing authority were very airy-fairy and weighted in favour of the Jockey Club.

I said, 'If you are going to set up this racehorse authority, you have got to have the Tote on it otherwise you won't be in touch with betting trends.'

Then I dashed off to the *News of the World* party, taking a book for dear little Patsy Chapman.

By the time I got to Number 11 where the Lamonts had a party it was something like twenty to eight and the party was nearing its end. John Major was there.

I told him about my conversation with Leon Brittan. He said it wasn't quite true what he said about inventing the system by which we could maintain control over our own defence and foreign policy in things we considered vital. At the conference there was a scheme by which that was worked out but he certainly did support it.

David Hart[18] was also there. He had never met John Major. I said, 'I'll take you over to introduce you,' but the chance was missed. He

---

17. The argument was that their competitors in Europe were allowed to have betting shops open on Sundays.
18. Property developer and newspaper columnist; see Vol. 1, pp. 404, 406, 436.

said he was very angry with them because they won't talk to him any more at Number 10.

I think Major does rather better than Margaret in this matter.

When nearly everybody had gone John Major began to talk to Petronella in a very flirtatious manner.

Then it was off to the Berkeley Hotel and a great party given by Drue Heinz in honour of Tony O'Reilly who has just married a Greek heiress.[19] (She was fairly attractive but in rather a dark, Charles Addams way.)

Mary Soames, sitting next to me, said it was absurd how people were now trying to say that her parents didn't have a happy marriage. They were married for over forty years and of course they had rows at times like everybody else. But now one of the things which was being said was that they didn't sleep in the same bedroom. They frequently didn't but most upper class people don't. They had different bedtimes. He went to bed so late and she liked to get up early, so what was the matter with that? It's just that people don't understand how civilized upper class people live.

Thursday 19 December

Talked to Norman. He was in a great state because of the *Evening Standard* article last night which said there was a rift between Norman and the Prime Minister. It was on the front page of the *Sun* as well and it is all very damaging. I said I would see what I could do.

So I immediately rang Andrew Turnbull at the Prime Minister's office and said, 'In my view you have got to put out a statement immediately to kill all these extraordinary stories before they stick and the lies last.'

Poor Norman is being blamed for the bad state of the economy which is not his fault at all. If anything, it is John Major's who was Chancellor before him and also Margaret's.

Sunday 22 to Saturday 28 December

Down to Cornwall.

Christopher Mayhew and his wife had already arrived.

James Mayhew came to Redruth to meet us. I had pulled the communication cord because the train had stopped with our coach door a few yards outside the platform. There was no way we could

---

19. He m 2 (1991) Chryss Goulandris.

carry our luggage, which was voluminous, down the gangway to get out further up the coach. James came along and so did the station-master who started complaining about my pulling the communication cord, saying it would have stopped later. I said, 'We've been had like that before. I don't think it would have done.' However, nobody suggested that I should pay the £50 fine for improper use.

I made a contribution, originally of £175, for the housekeeping.

Later I gave Tessa another £50 towards telephone calls and other little expenses and for buying newspapers.

Next year we propose to go to Hungary for Christmas and I don't think it will be much more expensive.

I did a lot on the wind farm and the Cornish Spring Water.

I sent off a fax on Christmas Eve to Tim Yeo's office (Environment Junior Minister) pointing out the terrific increase there had been in unemployment in the last two years leading to November 1991. It was therefore very important for employment reasons, if nothing else, to let us have our wind farm application go through without taking it to a public inquiry which would delay it for at least six months.

Tuesday 31 December
The ritual was revived of going to Andrew Knight's on New Year's Eve with fireworks and jolly games and weird presents.

It was two years since I had seen his daughters, Amaryllis and Afsaneh. I said, 'You've put away childish things,' meaning that they weren't so keen on the oddities I had brought with me as they used to be.

However, we had some fun with the fireworks which were put out of doors and let off at midnight.

There was a sad atmosphere in the house in the absence of Sabiha.

Andrew Knight thinks the *Times* is no good at all, is very dull and that Simon Jenkins hasn't really improved it. As he is in charge, I don't know why he doesn't do something about it.

1992

Thursday 2 January

Petronella rings to say there is an attack on me by Taki in reply to my contention in last Sunday's *News of the World* that he had got it all wrong about Maxwell.

He said in his article that I had been taken in by the casino owners and he knows a great deal more about it than I do. He was also childishly insulting, as below:

'I think it imperative to start the New Year right, and nothing starts it better than bringing down a pompous ass a peg or two, namely Woodrow Wilson Wyatt Weeford, a once pinko turned establishment lackey. WWWW recently wrote that I got it wrong about Maxwell's gambling . . .'

Tuesday 7 January

Good news about the wind farm on Goonhilly Downs from Tim Yeo, Parliamentary Under Secretary of State at the Department of the Environment. Our application will not now be called in, despite it being an area of outstanding natural beauty, and provided the council don't change their minds, which I don't think they will, we can go ahead.

Not having an inquiry has saved us £30,000. I am pretty sure that without my nagging and without my having sent a fax from Cornwall when I was there [at Christmas], saying about the growing unemployment in the area, we wouldn't have got this helpful decision from the Department of the Environment.

Tessa is proving tiresome. She read the agreements about Cornish Spring Water which we made with Dashwood, or Tag as they are called in this particular operation, Sirdar Aly Aziz's lot.[1] She said they were very unfavourable to us and we could have done much better. She blamed Alan Hall [WW's accountant] and said I had no authority to

---

1. See 16 January 1991.

sign while they were on honeymoon – though I'm the Chairman and Alan had Robbie's power of attorney.

If it hadn't been for me, Aly Aziz wouldn't have come in at all.

And if it hadn't been for me, the royalty payments he was finally prepared to pay would have been much less.

We wouldn't have got the wind farm going if it hadn't been for my going to Birmingham and getting very friendly with Professor Little-child, the man who determines whether or not you can go forward with a wind farm. We were not on the approved list of contractors till I persuaded Littlechild to put us on.

I went to act as a trade union representative of the Stable Lads' Association. I am one of the three Trustees.

I pounded on the trainers and pointed out to them what a bad image they are making of racing if they gave the poor little stable lads a rise of no more than two per cent for the whole of the year to 1st February and they had only got between five per cent and seven per cent last year, against an inflation rate of nine per cent.

I then discovered they hadn't the slightest idea of what the general finances of trainers are, though they are supposed to be representing them. Only Ian Balding made any sense. He is Priscilla Hastings' son-in-law. When I said, 'What percentage of the cost of running a stable is the stable lads staff?' He said, 'Perhaps fifty per cent.' I think he is probably overstating it. I said, 'Right. In that case if the training bills were say £350 a week, maybe a little more in some cases and less in others, you are talking about adding £5–£7 a week to the training bill. You should put a note at the bottom saying it is a surcharge owing to the increase in wages for the stable lads.'

Went to the Sears party.

I talked to Norman Tebbit and his wife.

He is a director of Sears.

On politics Norman was very difficult. I said, 'Did you agree with those people who wrote the letter in the *Times* this morning?' That was Alan Walters, Patrick Minford and their gang who were saying we should come out of the ERM. I said, 'You can't do that now.' He said, 'You could later.' I said, 'I don't think the single currency will ever happen. They'll never match the convergency tests and there will be a lot of trouble. They might have perhaps three in it but we would never join.' He said, 'Never underestimate the capacity of great men to make mistakes.' I said, 'Do you mean Kohl?' He said, 'Yes, and there will be a revolution. There will be ghastly scenes if we ever go into a single currency and he is determined to see that we all will.'

I said, 'Do you want the Tories to win?' He said, 'The Tories are going to win. They'll get in again.' I said, 'Yes, but do you want them to win?' He was rather [quiet] for a bit and then said, 'There isn't much difference.'

Wednesday 8 January

It was a busy Tote working day, including the board meeting.

There was some discussion about the Jockey Club proposals.

I said, 'The sahibs of the Jockey Club are trying to get control of racing's finances without actually surrendering any power.' David Swaythling agreed. He hates the Jockey Club. He would have liked to be a member and thinks he has not been made one because he is too outspoken. He can't claim that it's because he is Jewish because they have a number of Jews.

Thursday 9 January

I fixed up the contract and sent the cheque for £5,000 for the first year's one-quarter contribution to the partnership in Pyrrhic Dance. My old colours had never been taken by anyone so they have been re-registered for the Pyrrhic Dance partnership: red cap, white vest, yellow and green striped sleeves, very smart. They had belonged to the Hastings racing family. Fun to be back in this atmosphere of owning, even only as a lease-holder, with a decent racehorse for two years.

The main feature of the day was a jolly outing to *Jack and the Beanstalk* with little Genevra and Antonella Banszky. They made a fairish commotion in the excellent Italian style restaurant in Swallow Street.

Antonella is four and Genevra six.

Cilla Black was the star of *Jack and the Beanstalk*. She still has marvellous legs. She has great presence and style, quite a genius as an entertainer. Really high class. When they make these ladies dames [DBE] because they act in up-market plays, they shouldn't neglect somebody like Cilla Black who thoroughly deserves to be a dame.

When I went to the lavatory in the interval, for the first time in my life I was actually accosted by a homosexual. A young man in the next urinal to mine suddenly put his face near mine and said, 'Hello, hello.' He was offering to do something or other. I was absolutely horrified and glared at him and glared down at my penis and tried to finish peeing as fast as I could and bolt out of the lavatory.

Friday 10 January
Had an encouraging letter from the lady at French's. She wants to publish my play *The Unbelted Earl* for amateur production. I don't know if that will ever lead to it coming to London but at least she thinks more highly of it than Laurence Fitch did. Allan Davis glanced at it and didn't like it either.

I've been working on revising and improving my third play. I think I shall call it *No Wrinkles*.

Saturday 11 January
On the way to Ascot Robbie turned right straight across the traffic in Bishop's Bridge Road to move into Gloucester Terrace as a quick way to the A40.

I was reading the paper in the back when suddenly I saw out of the corner of my eye a car coming up very fast. It hit us just behind where I was sitting, smashed the left-hand side rear lamp and buckled the mudguard badly.

It transpired that the driver of the car which hit us and was going fast (though, as he rightly said, he had the right of way) was an employee of Ladbroke's. This made me laugh a lot. Could Cyril Stein[2] be so keen to get rid of me that I was to be killed by a hitman?

We arrived a bit late at Ascot and the Kenneth Baker house party were already sitting down for lunch. There was much solicitation.

I had to tell Verushka about my one-quarter share in the leasing partnership of Pyrrhic Dance because I knew Piers Bengough, who headed the syndicate which owns the horse and of which I am a member, would tell her.

We went to Dorneywood before the others started off from the racecourse. I walked right round the little park without an overcoat but I did have a warm vest on. It is an agreeable little park with a nice sunken garden at the left of the house as you look at it.

Stoker Hartington and his wife Amanda were of the party. Stoker is now immensely friendly and wants me to do all kinds of things. One of them is to see if we'd be able to have a Newmarket meeting on a

2. Chairman, Ladbroke Group, 1966–93.

Sunday without betting except by credit telephones on the side which is not part of the course. I said, 'That could be possible. It's not a bad idea but we mustn't do it in any way which is illegal.' He said, 'Ken Baker is keen on it.' I said, 'Yes. He once said to me we should have Tote betting on the course on a Sunday but he didn't seem to understand the implications. It would be a criminal offence.'

He asked me what I thought of the proposal for a horseracing authority. I said, 'You'll never get agreement on it and you'll never get it made a statutory body. Ken Baker or any other Home Secretary won't want to introduce this legislation because they would get flak from all directions.' Stoker said he had gathered that from Ken.

I decided to have a bath and wash my hair before dinner. This was a fatal decision. The water ran so cold it was barely lukewarm.

Some comforts are missing from this quite substantial house which was given by Sir Courtauld-Thomson[3] (made a peer in exchange) to the nation. He hoped Prime Ministers would use it but I don't think they ever would – too small. Usually the Foreign Secretaries have used it but latterly it has been Home Secretaries like Willie Whitelaw or Ken Baker now.

I sat next to Lady Tugendhat[4] who turned out interesting.

She is convinced it does have an effect on children when divorces take place, even when the children are grown up, because it shakes them to think that their parents could divide and behave in that manner.

I thought, 'Ho, that is what I said in my play *No Wrinkles* so I have probably got that right.'

There was a good deal of playing at a form of bagatelle, a slightly old fashioned one.

Anyone who scored a thousand or more is recorded in the special book kept for it. Winston Churchill, while using Dorneywood during the War no doubt for security reasons, recorded a thousand or more several times. This is all contained in a letter which Clemmie Churchill wrote to Sir Courtauld, as he was then, saying Winston's feats were

---

3. Colonel Courtauld Courtauld-Thomson (1865–1954) gave Dorneywood, with its contents and an endowment, to the nation in 1942, for the use of prime ministers or their secretary of state nominees; knight 1912, 1st Baron 1944.

4. Julia, née Dobson, m (1967) Christopher Tugendhat (Conservative MP, 1970–6; British EEC Commissioner, 1977–81; a vice-president, EEC Commission, 1981–5, with responsibility for budget, financial control, financial institutions and taxation; chairman, Abbey National, since 1991; knight 1990, life peer 1993).

correctly witnessed and entered in the record books. I started having a go as well but got nowhere near it. Verushka got up to 735 which wasn't bad.

Margaret didn't like Christopher Tugendhat because when she was Leader of the Opposition, Callaghan appointed him to be one of the European Commissioners without consulting her. It is hardly his fault. Margaret thought he ought not to have accepted without asking her first. He ended up as the EC Communications Director, an important job. He thought he should have been given a peerage, as other people who had EC jobs at that level were, but she wouldn't give him one. He only got a knighthood in 1990. He is still hoping for a peerage. He used to be a Tory MP. After his compliments and friendliness to me I decided I liked him.

John Patten and his very pretty wife came to dinner.

She has got a very good job.[5] She said, 'I have to have this job in order to keep John in a comfortable style.' He is very underpaid, as they all are, as Minister of State at the Home Office. She has a pretty back and was obviously determined that everyone should see it, as she wore a very low cut dress at the back.

Ken has an imaginative idea about Scotland: that we should let them have a parliament in Scotland and Scottish MPs shouldn't be allowed in Westminster to vote on English issues. I said, 'In that case there will never be another Labour majority.' He said, 'Exactly. That's the reason it should be done.'

I had a private talk with him about racing and Tote matters.

I told him that we were just about to sign the documentation with Coral/Bass. He is very interested and thinks it a very good idea.

Then I said, 'It was agreed with Waddington when I was given my last two years' appointment that it would be considered again at the end of the two years. That will be up next April. I have got so much to do pushing all this through – and it has not been easy making sure that this new arrangement with Coral works and that we attract all the other bookmakers in – that I would like another year.' He said, 'Right. I will have to speak to John Major about it. You would like it, wouldn't you, announced or given to you before the election, in case it goes wrong?' I said, 'That would be helpful.'

I said, 'As a public relations point, you might, when awarding your

---

levy determination, consider giving a little bit more while saying you hope they will use it to give the stable lads a decent wage.'

He said he would consider that.

Sunday 12 January

To lunch came the Baroness Cox[6] and her husband, Dr Murray Cox, who is a strange man. He is a resident psychiatrist and doctor at Broadmoor and gives his opinion on whether they should be let out or not.

He said he had seen a little old lady who said to him, 'Do you think I have got a chance when I see the parole board?' and he said, 'I suppose you might have one.' She had murdered her husband. When she got there she was asked what would be the first thing she would do if she were released. She replied, 'I'd look for my GP and kill him.' So it wasn't surprising she wasn't let out.

On the lottery, Ken was complaining to me that Norman wants to swipe the lot and then deduct the money to be given to the various arts and sports and so on. He said, 'That's the wrong way round.'

I rang Margaret. She said she had been in the Bahamas for nine days sorting out how to do her memoirs and going through some of the papers.

She started telling me about how she burned her notes on the way Nigel Lawson had resigned and so forth. She had told me all that before, but still there it was, she told me again.

Then she said, 'But you haven't rung me up to talk about that. You want to know what I think of the political situation. We will have to devalue or realign. We should have done it at once when the Germans put up their interest rates. We've got the highest interest rates in the world, still ten per cent, way above inflation and it's got to be done. It's no good Norman being like Stafford Cripps saying he's never going to devalue. He had to. They'll have to do it in January or February.' She means a kind of realignment in which the Germans go up and everybody else goes down.

I said, 'But that would put up the prices of our imports so much.' She said, 'No. Everybody is so anxious to sell they'll reduce their prices. That's what happened before.'

---

6. Caroline, née Cox, m (1959) Dr Murray Cox; director of Nursing Education Research Unit, Chelsea College, University of London, 1977–84; a deputy Speaker, House of Lords, at this time; life peer 1982.

And she ripped me off a bit for not telling what she called the truth. I don't really accept that. I think they are right to stick to their no devaluation. She wants them to drop interest rates by two per cent.

Then I rang Norman. He was getting rather despondent.

I told him what Margaret had said about devaluation. He said, 'It's terrible. She does enormous harm. I have to keep giving interviews to American papers and all round the world because she says we are going to devalue and we should devalue and she is undermining us. They take her seriously.'

He said it wasn't true we had the highest interest rate in the world. 'The Italians, for example, have got a much higher one.' I said, 'I suppose she doesn't take them seriously.'

He said, 'When do you think we should have the election?' I said, 'We'd better get the March Budget in and make it good and then have it.'

Monday 13 January

Wrote my *Times* article for Tuesday's publication. Told Margaret I thought she would like it and she should read it. It explains the lasting successes of the Thatcher years.

I also told her that Irwin Stelzer had written saying he would like to help create money for her foundation and he had got no answer on the subject. She was horrified, saying, 'I haven't seen such a letter. I will be in Washington next Sunday. Will you give me his telephone number?'

I got down to writing a letter to Norman which he had asked me for. It is on my theory that the rate of betting duty tax at eight per cent is actually producing less revenue in real terms for the Treasury than it would if they lowered it.

Thursday 16 January

Chiquita Astor[7] has died. She was six months younger than me. She was a glorious, warm-hearted girl, full of dash and style, a dark-haired, dark-eyed beauty. Her father was Argentinian Ambassador in London at one time. Many were in love with her. She married Jakie Astor when they were both young. Then she had a long affair with Tommy Clyde, with whom I was at Oxford before the War. He was tall, fair, beautiful to look at, slim. His son became a well known actor, Jeremy Clyde.

---

7. Anna Inex (Chiquita), daughter of Señor Dr Don Miguel Carcano, m (1944–72) the Hon. Jacob Astor.

Tommy was a pursuer of girls with vigour and enthusiasm from the moment he reached puberty.

I greatly amused her once by taking her shoe off in a restaurant where a number of us were dining and tickling her feet. After that particular dinner party when we stood by the car, to my amazement, she said, 'You were the most attractive man there,' though there had been people like David Somerset. She said, 'That's because you have life and interest and excitement.'

Dear Chiquita. She had a troubled life in many ways. She never married again but she was a gorgeous present to the world and made it sparkle.

I had a triple-decker toasted sandwich lunch with fizzy white water with Ian Chapman at the Waldorf. I showed him a chunk of this manuscript. He was delighted with it and laughed a lot.

The real purpose was to discuss the signing and completion of the contract. Their lawyers had a problem worrying about who owns the moral right when I am dead and who owns what they call the archives and the copyright to that, meaning all the material, the hundreds of pages with the million or so words which I will have written if I haven't written it already.[8] That I think will have to be done by the executors, Goodman Derrick, taking charge of it.

There could be quite a lot of money in it, perhaps around a quarter of a million eventually arising out of this manuscript.

To dinner came the Zarachs bringing J. S. Chipperfield. He neither drinks nor smokes. He is a great safari man and collector of animals. He runs circuses. He is making a lot of money at it. He said the London Zoo is incredibly badly run. I said, 'I wish you would do it. You'd do it better.' He said, 'We've made suggestions but they are very impractical. The research side must be detached from the commercial side.' I said, 'It used to be to some extent. If it were, then of course the zoo could pay for itself and attract more customers.'[9]

He is an inventor. He told me about a device he has invented for putting hoods on television screens so you can stand them in blazing sunlight and still see the pictures clearly as though you were in a dark

---

8. The number of words from the beginning of the journals in October 1985 to this date in January 1992 already totalled nearly 2 million.

9. WW was on the Council of the Zoological Society of London, 1968–71 and 1973–7.

room. I said, 'That's absolutely marvellous. It's just what we need for the Tote.'

Friday 17 January
Irwin Stelzer rang up.

Mrs Thatcher had rung him up with great apologies about the letter not being dealt with in which he had offered to help raise money for her foundation. They are going to meet when she gets to Washington.

Sunday 19 January
Dinner party at Number 11 Downing Street.

The champagne before dinner wasn't very good but poor Norman has to pay for it. The wine at dinner was so-so. The food, however, wasn't too bad.

David Mellor was there in a check coat and patent leather shoes. I have never liked him but as the evening went on I began to like him quite a lot, thinking there was much more to him than a conceited façade.

Monday 20 January
A hectic day. Began by pointing out to Manuel, who is utterly useless, that he was not only useless but a menace. I have been growing the Cypress Leylandii in the front of the house for twenty years. He decided to chop a number of huge branches off them, thus destroying the screen which prevented people looking into the garden and also enabled me in the summer to walk about with nothing on in the garden.

Between the two of them, Manuel and Rebecca, they cost me £780 a week with the taxes I have to pay on their salary. I have to pay their National Insurance and the employer's National Insurance for them, as well as feed them and house them. She is excellent but he is worth nothing at all.

After a hectic morning telephoning all and sundry about NERA's wish, at my instigation, to help the tobacco industry by analysing the costs in wages and to the economy of banning advertising for cigarettes and tobacco, not only on television but in newspapers, and various other things, I went to the Tote.

I went on to the Athenaeum Hotel for a party being given by Jansen, the Australian who has a business in Australia and who writes many interesting things in Australia of a gossipy nature. He has somehow got himself close to David Somerset and stays often at Badminton.

I asked David why he never took his seat in the Lords. He said, 'I don't believe in being a hereditary legislator. It's fine for people like you who take an interest in politics and always have done and know about them, but not for me because I don't think I am entitled to be there.'

I said, 'You might enjoy the atmosphere a bit.' He said he thought he wouldn't. He obviously thinks it would be far beneath him socially.

Nearby was his mistress of about fifteen years, Miranda Morley. She is a charming girl.

What is fascinating is that she is really very plain, and there is the great woman slayer, with all his elegance and male beauty, David, happy to link himself up with this quiet creature. She is very pleasant. I dare say she is a contrast to Caroline who has always been slightly off her rocker, even before David drove her to drink by his infidelities which were flaunted around London. Caroline was a sweet girl when I first knew her though there was something crazy in the Thynne family as indeed in her mother's – the Vivians.[10]

As I was talking to David, a fairly handsome, largish woman came up.

She was the daughter-in-law, at least at one time, of Nikita Hulton, the mad Russian woman whom I described as a predatory lady with claws but with great beauty and sex appeal, to which she agreed.

She is now married to the Duke of Hamilton.[11]

She lives on the Great Barrier Reef in Australia in a tower. She says the view is absolutely fabulous though it is getting crowded as people come closer and closer to it.

I think perhaps I would like to go to Australia before I die and also to New Zealand to see the great white colonies which sprouted from us. It would be like a visit from an Athenian to the Greek colonies of say Syracuse and Paestum, seeing how his old race and religion and culture were getting on.

I went to visit the Medical School at the Royal Free Hospital.

---

10. The Duchess of Beaufort (d 1992) was the daughter of the 6th Marquis of Bath and the Hon. Daphne Vivian (d 1997), daughter of 4th Baron Vivian, who m 2 the travel writer Xan Fielding; both her parents were unconventional.*

11. Jillian, daughter of Noel Robertson of Sydney, Australia, m 2 Edward, the son of Sir Edward Hulton (1906–88, proprietor of *Picture Post*) and his second wife Princess Nika Yourievitch; m 3 (1988) 15th Duke of Hamilton.

They explained to me why the Royal Free wanted more money. It comes to about £16 million to develop their medical school.

When Dr Pounder came into the room (he is my general physician) he said, 'You do look well.' I said, 'You look well, too. You seem to be thinner.' He said, 'Yes. I gave up drinking alcohol to get thinner.' I said, 'Well you should eat less. It's not a very good idea to drink less alcohol.'

While we were going around the pathological laboratory I said, 'How long would it take a liver to recover?' He said, 'If you stop drinking for a while, it will recover. But you can utterly destroy it. You can do almost anything to a liver and it will restore itself, if you don't keep pumping it with alcohol.'

They are very proud of their library where you can whistle up any medical communication or text you want. 'Have you ever written anything about medicine?' I was asked. I said, 'No.' They said, 'Let's see if you are on the computer,' and blow me down they found one reference to me. A story I had written in *Stories of the Forties* edited by Reginald Moore, published in 1945.

I am afraid they are hoping too much from me if they think I could seriously raise money in the sort of manner they require. But I will have a little go.

Thursday 23 January
A gala given by a Hong Kong troupe. Princess Diana was there. Before it began, as she did her rounds, she was brought over to me and the Governor, Wilson, said, 'Lord Wyatt is making a debate next week in the Lords about Hong Kong.'

She asked me how long it would take me to prepare the speech. I said, 'About an hour and a half but I have been thinking about it and looking at papers beforehand. You make a lot of speeches. Your impromptu ones are very good. You never strike a wrong note.' She said, 'I do sometimes.'

She was very friendly. But she didn't look as pretty as she used to. Her new hair style, rather short cropped, doesn't suit her. Her make-up made her face look too red. It contrasted uneasily with her lovely white skin. Her clothes were inappropriate in the sense that they were dark colours and they didn't suit her. Verushka said her hair used to be blonde and now it is kind of mousy brown. I said, 'Perhaps she has stopped dyeing it.' However, I like that girl. She has got more to her than any of them in the Royal Family bar the Queen and her mother.

Friday 24 January

After a hectic time finishing my article and dealing with all kinds of other matters we left for the airport [to go to Paris]. I lost Verushka. I thought she had gone to the Euro lounge and walked about two miles backwards and forwards and got into the wrong terminal, terminal one instead of terminal two. However, eventually we met up.

We were met by the car sent by Jacques Chartier from the trotting organization. We went to the Ritz.

We had been promised the same suite as we had a year ago but found we had been moved to another. There may have been some confusion with Mrs Oscar Wyatt who is the mother of the adopted son who has been having a fling with the Duchess of York.

Saturday 25 January

Lunch with Jean Romanet, Pierre Carrus and the German PMU man. We discussed a great deal about how to keep bookmakers out of France. I said, 'One of the things you've got to do is to allow cross-border trade between the pools. You are preventing that. It's not a very good advertisement against the bookmakers when you won't allow cross-border entry into other pools. You no longer let us bet into your pool and you won't bet into ours.'

I told them about the great new device which we are going to put into our betting shops jointly with Coral. I said, 'It is only going to cost about £580 apiece and it will do everything which your machines do in the cafés.' They confirmed that they still cost £3,000. I said, 'We could probably let you have them for £1,000 and still make a decent profit.'

If I can sell even ten thousand to the PMU people and make a £300 profit on each of them we're talking about a £3 million profit for our joint company with Bass.

Tuesday 28 January

Amidst all the other things I had to do I was obliged to go to a meeting of the Parliamentary All Party Racing Committee. Stoker and Christopher Haines were addressing it. I had to be there to support Stoker about Sunday racing.

Stoker made a little speech to begin with. It wasn't bad but he doesn't speak forcefully or totally convincingly. Christopher Haines then chipped in to elaborate which didn't add much to the price of tea.

Wednesday 29 January

The morning began at nine o'clock with Brian and John Heaton coming to discuss what we were going to say to Peter Sherlock and his people. They were niggling away, producing all kinds of new points which they want settled before the agreement is signed.

I told Peter Sherlock, who arrived at 9.30, that we were getting fed up with this and were they really serious. He said, 'Good heavens, yes, mad serious.'

When the meeting ended he asked to see me quietly alone. He then said Bass were still interested in selling Coral. They couldn't get the £200 million they wanted before because the profit figures wouldn't stand up and they were running into a very bad year. Would we be interested in it? There is no hurry in trying to do something more about it.

I said yes. He had a number of suggestions, one that we might buy a hundred per cent and another that Bass would keep forty-nine per cent and a declining amount if we wanted them to and we would work a price out. He said it was a natural merger. I agreed with that. He promised me he wasn't talking to anybody else.

As we were talking, he said Bass hoped to add to their profits £3 million a year as a result of the deal with us. I think he sincerely intends to carry that through.

When they had gone, about lunch time, I had to start preparing my speech for Hong Kong.

My unstarred question didn't come on until just a few minutes before eight.

Malcolm Caithness[12] was very disparaging. He spoke as though he hadn't even heard what I said and said I had got it all wrong, which was quite ridiculous.

By some confusion Petronella had agreed to have dinner with Damien Thompson, the religious correspondent of the *Daily Telegraph*, and Anna Pasternak, a great-niece of the great Boris Pasternak of *Dr Zhivago* fame.[13] They were waiting for me with Verushka in the Barry Room when I came out.

The half Russian girl had been at St Paul's School with Petronella

---

12. 20th Earl of Caithness; Minister of State, Foreign and Commonwealth Office, 1990–2.

13. Anna Pasternak's book *Princess in Love*, about Princess Diana, was published in 1994.

but was a year senior and didn't see much of her, such is the conventional enormity of the age gap at that stage in one's life. She had been working on 'Peterborough' with Petronella at one point. She has now gone off to the *Daily Express* which she doesn't like at all. She is a bright girl, particularly good-looking with a dark, round face and she had quite nice legs and dark hair which flowed on either side of her face.

She wasn't going to have a sexual permanent relationship with a live-in lover unless she wanted to marry the man. I said, 'That's a very good outlook. All the sleeping around does not improve a girl's attitude or her attraction and it is altogether too stressful.'

Thursday 30 January
Not surprisingly there was nothing in the newspapers about the Hong Kong debate. It started too late and people are not interested in Hong Kong any more. There was nothing on the wireless about it either. But Alastair Laing[14] said it was a fine thing I raised it all because Hong Kongers felt completely neglected by the British. There had been no debate for over a year or a year and a half in either House.

---

14. London head of Omelco, the organization comprised of members of the Hong Kong legislative and executive councils.

Saturday 1 February
We arrived at Donhead St Mary just after five o'clock. John Bowes Lyon was there.[1] Bindy Lambton came down from London with him. She was looking extremely groggy.

In the first-class second-hand bookshop at Shaftesbury, Anne [Tree] had found a book called *Mrs Markham's History of England* by Hilaire Belloc. She wanted me to look at the anti-semitism in it. There was just a little bit but it was a hilarious book and I started reading chunks of it aloud to her, all about how the police treat people and how you don't get a fair trial, which is exactly what you shouldn't have according to Mrs Markham talking to her children.

We had some decent Lynch-Bages at dinner and some very good champagne which had been given by Jeremy Tree, the famous trainer who is Michael Tree's brother, as a Christmas present. Jeremy rang and I answered the telephone. I said, 'How are you?' He said, 'Only fair.' The poor chap is very much wrecked by his illnesses and a brain tumour and he is drained out.

Khalid Abdullah was one of his owners. He is very kind to him, not that there is any great shortage of money. They inherited a lot from the Marshall Field side of the family, famous store owners in America [Chicago]. I think Michael has been losing a lot of money. He had set up a little factory on a nearby disused airfield, making pretty objects out of a tin-like material [Tôle] but it went bust in the recession. Also he is a big shareholder in Colefax & Fowler which went public and their shares have taken a heavy battering. He doesn't provide cigars any more. He always used to. I had taken the precaution of bringing a sufficient supply of my own.

I went on Sunday morning to the church where Anne said they were having a terrible row with the local priest, a new one, very left-wing and very High Church and utterly opposed to the ordination of women. He says if they ordain women, he will join the Roman church,

---

1. A director of Sotheby's, 1970–80.

which seemed to be the best argument they had heard for women being ordained in the Church of England.

At breakfast John Bowes Lyon was talking about the state of the monarchy. We were noting the usual attacks in the *Sunday Times*, saying the Queen ought to pay tax and all the rest of it. Basically the Crown is now in more disrepute than it should be because of the antics of some of the younger members. John is a near cousin to Queen Elizabeth the Queen Mother. He knows exactly what goes on at Buckingham Palace and the inner Royal talk.

The Duchess of York is utterly childish and low level, like a barmaid who has got into some money. She is bereft of education and taste. Andrew is furious with all her carryings on with other men and was particularly enraged with all the stuff which came out about her association with Wyatt. They are now not speaking to each other at all and, according to John, almost certainly heading for a divorce.

Prince Charles, John agrees with me, is a sensible, interesting man but he and Diana don't speak to each other either.

They have nothing in common of any kind whatever and the atmosphere between them is frozen. I said, 'But I think they will jog along and at the end they will survive all these difficulties and have a *modus vivendi* because she is a well brought up girl with proper standards and obviously he is, too. They are not going to do anything which is going to put the Crown in danger or become a most fearful scandal.'

I said, 'That girl has got a magic. She always says the right things and she is genuinely interested and compassionate. Whereas you always think that Fergie is showing off.'

Michael has an amazing collection of pictures left to him by Cecil Beaton.[2] One set is of the Countess of Rosse[3] whom he hated with deep malevolence. She is shown preening herself during various stages prior to the announcement of her son's engagement to Princess Margaret, and at the Abbey and so forth. When she hears the news of the pending divorce, her eyes pop out and her wig flies off. Right at the end there are views of the Countess of Rosse looking out of the

---

2. (1904–80); society photographer and designer; knight 1972; Hugo Vickers hints at Beaton's dislike of the Countess of Rosse (who died in 1992) in his 1985 *Cecil Beaton: The Authorised Biography*.

3. (d 1992); Anne, née Messel, m 1 Ronald Armstrong-Jones, m 2 (1935) 6th Earl of Rosse; her son by her first marriage, Antony Armstrong-Jones, photographer, m 1 (1960–78) Princess Margaret and was made 1st Earl of Snowdon in 1961.

window of an aeroplane as it is getting closer. She looks fairly pretty in the first one, plain in the second one as it gets closer, fifty feet away, and when it is only five feet away she is depicted as a horrible old hag.

He said did I think they were libellous? I said, 'They would be if you displayed them or published them in a magazine.' He said, 'But they were done by Cecil Beaton who is dead.' I said, 'But you are the owner of the copyright. It's all right to show them to friends. However, I suppose you could risk it if you wanted to. She would make an ass of herself, this go-getting, vain social climber, if she were to bring a libel action.'

Another set of pictures were of Violet Trefusis who was the lover of Vita Sackville-West.[4] There is a very funny one of her amusing 'les boys', gentlemen in white ties and tails, by balancing a glass of champagne on her bottom and kicking her leg out. Then you see Vita looking round the corner and putting an end to the fun. You also see Vita Sackville-West at the wedding of Violet, looking absolutely furious because her Lesbian lover had got married and liked men as much as she did women. It is extremely funny and well done.

Michael said, 'Do you think that could be libellous?' I said, 'No. All the participants are dead. In any case, Nigel (Nicolson) hasn't any grounds for complaint because he has written it all in his book about his mother and father.'

Bindy was in a much brighter state before lunch. She had slept well and seemed more like her old self. She has got far more brains than Claire and is more knowledgeable and entertaining.

Tuesday 4 February
I had been trying to get Margaret the night before. No answer. I also tried her on Sunday evening but no answer. I rang her at half past eight this morning. I hate to think she may feel I am neglecting her now she is no longer Prime Minister. She was in quite a hurry, waiting to go out.

Of her trip to America she said she got on very well but money is short for her foundation, partly due to the recession and partly because

---

4. Victoria Glendinning described their relationship and attempted elopement in *Vita* (1983), as did Nigel Nicolson, son of Vita and Harold Nicolson, in *Portrait of a Marriage* (1973); Violet, née Keppel, (1894–1972), m (1919) Denys Trefusis.

people were giving money to President Bush. She said he thinks he will be all right now because his opponents are weak and hopeless.[5]

She asked if I had read Alan Walters in the *Evening Standard* last night in the pink page section. She said it was very good. 'He says we are in for a worse recession than since the 1930s.'

When I told Norman what she had said he said, 'Good gracious, it's absolute rubbish what Alan Walters wrote last night.'

I am not very nice. I thought we should take a present to Hartley Shawcross for his ninetieth birthday.[6] The question was what? I thought I would look out some wine which I felt I could spare, like a magnum of Mouton Rothschild 1970. I thought, no it's rather too valuable. Then I came across a magnum, out of five I have, of Winston Churchill special cuvée 1979 with a picture of Winston on the bottle and a beautiful case. I thought shall I or shan't I because they are very precious to me and the older the champagne gets the better it is. It's Pol Roger, Winston's favourite.

I rang Christie's and found I paid £50 a magnum.

So that was a good bargain and he will think it is very much more expensive.

I thought to myself, 'What a shabby chap you are, resisting giving a generous, nice gesture because you are so mean and can't bear to sacrifice anything you really treasure to give pleasure to somebody else.'

The dinner was at the Café Royal Grill Room.

I duly left my present for Hartley Shawcross with the note stuck on the handsome presentation box. By this time I was feeling pleased with myself at my generosity – how feeble my mind is and so shallow.

Margaret was there, blooming and looking really beautiful. Her skin is lovely and I told her she looked wonderful and beautifully dressed. I told her, 'As you know, I adore you.' She wanted to know if I had read the Alan Walters article in the *Evening Standard*. I said, 'Yes but I can't take it so seriously as you.' She said, 'Right, we're all doomed,' but I don't believe that.

---

5. Clinton was elected US President on 4 November 1992.
6. Labour MP, 1945–58; Attorney General, 1945–51; m 1 (1924) Rosita Shyvers (d 1943); m 2 (1944) Joan Mather (d 1974); life peer 1959.

Quintin Hogg made a speech. He said they spent a lot of time in each other's houses although they were great political opponents and that Hartley had always been very fair in what he said about the Tory opposition when he was in Attlee's government.

Young William Shawcross, who is extraordinarily good-looking, tall and slim with his curly black hair, made an elegant speech. He said his father, though he never showed much direct emotion and was awesome, was also very kind.

There was some mention of Hartley's second wife, Joan. I talked at length to Joanna, his daughter, who is a doctor in general practice. She is a strikingly handsome woman, not quite as tall as Hartley but she has half Hartley's face and half Joan's. I told her she looked half like her mother and reminded me of her and how good Hartley had been to his first wife when he was a young lawyer, sitting by her bedside because she was very ill and dying. He sat with his work there, never leaving her alone. I said, 'He is a bit of a saint, your father, in a curious way.'

Hartley spoke with great vigour, not at all like a man of ninety. He is still elegant, still precise, still clear.

Wednesday 5 February
The lunch for the Mayor of Ulyanovsk on the Volga where Lenin was born. The Mayor's name was Stupnikov. He was accompanied by Mr Mikhaylov, President of the company in this town. It makes motor cars, refrigerators, engines, all kinds of things, plus having the biggest aircraft construction for cargo aeroplanes possibly in the world, certainly in Russia.

I talked to the Mayor through the interpreter while Mr Shapiro, from Skadden Arps, very senior indeed, number two to the head of Skadden Arps, who comes from a Russian family and speaks perfect Russian, engaged Mr Mikhaylov much of the time.

The Mayor is smart. He had boned up about me and knew what I wrote about Russia. He said he thought it was time for Gorbachev to go and asked what I thought of Yeltsin.

Mr Shapiro was desperately trying to get them to pay something up front for the Skadden Arps work on privatization and arranging a lot of matters thereto. But they wanted to leave it until everything was done and pay them out of the proceeds. I think Mr Shapiro made a great deal of headway because I conducted the whole affair with considerable verve and the Mayor obviously loved it.

Bumped into Ivor Richard[7] in the Lords. He was one of my candidates for Governor of Hong Kong. I said was he willing to be that, if he were asked. He said he thought he probably would. I said, 'But you have not had any discussions with the Tories?' He said no. I said, 'They have behaved disgracefully over the whole thing. It should be a bi-partisan matter and I think you would make a very good Governor. You have had great experience in the United Nations and as a Commissioner in Brussels and I have always had a great admiration for you. You have a lot of guts.' He was frightfully pleased.

Saturday 8 February
Off early for Newbury for the Tote Gold Cup Hurdle race which was at two o'clock.

Queen Elizabeth the Queen Mother came.

Before she came Martin Gilliat said to me, 'Would you please be kind to her today?' I said I thought I always was very kind to her. Martin said, 'Yes, but this is the day after her husband's death forty years ago and she is very sad. People forget that for her yesterday was not a day of rejoicing at forty years of the Queen's reign but one of sorrow.'

I think that is why the Queen, who loves her mother, doesn't ever want to make a great celebration of the day of her accession to the throne. However, the Queen Elizabeth became very jolly. Ian Balding, her trainer, was there. As we both talked to her, I told her how I had been the trade union representative making him and the trainers put the minimum wages up for the poor stable lads. She thought that was funny and he was very pleasant about it and laughed a lot.

Little Angela Oswald and her husband Michael were there. He is in charge of the Queen's stud. He seems to have little success with it. The Queen's horses are never much good.

Sunday 9 February
Henry, Tessa [the Keswicks] and I went off to Lambourn. The first stop was to see John Hills, the trainer of the horse I have leased with three others in the Pyrrhic Dance partnership.

---

7. Labour politician; MP, 1964–74; UK Permanent Representative to UN, 1974–79; EEC Commissioner, 1981–4; leader of the Opposition, House of Lords, 1992–7; leader of the House of Lords, 1997–8; life peer 1990.

John said it is coming on nicely but they don't know when it will be ready to run as a two-year-old.

It's very handsome with a lovely white streak on its face down to its nose and a couple of white fetlocks. Well built, brown and beautifully groomed. It was paraded and it moved beautifully and looked strong.

I enjoyed being back in the atmosphere of racing as I used to be when I had horses with David Hastings from 1956 to 1966. As I said to John Hills, 'This is the time for optimism. When it runs we may be thinking rather differently.'

I like John Hills a lot. He is young and keen and good-looking. Tessa thought the same, remarking what nice legs he has, which I thought amusing. His father was a stable lad who went on to be a head stable lad and then won a big bet, putting all his savings on a horse which won, and that was enough for him to start off as a trainer. That is how Barry Hills' career began and now he is one of the very top trainers. Young John Hills has got thirty-five horses in his stables, but like all other trainers he is feeling the pinch at the moment.

We then moved off in the rain to Seven Barrows, Lambourn, where David Hastings used to train, which I last saw in 1965. I used to have many jolly times with him in that house. It looked even more shambolic than it did then, a great deal worse. It was like Cold Comfort Farm.

Henry had been trying to get Peter Walwyn on the telephone but he only got an answering machine. We thought we would arrive anyway and find a stable lad or whatever and see his filly, Oare Sparrow. We rang the bell and eventually Peter Walwyn came to the door and said, 'We have just got back. We've been hunting in the south.' He looked absolutely dazed but he always does.

Tessa was annoyed when she found the filly was in what she called hospital. It had a cough and had to be separated from the other horses.[8]

Walwyn has only fifty horses there now and he should have seventy. Tessa said she didn't want Oare Robin, the next filly, sister of the one now at Lambourn, to go to Peter Walwyn.

She is quite a pretty girl though she is well past forty now. She has nice legs. That is why she appreciated John Hills' very long legs and slim body and good-looking, cheerful face.

We got back just in time to be there [at Oare House] for when Jacob and Serena Rothschild arrived. I was pleased to see my little

---

8. WW afterwards wrote 'a jingle' to Tessa Keswick: 'Where is my lovely horse? / In the hospital of course.'

Serena and we talked away about her horses She has got about twenty in all, including the mares she has for breeding purposes left by Aunt Dorothy. She said that Jacob is very generous and is paying for it all but she hasn't had any serious results yet. It would be terribly funny if Pyrrhic Dance turned out to be a really good horse, better than Oare Sparrow or any of Serena's, considering all the enormous wealth they have behind them, both Jacob and Henry.

It seems that Conrad Black is definitely going to marry Barbara Amiel.[9] I said, 'I don't think it will last very long because she is so erotic and intense, though attractive and a good writer. But I don't think he will put up with it. I think she was just a great change from his very pretty Joanna from whom he is getting a divorce. She was a bit of a flibbertigibbet with no brain who liked jolly parties and she didn't like England.'

When I got back I rang Margaret after having spoken to Norman who had rung in the morning while I wasn't there. He was rather gloomy because there is nothing promising on the horizon and he didn't think there would be before the Budget.

We were talking about the Paddy Ashdown affair.

I said, 'None of you are in any great danger now. You can now advertise you have got a couple of mistresses and rise in the polls.'[10]

Margaret said she doesn't think much of the policy initiatives John Major comes up with and she wants the election to happen as soon as possible because electioneering has gone on too long and everyone is getting bored. I said, 'Would you have it early in April?' She said 'Yes, as soon as they have got the Budget out of the way.'[11]

She said she is going to support a number of her friends during the election campaign and speak for them. She had a lot of invitations but she was not going on TV or to hold press conferences. All that could wait until after the election. She didn't want anybody thinking she was rocking the boat.

---

9. Canadian-born journalist; they married on 21 July 1992 and were still married in 1999.

10. Papers stolen from Ashdown's solicitors, concerning the affair he had five years previously with his secretary, had been leaked to the press. His rating as a potential prime minister jumped in the polls ahead of Kinnock's and to within two points of Major's.

11. The general election took place on 9 April.

Tuesday 11 February

In the afternoon Peter Paterson,[12] whom I know well (he is an old journalist), Graham Paterson's father, came to see me. We talked at length about George Brown[13] because he is writing a biography of him. I sent him away with *Confessions of an Optimist*, pointing out my references to him, and added a great deal besides in stories. When George Brown came to dinner at Tower House, Park Village West, he sat next to Edwina, Mrs Leo d'Erlanger, an attractive woman, the wife of the man who founded the Channel Tunnel company. After he had been talking to her for a while he turned and said, 'I've talked enough to you, you old hag. Now I'm going to talk to my neighbour. She is much better looking.'

At Pratt's I waited for Arnold who had never been there before, at least not by himself. He had been with Andrew. He is an Andrew Devonshire honorary member like me. I arrived there at twenty past eight, as I said I would. He turned up just gone nine. He had been talking to a parliamentary group from the Labour Party.

I said to Arnold, 'You're taking out an insurance policy against Labour winning and sometimes you say you want them to win.' William Waldegrave laughed and said, 'You're quite right. He always does that.' Arnold smiled and said, 'Well yes, there is something in that. It's sensible.'

William had worked about eight years for Arnold, learning about industry, sitting in his office with him, so he knows Arnold well and likes him very much, as I do. We talked about Victor Rothschild and how much we all miss him. William said he thinks about him almost every day and the funny things he said and the brilliant ideas he had. It's nice that people are remembered for their good qualities, not only for their bad.

We each named a few people with total arrogance from Winchester. There was Oswald Mosley, D. L. Pritt (the Communist and great lawyer), Stafford Cripps, Dick Crossman, Hugh Gaitskell. Arnold said, 'There aren't many Tories in that list.' I said, 'There's Willie Whitelaw and Toby Low.' He said, 'They were lucky to have got to Winchester

---

12. Then TV critic, *Daily Mail*; his biography *Tired and Emotional: The Life of Lord George Brown* was published in 1993; his son Graham was at this time an assistant editor on the *Times*.

13. (1914–85); Labour Foreign Secretary, 1966–8.

as they are not all that bright.' I said, 'They are cleverer than you think they are.'

He said it was extraordinary: the moment Verushka heard I was going to meet him at Pratt's, the telephone was buzzing between her and Netta. Netta came to have dinner at 19 Cavendish Avenue. He said, 'They can't bear to let us go out by ourselves.'

Michael Tree rang up. Could I intervene because he has sold two very valuable chairs for £150,000 but the export council which decides that marvellous works of art are not to be allowed to leave the country had put a stop on it and he has been waiting for four months. In the meanwhile he gets no interest on his £150,000, and isn't that a disgrace. Will I take it up for him? I said, 'Send me a letter and I will take it up with Tim Renton, Arts Minister, and see what can be done. But if those are the rules they most probably won't alter them.'

Tessa Lyle had a boy at 12.18 this morning. It is to be called Christopher. None of the Wyatt names of his father, his grandfather or his great-grandfather are to be used.[14] Bonython is rapidly becoming Mayhew land. I shall certainly not want to be buried in Cury Church in the family vault. I shall prefer to go to Weeford, the home of my ancestors, alongside the church built by James Wyatt, mainly at the expense of the family.

The baby weighed some enormous amount, nine and a half pounds. It is huge, like its mother.

To dinner with the Pejacsevichs.

Chips [Keswick] was extremely good and honest in his appraisal of what is going on in the economy. I thought he made an excellent impression on Norman [Lamont].

Mark [Pejacsevich] was so nervous that he spilt wine and coffee all over the bloody place and some of it went on to me and on to Rosemary [Lamont]. He kept saying that Norman didn't want to talk about serious matters. I said, 'Of course he does. He loves it. He wants to know what everybody's opinion is.'

Thursday 13 February
Chips rang to thank me for being so loyal to him and praising him to the Chancellor of the Exchequer.

I want Norman to make Chips a director of the Bank of England. I told Chips what Mark had said about not talking shop and trying to

---

14. But see later, 28 February.

stop us doing it. Chips said, 'He's got nothing else to talk about. It's his life and blood, meat and drink.' I said, 'Of course. It was hardly the place where we could chat about girlfriends with Norman present.'

Then I went off to see Douglas Hurd.

Oh me, oh my, my memory is getting so bad. I didn't mention, as I think I should have done and will do so, that I had sounded out Ivor Richard as to whether he would like to be the next Governor of Hong Kong and he said he would be willing. Douglas said he doesn't want to make it bi-partisan: 'I don't want to talk to Kaufman about it.'

It had to be a straight Britisher. Peking attached enormous symbolic importance to an Englishman hauling down the flag when the time comes.

In the evening Susan Crosland came to dinner. She was absolutely punctual because there was going to be a spinach soufflé. It was very good. I opened for her a bottle of 1937 Pichon-Longueville which is next to Château Latour. It was absolutely marvellous.

Susan said I was looking very much thinner. I said I weighed 11 stone or thereabouts, down from just over 12 and I weighed 10.10 in 1956. 'Do you think it makes me look old?' After some hesitation she said, 'Yes, it makes you look older than you are.' I said, 'Oh dear. Does that make me look less attractive?' She said, 'Yes. I like my men to have plump, solid bodies.'

Sunday 16 February

Spoke to Norman. I told him what I thought he should put in his Budget.

He said, 'What do you think would happen if there were an election tomorrow?' 'Absolute confusion,' I replied. 'Polling stations wouldn't be ready.'

Monday 17 February

Great meeting at 19 Cavendish Avenue, I hope it is the last, with Peter Sherlock and the Bass team. We agreed to sign the agreement by at least next Monday and have a press conference at ten o'clock on Tuesday, February 25th.

On Friday Michael Naylor-Leyland, son of Diana [Wilton], aged thirty-two and Assistant Manager, or Floor Manager, at the great new hotel at Hyde Park Corner [the Lanesborough], rang me up.

There had been a big story in the *News of the World* the previous Sunday about a commissionaire giving two journalists a telephone number (he didn't know they were journalists) at which they could enquire for a couple of girls to go upstairs to a bedroom at this new hotel and watch them perform and have sex with them. They had tried to get him, Michael Naylor-Leyland, involved.

Now the *News of the World* has started ringing again and pestering him because they have got a new angle. His wife is a Hanoverian Princess. What should he do? I said, 'Say, one, you have no further comment to make on the subject. Two, if they go on pestering you, you will get on to the Press Complaints Commission. Three, if they write anything on Sunday, your lawyers have been instructed to examine it extremely carefully to see if it is libellous.' He took my advice. In the event nothing was published on Sunday.

Poor Diana was frantic.

Wednesday 19 February
Spoke early to Ken Baker.

He said, 'I want to see you urgently, "très sensitivo". Nobody is to know you are coming to see me. Could you come at half past eight to the Home Office tomorrow morning?' I don't know what it is all about.

I told him the press conference was to take place on Tuesday announcing our venture with Bass.

The next thing I heard was that Peter Sherlock was at his old tricks again, saying there were many points which hadn't been agreed properly. He wanted to work all night tonight and maybe we wouldn't be able to conclude it, and so on, and so on, by next Tuesday.

I left a message with his secretary because he was at a board meeting, saying the Home Secretary had already been informed there was going to be a press conference on Tuesday next and that it would be very embarrassing if it doesn't happen.

Thursday 20 February
Most extraordinary. I was smuggled in secretly to see Ken Baker.

He wanted my advice on the levy to charge against the bookmakers.

I had wanted the Levy Board government members to ask for more than £42.6 million 'so that you would then in the good old fashioned English way give them something like £41 million or a little more'.

'You think the bookmakers can pay more?' I said, 'Yes. If you make it £41 million or a little more it will be fine.' I think he is going to do that. He doesn't have to do it until after the Budget. He is waiting to see whether they knock my suggested half per cent off the betting tax, about which he is not allowed to have any communication with Norman, though I have had. He said did I think bookmakers generally could be called upon to give the extra money? I said yes, but the top bookmakers could afford more and it could easily be arranged on a sliding [scale].

I was then smuggled out of the office to where the car had been put in a special place after the conversation which never happened.

To The Other Club. We had 1981 Brane-Cantenac. It had clearly not been opened long enough because it began acid with a nasty smell. It grew to be pleasant and mellow. Roy Jenkins described it as 'closed' till it got to its better condition. Michael Hartwell said, 'If Roy approves of a claret, then we know it is OK.' Such is his reputation, not wholly justified.

There was a lot of betting going on about who would be a Labour Lord Chancellor. Jeremy Hutchinson,[15] who was in the chair, said he thought Irvine of Lairg would be. Quintin Hogg said he would be a very bad lawyer. Of course they were talking about if Labour won.[16]

Friday 21 February
At last we got the word from the team sitting at Linklaters the solicitors (fabulously expensive), consulting with our own lawyers Simmons & Simmons (also fabulously expensive), that Bass had at last agreed to the press conference going ahead next Tuesday.

We sent out the invitations immediately so they couldn't change their minds on any points again.

It was then on to the House of Lords dining-room, wearing a black tie, to speak as the guest of honour at the annual dinner of Sir John Wheeler's North Westminster Conservative Party Association. I had only agreed because he was the Chairman of the Home Affairs Select Committee looking into racing and I need to keep him on my side.

Actually he is an extremely nice man. He ought to have been in the Cabinet or a senior Minister. He is able and pleasant. His wife, who is a physiotherapist and whom I sat next to, is also charming. She doesn't much like politics but she does her job beautifully.

In the Tory Party women are still treated as dear little things, fit to

---

15. QC, life peer 1978.
16. Lord Irvine of Lairg did become Lord Chancellor when Labour won in 1997.

make tea but not to make policy. Labour is now stealing a march on them in this area.

Saturday 22 February
Despite our agreement with Peter Sherlock and Bass that nothing would be said before the press conference on Tuesday, there were huge head-lines in the *Sporting Life*.

At the end it idiotically said this was my final passing shot before going at the end of April next year. When a man rang up from *Sporting Life* the next day I said that was something rather premature as I haven't decided yet whether I am going to retire then.

Monday 24 February
The gamesmanship and the attempts to put one over us by Bass con-tinued all day Sunday until 2.15 on Monday morning. I was in constant consultation with Brian and John Heaton as they argued at the lawyers' with the Bass people including Peter Sherlock.

I was amazed at how inefficient Bass is, even though it is a great conglomerate highly rated on the Stock Exchange. They think they have got a lot of brains because they hire a lot of lawyers and they think they are very cunning but they are not as cunning as they think they are. However, I like Peter Sherlock who is highly ambitious and doubt-less will become in charge of Bass or some other great conglomerate.

The idiotic story from the *Sporting Life* was repeated foolishly by the *Times* that he was now in the running to be the next Chairman of the Tote. They have to be insane. He must be earning at least £250,000 a year and all I get from the Tote is about £90,000, so he is far better where he is.

Journalists are so terribly uninformed, lazy, idle, ignorant. They write the most total piffle with a knowing air, misinforming their readers through their own carelessness in order to make what they think is a sensational point – which would explode in their faces, if anyone remembered later on when it was proved to be total nonsense.

We were supposed to sign all the documents and the final agreement at seven o'clock at Simmons & Simmons, our lawyers. Of course it didn't happen, as I knew it wouldn't.

So now I shall have to get up again tomorrow morning at 7.30 or earlier and bustle off to the office of Simmons & Simmons to the signing there before our press conference begins at around a quarter to eleven.

I popped into the House of Lords.

I had some tea and some anchovy toast with margarine underneath it which I have managed to get the House of Lords dining-room to provide. I found myself sitting next to Hugh Trevor-Roper. I am very fond of him. I asked him what he was writing now. He was quite mysterious. I said, 'Are you writing your memoirs?' and he said, 'Yes,' rather reluctantly. I said, 'To be published after your death?' He said, 'Yes.' I said, 'Do you write it every day or once a week?' He said, 'Intermittently but not all the time.' It was quite clear that, like me, he is writing a diary for publication after his death.

Tuesday 25 February

The lawyers from both sides were all congregated in the room at Simmons & Simmons. There were ladies there looking like prison officers, severely in black, not a good-looking one in sight. There was a strained atmosphere.

Than it was time to go to the press conference. I had seen at Simmons & Simmons that Peter Sherlock was very nervous and apprehensive, facing a press conference of this kind. There were forty to fifty journalists and lots of photographers. They only ever use one or two pictures so it is a total waste of time, as we were made to pose again and again.

Wednesday 26 February

There was very good coverage in the ordinary newspapers and tremendous coverage in the racing papers.

The best piece was Tony Fairbanks' from the *Racing Post*. He had understood that it would be the Placepots and the Jackpots which would swell to great sums with our new outlets in the thousand shops or so, including Coral's.

The *Times*, Richard Evans' gang, as usual were fairly monstrous. It said the whole project had been driven through by Peter Sherlock of Bass for Coral and he was the inspiration behind it. This is totally untrue. Peter Sherlock himself had said at the press conference that I had driven it through and it was due to my drive that we had got there. We have been developing the device for over a year, before we started talking to Coral about it.

Dinner in Pimlico with the Lennox-Boyds.

Mark said that during the election campaign Margaret would be staying with them so would I come up at the same time to stop her making trouble. I said, 'I don't think she is going to make any trouble.'

Thursday 27 February
Amanda Smith at French's has said she thinks the play *No Wrinkles* is no good in its present form. It is too much like a drawing-room comedy by William Douglas-Home. However, I shall bash away at it and see what I can do with it to make it rougher and more modern.

Norman Stone came to dinner to play bridge. Livia, my sister-in-law, sweet girl, arrived yesterday to stay with us. Norman speaks very good Hungarian. We learned this evening for the first time that his first marriage produced two quadroons, now in their twenties. That was with a Haitian girl, a niece of Papa Doc. He was terribly funny about living in Haiti, which he did for a couple of years, and being connected with its ruling murderous family.

He played bridge with a great deal of over-bidding which prevented us from overtaking Livia and Verushka.

Having polished off the best part of a bottle and a half of red wine and half a bottle of white wine and a bottle of champagne, he asked while we were playing bridge for some whisky. He had to stay the night here instead of going back to Oxford because of a meeting the next morning for which he had to leave the house at nine.

When we got up from the bridge table he almost fell on the floor and practically passed out. I had to feed him with anti-indigestion tablets and water.

He brought no pyjamas and slept naked. He had a toothbrush in his pocket and had forgotten to bring toothpaste. He had a razor in his pocket and some shaving soap and that was the lot.

Norman was fresh and bright in the morning. He is very attractive with his curly hair and quick, lively, dark face and the brilliance of his mind. I don't know anyone who doesn't like him, which is a pretty good tribute to someone who is never slow to criticize bitterly the failures of others.

I also drank too much.

Friday 28 February
Aly Aziz thinks they [Robbie and Tessa] have somebody else in mind [for Cornish Spring Water]. That is nonsense. Nobody else is going to take it over. They are just trying to be clever.

My brother would have been horrified. Which reminds me that at the wedding no mention was made at all at the reception or at the Apsley House wedding dinner of my brother or his wife, until I included them in my speech.

However, Robbie tells me his child is not going to be called only Christopher but also Robert David Wyatt as his Christian names.

Sunday 1 March

Went to Crockford's for dinner with the Zarachs.

Eva Zarach said to me, 'Have you got a lover?' With Verushka sitting next to her I said, 'That is not the sort of thing one discusses here.'

Tuesday 3 March

Told Ken Baker that I thought they could do a very good election ploy by announcing the internment of the terrorists in Northern Ireland again and also by announcing that we are going to have identity cards which everybody else in Europe does.

This would stop not only terrorists getting in and out so easily but it would also stop the flood of illegal immigrants pretending to be political refugees.

He disagreed about the internment. He thinks that if you did introduce it, it would simply make Southern Ireland a safe haven.

But he is attracted by the idea of the identity card.

I then asked him whether he had taken any further the proposal that I should get an extension at the Tote and he said he didn't know what John Major was doing about these things now but he would enquire about it. My guess is that they would want to leave it until after the election so if the Tories lose, I shall be done for immediately. A pity for the Tote as well as myself.

Brian McDonnell was at a meeting in the morning with the Labour group which is seeking to propose a horserace authority. Earlier they had been to see Stoker Hartington and Christopher Haines where they were given a very confidential briefing; they were told not to repeat it as it was solemnly secret. A large amount of it consisted of another attack on me, saying that I was quite useless, the Tote was useless and they gave a long exposition of already exploded figures, how we had a declining share of the market over the last twelve years, which is totally untrue.

I was very upset, unreasonably so, I suppose. I had begun to trust Stoker.

Not one word of congratulation from Stoker or Christopher Haines on this fantastic deal I have done with Bass, getting our Tote betting into the Coral betting shops via our new device. And they are so inefficient they haven't even progressed properly the initiative I started for them over Sunday racing in Brussels.

Stoker must be a bloody idiot to suppose that Alan Meale, who was very well disposed to the Tote and who was present at the meeting with Stoker and Christopher Haines, wouldn't tell Brian about it and warn him of our enemies.

Wednesday 4 March
Dinner at Roland Fuhrer's at No 5 Hyde Park Gardens. A huge house running laterally, joined at the same levels to the house next door. He said it was originally built by Nash in 1807.

It has very high ceilings on the ground floor, many handsome columns against the walls, beautifully gilded, fabulously decorated, full of pictures and strange and interesting art objects. He has a Torah made for the synagogue in Paris in 1775 and another Torah with a crown on it made in about 1745 in Paris. He is Jewish, of course, as is his wife.

There was some discussion about penises and their various sizes, which reminded me of an extraordinary conversation at dinner the night before when Eva said that Catherine the Great died when a pony was lowered on to her. She liked being stuffed by very large penises and the apparatus broke which was lowering the pony and she was crushed to death. I said I would try to find out whether this was right or not. It did seem from the books I could find immediately that the circumstances of her death after an abandoned sex life were somewhat mysterious.

Mrs Fuhrer, whose Christian name I didn't discover, is a Sabra (born in Israel).

She said her husband's family were very big in the steel business in Israel but he didn't like it, even though it was so profitable, because it was so boring making steel. So he decided to make money out of art. This she said he did by buying and selling objects all over the place at a profit.

She is a stunningly beautiful creature, well built, wonderful breasts, beautiful figure, elegant tapering slender legs, a mass of darkish hair circling a round face with life and laughter in it. She reminded me very much of the wonderful Jewish girl, Doris Kaplan, with whom I had the most exciting love affair of my life, during my second marriage and before and until my third marriage. I told her about that and said how fond I was of Jewish girls and that my second wife [Alix Robbins] was Jewish and half Russian.

The food was fantastic.

The only thing which wasn't good was the cigars. They were Davidoff made in the Dominican Republic and not Havana at all.

Simon Weinstock asked me whether Nicholas and Caroline were getting on all right. He had heard something disturbing. I said, 'Ask your mother. She knows everything. She knows every single thing that happens in our household or in our family. She and Verushka meet about twice a week and if they don't do that they talk on the telephone. They know every single thing about you, your wife, what Arnold does and what any member of the family has been doing on either side.'

He was astonished. I said, 'Didn't you know? You don't think they discuss politics over their regular lunches and on the telephone?'

Saturday 7 March
To Blenheim. It was the 26th Churchill Memorial Concert in aid of the Music Therapy Charity. This somehow induces the mentally disjointed to become more normal by having music played to them. Alexandra Trevor-Roper, who now looks a thousand years old, started it. Actually she was born in 1907 so she is only eighty-five. She is a nice woman but it is difficult to hear what she is saying or understand it sometimes and she doesn't hear what you are saying back to her.[1]

She and Hugh were slightly surprised to see us in the grand ducal party.

The tribute to Sir Winston Churchill in the interval was given by Professor R. V. Jones. Jones, who is now eighty, is a scientific genius. He is Emeritus Professor at Aberdeen of Natural Philosophy.

He was twenty-eight at the beginning of the War. He was sent for to the Cabinet Room by Churchill. He was asked to explain the way he had devised of countering a startling development by Germany who were getting through all our defences with their bombers, using a radio

---

1. Lady Alexandra (d 1997), eldest daughter of Field Marshal Earl Haig, m 1 (1941–54) Rear Admiral Clarence Dinsmore Howard-Johnston, m 2 (1954) Hugh Trevor-Roper, historian (Lord Dacre).

beam to guide them to their target. He was made Assistant Director of Intelligence, Air Staff, in 1941, and scientific adviser to MI6, the secret service, etc.

He was very funny about Winston wanting to go to Oxford after he had been in India (or to Cambridge, he didn't mind which) and being told he couldn't unless he passed the Latin and Greek tests. Winston said that having been commander of regular soldiers in India he didn't think he should have to try to command irregular verbs in Latin.

I gave Sonny what I had written about Churchill originally in *Encounter* which then went into *Harper's Bazaar* and then into a book for university [under]graduates in America.[2]

Sunday 8 March

I had my usual enormous country house breakfast of mushrooms and sausages and scrambled eggs and bacon.

Algy Cluff was staying. He had to dash off after breakfast to fly to Zimbabwe for the day. He had been summoned by Mugabe, the President of Zimbabwe, to be present when he visited Algy's great gold mine there which is making a fortune. He said he had to go otherwise there would be trouble. I said, 'Look out! He'll probably throw you down the ruddy mineshaft and confiscate your mine.' He said, 'I don't think there is any real danger.' Apparently a great deal of foreign currency goes into Zimbabwe from the mine.

Algy is a very amusing fellow.

He told me he has bought the copyright and all the rights in all E. Phillips Oppenheim's novels.[3] He wrote a hundred and fifty-seven books. He died in 1946. I said, 'How long has the copyright got to last?' He said until 1996. He might get films and television series made out of them. I said, 'You had better jolly well hurry up.'

They have a fair number of servants for these days. A number of footmen, a butler. I had to help me a rather effeminate valet who was kind and motherly and laid out all my clothes and packed them beautifully again. He had got special tissue paper to put everything in and little bags to put things like my wireless in. I gave him £10. I then

---

2. 'Churchill in His Element' was published in *Harper's Magazine*, September 1954.

3. (1866–1946); known as 'the Prince of Storytellers' and famous for his spy-fiction; the 1921 film of *The Great Impersonation* starred James Kirkwood; further versions were made in 1935 (with Valerie Hobson) and 1942.

had to find the senior butler in the kitchen to give him another £30 to distribute.

Spoke to Norman at twenty to eleven on Sunday night. He had been working on his Budget speech all day. I said, 'Restrain your schoolboy enthusiasm for jokes.'

Probably the date of the election will be announced on Thursday, Gold Cup day, for April 9th.

Monday 9 March

There was a jolly dinner at Cavendish Avenue. Ken and Mary Baker, Conrad Black and his new paramour, Barbara Amiel, Diana and John Wilton, Olga Polizzi and William Shawcross, Leonard and Estelle Wolfson.

The dinner was very good, a spinach soufflé – amazingly Olga and William arrived on time for it, though Conrad Black was late with Barbara.

Barbara Amiel is not so pretty as I recall her when I saw her last two years ago. I wasn't able to talk to her much because of the seating arrangements. She has rather larger breasts now. When I went round pouring the claret, which I do myself so they don't mix up the bottles because they all age differently, she leant back. I asked her if she would like some more claret. She had her head back and her mouth open so I kissed her. She liked that.

She had said I hadn't been talking to her so I said my nice kiss was in compensation.

Leonard told Diana that Ruth had left him in Barbados on a summer holiday. They were on the beach and it was twelve o'clock. Ruth said she wanted her lunch because she was hungry. Leonard said it was too early and he was staying on the beach. Angry, she went back to the hotel room, booked a plane immediately to Palm Beach and rang Jarvis Astaire to meet her when she got there.

She left no message for Leonard at all and he couldn't understand what had happened to her. She rang later and said it was the last straw when she couldn't have her lunch when she wanted it, she was bored with him and she had gone off with Jarvis Astaire. Leonard was shattered. He couldn't believe that she would do that after forty years of marriage.

He is now immensely happy with Estelle.

Her husband died of cancer at the age of fifty. She was a sad widow until fortune swung her way with Leonard.

I had a private talk with Ken. He will announce the levy determination tomorrow.

I asked him to make sure there would be something in the Lottery Act so that the Tote bidding for the lottery would be a hundred per cent OK. Basically we think it is going to be Bass and ourselves who will be making the tender in connection with Tote Direct.

Then I asked him about making sure that I got another year at least at the Tote because I have so much to see through, particularly Tote Direct. I didn't think anybody else had the drive and knowledge to do it. He said, 'I can't do it now till after the election. It's not a good moment. But I am a very great fan of yours and I will certainly do what I can.' He is quite convinced, clearly, that he is going to go on being Home Secretary.

There was talk about the election among the men when the women left the room.

Ken talked a little bit about the Political Asylum Bill. William Shawcross said he had got to let people come in. There were hordes of them moving all over Europe from all over the world. I said, 'Why should we change the whole nature of our society? Nobody wants a totally multi-cultural society.' William said, 'You're playing the race card.' I said, 'In a sense, yes. There is no reason at all why we should be completely swamped by coloured people. We have enough here already.' William seemed to be quite shocked.

Tuesday 10 March
Rang Norman to wish him luck with the Budget.

I went round to listen to the Budget speech, getting in very early to get a good place in the peers' gallery. There was Margaret sitting looking fairly disapproving in a back seat, listening intently to the Prime Minister beforehand. The Opposition asked a question or two to try and score party points. John Major is getting better at questions. He turns them very neatly.

Then along came Norman. He made an extremely good speech which put the Labour Party into a dilemma because of a skilful reduction of the standard rate of tax from twenty-five to twenty per cent for the first £2,000 of earned income.

He reduced the betting duty by a quarter per cent. In the context of his Budget, which was extremely cautious in some respects, I was glad that I had managed to persuade him to do that much. He said it was to help racing. Afterwards Ken Baker rang and told me that he had fixed the levy at £48 million. He thanked me for all my help. The .25 per cent would cost £15 million to the Exchequer. I said, 'It is not all going into that £48 million you have raised the levy to?' He said, 'No. We're not attributing any specific amount to it but I suppose you could say privately that perhaps £10 million or £11 million is.'

Alan Walters immediately after the Budget went on television to attack it, saying he shouldn't have cut taxes and it is disgraceful to run this enormous deficit. I think this was appalling. He is obviously doing it in tandem with Margaret. I am terrified to ring her up.

Wednesday 11 March

I listened to Norman prattling away to Brian Redhead, affectionately calling him Brian, which I think is a mistake, but he did quite well defending his Budget. I then screwed up my courage to ring Margaret.

She was against the reduction to twenty per cent tax at the bottom. She said, 'We got rid of those bands before. We had fifteen per cent when we came into power. It will be very difficult. That's why we got rid of it. And very costly to collect.' I said, 'But with modern computer techniques it ought to be quite simple.' She said, 'Oh no. People have still got to fill in their tax forms.'

She said, 'In any case it's another swingeing blow at the top tax-payers because the limit hasn't been raised in line with inflation. It therefore becomes a real tax increase. That's hitting our own supporters again.' She doesn't think the Budget will have any effect on the election. She thought it was 'clever' which is not necessarily a merit. 'They have saddled themselves with terrifying debt and I don't see how they are going to get out of it.'

I said, 'I have to support the Budget in the *News of the World* and the *Times*.' She broke in quickly, 'Of course you must support it but I'm just talking to you, dear. I'm just telling you what I think the real consequences are. Of course we must support it. I'm going off tomorrow to start helping various candidates.'

I then rang Norman and had quite a long talk with him. I told him she was going to support the Budget. He said, 'I wish you'd tell Alan Walters to do the same.'

I congratulated him on his delivery, on his jokes. He said, 'I disregarded you about jokes.' I said 'Yes, but I only meant the kind of jokes you could be taken up on, like the one you did about the Yuppies and their mobile telephones in restaurants and so forth.'[4]

I also said I was glad he had been able to do something about racing and he and Ken Baker had done it in a very imaginative way.

Of course it was all due to me, actually, but the world will never know it, this additional great levy of up to £48 million when even government members of the Levy Board had dared ask for only £42.6 million. But it is a sleight of hand to do it with the betting duty cut which I had hoped would be larger. He said it was the most he could do at the time.

Chips rang up and said he thought it was a clever Budget but it was not as well received in the City as Norman would expect because they are worried sick about this huge deficit. He said they must explain that it's not all just on social security benefits, tax relief and jolly pensions but a helluva lot of it is investment in long-term projects.

We arrived at Charlton Park when it had just got dark and found Micky Suffolk standing outside the house. He then took me down to his wine cellars in the big house.

We selected some fascinating-looking South African wines from the furthest south vineyards in Africa. It is a Hamilton vineyard, very famous. For dinner we had a 1964 Burgundy from a jereboam. There was some very good champagne before, too.

I don't really like Burgundy as much as claret but he particularly wanted to drink Burgundy so I obviously had to let him do so.

At breakfast time Micky Suffolk, who is now fifty-seven, gave me some ginseng from Korea. This is the red Asian one which the Chinese are very keen on. It holds up the ageing process and is very good in one's old age but, contrary to popular belief, it doesn't add anything to one's sexual activity. It is not an aphrodisiac. He had a little bottle which cost him £75, an extract of this stuff.

It's good for hangovers but I can't say it did a great deal of good to mine.

Then it was off to Cheltenham. I did my rounds. John Sparrow, Tristram Ricketts, John Sanderson and various other people all congratulated me on getting the levy up and the betting duty coming down by a quarter per cent.

Even Stoker Hartington said they knew how much they owed to me in getting this done. What a two-faced bugger he is.

---

4. The tax Lamont put on company mobile phones was repealed in the 1999 Budget.

As Queen Elizabeth the Queen Mother had a chill and couldn't come, Verushka made the presentation of the Tote Cheltenham Gold Cup.

Saturday 14 March
A charming letter from Queen Elizabeth the Queen Mother. She actually apologized for not being able to present the Tote Cheltenham Gold Cup after she had undertaken to do so. What exquisite manners. What thoughtfulness. What consideration and kindness. She is one of the two greatest *ladies* I have known, the other being Margaret Thatcher.[5]

Off to Uttoxeter. There was a very agreeable man called Stan Clarke who is the Chairman of Uttoxeter, a very go-ahead businessman making a great success of the course. He has been made a member of the Jockey Club. He is the sort of member they would not have dreamed of having even five years ago because he is not in the upper echelons. He is a practical man, sturdy, with a firm face and dark hair.

On Channel 4 they announced me as 'Lord Wyatt of Weeford' and said 'Weeford is not very far from here and we believe he is going on there after the meeting.'

I went to the church built by James Wyatt on the site of an old church which was tottering into collapse. He built it in 1802 and my family basically paid for it.

Several of my Wyatt ancestors are buried in and around it.

What with Robbie Lyle becoming a Mayhew and God knows what, I have decided to be buried there.

The Tories are getting the jitters. The opinion polls have not got any better for them since the election was announced. Not even Norman's very clever Budget has helped.

Sunday 15 March
I had a long talk with Margaret. She is very gloomy.

I said I thought it was very nice of John Major to send her flowers as soon as he announced the date of the election. She said, 'A bunch of flowers won't make up for a £28 billion deficit, Woodrow.'

Norman Lamont has got a new problem this time. The Labour Party, John Smith, is going to produce its alternative Budget tomorrow and not on Tuesday. The Tory Party, as usual, is unprepared for it.

---

5. The Queen Mother also said that she had seen on television that 'your dear one did it most gracefully' in her stead.

I said, 'I'll get on to Chips Keswick.' He said, 'That's marvellous.' I managed to get Chips at home.

He said he would get Sir Adam Ridley, ex Treasury, now at Hambros, on to the job first thing in the morning.

During the day I amused myself looking up my relationship with Dr Johnson. He was rather closer than I had thought. At a not too distant point (early 18th century) his ancestors are the same as mine. The wife of Benjamin Wyatt II was Sarah Ford, one of the co-heiresses of Ford, the big brewers of Burton-on-Trent. Her mother was sister to Dr Johnson's mother. Dr Johnson's father had a bookshop in Lichfield which eventually failed because he was not very good at business. Dr Johnson, when young, refused to go to the market at Uttoxeter with him and stand at his bookstall. Fifty years later he stood in the rain on the spot where his father's bookstall used to be for two hours as a penitence for not helping his father when he asked him to.

Monday 16 March

John Smith's Budget came out with great showmanship pretending to be the real one. Chips had mustered a fair number of pundits to blow off with their criticisms on the radio and TV.

Panorama was devoted to a kind of debate interview with Norman, John Smith and an idiot called Alan Beith[6] who is the Lib Democrat finance man – they had issued a silly Budget of their own as well, the same day. Norman did it incredibly badly. He missed every trick and let John Smith win handsomely on points.

I was so horrified that I rang Ken Baker. He agreed with me. I rattled off all the points I thought Norman had missed and said I didn't think they were conducting the campaign energetically enough. He said, 'No, it's not combative enough.' I said, 'I don't know who the inner circle is now. I suppose Richard Ryder is in it.' He said, 'John Wakeham is, possibly.' I said, 'I am going to send a memo to John Major in the morning.'

Tuesday 17 March

Spoke to Richard Ryder and told him what I thought.

Talked to Andrew Turnbull, Principal Private Secretary to John

---

6. Liberal and Liberal Democrat MP since 1973.

Major. I told him about my memo and he said, 'Good,' and to mark it for his attention so he could make sure he got it quickly.[7]

Then Ken Baker rang. He said he was on his way now to the helicopter for Newmarket and Cambridge. 'What I do for my party!'

I said, 'You have got to put at the top of the list the Asylum Bill and how the Labour Party would let in all these floods of immigrants of various colours, sizes and shapes.' He absolutely agreed and said it was coming out in the manifesto when it comes out tomorrow morning. I said, 'You've got to make a big issue of it. It's not racist. It's just common sense maintaining our society on the same balance as it is now and not promoting racial strife by introducing all kinds of other elements.'

I told him I had given John Major a list of effective TV broadcasters with him at the head of the list. He was rather pleased at that and I said, 'I also put Michael Heseltine in, shuddering, but he is pretty good at seizing on opponents' weaknesses.'

Andrew Turnbull and I talked briefly about Margaret. I said I had been doing my best to keep her on side and not voice her criticisms. He said, 'Her behaviour has been absolutely first class. Impeccable. We couldn't have asked for more. She's been wonderful.'

Thursday 19 March

Shaun Woodward,[8] who is in charge of much of the campaign for the Tories, has started ringing me to ask for advice and help. I sent a memo to Chris Patten underlining what I had said to the Prime Minister.

John Smith's so called Budget may have been a mistake. It is beginning to boomerang as people realize how deeply they are going to be hit.

There was a curious article in the *Racing Post* this morning saying 'wily old Wyatt' was responsible [for the increased levy] and that it was my dinner with old friends Kenneth Baker and Norman Lamont

---

7. WW began by predicting an overall majority of between thirty and fifty. It would be largely a 'presidential' choice between Major and Kinnock so Major should be prominent on TV. Their best other TV performers were Baker, Clarke, Heseltine and Hurd. The Tories should stress that increased taxes were counter-productive, attack the minimum wage and bring the Asylum Bill to the forefront: 'This is not a *race* card but calm common sense.'

8. Former BBC TV journalist; Director of Communications, Conservative Party, 1990–2; Conservative MP since 1997.

just before the Budget which had clinched the thing. Absolute rubbish, of course. I had clinched it but not at the dinner – I had dinner with Ken Baker but not with the two of them together.

Friday 20 March
My brother's birthday. He would have been seventy-seven today.

Though Robert was not always fair to me, particularly in influencing my mother to cut me out of her will and break her promise to my father that everything would be left equally between my brother and myself, he had his kind side to me, perhaps sometimes out of a sense of guilt.

My brother also winkled all the money from my Uncle Arthur. I was his favourite nephew and would have remained so if I hadn't joined the Labour Party. I might have made up with him later when I moved somewhat to the right.

I regard my stake in Cornish Spring Water as Robert's intended part recompense to me and I certainly regard the twenty-five per cent shareholding I have in the wind farm as my due for all I have done to put it on the road. Without me it would have been impossible to get anywhere. I am also paying a quarter of the pre-launch expenses. I may lose that altogether if nothing happens. It is fairly dodgy. The wind strength is only 6.8. It should be 7 to make sure of it as a reasonable financial proposition.

Sir Leon Brittan, the Competition Commissioner at Brussels, came to lunch. So did Chips Keswick, Chairman of Hambros.

Leon is brimming full of cleverness, shrewdness and intelligence. I always liked him though we fell out for a period when he was trying to push us into a political federation of Europe and shove on top of us a single currency and a single European bank.

On that subject Chips said there was still a chance for London to have that bank. Leon said, 'I think we have missed the boat now. It will probably go to Amsterdam because people don't want it to go to Germany. Of course, if you had been willing to join the single currency and had been willing to accept the European bank, it very likely would have gone to London.'

I said to Leon that one of the difficulties with the Commissioners appointed by their governments to Brussels is that though they take the oath to be loyal to the Commission and not to their own countries, they strive for them, whereas our people tend not to. He said, 'Yes, that is certainly true on the whole.'

On mergers he was very interesting. Any merger above a given sum of money has to be referred to Brussels. They get the answer from Brussels, from Leon's Department, in about a month whereas it can take six or nine months or even a year when it is referred here to the Monopolies and Mergers Commission. They are not as inefficient as I thought they were. This is to Leon's credit.

Leon is helping the Tories in their campaign, which he is allowed to do, in pointing out the need to have a Tory government if our position is to continue strong in the European Community.

He is very happy in Brussels. He says it is architecturally splendid, the restaurants are very, very good (he is very fond of his food), and so is the wine, though he politely said 'not as good as it is in your house'.

Chips arrived with a box of Ramon Allones cigars for me, my favourite. Verushka immediately said cheekily, 'Why have you brought Woodrow a present and not me?' 'Oh well,' he said, 'I often send you flowers and presents.' But after he had gone, an hour and a half later, an enormous quantity of orchids arrived.

Dear Chips, with his stocky, broad body, a little stout, and his round, lively and eager face. He is a loyal friend and I feel great warmth for him.

Saturday 21 March
Went to Wigan on the 8.15 train. I felt less tired than I thought I would. Maybe it is the ginseng I am taking. Patrick Meaney[9] takes it, too. He says he takes it all the time. I had asked at the Levy Board whether it could be given to horses as it is only a vegetable. I am told this is the case; it can be done without crossing the Jockey Club rules.

It was an interesting day from my point of view at Wigan. We met the Chief Executive, the man who runs the Wigan development of City Challenge. Twenty cities can win out of fifty-seven so they have a real chance and they are including us as part of their challenge.

We are getting increasingly liked at Wigan as a big employer and a good one.

In the evening after I had got back Norman rang. He wanted to know how I thought they were getting on. I said, 'You were very effective. I have just seen your press conference about Labour's high spending. I think it excellent.'

---

9. Chairman, the Rank Organization; knight 1981; he died in 1992 aged sixty-seven.

Dear Norman looks very odd on television. His hair stands up in a slightly Mephistopheles manner, his face looks blotchy and peculiar and he seems without authority, though he is brilliantly clever and did a most ingenious Budget. John Smith in all the opinion polls is streets ahead of him as the alternative Chancellor.

Sunday 22 March

On Thursday the Tories had a stroke of luck when the dreadful unemployment figures were put into second place in the press and on the air by the Duchess of York and the Duke of York splitting up.

David Somerset rang in the middle of our game of bridge with the Pejacsevichs, desperately wanting to know whether I still believe that the Tories will win an overall majority. I said yes and gave him my usual reasons. He is getting more and more nervous. I said, 'I expect you will be ringing me more and more as the election day approaches.' He said he certainly would be. I told him I had spoken to Michael Tree who had rung from Greece in a panic with enquiries.

Monday 23 March

John Major was a disaster at his press conference. He misunderstood entirely the point of the question about the burden of individual taxation, which it is true has risen from 34.8 per cent to about 37.1 per cent since 1979 or 1980. Clearly he didn't understand the answer, which he should have done as he was Chancellor of the Exchequer himself.

[It is that] you are much better off altogether and you have only got better off by the Tories making you better off. That is also how they funded all the extra spending on the Health Service, education, and every social security benefit you could think of.

In the afternoon I went to Rothschild's to talk about lotteries. They saw pretty quickly that we were an invaluable part of any consortium or scheme. Our machines, at £583 a time, startle them with their [low] cost. They had put in far, far more than that, five to ten times as much towards capital for equipment. I think maybe we should get them together with us. They would like to do that. They are also in touch with Peter Sherlock but that is fine.

Thursday 26 March

To the National Theatre as guests of Mary Soames to see *The Madness of George III*, a new play by Alan Bennett.

Before the performance began John Sainsbury[10] commented on the Cornish Spring Water and said how good it is. I said, 'I hear it is now in twenty Sainsbury stores.' He said, 'Yes. Of course I didn't use my influence over it.' I said, 'No, of course not.'

The play was superb. But when I looked him up in the *Dictionary of National Biography* it seems to have been pretty wildly inaccurate. George III was not as badly treated as portrayed, beaten and blistered and in agony and pain. There was fearful stuff on the stage, very riveting and moving, distressing.

Nicholas Soames should have been at the dinner but was away electioneering. I asked someone how big his majority was and they said twelve thousand at Crawley. I remarked, 'If he lost that, he'd have to be even more foolish than I think he could be.' Mary Soames thought that a somewhat derogatory remark and she was quite right. It was meant to be.

The dinner was extremely good, wonderful fillet steak, exactly right – that is, nice and bloody.

It is very agreeable going in such style to the National Theatre.

Friday 27 March
The Tory Party is getting very jagged. The polls continue to be bad. The campaign is being run dreadfully badly by Chris Patten, the Chairman, who is wet as hell.

Saturday 28 March
I spent a chunk, most of it, of Saturday morning rewriting parts of my article for the *News of the World* and putting in something about Patten.[11]

I had a long conversation with Margaret.

We both agreed that he, John, is a very dull man though no doubt very nice. She said she doesn't like to get through to them because she would be thought to be interfering.

Ronnie Millar[12] is supposed to be writing his speeches and giving him

---

10. Lord Sainsbury, chairman, J. Sainsbury, 1967–92, president since 1992.
11. 'The Tories' dismal campaign', began WW's first item on 29 March, 'is down to Chris Patten, their chairman. He should be replaced at once by someone more imaginative, determined and persuasive ... Patten should hop off to his shaky Bath seat and stay there.'
12. Playwright, screen and political writer; knight 1980.

jokes. She said, 'But of course you can't do it that way. Ronnie has to be there when the speech is written so you compose it together. Otherwise you get it wrong. John doesn't get it right and insofar as Ronnie Millar supplies him with jokes, he doesn't put them over or in the right places.'

Sunday 29 March
I talked to Norman Lamont.

I asked him what he thought of what I had written about Patten. He said, 'No comment.' I said, 'You mean you agree.' He didn't demur. He said, 'But it's too late now.' I said, 'I don't think so. It could be done quite quickly.'

The Tory campaign remains abysmal, with the Prime Minister standing in a tent, his back to half the audience, looking like a Sunday school teacher. Perhaps it makes him feel at home because it is like a circus tent. But it cost a fortune and they can't scrap it now, they tell me.

Richard Ryder says perhaps I could say in my article next Sunday that the campaign has improved because there is a great deal of distress at the Conservative Central Office at my saying that Patten ought to be dumped to win votes.

I shall have to consider that because when the Tories win, this might have so annoyed the Prime Minister that he won't give me my extra year which is essential for the benefit of the Tote. If Labour win, of course I am done for in any case because Roy Hattersley would be the Home Secretary. I shall just have to tell the truth, even though it is to my own personal disadvantage. It is far more important that we don't have five or six years of a Labour government wrecking everything which was done and putting Britain right back beyond where Mrs Thatcher started.

Monday 30 March
I spoke to Kenneth Baker and said, 'You have got to press immigration and make a big thing of it.' I pleaded with him again but nothing seems to be happening about it.

Dinner with Cita and Irwin Stelzer at the Connaught. There were the usual floods of Dom Pérignon champagne, wonderful white wine, two bottles of Beychevelle 1975.

Also present was Sir Sydney Lipworth.[13] I sat next to his wife

---

13. Chairman, Monopolies and Mergers Commission, 1988–93; chairman, Zeneca, since 1995; m (1957) Rosalie Liwarek; knight 1991.

at the Levers. She is a very jolly woman and a very keen bridge player.

She is no beauty but amusing. He is no beauty either. He is Chairman of the Monopolies and Mergers Commission. He disputed Leon Brittan's claim to me that Brussels was faster than he was when mergers were referred.

I hope very much that he is not going to be beastly to Rupert. If there is a Labour government, they will refer the ownership of Sky Television and cross-ownership with newspapers to the Monopolies and Mergers Commission. It might get to Brussels. I don't know whether Leon Brittan would be more sympathetic or otherwise.

The reason why Irwin had asked them to dinner was because he obviously wants to get on the right side of him for Rupert's sake, if challenged by a Labour government on the monopolies side. He had never met either of them before and was surprised that I knew them reasonably well.

Tuesday 31 March

Talked to Margaret after I had heard that three polls were coming out giving Labour substantial leads.

She agrees completely with me that Ken Baker must thump the immigration card and the Prime Minister is far too wet.

I said, 'A naughty thought occurred to me – don't be in too much of a hurry, if Labour wins, to go to the Lords.' She said, 'I had been thinking of that myself but I would be too old when the time came for the Tories to win the next election.'

Wednesday 1 April

At the board meeting David Sieff was in a panic saying, 'You can't still believe the Tories are going to win?' I said, 'I still believe the Tories will get an overall majority. It is a strange election. Watch the Liberal Democrat rating. When it gets to twenty-three per cent the Tories will be home and dry, if that happens.'

At two o'clock I spoke to Ken Baker.

I said I had been talking to Margaret and, 'When I told her the idea was that you were going to be asked a question by a friendly journalist and then make your answer, and make it pretty fierce, on the whole immigration question, she said, "He's got to do it at the beginning of his speech, when he makes his opening speech at the press conference, to make a greater impact." '

He said, 'You know who doesn't want me to' (meaning Major and of course Patten because they are scared of the whole thing). I said, 'She said be bold and make your opening speech with it in, then have the row afterwards when it is too late for them to do anything about it.' He said, 'I think I will do that.' I wonder if he will.

Thursday 2 April

Had a dreary meeting with Brian Wimble from Chipchase Jarvis, my accountants. They want to charge me £9,000 a year for doing my simple income tax. I pointed out to him that all the audit for the Tote, with a business of £250 million a year, is only £50,000.

Cita and Irwin Stelzer came to dinner. I look forward to seeing them. He is so acute in his brain and a very loyal friend. She is delightful.

Irwin is amazed at the wetness and feebleness of the Tory campaign. He also thinks nothing of Norman Lamont. I tell him he is wrong about that.

Friday 3 April
I don't know why they won't play the immigration card. A serious row broke out this evening between Willie Whitelaw and Sir Nicholas Fairbairn. The latter is the eccentric ex Solicitor General for Scotland, still a candidate. Willie Whitelaw was going to speak for him but cancelled when Nicholas Fairbairn made an attack on immigration and the floods of immigrants coming in. Fairbairn, although going a bit over the top, struck a chord and he was right. But Willie, in his usual wet way, said how awful and cancelled his promise to speak for him very publicly, with television reporters coming to him in Cumberland.

Saturday 4 April
The BBC sports programme, *Grandstand*, chose to come to Wigan to follow all the betting from our wonderful new complex. They gave us a long run at one o'clock and another one at two o'clock and another one at five o'clock. If we had tried to get this publicity for ourselves, it would have cost us half a million pounds. They were so pleased with what they did and it went down so well that they said they wanted to come back again next year.

To my great pleasure Oxford won the Boat Race, having been behind once or twice at the beginning. I took that as a good omen for the Tories to win, having been behind in the polls at the beginning. They are still behind. But I still think, as I have written in the *News of the World* for tomorrow, that they will pull it off in the end with an overall majority.

Sunday 5 April
Talked to Ken Baker who was apologetic that he couldn't persuade the Prime Minister and Chris Patten to let him have a really good go on immigration.

In my second conversation with him today Norman is still very gloomy. He can't see how we are going to win. He doesn't believe my calculations. I wondered whether to ring John Major but I suppose he probably wouldn't speak to me, particularly after my attack on Chris Patten.

I had a long conversation with Nick Lloyd (editor of the *Daily Express*) telling him, 'For God's sake push this immigration issue and also the wreck and ruin, with the increased interest rates that Smith is promising, which would bring everything to a juddering halt.'

As a campaigner Major has been a disaster. He is now spending his last few days rabbiting on about the constitution which nobody is interested in. The English couldn't give a damn what happens to the Scots and the Scots couldn't give a damn what happens to the English.

Monday 6 April

Sent memo to John Major.[1] Despite my praise of his new campaigning it is still pretty flat. He might not get his overall majority for lack of extra push and drive.

Then a calamity. Graham Paterson rang up [from the *Times*].

He said the editor had made a sudden decision this morning. He is going to take all the page on Tuesday and write about the different contenders' merits.

He said, 'So your column has got to go.' I said, 'This is absurd, I have planned it. I waited till the last moment because I knew it was my last shot before the election. I have also got to deal with the fact that just before Mrs Thatcher was deposed I said I would tell people to vote Labour if she were. I now have to explain why I haven't done so.'

Eventually, after a lot of ringing backwards and forwards I got hold of Ted Pickering who is the Vice Chairman of the *Times*.

I said, 'I don't write these articles for the money, you know, at least certainly not mainly for it. I have got a contract with you and I get paid whether I write them or not. But I write them to influence people and he has now taken my chance away. If I had been told in time, I could have written it for some other newspaper.'

He said, 'Have you spoken to the editor?' I said, 'I have been trying to get him but he won't speak to me. The warning had gone out from his office that he is so engrossed in writing his drivel' (at which point Ted laughed) 'that he can't speak to anyone. At least let me write the damn thing tomorrow.'

Ted said, 'It is the editor's prerogative.'

Ted said he would do what he could about it and speak to him.

In the meanwhile I took advantage of the moment to say I would like £1,500 expenses to go to Hungary on May 8th so I can find out

---

1. This second memo began by saying Major was doing fine but should smile more often in his interviews on TV. It was vital to instil fear of *socialist* government and to make a big feature of immigration, 'not in the dotty Fairbairn way but as in my *News of the World* article of yesterday'.

what their reaction is to our election and what is going on in Eastern Europe.

He said he was sure that would be all right.

I am reading an absorbing book by Mary Wesley. I tried one before and didn't think much of it but that was her first. This one, called *Not That Sort of Girl*, is utterly fascinating. It reminds me of many things which happened to me in the War and it is beautifully written with lots of jolly sex in it, too. I am much heartened by the fact that she didn't start writing novels until she was in her seventies. She is now eighty and she has written three extraordinarily successful ones. One is called *The Camomile Lawn* which has been an enormous success on TV.

Later on in the afternoon came some better news. Obviously Pickering had got to work well. Graham Paterson rang me. He said he had told the editor I was very upset and they are going to let me write my article tomorrow, the final article before the election.

Tuesday 7 April
Had a great triumph. Having energized the *Daily Express* over the immigration issue they made a great front page splash of Baker's somewhat muddled speech about it yesterday.

Though he talked unimportant muddle about proportional representation, he led on from this through to saying that's how you got extremist parties rising, as in France and Germany, and that's how you get racism, and that's why all this immigration must be legislated for properly, and that is what the Labour Party is not going to do, etc.

At the Tory press conference Major was challenged about Baker's speech. He said he agreed with it completely, that he didn't want the situation developing here as in Marseilles (where there is a lot of racial violence) and he was going to stick to firm and fair immigration.

Paddy Ashdown immediately called foul and said Baker was sinking into the gutter. God knows why he's so idiotic.

Norman rang later and said that a lot of people were defecting to the Lib Democrats in Kingston. I said, 'Are you worried?' he said, 'No. I got fifty-five per cent of the vote last time.'[2]

I told him, 'You are going to get an overall majority,' and he thinks

2. Lamont got 51.6 per cent of the vote this time, but lost the seat to the Liberal Democrats in 1997.

that now may be possible because of regional differences and the way the votes stack up in different places.

Dinner with David Montagu [Swaythling]. John Freeman[3] was there with his wife, Judy. John is looking emaciated. He is taller and thinner than I am. He is seventy-eight. He did have some sort of cancer but that has gone out of his system. He now lives in complete retirement in Barnes. I said, 'What do you do all day?' He replied that he looked after the children, such as there were. He has got children by [almost] every marriage and he has been married four times. He does the household chores and washes up and a lot of the cooking instead of his wife. He said, 'I send her out to work to earn some money.'

I said, 'You could have been Prime Minister if you hadn't disdained the mucky, grubby world of politics.' He said it was true, he'd hated it.

I said, 'You are a little bit like Hartley Shawcross in that respect. He, too, could have been Prime Minister and Leader of the Labour Party.' John said, 'But he was much more ambitious than I was. He made a lot of money at the Bar. I never wanted to make a lot of money.'

John claimed not to be eccentric but said that I was. I said, 'Me?' with surprise. Verushka said, 'Yes. You're very eccentric.' I said, 'Why?' She said, 'I could tell them but I am not going to.' David said I was very eccentric and conducted my board meetings in a very eccentric way; they were the jolliest things he had ever been to in a boardroom and he would not for a moment stay as a board member if I wasn't the Chairman.

I said, 'I merely state the obvious, which is considered to be very eccentric in England because nobody ever states the obvious, and what is the real truth.' John said, 'Yes, that is your real strength. You have never been afraid to get up and say the emperor has no clothes on, however unpopular it makes you. You have great courage.'

So we had a pleasant time praising each other.

---

3. Former Labour politician (MP, 1945–50) and journalist (editor, *New Statesman*, 1961–5); British High Commissioner in India, 1965–8; Ambassador to the US, 1969–71; chairman, London Weekend Television, 1971–84; Visiting Professor of International Relations, University of California at Davis, 1985–90; m 1 (1938–48) Elizabeth, née Johnston; m 2 Margaret, née Abbot (d 1957); m 3 (1962–76) Catherine Wheeler, née Dove; m 4 (1976) Judith, née Mitchell; children by all but his first marriage.

Wednesday 8 April

John Major has been smiling more. I saw him this morning doing a phone-in election call. He handled it very well. People go rabbiting on about whether they are going to get free dentists or not instead of thinking of the big issues and the calamity which would befall them and Britain if Labour won. They can't see beyond the end of their teeth.

Excitement now building up. Polls coming out show the Tories a half per cent ahead in the *Telegraph*. But they have still got the Lib Democrat vote too low in my view.

Norman rang in a great state of excitement. I said, 'You are going to do it all right.' He said he was getting a bit more confident.

I rang, rather late, the *Sun* and the *Express* and said, 'For Christ's sake do that immigration thing on the front page,' but I think I was too late for it. Rupert rang at the same time. He started blowing up about the appalling Tory campaign, how they didn't have enough money to put proper advertisements in.

I told him what I wanted the *Sun* to do. He said he would ring them straight away and started dialling on another telephone while I was talking to him.

Thursday 9 April

A beautiful sunny day over most of England. Whether that will give a cheerful spirit to make them vote Tory, or make them vote Labour, for what they think is a better world, I have no idea. I think it may slightly help the Tories.

Went out to Kempton to see the new hood designed by the Chipperfield chap of Chipperfield circuses. It is quite good. It is designed to prevent the sun affecting what you see on the television, as many of our televisions, a thousand of them, are outside and punters can't read them properly when it's a sunny day. It's not too bad but it's not good enough at £280 a shot. I had to ring him and tell him.

Chips rang early and said, 'The mood is much better in the City. They are now expecting a Tory victory and already (this was at ten to nine) the market has gone up twenty-four points.'

Chips was very surprised that the *Financial Times* had come out this morning saying vote Labour. I wasn't. As I told him, it has always been run editorially by these weird people from Central Europe or people in the same mould who are very left-inclined.

Rupert was ringing from Los Angeles. Obviously he was wishing he was here. I wish he had been. He would have stirred the *Sun* and the *Express* up better on my immigration point.

We went to four parties. The first was a dinner at Geoffrey Ampthill's.

The Wolfsons' was at Claridge's.

Usually Leonard has his post election parties at his great flat in Portman Place, opposite where Arnold Goodman lives. He has really splashed out this time. He is becoming much less stingy in his second marriage state.

Margaret was at the *Daily Telegraph* party at the Savoy, as she was at the Wolfson party.

On the screen the ridiculous Peter Snow of *Newsnight* was dancing around his idiotic swingometer. He looked like a mad professor as he kept shrieking and yelling, trying always to push his swingometer far enough to show a Labour overall majority and then gradually reducing it in dismay, as it stubbornly kept hanging around a far too small swing away from the Tories.

On my way out I met John Mortimer and his wife looking glum.

John said, 'We're just going off to the BBC.' 'Ah,' I said, 'you'll be among friends there.'

I said to Julian Amery, 'Your peerage is looking brighter now.'

The final election party at Alistair McAlpine's house in College Street was far more amusing than any of the other parties.

It was about one o'clock. Margaret was right at the top of the house in a fairly small room with two television screens on either side. There was an empty chair beside her and she asked me to sit with her.

She was quite cross with me when the news of Chris Patten's defeat at Bath came up. I said, 'That's a small sacrifice to pay for getting an overall Tory majority.' Margaret said, 'You're not being very generous.' I replied, 'He was never a friend of yours.' She was in a magnanimous mood. I said, 'I will write something of condolence for him in the *News of the World* just to show that I'm not really anti him.'

Margaret was also cross, a little bit, with Alexander Hesketh, when he was agreeing heartily with me about how terrible Christopher Patten is.

She said, 'You shouldn't talk like that, either of you.'

When we were talking about Mr and Mrs Kinnock I said, 'She is very pretty.' Margaret said, 'Do you think so?' I said, 'Yes, I have always had a soft spot for her in my heart.' Nick Ridley called out from the other side of the room, 'You mean much lower down, don't you?' Margaret laughed. I thought it quite a coarse observation but she doesn't mind that kind of a joke. I forbore to reply, 'It wouldn't be soft lower down.'

Margaret got more and more pleased as the evening wore on.

I had told her during the evening that they would have won even more votes and more seats if she had been conducting the campaign. This is what I really felt. Not surprisingly, she agreed.

She left at about a quarter to four when there were no more results coming in.

When she finally got up to go I gave her a great hug and whispered in her ear, 'I adore you. You are marvellous.'

She behaved with great dignity throughout the night with no carping criticisms. They will doubtless come later. As she went out the photographers, who were waiting and who had been photographing everybody going in, took masses of photographs of her and the television was there asking for her comment. She said, 'It is a great night. It is the end of Socialism.' That is, after all, what she has been aiming at.

The Conservatives won the 1992 election with an overall majority of twenty-one, and forty-two per cent of the votes.

Chronology

1989

11 January	Political parties allowed in Hungary
17 January	Government proposes football fans should carry ID cards; plan later shelved
20 January	George Bush inaugurated as US President
26 January	Windlesham report clears Thames TV over *Death on the Rock* programme but government rejects findings
3 February	F. W. de Klerk succeeds P. W. Botha as leader of South Africa's National Party
5 February	Murdoch launches Sky TV satellite network
15 February	Ayatollah Khomeini's *fatwa* against Salman Rushdie
3 March	Mrs Thatcher becomes a grandmother
4 March	Train crash near Purley
26 March	First multi-party elections in Soviet Union
27 March	Mrs Thatcher begins visit to Africa
1 April	Poll tax introduced in Scotland
5 April	Leon Brittan reveals PM's Private Secretary and Press Officer as sources of leaked letter in the Westland affair
6 April	Abolition announced of the National Dock Labour Scheme
15 April	Hillsborough football ground disaster – ninety-six crushed to death at FA Cup semi-final

3 May	Mrs Thatcher's tenth anniversary as Prime Minister
5 May	Labour win Vale of Glamorgan by-election
17 May	Government rejects the EC's Social Charter
3 June	Massacre of pro-democracy supporters in Tiananmen Square, Peking
12 June	Chancellor says UK will not join EMS before 1990
26 June	Madrid European summit; Britain agrees to enter ERM when three conditions are met
14–16 July	French Revolution bicentennial celebrations
19 July	Government proposals to reform the legal profession
24 July	Government reshuffle: Howe becomes Lord President of the Council, Leader of the House of Commons and Deputy Prime Minister; Major becomes Foreign Secretary
31 August	Buckingham Palace announces separation of Princess Anne and Captain Mark Phillips
13 September	Ambulance staff ban overtime
19–22 September	Mrs Thatcher visits Japan
2 October	Labour conference abandons commitment to unilateral nuclear disarmament
4–21 October	WW's play *The Division Belle* at Theatre Royal, Margate
6 October	UK interest rates 15 per cent
16 October	SLD change name to Liberal Democrats
19 October	Court of Appeal frees Guildford Four, fourteen years after their imprisonment for pub bombing
22 October	Mrs Thatcher refuses to join Commonwealth sanctions against South Africa
26 October	Lawson resigns as Chancellor of the Exchequer,

	replaced by Major; Hurd becomes Foreign Secretary; Alan Walters also goes
9 November	Government announces nuclear power stations will not be privatized
10 November	Demolition of Berlin Wall begins
21 November	Televising of Parliament begins; ambulance dispute escalates
5 December	Mrs Thatcher defeats Sir Anthony Meyer in Conservative Party leadership contest, 314 to 33 with twenty-seven abstentions
7 December	Broadcasting Bill published
12 December	House of Commons votes to prosecute alleged war criminals in Britain
20 December	Banks refuse to continue Government's plans for student loans
22 December	Government announces it will grant UK citizenship to 225,000 from Hong Kong
25 December	Former Romanian dictator Nicholae Ceauşescu and his wife executed
29 December	Václav Havel elected Czechoslovakian President

1990

2 February	African National Congress unbanned in South Africa
11 February	Nelson Mandela released from prison in South Africa
23 February	Ambulance dispute settled
11 March	Lithuania first Soviet republic to declare independence
22 March	Labour win Mid-Staffordshire by-election

25 March	Dr Runcie announces his retirement as Archbishop of Canterbury in January 1991
31 March	Riots in Trafalgar Square against the poll tax
1 April	Prisoners seize control of Strangeways Prison, Manchester; poll tax starts in England and Wales
19 April	Forty-four Conservative MPs rebel against Hong Kong Citizenship Bill
4–5 May	Latvia and Estonia vote to secede from the USSR
29 May	Yeltsin elected President of Russian Federation
3 June	SDP formally disbanded; David Owen, John Cartwright and Rosie Barnes continue as Independent Social Democrat MPs
4 June	House of Lords rejects War Crimes Bill
25 June	IRA bomb at the Carlton Club, London
9 July	G7 summit at Houston
14 July	Nicholas Ridley resigns from the government after *Spectator* interview
19 July	Government gives £3,000m to reduce impact of poll tax
25 July	Dr George Carey announced as next Archbishop of Canterbury; defence review indicates 18 per cent cut in armed forces
30 July	IRA murder Ian Gow
2 August	Iraq invades Kuwait
4 August	Queen Mother's ninetieth birthday
7 August	US orders troops to the Gulf
27 August	Ernest Saunders and two others found guilty of charges arising from the Guinness takeover of the Distillers Group
17–19 September	Mrs Thatcher visits Czechoslovakia and Hungary

3 October	German reunification
8 October	Britain joins European Exchange Rate Mechanism (ERM)
12 October	Inflation rises to 10.9 per cent
18 October	Liberal Democrats win Eastbourne by-election
27–28 October	Rome European Council summit agrees timetable for monetary union which Mrs Thatcher denounces
1 November	Howe resigns
2 November	Sky and BSB announce merger
13 November	Howe's resignation speech in the House of Commons
14 November	Heseltine launches his challenge for the Conservative leadership
19–21 November	Paris Conference on Security and Co-operation in Europe
20 November	Conservative leadership first ballot: Thatcher 204, Heseltine 152, sixteen abstentions
22 November	Mrs Thatcher announces she will not contest second ballot; Major and Hurd enter the contest
27 November	Major wins 185 votes, Heseltine 131, Hurd 56; Heseltine and Hurd stand down
28 November	Mrs Thatcher resigns as Prime Minister; Major takes over, with Lamont as Chancellor of the Exchequer, Baker Home Secretary, Heseltine at the Environment and Chris Patten Chairman of the Conservative Party
5 December	Electricity privatization launched
7 December	Mrs Thatcher awarded OM; Denis Thatcher made a baronet

1991

16 January	US air attack on Baghdad begins Gulf War
29 January	Iraq invades Saudi Arabia
7 February	IRA mortar attack on Downing Street
22 February	Iraqi troops set fire to Kuwait oil wells
24 February	Allied land offensive begins against Iraq
28 February	Ceasefire in Iraq and Kuwait as Iraqis accept UN resolutions
7 March	Liberal Democrats win Ribble Valley by-election
19 March	Budget raises VAT to 17.5 per cent to finance cuts in poll tax
21 March	Heseltine announces poll tax will be replaced by council tax
17 April	US troops enter Iraq to establish centres for Kurdish refugees
30 April	House of Lords rejects War Crimes Bill for second time
9 May	Government uses Parliament Act to pass War Crimes Bill
16 May	Labour wins Monmouth by-election
30 May	George Walker replaced as chief executive of Brent Walker group
18 June	Mrs Thatcher (in US) criticizes EC
28 June	Mrs Thatcher announces she will not stand at next election
2 July	John Birt appointed BBC Director General from 1993
10 July	International Cricket Commission admits South Africa to full membership
22 July	John Major launches Citizen's Charter

31 July	Bush and Gorbachev sign Strategic Arms Reduction Treaty
19 August	Soviet coup; Gorbachev ousted; Yeltsin announces he is taking control of Russia
20 August	Russian troops defect to Yeltsin and coup collapses
23 August	Gorbachev resumes presidency in Moscow
27 August	EC recognizes independence of Estonia, Latvia and Lithuania, as does US on 2 September
27 September	Bush announces cuts in US nuclear weapons
6 October	Gorbachev announces nuclear cuts; Major says Britain will keep Trident
16 October	Thames, TVS and TV-AM lose their television franchises
5 November	Robert Maxwell dies at sea
6 November	Chancellor's Autumn Statement announces £11m more on public spending
3 December	Disclosures about unauthorized loans from the Mirror pension fund to private Maxwell companies
10 December	Britain secures opt-out on single currency and Social Charter at Maastricht EC summit
25 December	Gorbachev resigns

1992

5 February	Ashdown admits affair
11 March	General election announced
9 April	General election – Conservative majority twenty-one

Biographical Notes

Names in italics are of people WW mentions in this volume.

Amery, Julian (life peer 1992), b 1919, Conservative politician, son of Leo Amery (Conservative politician and writer), m (1950) *Lady Catherine Macmillan* (d 1991), daughter of *Harold Macmillan*, 1st Earl of Stockton, Prime Minister, 1957–63. One son, three daughters (*Elizabeth*, b 1956, m (1988) Alan, son of *Alan Hare*). Secretary of State for Air, 1960–2; Minister of Aviation, 1962–4; Minister for Housing and Construction, DoE, 1970–2; Minister of State, FCO, 1972–4.

Amis, Kingsley (1922–95, knight 1990), novelist, poet, critic and *bon viveur*, m 1 (1948–65) Hilary (Hilly), née Bardwell (two sons, one being Martin, also a novelist, one daughter). Hilly married 2 the 7th Baron Kilmarnock; Amis lodged in their house for his latter years, lunching regularly at the Garrick Club. He was married 2 (1965–83) to the novelist Elizabeth Jane Howard. He won the 1986 Booker Prize.

Archer, Jeffrey (life peer 1992), b 1940, Conservative politician and best-selling author, was MP for Louth, 1969–74, and Deputy Chairman of the Conservative Party, 1985–6. He published *As the Crow Flies* in 1991. His play *Exclusive* was at the Queen's theatre in 1990. He married (1966) *Mary*, née Weeden, scientist; Fellow of Newnham College, Cambridge, and Lector in Chemistry, Trinity College, Cambridge, 1976–86; Visiting Professor, Dept of Biochemistry, Imperial College, London, since 1991; member, Council of Lloyd's, 1989–92; a director, Anglia Television, 1987–95; she published *Rupert Brooke and the Old Vicarage, Grantchester* in 1989.

Astor, Major Hon. Sir John Jacob (*Jakie*), b 1918; Conservative politician, MP 1951–9; member of the Tote Board, 1962–8, of the Horserace Betting Levy Board, 1976–80, and Steward of the Jockey Club, 1968–71 and 1983–85. The fourth son of 2nd Viscount Astor, he married 1 (1944–72) Ana Inez (*Chiquita*), née Carcano (d 1992), 2 (1976–85) *Susan*, née Eveleigh; 3 (1988) *Marcia de Savary* (m 1 Peter de Savary). His older brother, the *Hon. Michael Astor* (1916–80), m 2 (1961–8) as her second husband *Pandora* née Clifford. Pandora had previously married Timothy Jones, son of Sir Roderick Jones of Reuters and the writer Enid Bagnold; *Annabel*, daughter of Pandora and Timothy Jones, m (1976) *William 4th Viscount Astor*, a government whip 1990–3 and spokesman in the House of Lords for the DE, 1990–1, on home affairs, 1991–2; Parliamentary Under-Secretary of State, Department of Social Security, 1993–4, Department of National Heritage, 1994–5. Michael Astor m 3 *Judy*, née *Innes*. The *Hon David Astor* (b 1912), older brother of Jacob and Michael, was editor of the *Observer*, 1948–75.

Avon, Clarissa Countess of, b 1920, widow of the 1st Earl of Avon (Sir Anthony Eden (1897–1977), Prime Minister 1955–7, his 2nd marriage; they married 1952), and niece of Sir Winston Churchill.

Beaufort, 11th Duke (*David Somerset*), b 1928, chairman, Marlborough Fine Art Ltd since 1977. He succeeded his cousin the 10th Duke ('Master') in 1984. M (1950) Lady Caroline Jane Thynne (*Caroline*), daughter of the 6th Marquess of Bath and the *Hon. Daphne Fielding* (1904–97), writer. (Daphne Fielding, daughter of 4th Baron Vivian, m 2 Xan Fielding, travel writer; she was famous for her beauty, affairs and courage in breaking convention; her books include biographies of Rosa Lewis, Emerald and Nancy Cunard, Iris Tree and Gladys Deacon, 9th Duchess of Marlborough.) Caroline, who died in 1995, was Petronella's godmother. Badminton is the Beaufort seat. The Beauforts' heir is the *Marquess of Worcester* (*Harry*), b 1952, m (1987) *Tracy Ward* (b 1958, daughter of the Hon. Peter Ward, son of the 3rd Earl of Dudley, and *Claire Ward*, née Baring, Tony Lambton's companion; Tracy Worcester is a trustee of Friends of the Earth). Their other children include Lord Edward Somerset, m (1982) the Hon. Caroline Davidson, daughter of Viscount Davidson; and Lady Anne Somerset, writer, m (1988) Matthew Carr, younger son of Raymond Carr (historian, Warden, St Antony's College, Oxford, 1968–87, knight 1987).

Black, Lady Moorea, see Note on Woodrow Wyatt, p. xvii.

Brittan, Leon QC (knight 1989), b 1939, Conservative politician, Chief Secretary to the Treasury, 1981–3; Home Secretary, 1983–5; Secretary of State for Trade and Industry, 1985–6, when he resigned over the Westland affair; appointed UK member of the European Commission 1989 and since then a Vice-President; m (1980) *Diana* (m 1 Dr Richard Peterson, member of Equal Opportunities Commission, 1988–96, deputy chairman,

1994–6); *Sir Samuel Brittan* (knight 1993), principal economic commentator, *Financial Times*, is his older brother.

Cranborne, Viscount Robert, b 1946, heir to the 6th Marquess of Salisbury, m (1970) Hannah, née Stirling. Conservative politician; MP, 1979–87, when he left the Commons over opposition to the Anglo-Irish Agreement. Entered the House of Lords 1992; Parliamentary Under-Secretary for Defence, 1992–4; Lord Privy Seal and Leader of the House of Lords, 1994–7; shadow Leader, House of Lords, 1997–8.

Crawley, Aidan (1909–93), politician and journalist; Labour MP, 1945–51, Parliamentary Under-Secretary for Air, 1950–1; resigned from Labour, 1957, and became Conservative MP, 1962–7; editor-in-chief, Independent Television News, 1955–6; president, MCC, 1973. M (1945) *Virginia Cowles* (d 1983), writer; their two sons *Andrew* and *Randall* were killed in an air crash in 1988; one surviving daughter, *Harriet*, writer and politician.

Derby, Isabel, Countess of, JP (d 1990), née Milles-Lade, m (1948) 18th Earl of Derby (*John*, 1918–94). No children. Their houses were Knowsley in Merseyside and Stanley House at Newmarket, Suffolk. Lord Derby was a member of the Jockey Club.

Devonshire, 11th Duke (*Andrew*), b 1929; he succeeded his father in 1950, his older brother having been killed in the Second World War; m (1941) Deborah (*Debo*), née Freeman-Mitford, daughter of 2nd Baron Redesdale, writer; their eldest son and heir is the *Marquess of Hartington* (*Stoker*), b 1942, senior steward of the Jockey Club, 1989–94, m (1967) *Amanda*, née Heywood-Lonsdale, their son being the *Earl of Burlington* (b 1969); Andrew Devonshire's sister *Lady Anne Cavendish* m (1949) *Michael Tree* (1921–99), painter. Conservative Parliamentary Under-Secretary for Commonwealth Relations, 1960–2, and Minister of State CRO, 1962–4; he was a member of the SDP at the time of the last volume. He was a member of the Tote Board, 1977–86, and chairman, Thoroughbred Breeders' Association, 1978–81. Chatsworth is the Devonshire seat.

Dudley, 4th Earl, William (*Billy*), b 1920, son of 3rd Earl and his first wife. (The 3rd Earl m 2 (1943–54) *Laura*, née Charteris (died 1990), her second marriage; she m 1 (1933–43) 2nd Viscount Long, their daughter being the Hon. *Sara Morrison*, 3 Michael Canfield of New York and London, 4 (1972) 10th Duke of Marlborough (d 1972). Laura's sister

Anne (*Annie*, 1913–81) m (1952) *Ian Fleming*, the writer, having married 1 (1932) 3rd Baron O'Neill (d 1944) and 2 (1945–52) 2nd *Viscount Rothermere* (*Esmond*, d 1978). Rothermere m 3 (1966) *Mary* Ohrstrom, née Murchison, of Dallas, Texas. Mary Rothermere died in 1993.) 'Billy' Dudley m 2 (1961) *Maureen Swanson*, the actress.

Fielding, Daphne, see under **Beaufort**.

Forte, Charles (life peer 1982), b 1908, was chief executive, chairman and president of Trusthouse Forte and Forte (which he began as a milk bar in Regent St in 1935), retired 1996; m (1943) *Irene*, née Chierico; the Fortes had five daughters and one son, *Rocco Forte* (knight 1995), b 1945, m (1986) *Aliai*, daughter of *Professor Giovanni Ricci* of Rome, one son, two daughters; chairman and chief executive RF Hotels since 1996, of Forte 1983–96. Their daughter *Olga*, hotelier, formerly director of Forte and managing director of design, m 1 Alessandro Polizzi (d 1980), 2 (1993) the Hon. *William Shawcross*, b 1946, writer, son of Lord (*Hartley*) *Shawcross* (Labour Attorney-General, 1945–51).

Goodman, Arnold (1913–95, life peer 1965), solicitor, founder Goodman Derrick and Co.; Master of University College, Oxford, 1976–86; director, Royal Opera House, 1972–83; chairman, English National Opera, 1977–86; president, National Book League, 1972–85; chairman, *Observer* editorial trust, 1967–76, director, *Observer*, 1976–81, etc.

Hare, the Hon. Alan (1919–95), son of 4th Earl of Listowel, m (1945) *Jill*, née North; their son Alan m (1988) *Elizabeth Amery*. Oxford friend of WW; chairman, *Financial Times*, 1978–84, and chief executive, 1975–83; director, Pearson Longman, 1975–83, the *Economist*, 1975–89, English National Opera, 1982–8; president, Société Civile du Vignoble de Château Latour (owned by Pearson), 1983–90.

Henderson, John (*Johnnie*), b 1920, m 2 (1976) *Catherine* Christian, née Barford; chairman, Henderson Administration, 1983–90; Lord Lieutenant of Berkshire, 1989–95; member of the Jockey Club.

Henderson, Nicholas (*Nicko*) (knight 1972), b 1919, diplomat; Ambassador to Poland, 1969–72, Federal Republic of Germany, 1972–5, France, 1975–9, Washington, 1979–82, chairman, Channel Tunnel Group, 1985–6; director, Hambros, 1983–9, Eurotunnel 1986–8.

Heseltine, Michael, b 1933, Conservative politician and publisher; m (1962) Anne, née Williams; MP since 1966; Secretary of State for the

Environment, 1979–83; Secretary of State for Defence, 1983–6, when he resigned over the Westland affair; candidate in the Conservative Party leadership contest, November 1990; Secretary of State for the Environment, November 1990–2, for Trade and Industry, 1992–5, Deputy Prime Minister, 1995–7; chairman, Haymarket Press, 1966–70, director, Haymarket Group, since 1997.

Hesketh, Alexander, 3rd Baron, b 1950, m (1977) the Hon. *Claire*, daughter of 3rd Baron *Manton*. Conservative politician, a government whip in the House of Lords, 1986–9, Parliamentary Under-Secretary, DoE, 1989–90, Minister of State DTI, 1990–1, Government Chief Whip, House of Lords, 1991–3.

Howard de Walden, John, 9th Baron (*Johnnie*), (1912–99), m 2 (1978) Gillian (*Gillie*) Viscountess Mountgarret. Member of the Jockey Club (senior steward, 1957, 1964, 1976), racehorse owner (including Slip Anchor, 1985 Derby winner).

Howe, Geoffrey QC (knight 1970, life peer 1992), b 1926, m (1953) *Elspeth*, née Shand, JP (deputy chairman, Equal Opportunities Commission, 1975–9, subsequently chairman Opportunity 2000, Broadcasting Standards Commission, BOC Foundation, and president, UNICEF UK). Conservative politician, MP 1964–6 and 1970–92. Reached the second ballot in the 1975 Conservative leadership contest and was made shadow Chancellor of the Exchequer by Mrs Thatcher after she won. He was Chancellor of the Exchequer, 1979–83, Secretary of State for Foreign and Commonwealth Affairs, 1983–9, Lord President of the Council, Leader of the House of Commons and Deputy Prime Minister from 1989 until he resigned in 1990, precipitating Mrs Thatcher's fall.

Hurd, Douglas (life peer 1997), b 1930, Conservative politician; eldest son of Lord Hurd (life peer 1964, d 1966, farmer, Conservative MP, 1945–64, and agricultural correspondent of the *Times*), m 1 (1960–82) Tatania, née Benedict Eyre, m 2 (1982) *Judy*, née Smart (sister-in-law of racehorse trainer *Jeremy Hindley*). After leaving the diplomatic service in 1966 he joined the Conservative Research Department and in 1968 became Private Secretary to *Edward Heath* when Leader of the Opposition, continuing when Heath became Prime Minister. He entered Parliament in 1974 and although closely associated with Heath became Minister of State at the FCO, 1979–83, in the first Thatcher government. As Home Secretary (1985–9) he was responsible for legislation about betting and opening hours, and for the Tote. He was Secretary of State for Foreign and Commonwealth Affairs from 1989 until 1995, retiring from Parliament in 1997. He also writes thrillers, some with *Andrew Osmond* (d 1999).

Jenkins, Roy (life peer 1987, OM 1993), b 1920, politician. His father, Arthur Jenkins, was a South Wales miner who became a Labour MP and junior minister. Roy Jenkins entered Parliament as a Labour MP in 1948, having lost the selection for Aston in 1945 to WW. He was a reforming home secretary, 1965–67 and 1974–6; Chancellor of the Exchequer, 1967–70; Deputy Leader of the Labour Party, 1970–2. After failing in the Labour leadership contest on Harold Wilson's resignation, he became the first British President of the European Commission, 1977–81, presiding over the creation of the EMS. He left the Labour Party with *David Owen*, Shirley Williams and Bill Rodgers, the 'Gang of four', in 1981 to form the SDP, becoming its first sole Leader, 1982–3. He won Glasgow Hillhead for the SDP in a by-election in 1982, remaining its MP until his defeat in the 1987 general election. Elected Chancellor of the University of Oxford in 1987, he became Leader of the Social and Liberal Democrat Peers in 1988. M (1945) *Dame Jennifer* née Morris (chairman, National Trust, 1986–91), and has written biographies of Balfour, Dilke, Asquith, Baldwin, Truman and Gladstone. His autobiography *A Life at the Centre* was published in 1991.

Keswick, Henry, b 1938, chairman, Matheson & Co., since 1975; Jardine, Matheson Holdings, Hong Kong, and Jardine Strategic Holdings since 1989; proprietor, the *Spectator*, 1975–81; director, *Daily Telegraph*, since 1990; chairman, Hong Kong Association, since 1988. M (1985) the Hon. *Tessa* Lady Reay (née Fraser, daughter of 15th Baron Lovat, m 1 (1964–78) 14th Lord Reay), whose early career was in journalism. She has been director, Cluff Investments and Trading, 1981–95; special adviser (1989–95) to Kenneth Clarke when he was Secretary of State for Health, then for Education and Science, Home Secretary and Chancellor of the Exchequer; executive director, Centre for Policy Studies, since 1995.

Chips Keswick (John Chippendale, knight 1993) is Henry Keswick's younger brother, b 1940; chairman and chief executive, Hambros Bank, 1986–95, non-executive chairman, 1995–7, chairman since 1997; director, Bank of England, since 1993; m (1966) Lady *Sarah* Ramsay, daughter of 16th Earl of Dalhousie.

Lambton Viscount Antony (*Tony*), b 1922, disclaimed his peerages 1970; m (1942) Belinda (*Bindy*), née Blew-Jones; one son, Edward (m (1983)

Christabel daughter of *Rory McEwen*, painter); five daughters including *Lucinda*, writer, photographer and broadcaster (b 1943, m 1 (1965) Henry Mark Harrod, son of Sir Roy Harrod, m 2 (1986) Sir Edmund Fairfax-Lacy, m 3 (1991) Sir Peregrine Worsthorne (b 1923, m 1 (1950) Claudie Baynham, who died 1990)), *Anne* and *Rose*, actresses. Conservative MP, 1951–73, Parliamentary Under-Secretary, MoD, from 1970 until 1973 when he resigned after photographs of him with a prostitute were offered to the press. Owner of Villa Cetinale near Siena, Italy, and La Cerbaia which the Wyatts used to rent.

Lamont, Norman (life peer 1998), b 1942, m (1971–99) *Rosemary* née White (daughter *Sophie*, b 1980, son, *Hilaire*, b 1977). Conservative politician. Merchant banker at N. M. Rothschild & Sons, 1968–79, non-executive director, 1993–5; currently director, Jupiter Asset Management. MP from 1972 until 1997 when defeated in the general election. Minister of State, DTI, 1981–5, for Defence Procurement, 1985–6; Financial Secretary to Treasury, 1986–9; Chief Secretary to Treasury, 1989–90; Chancellor of the Exchequer, 1990–3.

Lawson, Nigel (life peer 1992), b 1932, m 1 (1955–80) Vanessa, née Salmon (who m 2 (1983) Sir Freddie Ayer, philosopher, and died 1985), m 2 (1980) *Thérèse*, née Maclear. Conservative politician and journalist (*Financial Times*, *Sunday Telegraph* and editor, *Spectator*, 1966–70). MP, 1974–92; Chancellor of the Exchequer, 1983 until he resigned in October 1989 over differences with Mrs Thatcher about Europe, the EMS and her adviser Alan Walters. Director, Barclays Bank, since 1990. *Dominic*, his son by his first marriage, edited the *Spectator*, 1990–5, and has been editor, *Sunday Telegraph*, since 1995; *Nigella*, one of his daughters by his first marriage, is a journalist (the *Times* since 1995) and cookery writer.

Lever, Harold (1914–95, life peer 1979), m 3 (1962) *Diane*, née Bashi. Labour politician; MP, 1945–79, Financial Secretary to the Treasury, 1967–9, Paymaster General, 1969–70, Chancellor of the Duchy of Lancaster, 1974–9; chairman, SDS Bank, 1984–90.

Macmillan, Katherine Viscountess DBE (*Katie*), née Ormsby-Gore, widow of Viscount Maurice Macmillan (1921–84, Conservative politician, Oxford friend of WW and son of Harold Macmillan, 1st Earl of Stockton, Prime Minister, 1957–63). Mother of 2nd Earl of Stockton (*Alexander*), b 1943, m (1970–91) Birgitte (*Bitte*), née Hamilton, succeeded his grandfather in 1986; of Adam Macmillan, b 1948; and David Macmillan, b

1957; also Joshua (d 1965) and Rachel (d 1987). The family estate was Birch Grove in East Sussex.

Marlborough, 11th Duke (*Sonny*), b 1926, son of 10th Duke (Bert) by his first wife; (*Laura* Duchess of Marlborough (d 1990) was his stepmother, see under **Dudley**); m 3 (1972) *Rosita*, née Douglas. His heir is the Marquess of Blandford (Jamie). The Marlborough seat is Blenheim Palace, Woodstock, Oxfordshire.

Montagu, the Hon. David (1928–98), succeeded father as 4th Baron Swaythling in 1990; m (1951) *Ninette*, née Dreyfus; son, Charles, b 1954, daughter, b 1956 and daughter, b 1952, d 1982. Merchant banker: chairman, Samuel Montagu, 1970–3; chairman and chief executive, Orion Bank, 1974–9; chairman, Ailsa Investment Trust, 1981–8; director (latterly deputy chairman), J. Rothschild Holdings, 1983–9; chairman, Rothmans International, 1988–98. Member of Tote Board for twelve years. Director, *Daily Telegraph*, 1985–96, British Horseracing Board, from 1993.

Murdoch, Rupert, b 1931, newspaper and media proprietor, son of Sir Keith Murdoch, Australian newspaper owner, and Dame Elisabeth Murdoch; educated Geelong GS and Worcester College, Oxford; m 1 (1956–66) Patricia Booker, one daughter, Prudence (*Prue*, m 1, Crispin Odey, m 2 Alisdair MacLeod, general manager, Times Newspapers); m 2 (1967, divorced 1999) *Anna*, née Torv, novelist, two sons, *Lachlan* and *James*, one daughter *Elisabeth*; m 3 (1999) Wendy, née Deng. Chairman since 1991 and group chief executive since 1989, the News Corporation, Australia; director, News International UK, since 1969 (chairman, 1969–87 and 1994–5); chairman and president, News America Publishing; director, Times Newspapers Holdings, since 1981 (chairman, 1982–90 and since 1994); director, HarperCollins Publishers, since 1989; British Sky Broadcasting since 1990; chairman and chief executive officer, 1992–6, then director, Twentieth Century Fox. His UK newspapers include the *Times* and *Sunday Times* (acquired 1981), *News of the World* (1968) and *Sun* (1969). His newspapers supported Harold Wilson (Labour) in the 1970 general election but in 1973 switched to the Conservatives and back again to Labour in 1997. He is a US citizen.

Parkinson, Cecil (life peer 1992), b 1931, m (1957) *Ann*, née Jarvis. Conservative politician; Paymaster General, 1981–3; Chancellor of the Duchy of Lancaster, 1982–3; Secretary of State for Trade and Industry from June to October 1983 when he resigned on the revelation that his secretary Sara Keays was pregnant with his child. He returned as Secretary of State for Energy, 1987–9, for Transport 1989–90. He was Chairman of the Conservative Party, 1981–3.

Polizzi, Olga, see under **Forte.**

Quinton, Anthony (*Tony*) (life peer 1982), b 1925, m (1952) *Marcelle*, née Wegier of New York, sculptor. Philosopher and broadcaster (*Round Britain Quiz*). Fellow, All Souls College, Oxford, 1949–55, New College, Oxford, 1955–78; President, Trinity College, Oxford, 1978–87; member, Arts Council, 1979–81; chairman of the board, British Library, 1985–90.

Rothermere, Mary, Viscountess, see under **Dudley.**

Rothschild, Victor 3rd Baron (1910–90), succeeded his uncle in 1937, m 1 (1933–45) Barbara, née Hutchinson, 2 (1946) Teresa (*Tess*), née Mayor. Scientist and banker. Prize-Fellow, Trinity College, Cambridge, 1935–9; in military intelligence during the Second World War; chairman, Agricultural Research Council, 1948–58; Assistant Director of Research, Dept of Zoology, Cambridge, 1950–70; chairman, Shell Research, 1963–70; director-general and first Permanent Under-Secretary, Central Policy Review Staff, Cabinet Office, 1971–4; director, Rothschilds Continuation (chairman, 1976–88), N. M. Rothschild & Sons (chairman, 1975–6); chairman, Royal Commission on Gambling, 1976–8.

Succeeded in 1990 by his eldest son by his first marriage, *Jacob*, b 1936, m (1961) *Serena* (elder daughter of *Sir Philip Dunn* (d 1976) and sister of Nell Dunn, writer), one son, three daughters. Banker; chairman, St James's Place Capital (formerly J. Rothschild Holdings), 1971–97; chairman, Trustees National Gallery, 1985–91, National Heritage Memorial Fund, 1992–4, National Heritage Lottery Fund, 1994–8.

Evelyn de Rothschild (knight 1989), second cousin of Victor – their grandfathers were brothers – succeeded Victor as chairman of N. M. Rothschild & Sons. Chairman, Economist Newspaper, 1972–89; a director, *Daily Telegraph*, 1990–6 and since 1997; chairman, United Racecourses Ltd, 1977–94; member of the Jockey Club.

Sinclair, Sonia, b 1928, née Graham, m 1 (1947) the Hon. *Julian Mond*, later 3rd Baron *Melchett* (grandson of the founder of ICI; chairman, British Steel Corporation, from 1967, d 1973), 2 (1984) Dr *Andrew Sinclair*, b 1935, writer and former academic, his third marriage. Her books are *Tell Me, Honestly* (1964), *Someone is Missing* (1987), *Passionate Quests* (1991). She has been a board member, Royal Court Theatre, since 1974, Royal National Theatre 1984–94. Andrew Sinclair's books include *The Breaking of Bumbo* (1958), *The Red and the Blue* (1986), *Spiegel* (1987), *War Like a Wasp* (1989); he edited *The War Decade: An Anthology of the 1940s* (1989); managing director, Timon Films, since 1967.

Soames, Lady (Mary), DBE, b 1922, writer; chairman, Royal National Theatre, 1989–95; daughter of Sir Winston Churchill; m (1947) *Christopher Soames* (1920–87, life peer 1978; Conservative politician, MP, 1950–66; Ambassador to France, 1968–72, Governor Southern Rhodesia, 1979–80, chairman ICL from 1984). Their son the Hon. *Nicholas Soames*, b 1948, m 1 (1981–90) Catherine, née Weatherall, 2 (1993) Serena, née Smith; Conservative politician, MP since 1983; PPS to Secretary of State, DoE, 1987–9; Parliamentary Secretary, MAFF, 1992–4; Minister of State for the Armed Forces, 1994–7.

Somerset, David, see under **Beaufort**.

Stelzer, Irwin, b 1932, m (1981) Marian Faris Stuntz (*Cita*); American economist and journalist living partly in London. President, NERA (National Economic Research Associates), 1961–85; director of regulatory studies at the American Enterprise Institute for Public Policy Research, Washington; columnist, *New York Post* and *Sunday Times* (since 1986).

Stockton, see under **Macmillan**.

Swaythling, see under **Montagu**.

Tree, Michael (1921–99), painter, director of Christie's and Colefax & Fowler; son by his first marriage of Ronald Tree (d 1976, Conservative politician who m 2 *Marietta* (1917–91), actress and US representative to the UN Human Rights Commission), brother of *Jeremy*, racehorse trainer; m (1949) Lady *Anne*, née Cavendish, daughter of the 10th Duke of Devonshire, sister of the 11th Duke (*Andrew*).

Trethowan, Sir Ian (1922–90, knight 1980), joined BBC, 1963, from newspaper journalism (political commentator) and Independent Television News (1958–63); managing director, radio, BBC, 1969–75; managing director, television, BBC, 1976–7; Director General, BBC, 1977–82; director, Barclays Bank, 1982–7; chairman, Thames Television, from 1987; director, Times Newspapers, from 1982; chairman, Horserace Betting Levy Board, 1982–90.

Trevor-Roper, Hugh (life peer 1979, Lord Dacre), b 1914, m (1954) Lady Alexandra (*Xandra*) Howard-Johnston (d 1997, daughter of Field Marshal

Earl Haig); Regius Professor of Modern History, Oxford University, 1957–80; Master of Peterhouse, Cambridge, 1980–7; director, Times Newspapers, 1974–88.

Ward, Claire, see under **Beaufort.**

Weidenfeld, George (life peer 1976), b 1919, m 1 (1952) Jane Sieff; 2 (1956–61) *Barbara*, née *Skelton*, former wife of *Cyril Connolly*, writer and critic; 3 (1966–76) Sandra née Payson Meyer; 4 (1992) Annabelle, née Whitestone. Publisher; founded Weidenfeld & Nicolson 1948, chairman, Weidenfield & Nicolson and associated companies, since 1948. Member, South Bank board, since 1986, ENO board, since 1988; trustee, National Portrait Gallery, 1988–95.

Weinstock, Arnold (knight 1970, life peer 1980), b 1924, m (1949) *Netta*, daughter of *Sir Michael Sobell* (chairman, Radio and Allied Industries, television set manufacturers, and racehorse owner, d 1993); son *Simon* (1952–96), daughter, *Susan* (b 1955, m Charles Lacroix). The electrical group GEC bought RAI and its management team, making the Sobell and Weinstock families GEC's largest shareholders. Weinstock became a director of GEC in 1960 and then managing director from 1963 to 1996, building GEC into one of Europe's major electronics companies and a principal defence supplier to the government. Sits as an independent in the House of Lords. Honorary Master of the Bench, Gray's Inn, since 1982; trustee, British Museum, since 1985; racehorse owner and breeder, member of the Jockey Club. Owns Bowden Park, Wiltshire, a James Wyatt house.

Wolfson, Leonard (knight 1977, life peer 1985), b 1927, son of Sir Isaac Wolfson (founder, Great Universal Stores, d 1991), m 1 (1949–91) Ruth, née Sterling, 2 (1991) Estelle, née Feldman, widow of Michael Jackson. Chairman, Great Universal Stores, 1981–96. Founder trustee and chairman, Wolfson Foundation.

Appendix on Racing

Horserace Totalisator Board (the Tote)
The Tote was set up by Act of Parliament in 1928 to provide an alternative means of betting other than with bookmakers and to give financial support to racing.

The term 'totalisator' originates from the machines used for the aggregation of bets under a 'pool' system of betting, whereby an organization acts as stakeholder to enable people to bet among themselves. The Tote's original name under the 1928 Act was the Racecourse Betting Control Board, changed to its present name by the Betting Levy Act 1961. The Tote was given an exclusive licence to run pools betting on horseracing. In 1972 the Tote was allowed to open high street betting offices with betting also at starting prices, eleven years after high street betting offices were made legal for ordinary bookmakers.

Today the Tote offers a full betting service to all fifty-nine racecourses in the UK. Its 1997 annual report, the last with WW as its chairman, stated that on average two-thirds of the Tote's profits went back into British racing, £7.9m in that year. In 1997 it had 209 high street betting shops and was Britain's fifth biggest bookmaker, running the world's largest credit betting operation.

The chairman of the Tote board is appointed by the Home Secretary, who approves the appointment of board members. WW joined the board in 1975 and in May 1976 was appointed chairman by the then Home Secretary, Roy Jenkins. He was reappointed by all subsequent home secretaries until his retirement at the end of July 1997 at the age of seventy-nine.

WW succeeded Lord Mancroft as chairman and was succeeded by Peter Jones, a director of the British Horseracing Board and a council member of the Racehorse Owners' Association.

At the time of this volume Tote board members included Prince Michael of Kent and Frank Chapple (Lord Chapple), until 1990; Mrs Priscilla Hastings, the Hon. David Montagu (Lord Swaythling), John Sanderson, David Sieff (from 1991) and Peter Winfield. On the staff were Brian McDonnell (chief executive from 1981), John Heaton (secretary from

1983 – he succeeded McDonnell as chief executive in November 1996) and Geoffrey Webster (public relations director from 1976).

The Tote's high-tech headquarters are at Wigan and its offices in Putney, south-west London.

During this period the government was considering privatization of the Tote. The affairs of the Tote were scrutinized first by Lloyds Merchant Bank, commissioned in 1988 by the Home Office to make a feasibility study on privatization, and then by the House of Commons Home Affairs Select Committee, chaired by Sir John Wheeler. WW fought to keep the Tote's different operations – on-course betting, credit betting and betting shops – under the single Tote umbrella. In his speech at the 1990 Tote Annual Lunch he said, 'Selling Tote Bookmakers would be like cutting off a leg and half an arm.'

On the other hand, WW supported the suggestion mooted for a racing trust, or Horserace Advisory Council, to take over the Home Office's role vis-à-vis the Tote, appointing its board and chairman, as long as the existing arm's-length relationship with the board (and its chairman) was maintained. He thought such a transfer of the Home Office's responsibilities would have the advantage of enabling the Tote to offer bets on non-sporting events and increase the amount contributed to racing, whereas privatization would take profits away from racing. Nothing was resolved during this period but WW was troubled by attacks on the Tote in the press and speculation about his own position.

In addition, an attempt to buy Coral, one of the Big Four bookmakers, was made in 1991. The talks in the end floundered but the alternative plan succeeded for Coral to buy the Tote's new technology, linking terminals in its betting shops to the Tote on course. WW also talked to Pari Mutuel, trying to link the Tote with Europe by a similar system.

WW was an *ex officio* member of the Horserace Betting Levy Board, a director of Satellite Information Services (Holdings) and a trustee of the Stable Lads' Welfare Trust.

Horseracing Betting Levy Board

Established in 1961 by the Betting Levy Act to levy money for the benefit of racing, it works by taking a percentage of turnover from all bookmakers (including the Tote) who in turn pass this charge to the punters along with betting tax.

Sir Ian Trethowan (former Director General of the BBC) was chairman of the Levy Board from 1982 until shortly before his death in 1990. He was succeeded by Sir John Sparrow. The chief executive at this time was Tristram Ricketts (subsequently chief executive of the British Horseracing Board). Other executives included Rodney Brack (finance director, now chief executive in succession to Ricketts). Former chairmen included Lord (George) Wigg, Labour politician, and Lord (Desmond) Plummer, Conservative Leader of the Greater London Council.

The money raised by the levies goes towards prize money, improving racecourses, technical services at racecourses, training of stable staff, veterinary research, improvements to breeding, security, and grants for point-to-point races.

United Racecourses (Epsom, Kempton Park and Sandown Park) was at this time a subsidiary of the Levy Board. Its chairman (1977–94) was Sir Evelyn de Rothschild.

The Big Four Bookmakers
At the time of this volume the 'Big Four' were Coral (represented by Mike Snapes), Ladbroke's (Peter George), Mecca (Bob Green), and William Hill (Len Cowburn).

The Jockey Club
The oldest regulatory body of racing in the world, the Jockey Club 'sets and maintains standards for racing'. Its rules and the supervision by its stewards govern the state of the course, starting procedures, discipline on course, the determination of winners and inquiries.

Jockey Club members are elected for life. Those mentioned in this volume include the Hon. Sir John 'Jakie' Astor, Colonel Sir Piers Bengough, the Duke of Devonshire, Lord Fairhaven, the Marquess of Hartington, Mrs Priscilla Hastings, John Henderson, Lord Howard de Walden, Sir Evelyn de Rothschild, Sir Michael Sobell, Christopher Spence, Christopher Sporborg, J. J. Warr, Lord Weinstock, the Marquess of Zetland and (honorary) HH Prince Khalid bin Abdullah.

Christopher Foster was secretary of the Jockey Club, 1983–90, and has been executive director since 1993; Christopher Haines was chief executive, 1989–93.

The Racecourse Holdings Trust, the Jockey Club's subsidiary established in 1964, owns and operates twelve racecourses, including Aintree, Cheltenham, Newmarket (and since the time of this volume Epsom, Kempton Park and Sandown Park). Captain Miles Gosling (d 1997) was its chairman from 1989; Tommy Wallis (d 1992) was its managing director, 1975–89.

Pari Mutuel

The first system of betting by means of a totalisator was introduced in France in 1872 and became known as the *pari-mutuel*; hence the name of the French equivalent of the Tote. Its head at the time of this volume was André Cormier.

Racecourse Association Ltd

All fifty-nine UK racecourses belong. Its chairman at the time of this volume was J. J. Warr.

Satellite Information Services

The Tote had secured a 5 per cent holding in SIS when it was founded in 1986/7.

List of Abbreviations

ANC	African National Congress
BSB	British Satellite Broadcasting, later British Sky Broadcasting
BUPA	British United Provident Association
CBI	Confederation of British Industry
CEGB	Central Electricity Generating Board
DHSS	Department of Health and Social Security
DoE	Department of the Environment
DTI	Department of Trade and Industry
EBRD	European Bank for Reconstruction and Development
EC	European Community
EETPU	Electrical, Electronic, Telecommunication and Plumbing Union
EMS	European Monetary System
ERM	Exchange Rate Mechanism (of the EMS)
FCO	Foreign and Commonwealth Office
GAM	Global Asset Management
GATT	General Agreement on Tariffs and Trade
GEC	General Electric Company
GLC	Greater London Council
IBA	Independent Broadcasting Authority
IMF	International Monetary Fund
ITC	Independent Television Commission
MAFF	Ministry of Agriculture, Fisheries and Food
MCC	Marylebone Cricket Club
MoD	Ministry of Defence
NERA	National Economic Research Associates
NUM	National Union of Mineworkers
PLO	Palestine Liberation Organization
PMU	Pari Mutuel
PPS	Parliamentary Private Secretary
RAC	Royal Automobile Club
RPI	Retail Price Index
SDI	Strategic Defence Initiative

SDP	Social Democratic Party
SIB	Security and Investments Board
SIS	Satellite Information Services
SP	Starting Price
Tote	Horserace Totalisator Board
TUC	Trades Union Congress

Index